JAVA™
SECRETS®

Java™
SECRETS®

Elliotte Rusty Harold

IDG Books Worldwide, Inc.
An International Data Group Company

Foster City, CA ♦ Chicago, IL ♦ Indianapolis, IN ♦ Southlake, TX

Java™ SECRETS®

Published by
IDG Books Worldwide, Inc.
An International Data Group Company
919 E. Hillsdale Blvd.
Suite 400
Foster City, CA 94404
http://www.idgbooks.com (IDG Books Worldwide Web site)

Library of Congress Catalog Card No.: 97-72189

ISBN: 0-7645-8007-8

Printed in the United States of America

10 9 8 7 6 5 4 3 2 1

1B/RZ/QV/ZX/FC

Distributed in the United States by IDG Books Worldwide, Inc.

Distributed by Macmillan Canada for Canada; by Transworld Publishers Limited in the United Kingdom and Europe; by WoodsLane Pty. Ltd. for Australia; by WoodsLane Enterprises Ltd. for New Zealand; by Longman Singapore Publishers Ltd. for Singapore, Malaysia, Thailand, and Indonesia; by Simron Pty. Ltd. for South Africa; by Toppan Company Ltd. for Japan; by Distribuidora Cuspide for Argentina; by Livraria Cultura for Brazil; by Ediciencia S.A. for Ecuador; by Addison-Wesley Publishing Company for Korea; by Ediciones ZETA S.C.R. Ltda. for Peru; by WS Computer Publishing Company, Inc., for the Philippines; by Unalis Corporation for Taiwan; by Contemporanea de Ediciones for Venezuela. Authorized Sales Agent: Anthony Rudkin Associates for the Middle East and North Africa.

For general information on IDG Books Worldwide's books in the U.S., please call our Consumer Customer Service department at 800-762-2974. For reseller information, including discounts and premium sales, please call our Reseller Customer Service department at 800-434-3422.

For information on where to purchase IDG Books Worldwide's books outside the U.S., please contact our International Sales department at 415-655-3023 or fax 415-655-3299.

For information on foreign language translations, please contact our Foreign & Subsidiary Rights department at 415-655-3021 or fax 415-655-3281.

For sales inquiries and special prices for bulk quantities, please contact our Sales department at 415-655-3200 or write to the address above.

For information on using IDG Books Worldwide's books in the classroom or for ordering examination copies, please contact our Educational Sales department at 800-434-2086 or fax 817-251-8174.

For press review copies, author interviews, or other publicity information, please contact our Public Relations department at 415-655-3000 or fax 415-655-3299.

For authorization to photocopy items for corporate, personal, or educational use, please contact Copyright Clearance Center, 222 Rosewood Drive, Danvers, MA 01923, or fax 508-750-4470.

IDG BOOKS WORLDWIDE is a trademark under exclusive license to IDG Books Worldwide, Inc., from International Data Group, Inc.

ABOUT IDG BOOKS WORLDWIDE

Welcome to the world of IDG Books Worldwide.

IDG Books Worldwide, Inc., is a subsidiary of International Data Group, the world's largest publisher of computer-related information and the leading global provider of information services on information technology. IDG was founded more than 25 years ago and now employs more than 8,500 people worldwide. IDG publishes more than 275 computer publications in over 75 countries (see listing below). More than 60 million people read one or more IDG publications each month.

Launched in 1990, IDG Books Worldwide is today the #1 publisher of best-selling computer books in the United States. We are proud to have received eight awards from the Computer Press Association in recognition of editorial excellence and three from *Computer Currents'* First Annual Readers' Choice Awards. Our best-selling ...*For Dummies®* series has more than 30 million copies in print with translations in 30 languages. IDG Books Worldwide, through a joint venture with IDG's Hi-Tech Beijing, became the first U.S. publisher to publish a computer book in the People's Republic of China. In record time, IDG Books Worldwide has become the first choice for millions of readers around the world who want to learn how to better manage their businesses.

Our mission is simple: Every one of our books is designed to bring extra value and skill-building instructions to the reader. Our books are written by experts who understand and care about our readers. The knowledge base of our editorial staff comes from years of experience in publishing, education, and journalism — experience we use to produce books for the '90s. In short, we care about books, so we attract the best people. We devote special attention to details such as audience, interior design, use of icons, and illustrations. And because we use an efficient process of authoring, editing, and desktop publishing our books electronically, we can spend more time ensuring superior content and spend less time on the technicalities of making books.

You can count on our commitment to deliver high-quality books at competitive prices on topics you want to read about. At IDG Books Worldwide, we continue in the IDG tradition of delivering quality for more than 25 years. You'll find no better book on a subject than one from IDG Books Worldwide.

John Kilcullen
CEO
IDG Books Worldwide, Inc.

Steven Berkowitz
President and Publisher
IDG Books Worldwide, Inc.

VIII WINNER
Eighth Annual Computer Press Awards ≥1992

IX WINNER
Ninth Annual Computer Press Awards ≥1993

X WINNER
Tenth Annual Computer Press Awards ≥1994

XI WINNER
Eleventh Annual Computer Press Awards ≥1995

IDG Books Worldwide, Inc., is a subsidiary of International Data Group, the world's largest publisher of computer-related information and the leading global provider of information services on information technology. International Data Group publishes over 275 computer publications in over 75 countries. Sixty million people read one or more International Data Group publications each month. International Data Group's publications include: **ARGENTINA:** Buyer's Guide, Computerworld Argentina, PC World Argentina; **AUSTRALIA:** Australian Macworld, Australian PC World, Australian Reseller News, Computerworld, IT Casebook, Network World, Publish, Webmaster; **AUSTRIA:** Computerwelt Osterreich, Networks Austria, PC Tip Austria; **BANGLADESH:** PC World Bangladesh; **BELARUS:** PC World Belarus; **BELGIUM:** Data News; **BRAZIL:** Annuário de Informática, Computerworld, Connections, Macworld, PC Player, PC World, Publish, Reseller News, Supergamepower; **BULGARIA:** Computerworld Bulgaria, Network World Bulgaria, PC & MacWorld Bulgaria; **CANADA:** CIO Canada, Client/Server World, ComputerWorld Canada, InfoWorld Canada, NetworkWorld Canada, WebWorld; **CHILE:** Computerworld Chile, PC World; **COLOMBIA:** Computerworld Colombia, PC World Colombia; **COSTA RICA:** PC World Centro America; **THE CZECH AND SLOVAK REPUBLICS:** Computerworld Czechoslovakia, Macworld Czech Republic, PC World Czechoslovakia; **DENMARK:** Communications World Danmark, Computerworld Danmark, Macworld Danmark, PC World Danmark, Techworld Denmark; **DOMINICAN REPUBLIC:** PC World Republica Dominicana; **ECUADOR:** PC World Ecuador; **EGYPT:** Computerworld Middle East, PC World Middle East; **EL SALVADOR:** PC World Centro America; **FINLAND:** MikroPC, Tietoverkko, Tietoviikko; **FRANCE:** Distributique, Hebdo, Info PC, Le Monde Informatique, Macworld, Reseaux & Telecoms, WebMaster France; **GERMANY:** Computer Partner, Computerwoche, Computerwoche Extra, Computerwoche FOCUS, Global Online, Macwelt, PC Welt; **GREECE:** Amiga Computing, GamePro Greece, Multimedia World; **GUATEMALA:** PC World Centro America; **HONDURAS:** PC World Centro America; **HONG KONG:** Computerworld Hong Kong, PC World Hong Kong, Publish in Asia; **HUNGARY:** ABCD CD-ROM, Computerworld Szamitastechnika, Internetto online Magazine, PC World Hungary, PC-X Magazin Hungary; **ICELAND:** Tolvuheimur PC World Island; **INDIA:** Information Communications World, Information Systems Computerworld, PC World India, Publish in Asia; **INDONESIA:** InfoKomputer PC World, Komputek Computerworld, Publish in Asia; **IRELAND:** ComputerScope, PC Live!; **ISRAEL:** Macworld Israel, People & Computers/Computerworld; **ITALY:** Computerworld Italia, Macworld Italia, Networking Italia, PC World Italia; **JAPAN:** DTP World, Macworld Japan, Nikkei Personal Computing, OS/2 World Japan, SunWorld Japan, Windows NT World, Windows World Japan; **KENYA:** PC World East African; **KOREA:** Hi-Tech Information, Macworld Korea, PC World Korea; **MACEDONIA:** PC World Macedonia; **MALAYSIA:** Computerworld Malaysia, PC World Malaysia, Publish in Asia; **MALTA:** PC World Malta; **MEXICO:** Computerworld Mexico, PC World Mexico; **MYANMAR:** PC World Myanmar; **NETHERLANDS:** Computer! Totaal, LAN Internetworking Magazine, LAN World Buyers Guide, Macworld Netherlands, Net, WebWereld; **NEW ZEALAND:** Absolute Beginners Guide and Plain & Simple Series, Computer Buyer, Computer Industry Directory, Computerworld New Zealand, MTB, Network World, PC World New Zealand; **NICARAGUA:** PC World Centro America; **NORWAY:** Computerworld Norge, CW Rapport, Datamagasinet, Financial Rapport, Kursguide Norge, Macworld Norge, Multimediaworld Norge, PC World Ekspress Norge, PC World Nettverk, PC World Norge, PC World ProduktGuide Norge; **PAKISTAN:** Computerworld Pakistan; **PANAMA:** PC World Panama; **PEOPLE'S REPUBLIC OF CHINA:** China Computer Users, China Computerworld, China InfoWorld, China Telecom World Weekly, Computer & Communication, Electronic Design China, Electronics Today, Electronics Weekly, Game Software, PC World China, Popular Computer Week, Software Weekly, Software World, Telecom World; **PERU:** Computerworld Peru, PC World Profesional Peru, PC World SoHo Peru; **PHILIPPINES:** Click!, Computerworld Philippines, PC World Philippines, Publish in Asia; **POLAND:** Computerworld Poland, Computerworld Special Report Poland, Cyber, Macworld Poland, Networld Poland, PC World Komputer; **PORTUGAL:** Cerebro/PC World, Computerworld/Correio Informático, Dealer World Portugal, Mac*In/PC*In Portugal, Multimedia World; **PUERTO RICO:** PC World Puerto Rico; **ROMANIA:** Computerworld Romania, PC World Romania, Telecom Romania; **RUSSIA:** Computerworld Russia, Mir PK, Publish, Seti; **SINGAPORE:** Computerworld Singapore, PC World Singapore, Publish in Asia; **SLOVENIA:** Monitor; **SOUTH AFRICA:** Computing SA, Network World SA, Software World SA; **SPAIN:** Communicaciones World España, Computerworld España, Dealer World España, Macworld España, PC World España; **SRI LANKA:** Infolink PC World; **SWEDEN:** CAP&Design, Computer Sweden, Corporate Computing Sweden, Internetworld Sweden, it.branschen, Macworld Sweden, MaxiData Sweden, MikroDatorn, Nätverk & Kommunikation, PC World Sweden, PCaktiv, Windows World Sweden; **SWITZERLAND:** Computerworld Schweiz, Macworld Schweiz, PCtip; **TAIWAN:** Computerworld Taiwan, Macworld Taiwan, NEW ViSiON/Publish, PC World Taiwan, Windows World Taiwan; **THAILAND:** Publish in Asia, Thai Computerworld; **TURKEY:** Computerworld Turkiye, Macworld Turkiye, Network World Turkiye, PC World Turkiye; **UKRAINE:** Computerworld Kiev, Multimedia World Ukraine, PC World Ukraine; **UNITED KINGDOM:** Acorn User UK, Amiga Action UK, Amiga Computing UK, Apple Talk UK, Computing, Macworld, Parents and Computers UK, PC Advisor, PC Home, PSX Pro, The WEB; **UNITED STATES:** Cable in the Classroom, CIO Magazine, Computerworld, DOS World, Federal Computer Week, GamePro Magazine, InfoWorld, I-Way, Macworld, Network World, PC Games, PC World, Publish, Video Event, THE WEB Magazine, and WebMaster; online webzines: JavaWorld, NetscapeWorld, and SunWorld Online; **URUGUAY:** InfoWorld Uruguay; **VENEZUELA:** Computerworld Venezuela, PC World Venezuela; and **VIETNAM:** PC World Vietnam. 3/24/97

CREDITS

Senior Acquisitions Editor
John Osborn

Development Editors
Nancy Stevenson
Susan Pines

Copy Editors
Faithe Wempen
Kerrie Klein

Technical Editor
Sundar Rajan

Project Coordinator
Katy German

Graphics and Production Specialists
Mario F. Amador
Laura Carpenter
Ed Penslien
J. Christopher Pimentel
Andreas Schueller

Proofreader
Carrie O'Neill

Indexer
Elizabeth Cunningham

Cover Design
Jim Donohue
Peter Kowaleszyn
Deborah Mills
Eunice Ockerman

ABOUT THE AUTHOR

Elliotte Rusty Harold

Elliotte Rusty Harold is an internationally respected writer, programmer, and educator, both on and off the Internet. He got his start by writing FAQ lists for the Macintosh newsgroups on Usenet and has since branched out into books, Web sites, and newsletters. He's currently fascinated by Java, a preoccupation which is beginning to consume his life. He lectures about Java at Polytechnic University in Brooklyn, and his Cafe Au Lait Web site at http://sunsite.unc.edu/javafaq/ has become one of the most popular independent Java sites on the Internet.

Elliotte is originally from New Orleans, where he returns periodically in search of a decent bowl of gumbo. He currently resides in New York City's East Village with his wife Beth and cat Charm (named after the quark). When not writing about Java, he enjoys working on genealogy, mathematics, and quantum mechanics. His previous books are *The Java Developer's Resource* from Prentice Hall and *Java Network Programming* from O'Reilly & Associates.

To my parents.

PREFACE

*T*here are more than 100 books about Java on bookstore shelves today, and at least 90 of them are completely predictable and more or less interchangeable. It's as if they had all been written from the same outline but by different authors.

Each book begins with a chapter about what's special about Java and how it differs from other programming languages. Each book shows how to write Hello World and other command-line applications to teach Java's syntax. There is a chapter or two on object-oriented programming, a chapter on threads, a chapter on exceptions, and a few chapters on the AWT. I know. I wrote one of these books.

WHY *Java SECRETS?*

This book is different. It starts where the other books stop. This book assumes that you already know Java's syntax and what an object is. This book assumes that you're comfortable with the AWT. Instead of rehashing these topics, this book delves into the parts of Java that are not documented by Sun, that are not generally accessible to anyone with a Web browser, and that are not already in a hundred other books.

I had some reservations about writing this book. I still do. This book reveals cutting edge secrets: knowledge that can easily be abused. Improper use of the secrets revealed herein can easily tie Java programs to specific platforms or implementations. As a longtime Mac user, I know the agony of watching all the best software come out on Windows first and the Mac much later, if at all. I do not want to extend this trend to Java-based software.

Nonetheless, I have come to the conclusion that a book like this is necessary if Java is to move out of its niche of creating applets for Web pages and into the broader software development market. There are many applications for which Java is ideal, but which cannot be written without more information than Sun has chosen to reveal. These include stand-alone executable applications. HotJava and javac are stand alone applications, so it must be possible to write them, but until now, Sun has not revealed how. This book reveals that secret among others.

There are other reasons programmers want to know these details. Just as in the early days of DOS when you needed to use undocumented functions to load a program without executing it so you could write a debugger, so too will you need to use undocumented parts of Java if you're working on development or runtime environments.

However, rationalize though I might (and I'm quite good at rationalizing, I admit), the real reason this book is being written is that it seemed like a neat thing to do at the time. This is far and away the most exciting book I've ever written. The sheer number of "Aha!" experiences I've had while researching and writing it is phenomenal. I hope you'll get the same feeling while reading it. I know the information I present here will be misused. I accept that. Nonetheless, I firmly believe that in the long run, more knowledge is a good thing, dangerous though it may be; and that secrets are meant to be revealed.

What's in This Book?

There are three different ways a Java program can become dangerous. It can rely on the internal structure of Java objects; it can use classes it isn't supposed to know about; or it can be platform-specific. This book covers all three.

Part I: How Java Works

After a brief introduction, Part I begins with six chapters on Java internals. You learn how objects and primitive data types are laid out in memory, how arguments are passed to and values returned from methods, what a variable really is, and more. Java's implementation of arrays and strings will be explored. Different possible models for threads and algorithms for garbage collection are discussed and compared, shedding some light on why Java uses the data structures and algorithms it does and why it sometimes behaves in unexpected ways. This is all tied to the Java .class file format in Chapter 5, where you learn how to read and disassemble Java byte code. You also learn some details about Java's thread model and garbage collection algorithms.

Finally, you learn how an applet runs and what really happens when a Web browser loads an applet. This section is dangerous because none of it is guaranteed. Tomorrow, Sun could change Java's thread model from cooperative to preemptive or make strings null-terminated. Worse yet, Java might be implemented one way on one system and another way on another. Writing code that depends on implementation issues is always dangerous but sometimes necessary.

Nonetheless, it often helps to know what's going inside a class or method even if you don't explicitly use that information. For example, knowing whether the Vector class is implemented with a growable array or a linked list has a lot to do with whether you choose to use it in a program that performs thousands of insertions in the middle of a list. You can drive a car without knowing the first thing about carburetors or transmissions, but it certainly doesn't hurt to know about them, especially when things go wrong. Knowing what goes on the under the hood but ignoring it when it isn't relevant is a good technique for both programmers and drivers. Not knowing isn't.

Some may object that this goes against the philosophy of object-oriented programming. Objects are supposed to be black boxes into which data is sent and out of which a result flows. You aren't supposed to need to know what happens inside the box. However, objects aren't everything, and practical experience shows that time and time again, the black box doesn't do exactly what it's supposed to and you need to open it up and fix it. Part I opens up many black boxes to expose their inner workings.

Part II: The Sun Classes

Part II delves into the sun classes, a group of undocumented packages that add considerable power to Java programs. The following are just a few of the undocumented classes that will be covered in this section:

- More LayoutManagers
- Communicating with ftp, mail and news servers

- Data encoding and decoding
- Character set conversion
- Protocol and content handlers

As you can see, Sun has hidden a lot of functionality inside the Sun classes. This book reveals it.

Part II is full of classes that provide tremendous additional power. They may not even be present in Java implementations not written by Sun. If they are present, their public methods may not have the same signatures. Nonetheless, they provide too much additional power to be ignored, and there are some very simple techniques that allow one to use these packages safely in even non-conforming implementations.

Part III: Platform-Dependent Java

Part III explores the possibilities opened by platform-dependent code. It demonstrates how to call the native API and how to create stand-alone executable programs.

This part is dangerous because it limits the audience of a program. It's also dangerous because it violates many of the security restrictions normally imposed on Java programs. Nonetheless, not all programs are applets on Web pages. Many programs can benefit from taking advantage of native code, either for speed or to add additional functionality not present in the AWT. There are ways to use platform-dependent code to enhance your application without making your program inaccessible to users on all other platforms. This section will explore these possibilities.

Part IV: Appendixes

Part IV provides several appendixes to help supplement those skills you learn from Parts I through III. You can use these appendixes as handy references to relevant information as you learn. Included is an appendix that describes the contents of the accompanying CD-ROM.

Icons used in this book

You'll notice some special icons sprinkled throughout this book to draw your attention to the information at hand. The following briefly describes the use of these icons:

This icon identifies information that is particularly noteworthy or helpful.

This icon alerts you to information that, for one reason or another, is undocumented or is not common knowledge. This information can contain time-saving tricks and techniques or nifty facts that will enhance your understanding and learning of Java.

WHO YOU ARE

This is not an introductory book. It is for the programmer who has learned enough about Java to be frustrated by its limitations. You should have a solid grasp of the fundamentals of both the Java language and the AWT, including advanced topics like threads. Although every effort has been made to make this book accessible to as broad a range of readers as possible, this is not an introductory book and does require more of its reader than most books on the market.

On the other hand, this book does not assume prior experience with assembly language, Java byte code, compiler design, or even pointers. In fact, this book may serve as a first taste of some of these to a reader who's never seen them before, in Java or any other language. Nonetheless, low-level programmers who are familiar with pointers, assembly language and compiler design should find the discussion of Java's implementation of these topics to be useful. They'll simply find the book easier going than a programmer encountering these topics for the first time.

HOW TO USE THIS BOOK

As mentioned earlier, this book is broken into four main parts. I recommend that you begin by reading or at least skimming Part I more or less in its entirety. This section introduces many deep concepts you'll need later and that the rest of the book depends on. These include bit-shift operators, Unicode, the nature of strings, the virtual machine, the class file format, and Java byte code. These are the tools you'll need to understand the internals of Java. The remainder of the book (Chapters 6 through 20) can be read in pretty much any order that interests you. As a general rule, these chapters are pretty much independent of each other. While each chapter should probably be read from start to finish, the chapters themselves are mostly self-contained.

BUGS

This book is so far out on the bleeding edge, I've got a personal account rep at the New York Blood Bank. I've done my best to try to provide useful and accurate information. All the code in his book has been verified on at least one virtual machine (VM). Most of the code has been tested on two or more. However, because Java runs on so many different platforms and because it is changing in Internet time, it is impossible to be completely precise and accurate in all instances. Furthermore, precisely because the material in this book is secret, it's been extremely hard to verify.

Please use this information carefully and read it with a critical eye. If you do find mistakes or inaccuracies, let me know by sending e-mail to `elharo@sunsite.unc.edu`, and I'll correct them in future editions. I will also post corrections and updates on my Web site at `http://sunsite.unc.edu/javafaq/secrets/`, so you may wish to look there first before sending me e-mail. When you communicate with me about a problem you've found, please let me know the VM, version of Java, vendor, processor, and operating system you're testing with. By early 1997, there were already more than 100 slightly different virtual machines is use, so it's important to be as precise as possible.

Elliotte Rusty Harold
`elharo@sunsite.unc.edu`
`http://sunsite.unc.edu/javafaq/`

ACKNOWLEDGMENTS

Many people were involved in the production of this book. Andrew Schulman's *Undocumented DOS* and *Undocumented Windows* inspired me to write this book in the first place, and Andrew's comments on the early proposals and outlines were extremely helpful. My editors, John Osborn, Nancy Stevenson, Sundar Rajan, and Faithe Wempen, all provided important assistance at various stages of development. My agent, David Rogelberg, convinced me it was possible to make a living writing computer books instead of writing code in a cubicle. All these people deserve much thanks and credit. Finally, I'd like to save the largest thanks for my wife, Beth — without her support and assistance, this book would never have happened.

CONTENTS

PART III: PLATFORM-DEPENDENT JAVA 597

HOW JAVA WORKS

INTRODUCING JAVA *SECRETS*

*T*here are close to a hundred books about Java programming on bookstore shelves today, and at least 70 of them are completely predictable and more or less interchangeable. It's as if they had all been written from the same outline but by different authors. Each book begins with a chapter about what's special about Java and how it differs from other programming languages. Each book shows how to write Hello World and other character mode applications to teach Java's syntax. There is a chapter or two on object-oriented programming, a chapter on threads, a chapter on exceptions, and a few chapters on the AWT.

This book is different. It starts where the other books stop. This book assumes you already know Java's syntax and object-oriented programming basics. This book assumes that you're comfortable with the AWT. Instead of rehashing these topics, this book delves into the parts of Java that are not documented by Sun, that are not generally accessible to anyone with a Web browser, and that are not already covered in a hundred other books.

A Little Knowledge Can Be a Dangerous Thing

I had some reservations about writing this book. I still do. This is a dangerous book. It reveals knowledge that can easily be abused. Improper use of the secrets revealed herein can easily tie Java programs to specific platforms or implementations. As a longtime Mac user, I know the agony of watching all the best software come out on Windows first and the Mac much later, if at all. I do not want to extend this trend to Java-based software.

Nonetheless, I have come to the conclusion that a book like this is necessary if Java is to move out of its niche of creating applets for Web pages and into the broader software development market. There are many applications for which Java is ideal, but that cannot be written without more information than Sun has chosen to reveal. Among other things, this includes stand-alone executable applications. HotJava and javac are such applications, so it *must* be possible to write them, but until now Sun has not revealed how. This book reveals that secret, among others.

There are other reasons why programmers need to know these details. For example, a programmer writing development tools requires a much deeper understanding of Java's internals than does the average application developer. Programmers merely writing applets don't need to know exactly how and when the ScreenUpdater thread calls the various paint() and update() methods in different components and containers. A programmer adding applet support to a Web browser, however, absolutely has to understand this.

Rationalize though I might, however (and I'm quite good at rationalizing, I admit), the real reason why I am writing this book is that it seems like a neat thing to do. I know that the information I present here will be misused. I accept that. Nonetheless, I firmly believe that, in the long run, more knowledge is a good thing, dangerous though it may be, and that secrets are meant to be revealed.

What's in This Book?

There are three ways that a Java program can become dangerous. It can rely on the internal structure of Java objects; it can use classes that it isn't supposed to know about; or it can be platform-specific. This book covers all three.

Part I: How Java Works

After a brief introduction, Part I begins with seven chapters on Java internals. You will learn how objects and primitive data types are laid out in memory, how arguments are passed to and values returned from methods, what a variable really is, and more. Java's implementation of arrays and strings will be explored. I will discuss and compare different possible models for threads and algorithms for garbage collection, shedding some light on why Java uses the data structures and algorithms that it does and why it sometimes behaves in unexpected ways. You'll learn how a Web browser loads applets and what it needs to provide for them so that you can add applet support to your own programs. All of this is tied to the Java virtual machine and .class file format, so you'll learn how to read and disassemble Java byte code.

This section is dangerous because none of it is guaranteed. Tomorrow Sun could change Java's thread model from cooperative to preemptive or make strings null-terminated. Worse yet, it might be one way on one system and another way on another. (In fact, in the case of threading this is already true.) Writing code that depends on implementation issues is always dangerous but sometimes necessary. And it often helps to know what's going on inside a class or method even if you don't explicitly use that information. For example, knowing whether the Vector class is implemented with a growable array or a linked list influences whether or not you would use it in a program that will perform thousands of insertions in the middle of a list.

You can drive a car without knowing the first thing about carburetors or transmissions, but it certainly doesn't hurt to know about them, especially when things go wrong. Knowing what goes on under the hood, but ignoring it when it isn't relevant, is a good technique for both programmers and drivers; it is a very different technique from not knowing at all.

Some may object that this technique goes against the philosophy of object-oriented programming. Objects are supposed to be black boxes into which data is sent and out of which a result flows. You aren't supposed to need to know what happens inside the box. Objects aren't everything, however, and practical experience shows that sometimes the black box doesn't do exactly what it's supposed to, and you need to open it up and fix it. Part I opens up many black boxes to expose their inner workings.

Part II: The sun Classes

Part II delves into the sun packages, a group of undocumented classes that add considerable power to Java programs. The java packages provide the public API that most programmers use, but the sun packages work behind the scenes. Many of Sun's Java development tools, like javac and the appletviewer, are built from Sun classes. Furthermore, many of the public classes and interfaces in the JDK privately use the sun classes.

The following are just a few of the capabilities hidden inside the sun classes:

- Running applets
- Communicating with ftp, mail, Web and news servers
- Data encoding and decoding
- Playing audio files

As you can see, Sun has hidden a lot of functionality inside the sun packages. This book reveals it.

Part II is dangerous because these classes may not be present in future releases of Java. They may not even be present in Java implementations not written by Sun. Even if they *are* present, their public methods may not have the same signatures. Classes that are public in one version may have only package access in the future. They may even move from one package to another. Nonetheless, these classes provide too much additional power to be ignored, and there are some very simple techniques provided here that enable you to use these packages safely in even non-conforming implementations.

Part III: Platform-Dependent Java

Part III explores the possibilities opened by platform-dependent code. It demonstrates how to call the native API and how to create stand-alone executable programs that take advantage of unique abilities of the local platform.

This part is dangerous because it limits the audience of a program. It's also dangerous because it violates many of the security restrictions normally imposed on Java programs. Nonetheless, not all programs are applets on Web pages. Many programs can benefit from taking advantage of native code, either for speed or to add additional functionality not present in the AWT. There are ways to use platform-dependent code to enhance your application without making your program inaccessible to users on all other platforms. This section explores these possibilities.

WHY JAVA SECRETS?

Relying on implementation-specific details opens up the possibility that your programs may stop working when Sun revises Java. Using the sun packages means that not all Java environments may be able to run your programs. Using native code limits your audience, increases the time-to-market, and makes your program buggier. There are ways you can limit these bad effects, but they are real, and they must be considered. Given these problems, why would anyone want to learn about the material in this book? I can think of several reasons.

Broader applicability

In some cases, the design of Java limits you to a very small portion of the programs you might want to write. For example, the getAudioClip() and loop() methods of the Applet and AppletContext classes let your applets play sounds. Only applets can play sounds, however. In fact, it's a little worse than that. Only applets that run in a Web browser or an applet viewer can play sounds. Applet subclasses that you instantiate in main() or embed in your own programs cannot play sounds because they don't have an AppletContext.

Secret

There really isn't any good reason for restricting sound playing to applets. Applications of all sorts often need to play sounds. By using the sun.audio classes, you can play sounds in all your Java programs, not just your applets.

More power

Secret

The sun packages let you do things you just can't do otherwise. For example, suppose you wanted to build an IDE for Java development and actually use Java. To accomplish this, you need to compile files, debug them, and run them. All the hooks to do that are in the undocumented sun.tools package.

Inspiration

The sun classes are often a fertile source of ideas. Although many of the classes and packages are incomplete, they often provide a pattern on which you can model your own, more functional classes.

Secret

For example, the sun.net.nntp.NntpClient class lets you open groups, list the articles in the groups, request specific articles, and post new articles. That's useful, but some obvious methods are missing. There is no method to get a list of all the newsgroups on the server, for example. You can use the sun.net.nntp.NntpClient class as a model for your own NNTP class that does know how to get a list of all the available newsgroups and a lot more. Furthermore, your class can fix some of the bugs in Sun's NntpClient class.

Sometimes you can create your own classes by extending Sun's; sometimes you'll copy and paste; sometimes you'll write your own classes from scratch using a similar API. Whichever you choose, it's almost always easier to start with a good design and correct some minor deficiencies than it is to design a class from scratch.

Of course, not all of Sun's designs are good. Sometimes you can learn from the mistakes made in the sun classes so you don't repeat them. Not every class described in this book actually performs as advertised, and I'll be sure to tell you when that's so. One reason that some classes and packages are undocumented is that they're buggy, poorly designed, or incomplete. Learning from your mistakes is good. Learning from someone else's mistakes is even better. You can learn from Sun's mistakes.

WHERE DID THE SECRETS COME FROM?

Some people have asked how I discovered this information. To be perfectly honest, it really wasn't that hard. Sun has not gone to particularly great lengths to hide Java's internal structure from nosy eyes.

Where is the documentation?

Until this book, there have been three main sources for information about Java internals. The first source is alpha releases. Far more of Java's internals tend to be exposed and documented in alpha versions than in later releases.

Although many details have since changed, the HotJava 1.0a3 release provides a broad picture of many otherwise undocumented features that remain in Java 1.1. Alpha versions of other technologies like the Java Web Server (originally called Jeeves) and Remote Method Invocation (RMI) can be similarly useful.

While a technology is being developed, it's often completely open for inspection because Sun hasn't yet decided which parts to document and which to hold to themselves. Once the product is shipped, however, previously open classes can be closed off. This is one reason why the alpha versions of Java still reveal a great deal of information that is otherwise unavailable. Of course, as time passes, these alpha versions become a progressively less reliable guide to current technology, so any information garnered in this fashion must be verified and tested. Nonetheless, an alpha version is often a useful starting point.

The second source of information is the source code itself. The JDK includes source code for all the classes in the java packages. Furthermore, Sun freely licensed the full source code for Java 1.0 for non-commercial use, such as for education and personal edification. Regrettably, this commendable policy of openness has been rescinded with Java 1.1. Now, source code for the sun classes is available only to commercial licensees willing to shell out big money. Nonetheless, the available source code for the java packages and for Java 1.0 still reveals much that is not obvious from the official documentation.

The third source of information is first-hand communication with Sun's Java team. Regrettably, but necessarily, this access has so far been restricted mostly to Sun commercial licensees lsuch as Netscape and Symantec. It is not reliably available to the general public. However, many members of the Javasoft team do participate in various Java newsgroups and mailing lists and do post information that hasn't been revealed through more official channels. The Sun-sponsored mailing lists for unreleased products seem to be particularly fertile sources for direct interaction with Javasoft team members. Programmers are often more loquacious about their thoughts, ideas, and problems when they're still looking for a solution than they are once they've found it.

Although these are all useful things to avail yourself of, the average programmer should hardly be expected to use these informal and incomplete mechanisms as his or her sole source of information. This book is therefore designed to collect and organize much information that has been previously either inaccessible or inconvenient to come by for the vast majority of Java programmers.

The source code

Prior to Version 1.1, Sun made the source code for the Java Development Kit (JDK) fairly freely available. It was not difficult to get a source code license for personal or educational use. In addition, both Java 1.0 and 1.1 included the source code for the Java classes in the base distribution. However, full source code for the JDK 1.1 is now available only to Java's commercial licensees and a few, select others such as the Linux development team. Apparently the commercial licensees were more than a little peeved that Sun was giving away what they had paid substantial sums of money for, so Sun began restricting access to the source to make them happy. This policy may or may not be relaxed in the future.

Nonetheless, you should get a license to the source code for whatever version you can come by, even if it's a few releases out of date. Some classes have changed a great deal, but many are substantially unchanged since the early alphas.

The API documentation

The javadoc documentation generally covers only the public and protected members of a class. This is not enough, especially when you're trying to do things Java's designers didn't mean for you to do.

In particular, methods and fields that have default or package access may in fact be relevant to your classes. These are the members that do not have an access specifier; they are not declared as public, private, or protected. For example,

```
int value;
InputStream getData();
Vector tokenize();
```

There are probably more members with package access in the classes in the Java class library than there are members with protected and private access combined. Methods and fields with no access specifiers are accessible only from within the package in which they're declared.

In versions of Java before 1.1b3, although these package access members could be invoked only by other classes in the same package, subclasses in different packages could override these methods and fields. In these cases, another method in the package might call one of the overridden methods. The superclass's behavior could be affected by the change in the overridden method, so by overriding a package member, you could change how any method that used the member behaved. Sun eventually decided this was a bug and fixed it in Java 1.1b3. This behavior is still present in virtual machines based on Java 1.0, however, and there are times when this is the best option. For example, you see in Chapter 12 that creating new encoders and decoders requires you to override these package access methods. In fact, the class was designed under the assumption that you would do this. Now that this is no longer possible, you have to create new classes in the sun.misc package instead.

Why bring this up now? Because often the only way to ensure that your overriding method does not unexpectedly interfere with the proper workings of a class is to carefully inspect the source code. By looking at the source, you can see what a method is supposed to do and what will change if you make it do something else.

Furthermore, although applets are expressly prohibited from adding new classes to existing packages, applications are not. When you build a stand-alone application, you can build it in such a way that you add new classes to existing sun or java packages. You can even completely replace existing classes if you prefer to use one of your own devising. It's better to avoid this if you can, but there are times when you have no other choice. In Java 1.0, the only way to do a reverse lookup on an IP address (that is, to convert a dotted quad address like 204.178.32.1 into an Internet hostname like utopia.poly.edu) was to add a new package to the java.net package. You should try to avoid doing this if you can, but when you have to do it, you might as well do it right. The more you know about the internal workings of the classes with which you'll be interfacing, the less likely you are to unintentionally break something else.

The bug that required this hack is fixed in Java 1.1.

WHAT VERSIONS OF JAVA ARE COVERED?

You may rightly ask what versions of Java this book covers. The answer is "quite a few." Although the documented parts of Java are well defined with version numbers and release dates, the undocumented parts described here are much less clear.

Nonetheless, I've chosen to focus on Java roughly as found in Sun's JDK 1.1. I've chosen to focus on Sun's JDK because it is the most widely distributed implementation of Java, especially when all of the other Java environments derived from it are factored in. Netscape's Java virtual machine is based on Sun source code, for example. Even virtual machines that were written independently such as Roaster Technologies' Roaster VM for the MacOS use Sun's JDK class library with a few modifications.

I'm focusing on Version 1.1 because it's the most current version of Java at the time of this writing. Even though right now 1.0.2 VMs are built into most Java-aware browsers, the life span of Java software is considerably shorter than the life span of Java books. The only way to avoid getting drowned by the fast-moving Java tidal wave is to stay as close to the front of the wave as possible. I expect that by the time you're reading this, Java 1.1 will be in common use everywhere, and I hope that any further developments won't make too much of what's described here obsolete.

During the four months I spent writing this book, Sun's Java JDK went through three beta releases and two release versions (1.0.2, 1.1b1, 1.1b2, 1.1b3, and 1.1), and this doesn't even count any of the many releases by third parties. This has given me some practical experience at gauging what is and what is not likely to change. Surprisingly, I've discovered that the undocumented parts of Java change far more slowly than the documented parts.

Between 1.0.2 and 1.1, the .class file format and the virtual machine barely changed at all. The sun packages were expanded and some bugs were fixed, but very few classes were deleted or changed in incompatible ways. To the best of my knowledge, nothing in the sun classes was marked as deprecated, compared to many extremely common methods like action() and readLine() in the java packages. In fact, some of the sun classes appear to have been unchanged, aside from recompilations, since the 1.0 pre-beta. They probably would have lasted even longer had not changes to the language specification between alpha and beta broken more or less all of the existing source code. It does not appear that anybody is actively working on many of these classes. It therefore seems unlikely that they'll change suddenly and unexpectedly.

SOME OBJECTIONS

Even the idea of *Java SECRETS* disturbs some people. Java is not supposed to need a book of secrets. It is supposed to be a truly open system that anyone can implement from freely available, well-documented specifications. It is supposed to provide everything a programmer needs. This is only partially true, however.

Java is supposed to be platform independent

If I had to pick one issue in this book that I think is most controversial, it would be platform-dependent applications. From what I read on the newsgroups and in the press, I think that many programmers agree with me. As you'll see in Part III, I myself am quite torn about the whole idea.

Much of this concern is misguided, however. If Java is to fulfill its promise as a full-powered environment for developing applications, then it cannot be hobbled by requirements that are intended for applets on Web pages. Only by taking advantage of undocumented packages and the native API can Java programmers level the playing field with their C and C++ counterparts and produce commercial-quality applications.

The advent of Java-based network computers only extends the problem. On a network computer, anything you want to do must be done in Java. You cannot drop out to a native method in C. Therefore it is even more important to have full access to all the capabilities of Java.

What went wrong? What happened to the dream of applets moving transparently and easily between platforms? The answer is that Java succeeded. In fact, it succeeded wildly, much faster and far beyond the expectations of its designers. What was a simple language for consumer electronics has become the most rapidly adopted programming language in history. It is being used for applets on Web pages, for database front ends, for numerical analysis, for multi-player networked games, and for much, much more. It is no wonder that many of these programmers need capabilities and knowledge that were not originally planned for Java.

Why aren't these things documented?

A question may occur to the inquiring mind: If these classes and methods aren't documented, is there perhaps a good reason for that? Maybe these are things human beings were not meant to know.

Poppycock. Given the relatively few people working on Java, especially in its early days, combined with the large size of the API, it's surprising that there aren't *more* undocumented features. Indeed, there are many methods in the allegedly documented Java packages that literally qualify as undocumented by virtue of their poor documentation, but they are not discussed in this book.

There are four main reasons that certain parts of Java were left undocumented. The first and the most important for Java programmers to remember is that not all implementations of Java can be guaranteed to support these features. What works in Netscape may not work in Internet Explorer. Even more likely, what works in the appletviewer or HotJava may not work in Netscape. This is sometimes a problem for applets, but it is a fully surmountable problem for applications.

The second common reason why a Java class is undocumented is that the source code is in rather poor shape. Many parts of Java are held together by bubble gum and bailing wire. Java is full of quick fixes to unexpected problems pieced together by overworked programmers with insufficient resources. The Java team was simply not prepared for the stunning success of Java, and Javasoft has been desperately trying to catch up to itself. There simply hasn't been enough time to whip the source code into shape while simultaneously fixing bugs, writing documentation, negotiating licensing agreements, adding features, and planning for the future. Some classes that were undocumented in Java 1.0, such as sun.net.MulticastSocket, became documented in Java 1.1, just as soon as Javasoft had time to do it. This code is nonetheless useful now, and it is available to you even if it's not documented.

The third and related reason why these features are undocumented is the fear that making them public hinders future modifications. In many cases, JavaSoft may clean up the messy classes and quick fixes in the future and document them. Until then, however, they would rather not get tied to their original ad hoc solutions that were never properly thought out. It is believed that Java is in a much too early state of development to be locked into a half-baked API. This is almost certainly true. Java's original event model was completely revised between Java 1.0 and Java 1.1. However, because the 1.0 model was documented and in widespread use, Sun was forced to continue to support it. Sun would rather limit the number of APIs locked into to the bare minimum until they feel more confident that they've made the right decisions. This attitude places the focus on what may happen in the future rather than on what is shipping today. At the speed at which the Web moves (One calendar month equals one Web year), programmers need solutions today, not next month or next year.

According to Sun (`http://java.sun.com/products/JDK/1.1/ compatibility.html` [as of January 14, 1997]), when discussing the changes from Java 1.0 to Java 1.1:

> Some APIs in the sun.* packages have changed. These APIs are not intended
> to be used directly by developers. They are there to support the java.*
> packages. Developers importing from sun.* do so entirely at their own risk.

The fourth and final reason that the topics of this book aren't properly documented is the mistaken belief that Java programmers simply don't need to know. This confuses the issue of "need to know" with "need to use." These are two different things. A deeper understanding of how Java operates leads only to more efficient programs. You don't absolutely have to know exactly how a Web browser loads and instantiates an applet on a Web page to write applets, but if you do understand this, you'll be able to write applets that play more smoothly and load more quickly. You won't actually call any of the undocumented methods and classes in your own source code, but by knowing how they operate behind the scenes, you can map your use of the documented methods to work with them instead of against them.

Finally, both what programmers need to know and what programmers need to use are closely tied to the sorts of applications that programmers are building. What Javasoft has chosen to document so far assumes that programmers are building simple applets for Netscape. In reality, this is a plurality but still a minority of the programs that people are actually writing. Many other things that people are writing, especially development tools, need much more information than is required by a simple applet.

FUD (fear, uncertainty, and doubt)

There is a certain amount of fear, uncertainty, and doubt about using undocumented Java classes. Is it safe? To borrow terminology from AIDS educators, there's no such thing as safe or unsafe Java. All Java programs are safe or less safe with varying degrees of safety. Naturally you should always strive to have safer Java.

First of all, remember that Java has more built-in safeguards than almost any other language. A Java program is not going to work today and crash your system tomorrow. Further, as long as users don't change their Java environments, the programs that run today should still run tomorrow.

Java will change. Methods that work today may not be present in future releases. Worse yet, they may be changed in future releases. Early adopters have already been through several gut-wrenching transitions — worst of all the transition from alpha to beta — and they survived. Time simply needs to be allotted for code to be rewritten.

There are many ways to guard against these problems. Java's robust exception-handling mechanism provides an easy means to deal with classes or methods that unexpectedly disappear between versions of Java. Code from the sun classes can be copied into your own package or placed on your server so that it's guaranteed to be available to an applet. Native methods can be backed up by Java-only alternatives that are invoked if the native methods can't be found. Versions can be checked to make sure an application is running in a known environment.

However, that's all in the future. Today, the programs that you write with the Sun classes and native code are safe. You should of course try to use garden-variety, safe Java whenever possible, but don't *not* write the next killer application simply because it requires you to use a native method or to instantiate a sun class.

How secret is this, anyway?

Some people have questioned whether the title *Java SECRETS* is truly appropriate for this book. Certainly a lot of the material here is less secret than the internals of Microsoft Windows. Sun licenses the source code very freely (at least the code prior to Java 1.1), and, as you'll learn, the byte code is comparatively trivial to disassemble.

Source code may be a precise form of documentation, but it is hardly the easiest form to understand. Java source code has been available since the earliest days, but it's still left many people confused about exactly how to accomplish their goals. The content of this book may not exactly be secret, but it certainly contains information that is not widely known. Frankly, given the quality of information about these topics that is available, many of them might as well be secret. I expect this book to generate a phenomenal level of interest among Java programmers, most of whom have only a vague idea that this sort of programming is possible in Java, much less the knowledge to do it.

SUMMARY

In this chapter, you learn about the following:

- A deeper understanding of how the Java runtime operates helps you write better programs, even if you don't use that knowledge explicitly in your source code.

- The sun packages are a group of classes included in Sun's JDK and many other Java implementations that provide extra capabilities to Java programs. They also support much of the Java infrastructure that applet programmers don't always need to think about.

- Native methods may not be pleasant, but they are often necessary. If you want to write classic, stand-alone applications in Java that can compete with applications written in C and C++ in both speed and features, you will need to use native methods.

- The techniques described in this book are powerful tools, but they are also more than a little dangerous. Using them naïvely can and will produce unintended consequences. But with proper forethought and planning, you can prepare for these problems and avoid them.

PRIMITIVE DATA TYPES

2

*T*he Java virtual machine defines eight primitive data types: five integer types, two floating-point types, and one boolean type. The types are byte, short, int, long, float, double, char, and boolean. This chapter explores how these different primitive types are stored in memory and used in calculations. You'll learn how one can be converted to another and what can go wrong in this conversion. You'll also learn how to use the bit-level operators to reach down to the lowest level of the virtual machine and to change what you find there.

BYTES IN MEMORY

All data in Java (or any digital computer) must be represented as a particular sequence of bits in the computer's memory. A bit is an abstract quantity that can have exactly two values. These two values are commonly called 0 and 1. However, as you'll see shortly, these are not the same as the numbers zero and one.

At the very low level of electronic circuits, a transistor that is charged to a particular value — generally 5.0 or 3.3 volts relative to ground — is said to be *on* and to have the value "one." A transistor that is uncharged — at the value of 0.0

volts relative to ground — is said to be *off* and have the value "zero." However, when you consider matters at this low a level, the real world is analog, not digital. It is possible for transistors to have voltages of 2.5 volts, 1.2 volts, -3.4 volts, or just about any other value you can imagine. Most digital electronic circuits have some tolerance so that a transistor that's on at 3.3 volts will still be on at 3.2 volts. Past that tolerance, however, the transistor is said to be *three-stating*. This is a problem for the electrical engineers that design integrated circuits, but it shouldn't be a problem for a software engineer. If your computer starts three-stating when it isn't supposed to, send it back to the shop to be replaced.

Modern computers, including the Java virtual machine, organize bits into groups of eight called *bytes*. A group of eight bits is also sometimes referred to as an *octet*. The single byte is normally the lowest level at which you can interact with a computer's memory. You always work with at least eight bits at a time. Bits are like hot dog buns. You can't go to a grocery store and buy one hot dog bun or 13 hot dog buns. Because hot dog buns come in packs of 8, you can get 8, 16, 24, or any other multiple of 8, but not any number of buns that isn't a multiple of 8. There is no keyword or operator in Java that enables you to read from or write to one bit of memory at a time. You have to work with at least seven more bits adjacent to the bit you're interested in at the same time, even if you aren't doing anything to those bits.

This wasn't always the case. Some early computers used 12-bit words. However, these computers have long since become extinct.

Although you can buy as few as eight hot dog buns at a time, it's sometimes cheaper to buy them by the case. The case size often depends on where you buy them. At the corner convenience mart, 32 hot dog buns probably cost you four times as much as eight hot dog buns. However, at Benny's Super Discount Warehouse Store, buns may be cheaper by the gross. Similarly, different computers pack different numbers of bytes into a *word*. Computers based on the Intel 8088 chip use 8-bit, 1-byte words. Computers based on the 286 architecture, however, use 16-bit words and can therefore move data around at (very roughly) twice the speed of an 8088 computer at the same clock rate. Most modern CPUs use 32-bit words. The 32-bit processors include the 80386, 80486, Pentium, Pentium Pro, Sparc, PowerPC 601, PowerPC 603, and PowerPC 604 CPUs. Some 64-bit processors are just starting to appear, including Digital's Alpha line, Sun's UltraSparc chip, and the forthcoming HP/Intel Merced. All of these chips can still run old 8-bit or 16-bit software, but they run faster and more efficiently with software that moves data around in words that match the native size of the processor.

So which is Java? 8-bit? 16-bit? 32-bit? In fact, it's really none of the above. Because Java uses only a virtual machine, it needs to be able to run on any and all of the mentioned architectures without being tied to a particular word size. In one sense, you can argue that the Java virtual machine is an 8-bit machine because each instruction is exactly one byte long. However, the native integer data type for Java is 32-bit, so in that respect, Java is a 32-bit computer. The interpreter or JIT will likely convert the Java instructions and data into whichever format is appropriate for the machine on which it's running.

VARIABLES, VALUES, AND IDENTIFIERS

Variables, values, and identifiers are closely related to each other. In common use, the three words are used interchangeably. However, each word does have a slightly different meaning, and when you discuss computers at the CPU or virtual machine level, these differences become important.

Consider this Java statement:

```
int j = 2;
```

The letter "j" is an *identifier*. It identifies a variable in Java source code. The identifier, however, does not appear in the compiled byte code. It is a mnemonic device to make programmers' lives easier. The number 2 is the *value* of the variable. To be more precise, the bit pattern 00000000000-00000000000000000010 is the value of the variable. The four bytes of memory where this pattern is stored are the variable.

A *variable* is a particular group of bytes in the computer's memory. The value of a variable is the bit pattern stored in those bytes that make up the variable. How the bit pattern is interpreted depends on the type of the variable. The rest of this chapter discusses the interpretation of the bit patterns that make up different primitive data types.

You can change the value of a variable by adjusting the bits that live in those bytes. This does not make it a new variable. Conversely, two different variables can have the same value.

An identifier is a name for a particular group of bytes in memory. Some programming languages allow a single variable to have more than one name. However, Java does not. In a Java program, an identifier always points to a particular area of memory. Once an identifier has been created, there is no way to change where it points.

> **Note** This may sound a little strange to experienced Java programmers. In particular, you may think that this is true for primitive data types like int but not for object types like String. In fact, this is true for *all* Java data types. You'll have to wait till the next chapter to see why.

PLACE-VALUE NUMBER SYSTEMS

The bits in memory aren't just random voltages. They have meanings, and the meanings depend on the context. In one context, the bit sequence 0000000000100001 means the letter "A." In another context, it means the number 65. Let's explore how you get the number 65 out of the bits 0000000000100001.

When you write a number like 1406 in decimal notation, what you really mean is one thousand, four hundreds, no tens, and six ones. This may seem trivially obvious to you. After all, you've had this system drilled into you since early childhood. However, the place-value number system in which there are exactly ten digits and numbers larger than nine are represented by moving the digits further to the left is far from obvious. It took humanity most of its existence on this planet to develop this form of counting, and it didn't become widespread, even in Eurasia, until well into the second millennium. It's even less obvious that the digits on the left represent bigger numbers than the digits on the right. You could just as easily write the number as 6041 with the understanding that the first place is the ones place, the second place the tens place, the third place the hundreds, and so on.

> **Note** Classical Hebrew writes numbers from right to left. However, it doesn't use a place-value system.

Binary notation

The number 0000000000100001 that you saw in the preceding section is written in a place-value system based on powers of two called *binary notation*. Each place is a power of two, not of ten, and there are only two digits — 0 and 1. Moving from right to left, therefore, we have one one, zero twos, zero fours, zero eights, zero sixteens, zero thirty-twos, and one sixty-four. Therefore, 0000000000100001 is equal to 64 + 1, or 65, in decimal notation.

There are extra zeroes on the left side because Java uses bits only in groups of eight at a time, although the individual bits do have meaning. Furthermore, as you'll see below, characters like A are always 16 bits wide. You could use 0100001 to represent the value 65, but unlike 0000000010-0001, it would not also mean the letter A.

Java has several methods to convert between binary and decimal notation. The Integer and Long classes each have a static toBinaryString() method which converts ints and longs respectively to binary strings of ones and zeroes. For example, to print the int value 65 as a binary string, you could write

```
System.out.println(Integer.toBinaryString(65));
```

Longs are converted similarly:

```
System.out.println(Long.toBinaryString(5000000000L));
```

The Byte and Short classes do not have toBinaryString() methods, but bytes and shorts can be converted using the Integer.toBinaryString() method.

Given a binary string of ones and zeroes, the Byte, Short, Integer, and Long classes each have static valueOf() and parse methods that convert binary strings into integers of the specified width.

The Byte.parseByte(String s), Short.parseShort(String s), Integer.parseInt(String s), and Long.parseLong(String s) methods convert a string like "28" into a byte, short, int, or long value respectively. These methods presume that the string is written in base 10. However, you can change the base that's used to make the conversion by passing an additional int containing the base to the method, like this:

```
int m = Integer.parseInt("100001", 2);
```

To convert the binary string 00000000100001 into byte, short, int, and long values of 65, you would write

```
byte b = Byte.parseByte("0100001", 2);
short s = Short.parseShort("00000000100001", 2);
int i = Integer.parseInt("00000000100001", 2);
long l = Long.parseLong("00000000100001", 2);
```

If the string does not have the form appropriate for the base you specify in the second argument (for example, if you try to convert the string "97" in base 2), then a NumberFormatException will be thrown.

The static valueOf() methods in the Byte, Short, Integer, and Long classes are very similar except that they return objects of the type-wrapper classes rather than primitive data types. For example:

```
Byte B = Byte.valueOf("0100001", 2);
Short S = Short.valueOf("00000000100001", 2);
Integer I = Integer.valueOf("00000000100001", 2);
Long L = Long.valueOf("00000000100001", 2);
```

Hexadecimal notation

One reason why humans use a system with ten digits instead of one with two digits is that it's quite hard to read numbers like 00000000100001. Converting between binary and decimal notation requires substantial arithmetic, but converting between binary and hexadecimal notation can be done with the much faster table-lookup approach.

Counting on Our Fingers

Undoubtedly, the main reason humans use decimal notation instead of binary notation is that we have ten fingers on our hands. Indeed that's why the word *digit* is used to refer to both the characters between 0 and 9 and our fingers and toes. Humans use both things to count with. Doubtless if we ever encounter a sentient alien race, their number system will be based on the number of fleshy protuberances they count with.

However, not all human societies have used decimal notation. The Mayans used a system with twenty digits, and the Babylonians had an unbelievable 60 different digits, although only two symbols were used to form each of the 60 digits in a predictable way.

Hexadecimal notation uses 16 digits and a place-value system based on powers of 16. As well as the customary 0 through 9, there are also A (10), B (11), C (12), D (13), E (14), and F (15). These extra digits are normally written using uppercase letters, but the lowercase a, b, c, d, e, and f are sometimes used instead. Thus in hexadecimal notation, 65 is written as 41; that is, four times 16 plus one times 1. The hexadecimal number E3 is decimal 227; 14 times 16 plus 3.

There are always exactly four bits in one hexadecimal digit, so binary 0000 is always hex 0, binary 1000 is always hex 8, and binary 1111 is always hex F. This is in contrast to decimal notation, where the digits 0 through 7 can be encoded in three bits but the digits 8 and 9 require four bits. If you do use four bits for each decimal digit, you also have six 4-bit patterns that don't correspond to a digit. Table 2-1 lists the binary equivalents of the 16 hexadecimal digits. You can convert a number from binary to hexadecimal and vice versa by simple substitution of bit patterns according to this table. Conversion to decimal requires quite a bit more effort.

Table 2-1

Hexadecimal digit binary bit patterns

4-bit binary pattern	Hexadecimal digit
0000	0
0001	1
0010	2
0011	3
0100	4
0101	5
0110	6
0111	7
1000	8
1001	9
1010	A
1011	B
1100	C
1101	D
1110	E
1111	F

There's one more advantage to a hexadecimal number system: Two hexadecimal digits equal one byte. Any single-byte value can be written as exactly two hexadecimal digits, and any pair of hexadecimal digits is exactly one byte. Therefore, hexadecimal digits are often used to represent the state of a computer's memory in a compact and relatively easy-to-read fashion. Disk editors can display the contents of hard drives as sequences of hexadecimal numbers. And, as you soon learn, you can read and write Java .class byte code files by treating them as sequences of hexadecimal numbers.

Hexadecimal digits are so useful in computer programming that Java even lets you write integer literals as hexadecimal digits. To use a hexadecimal literal instead of a decimal literal, prefix it with 0x or 0X. Java does not care whether you use small letters or capital letters in your hexadecimal literals. For example, the following five lines of code each say the same thing:

```
int n = 227;
int n = 0xE3;
int n = 0xe3;
int n = 0Xe3;
int n = 0XE3;
```

When using hexadecimal numbers, most programmers choose the form 0xE3 with a small x and capital hex digits. This is slightly easier to read and understand than the other three forms.

Java has several methods to convert between decimal and hexadecimal notation. The Integer and Long classes each have a static toHexString() method that converts ints and longs respectively to hexadecimal strings. For example, to print the int value 1024 as a hexadecimal string, you could write

```
System.out.println(Integer.toHexString(1024));
```

Longs are converted similarly:

```
System.out.println(Long.toHexString(5000000000L));
```

Secret

The Byte and Short classes do not have toHexString() methods, but bytes and shorts can be converted using the Integer.toHexString() method.

You can convert a hexadecimal string to a numeric value using the parse and valueOf() methods described in the last section. Just pass 16 as the base argument instead of 2. For example:

```
byte b = Byte.parseByte("3F", 16);
short s = Short.parseShort("78A2", 16);
int i = Integer.parseInt("90087FA2", 16);
long l = Long.parseLong("02087FA290087FA2", 16);
Byte B = Byte.valueOf("3F", 16);
Short S = Short.valueOf("78A2", 16);
Integer I = Integer.valueOf("90087FA2", 16);
Long L = Long.valueOf("02087FA290087FA2", 16);
```

Octal notation

Java also allows the use of a base-eight notation with eight digits called *octal notation*. An octal digit can be represented in three bits. For example, 011 is octal 3. Table 2-2 lists all the octal digits and their equivalent binary patterns. Notice that this is the same as the first eight rows of Table 2-1 with the initial zero removed from each bit pattern.

Table 2-2
Octal digit binary bit patterns

3-bit binary pattern	Octal digit
000	0
001	1
010	2
011	3
100	4
101	5
110	6
111	7

Although the words *octal* and *base eight* sound like they should be closely related to the eight bits in a byte, in reality they're not. You cannot write a byte value as a certain number of octal digits because the three bits in an octal digit do not evenly divide the eight bits in a byte. Therefore, octal numbers aren't nearly as useful in practice as hexadecimal numbers. Their presence in Java is a holdover from their presence in C. Octal numbers were included in C because they are quite useful on machines with 12-bit words. The three bits in an octal number divide evenly into 12 bits, and computers with 12-bit words were still being used when C was created.

To use an octal literal in Java code, just prefix it with a leading 0. For example, to set n to decimal 227, you could write

```
int n = 0343;
```

I can think of no reason why you might want to do this. If you do this, please write and tell me why.

Java has several methods to convert between decimal and octal notation. The Integer and Long classes each have a static toOctalString() method which converts ints and longs respectively to octal strings. For example, to print the int value 1024 as an octal string, you could write

```
System.out.println(Integer.toOctalString(1024));
```

Longs are converted similarly:

```
System.out.println(Long.toOctalString(5000000000L));
```

Secret

The Byte and Short classes do not have toOctalString() methods, but bytes and shorts can be converted using the Integer.toOctalString() method.

You can convert an octal string to a numeric value using the parse and valueOf() methods described in the last section. Just pass 8 as the base argument instead. For example:

```
byte b = Byte.parseByte("30", 8);
short s = Short.parseShort("7002", 8);
int i = Integer.parseInt("30047132", 8);
long l = Long.parseLong("0108755260027112", 8);
Byte B = Byte.valueOf("30", 8);
Short S = Short.valueOf("7002", 8);
Integer I = Integer.valueOf("30047132", 8);
Long L = Long.valueOf("0108755260027112", 8);
```

INTEGERS

An integer is a mathematical concept that describes a whole number. One, two, zero, 72, -1,324, and 768,542,188,963,243,888 are all examples of integers. There's no limit to the size of an integer. An integer can be as large or as small as it needs to be, although it must always be a whole number like seven and never a fraction like seven and a half.

Java's integer data types map pretty closely to the mathematical ideal, with the single exception that they're all of finite magnitude. The four integer types — byte, short, int, and long — differ in the size of the numbers they can hold, but they all hold only a finite number of different integers. Most of the time this is enough.

ints

In Java, an int is composed of four bytes of memory — that is, 32 bits. Written in binary notation, an integer looks like

```
01001101000000001110010101010001101
```

In hexadecimal notation, this same number is

```
8D01BA8D
```

Each of the rightmost 31 places is a place value. The rightmost place is the one's place, the second from the right is the two's place, the third from the right is the four's, the fourth from the right is the eight's, and so on, up to the 31st place from the left, which is the 1,073,741,824's place.

The largest possible int in Java has all bits set to one except the leftmost bit. In other words, it is 01111111111111111111111111111111, or, in decimal, 2,147,483,647.

You're probably thinking that we could set the leftmost bit to one, and then have 11111111111111111111111111111111 as the largest number, but the leftmost bit in an int isn't used for place value. It's used to indicate the sign of the number and is called the *sign bit*. If the leftmost bit is one, then the int is a negative number. Therefore, 11111111111111111111111111111111 is not 4,294,967,295 but rather -1.

Java, like most modern computers, uses two's complement binary numbers. In a two's complement scheme, to reverse the sign of a number, you first take its complement — that is, convert all the ones to zeroes and all the zeroes to ones — and then add one. For example, to convert the byte value 0100001 (decimal 65) to -65, you would follow these steps:

65:	0100001
65 complement:	1011110
Add 1:	+0000001
-65:	1011111

Here I've worked with 8-bit numbers instead of the full 32-bit ints used by Java. The principle is the same regardless of the number of bits in the number.

To change a negative number into a positive number, do exactly the same thing. For example:

-65:	1011111
-65 complement:	0100000
Add 1:	+0000001
65:	0100001

One of the advantages of two's complement numbers is that the procedure reverses itself. You don't need separate circuits to convert a negative number to a positive one.

Computer integers differ from the mathematical ideal in that they have maximum and minimum sizes. The largest positive integer has a zero bit on the left side and all remaining bits set to one — that is, 0111111111111111-111111111111111, or 2,147,483,647 in decimal. If you try to add one to this number as shown here, the one carries all the way over into the leftmost digit. In other words, you get 10000000000000000000000000000000, which is the smallest negative int in Java, decimal -2,147,483,648.

```
  0111111111111111111111111111111
+ 0000000000000000000000000000001
  ————————————————————————————————
  1000000000000000000000000000000
```

Further addition will make the negative number count back up to zero and then into the positive numbers. In other words, if you count high enough, eventually you wrap around to very small numbers. The next int after 2,147,483,647 isn't 2,147,483,648. It's -2,147,483,648. If you need to count higher than 2,147,483,647 or lower than -2,147,483,648, then you need to use a long or a floating-point number, as I discuss in the next sections. These numbers have maximums and minimums of their own; they're just larger ones.

Long, short, and byte

So far we've worked with 32-bit ints. Java provides three other integer data types: byte, short, and long. These have different bit-widths, and they're not as easy to use as literals in Java source code, but their analysis is exactly the same as that of ints.

One's Complement

Some early computers used one's complement arithmetic instead. In one's complement, you invert all the bits to change the sign of a number, as you do in two's complement, but you don't add 1. Thus, since 65 is 0100001 and -65 is 1011110. This seems simpler. However, you encounter a problem with zero. Zero itself is 00000000. Negative zero is 11111111. But negative zero is supposed to be the same as positive zero.

Adding one to 11111111, as you do in two's complement, flips all the bits back to 0 as the one carries across to the left and disappears. In two's complement notation, therefore, 0 and -0 have the same bit pattern. This advantage has led to the triumph of two's complement computers in the marketplace. One's complement computers died off even before 12-bit word machines did.

A byte is eight bits wide. The largest byte is 01111111, or 127 in decimal. The smallest byte is 10000000, or -128 in decimal. Bytes are the lowest common denominator for data interchange between different computers, and Java uses them extensively in input and output. However, it does not use byte values in arithmetic calculations or as literals. The Java compiler won't even let you write code like the following:

```
byte b3 = b1 + b2;
```

If you try this, where b1 and b2 are byte variables, you'll get an error message that says `Error: Incompatible type for =. Explicit cast needed to convert int to byte.` This is because the Java compiler converts bytes to ints before doing the calculation. It does not add b1 and b2 as bytes, but rather as ints. The result it produces and tries to assign to b3 is also an int.

Shorts are 16 bits wide. The largest short is 0111111111111111, or 32,767 in decimal. The smallest short is 1000000000000000, or -32,768 in decimal. There is no way to use a short as a literal or in arithmetic. As with bytes, if you write code like

```
short s3 = 454 + -732;
```

you'll get an error message that says: `Error: Incompatible type for =. Explicit cast needed to convert int to short.` The Java compiler converts all shorts to ints before doing the calculation. The only time shorts are actually used in Java is when you're reading or writing data that is interchanged with programs written in other languages on platforms that use 16-bit integers. For example, some old 680X0 Macintosh C compilers use 16-bit integers as the native int format. Shorts are also used when very many of them need to be stored and space is at a premium (either in memory or on disk).

The final Java integer data type is the long. A long is 64 bits wide and can represent integers between -9,223,372,036,854,775,808 and 9,223,372,036,854,775,807. Unlike shorts and bytes, longs are directly used in Java literals and arithmetic. To indicate that a number is a long, just suffix it with the letter L — for example, 2147483856L or -76L. Like other integers, longs can be written as hexadecimal and octal literals — for example, 0xCAFEBABEL or 0714L.

You can use either a small l or a capital L to indicate a long literal. However, a capital L is strongly preferred because the lowercase l is easily confused with the numeral 1 in most typefaces.

Note

FLOATING-POINT NUMBERS

Integers aren't the only kind of number you need. Java also provides support for rational numbers — numbers with a decimal point like 106.53 or -78.0987. For reasons you'll learn shortly, these are called *floating-point numbers*, and Java has two primitive data types for them: the float and the double.

Floating-point literals can be made quite large or quite small by writing them in exponential notation — for example, 1.0E89 or -0.7E-32. The first is 1.0×10^{89}, in other words 1 followed by 89 zeroes. The second is -0.7×10^{-32} or -0.000000000000000000000000000000007.

A floating-point number can be split into three parts: the sign, the mantissa, and the exponent. The *sign* tells you whether the number is positive or negative. The *mantissa* tells you how precise the number is. Generally, the more digits a number has, the more precise it is. Finally the *exponent* tells you how large or small the number is. In the number 0.7E-32, the sign is -, the mantissa is 7, and the exponent is -32. In 1.0E89, the sign is +, the mantissa is 1, and the exponent is 89.

Although Java does not put any particular limits on the number of digits a float or double literal can have before the decimal point, it is customary to place exactly one non-zero digit before the decimal point and all the rest after it and adjust the exponent to compensate. Thus, instead of writing 15.4×10^{89}, you would write 1.54×10^{90}. This is called *scientific notation*. An alternative custom called *exponential notation* places the first non-zero digit immediately following the decimal point. In exponential notation, 15.4×10^{89} becomes 0.154×10^{91}.

The advantage to such a custom is that you no longer actually have to write the decimal point. If you know that the decimal point is always going to be immediately after the first non-zero digit, as it is in scientific notation, then why bother writing it down? Of course, not writing it makes it harder for human beings to read and understand the number, so the decimal point is required in Java source code. Computers can do quite well without an explicit decimal point as long as the byte code sticks to a form of scientific notation.

Once we've agreed that floating-point numbers will always be written in scientific notation, the mantissa, exponent, and sign of a floating-point number can all be written as integers. Just like the sign bit in integer data types, 1 represents a positive number and 0 represents a negative number. For example, 15.4 has sign 1, mantissa 154, and exponent 1. The number -0.7×10^{-32} has sign 0, mantissa 7, and exponent -32.

Representing floating-point numbers in binary code

To represent a floating-point number in a computer, you must convert each of these values into bits and binary notation. Converting a number with a decimal point into binary notation is only slightly harder than converting a number without a decimal point. When you write the number 10.5, you mean one ten, no ones, and five tenths. In binary notation you use a binary point rather than a decimal point (though they look exactly the same on the printed page.) Thus, a real number in binary notation looks like 1010.1. This means a number with one eight, no fours, one two, no ones, and one half. In other words, this is $8 + 2 + 0.5 = 10.5$ in decimal notation.

Binary floating-point numbers in Java are written in *normalized form*. This means that the leftmost one is shifted to the immediate right of the binary point. An exponent is then added as a power of two. Thus 1010.1 becomes 0.10101×10^{100} (where 10^{100} is 2^4 in decimal). The sign is 1, the mantissa is 10101, and the exponent is 100.

But wait! It gets better. When you're using binary notation, the only non-zero digit is 1. The first non-zero digit after the binary point must be 1 because it can't be anything else. Therefore, you don't need to write it down either. You get an extra bit of precision, essentially for free. To store the mantissa 10101, you only need to write the bits 0101.

The next step is to determine how these numbers will be stuffed into bytes. Java allots four bytes for each float and eight bytes for each double. The first bit of each float is used for the sign bit. A 1 bit is negative and a 0 bit is positive, exactly as with integers.

The next eight bits are used for the exponent. These eight bits are treated as an unsigned integer between 0 and 255. The numbers 0 and 255 have special meanings that I discuss shortly. Otherwise, the exponent is *biased* by subtracting 127 from it. Therefore, float exponents have values between -126 (1 - 127) and +127 (254 - 127). Here's what this arrangement looks like:

```
0111111111111111111111111111111111
0000000000000000000000000000000001
1000000000000000000000000000000000
```

The final 23 bits are used for the mantissa. The mantissa is given as a fractional number between 1 and 2. As discussed earlier in this chapter, the first bit is assumed to be one, so the mantissa effectively has 24 bits of precision. Extra zeroes are appended if necessary. This doesn't change the number, though, because 1.0101000000000000000000 is exactly the same as 1.0101. In other words, you can always add extra zeroes at the end of the mantissa to fill space. Figure 2-1 shows the bits in a float.

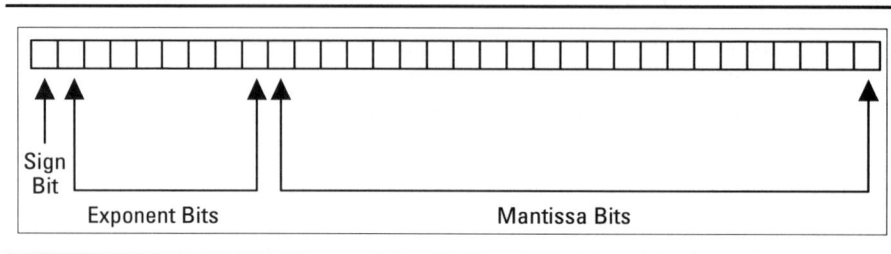

Figure 2-1
The bits in a float.

Note

The description that I've adopted here is the one used by the IEEE 754 specification. In this description, the mantissa is a normalized, binary, rational number — that is, its value is a fraction between 1 and 2. The Java Language Specification uses an alternate but equivalent description in which the mantissa is interpreted as an integer between 2^{23} and 2^{24-1}. In this description, the bias used on the exponent is 150 — that is 127 + 23. A little thought should convince you that these descriptions are equivalent.

Finite precision

It's important to understand that not all floating-point numbers can be exactly represented in a finite number of bits. For example, whereas one half is exactly 0.1 (binary) or 0.5 (decimal), one third in binary is 0.0101010101 . . . where the pattern repeats indefinitely. One third also repeats in decimal notation where it's 0.33333333 . . . . Whether or not a number repeats or terminates depends on the base of the number system. One fifth is exactly 0.2 in decimal, but is 0.0011001100110011 . . . in binary. Some numbers, most famously Π, neither terminate nor repeat. Because computer arithmetic must truncate these infinite mantissas to just 24 bits, computer arithmetic on floats is often imprecise. The best Java can do with a number like Π is approximate with an accuracy of 24 bits.

Doubles

If a float is not precise enough or large enough, you can use a double instead. A double has eight bytes, of which 1 bit is used for the sign, 11 bits for the exponent, and 53 bits for the mantissa. If you're sharp, you'll notice that this adds up to 65 bits. Don't forget that the first bit of the mantissa is always 1, so you don't need to store that bit. The exponent is biased by subtracting 1023.

Special values

Java's floating-point numbers aren't limited to the rational numbers you learned in high school. There are several special numbers that, while not true numbers in the traditional sense of the word, are produced by some calculations. If the non-biased exponent is 255, then the number takes on one of several special meanings.

Inf

Java has two special floating-point values to represent positive and negative infinity. There's no literal for these infinities, but the public final static float values java.lang.Float.POSITIVE_INFINITY and java.lang.Float. NEGATIVE_INFINITY allow you to use them in source code.

More commonly you'll bump across these values unexpectedly when a calculation goes in a direction that you didn't anticipate. Positive infinity is produced when a positive float or a double is divided by zero. Dividing a negative float or double by zero gives negative infinity. For example:

```
double x = 1.0/0.0;
```

There's little reason to deliberately create a float or double that's infinite. However, it is a rather common thing to create one accidentally in more complicated programs where all possible divisors aren't determined until runtime. The Inf value lets your programs continue without crashing or throwing an exception.

You can get the value Inf only in a floating-point calculation. If you try to divide an integer by integer zero, an ArithmeticException is thrown instead. For example:

```
int i = 1/0;
```

In a comparison test with <, <=, >, or >=, -Inf is smaller than any other number and Inf is larger than any other number. Each is equal only to itself.

The bit patterns for positive infinity and negative infinity are formed by the appropriate sign bit (1 for negative, 0 for positive), an unbiased exponent of 255 (11111111), and a mantissa of zero. Thus, positive infinity is 01111111100000000000000000000000, or in hexadecimal, 7F800000. Negative infinity is 11111111100000000000000000000000, or in hexadecimal, FF800000.

Double positive and negative infinity are formed in the same way. Choose the appropriate sign, fill the exponent with one bits, and set the mantissa to zero. Thus, positive double infinity is 7FF0000000000000 and negative double infinity is FFF0000000000000.

NaN

NaN is an acronym for "Not a Number." A floating-point calculation returns NaN if it divides zero by zero. For example:

```
double z = 0.0/0.0;
```

You can also get NaN values in certain other undefined arithmetic operations, such as taking the square root of a negative number or raising zero to the zeroth power.

There is no literal that lets you type NaN into Java source code, but you can get the same effect with the public, final, static float constant java.lang.Float.NaN.

More commonly, NaN will pop up unexpectedly. For example, the following code fragment divides 0.0 by 0.0 when x is equal to 5.0:

```
double y = 10.0;
for (double x = 0.0; x <= y; x+=1.0, y -= 1.0) {
  double z = x - 5.0;
  double result = (x - y)/z;
  System.out.println(x + " " + y + " " + z + " " + result);
}
```

NaN is unordered, so the result will always be false if you compare it to other numbers with <, <=, >, >=, or ==. The only comparison that can return true is !=, which always returns true if one or both of the operands is NaN. In other words, NaN is never equal to any number (including itself), never greater than any number, and never less than any number.

Although division by zero does not crash your program like it does in some programming languages, the unexpected appearance of NaNs or Infs in program output generally indicates a bug that needs to be stomped. Real world quantities shouldn't be infinite or "Not a Number." If you see NaNs or Infs, it may be an indication that a small factor you left out of your analysis, friction for example, is becoming important in a special case because everything else is canceling out.

NaN is represented by any float or double bit pattern in which the exponent is all ones and the mantissa is non-zero. (If the mantissa is zero, then the number is either positive or negative infinity.) The sign bit is ignored because NaN is not signed. Thus, all floats from 7F800001 to 7FFFFFFF and from FF800001 to FFFFFFFF correspond to NaN. All doubles from 7FF0000000000001 to 7FFFFFFFFFFFFFFF and from FFF0000000000001 to FFFFFFFFFFFFFFFF also correspond to NaN.

Positive and negative zero

The smallest value that you can represent in Java is java.lang.Double. MIN_VALUE, 4.94065645841246544e-324. Numbers with absolute values smaller than this are set to zero. However, the sign of the number can be retained if the number is in fact non-zero. The normal 0.0 you type in source code is positive zero. You get negative zero when you multiply a negative number by zero. For example:

```
double x = -1.0 * 0.0;
```

In direct comparisons, negative zero and positive zero appear to be equal. However, some other operations will produce different results depending on whether positive zero or negative zero is used. For example, 1.0 divided by positive zero is positive infinity, but 1.0 divided by negative zero is negative infinity.

The zero literal you type into source code with 0.0 or 0.0F is always positive zero. You can get negative zero only if it shows up in a calculation.

Positive zero is, as you would expect, the float or double value whose bits are all zero. In other words, float positive zero is 0000000000000000-0000000000000000, or 00000000 in hexadecimal. Negative zero is the same, except that the sign bit is one. Thus, float negative zero is 10000000-0000000000000000000000000, or 80000000 in hexadecimal. Double positive zero is 0000000000000000 in hexadecimal, and double negative zero is 8000000000000000.

Denormalized floating-point numbers

Numbers whose unbiased exponent is zero but whose mantissa is not zero are *denormalized*. Denormalized numbers do not have an implied first bit with value one. All of the bits that a denormalized number has are present in the mantissa. The mantissa is presumed to be multiplied by 2^{-127} In other words, it acts like it has a biased exponent of -127, or an unbiased exponent of zero. In fact, this is exactly what it does have, so the only real difference between normalized and denormalized floating point numbers is the implied first bit.

Unlike Inf, NaN, and positive and negative zero, all of which can appear in one form or another in Java source code or output, denormalized numbers don't look any different from regular floating point numbers. However, being able to recognize and decode them will become important when you learn how to disassemble Java byte code in Chapters 4 and 5.

CHAR

The char data type in Java is considered to be a number, but it's a funny one. Most obviously, when you try to print a char, you don't get a number. Rather you get a character like "a" or "#". Secondly, char literals don't look like numbers in source code. You normally enter a char like this:

```
char c = 'r';
```

You can, however, use integer literals to assign values to char variables. The following statement does exactly the same thing as the previous one:

```
char c = 114;
```

You don't often see Java source code that initializes chars with integer literals, because most programmers don't walk around with the entire ASCII chart in their head. The meaning of the first statement is much more obvious than the meaning of the second, but they produce identical byte code.

Chars are two bytes wide-they take up the same space as a short. However, chars are not shorts. Shorts are signed and chars are unsigned. The first bit in a char is the 32,768 place, not a sign bit. Thus, while 1000000000000001 interpreted as a short is -32,768, 1000000000000001 interpreted as a char is 32,769. Chars range from 0 to 65,535.

The Java compiler has to work a little magic to handle this. The line

```
char c = 114;
```

compiles without problem. So does the line

```
char d = 45000;
```

Both 114 and 45000 are within the range of a char. However, the following two lines produce compile-time error messages, telling you an explicit cast is needed to convert an int to a char:

```
char e = -123;
char f = 65536;
```

Java characters are understood to be part of the Unicode character set. The Unicode character set has, at the time of this writing, 38,885 characters, each two bytes wide. Unicode scripts include alphabets used in Europe, Africa, the Middle East, India, and many other parts of Asia, as well as the unified Han set of East Asian ideographs and the complete ideographs for Korean Hangul. Some scripts are not yet supported or are only partially supported, primarily because these scripts are not yet well understood.

Unsupported scripts include Braille, Cherokee, Cree, Ethiopic, Khmer (a.k.a. Cambodian), Maldivian (a.k.a. Dihevi), Mongolian, Moso (a.k.a. Naxi), Pahawh Hmong, Rong (a.k.a. Lepcha), Sinhalese, Tagalog, Tai Lu, Tai Mau, Tifinagh, Yi (a.k.a. Lolo), and Yoruba. Cherokee, Ethiopic, Braille, and possibly Khmer are likely to be added in the near future. Some of these languages can be written with other scripts that Unicode does support. For example, Mongolian is commonly written using the Cyrillic alphabet, and Hmong can be written in ASCII.

Furthermore, Unicode does not support many archaic alphabets, including Ahom, Akkadian Cuneiform, Aramaic, Babylonian Cuneiform, Balinese, Balti, Batak, Brahmi, Buginese, Chola, Cypro-Minoan, Egyptian hieroglyphics, Etruscan, Glagolitic, Hittite, Javanese (a particularly galling omission), Kaithi, Kawi, Khamti, Kharoshthi, Kirat (Limbu), Lahnda, Linear B, Mandaic, Mangyan, Manipuri (Meithei), Meroitic (Kush), Modi, Numidian, Ogham, Pahlavi (Avestan), Phags-pa, Pyu, Old Persian Cuneiform, Phoenician, Northern Runic, Satavahana, Siddham, South Arabian, Sumerian Cuneiform, Syriac, Tagbanuwa, Tircul, and Ugaritic Cuneiform. Runic and Ogham are likely to be added in the near future. Some of the rest of these languages, such as Linear B, are still areas of active research among linguists. Of the remainder, few (if any) are likely to be added to Unicode in the foreseeable future, even those that are fairly well understood.

Theoretically, Unicode can be expanded to cover up to 65,536 different characters. This is not quite enough to handle every character from all the world's alphabets, primarily because of the large number of characters in the pictographic alphabets used for Chinese, Japanese, and historical Vietnamese. The Chinese alphabet alone has more than 80,000 different characters. However, by combining similar characters in these four alphabets so that some chars represent different words in different languages, all of the alphabets and the most commonly used pictographs can be squeezed into two bytes.

ASCII

Unicode is based on two character sets that predate it: ASCII and ISO Latin-1. ASCII is a 7-bit character set with 128 different characters. ASCII was designed for communication in United States English. It therefore contains the lowercase letters a-z, the capital letters A-Z, the digits 0-9, various punctuation marks, and a number of non-printing control characters, many of which are closely related to the types of terminals and printers that were in use when ASCII was invented. The characters in ASCII are numbered from 0 to 127. Character 0 is the non-printing null character. Character 127 is the delete character. Characters 48 through 57 are the digits 0 through 9. Characters 65 through 90 are the capital letters A through Z. Characters 97 through 122 are the lowercase letters a through z. The remaining ASCII characters are various punctuation marks and non-printing characters. Table 2-3 is a complete list.

ISO Latin-1

As I said, ASCII is designed to handle U.S. English. It can do a reasonable approximation of other dialects of English, but it begins to have problems with many other European languages, like French and German. There are no cedillas, umlauts, or any of the other characters not used in English, but present in these languages.

The first bit of each ASCII character is 0. You can define another 128 characters by using the bytes whose first bit is one. Indeed, this is the scheme used in most modern computers. The characters with numeric values between 128 and 255 are used to encode the additional characters needed by most languages that are written in some approximation of the Latin alphabet. There are at least two common ways ASCII is extended into the upper 128 characters. The one around which Unicode and Java are built is the ISO 8859-1 Latin-1 character set, often just referred to as ISO Latin-1. Table 2-4 lists the upper 128 characters of the ISO Latin-1 character set. The lower 128 characters are exactly the same as they are for ASCII.

Programs that don't support ISO Latin-1 characters often operate by ignoring the most significant bit of each character; that is, they presume that each byte begins with a zero bit. For example, the umlaut (ü), ISO Latin-1 character 252, would be reduced to ASCII character 252-128, which is character 124, the vertical bar, |. This can be a reasonable approximation if most of the text is ASCII.

Table 2-3

The ASCII character set

Code	Character	Code	Character	Code	Character	Code	Character
0	null	32	space	64	@	96	`
1	soh	33	!	65	A	97	a
2	stx	34	"	66	B	98	b
3	etx	35	#	67	C	99	c
4	eot	36	$	68	D	100	d
5	enq	37	%	69	E	101	e
6	ack	38	&	70	F	102	f
7	bell	39	'	71	G	103	g
8	backspace	40	(	72	H	104	h
9	tab (\t)	41	)	73	I	105	i
10	linefeed (\n)	42	*	74	J	106	j
11	vertical tab	43	+	75	K	107	k
12	formfeed (\f)	44	,	76	L	108	l
13	carriage return, (\r)	45	-	77	M	109	m
14	so	46	.	78	N	110	n
15	si	47	/	79	O	111	o
16	dle	48	0	80	P	112	p
17	dc1	49	1	81	Q	113	q
18	dc2	50	2	82	R	114	r
19	dc3	51	3	83	S	115	s
20	dc4	52	4	84	T	116	t
21	nak	53	5	85	U	117	u
22	syn	54	6	86	V	118	v
23	etb	55	7	87	W	119	w
24	can	56	8	88	X	120	x
25	em	57	9	89	Y	121	y
26	sub	58	:	90	Z	122	z
27	escape	59	;	91	[	123	{
28	is4	60	<	92	\	124		
29	is3	61	=	93	]	125	}
30	is2	62	>	94	^	126	~
31	is1	63	?	95	_	127	delete

Table 2-4
Upper 128 characters of the ISO Latin-1 character set

Code	Character	Code	Character	Code	Character	Code	Character
128		160	non-breaking space	192	¿	224	‡
129		161	¡	193	¡	225	·
130	bph	162	¢	194	¬	226	,
131	nbh	163	£	195	∨	227	„
132		164	¤	196	ƒ	228	‰
133	nel	165	¥	197	˜	229	Â
134	ssa	166	¦	198	?	230	Ê
135	esa	167	§	199	«	231	Á
136	hts	168	¨	200	»	232	Ë
137	htj	169	©	201	…	233	È
138	vts	170	ª	202		234	Í
139	pld	171	«	203	À	235	Î
140	plu	172	¬	204	Ã	236	Ï
141	ri	173	shy	205	Õ	237	Ì
142	ss2	174	Æ	206	Œ	238	Ó
143	ss3	175	Ø	207	œ	239	Ô
144	dcs	176	8	208	-D	240	?
145	pu1	177	±	209	—	241	Ò
146	pu2	178	2	210	”	242	Ú
147	sts	179	3	211	“	243	Û
148	cch	180	¥	212	‘	244	Ù
149	mw	181	µ	213	õ	245	
150	spa	182	¶	214		246	ˆ
151	epa	183	·	215	×	247	˜
152	sos	184	,	216	ÿ	248	—
153		185	1	217	Ÿ	249	?
154	sci	186	•	218	/	250	?
155	csi	187	»	219	¤	251	°
156	st	188	1/4	220	‹	252	,
157	osc	189	1/2	221	Ý	253	ý
158	pm	190	3/4	222	capital thorn	254	little thorn
159	apc	191	¿	223	?	255	?

Unicode

Just as ISO Latin-1 extends ASCII by adding an extra high-order bit, so too does Unicode extend ISO Latin-1 by adding an extra high-order byte. If the high-order byte is zero (00000000), then the Unicode character is identical to the ISO Latin-1 character in the low-order byte. You can do an approximate conversion from Unicode to ISO Latin-1 by chopping off all the high-order bytes. This works as long as all the text is composed only of ISO Latin-1 characters. Most of the time, especially when you're working in English, this is a reasonable assumption. Many of Java's classes that output text make this assumption, most notably PrintStream, which includes System.out.

Note
I'd love to show you a table of all the extra characters in Unicode, but it would be so lengthy that this book would be mostly that table and not much else. If you need to know more about the specific encodings of the different characters in Unicode, you should check out *The Unicode Standard*, Second edition, ISBN 0-201-48345-9, from Addison-Wesley. This 950-page book includes the complete Unicode 2.0 specification. Errata for this volume are on the Web at http://www.unicode.org/.

Mac Roman

Remember that I said there were two ways to encode these extra characters in the upper 128 bytes? The Macintosh uses a completely different character-encoding scheme called Mac Roman. It has most of the same glyphs as the ISO Latin-1 character set, but different glyphs are mapped to different numbers. If Java programs try to print the upper 128 characters on a Macintosh, they come out in the Mac Roman character set, not the ISO Latin-1 character set like they are supposed to.

This is a royal pain for more than just Java programs because it makes file translation between platforms excessively difficult. In fact, Java 1.1 provides one of the few class libraries that can translate between the Mac Roman and ISO Latin-1 character sets. This is especially painful to authors trying to write about ISO Latin-1 on a Macintosh.

When the Macintosh was created in the early 1980s, it was one of the very few computers that could handle non-ASCII text. ISO Latin-1 was not yet established. Therefore, Apple had to invent their own scheme for encoding the extra characters. Regrettably, backward-compatibility means that Macs will never get in sync with the rest of the world. That's one of the disadvantages of pioneering new technology.

To make matters worse, it's happening again. Apple developed their 2-byte WorldScript technology before Unicode was ready. Everyone who came after Apple standardized on Unicode. This means that we're probably stuck with ASCII as the lowest common denominator for text data for the foreseeable future.

Because very few text editors are available that allow you to write in Unicode, Java source code files are written in ISO Latin-1. Furthermore, the Java compiler expects to see source code written in ISO Latin-1. If you actually have a text editor that works in Unicode and try to write Java files with it, the compiler will get hopelessly confused when it tries to compile your files.

In fact, Java can be written perfectly well with only ASCII. All Java keywords, operators, and literals, as well as all method, class, and field names in the java packages, can be written in pure ASCII. Because ISO Latin-1 makes your source code difficult to move between Macs and other platforms, you should probably restrict yourself to ASCII in your programs.

You can use Unicode characters in Java string and char literals as well as in identifiers. To embed a non-ASCII character in a string, prefix the hexadecimal number for the character with \u. For example, the division sign is Unicode character 247. Therefore, you can make it part of the string by writing \u00F7. The Greek letter π is Unicode character 12,480 or hexadecimal \u03C0. Thus,

```
double \u03C0 = 3.141592;
```

All Unicode characters can be encoded in this fashion, even those you could type literally. For example, the small letter t can also be written as \u0074. The backslash itself can be written as \u005C. Writing code this way is a very bad idea unless you're deliberately trying to make it obscure.

When a Java compiler reads Java source code, it first converts all such \u escapes to the actual characters, taking into account double backslash escapes as well. This pre-processing happens before anything else. For example, consider this statement:

```
System.out.println("This is not a \\u0074");
```

The double backslash is interpreted as a literal backslash, not as the start of an escape sequence. Thus you get "This is not a \u0074" instead of "This is not a \t." To get the second effect, you would have to write

```
System.out.println("This is not a \\\u0074");
```

or better yet, just

```
System.out.println("This is not a \\t");
```

Unicode escape translation is not cumulative. "\u005Cu0074" is translated to the six characters "\u0074" rather than the single character "t."

As if Unicode input to Java weren't complex enough, Unicode output is equally troublesome. You already know that PrintStreams like System.out just chop off the high byte of a Unicode character. Although it varies from platform to platform, different output classes in the java package either chop off the high byte like PrintStream or output \u escapes.

UTF8

To summarize what you have learned so far, characters in Java source code are 8-bit ISO Latin-1 characters. Internally, Java translates these characters and any embedded \u escapes into 16-bit Unicode characters.

Using 16-bit characters is relatively inefficient, however, when almost all the text you're working with is likely to be regular 7-bit ASCII. Therefore, Java byte code embeds string literals in an intermediate format called "Universal Character Set Transformation Format 8-bit form." Since that's way more than a mouthful, this is almost always written as the acronym UTF8.

UTF8 encodes the most common characters (the ASCII character set) in a single byte for each character. However, less-common characters use two bytes, including the upper 128 ISO Latin-1 characters (which normally only take one byte apiece). The least common characters of all — the upper 32,768 Unicode characters — are encoded in three bytes.

The details are as follows. Characters between 1 and 127 (\u0001 and \u007F) — that is, ASCII characters except null — are encoded as their low-order byte. The high byte (which is just zeroes anyway) is discarded. If the Unicode character is between 128 and 28,927 (\u0080 to \u07FF) — that is, if its top five bits are zero — then it has 11 bits of data. These 11 bits are encoded as a pair of bytes like this

```
1 1 0 x x x x x 1 0 x x x x x x
        bits 6-10     bits 0-5
```

The null character is also encoded in two bytes as 1100000010000000.
Characters in the range \u0800 to \uFFFF have a full 16 bits of data. These are encoded in three bytes, like this:

```
1 1 1 0 x x x x x 1 0 x x x x x x 1 0 x x x x x x
        bits 12-15     bits 6-11     bits 0-5
```

Note

This is not exactly the official UTF8 encoding. Java differs from the formal standard in that it uses two bytes to encode the null character (\u0000) rather than one. Furthermore, the real UTF8 standard has several more formats to handle four byte characters as well. By using a 4-byte character set, it's no longer necessary to unify the Chinese, Japanese, and Vietnamese scripts.

This encoding scheme is designed to be easy and quick to parse. Any byte that begins with a 0 bit is a 1-byte ASCII character. Any byte that begins with 110 starts a 2-byte character. Any byte that starts with 1110 is a 3-byte character. Finally, any byte that starts with 10 is the second or third byte of a multi-byte character.

The more ASCII characters in a text string, the more space that can be saved by UTF8. Pure ASCII text is only half as large in UTF8 as it is in true Unicode. In the worst case, where all characters occupy three bytes, a UTF8 string is only 50 percent larger than the equivalent Unicode string. However, the worst case is rarely seen in practice.

The DataInputStream and DataOutputStream classes have writeUTF() and readUTF() methods to handle UTF8 data. readUTF() first reads two bytes from the underlying stream. These are interpreted as an unsigned short specifying the number of bytes to read from the stream (*not* the number of characters to read from the stream). These bytes are then read and translated from UTF8 into Unicode, and a String containing the translated data is returned. We use this method in Chapter 4 to read the UTF8 strings stored in the constant pool of a byte code file.

The DataOutputStream writeUTF(String s) method writes a Unicode string onto the underlying output stream after translating the string to UTF8 format. The string is preceded by an unsigned short that gives the number of bytes that will be written.

BOOLEAN

The final primitive data type is the only one that cannot be interpreted as a number. This is the boolean. A boolean has two possible values: true and false. In Java source code, these are boolean literals. They are not the same as 1 and 0. They are not the same as the strings "true" and "false." They are simply true and false. That's all.

At the level of the virtual machine, things are a little different. The virtual machine does not have instructions that operate on boolean data. Instead, expressions that involve booleans are compiled using integer instructions. The integer constant 1 is used to represent true, and the integer constant 0 is used to represent false. Don't try to take advantage of this when writing Java source code, though. It won't work.

However, for the purposes of efficiency, Java does allow arrays of booleans to be stored more compactly than arrays of ints. Sun's virtual machines make arrays of booleans out of arrays of bytes. In these arrays, true is 01 and false is 00. Other implementations are free to use even more compact representations for boolean arrays, perhaps as little as one bit per value.

Cross-Platform Issues

The preceding section described how primitive data types are represented in Java. This matches fairly closely how numbers are represented on Sparc-Solaris systems. This shouldn't be surprising, given that Java was created by Sun Microsystems programmers who were accustomed to Sparc-Solaris systems.

However, not all systems represent data in the same way. Most annoyingly, roughly half of computer architectures are Little-Endian rather than Big-Endian. (Little-Endian and Big-Endian architectures are discussed shortly). Furthermore, some programming languages allow the use of unsigned numeric quantities. And although Java's native integer format is 32 bits, many other systems prefer 16-bit or 64-bit ints. Although Java is supposed to be above such concerns, when you have to deal with legacy data from programs written in other languages, you need to be aware of these differences.

Byte order

Which two mighty powers have, as I was going to tell you, been engaged in a most obstinate war for six and thirty moons past. It began upon the following occasion. It is allowed on all hands, that the primitive way of breaking eggs, before we eat them, was upon the larger end: but his present Majesty's grandfather, while he was a boy, going to eat an egg, and breaking it according to the ancient practice, happened to cut one of his fingers. Whereupon the Emperor his father published an edict, commanding all his subjects, upon great penalties, to break the smaller end of their eggs. The people so highly resented this law, that our histories tell us there have been six rebellions raised on that account; wherein one Emperor lost his life, and another his crown. These civil commotions were constantly fomented by the monarchs of Blefuscu; and when they were quelled, the exiles always fled for refuge to that empire. It is computed that eleven thousand persons have, at several times, suffered death, rather than submit to break their eggs at the smaller end. Many hundred large volumes have been published upon this controversy: but the books of the Big-Endians have been long forbidden, and the whole party rendered incapable by law of holding employment. During the course of these troubles, the Emperors of Blefuscu did frequently expostulate by their ambassadors, accusing us of making a schism in religion, by offending against a fundamental doctrine of our great prophet Lustrog, in the fifty-fourth chapter of the *Blundecral* (which is their *Alcoran*). This, however, is thought to be a mere strain upon the text: for the words are these: *That all true believers shall break their eggs at the convenient end*: and which is the convenient end, seems, in my humble opinion, to be left to every man's conscience, or at least in the power of the chief magistrate to determine. Now the Big-Endian exiles have found so much credit in the Emperor of Blefuscu's court, and so much private assistance and encouragement from their party here at home, that a bloody war has been carried on between the two empires for six and thirty moons with various success; during which time we have lost forty capital ships, and a much greater number of smaller vessels, together with thirty thousand of our best seamen and soldiers; and the damage received by the enemy is reckoned to be somewhat greater than ours.

Jonathan Swift, Gulliver's Travels, Chapter IV

I made an implicit assumption in the preceding section: that the leftmost byte of a multi-byte number is the most significant one. Of course, spatial concepts like *left* and *right* really don't apply to computer memories. In this context, left means lower in memory, and right means higher. Of course, lower and higher are also spatial terms. By lower, I mean "has a smaller address," and by higher, I mean "has a bigger address." Thus, if the bytes in a computer memory with n bytes of memory are organized from byte 0 to byte n-1, then byte 0 is the lowest, or leftmost, byte and byte n-1 is the highest, or rightmost, byte.

We associate left with lower addresses in memory because computer programs start executing the instruction at a lower address and then proceed through the instructions to a higher address. In other words, first the instruction in byte 0 is executed, and then the instruction at byte 1, and then the instruction at byte 2, and so on.

This is a little over-simplified. Not all bytes contain instructions; not all instructions are one byte long (though they are in Java); and some instructions jump backward or forward in memory. However, none of this changes the point I'm making here about associating lower addresses in memory with left and higher addresses with right.

When people who speak English write sequences of numbers they automatically put 0 on the left as shown here:

0   1   2   3   4   5   6   7   8   9   10   11

Because English is a left-to-right language and most of the people who developed the first computers spoke English, the spatial concept of left came to be implicitly associated with lower addresses in memory. If the first digital computers had been invented in Arabic- or Hebrew-speaking cultures, which use right-to-left scripts, we'd probably speak of byte 0 as the rightmost byte.

Consider the number 6401. This is shorthand for six *thousands*, four *hundreds*, zero *tens*, and one *one*. The leftmost digit, 6, is the most important. It tells you to within a thousand how big the number is. Subsequent digits improve on the precision, but don't change the big picture. In jargon, it's said that 6 is the *most significant* digit. Similarly, the rightmost digit, 1, is the *least significant* digit.

The most significant digits are read first. Therefore, this is a *Big-Endian* number system. The big end of the number (the thousands) comes before the little end (the ones) of the number. This assumption seems to be perfectly reasonable unless and until you encounter a script in which numbers are stored differently.

A number system in which 6401 means 6 ones, 4 tens, 0 hundreds, and 1 thousand is called *Little-Endian* because the least significant digits come first. There's no reason why 6401 couldn't mean 6 ones, 4 tens, 0 hundreds, and 1 thousand. That's just not the way European scripts count. There's no mathematical reason for Big-Endian numbers. It's purely a convention enforced by centuries of common practice. It's no more right or wrong than the grammatical convention that adjectives tend to come before the nouns they modify. In English and many other languages, adjectives come first. In Latin and many other languages, the nouns come first. Neither is right or wrong. They're just different.

Bringing this discussion back to the level of computers, recall that a Java int can be thought of as made out of four hexadecimal digits. For example, decimal 6401 is 0x1901. Java follows a Big-Endian scheme. The most significant digit comes first, followed by the second most significant digit, followed by the third most significant digit, followed by the least significant digit.

Macs and most UNIX machines, including Sun's, also support a Big-Endian architecture, where the digit with the highest place value in a number is in the leftmost (lowest addressed) byte in the number. However, computer architectures based around the Intel X86 and VAX architectures do things exactly the opposite way. Those machines are *Little-Endian*; the least significant byte in a number comes first. On an X86 system, the decimal number gets laid out in memory as 1091.

Now let's suppose we have to store the 4-byte integer 1,870,475,384 in this memory. All computer architectures would use four contiguous bytes. First, the integer is converted into its hexadecimal form, 6F7D3078; each 2-digit pair is exactly one byte. Working from the bottom up, as is customary in a stack, the first byte can go to address A, the second byte to address A+1, the third to A+2, and the fourth to A+3. Figure 2-2 shows this arrangement.

A + 3	78
A + 2	30
A + 1	7D
A	6F

■ Figure 2-2
The number 0x6F7D3078 stored at address A in memory in Big-Endian order.

This is a classic Big-Endian ordering of bytes. However, not all architectures do it like this. In particular, X86 and VAX architectures use a Little-Endian ordering. They put the most significant byte at address A+3, the second most significant byte at address A+2, the third most significant byte at address A+1, and the least significant byte at address A. Figure 2-3 shows this arrangement.

As long as you're on only one computer system, you don't need to worry about this. All the routines are designed to work with the native data format. However, as soon as you start trying to transfer data between systems, you need to worry about converting between byte orders. Otherwise, the integer you write to a file in Big-Endian format on your Sun as 6F7D3078 (1,870,475,384) will be read in Little-Endian format as 78307D6F (2,016,443,759) on your PC — not the same thing at all.

A + 3	7D
A + 2	6F
A + 1	30
A	78

Figure 2-3
The number 0x6F7D3078 stored at address A in Little-Endian order.

Some older computer systems used neither Big-Endian nor Little-Endian byte orders. DEC's PDP-11 wrote 4-byte integers in this order: second-least-significant byte, least-significant byte, most-significant byte, and second-most-significant byte. Other computers did even stranger things. Fortunately, these architectures have all died out, and we're now left to deal with only the confusion between Little-Endian and Big-Endian.

Java was first designed by Big-Endian engineers at Sun Microsystems. It was also designed for the Internet, where almost all protocols specify Big-Endian byte orders. Therefore, it should come as no surprise that Java's virtual machine uses Big-Endian format for all data types. Little-Endian systems, like the X86, have to translate the Big-Endian data in Java byte code into their native Little-Endian format before executing it.

You need to worry about byte order only when you're reading data that comes from a Little-Endian source. The readByte(), readShort(), readInt(), readLong(), readFloat(), and readDouble() methods of java.io. DataInputStream all assume the data is Big-Endian. Similarly the writeByte(), writeShort(), writeInt(), writeLong(), writeFloat(), and writeDouble() methods of java.io.DataOutputStream write Big-Endian data. To read Little-Endian data in Java, you have to read each byte separately and then reconstruct the int or long from the bytes that make it up. To write Big-Endian data, you have to break the ints or longs apart into bytes and then write the bytes separately. There are several ways to accomplish this, but the most efficient use the bit-level operators discussed later in this chapter. I revisit this topic there.

Unsigned integers

Many traditional programming languages, notably C, allow the use of unsigned quantities. An unsigned number uses its high-order bit for data so it can count twice as high as a number that has to reserve one bit for the sign. However, it can only count positive numbers, not negative numbers. Recall that the largest signed byte is 01111111, which is 127 in decimal. 11111111 is not 255 but rather -128. However, by reading 11111111 as an unsigned quantity, the first 1 bit is interpreted as 128, not the - sign. Thus, as unsigned quantity, 11111111 is indeed 255. On the other hand, there's no way to express negative numbers as unsigned numbers.

All Java numeric data types except char use signed integers exclusively. However it's not unlikely that you'll run across data from programs written in other languages that do have unsigned integers. java.io.DataInputStream has two methods that read unsigned quantities. readUnsignedByte() reads a single byte off the stream and returns an int between 0 and 255. An int is returned instead of a byte or a short because a byte can go only as high as 127, whereas an unsigned byte can go as high as 255. Similarly readUnsignedShort() reads two bytes from the input stream and returns an int between 0 and 65,535.

There is no similar readUnsignedInt() method. If you want to, it's easy enough to write one yourself. You'll need to read four bytes and return a long between 0 and 4,294,967,295. Again, the most efficient way to do this uses bit-level operators, so we'll defer the details until the end of this chapter.

An unsigned long — that is, an 8-byte unsigned integer — is relatively uncommon in practice. No primitive Java data type is large enough to handle unsigned longs. You can, however, use the java.math.BigInteger class instead.

Integer widths

You've probably heard a lot of hype about 32-bit computing and 32-bit clean code. You'll be hearing more about 64-bit platforms in the near future, if you haven't already. What's being referred to is, very roughly, the preferred size of an integer on a given computer architecture and the number of bits that can be transferred from main memory to the CPU in one clock cycle. Generally, the higher the number of bits, the faster the computer will run. However, you need to rewrite (or at least recompile) the software to accommodate the proper bit width before you can see the performance gain.

Much legacy code is written in languages like C that do not guarantee the width of an integer. The same C program may use 32-bit ints on a Sparc, 16-bit ints on a Mac, and 64-bit ints on a DEC Alpha. Although these all have Java equivalents, you have to know which one you're dealing with before you write the code to handle it! Trying to read 16-bit ints with Java's readInt() method is a sure path to failure.

There's no guaranteed way to look at a file in the absence of outside information and tell solely from the contents of the file whether it was written using 16-bit integers or 32-bit integers. Similarly, you can't tell whether or not it uses Big-Endian or Little-Endian data. In an ideal world, you'd have access to a specification that describes the data format used. If you don't, perhaps you have access to the source code that was used to write the file. If not, you'll have to do some testing. Try to read the file as 16-bit ints. Do the results make sense? What if you read it as 32-bit ints? Do those results make sense? If you seem to have an excessive number of zeroes appearing in your data, especially if they tend to alternate with non-zero values, that may indicate that you are reading the data using too short an integer. For example, if the data file is full of numbers mostly between 10 and 1000, then if it's written with 32-bit ints, the high two bytes of each int will be zero.

CONVERSIONS AND CASTING

With seven different numeric types that may be freely intermixed in expressions, it's important to understand the rules by which this intermixing takes place. Java converts between primitive data types in expressions, in assignment statements, as a result of explicit casts, and during method invocations. You need to understand when conversion can occur and what happens when it does.

Using a cast

Java enables you to explicitly change the type of a value using a cast. A *cast* is just the name of the type to which you wish to change the value, enclosed in parentheses. For example, suppose you've read a byte into the byte variable b, perhaps using DataInputStream's readByte() method. Then you can cast that variable to the int type like this:

```
int n = (int) b;
```

This doesn't permanently change the type of b. It just makes a temporary copy of the value of b and puts it in an int. This int is then assigned to the int variable n.

The second place in which conversion of primitive types takes place is in arithmetic expressions. Expressions range from simple ones, like a + b, to considerably more complex ones such as 1.65 * (32 / -9.8 - c++)/0.65. The expression is evaluated using the widest type present in the expression, where doubles are wider than floats, which are wider than longs, which are wider than ints. Thus, if any of the operands are doubles, all operands are promoted to doubles. If no operands are doubles but some are floats, then all operands are promoted to floats. If no operands are floats or doubles but some are longs, then all operands are promoted to longs. Finally, if an expression contains no floats, doubles, or longs, then all operands are promoted to ints. All arithmetic in Java uses at least ints. Shorts, bytes, and chars are never used directly in arithmetic expressions.

The third place in which conversions take place is in assignment statements; that is statements like

```
long a = 3 + 4;
```

In this example 3 is an int, 4 is an int, and the result of their addition is the int value 7. This must be promoted to a long before being assigned to a. Conversions in the other direction may lose information. Not all longs have equivalent int values. For example, 5294967295L is a valid long, but it's more than two times larger than the largest int:

```
int n = 5294967295L;
```

If you try to assign 5294967295L to an int variable, you get the compile-time error Error: Incompatible type for declaration. Explicit cast needed to convert long to int. The compiler sees that you may lose information and warns you about it. However, the compiler isn't that smart. The following assignment, which does not lose information, also causes a compiler error:

```
int m = 3L;
```

In both of these cases, you can tell the compiler that you're aware of the problem, that you accept that your assignment may lose information, and that you want it to go ahead anyway. You do this with an explicit cast to the type on the left side. For example:

```
int m = (int) 3L;
int n = (int) 5294967295L;
```

This tells the compiler that you know what you're doing, that you've given thought to whether this cast will lose data. Java tries to prevent you from performing operations that may lose data, but it does allow you to do so if you use a cast to tell it that you know what you're doing.

The final place where conversions take place is in method calls. Suppose you try to call MethodA(24). The compiler first tries to find a perfect match, a version of MethodA that takes as an argument a single int. However, if it fails in this effort, it will next look for a MethodA that takes a long as an argument. If it finds one, it promotes 24 to 24L and calls MethodA(long). Failing to find a MethodA that takes a long, Java next looks for one that takes a float. Failing to find that, it looks for one that takes a double. Only if it can't find any of these will Java produce a compile-time error.

The mechanics of conversion

Now that we've seen when conversions may take place, let's investigate how. Some conversions, such as an int to a long, are easy and never lose information. Others, such as a long to an int, are trickier because not all longs have int equivalents. For example, suppose that a byte variable b holds the value 92. In binary notation, this is 01011100. Because an int needs 32 bits, three extra zero bytes are added to the front of b, making it 000000000000-0000000000001011100.

Now suppose instead that the value of b is -92. Using two's complement arithmetic, we see that the binary expansion of -92 is 10100011 + 00000001 = 10100100. Now if you just attach three bytes of zeroes on the left side of this number, you get 00000000000000000000000010100100, which is not -92 (since the sign bit is zero, the number must be positive) but rather 164, not the same thing at all. In fact, it's not even off by a sign. If that were the problem, it would be simple enough to change the leftmost bit to 1. However, here that gives you -164, which isn't -92 any more than 164 is.

On the other hand, look what happens if you extend -92 with three bytes full of ones. You get 11111111111111111111111110100100. This is obviously a negative number since the leftmost bit is one. Using two's complement arithmetic to find out which number it is, you invert the number and add one:

```
  00000000000000000000000001011011
+ 00000000000000000000000000000001
  _____
  00000000000000000000000001011100
```

which, lo and behold, is 92! Thus, the proper way to convert an integer type to a wider format is *sign extension*. That is, take whatever bit is in the sign bit and add as many extra bytes as you need filled with that bit. This works for other widening casts between integer types as well. For example, to change a positive int to the equivalent long, just add four bytes of zeroes to the front. To change a negative int to the equivalent long just attach four more bytes of ones to the front of the int. Performed in this fashion, widening integer casts — that is, casts that go from a smaller type to a larger type — never lose information.

The same cannot be said for narrowing casts. A narrowing cast moves from a wider type, like int, to a narrower type, like byte. To do this, the extra bytes are just cut off the front of the wider type. Thus, to move from the int 92 to the byte 92, remove the first three bytes from 000000000000-00000000000001011100, leaving 01011100. This cast doesn't lose information, but other casts can. For example, the int 192 is 00000000000-00000000000011000000. If you cast this to a byte by removing the first three bytes, you get 11000000. Notice the sign bit. This is a negative number, specifically -64. There is no easy way around this problem. The numbers you get in a narrowing cast are not guaranteed to make sense. The simple fact is that you cannot fit 192 into a signed byte.

The two basic rules for conversion between integer data types are as follows:

1. If the type to be converted to is wider than the type you're converting from, sign extend the narrower type.

2. If the type to be converted to is narrower than the type you're converting from, truncate the most significant bytes of the integer you're converting.

Conversions to and from the char type behave similarly, once you take account of the fact that char is unsigned. To convert a char to a byte, the high-order byte is truncated. To convert a char to a short, the char is left as is, but is now interpreted as a signed 2-byte integer. To convert to an int or a long, the char is sign extended by two or six bytes respectively. This may produce a negative number where there wasn't one before if the char value is greater than 32,767 — that is, if its high-order bit is one.

To convert a byte to a char, the byte is sign extended one byte. To convert a short to a char, the short is merely reinterpreted as a signed, 2-byte integer. Finally, to convert an int or long to a char, all but the least-significant 16 bits are truncated. Although converting a char to a short, int, or long may play funny games with the sign, converting it back will return the original char.

The rules for conversions to and from floating-point numbers are more complex. A float can be cast to a double with no loss of precision whatsoever. Double to float conversion presents some problems, though. Some doubles can be exactly represented as floats, but some are too large, some are too small, and some have more precision (that is, a longer mantissa) than a float allows. If the absolute value of the double is larger than can fit in a float, the float becomes infinity — positive or negative depending on the sign of the double. If the absolute value of the double is smaller than can fit in a float (that is, closer to zero), the float becomes zero — positive or negative depending on the sign of the double.

Floats and doubles that are small enough to be represented as ints must fall between two ints; that is, there is an int value larger than the float and an int value smaller than the float. The float is rounded to the int in the pair between which it falls that is closest to zero. Thus, 7.5 is rounded to 7; 7.6 is also rounded to 7, but -7.5 is rounded to -7, not to -8. If the float or double is too large to be represented as an int, for example 6.73E14, then it is rounded to the largest possible int, 2,147,483,647. Similarly, if the float is too small and negative, for example -6.73E14, then it is rounded to the smallest possible int, -2,147,483,648. NaN is rounded to zero. Rounds to longs behave similarly except that the largest and smallest values are quite a bit larger.

Conversions of floats and doubles to shorts and bytes involve a two-step procedure. First the float or double is converted to a double, as described earlier in this chapter. Then the int is converted to a byte or short in the normal way, by truncating the excess bytes in the int. Thus, casting the float 7.5 to a byte results in the value 7. However, casting 175.5 to a byte results in the value -47. This occurs by first rounding 175.5 to 175, 0x000000AF, and then by truncating this to AF, 10101111 in binary. Of course, a byte is signed, so this is equal to -47.

I can think of little reason to want to convert a float or a double to a char, but you can if you need to. The conversion takes place much as with conversions to shorts: the float or double is first converted to an int, which is then converted to a char.

BIT-LEVEL OPERATORS

The 13 bit-level operators are among the more obscure in Java. They nonetheless have their uses. The bitwise operators operate on a number or boolean at the bit level, generally by comparing the bits in two quantities and returning a result that depends on the bits in each. The single exception is ~, the NOT, or complement, operator. It takes a single argument and inverts all its bits. The bitshift operators take two operands: the number to be shifted and the number of places to shift it. Except for ~, these operators have "operate and assign" equivalents as well. Table 2-5 lists all the bit-level operators in Java.

Table 2-5
The bitwise operators

Operator	Meaning
&	AND
|	OR
^	Exclusive OR
~	NOT (complement)
<<	Shift bits left
>>	Shift bits right
>>>	Shift bits right without sign extension
&=	AND and assign
|=	OR and assign
^=	Exclusive OR and assign
<<=	Shift bits left and assign
>>=	Shift bits right and assign
>>>=	Shift bits right without sign extension and assign

Some terminology

We'll need some shorthand to discuss these operators. First, given a value with n bits, the rightmost, least-significant bit is bit 0. The second-rightmost bit is bit one, and so on, up to the leftmost and most significant bit, which is bit n-1. For example, the byte value 37, 00010101 in binary, would have bits shown in Figure 2-4.

Bit:	0	0	0	1	0	1	0	1
Bit Position:	7	6	5	4	3	2	1	0

Figure 2-4
Bit positions in a byte.

Next, when I write that a bit is "set," or "on," that means the bit is 1. When I write that a bit is "not set," "unset," or "off," that means the bit is 0. You'll also hear these states referred to as "true" and "false" in other books, but I avoid that terminology here to avoid confusion with the boolean literals.

Finally, note that a lot of the examples in this book will be with bytes, simply because it's easier to follow what's going on when you only have to keep track of eight bits. However, just as Java performs arithmetic only on int and larger data types, and promotes the operands as necessary, so too will it promote the operands of a bitwise operator and return an int or larger result. For example, even if b1 and b2 are bytes, b1 & b2 is an int; both b1 and b2 are promoted to ints before the bitwise and is performed.

Bitwise operators

The bitwise operators — &, |, and ^ — combine two numbers according to their bit patterns. The bitwise not operator ~ inverts a single number's bit pattern.

The & operator

The & operator is the bitwise AND operator. It takes two numeric arguments, compares their bits, and sets the bits in the result that are set in both of the arguments. For example, let b1 be a byte with value 78 and b2 be a byte with the value -23. In binary, 78 is 01001110 and -23 is 11101001. Lay these values on top of each other as shown in Figure 2-5. The result, shown in the bottom row, is 01001100, that is, 76.

	0	1	0	0	1	1	1	0
	1	1	1	0	1	0	0	1
= 76	0	1	0	0	1	0	0	0

Figure 2-5
78 & -23.

The bits that are equal to one in both 78 and -23 are equal to one in the result. All other bits are zero.

As mentioned earlier, Java actually performs this calculation using 32-bit ints. Because the high-order three bytes of a positive int are just full of zeroes, the real result of 78 & -23 must be 00000000000000000000000001001000. If either argument of & has a zero bit in a particular position, that bit must be 0 in the result, regardless of the value of the bit in the second argument. Therefore, 0 & anything is always 0.

The & operator can also be used with two booleans: true & true is true, true & false is false, and false & false is false. At the level of the virtual machine, the boolean value true is the int 00000001 and false is the int 00000000. Thus, true & true is the same as 00000001 & 00000001 equals 00000001 or true. Conversely, false & false is 00000000 & 00000000 equals 00000000 or false. And finally, true & false is 00000001 & 00000000 equals 00000000 or false.

This is often used to avoid short-circuiting expression evaluation. Suppose isConditionOne() and isConditionTwo() are methods that return booleans and have some side effect such as printing output on System.out. Now suppose you write this statement:

```
if ( isConditionOne() && isConditionTwo() ) doSomething();
```

If isConditionOne() returns false, then isConditionTwo() is never called. Because isConditionOne() is known to be false, Java knows the result will be false, regardless of the value of isConditionTwo(). This can be a problem when isConditionTwo() has side effects, and you need it to be called regardless of condition one. To force isConditionTwo() to be called, use the bitwise & instead. That is

```
if ( isConditionOne() & isConditionTwo() ) doSomething();
```

The truth value of (isConditionOne() & isConditionTwo()) is the same as the truth value of (isConditionOne() && isConditionTwo()), but now both methods will be called.

The | operator

The | operator is the bitwise OR operator. It takes two numeric arguments, compares their bits, and sets the bits in the result that are set in either or both of the arguments. For example, let b1 be a byte with value 78 and b2 be a byte with the value -23. In binary, 78 is 01001110 and -23 is 11101001. Lay these values on top of each other as shown in Figure 2-6. The result, shown in the bottom row, is 11101111, that is -17.

	0	1	0	0	1	1	1	0
	1	1	1	0	1	0	0	1
= -17	1	1	1	0	1	1	1	1

Figure 2-6
78 | -23.

The bits that are equal to one in either 78 or -23 or both are equal to one in the result. All other bits are zero.

Of course, Java actually performs this calculation using 32-bit ints. Because the high-order three bytes of a positive int are just full of zeroes, the real result of 78 & -23 is 11111111111111111111111111101111. If either argument of | has a one bit in a particular position, that bit must be 1 in the result, regardless of the value of the bit in the second argument.

The | operator can also be used with two booleans: true | true is true, true | false is true, and false | false is false.

The AWT sometimes uses this to set a series of flags. If you have an item that has up to 32 boolean characteristics, then you can stuff all the values of those characteristics into an int.

For example, consider the java.awt.Font class. To create a new font, you use this constructor:

```
public Font(String name, int style, int size)
```

The name is the name of the typeface, like Times or Arial. The size is the size of the font in points, such as 12 or 24. The style, however, is one of a special set of mnemonic constants. These constants are

```
Font.BOLD = 1
Font.PLAIN = 0
Font.ITALIC = 2
```

You can pass one of these constants in the style argument of the Font constructor to get that style. However, what if you want a Font that is both bold and italic? Then, you pass Font.BOLD | Font.ITALIC. This means that the bold bit and the italic bit are both set in the style argument. Notice that Font.BOLD is 00000001 whereas Font.ITALIC is 00000010. Each bit in the number is a binary flag indicating the value of the binary characteristic; for example, is this or is this not bold? Other classes that use this scheme can have many more such constants, all of which are powers of two: 4, 8, 16, 32, 64, and so on. Each power of two is a 32-bit int with exactly one bit set and the rest unset.

As with &, | can also prevent the short-circuiting of expression evaluation. Consider the statement

```
if ( isConditionOne() || isConditionTwo() ) doSomething();
```

If isConditionOne() returns true, then isConditionTwo() will not be called because Java knows the result will be true, regardless of the value of isConditionTwo(). To force isConditionTwo() to be called, use the bitwise | instead. That is

```
if ( isConditionOne() | isConditionTwo() ) doSomething();
```

The truth value of (isConditionOne() | isConditionTwo()) is the same as the truth value of (isConditionOne() || isConditionTwo()), but now both methods are called.

The ^ operator

The ^ is the bitwise EXCLUSIVE-OR operator. The operator | does not behave like many people expect, based on its English meaning. Many people think the "A or B" is true if A is true and B is not true, or vice versa, but that "A or B" is not true if both A and B are true. ^ is the bitwise equivalent of this idea. The ^ operator takes two numeric arguments, compares their bits, and sets the bits in the result that are set in exactly one of the arguments.

Returning to the example where b1 is a byte with value 78 and b2 is a byte with the value -23, lay these values on top of each other as shown in Figure 2-7. The result, shown in the bottom row, is 10100111-89. The ^ operator can also be used with two booleans: true ^ true is false, true ^ false is true, and false ^ false is false.

78	0	1	0	0	1	1	1	0
-23	1	1	1	0	1	0	0	1
78 ^ -23 = -17	1	0	1	0	0	1	1	1

▌Figure 2-7
78 ^ -23.

The ~ operator

The ~ is the bitwise NOT or *complement* operator. It is unary; that is, it acts on a single number or boolean, and it flips all the bits in that value. As a result, all ones turn to zeroes and zeroes turn to ones. Figure 2-8 shows 78 and ~78.

78	0	1	0	0	1	1	1	0
~78 = -79	1	0	1	1	0	0	0	1

Figure 2-8
78 ~ -23.

By the nature of two's complement arithmetic, if b is an int or a long, then ~b equals -b - 1.

Assignment operators

The &=, |=, and ^= operators behave like their arithmetic cousins, *=, +=, -=, %= and /=. In other words, they combine the value on the left side of the operator with the value on the right side, and then assign it to the left side. For example:

```
int a = 78;
a &= -23;
```

This makes a equal to 76. |= and ^= behave similarly except they use bitwise OR and bitwise XOR respectively.

Bit shift operators

The bit shift operators shift the bits in an integer type by a specified number of places to the right or left. Bit shift operators cannot be used on floats, doubles, or booleans. For example, << is the left shift operator. The integer 78 is 00000000000000000000000001001110 in binary. Table 2-6 shows the result of shifting it progressively leftward. Notice that at each step the pattern of ones and zeroes appears to move one bit further left.

Table 2-6

Left-shifting 78

Value	Bit Pattern
78	00000000000000000000000001001110
78 << 1 = 156	00000000000000000000000010011100
78 << 2 = 312	00000000000000000000000100111000
78 << 3 = 624	00000000000000000000001001110000
78 << 4 = 1248	00000000000000000000010011100000
78 << 5 = 2496	00000000000000000000100111000000
78 << 6 = 4992	00000000000000000001001110000000
78 << 7 = 9984	00000000000000000010011100000000
78 << 8 = 19,968	00000000000000000100111000000000
78 << 9 = 39,936	00000000000000001001110000000000
78 << 10 = 79,872	00000000000000010011100000000000
78 << 11 = 159,744	00000000000000100111000000000000
78 << 12 = 319,488	00000000000001001110000000000000
78 << 13 = 638,976	00000000000010011100000000000000

Also notice that at each step, the value of the number is doubled. A 1-bit shift left is exactly equivalent to multiplication by two. Depending on the compiler, the virtual machine, and the CPU, it may be mildly quicker to shift an int to the left by the appropriate number of bits rather than to multiply by two. Similarly, shifting an int to the right can replace dividing by two or a power of two. However, this optimization may well not be worth the decrease in the legibility of your code, even on platforms where it makes a difference in performance.

What happens when the pattern of ones reaches the left side? Does it wrap around? No. The ones just march off to the left as the right side fills with zeroes. Note that once you hit 25 left shifts, you lose the multiplication by two property and drop over into negative numbers. If you had started with a larger number, this might have happened sooner. From that point on, the results bear little numerical relation to the original 78. Table 2-7 demonstrates.

Table 2-7
Left-shifting 78 by 22 to 31 places

Value	Bit Pattern
78 << 22 = 327,155,712	00010011100000000000000000000000
78 << 23 = 654,311,424	00100111000000000000000000000000
78 << 24 = 1,308,622,848	01001110000000000000000000000000
78 << 25 = 1,677,721,600	10011100000000000000000000000000
78 << 26 = 939,524,096	00111000000000000000000000000000
78 << 27 = 1,879,048,192	01110000000000000000000000000000
78 << 28 = -536,870,912	11100000000000000000000000000000
78 << 29 = -1,073,741,824	11000000000000000000000000000000
78 << 30 = -2,147,483,648	10000000000000000000000000000000
78 << 31 = 0	00000000000000000000000000000000

However, if you keep going, something interesting happens. The next shift, by 32, appears to bring the number back, as Table 2-8 demonstrates.

Table 2-8 should look familiar. Except for the number of bits by which 78 is shifted, it's an exact copy of Table 2-6. Did it just take a little extra time to wrap around? Not exactly. Java limits the right side of the shift operator to five bits (six bits if the left side is a long). Extra bits are truncated. This means that you can only really shift an int (or a byte, or a short) between 0 and 31 bits. Longs can be shifted between 0 and 63 bits. If you try to shift by more than that, Java throws away the higher-order bits. Thus, in the last line of Table 2-8, 78 is really being shifted by 45 - 32 = 13 bits, not by 45 bits.

Table 2-8
Left-shifting 78 by values greater than 31

Value	Bit pattern
78 << 32 = 78	00000000000000000000000001001110
78 << 33 = 156	00000000000000000000000010011100
78 << 34 = 312	00000000000000000000000100111000
78 << 35 = 624	00000000000000000000001001110000
78 << 36 = 1248	00000000000000000000010011100000
78 << 37 = 2496	00000000000000000000100111000000
78 << 38 = 4992	00000000000000000001001110000000
78 << 39 = 9984	00000000000000000010011100000000
78 << 40 = 19,968	00000000000000000100111000000000
78 << 41 = 39,936	00000000000000001001110000000000
78 << 42 = 79,872	00000000000000010011100000000000
78 << 43 = 159,744	00000000000000100111000000000000
78 << 44 = 319,488	00000000000001001110000000000000
78 << 45 = 638,976	00000000000010011100000000000000

In this example, we used an int. You can also shift bytes, shorts, chars, and longs. Bytes, chars, and shorts are promoted to ints before being shifted. Floats, doubles, and booleans cannot be shifted.

Making Floats from Bits

If you really need to create a float from a series of bits, there are a couple of workarounds. You can shift the bits around in an int and use the static java.lang.Float.intBitsToFloat() method to convert the int into a float. For example, suppose data is a byte array with four components that correspond to the four bytes in a float. (You'll see exactly this in Chapter 4.) You can read the float out of the byte array by first shifting the bytes into an int called bits and then calling the java.lang.Float. intBitsToFloat(int bits) method like this:

```
int bits = data[0] << 24 | data[1] << 16 | data[2] << 8 | data[3];
float f = Float.intBitsToFloat(bits);
```

You can make doubles from longs in a similar fashion with the java.lang.Double.longBitsToDouble(long bits) method.

```
long bits = (long) data[0] << 56 | (long) data[1] << 48
 | (long) data[2] << 40 | (long) data[3] << 32
 | (long) data[4] << 24 | (long) data[5] << 16
 | (long) data[6] << 8 | (long) data[7];
double d = Double.longBitsToDouble(bits);
```

Alternately, you can construct a ByteArrayInputStream from the byte array, chain the ByteArrayInputStream to a DataInputStream, and then call the readFloat() or readDouble() method of the DataInputStream. For example,

```
ByteArrayInputStream bis = new ByteArrayInputStream(data);
DataInputStream dis = new DataInputStream(bis);
float f = dis.readFloat();
```

In most Java implementations, this is less efficient than the first alternative. However, it produces slightly more intelligible code.

The >> operator shifts numbers to the right with *sign extension*. This means that vacated bits on the left are filled with the sign bit: 0 for a positive number or 1 for a negative number. Otherwise, right shifts carry the same caveats as left shifts: The left side must be an integral type and will be promoted to an int if necessary before shifting. The left side must be between 0 and 31 (0 to 63 if the left hand side's a long) and will be truncated to that value if necessary. For example, the int -23 is, in binary notation, 11111111111111111111111111101001. Table 2-9 shows what you get when this is right shifted by various numbers of bits. Note that the vacated spots are filled with sign bits and that right shifting is equivalent to division by two.

Sometimes you don't want to fill with the sign bits, but rather with 0. The >>> operator does an unsigned shift right. In other words, it fills the vacated spaces with zeroes regardless of the sign bit. Table 2-10 demonstrates this.

Table 2-9
Right-shifting –23

Value	Bit Pattern
-23	11111111111111111111111111101001
-23 > 1 = -12	11111111111111111111111111110100
-23 > 2 = -6	11111111111111111111111111111010
-23 > 3 = -3	11111111111111111111111111111101
-23 > 4 = -2	11111111111111111111111111111110
-23 > 5 = -1	11111111111111111111111111111111
-23 > 6 = -1	11111111111111111111111111111111

Table 2-10
Unsigned right-shifting of –23

Value	Bit Pattern
-23	11111111111111111111111111101001
-23 >> 1 = 2,147,483,636	01111111111111111111111111110100
-23 >> 2 = 1,073,741,818	00111111111111111111111111111010
-23 >> 3 = 536,870,909	00011111111111111111111111111101
-23 >> 4 = 268,435,454	00001111111111111111111111111110
-23 >> 5 = 134,217,727	00000111111111111111111111111111
-23 >> 6 = 67,108,863	00000011111111111111111111111111

The >>=, <<=, and >>>= behave as you might expect, shifting the left argument by the number of bits specified in the right argument and in the direction specified by the operator, and then assigning the result to the left side.

Little-Endian data

To read Little-Endian data, you first read the necessary number of bytes into an array. Then you use the << bit shift operator and the | operator to put the parts of the Little-Endian number back together in the right order.

```
public static int readLittleEndianInt(InputStream is) throws IOException {

    int result;
    byte[] buffer = new byte[4];

    int check = is.read(buffer);
    if (check != 4) throw new IOException("Unexpected End of Stream");

    result = (buffer[3] << 24) | (buffer[2] << 16) | (buffer[1] << 8) |
buffer[0];

    return result;

}
```

Longs are just the same except you have to use an 8-byte buffer and put eight pieces back together.

To write Little-Endian data, you create a buffer for the bytes in an int. The bytes are extracted from the int by a simple cast. Recall that casting an int to a byte truncates the int to its least significant byte. Before the cast is done, the right shift operator >> moves the needed byte into position in the least significant byte.

```
public static void writeLittleEndianInt(int i, OutputStream os) throws
IOException {

    int result;
    byte[] buffer = new byte[4];

    buffer[0] = (byte) i;
    buffer[1] = (byte) (i >> 8);
    buffer[2] = (byte) (i >> 16);
    buffer[3] = (byte) (i >> 24);

    os.write(buffer);

}
```

Unsigned integers

java.io.DataInputStream has methods to read unsigned bytes and unsigned shorts, but nothing to read an unsigned int. To do that, you must read four bytes and use them to construct the lower four bytes of a long. The upper four bytes of the long will be zero. For example:

```
public static long readUnsignedInt(InputStream is) throws IOException {

  byte[] buffer = new byte[4];

  int check = is.read(buffer);
  if (check != 4) throw new IOException("Unexpected End of Stream");

  long result = 0L;

  // move the bytes into position
  result = (buffer[0] << 24) | (buffer[1] << 16) | (buffer[2] << 8) |
buffer[3];
  // zero out the upper four bytes
  result &= 0xFFFFFFFF;

  return result;

}
```

It's necessary to combine the result with 0xFFFFFFFF using a bitwise and to make sure that none of the bytes were sign extended into negative numbers when left-shifted.

Image manipulation with bit shift operators

Bit shift operators are fairly obscure. One of the few areas of Java where they're useful is working with images and image filters.

Java images are built with a 32-bit color model. Each color has four channels: alpha, red, green, and blue. The alpha channel represents transparency. The other three channels are the primary colors for an additive color system. Each of the four channels has a value from 0 to 255 (in other words, one unsigned byte). For the color channels, the higher the value, the brighter the color. For the alpha channel, the higher the value, the more opaque the image is.

Java 1.0's support for transparency is mainly theoretical. A value of 255 is fully opaque. Anything less is 100 percent transparent (invisible).

Figure 2-9 shows a color that is 50 percent gray. The alpha channel is 255 (11111111), which is fully opaque, while each of the red, green, and blue channels is set to 127. This means the color is equal to the integer 11111101111111011111101111111. The integer value has little meaning here, though; it's the individual bytes that matter.

When the red channel, green channel, and blue channel have the same value, the resulting image varies from black (all three 00000000) to white (all three 11111111). It passes through various shades of gray in between. By varying the colors disproportionately, you can produce the different colors of the visible spectrum. For example, pure blue is 11111111000000-001111111100000000.

01111111	01111111	01111111
Red	Green	Blue

Figure 2-9
The layout of a 32-bit color

So how do you create these colors? It's simple, really. Just initialize ints to the values you want for each of the four channels, shift them into place, and combine them with the bitwise OR operator, |. For example, to create a pure blue, do the following:

```
int alpha = 255 << 24;
int red = 0 << 16;
int blue = 255 << 8;
int green = 0;
int pureblue = alpha | red | green | blue;
```

If you prefer, you can combine these on one line. For example, to create the 50 percent gray of Figure 2-9, use this command:

```
int halfgray = (255 << 24) | (127 << 16) | (127 << 8) | 127;
```

SUMMARY

In this chapter you learn how a computer stores numbers. You learn what a place-value number system is, and about the binary and hexadecimal place-value number systems computers use. You learn how the primitive Java data types like int and float are laid out in memory and how this affects operations with those types.

You also learn how Java stores characters and the different character sets used for this purpose, particularly ASCII, ISO Latin-1, Unicode, and UTF8. You learn when and for what purposes these different but related character sets are used and how to convert from one to another.

Finally, you learn how to use the bit-level operators to operate on numbers at a very low level. The bitwise operators combine values in memory, while the bitshift operators move the bits in data back and forth.

CLASSES, STRINGS, AND ARRAYS

3

*T*he last chapter explored Java's primitive data types. This chapter explores Java's reference data types. A *primitive* data type is one whose value is stored directly in memory. A *reference* data type stores only a reference to the place where the actual data can be found. There are two reference data types: objects and arrays. Objects and arrays are normally explained very abstractly and at a very high level. It's my goal in this chapter to explain them very concretely and at a very low level. By understanding the low-level structure you can make sure you're that working *with* Java rather than against it and substantially speed up your programs.

THE HEAP

The *heap* is a large block of memory that Java uses to store objects and arrays. Memory in the heap can be allocated discontiguously. When a new object or array is created, the space comes from somewhere in the heap. Exactly where isn't important, or even defined. When an object or array is garbage-collected, the memory that it occupied in the heap is freed. That is, the memory is marked as unused and made available for reuse by other objects.

An object has two parts: its fields and its methods. Each field requires memory to hold a value appropriate to its type. Each method requires memory to hold its arguments and return values and code. However, the memory for the method is needed only when the method is invoked. Furthermore, methods are the same for each instance of the class. Methods therefore are allocated on an as-needed basis in an area of memory called the *stack*.

Consider the following 3DPoint class:

```
public class 3DPoint {

    double x;
    double y;
    double z;

    //  various methods...

}
```

This class has three double fields. Each double occupies eight bytes. Therefore, each instance of this class needs 24 bytes of memory in the heap. If there is one 3DPoint object in existence, then exactly 24 bytes of heap memory are needed. If there are two 3DPoint objects in existence, then 48 bytes of heap memory are needed. If there are three 3DPoint objects, then 72 bytes of heap memory are needed, and so on.

Arrays are similar. To determine how much heap memory that an array requires, multiply the length of the array by the width of the data type stored in the array. A float array of length 10 thus needs 40 bytes of heap memory; a char array of length 10 needs 20 bytes of heap memory; and a byte array of length 10 needs 10 bytes of heap memory.

When a new object or array is created, the necessary amount of space is set aside for it in the heap. The new operator returns a reference to the block of memory in the heap where the object or array is stored. The virtual machine is responsible for managing the heap and making sure that the same block of memory is not used for two different objects or arrays at the same time.

The exact size of the heap is system-dependent. However, the heap is finite on all systems. In some Java implementations, the heap can grow if more space is needed. On others the size of the heap is fixed when the virtual machine starts up. Nonetheless, the heap is definitely smaller than the memory (physical or virtual) available on the host computer. If the heap fills up, the runtime system throws an OutOfMemoryError.

Garbage collection attempts to prevent this from happening by purging objects and arrays from the heap when they're no longer necessary. Exactly how the garbage collector decides what can and cannot be purged from the heap is one of the topics in Chapter 6. For now, all you need to know is that the garbage collector is quite reliable and won't purge anything that you might actually need to use.

Objects of different types require different amounts of memory. The more fields that an object has, the more memory that it needs in the heap. Objects can contain other objects as fields. For example, consider this class:

```
public class GridPoint {

  Integer i1;
  Integer i2

  //  various methods...

}
```

The GridPoint class contains two Integer objects. A GridPoint object does not store the Integer objects themselves in its own block of memory; it stores only references to the Integer objects. References take up four bytes. Therefore, the GridPoint object needs eight bytes of heap memory, regardless of how much heap memory an Integer object requires. Of course, the total memory used by a program will include the memory used by all of the GridPoints, all of the Integers, and all of the other objects stored in the heap.

POINTERS, HANDLES, AND REFERENCES

There's a lot of confusion about whether Java does or does not have pointers. If you've never programmed in a pointer-based language like C or Pascal, then you will probably never need to understand pointers. You can rest assured that Java lets you do everything that you normally use pointers to do, especially with respect to data structures. However, if you're accustomed to a pointer-based language like C, then you probably need to be convinced of this statement.

What is a pointer?

A *pointer* is the address of a particular byte of a computer's memory. For example, a computer with eight megabytes of memory has 8 * 1024 * 1024 = 8,388,608 bytes of memory. Therefore, the valid pointers on this system begin at zero and count up to 8,388,607. The first byte of memory has the address zero. The last byte of memory has the address 8,388,607. With a pointer, you can inspect the contents of any byte or group of bytes. Similarly, you can write any value you like at any point in memory. For example, in C, to write the int 768 in the four bytes starting with byte 4,324,682, you would write

```
int n = 4324682;
int* m = (int*) n;
*m = 768;
```

No check is performed to make sure that it makes sense to put the value 768 at memory location 4324682. If you put the wrong value in the wrong place, it can crash your program, your machine, or worse.

These sorts of bugs are common in C programs. Java has eliminated pointers in order to prevent them. Furthermore, pointers open up many security holes, because they allow any program more or less unrestricted access to all parts of the system.

What is a handle?

A *handle* is a pointer to a pointer. That is, a handle points to a location in memory where the address of the actual data can be found. The advantage of handles over raw pointers is that an object can be moved in memory and the pointer to it updated while the handle for the program remains valid. This has significant advantages for keeping memory clear and defragmented.

For example, after a program has run for some time, many objects will have been constructed and garbage collected. This can make a heap very fragmented, as shown in Figure 3-1. Each block is a word. The gray blocks are words in use. The white blocks are free words. Of course, real heaps have many more words than this, but this is sufficient for a demonstration.

Figure 3-1
A fragmented heap.

Suppose, with the heap in this state, that you need four words for an object. There is plenty of space in the heap, but it's fragmented. There is no one place where you can get four words of contiguous memory. To make space for the new object, you have to move some of the allocated blocks around in memory. However, this can cause problems if the running program has pointers straight into the heap. For example, consider Figure 3-2. This is the same heap, with object variables shown as ovals. The arrows are pointers into the heap. Each object has at least one pointer (to its own data), and some have multiple pointers if they themselves contain references to other objects. Furthermore, one object may be pointed to from several different places. This interconnected web of pointers makes it very difficult to move objects in the heap, because you have to update all of the different pointers that can exist in hundreds of different objects, methods, and threads.

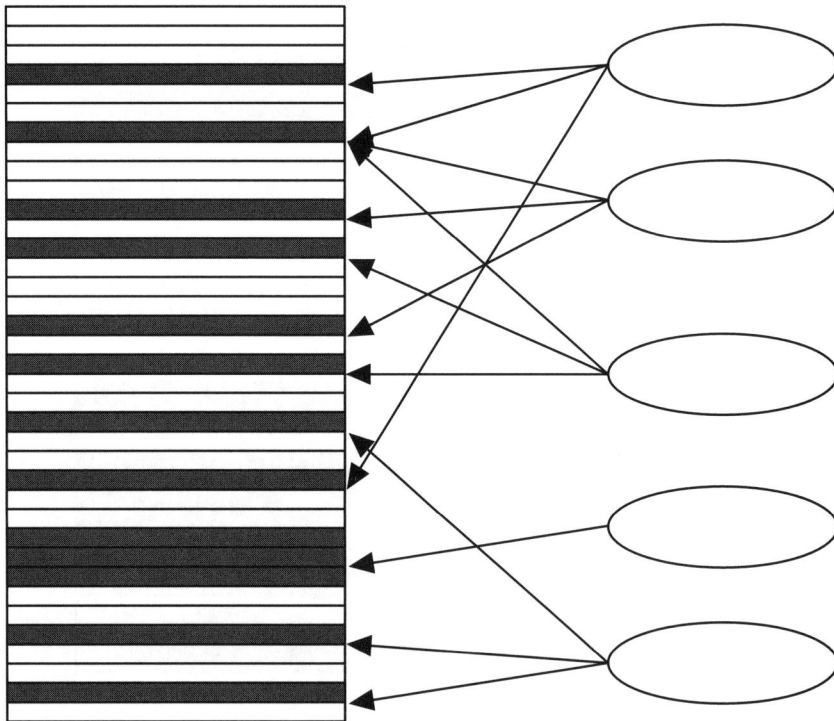

Figure 3-2
A heap with pointers.

Now look at what happens if you just willy-nilly compact the heap by moving all the data down to the bottom. Figure 3-3 shows the result. Now there is space for a four-word object. However, many — perhaps most — of the pointers are broken. Some now point to the wrong object. Others point to nowhere in particular. The VM can try to identify every reference to each moved object in the running program and update it with the new address of its data, but there can be thousands of these, and the operation can be extremely time-consuming in a large program.

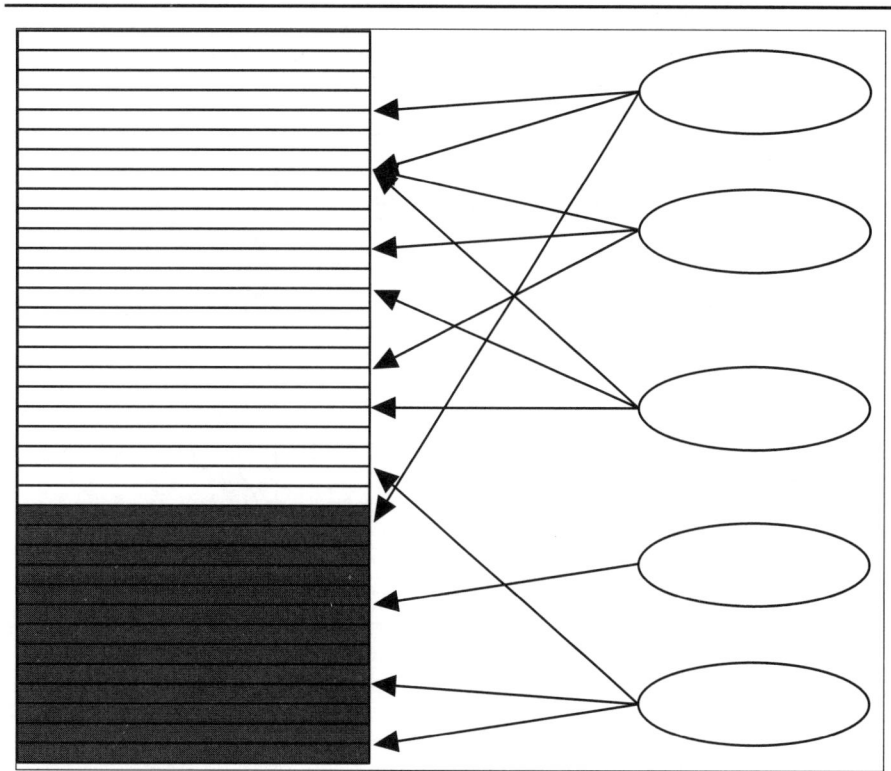

Figure 3-3
A compacted heap.

How can the references be arranged in such a way that they don't break when the heap is defragmented? One way to look at the problem is that references point to areas of different sizes in the heap. If you could somehow arrange it so that every object needed exactly the same amount of space in the heap, then fragmentation would not be a problem. As long as there was any free space at all, it could be used.

Of course, different objects do take different amounts of space, but references always take four bytes (one word). The solution is to insert an extra block of references between the references in your source code and the heap. When an object is moved in the heap, only one link needs to be updated: the one between the offset table and the data in the heap. The many more pointers to the offset table do not need to be updated. Furthermore, it's relatively easy to find the pointers in the offset table that need to be updated. The VM does not need to search the entire memory space of the running program looking for anything that might be a pointer.

Figure 3-4 shows this scheme. To find an object's data, you follow the first arrow into the offset table. Then you follow the second arrow out to the actual data in the heap.

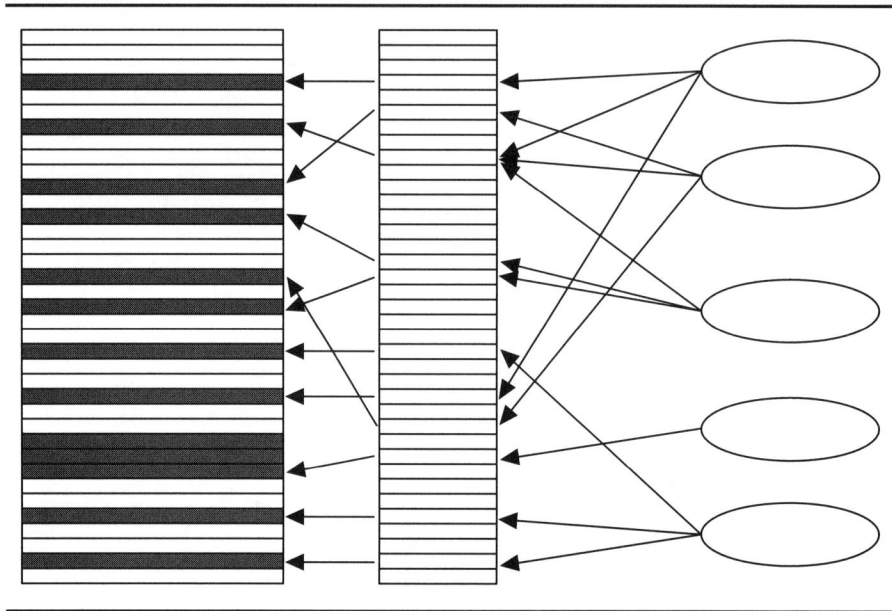

Figure 3-4
A fragmented heap with handles.

At first glance this appears more complicated than the method in Figure 3-2. However, consider what happens when the heap is compacted. Figure 3-5 shows the result. The object pointers don't need to be changed. Only one pointer needs to be adjusted for each object, not one pointer for each reference, as in the previous case. Because there's a one-to-one relationship between filled entries in the offset table and objects in the heap, once you've adjusted the pointer from the offset table to the object, you'll never have to adjust another pointer to the same object later. If you're moving only one object in the heap, you can stop looking as soon as you find the pointer to it in the offset table.

There are many optimizations that can be made to this scheme. For example, each object in the heap can contain the index of its pointer in the offset table, so when the memory manger needs to move it, the memory manager can adjust the pointer in constant time.

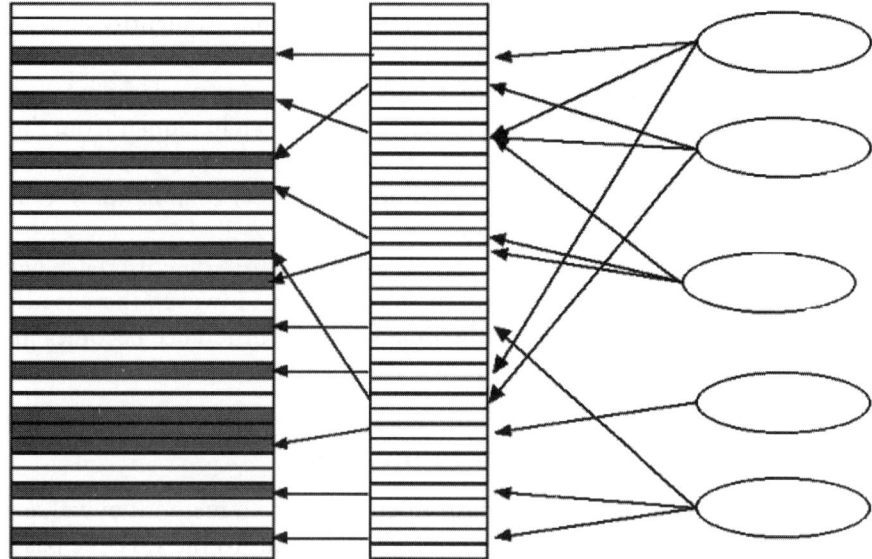

Figure 3-5
A compacted heap with handles.

Secret

This all happens behind the scenes, so you normally don't need to worry about it. Sun's virtual machines use handles, but this isn't absolutely necessary. Microsoft's VM implements references as pointers, not doubly indirected handles.

Of course, double indirection is useful not only in virtual machines. This scheme, or variants of it, can be used in situations where moving objects in the heap is very expensive but moving objects in the offset table is cheap. For example, if the heap is actually a file on disk but the offset table is in memory, then you can reorganize the structure of a file by changing the offset table. Variations on this scheme are used in most relational databases.

What is a reference?

Reference is strictly a Java term. There are no references in C or Pascal. A *reference* is an abstract identifier for a block of memory in the heap. Furthermore, a reference has a type like string or double[]. At the level of the non-virtual host machine, references may be implemented as handles, pointers, or something else entirely. However, references are not pointers; they are not handles; they are merely a means of identifying a particular block of memory in the heap.

How exactly the virtual machine implements references at the level of machine code is VM-dependent and completely hidden from the programmer in any case. Most VMs — including Sun's — use handles, not pointers. Microsoft's VM uses pointers rather than handles. Other schemes are possible.

Ninety percent of the time, you can ignore the difference between a reference to an object and the object itself. However, there is always that annoying 10 percent of the time when the difference becomes important. This 10 percent occurs mostly when passing arguments to methods.

Passing arguments to methods

There are two ways to pass an argument to a method: by value and by reference. The difference is in what happens to the variable passed in the calling method as a result of what's done to it in the called method. For example, consider this code fragment:

```
int a = 7;
changeVariable(a);
System.out.println(a);
```

Now suppose the changeVariable() method looks like this:

```
public void changeVariable(int a) {
  a = 10;
}
```

What value gets printed — 7 or 10? If the argument a is passed by value, then a copy of variable a's value is used by the changeVariable() method. The changeVariable() method never gets access to the original variable a in the calling method. It has a different variable, also named a. Therefore, the calling method prints the value 7.

On the other hand, if a is passed by reference, then the changeVariable() method does not get a copy of the variable named a. It gets the real thing. The name a in the calling method and the name a in the changeVariable() method refer to the same variable. Therefore, System.out.println() prints 10.

Note that the names aren't important here. If changeVariable() were written using i or some name other than a for its argument, the result would be the same. What makes the difference is whether the variable is passed by reference or by value. If a variable is passed by reference, it can change in the calling method. If it's passed by value, it cannot. Java passes all arguments by value, not by reference.

Because object and array variables in Java are references to the object or array, it can appear as if an object is passed by reference if you modify only the fields of the object or array, but do not change the reference itself. For example, consider this program:

```java
import java.awt.Point;

class changePoint {

  public static void main(String args[]) {

    Point p1 = new Point(0, 0);
    changePoint(p1);
    System.out.println(p1);

  }

  static void changePoint(Point p) {

    p.x = 38;
    p.y = 97;

  }

}
```

This program prints

```
java.awt.Point[x=38,y=97]
```

The point has therefore been changed. However, the reference, which is what was really passed, has not been changed. To see that, consider the following program:

```java
import java.awt.Point;

class dontChangePoint {

  public static void main(String args[]) {

    Point p1 = new Point(0, 0);
    dontChangePoint(p1);
```

```
        System.out.println(p1);

    }

    static void dontChangePoint(Point p) {

        p = new Point(38, 97);

    }

}
```

It prints the following:

```
java.awt.Point[x=0,y=0]
```

Once and for all: Does Java Have Pointers?

The issue of whether Java really has pointers seems to generate countless flame wars on Usenet, almost as many as are generated by Star Trek trivia. Some of this confusion is a result of incorrect or incomplete knowledge. Even more of the confusion is a result of using the same word to mean two different things.

In this book, I use the word *pointer* to mean the address of a byte of memory on the computer. This is the definition of pointer used by assembly language, C, and C++ programmers. Java has no equivalent for this kind of pointer.

Some programmers, particularly those accustomed to pointerless languages like Fortran 77 and Basic, use the word *pointer* in a very abstract sense, in which it is just about anything that gives a reference to or points to a block of data. Thus, an array that contains indexes of entries in another array is often said to be an array of pointers, although C programmers would not recognize it as such. In this sense, Java does have pointers.

Some programmers also claim that Java has pointers because the virtual machine may use pointers in the same sense as used by assembly language programmers to implement Java's references. In fact, some implementations of Java, particularly Microsoft's, do use pointers in exactly this fashion. However, the .class file verifier severely restricts what you can do with these pointers. In particular, you cannot use them as freely as you can in C or assembly language. You cannot perform arithmetic on them. You cannot convert them to and from numeric data types like int. Furthermore, the virtual machine need not implement references as pointers. Sun's virtual machines use handles instead. Others may use something completely different, like numeric indexes into a large, static array.

The bottom line is that Java doesn't have pointers in the sense that 95 percent of the people who talk about pointers mean. It's best just to use the term *reference*, and try to stay out of flame wars when possible.

In this example, a copy of the reference p1 was passed to the dontChangePoint() method. A new Point object was then assigned to that copy. This, however, did not change the old reference in the main() method. In the previous example, the reference p in the changePoint() method and p1 in the main() method both referred to the same object. In this example, p and p1 refer to different objects after the new Point is assigned to p.

Special references

There are three special references in Java source code: null, this, and super. The meaning of these references generally depends on their context.

The null reference

The null reference is an invalid reference. It has no type, and thus may be assigned to a variable of any reference type. When a reference variable is declared but not constructed, it is initially equal to null.

The this reference

The special reference this always refers to the current object. For example, the statement

```
int j = this.x;
```

sets the variable j equal to the x field of this object. Using the this reference is normally optional. Using "int j = x" would work equally well. However, on occasion, a variable declared inside a method can shadow a field. This is most common in constructors. For example, consider this elaboration of the 3Dpoint class:

```
public class 3DPoint {

  double x;
  double y;
  double z;

  public 3DPoint (double x, double y, double z) {

    this.x = x;
    this.y = y;
    this.z = z;

  }
```

```
// other methods...

}
```

The three arguments to the constructor — x, y, and z — shadow the fields of the same name. Inside the 3DPoint constructor, x, y, and z no longer refer to the fields of the object but rather to the arguments to the method. However, this.x, this.y, and this.z still refer to the fields x, y, and z.

The this keyword can also be used to call a different constructor in the current class. With this usage, this is not, strictly speaking, a reference. The this keyword can be used this way only in the first statement of another constructor. For example, to call the 3DPoint (double x, double y, double z) constructor from the noargs 3DPoint() constructor, you would write

```
public 3DPoint () {

    this(0, 0, 0);

}
```

This technique is especially common in polymorphic constructors. Arguments not passed to one constructor are filled in with default values as a call to another constructor.

The super reference

The this reference refers to methods and fields of the current object. The super reference refers to the methods and fields of the immediate superclass. You need to use the super prefix only if a field or method in the subclass has the same name as a field or method in the superclass.

For example, the java.awt.Component class has a handleEvent() method, so its subclasses do, too. Specifically, java.awt.Container has a handleEvent() method; java.awt.Frame() has a handleEvent() method; and any subclass of java.awt.Frame that you write has a handleEvent() method. Now let's suppose that you want to write a subclass of Frame that allows the window (that is, the Frame) to be closed. One way to do this is to override handleEvent() in your subclass of Frame so that it handles WINDOW_DESTROY events. That method might look like this:

```
public boolean handleEvent(Event e) {

    if (e.id == Event.WINDOW_DESTROY) {
        hide();
```

```
        return true;
    }
    else return false;

}
```

This method will close the window (by calling the Frame's hide()
method), but it doesn't handle any other events. It completely misses mouse
clicks, key presses, action events, and more. This would normally be
handled by the handleEvent() method of the Component class, but we've
shadowed that method with our own handleEvent(). Once we've finished
our custom processing of the WINDOW_DESTROY event, we want to pass
all other events to the handleEvent() method of java.awt.Component. The
super keyword acts like a reference to that class that lets us do that. Instead
of writing "else return false;", write "else return super.handleEvent(e);".
This calls the handleEvent() method in the superclass rather than the
handleEvent() method in this class. Here's the complete method:

```
public boolean handleEvent(Event e) {

    if (e.id == Event.WINDOW_DESTROY) {
        hide();
        return true;
    }
    else return super.handleEvent(e);

}
```

Using the super keyword like this finds the nearest method with a
matching signature. In this case, it's the handleEvent() method in
java.awt.Component. If there were a handleEvent() method in
java.awt.Frame or java.awt.Container, that would be called instead.

Like the this keyword, super also has a non-reference meaning inside a
constructor. If you use super() as the first statement in a constructor, it calls
the matching constructor in the immediate superclass.

If you do not include an explicit call to super() as the first statement in
your constructor, then the compiler will insert such a call into the byte code.
The compiler always chooses the noargs super() constructor if you don't
explicitly choose a different one. This can lead to annoying bugs that
prevent you from instantiating a subclass if the superclass doesn't have a
public or protected noargs constructor. For example, consider this incorrect
Java program:

```
public class superclass {

  public superclass(int i) {

  }

}


class subclass extends superclass {

  subclass() {

  }

}
```

If you try to compile this program, you get the error message "No constructor matching superclass() found in class superclass: superclass.java line 12". This is a common problem for novices. What you should do to fix this is completely un-obvious, because you never actually called the superclass() constructor that you're being warned doesn't exist. The solution is either add a noargs constructor to the superclass or to call the superclass(int i) constructor in the first line of the subclass. For example,

```
class subclass extends superclass {

  subclass() {
    super(0);
  }

}
```

THE CLASS CLASS

Introductory texts and classes about object-oriented programming spend a lot of time trying to explain the difference between objects and classes. If there is a single thing that separates people who understand object-oriented programming from the people who merely know a few buzzwords, it's the proper use of the words *object* and *class*. It's drilled into students that they are two different things, as different as the recipe for a cake and the cake itself. However, now that you are a more advanced student of object-oriented programming, I can tell you the truth. Classes really *are* objects, at least in Java.

A Java .class file contains the byte code for a particular class. When the Java VM loads a class, a ClassLoader object reads the byte codes and uses them to instantiate a new object of type java.lang.Class — in other words, a Class object. A Class object has methods that are useful for deducing information about the class at runtime.

There are two primary ways that your program can bootstrap a reference to a Class object: a ClassLoader object can load the class from bytes, or your program can call the static method Class.forName(String s) to load the class given its name. For example:

```
Class threadClass = Class.forName("java.lang.Thread");
```

The name of the class must be the fully qualified name, including the entire package. For example, you must write java.lang.Thread and not just Thread. This is true regardless of the import statements in the program or whether the class is in the java.lang package.

Once you have a Class object, you can use the newInstance() method to create instances of the class. Its signature is

```
public Object newInstance() throws InstantiationException,
IllegalAccessException
```

For example:

```
try {
  Object o = threadClass.newInstance();
}
catch (InstantiationException e) {
}
catch (IllegalAccessException e) {
}
```

The object is returned without any type information, though. In other words, it's a raw java.lang.Object, not a java.lang.Thread. You can cast the created object to the appropriate type like this:

```
Thread t = (Thread) o;
```

You often see these three steps combined on one line like this:

```
Thread t =(Thread) Class.forName("java.lang.Thread").newInstance();
```

You need to know what the object will be before you can cast it. There's no convenient way to determine the most specific type of an object created at runtime. If you know roughly what sort of objects are likely to be created, then you can check the possibilities with the instanceof operator and respond accordingly. For example,

```
if (o instanceof Thread) {
  Thread t = (Thread) o;
  // ... work with the Thread
}
else if (o instanceof Applet) {
  Applet a = (Applet) o;
  // work with the Applet
}
```

In general, though, it's much easier if you know your objects' types at compile time.

Aside from the type change, the newInstance() method behaves exactly like using the new operator with the noargs constructor for the class. The following lines produce identical byte code:

```
Thread t =(Thread) Class.getClass("java.lang.Thread").newInstance();
Thread t = new Thread();
```

If a class doesn't have a noargs constructor, you can't instantiate it with the newInstance() method. For example java.lang.Integer has two constructors:

```
public Integer(int  value)
public Integer(String  s)
```

It does not have a constructor with the signature

```
public Integer()
```

Therefore, you should not write

```
Integer i =(Integer) Class.getClass("java.lang.Integer").newInstance();
```

If you try this, a java.lang.NoSuchMethodError will be thrown at runtime. Integers and other classes that do not have noargs constructors must be instantiated with the new operator.

Once you have a Class object, there are several other methods to help you determine runtime type information.

The getName() method returns the full package and class name of the class of this object. Its signature is

```
public String getName()
```

This is primarily useful for debugging. For example,

```
public void printname(Object o) {
  System.out.println("I got an object of class " + o.getname());
}
```

The name returned is always the most specific type possible, never a superclass or an interface.

The getSuperclass() method returns a Class object representing the class of the immediate superclass of this object. Its signature is

```
public Class getSuperclass()
```

You can use this to walk the class hierarchy of an object. For example, given a Class object c,

```
while ((c = c.getSuperclass()) != null) {
  System.out.println("extends " + c.getName());
}
```

However, java.lang.Object does not have a superclass, so if the Class object is of type java.lang.Object, then null is returned. Thus, the last name printed by this loop will always be java.lang.Object because that's the ultimate superclass of all Java objects. Also, null is returned if the object is an interface.

Interfaces are also loaded into the VM as objects of type Class. You can test whether a Class object in fact represents an interface with the isInterface() method. It returns true if the Class object in question represents an interface and false if it doesn't. Its signature is

```
public boolean isInterface()
```

The getInterfaces() method returns an array containing Class objects that represent interfaces. Its signature is

```
public Class[] getInterfaces()
```

If the Class object represents a class, then the array contains Class objects representing all interfaces implemented by the class. However, if the Class object represents an interface, then the array contains objects representing all the interfaces extended by this interface. This array may be of length zero if the Class object neither implements nor extends any interfaces.

The one remaining piece of information about a Class object is the ClassLoader that was used to load the class from bytes on disk or on the network. The getClassLoader() method returns the ClassLoader object which loaded this class. It returns null if the class was not created by a ClassLoader. Its signature is

```
public ClassLoader getClassLoader()
```

Finally, there's the usual toString() method for creating a string representation of the Class object. The string is the word class or interface followed by the full, package-qualified name of the class. Some examples are "class java.lang.Integer" and "interface java.io.Serializable."

Listing 3-1 is a program that demonstrates most of these methods. The static printRTTI(Object o) method is the heart of it. This method checks all the possible type information about the object that it has passed and prints it on System.out. This can be very useful for debugging. The main() method tests the program on two objects: an Integer and a DataOutputStream. The three methods printHierarchy(), printInterfaces(), and printClassLoader() break up the code to make it a little more legible. Each one handles a particular aspect of the runtime type.

Listing 3-1
RTTI

```
import java.io.*;

public class RTTI {

    public static void main(String args[]) {
      printRTTI(new Integer(7));
      printRTTI(new DataOutputStream(System.out));
    }

    public static void printRTTI(Object o) {

    if (o == null) {
      System.out.println("This object is null");
      return;
    }
    Class c = o.getClass();
    printHierarchy(c);
    printInterfaces(c);
    printClassLoader(c);

    }
```

(continued)

RTTI *(continued)*

```
static void printHierarchy(Class c) {

 System.out.println(c.getName());
  while ((c = c.getSuperclass()) != null) {
    System.out.println("extends " + c.getName());
  }

}

static void printInterfaces(Class c) {

  Class[] ci = c.getInterfaces();
  if (ci.length > 0) {
    if (c.isInterface()) {
      for (int i = 0; i < ci.length; i++) {
        System.out.println("extends" + ci[i].getName());
      }
    }
    else {
      System.out.println("implements ");
      for (int i = 0; i < ci.length; i++) {
        System.out.println(ci[i].getName() + ",");
      }
    }
  }

}

static void printClassLoader(Class c) {

  ClassLoader cl = c.getClassLoader();
  if (cl != null) System.out.println("This object was loaded by " + cl);

}

}
```

THE OBJECT CLASS

Now that you know that classes are objects, I'll confuse you a little more by
telling you that objects are classes, too. As with the Class class, there is,
however, a difference between the big O Object (which is a class) and the
little o object (which is an object).

The java.lang.Object class is the common superclass for all Java classes. All classes eventually extend java.lang.Object. Thus, all classes have access to the methods of java.lang.Object. The primary purpose of java.lang.Object is to provide several useful methods that the programmer can count on all classes having. These are clone(), equals(), finalize(), getClass(), hashCode(), notify(), notifyAll(), toString(), and wait(). Furthermore there's a single constructor, Object(), but you'll rarely (if ever) call it directly.

What these methods have in common is that they represent internal details of Java objects, not anything external to Java like a window, a mouse, a motorcycle, a supernova, or anything else that exists outside the virtual machine. Objects normally represent real world entities. However, the java.lang.Object class is something of a meta-class — that is, a class that represents objects. The clone() method copies objects. The equals() method compares objects. The getClass() method returns the class of an object. The hashCode() method computes a unique integer for an object. The toString() method creates a string representation of an object. The notify(), notifyAll(), and the wait() methods interface between objects and threads. What all these methods have in common is that they treat objects as computer-based abstractions, not as real world things. Let's take a closer look at these methods.

Cloning

The clone() method makes a bitwise copy of an object in memory and returns the copy. In other words, it creates a new instance of the object's class and copies the values of each field of the object into the new object. It copies all fields, whether they're public, private, protected, or package protected.

Not all objects can be cloned. In fact, by default an object may not be cloned. Only objects that implement the java.lang.Cloneable interface may be cloned. The Cloneable interface does not actually declare any methods. It just tells the clone method in java.lang.Object that it's okay to clone this object. If you try to clone an object that does not implement the Cloneable interface, a CloneNotSupportedException is thrown.

Equality

The equals() method compares two objects for equality. Because equals() is a method of java.lang.Object, any object can be compared for equality to any other object. That is, every object at least inherits an equals() method.

The equals() method has this signature:

```
public boolean equals(Object  obj)
```

The java.lang.Object.equals() method just checks to see if two reference variables refer to the same object. For example, consider the following three reference variables:

```
Integer i1 = new Integer(7);
Integer i2 = new Integer(7);
Integer i3 = i2;
```

Using the equals() method in java.lang.Object, i1 is not equal to i2 because i1 and i2 refer to two different objects, even though those objects have the same value. On the other hand, i2 and i3 are considered equal to each other because they refer to the same object.

This is often not the behavior you want. Therefore, most classes override equals() with a method that is more appropriate to the specific class. For example, the equals() method in java.lang.Integer does in fact test the values of the Integer objects to see if they're the same. Thus, i1.equals(i2) returns true because the equals() method in java.lang.Integer behaves differently than the equals() method in java.lang.Object.

It's nonetheless important to realize that there are often multiple, sensible ways to decide whether two objects are equal. For example, consider these two URL objects:

```
URL u1 = new URL("http://www.inch.com/");
URL u2 = new URL("http://worm.inch.com/");
```

www.inch.com and worm.inch.com are different names for the same machine, so these URLs point to the same page. But are the URLs the same? Maybe not. After all, one of the host names could be moved to a different machine while the other one stayed behind. Or consider these two URLs:

```
URL u3 = new URL("http://sunsite.unc.edu/javafaq/");
URL u4 = new URL("http://calzone.oit.unc.edu/javafaq/");
```

These two URLs point to the same page on the Web. However the first URL goes over a 100 Megabit per second (Mbps) FDDI connection and the second over a 10 Mbps Ethernet connection. So these URLs are probably best considered to be unequal.

In fact, Java considers all four of the URLs above to be unequal. The equals() method in the URL class, like most of the equals() methods in the java packages, is relatively shallow. It does not attempt to discover whether two different objects might mean the same thing if they are superficially different.

This isn't all. What about these two URLs?

```
    URL u5 = new
URL("http://sunsite.unc.edu/javafaq/javafaq.html#xtocid1902930");
    URL u6 = new
URL("http://sunsite.unc.edu/javafaq/javafaq.html#xtocid1902931");
```

These point to different sections of the same page. Although they are different in one sense, Java considers them to be equal because they point to the same page.

The bottom line is that there are few guarantees about how the equals() method behaves. The only thing you can be reasonably confident about is that references to the same object will be equal to each other. Otherwise, you have to do the best you can. Regrettably, the documentation for the equals() methods is often incomplete. The only real way to find out what a particular equals() method really does is to look at the source code. If that's not possible, equals() methods tend to be simple enough to understand from decompiled or disassembled byte code. If for some reason you can't disassemble or decompile a class, then you have to run as many tests as you can think of to determine what's really going on.

Finalization

The finalize() method is called when an object is garbage-collected. The finalize()method is the programmer's last chance to do something with an object. The finalize() method of the java.lang.Object class is an empty method; that is, it does absolutely nothing. It looks something like this:

```
protected void finalize() throws Throwable {

}
```

You may ask yourself, why even have a finalize() method in java.lang.Object if it never does anything? The reason is so that the runtime knows that it can always call an object's finalize() method. A method doesn't have to do anything to be called. Subclasses of java.lang.Object may override finalize(). If they do, their finalize() method is called. Otherwise the finalize() method in java.lang.Object is called. It's much simpler to know

you can always call finalize() for any object at all than to have to check
whether an object has a finalize() method before calling it.

Runtime type information

In Java, an object can tell you what class it belongs to via the getClass()
method of java.lang.Object, which has the following signature:

```
public final Class getClass()
```

getClass() returns a Class object (an object of type Class) that can be
manipulated with the methods of the last section.

There's little reason to override this method in your own classes.

Hash codes

Hash codes are integers used as keys in hash tables. Each object that can
serve as a key in a hash table must be associated with a precise integer. The
list of items in the hash table is then indexed with these integer keys. Equal
objects — objects which compare equal to each other with the equals()
method — are supposed to have identical hash codes. Unequal objects
normally have different hash codes, although this is not always true. The
efficiency of a hash table is closely related to the percentage of objects in the
table with unique keys.

The default hashCode() method used by java.lang.Object is the numeric
value of the reference to the object. Although Java programs aren't allowed
to convert 32-bit references to 32-bit ints, you can do this in native C code,
and that's exactly what Java does, at least on 32-bit platforms. (Porting Java
to 64-bit platforms like the DEC Alpha or 16-bit platforms like Windows
3.1 is decidedly non-trivial, for this and many other similar reasons.)

No reference can point to two different objects. Therefore, hash codes
calculated in this fashion will always be unique. Conversely, no object can
have two different addresses, so an object always has the same hash code.
(An object can be referred to by two different reference variables, but these
two variables will still have the same value.)

The hashCode() method is closely tied to the equals() method. When
you override equals(), you need to override hashCode(), too. Remember
that all objects that are equal according to the equals() method must have
the same hash code.

Threading

Discussion among many people in the same place at the same time tends to degenerate rapidly into babble as everyone begins talking at once. To make discussion possible among large groups of people, a special object, sometimes called a "magic feather," is created and endowed with the special power that only the person holding the magic feather may speak. Because no more than one person can hold the magic feather at a time, no more than one person can talk at one time.

Many different threads talking at the same time can be a huge problem for Java programs as well. It is extremely important to guarantee that two different threads don't modify the same object at the same time. Therefore, each object is created with its own magic feather. The magic feather for an object can be held by at most one thread at any given time. As long as a thread holds an object's magic feather, it can do anything it's normally allowed to do with the object. All other threads that want to use the object have to wait until they get the object's magic feather.

I should note that "magic feather" isn't a sufficiently impressive technical term for most programmers. Instead, the commonly used word is *monitor*.

If you search the java packages, you won't find any class called monitor or magic feather. A monitor is not a separate object. It is a part of each individual object. Threads ask for an object's monitor when they execute a synchronized instance method of the object, execute the body of a synchronized statement that synchronizes on the object, or invoke a synchronized static method of a class. (In the latter case, the Class object associated with the class is synchronized.) Threads give back the monitor when they finish executing the synchronized code.

By calling one of an object's wait() methods, a thread can yield possession of the monitor and put itself to sleep until the monitor is available again. The thread can then be awakened with the object's notify() or notifyAll() methods. There are three polymorphic wait() methods. These are

```
public final void wait() throws InterruptedException
public final void wait(long  ms) throws InterruptedException
public final void wait(long  ms, int  ns) throws InterruptedException
```

Each of these methods causes the calling thread to release the object's monitor and go to sleep until another thread notifies threads waiting on this object's monitor to wake up. At that point, the thread wakes up, waits until it can regain the object's monitor, and then resumes running. The first wait() method, with no arguments, sleeps indefinitely. The second, with a single long argument, sleeps for at most the specified number of milliseconds and then wakes up whether it has been notified or not.

The third and final wait() method allows more finely grained control, down to a nanosecond. The first argument is the number of milliseconds to wait before waking, and the second argument is the number of nanoseconds to add to that. Not all architectures allow such finely grained timing. You shouldn't rely on accuracy of more than a millsecond or two.

There are two notify methods: notify() and notifyAll(). Their signatures are

```
public final void notify()
public final void notifyAll()
```

The notify() method wakes up a single thread that's waiting on this object's monitor. The notifyAll() method wakes up all threads waiting on this object's monitor. Both of these methods should be called only in a thread that owns the object's monitor.

Strings

The final thing that all objects must be able to do is to provide a string representation of themselves. They can do this with the toString() method. The default toString() method from the java.lang.Object class merely prints the name of the class of the object. Most classes will override this method with one that provides more information.

The toString() method is rarely called explicitly. It is instead invoked implicitly when an object is passed as an argument into a print() method or is concatenated with a string using a + sign. I'll talk more about strings and toString() methods later in this chapter.

ARRAYS

What is an array? To a high-level programmer, an array is an indexed list of values of the same type with a fixed length. The most important feature of an array is that you can retrieve any particular element of the array in constant time. In other words, it takes no more or less time to retrieve the seventh component of the array than it takes to retrieve the 70th or the 700th.

Secret

Internally, arrays are contiguous blocks of memory in the heap. To find the size of an array, multiply the size of the array's type by the length of the array. For example, an int[] array with length 60 takes up 240 bytes of heap memory because it has space for 60 four-byte ints. The memory is used even if the space isn't occupied.

Primitive data types like shorts and ints are stored directly in the array. They take up no more space than the array itself. In fact, an array of shorts, bytes, or chars takes up less space than the same number of short, byte, or char variables. Individual variables of these types are always promoted to ints. Thus, a byte variable occupies four bytes, and four byte variables occupy 16 bytes because each byte is promoted to an int. However, promotion does not occur inside arrays, so an array of four bytes occupies exactly four bytes. Similarly, an array of four shorts or an array of four chars occupies exactly eight bytes.

Arrays of objects are a little different. Each entry in the array is not the object itself but rather a reference to the object. Each reference requires four bytes, whether or not that reference is null. However, if a component of the object array is indeed non-null, then somewhere else in the heap is an object that also needs memory. When you calculate the total memory needed for an array of objects, you have to account for the array and the objects themselves separately. For example, consider this array:

```
Integer[] iarray = new Integer[10];
for (int i = 0; i < iarray.length; i++) {
  iarray[i] = new Integer(i);
}
```

By looking at the source code for the Integer class, you discover that each Integer object has a single non-static int field. Thus, each Integer object occupies four bytes of heap memory. When the Integer[] array iarray is created, it has space for ten references. This takes up 40 bytes. As new Integer objects are created and added to the array in the for loop, each of these takes an additional four bytes. When the loop is complete, the array occupies 80 bytes of the heap. If you then set some of the array components to null, the corresponding Integer objects would eventually be garbage-collected, and the array would shrink to somewhere between 40 and 80 bytes of the heap.

Whether the array ever really occupies more than 40 bytes is a semantic question. You could just as reasonably say that the array always occupies 40 bytes and additional space may be occupied by the objects to which the array's components refer. As long as you understand what's really going on, you can say it however you want.

Multidimensional arrays

Java does not have true multidimensional arrays like Fortran does. Instead, it fakes them with one-dimensional arrays of references to one-dimensional arrays, much in the fashion that C does. For example, consider a two-dimensional array of doubles like this:

```
double[][] matrix = new double[4][3];
```

This is allocated in two parts. First, a one-dimensional, length four array of references is allocated; then, each of these is pointed at a one-dimensional, length three array of doubles. In other words:

```
matrix = new double[4][];
for (int i = 0; i < 4; i++) matrix[i] = new double[3];
```

As you'll see in Chapter 5, Java can accomplish this with one byte code instruction that has the same effect as the above code.

This means that even though matrix is declared as a two-dimensional array of doubles, matrix[0], matrix[1], matrix[2], and matrix[3] are all legitimate Java entities. For example, you can copy the first row of matrix into the third row using System.arraycopy() like this:

```
System.arraycopy(matrix[1], 0, matrix[3], 0, 3);
```

You can use matrix[0], matrix[1], matrix[2], and matrix[3] anywhere a one-dimensional array of doubles is expected. This also means you can create ragged arrays — that is, arrays that do not have a fixed length in one dimension. For example,

```
int[][] triangle = new int[12][];
for (int i = 0; i < 12; i++) {
  triangle[i] = new int[i+1];
}
```

The zeroth row of the triangle array has length one, the first row has length two, the second row has length three, and so on.

Higher dimensional arrays just have additional levels of indirection. For example,

```
double[][][] Datacube = new double[4][3][7];
```

Datacube[0] through Datacube[3] are references to two-dimensional arrays of doubles; more precisely, they're references to arrays of references to one-dimensional arrays of doubles. Datacube [0][2] is a reference to a one-dimensional array of doubles and can be used anywhere a one-dimensional array of doubles is needed.

Array classes and objects

Arrays are objects. They extend the java.lang.Object class, and you can call toString(), equals(), hashCode(), wait(), notify(), and all the other methods of the object class on a reference variable of array type. An array can be assigned to variables of type Object and passed to methods that expect a reference to an Object type. Arrays live in the heap like all other objects do; therefore, you use reference variables to refer to arrays.

However, there is no java.lang.Array class. Each array has an implicit type of the most primitive type it holds, followed by a number of left-bracket signs ([) equal to its dimension. Thus, an int[][] has type int[[and a String[] array has type String[. These are not legal Java identifiers, and you won't find them in Java source code, but you will find them in Java byte code.

As well as the methods inherited from java.lang.Object, arrays have a single field called length. This field contains the length of the array. I used this field above in the line

```
for (int i = 0; i < iarray.length; i++) {
```

Other than this field, arrays mostly inherit the methods of java.lang.Object. The one they override is clone(). Arrays implicitly implement Cloneable, so you can call clone() without getting a CloneNotSupportException. However, the clone of a multidimensional array is a shallow copy. Only the initial references to the sub-arrays are copied, not the sub-arrays themselves.

System.arraycopy()

The System class contains one important method for working with arrays:

```
public static void arraycopy(Object src_array, int src_index, Object
dst_array, int dst_index, int length)
```

The System.arraycopy() method copies length values from the source array into the destination array. This is used in the StringBuffer and Vector classes as well as many other places. The basic algorithm looks like this:

```
for (int i = 0; i < length; i++) {
    dst_array[dst_index+i] = src_array[src_index+i];
}
```

In other words, the length components of src_array starting with component src_index are copied in order into the length components of dst_array starting at dst_index. The arrays src_array and dst_array can be the same array. If so, the copy is made as if the source components were first copied into a temporary array and then copied back into the array. This allows overlapping copies to work. If the arrays have reference types, then the copy is a shallow copy. That is, only the references are copied. The objects to which the references point are not copied.

If the arrays to be copied contain primitive data types, they must contain the same primitive data type. For example, an array of shorts can only be copied to another array of shorts, not to an array of ints or longs. This is one of the few places in Java where arithmetic promotion does not take place. If you try to copy an array of one primitive type such as short to an array of a wider primitive type such as int, then an ArrayStoreException is thrown and the destination array is left unchanged. Similarly if you try to copy an array of a reference type to an array of primitive type or vice versa, an ArrayStore-Exception is thrown, and the destination array is left unchanged.

Copies between arrays of reference types are a little more complex. As long as the reference type in one array can be converted to the reference type of the other array, the copy takes place. Thus, it is acceptable to copy a Float[] array to a Number[] array or an Object[] array to a String[] array because Floats can be cast to Numbers and Objects can be cast to Strings. (The latter cast works only if the Objects are in fact Strings. Otherwise, an ArrayStoreException will be thrown.) However if the reference types are incompatible — for example, Float and String — then an ArrayStoreException will be thrown.

It's possible for some of the components of the source array to be compatible with the type of the destination array and some to be incompatible. For example, if src_array has type Object[], then it can contain both Floats and Strings. If dst_array has type String, then you can copy the Strings from src_array to dst_array but not the Floats. In this case, the components of the src_array that can be copied starting with component 0 are copied. However, as soon as an incompatible component is encountered, an ArrayStoreException is thrown, and no further components are copied, compatible or incompatible.

This method can also throw an ArrayIndexOutOfBoundsException, in which case the destination array is not changed. (The source array is never changed.) An ArrayIndexOutOfBoundsException is thrown if srcIndex, dstIndex, or length is negative, if srcIndex+length is greater than srcArray.length, or if dstIndex+length is greater than dst.length.

The System.arraycopy() method is normally implemented in native code for maximum performance. While it would be possible to write an equivalent routine in pure Java, most architectures have extremely efficient native instructions for copying large blocks of memory from one place to another. Because an array is natively a large block of memory, this is one of the places where native code helps a lot.

STRINGS

Strings are objects like any other object in Java. There is a java.lang.String class. However, the compiler has special support for a number of things you might want to do with strings. For example, you can create a new String object like this:

```
String s="Hello world! ";
```

You don't need to write

```
String s = new String("Hello world! ");
```

although you could. You can't do that with any other kind of object. For example, if you write

```
Double d = 7.5;
```

you get this compiler error:

```
    Error:   Incompatible type for declaration. Can't convert double to
java.lang.Double.
```

Strings are the only class that can be initialized from literals without an explicit constructor call. In point of fact, what's really happening is that the compiler figures out that it needs to call a String constructor. It translates the statement "String s="Hello world! ";" into the following code:

```
StringBuffer sb = new StringBuffer("Hello world! ");
String s = new String(sb);
```

This is not the only way the String s="Hello world! "; statement could be compiled. However, somewhere there has to be a call to a String() constructor, even if you didn't write one in the source code.

Actually, depending on what use is made later of the String objects, an optimizing compiler may include only the String literal in the byte code and not actually create an object.

The Java compiler handles many other idioms for manipulating strings. For example, you probably know that you can concatenate strings with a plus sign (+) like this:

```
String s3 = s2 + s1;
```

The compiler translates that into a sequence of statements like this:

```
StringBuffer sb = new StringBuffer();
sb.append(s1);
sb.append(s2);
s3 = sb.toString();
```

Everything is accomplished with method calls. There are no additive operators that truly operate on strings. That's an illusion supported by the compiler. Several other illusions are also supported by the compiler. Consider this common statement:

```
System.out.println("Count is: " + i);
```

Here you have a String literal concatenated with an int variable. The compiler will translate this into something like this:

```
StringBuffer sb = new StringBuffer("Count is ");
sb.append(i);
String s = sb.toString();
System.out.println(s);
```

It is much simpler to just write System.out.println("Count is: " + i); than to put all the pieces together inside a StringBuffer yourself. That's why this intelligence was built into the compiler and the language specification. Much more complex concatenations are compiled similarly.

String implementation

In Java, at least the version of Java written by Sun, Strings are implemented as arrays of chars. The String class has three non-static fields: value (an array of chars), offset (an int), and count (also an int). Every string therefore takes up at least 12 bytes of heap memory. However, you also need space for the char array.

The char array value has one space for each character in the string. In theory, using the offset and length fields, the value array can have slots for more chars than are actually present in the string. The offset field says which part of the string contains the first character of the string, and the length field says how many characters there are in the string. In practice, there's no way for that to happen. The value array for the string "Hello world!" thus has length 12.

Strings are immutable. Once a string is created, it is never changed. A String variable may change, but a String object never changes. Consider the following code fragment:

```
String s;
s = "Hello World!";
s = "Goodbye World";
```

Here the String variable s is first null. It then refers to an object with the value "Hello World!" and then to a String object with the value "Goodbye World". However, these are two different objects, not different versions of the same object.

Similarly, if you were to concatenate another string to s, it would require the creation of still another String object. For example,

```
String s;
s = "Hello World!";
s += " Isn't it a beautiful morning?";
```

This compiles to this sequence of statements:

```
StringBuffer sb = new StringBuffer("Hello World!");
sb.append(" Isn't it a beautiful morning?");
s = sb.toString();
```

Note that the string itself is never changed.

However, in general, Java compilers are fairly smart about optimizing out unnecessary transformations to String objects. If you actually did something with the string between the second and third lines, then the compiler would be forced to actually create the String objects. For example, consider this code fragment:

```
String s;
s = "Hello World!";
System.err.println(s);
s += " Isn't it a beautiful morning?";
```

This compiles to this sequence of statements:

```
String s1 = new String("Hello World!");
System.out.println(s1);
StringBuffer sb = new StringBuffer();
sb.append(s1);
String s2 = new String(" Isn't it a beautiful morning?");
sb.append(s2);
String s3 = sb.toString();
```

Three separate strings are created while this program runs. In the source code, however, it looks like one string is being changed. This is an illusion supported by the compiler.

StringBuffers

Java strings are immutable; that is, a string's value may not be changed after the string is constructed. This makes strings very thread-safe and fairly fast, but also makes them excessively inefficient for many operations. For example, suppose you write

```
String s = "one";
s += " two";
s += " three";
s += " four";
s += " five";
```

Compiling these statements with only immutable strings would require the construction of five separate strings: first "one," then "one two," then "one two three," then "one two three four," and finally "one two three four five." There's no way, using only strings, to create one string and then append the new parts to it.

A StringBuffer is a string that can be changed. You can add additional characters to the end or the beginning or the middle of a StringBuffer without creating new objects. On the other hand, because StringBuffers are mutable, they're not inherently thread-safe, and thus many of the methods of the StringBuffer class are synchronized. This can slow down the execution of a program when Strings aren't changing.

In short, the String class is optimized for strings that don't change; the StringBuffer class is optimized for strings that *do* change. In general, the Java compiler is fairly smart about figuring out which class to use where. Nonetheless, the more manipulation of a string you're doing, the more efficient it becomes to use a StringBuffer and convert it to a string only when you're done.

The main methods of the StringBuffer class are append() and insert(). These methods are polymorphic, so they can accept any type or class of data. The append() method adds characters at the end of the StringBuffer; insert() places the new characters at a specified position in the StringBuffer. These methods are sufficiently polymorphic to handle all Java data types. There are ten different append()methods:

```
public StringBuffer append(boolean b)
public StringBuffer append(char   c)
public StringBuffer append(double d)
public StringBuffer append(float  f)
public StringBuffer append(int    i)
public StringBuffer append(long   l)
public StringBuffer append(String str)
public StringBuffer append(Object obj)
public StringBuffer append(char   str[])
public StringBuffer append(char   str[], int offset, int length)
```

Each of these methods converts its argument to a string format and appends it to the StringBuffer. The first six of these methods handles the primitive data types. Shorts and bytes are promoted to ints before conversion. Strings are also appended directly. All other object types are converted to a String object, using their toString() method, and then appended. The final append() method appends an array of chars to the StringBuffer. The second-to-last method appends the entire array, while the last method appends only the length characters in the array beginning with the character at offset. The only thing that you cannot append to a StringBuffer is an array of type other than char[].

The insert() methods are almost equally polymorphic with the exception of the methods to handle arrays of chars. These methods are

```
public StringBuffer insert(int  offset, boolean  b)
public StringBuffer insert(int  offset, char  str[])
public StringBuffer insert(int  offset, double  d)
public StringBuffer insert(int  offset, float  f)
public StringBuffer insert(int  offset, int  i)
public StringBuffer insert(int  offset, long  l)
public StringBuffer insert(int  offset, Object  obj)
public StringBuffer insert(int  offset, String  str)
```

These methods insert the string representation of their second argument beginning at the offset specified in the first argument. All characters after offset are shifted to the right. How far they're shifted is completely dependent on the length of the string format of the second argument.

Like Strings, a StringBuffer is fundamentally a private array of chars called value:

```
private char[] value;
```

It helps to keep this array in mind when considering where to insert an item. Because a StringBuffer is an array, the first character of the StringBuffer is number zero, not number one.

Also like with Strings, the length of the value array is set when the StringBuffer object is first constructed. There are three constructors:

```
public StringBuffer()
public StringBuffer(int  length)
public StringBuffer(String  s)
```

The noargs constructor starts with an array of length 16. The second constructor initializes the array to the specified length. The third constructor starts with an array of length s.length() + 16 — that is, the length of the string plus 16 empty spaces. This is because of the expectation that whatever length of the string that the StringBuffer initially holds, it will be expanded later.

So far this is very much like the String class. The difference, however, is that the buffer can expand as necessary to hold more characters. Suppose you have the following code:

```
StringBuffer sb = new StringBuffer(6);
sb.append("Hello world!");
```

The string "Hello world!" has 12 characters. Because 12 characters is six too many for the six character StringBuffer sb, Java expands the array with the ensureCapacity() method:

```
public synchronized void ensureCapacity(int minimumCapacity)
```

The ensureCapacity() method expands the array to two times the current capacity plus one (2 * (capacity() + 1)) or to the requested minimum capacity, whichever is greater. A new array is allocated of the appropriate size; the old value array is copied into the new value array with the System.arrayCopy()method; and the reference is set to the new array. In code, it looks something like this:

```
char[] value;
...
char[] newValue = new char[Math.max(minimumCapacity, 2*(value.length +
1))];
    System.arraycopy(value, 0, newValue, 0, value.length);
    value = newValue;
```

Notice that the length of the value array is at least doubled. It is not nearly expanded to the minimum necessary length. Although you don't want to waste space unnecessarily, it's even more important not to waste CPU cycles by growing the array every time you have to add a character to it. You will see this scheme for growing arrays again very shortly. The java.util.Vector class does almost exactly the same thing.

Note Although ensureCapacity() is public, you rarely need to call it directly. The insert() and append() methods of the StringBuffer class will call it when they need to.

The value array is also expanded when an item is inserted into the middle of a StringBuffer with one of the insert() methods. However, the value array will not be expanded to provide additional space if you try to insert an item past the end of the StringBuffer. If you try, a StringIndexOutOf BoundsException will be thrown.

There are a few other useful methods in the StringBuffer class. The charAt(int i) method returns the *ith* char in the StringBuffer. This is easy to do because you can just return the ith char in the value array.

The setCharAt(int i, char c) method changes the character at index i in the StringBuffer to the char c. This differs from the insert(int i, char c)method because it actually replaces the character at i rather than shifting it and all following characters to the right. A StringIndexOutOfBounds Exception is thrown if i equals or exceeds the length of the string.

The length() method returns an int giving the number of characters currently present in the StringBuffer. This is generally not the same as the length of the value array. That number is called the StringBuffer's capacity and is accessed with the capacity() method.

The ensureCapacity() method already discussed changes a StringBuffer's capacity. This is not the same as a StringBuffer's length. The capacity of a StringBuffer is the number of characters that can be stored in it without taking time to expand the internal value array. The length of a StringBuffer is the number of characters currently stored in the internal value array. To change a StringBuffer's length, invoke its setLength(int i) method. This does one of two things: if i is less than the current length of the StringBuffer, then the StringBuffer is truncated to the length i; however, if i is greater than the current length of the StringBuffer, then it is expanded with null characters to the requested length.

The reverse() method reverses the characters in the StringBuffer in place. For example, if sb contains the string "dam", after calling sb.reverse() it will contain the string "mad".

The getChars() method copies characters from the StringBuffer into an array. Its signature is

```
public void getChars(int srcBegin, int srcEnd, char dst[], int dstBegin)
```

A substring of characters from the StringBuffer is copied into the char array dst. The substring to be copied is delineated on the left by the index srcBegin and on the right by srcEnd-1. The characters of this substring are copied into the subsection of the char array dst beginning at dstBegin. A StringIndexOutOfBoundsException is thrown if either srcBegin or srcEnd is less than zero or greater than or equal to the length of the string. An ArrayIndexOutOfBoundsException is thrown if dstBegin is less than zero or greater than or equal to the length of the array or if the substring exceeds the bounds of the array.

Finally, like most other classes, StringBuffer contains a toString() method. This method is often invoked as the last step in a long sequence of string operations.

JAVA.UTIL DATA STRUCTURES

The java.util class includes several abstract data structures to hold collections of objects. On one level, the programmer is supposed to be shielded from the internal workings of these classes. The whole point of a class library and abstract container classes is to shield the programmer from low-level details.

However, there are performance issues that can be addressed only by learning how a class is implemented. For example, if the Vector class is implemented as a linked list, then insertions into the list will be very fast.

However, finding a particular element in the list will be rather slow. On the other hand, if the Vector class is really an array, then insertions into the middle of the list may be quite slow but retrieving an element from the list can be quite fast.

If you're writing an applet or application for public distribution, you may not wish to rely on what I say here about the internals of these classes. Although these data structures are implemented similarly on all Java implementations to which I have access, it is possible (though unlikely) that the implementation details will change in the future. If the performance of your program depends on a specific implementation of a class, then you may wish to copy the source code for the class, change its name, and recompile it. Then you would use your modified class instead of the original. Of course, this will increase the size of the program you have to distribute. This could be important for an applet, but is unlikely to be significant for an application. As with many other things, you must make the tradeoffs that are appropriate for your situation. You have to decide what's more important to you, guaranteed performance characteristics or smaller download size.

Vectors

A Vector is Java's basic list class. A list is an ordered collection of items. The fundamental operations on a list are

- Creating a new list
- Adding an element to the list
- Removing an element from the list
- Finding the nth element in the list

The main difference between a list and an array is that a list generally doesn't have a fixed size. It can grow or shrink as needed. Furthermore, a list doesn't have empty spaces. If you remove a component from the middle of an array, you leave an empty space. All the other components stay where they are. On the other hand, if you remove an item from a list, all the items above it in the list are moved down to fill the space left.

Implementation

There are many different data structures that you can use to implement these operations. The very word *list* suggests a linked list data structure to many programmers. However, the Vector class is not a linked list, although you can do with a Vector anything you can do with a linked list. Instead, a Vector is a growable array.

If that sounds funny to you, it should. Java arrays are not growable. You cannot take an array that was initialized with space for ten doubles and expand it so that it has space for twenty doubles. Once an array is created, its size is fixed.

However, you can, memory permitting, create a new array with space for 20 doubles. Then you can copy the components of the original array into the new array. If you then adjust all references to the old array to point to the new array instead, it's as if you grew the old array.

The hard part of this procedure is finding all the references to the old array. Java solves this problem by making the array you want to grow a protected field in a public class: Vector. Only the Vector class ever holds any references to the array, and it has only one reference to the array. Other objects have references only to Vector objects. Therefore, when the array needs to be grown, you need to adjust only a single reference in the Vector class. This sort of data encapsulation is one of the primary advantages of object-oriented programming.

You should recall that this is almost exactly what the StringBuffer class does when it needs to expand. StringBuffers use an array of chars instead of an array of objects like Vectors, but otherwise the logic is the same.

```
Object[] elementData;
...
// double the vector's capacity
Obj ect[] newData = new Object[2*elementData.length];
System.arraycopy(elementData, 0, newData, 0, elementData.length);
elementData= newData;
```

The array that grows is a protected field of the Vector class called elementData; the number of elements currently stored in the array is a protected int field called elementCount. The elementCount, the number of elements in the array right now, should not be confused with the capacity of the array, which is the number of elements that can be stored in elementData before you need to grow it. In other words, the capacity is elementData.length.

The fact that vectors are really just arrays behind the scenes has many implications for the performance and efficiency of the fundamental list operations. It means that insertions at the end of the list are quick, unless the vector has run out of space, in which case they can be quite slow. Insertions into the middle of the list are always slow. Finding the item at a given position in the list is fast.

The array implementation of the Vector class also sets an upper limit on how many items you can place in a Vector. A Vector can hold up to 2,147,483,647 objects because an array is indexed with a signed int. In practice, you'd run out of memory before you ever stuffed that many objects into a Vector.

Creating a new Vector

There are three constructors that create a new Vector:

```
public Vector()
public Vector(int  initialCapacity)
public Vector(int  initialCapacity,  int  capacityIncrement);
```

Every Vector has a capacity — that is, the number of objects it can hold before it must be expanded. Because it takes time to expand a Vector, you generally want to have some empty space in a Vector so you don't need to expand it every time you add an element to it. However you don't want to waste space if you can avoid it.

The noargs Vector() constructor creates a new Vector with an initial capacity of ten. When that capacity is exceeded, the Vector doubles in size. That is, when you add the eleventh element to the Vector, it expands itself to a capacity for 20 elements. When you add the 21st element, the Vector expands itself to a capacity for 40 elements, and so on.

If you know how many elements that the Vector will probably need to hold when you construct it, you can speed up your program by using the Vector(int initialCapacity) constructor. For example, if you know you're going to put about 30 elements in a Vector, give or take five, then you should construct it like this:

```
Vector myVector = new Vector(35);
```

Unless the maximum number of elements you'll place in the Vector is substantially greater than the average number of elements you'll put there, you should always construct a Vector with the maximum number of elements you expect. Each empty space in a Vector only takes up four bytes. Therefore, unless you're really pressed for space, it's much more important to avoid unnecessary resizing than to worry about the space wasted by a few empty slots.

If you don't want a Vector's capacity to double every time it needs to be expanded, you can also pass a capacity increment to the constructor. For example, to create a Vector whose capacity increases in blocks of ten at a time and has an initial capacity of 35, you would write:

```
Vector tenVector = new Vector(35, 10);
```

It's rather unusual to do this, however. Most of the time the disadvantage of the CPU time you'll lose to the extra resizing outweighs the small intermediate space savings you'll achieve.

Inserting and removing elements

There are two methods to put a new object into a vector, addElement() and insertElementAt(). Their signatures are

```
public final void addElement(Object o)
public final void insertElementAt(Object o, int index)
```

addElement() places the object at the end of the Vector. This method takes essentially constant time as long as there's empty space left in the vector. It takes slightly longer if the Vector first needs to be grown.

insertElementAt() places the object at the specified position in the vector. All elements of the vector at or beyond the specified index are moved up one to make room for the newcomer. The efficient native method System.arraycopy() is used to move the remaining elements up, but it's still less than ideal. If a program requires frequent insertions into the middle of a list, you may well be better off writing your own linked list class.

You can also replace elements in vectors. Because the size of the vector stays the same, this is always quite fast. The relevant method is:

```
public final void setElementAt(Object o, int index)
```

The object that was previously at index is no longer there. Instead, it is replaced by the new Object o. If there are no other references to the old object, then it will eventually be garbage-collected.

Elements can also be removed from a vector. This generally requires moving elements down that were above the object. Again this can be done with the System.arraycopy() method, but if you're doing a lot of this, you should consider using a linked list instead. The method is

```
public final void removeElementAt(int  index)
```

You can also remove an object from a Vector without knowing its index. The method to do this is

```
public final boolean removeElement(Object  o)
```

However, this method requires Java to traverse the entire Vector, searching for the requested object. Thus, its execution time is proportional to the length of the array. In computer science terms, this is an O(n) (pronounced "order en") operation where n is the number of elements in the Vector.

Furthermore, only the first occurrence of the object in the Vector is removed. This may or may not be what you expect. Removing all references to the object from the Vector requires multiple passes through the vector. If the object is found and removed, removeElement() returns true. Otherwise, it returns false. You can remove all references to an object o from a Vector v in one line of code like this:

```
while (v.removeElement(o)) {;}
```

However, this is deceptively simple. If there are n references to o in v, then this single line of code requires n+1 passes through the vector to remove them all.

The removeAllElements() method deletes every element in the Vector. Its signature is

```
public final void removeAllElements()
```

In the current implementation, Java deletes all elements from a Vector by looping through the Vector and setting each element to null. This is an O(n) operation, but it's less than optimally efficient. It looks something like this:

```
for (int j = 0; j < elementCount; j++) elementData[j] = null;
elementCount = 0;
```

Other implementations are possible. For example, you could simply reallocate a new elementData array like this:

```
elementData = new Object[elementData.length];
elementCount = 0;
```

This only takes constant time; this is an O(1) operation.

You could even leave the elementData array untouched and change only the elementCount field. This is even quicker. The old elementData array components will simply be overwritten as necessary. However, this has the potential to cause memory leaks because references to the old components still exist in the array, and thus those objects will not be garbage-collected.

Finding Objects in Vectors

In addition to the above methods for manipulating the contents of a Vector, there are several methods to find objects in a Vector. The elementAt(int i) method returns a reference to the Object at index i in the Vector. If i is not a valid index into the Vector, an ArrayIndexOutOfBoundsException is thrown.

```
public final Object elementAt(int  i)
```

The firstElement() and lastElement() methods return references to the first and last elements in the Vector respectively. If the Vector has no elements, and thus no first or last element, a NoSuchElementException is thrown.

```
public final Object firstElement()
public final Object lastElement()
```

Five methods search for a particular object. Because this requires a traversal of the array, these methods are proportional to the number of elements in the Vector. These methods are:

```
public final boolean contains(Object  o)
public final int indexOf(Object  o)
public final int lastIndexOf(Object  o)
```

The contains() method returns true if o is in the Vector and false if it isn't. The indexOf() and lastIndexOf() methods return the first and last indices of the specified object in the Vector respectively. If the object is not found in the Vector, then -1 is returned.

You can pass an extra int to these methods to indicate the element at which to begin searching.

```
public final int indexOf(Object  o, int  index)
public final int lastIndexOf(Object  o, int  index)
```

The indexOf() method searches forward beginning at that index, and lastIndexOf() searches backward beginning at that index. An ArrayIndex OutOfBoundsException is thrown if the index is less than zero or greater than or equal to the number of elements in the Vector.

Miscellaneous methods

There are three other useful methods in the Vector class. The isEmpty() method returns true if the Vector has no elements and false if it has one or more elements.

```
public final boolean isEmpty()
```

The setSize() method either shrinks or expands the Vector to a given non-negative size. If the vector is expanded, then the new elements are set to null. If the vector is shrunk, then elements past the requested size are removed from the Vector.

```
public final void setSize(int  newSize)
```

Finally, the elements() method returns a reference to an object which implements the Enumeration interface. This provides a convenient way for external classes to process each and every element of the Vector. For example,

```
Enumeration e = v.elements();
while (e.hasMoreElements()) {
  Object o  = e.nextElement();
  // work with o
}
```

When should you use a Vector?

Vectors are one of the most useful container classes in the java.util package. However, they're not right for everything. In particular, Vectors are slower than raw arrays; they can't handle primitive data types, and they can be quite slow when inserting or removing objects from any place except the end of the Vector.

If you can use a fixed array instead of a Vector, you should. As a rough rule of thumb, any operation that uses a Vector is about three times slower than the same operation performed with a plain array. That's primarily a result of the extra method calls needed to perform basic insertions, deletions, and accesses. It's always better to do it directly if you can.

The most common reason to use a Vector is that you don't know how many objects you'll need to deal with at compile time, only at runtime. However, if the Vector is going to be filled only once and then not modified, you're better off using a real array.

For example, one place common place vectors are used unnecessarily is in processing <PARAM> tags passed to an applet. It's quite common to pass an undetermined number of parameters to an applet like this:

```
<PARAM NAME="String1" VALUE="Kalel">
<PARAM NAME="String2" VALUE="Kara">
<PARAM NAME="String3" VALUE="Jorel">
<PARAM NAME="String4" VALUE="Lara">
<PARAM NAME="String5" VALUE="Lois">
```

You may not know when you compile an applet how many of these parameters there will be. At first glance this appears to be a perfect place for a Vector. You can read these parameters into the Vector in your applet's init() method like this:

```
Vector v = new Vector();
String name = null;
int i = 0;
while ((name = getParameter("String" + ++i)) != null) {
  v.addElement(name);
}
```

However, this is overkill. You do not need the full power of a Vector just to collect an undetermined number of quantities. There are several alternative solutions to this problem that don't involve the overhead of a Vector. For example, you could create the Vector as above, then copy it into an array with an Enumeration, like this:

```
String[] names = v.size();
Enumeration e = names.elements();
int i = 0;
while (e.hasMoreElements()) {
  names[i++] =(String) e.nextElement();
}
```

Alternatively, you could just use the first loop to determine how many PARAM tags you have to deal with, then use a second loop to read them, like this:

```
String name = null;
int i = 0;
while ((name = getParameter("String" + ++i)) != null) {
}
String[] names = new String[i];
for (int j = 0; j <= i; j++) {
  names[j] = getParameter("String" + (j+1));
}
```

There are some other more complicated solutions, such as implementing your own growable array, but the bottom line is that you shouldn't use a Vector as merely an array whose size will be determined at runtime. You should use a Vector only when the array is going to be constantly changing size and having elements removed and deleted. If you're only calling addElement() and never insertElementAt(), contains(), removeElement(), or the other such methods of the Vector class, then using a Vector instead of a plain array will make your program slower than it needs to be.

Bitsets

The Bitset class is an indexed list of bits. Each component of a Bitset has a boolean value: true or false. A one or set bit is considered to be true and a zero or unset bit is considered to be false. The primary purpose of a Bitset is to provide an extremely space-efficient means of storing many binary values. Bitsets are not necessarily very fast, but they should be very small.

Java implements Bitsets as arrays of longs. The first 64 bits — that is, bits 0 through 63 — are stored in the zeroth component of the array. The second 64 bits — that is, bits 64 through 127 — are stored in the first component of the array, and so on.

Extensive manipulation of these longs with the bit-level operators discussed in Chapter 2 is used to extract and set the values of individual bits. For example, consider the process of extracting the value of bit 97 from the Bitset bs. At the high level, all you need to do is this:

```
boolean b = bs.get(97);
```

Now consider what you have to do to get the value of the 97th bit from an array of longs called la:

```
boolean b;
long L = la[1];  // the 97th bit is in the first component
L = L & 0x00008000; // mask off the 97th bit
if (L == 0) b = false; // bit 97 wasn't set
else b = true; // bit 97 was set
```

That's a lot more complex, which is why this is hidden inside a class in the first place. Of course you want a general method for finding an arbitrary bit. That takes even more effort, such as this:

```
long[] la;

public boolean get(int i) {

    int index = i / 64; // find the right component of the array
    long bit = 1L << (i % 64); // find the right bit
    long result = la[index] & bit; // mask off the desired bit
    if (result == 0) return false; bit wasn't set
    else return true;

}
```

Sun's actual code is a little faster than this, but a little harder to understand.

Some operations are easier. For example, the logical operations and, or, not, and xor simply require performing the equivalent bitwise operations between each corresponding component of the arrays forming the two Bitsets. The only catch is that you may need to expand one array if it's smaller than the other is.

Stack

The Stack class implements a classic stack data structure, that is a last-in-first-out (LIFO) set of objects. There are three fundamental operations you can perform with a stack:

1. Put an object on the top of the stack. This is called *pushing*.

2. Take an object off the top of the stack. This is called *popping*.

3. Look at the object on the top of the stack, but leave it there. This is called *peeking*.

Notice that all three of these operations operate only on the top of the stack. To see what's further down in the stack, you must first remove everything that's on top of it.

Note

Some people claim that there are only two fundamental stack operations: pushing and popping. Peeking can be considered to be a pop followed by a push of the object back onto the stack.

Java provides methods to perform all three fundamental operations: pushing, popping, and peeking. They are

```
public Object peek()
public Object pop()
public Object push(Object  item)
```

When an object is placed in a stack, it loses its type information. Therefore, when you retrieve it from the stack, you have to cast it back. For example,

```
String s = (String) theStack.pop();
```

Java has two more utility methods that, while useful, are not part of the minimal requirements for a stack. They are

```
public boolean empty()
public int search(Object  o)
```

The empty() method returns true if the Stack contains no elements or false if it does not.

The search method returns an int that tells you how deep in the stack the object o is. The object on the top of the stack is at position 0; the second to the top object is at position 1, and so on. If the object is not found in the stack search() returns -1.

Objects are tested for their presence in the stack with the equals() method, not with ==. Thus, in some sense, search() is looking for an object equivalent to the requested object, not necessarily the same object. For example, consider the following code:

```
        Stack theStack = new Stack();
        URL u1 = new
URL("http://sunsite.unc.edu/javafaq/javafaq.html#xtocid1902961");
        URL u2 = new URL("http://sunsite.unc.edu/javafaq/javafaq.html");
        theStack.push(u1);
        theStack.push("Here's a string");
        theStack.push("Here's another string");
        theStack.push(u2);
```

When this code has finished, the stack looks like this:

```
0 (URL u2) http://sunsite.unc.edu/javafaq/javafaq.html
1 (String) "Here's another string"
2 (String) "Here's a string"
3 (URL u1) http://sunsite.unc.edu/javafaq/javafaq.html#xtocid1902961
```

Now suppose you search for u1 like this:

```
int result = theStack.search(u1);
```

If you print out the result, you will see that it's 0, not 3, even though u1 is at position 3 in the stack, not position 0. The stack is searched from top to bottom for the first object for which o.equals(u1) is true. In this example that's u2, http://sunsite.unc.edu/javafaq/javafaq.html, because the URL class's equals() method does not consider the ref to be part of a URL.

In Java, the Stack class extends the Vector class. Therefore, you can do anything with a stack that you can do with a Vector. Most significantly this means that you can use the at methods: elementAt(), insertElementAt(), removeElementAt(), and setElementAt(). This is unfortunate because it allows the integrity of a stack to be violated. The whole point of a stack is that operations always take place only on the top of the stack. Many algorithms depend on this assertion. It is extremely bad style to violate this directive.

It is certainly true that there are situations in which it is useful and convenient to operate on elements in the middle of a list. However, if this is what you need to do, you should use a raw Vector, not a stack.

The Stack class was written by Jonathan Payne. My best guess is that he decided to implement Stack as a subclass of Vector in order to save time through code reuse. However, what he probably should have done was to have used the Vector class via encapsulation rather than inheritance. Listing 3.2 demonstrates how the Stack class could have been quickly written without allowing too much access to the nether regions of the stack.

Listing 3-2

An alternative vision for the Stack class

```
/*
 * @(#)Stack.java 1.12 96/12/09
 *
 * Copyright 1996 Elliotte Rusty Harold.
 *
 * Permission to use, copy, modify, and distribute this software
 * and its documentation for all purposes and without
 * fee is hereby granted provided that this copyright notice
 * appears in all copies.
 */

package com.macfaq.util;

import java.util.*;

/**
 * A stack that guarantees its own integrity.
 *
 * @version   1.0, 12/09/96
 * @author   Elliotte Rusty Harold
 */
public class Stack {

  Vector theStack = new Vector();

  public Object push(Object o) {

    theStack.addElement(item);
    return o;

  }

  public Object pop() {

    Object  o;

    int len = theStack.size();
    o = peek();
    theStack.removeElementAt(len - 1);
    return o;

  }

  public Object peek() {
```

(continued)

An alternative vision for the Stack class *(continued)*

```
    Object   o;

    int len = theStack.size();
    if (len == 0) throw new EmptyStackException();
     return theStack.elementAt(len - 1);

  }

  public boolean empty() {

    if (theStack.size() == 0) return true;
    else return false;

  }

  public int search(Object o) {

    int i = theStack.lastIndexOf(o);

    if (i >= 0) return theStack.size() - i;
    return -1;

  }

}
```

This Stack class performs all the necessary stack operations; it's still based on the Vector class, so it can take advantage of any optimizations made there, but it does not allow other classes to violate the stack structure.

SUMMARY

This chapter is really about distinctions between concepts and words that are very closely related.

■ You learn what Java objects really are: chunks of memory in the heap. You also learn that Java uses references to locate those areas of memory in the heap and that all access to objects takes place through references. You learn how a reference to an object differs from the object itself.

- There is a class for objects (java.lang.Object), and classes are themselves objects of type java.lang.Class. A little-c class is not quite the same thing as a capital-C Class, nor is a little o-object quite the same thing as a capital-O Object. You learn about the methods of the java.lang.Object class and how you use and override those in classes you write.

- You learn that Strings are immutable arrays of Unicode characters. You also learn that StringBuffers are growable arrays of Unicode characters and that behind the scenes, many String operations are performed with StringBuffers.

- One-dimensional arrays of primitive data types are contiguous blocks of memory containing primitive values. However, one-dimensional arrays of reference data types contain only references to objects that live elsewhere in the heap; Multidimensional arrays are arrays of arrays, and all arrays implicitly subclass java.lang.Object.

- Finally, you learn about the internal structure of several common Java container classes: Vector, Stack, and Bitset. By understanding how these classes operate, you can now make intelligent decisions about when and whether these classes are appropriate for your needs and when you should rewrite or replace them with classes of your own devising.

THE JAVA VIRTUAL MACHINE

4

*J*ava source code files are compiled into .class byte code files. The .class file will often be available for a class but the corresponding .java source code file will not be. In these cases, with a little effort, it's possible to derive an astounding amount of information from the .class file alone.

READING COMPILED FILES

Does the program in Listing 4-1 look familiar? I guarantee you've seen it before, probably many times.

Listing 4-1
Mystery code, Version 1

```
CAFEBABE0003002D002008001D07001E07000E07001C0700160A00030009090004
000A0A0005000B0C000C00150C0014001B0C001A001F0100077072696E746C6E01
000D436F6E7374616E7456616C756501000136A6176612F696F2F5072696E745374
7265616D01000A457863657074696F6E301000F4C696E654E756D626572546162
6C6501000A536F7572636546696C6501000E4C6F63616C5661726961626C657301
0004436F64650100036F7574010015284C6A6176612F6C616E672F537472696E67
3B29560100106A6176612F6C616E672F4F626A6563740100046D61696E6501000F48
656C6C6F576F726C642E6A61766101010016285B4C6A6176612F6C616E672F537472
696E673B29560100063C696E69743E0100154C6A6176612F696F2F5072696E74534
7472656D3B0100106A6176612F6C616E672F53797374656D01000C48656C6C6F
```
(continued)

Mystery code, Version 1 *(continued)*

20576F726C642101000A48656C6C6F576F726C6401000328295600000002000500000000000020009
0017001900010013000000250002000100000009B200071201B60006B10000000100100000000A00
0200000005000800030001001A001F000100130000001D000100010000000052AB70008B100000001
0010000000060001000000001000100110000000020018

No? What if I write it like Listing 4-2?

Listing 4-2
Mystery code, Version 2

```
  ??æ___-_ __"__-____"___

  ___                ___


___@sr_____println__
ConstantValue___java/io/PrintStream__
Exceptions___LineNumberTable__
SourceFile__LocalVariables___Code___out__(Ljava/lang/String;)V___java/lang/Obje
ct___main__HelloWorld.java___([Ljava/lang/String;)V___<init>___Ljava/io/PrintSt
ream;___java/lang/System__Hello World!__
HelloWorld___()V_____        _____%_____
=____?_±_____
_____"_____*?__±_____
```

That's a little better. You can guess that this has something to do with Java because the word Java and various Java keywords seem to show up. There's also the string "Hello World" repeated a couple of times. This code isn't very long, so just maybe this is a hello world program. Then again, maybe not. Let's look at this same program another way in Listing 4-3.

Listing 4-3
Mystery code, Version 3

```
Compiled from HelloWorld.java
class HelloWorld extends java.lang.Object
    /* ACC_SUPER bit set */
{
    public static void main();
    HelloWorld();

Method void main()
    0 getstatic #7 <Field java.lang.System.out Ljava/io/PrintStream;>
    3 ldc #1 <String "Hello World">
```

(continued)

Mystery code, Version 3 *(continued)*

```
    5 invokevirtual #8 <Method java.io.PrintStream.print(Ljava/lang/String;)V>
    8 return

Method HelloWorld()
    0 aload_0
    1 invokespecial #6 <Method java.lang.Object.<init>()V>
    4 return

}
```

Now we're getting somewhere. This is obviously a class called HelloWorld. It extends java.lang.Object. The class has two methods. The main() method is public static and void and takes an array of strings as arguments. The constructor HelloWorld() is public and takes no arguments.

However, what are all those funky lines like these?

```
    0 getstatic #7 <Field java.lang.System.out Ljava/io/PrintStream;>
```

and

```
    5 invokevirtual #8 <Method
    java.io.PrintStream.print(Ljava/lang/String;)V>
```

That doesn't look like Java!

Finally, let's look at the same program one more way in Listing 4-4.

Listing 4-4
Mystery code, Version 4

```
class HelloWorld {

  public static void main (String args[]) {

    System.out.println("Hello World!");

  }

}
```

Listing 4-4 is obviously the classic Hello World program in Java, although it seems not nearly as complex as the last example. Believe it or not, all four of these programs are the same, just viewed differently.

Listing 4-1 is pure hexadecimal and comes from the file HelloWorld.class. This is what you'd see by looking at the file with a disk editor such as Norton Disk Editor. Listing 4-5 is a simple application that you can use to read files as hexadecimal digits.

Listing 4-5
HexReader

```
import java.awt.*;
import java.io.*;

public class HexReader extends Frame {

   TextArea output = new TextArea();
   Button OpenFile = new Button("Open File");

   public static void main (String[] args) {

      HexReader h = new HexReader();
      Toolkit t = Toolkit.getDefaultToolkit();
      Dimension d = t.getScreenSize();

      h.init();
      h.resize(d.width/2, d.height/2);
      h.move(d.width/4, d.height/4);
      h.show();

   }

   public HexReader() {

      super("HexReader");

   }

   public void init() {

      Panel p = new Panel();
      p.setLayout(new FlowLayout());
      p.add(OpenFile);
      add("South", p);
      add("Center", output);
```

(continued)

HexReader *(continued)*

```
    }

    public boolean action(Event e, Object what) {

      if (e.target == OpenFile) {
        File f = chooseFile();
        printFile(f);
        return true;
      }

      return false;

    }

    public File chooseFile() {

      FileDialog fd = new FileDialog(new Frame(),
       "Please choose a file:", FileDialog.LOAD);
      fd.show();

      return new File(fd.getDirectory(), fd.getFile());

    }

    public void printFile(File f) {

      try {
        output.setText("");
        FileInputStream fin =  new FileInputStream(f);
        byte[] buffer = new byte[(int) f.length()];
        int bytesread = fin.read(buffer);
        output.setText(hexprint(buffer));
      }
      catch (Exception e) {
      }

    }

    public String hexprint(byte[] b) {

     StringBuffer sb = new StringBuffer(b.length * 2);
     for (int i = 0; i < b.length; i++) {
       sb.append(BitsToChar(b[i] >> 4));
       sb.append(BitsToChar(b[i] & 0x0000000F));
```

(continued)

Listing 4-5

HexReader *(continued)*

```
    }
    return sb.toString();
  }

  public char BitsToChar(int bits) {

    int j = bits & 0x0000000F;
    switch (j) {
      case 0: return '0';
      case 1: return '1';
      case 2: return '2';
      case 3: return '3';
      case 4: return '4';
      case 5: return '5';
      case 6: return '6';
      case 7: return '7';
      case 8: return '8';
      case 9: return '9';
      case 10: return 'A';
      case 11: return 'B';
      case 12: return 'C';
      case 13: return 'D';
      case 14: return 'E';
      case 15: return 'F';
      default:
      throw new IllegalArgumentException(j +
        " is not a valid value for a hexadecimal digit.");

    }

  }

}
```

The main() method initializes the Frame shown in Figure 4-1. It has a TextArea field called output where the actual hex data appears and a single button with the label "Open File." When the users click the Open File button, they see a file dialog box in which they can choose a file. The program passes the chosen file to the printFile() method. The printFile() method opens the file, connects an input stream to it so that the contents can be read, and reads the contents into a byte array called *buffer*. Then the buffer is passed to the hexprint() method to get a hexadecimal string that is displayed in the output TextArea.

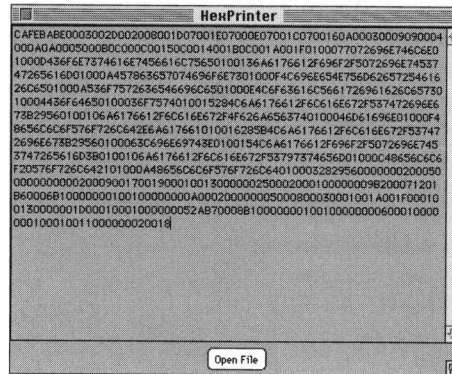

Figure 4-1
The HexReader application.

Our main interest here is in the hexprint() method, so let's take a closer look at it. The argument to hexprint() is a byte array, b. It returns a string that contains a hexadecimal printout of those bytes. Each byte in the array is read in order and converted to two hexadecimal digits.

To convert a byte to two hex digits, it is first split into its first four bits (b[i] >> 4) and its last four bits (b[i] & 0x0000000F). The result of each of these calculations is an int. This int is passed to BitsToChar(). BitsToChar() is little more than a switch statement that converts a single int between 0 and 15 to a hexadecimal digit between 0 and F. Numbers outside the acceptable range (greater than 15 or less than 0) cause a new IllegalArgumentException to be thrown. This is a RuntimeException, so you don't need to catch or declare it. Each of the chars is appended to the temporary StringBuffer sb. Finally sb.toString() is returned.

A raw hex dump of a file is not very informative, although you can learn a little from it. All Java .class files should begin with the 4-byte magic number 0xCAFEBABE — that is -889,275,714 in decimal. If you don't see this number at the beginning of the file, then you know it's not a valid Java byte code file, even if the file name ends in .class.

Bytes four and five of a .class file (the two bytes immediately following CAFEBABE) show the minor version of the compiler that produced this file. The two bytes after that show the major version of the compiler. In this example, the minor version is 0x0003 (3), and the major version is 0x002D j(45). When a Java virtual machine reads a .class file, it checks to see if it understands that version of the format. A virtual machine can generally read all of the minor versions in a major version, but if the major version changes, a new virtual machine is required. Some virtual machines may also understand older major versions, but they should not attempt to read files with newer major versions. The .class file format is actually more stable than the language and the API. Both Java 1.0.2 and Java 1.1 use the 45.3 .class file format.

The remaining digits all have meanings, but pulling them out by hand is excruciatingly painful. In fact, even in total disaster situations (such as when your hard disk has crashed, taking with it three months of un-backed-up, mission-critical .class files while the corresponding .java files are completely lost), you would probably copy the byte codes out of the file by hand and manually enter them into another computer where you could decompile them.

The next variant, Listing 4-2, was obtained by forcing the file open in a text processor (specifically BBEdit). The printout here has thrown away a few characters, such as page break (ASCII), that would have completely screwed up the formatting of this book. This looks awful, but it's a quick-and-dirty way to get a look at the String constants in a file.

I remember a stock trader in the early days of PCs who didn't like one of the messages that his program gave him, so he opened up the DOS .exe file in WordPerfect, searched for the offending string, replaced it, and saved the file. Amazingly, the program worked with his "user modification." I do not recommend this as general practice. There's not much else to be learned here, so let's move on.

Listing 4-3 is composed of disassembled byte code. This is much more useful than Listing 4-2. You get to see the name of the class, all imported classes, and all methods and fields. With a little effort, you can learn to read the byte codes as you would read someone else's source code. This listing was produced with the JDK's javap program with the -c command line flag — that is:

```
% javap -c HelloWorld
```

I'll develop a different byte code disassembler later in this chapter and the next.

Why would you want to do this when you can look at the .java source code file instead? The short answer is that you'll almost never do this *instead* of looking at the .java file. However, it's not uncommon to want to investigate the code of a class for which you do not have original source code. You've probably become accustomed to using your Web browser's View Source command to find out how someone did a neat HTML trick.

With the techniques and tools you'll develop in this chapter, you'll have an effective View Source equivalent for Java .class files.

Let's begin by looking at the source and byte codes for the main() method of the HelloWorld class.

```
public static void main (String args[]) { Method void main()

        System.out.println("Hello World!");    0 getstatic #7 <Field
java.lang.System.out Ljava/io/PrintStream;>
            3 ldc #1 <String "Hello World">
              5 invokevirtual #8 <Method
java.io.PrintStream.print(Ljava/lang/String;)V>
              8 return
    }                                               }
```

Lining them up side-by-side, you can see that these four lines

```
        0 getstatic #7 <Field java.lang.System.out Ljava/io/PrintStream;>
        3 ldc #1 <String "Hello World">
        5 invokevirtual #8 <Method
java.io.PrintStream.print(Ljava/lang/String;)V>
        8 return
```

are probably somehow equivalent to the single source code line:

```
System.out.println("Hello World!");
```

See if you can figure out how. The numbers on the left of each line start counting at zero. They're indices into the byte codes for this method. This is just a series of bytes in a particular place in memory.

The first byte is an instruction: getstatic. The argument to this instruction is #7. This refers to the seventh entry in the constant pool for this class. It so happens that the seventh entry in this particular pool is java.lang.System.out, an instance of java.io.PrintStream. You know that System.out is a static field in the System class of type PrintStream, so it seems logical to interpret getstatic as a command to retrieve a reference to a static class. In this case, it retrieves a reference to the System.out class and places it on the stack.

The next instruction is ldc, which stands for "load constant." It has one argument: the integer constant #1. The 1 tells it which constant to load from the constant pool. In this case, it loads the first constant in the pool, which happens to be the string "Hello World!" Because "Hello World" is the only constant literal in HelloWorld.java, it's not surprising that it's the first one in the pool. A reference to this string is placed on the top of the stack.

The next instruction is invokevirtual. This instruction calls instance methods. In this case, it calls the eighth entry in the constant pool, the method println() of the java.io.PrintStream class. The arguments for println() are taken from the stack. In this case, the top of the stack has a reference to the String object HelloWorld. The object whose method it should call is one level deeper in the stack. That's the reference to System.out placed there by getstatic.

The last instruction is return. There was no return statement in main(), but Java puts one here anyway. Writing return is optional in void methods. The compiler is smart enough to add a blank return for you if your void method requires one. However, in a non-void method, you have to return explicitly, because the compiler, although it knows you have to return, does not know what value you want to return.

The next method is the constructor HelloWorld(). The .java source code file did not include a constructor. However, the compiler puts a default constructor that takes no arguments in the byte code anyway.

```
Method HelloWorld()
   0 aload_0
   1 invokespecial #6 <Method java.lang.Object.<init>()V>
   4 return

}
```

The aload instruction loads a reference from a local variable. In this case, it loads the zeroth local variable. This local variable is the string "java.lang.Object()". This becomes the argument to the next instruction. The next instruction, invokespecial, is used to call the superclass's constructor from the subclass's constructor. Finally, the return instruction transfers control back to the calling method.

What's most interesting about this method is that none of it is in the Java source code. All Java classes have a constructor that takes no arguments if there are no other explicit constructors. Furthermore, all constructors call their superclass's constructor before they do anything else, even if there isn't an explicit super() call in the first line of the subclass's constructor.

In the remainder of this chapter, you'll explore the Java .class file format to see how you change raw hexadecimal bytes such as those in Listing 4-1 into something more intelligible like the byte code in Listing 4-4.

READING CLASS FILES

A Java .class file has 16 parts. Eleven of the parts always occupy the same number of bytes. For example, the magic number 0xCAFEBABE is always four bytes, never two bytes and never eight bytes. Five of the parts are of varying length. For example, longer methods must have more byte codes than shorter methods. Table 4-1 lists the 16 parts of every Java .class file in order. These parts always occur in exactly this order. The first step to disassembling a Java .class file is to break it up into these parts.

Table 4-1
The 16 parts of a .class file

Field	Width (bytes)	Meaning
magic	4	This identifies the .class file format. It should be 0xCAFEBABE. If it's anything else, you're dealing with a format more recent than this book.
minor version	2	The minor version of the compiler
major version	2	The major version of the compiler
constant pool	variable	The first two bytes give the number of entries in the constant pool. Then, as many bytes as are necessary to fill that many entries are read. The constant pool is a table of constant values used by this class.
access flags	2	These bit flags tell you whether the class is public, final, abstract, an interface, and a few other things.
this class	2	This tells you which entry in the constant pool holds this class's class info.
superclass	2	If this is zero, then this class's only superclass is java.lang.Object. Otherwise, this is an index into the constant pool for the superclass class info.
interfaces	variable	The interface table holds two byte indices into the constant pool table, one for each interface that this class implements. The first two bytes give the number of entries in the interface table. Therefore, after reading the first two bytes, you have to read twice as many bytes as the number stored in the first two bytes.
fields	variable	The fields table includes one field's info structure for each field in the class.
methods	variable	The method table contains the byte codes for each method in the class, the return type of the method, and the types of each argument to the method.
attributes	2	The attributes of the class

Listing 4-6 is a skeleton of a program that will disassemble byte code files. It reads the name of a file from the command line, opens a FileInputStream to the file, chains a DataInputStream to that FileInputStream, and then proceeds to read bytes out of the file. Or at least it will as soon as the skeleton is filled out. It would be simple enough to add a graphical interface to this program, as I did with Listing 4-5, but let's leave that as an exercise for you to explore.

Listing 4-6
Disassembler skeleton

```
import java.io.*;
import java.awt.FileDialog;
import java.awt.Frame;

public class Disassembler {

  DataInputStream theInput;
  PrintStream theOutput;

  public static void main (String[] args) {

    try {
      Disassembler d = new Disassembler();
      d.disassemble();

    }
    catch (Exception e) {
      System.err.println(e);
      e.printStackTrace();
    }

  }

  public Disassembler (String theFile, OutputStream os) throws IOException {

    this(new File(theFile), os);

  }

  public Disassembler (File theFile, OutputStream os) throws IOException {

    FileInputStream fis = new FileInputStream(theFile);
    theInput = new DataInputStream(fis);
    theOutput = new PrintStream(os);

  }
```

(continued)

Disassembler skeleton *(continued)*

```
public Disassembler (OutputStream os) throws IOException {

  this(chooseFile(), os);

}

public Disassembler () throws IOException {

  this(chooseFile(), System.out);

}

public static File chooseFile() {

  FileDialog fd = new FileDialog(new Frame(),
   "Please choose a file:", FileDialog.LOAD);
  fd.show();

  return new File(fd.getDirectory(), fd.getFile());

}


public void disassemble() throws IOException {

  try {
    readMagic();
    readMinorVersion();
    readMajorVersion();
    readConstantPool();
    readAccessFlags();
    readClass();
    readSuperclass();
    readInterfaces();
    readFields();
    readMethods();
    readAttributes();

    // Output the file
    writeImports();
    writeAccess();
    writeClassName();
    writeSuperclass();
    writeInterfaces();
    writeFields();
    writeMethods();
```

(continued)

Listing 4-6

Disassembler skeleton *(continued)*

```
      theOutput.println("}");
      theOutput.println("\n/*\n" + thePool + "\n*/");

  }
  catch (ClassFormatError e) {
    System.err.println(e);
    return;
  }

}

int magic;

void readMagic() throws IOException {

}

void readMinorVersion() throws IOException {

}

void readMajorVersion() throws IOException {

}

void readConstantPool() throws IOException {

}

void readAccessFlags() throws IOException {

}

void readClass() throws IOException {

}

void readSuperclass() throws IOException {

}

void readInterfaces() throws IOException {

}

void readFields() throws IOException {
```

(continued)

Disassembler skeleton *(continued)*

```
    }

    void readMethods() throws IOException {

    }

    void readAttributes() throws IOException {

    }

    public void writeAccess() {

    }

    public void writeClassName() {

    }

    public void writeSuperclass() {

    }

    public void writeImports() {

    }

    public void writeInterfaces() {

    }

    public void writeFields() {

    }

    public void writeMethods() {

    }

    public String getExceptions(MethodInfo mi) {

    }

    public String getCode(MethodInfo mi) {

    }
```

(continued)

Listing 4-6
Disassembler skeleton *(continued)*

```
    public String getReturnType(MethodInfo mi) {

    }

    public String getArguments(MethodInfo mi) {

    }

    public String decodeDescriptor(String d) {

    }

}
```

The key method of this program is disassemble(). This is the method that actually reads the bytes. It does this by calling the 11 methods — readMagic(), readMinorVersion(), readMajorVersion(), readConstantPool(), readAccessFlags(), readClass(), readSuperclass(), readInterfaces(), readFields(), readMethods(), and readAttributes() — in that order. You have to call them in that order because, except for the first few parts, the parts don't start on any particular byte. For example, to find where the seventh part begins, you have to pick up where the sixth ended, and so on.

Once all the pieces have been read, you write them back out with writeImports(), writeAccess(), writeClassName(), writeSuperclass(), writeInterfaces(), writeFields(), and writeMethods(). You must write these in the order in which they normally appear in a .java source code file, not in the order in which they were read in the byte code file. Indeed, some of these parts, like the import statements, are not specifically included in the compiled file but can be deduced from it.

In the event that there's a problem with a .class file, a java.lang.ClassFormatError appears. Once this program encounters an invalid file, it prints out an error message and stops executing.

It is rather unusual to catch an error rather than an Exception. You can't normally recover from a ClassFormatError because it means that one of the classes that the program needs will not be available. However, because you're not loading the class, but just parsing it, you have a little more leeway. This might get you into trouble if a ClassFormatError that you did not create yourself bubbles up during the file parsing. This is rather unlikely, but a somewhat more robust solution would provide a means to distinguish between the ClassFormatErrors that indicate a problem with the file being parsed and the ClassFormatErrors thrown by the Java VM when it fails to load a requested class.

The following sections explain each part in detail and fill in the code needed to make these methods work. The next chapter, Chapter 5, expands the readMethods() method to provide a better analysis of the code inside method bodies.

Magic number

All Java .class files are supposed to begin with the four-byte magic number 0xCAFEBABE, that is -1,258,207,934 in decimal. If you don't see this at the beginning of the file, then you know that it's not a valid Java byte code file, even if the file name ends in .class. In this event, the disassembler should throw a ClassFormatError and bail out. The easiest way to read the number is with the java.io.DataInputStream.readInt() method. Listing 4-7 shows the filled-out readMagic() method.

Listing 4-7
A method that reads the magic number and verifies that it is 0xCAFEBABE

```
int magic;

void readMagic() throws IOException {

    magic = theInput.readInt();
    if (magic != 0xCAFEBABE) {
      throw new ClassFormatError("Incorrect Magic Number: "
       + magic);
    }

}
```

Magic numbers are pure byte code phenomena. They do not appear anywhere in the .java source code file. Therefore, there's no corresponding writeMagic() method.

Minor version

Bytes four and five of a .class file (the two bytes immediately following CAFEBABE) are the minor version of the compiler that produced this file. This is an unsigned 2-byte int (like a char) and can have a value between 0 and 65,535. This book documents minor version 3. The easiest way to read

an unsigned 2-byte int is with java.io.DataInputStream.read
UnsignedShort() method.

> **Note**
>
> It's important to realize that although readUnsignedShort() reads a short, it
> returns an int. A normal signed Java short can't hold values up to 65,535 as
> an unsigned short can.

Listing 4-8 is the fleshed readminorVersion() method.

Listing 4-8
The readMajorVersion() method

```
void readMinorVersion() throws IOException {

    minor_version = theInput.readUnsignedShort();
    if (minor_version != 3) {
      throw new ClassFormatError("Minor Version not 3");
    }

  }
```

Like magic numbers, minor and major versions are part of only the byte
code, not the source code. Therefore, this method checks only that the
minor version is what it's expected to be. It doesn't need to be saved because
it doesn't have any effect on what comes after it.

Major version

The next two bytes are the major version of the compiler. Like the minor
version, the major version is a 2-byte, unsigned integer. The major version
you expect is 45. The parser is unlikely to be able to read anything different,
so the program throws a ClassFormatException and bails out. Listing 4-9
fleshes out this method:

Listing 4-9
The readMajorVersion() method

```
void readMajorVersion() throws IOException {

    major_version = theInput.readUnsignedShort();
    if (major_version != 45) {
      throw new ClassFormatError("Major Version not 45");
    }
  }
```

Constant pool

The constant pool is a data structure that stores all the constants in a program, not just literals like 1.0 or 72, but also class structures, method references, and the names and types of variables. The disassembler needs to make frequent reference back to this data structure when parsing later parts of the file. Many other entries in the .class file simply refer back to constants stored in the constant pool. It is therefore necessary to create a data structure to hold the constants for later reference.

The largest difficulty in this endeavor is that the constant pool has to hold values of 11 different types. To make matters worse, six of those types are reference types and five are primitive types. Because this is relatively complex, I'm going to push all the details into a new class called ConstantPool. The Disassembler class will simply call the ConstantPool() constructor, as shown in Listing 4-10. The ConstantPool() constructor will read the data out of theInput and parse it, and a new ConstantPool object will be stored in the field thePool.

Listing 4-10
The ConstantPool() constructor

```
ConstantPool thePool;

void readConstantPool() throws IOException {

  thePool = new ConstantPool(theInput);

}
```

The exact size of the constant pool depends on what's inside it. The first two bytes of this part of the file are an unsigned short specifying the number of entries in the constant pool. This number must be greater than zero. The first constant pool entry is reserved for the virtual machine's use. Therefore, there is actually one less than this number of actual entries to be read. However, entries of different types can have different sizes.

Listing 4-11 is the ConstantPool class. This class does two things: first, it reads the constant pool from the file; second, it responds to requests for items from the constant pool.

The ConstantPool class is implemented as an array of PoolEntry objects. Listing 4-12 is the PoolEntry class. A PoolEntry object can hold one item that has one of the 11 different types and classes that can be stored in the constant pool. The ConstantPool constructor first reads two bytes from the InputStream as an unsigned short. This specifies the number of entries in the ConstantPool so that it can decide how large to make the PoolEntry array. Then, it passes InputStream to the PoolEntry() constructor enough times to fill the array. The PoolEntry() constructor determines the type of that entry in the pool and reads the right number of bytes for that type.

To read a particular entry from the constant pool, you call the properly typed read method of ConstantPool — for example, readDouble(int i) to get a double constant from the pool. These methods retrieve the right PoolEntry from the array and then call that entry's matching read method.

All information about the type of a PoolEntry is stored in the PoolEntry itself. The user, however, will generally need to know the type of the entry being requested. If the user requests the wrong type from a PoolEntry, then the PoolEntry will throw a ClassFormatError.

Note

This is not the only way that I could have structured this program. Another possibility would have been to make PoolEntry an abstract class with an abstract read method. There would be subclasses for double, float, ClassInfo, and the other types.

Listing 4-11
The ConstantPool class

```
import java.io.*;


public class ConstantPool {

  PoolEntry[] thePool;

  public ConstantPool(DataInputStream dis) throws IOException {
    int length = dis.readUnsignedShort();
    thePool = new PoolEntry[length];
    for (int i = 1; i < length; i++) {
      thePool[i] = new PoolEntry(dis);
      // Doubles and longs take two pool entries
      // see Java VM Spec., p. 98
      if (thePool[i].tag == PoolEntry.cDouble || thePool[i].tag ==
PoolEntry.cLong)
        i++;
    }

  }

  public PoolEntry read(int i) {
    return thePool[i];
  }
```

(continued)

The ConstantPool class *(continued)*

```java
public String readUTF8(int i) {
  return thePool[i].readUTF8();
}

public int readInteger(int i) {
  return thePool[i].readInteger();
}

public float readFloat(int i) {
  return thePool[i].readFloat();
}

public double readDouble(int i) {
  return thePool[i].readDouble();
}

public ClassInfo readClassInfo(int i) {
  return thePool[i].readClassInfo();
}

public RefInfo readMethodRef(int i) {
  return thePool[i].readMethodRef();
}

public RefInfo readInterfaceMethodRef(int i) {
  return thePool[i].readInterfaceMethodRef();
}

public NameAndType readNameAndType(int i) {
  return thePool[i].readNameAndType();
}

public int howMany() {
  return thePool.length;
}

public String toString() {
  String result = "";
  for (int i = 1; i < thePool.length; i++) {
    result += i + ":  " + thePool[i].toString() + "\n";
    // Doubles and longs take two pool entries
    // see Java VM Spec., p. 98
    if (thePool[i].tag == PoolEntry.cDouble || thePool[i].tag ==
PoolEntry.cLong) i++;
  }
```

(continued)

Listing 4-11
The ConstantPool class *(continued)*

```
    return result;

  }

}
```

The PoolEntry class begins with 11 constants to represent the 11 types that may appear in the constant pool. That is, every constant pool entry is preceded by one unsigned byte that signals its type.

The PoolEntry() constructor reads this tag to determine how many bytes it should read. It reads four bytes for integer, float, ClassInfo, FieldRef, MethodRef, NameAndType, and InterfaceMethodRef types. It reads eight bytes for long and double types. ClassInfo and String types take two bytes. Finally, the UTF8 type requires a variable number of bytes, so first you must read one more unsigned short to learn how many bytes are in the UTF8 structure. Once you know how many bytes you need to read, reading them is almost trivial. Just use the read(byte[] b) method of the DataInputStream.

Note

I decided to store the data as a byte array that will be converted to the appropriate type when requested. I could have performed the conversion immediately in the constructor and stored the converted values rather than the raw bytes. However, this would require many excess fields for each PoolEntry object. For example, if a PoolEntry object is a float, then the UTF8, integer, long, double, and all other fields would be empty. This seems excessively wasteful. However, if you anticipate repeatedly requesting the same entry from the constant pool, then you might want to trade off the extra memory in exchange for reduced CPU time.

Listing 4-12
The PoolEntry class

```
import java.io.*;


public class PoolEntry {

  public final static int cUTF8 = 1;
  public final static int cInteger = 3;
```

(continued)

The PoolEntry class *(continued)*

```
public final static int cFloat = 4;
public final static int cLong = 5;
public final static int cDouble = 6;
public final static int cClassInfo = 7;
public final static int cString = 8;
public final static int cFieldRef = 9;
public final static int cMethodRef = 10;
public final static int cInterfaceMethodRef = 11;
public final static int cNameAndType = 12;

int tag;
byte[] data;

public PoolEntry(DataInputStream dis) throws IOException {

    tag = dis.readUnsignedByte();
    int bytesToRead;
    switch (tag) {
      case cLong:
      case cDouble:
        bytesToRead = 8;
        break;
      case cInteger:
      case cFloat:

      case cFieldRef:
      case cMethodRef:
      case cNameAndType:
      case cInterfaceMethodRef:
        bytesToRead = 4;

        break;
      case cClassInfo:
      case cString:
        bytesToRead = 2;
        break;
      case cUTF8:
        bytesToRead = dis.readUnsignedShort();
        break;
      default:
        throw new ClassFormatError("Unrecognized Constant Type " + tag);
    }

    data = new byte[bytesToRead];

    int check = dis.read(data);
    if (check != data.length) {
```

(continued)

Listing 4-12
The PoolEntry class *(continued)*

```
         throw new ClassFormatError("Not enough data to fill array");
      }

   }

   public String readUTF8() {
    if (tag != cUTF8) {
       throw new ClassFormatError
         ("This is not a UTF8 string ");
    }
    try {
      // first put length of string back in string
      int len = data.length;
      byte[] newdata = new byte[len+2];
      newdata[0] = (byte) (len >> 8);
      newdata[1] = (byte) len;
      System.arraycopy(data, 0, newdata, 2, data.length);
      ByteArrayInputStream bis = new ByteArrayInputStream(newdata);
      DataInputStream dis = new DataInputStream(bis);
      return dis.readUTF();
    }
    catch (IOException e) {
      throw new ClassFormatError(e + " Bad UTF8 string");
    }

   }

   public int readInteger() {
     if (tag != cInteger) {
        throw new ClassFormatError
          ("This is not an integer.");
     }
     return data[0] << 24 | data[1] << 16 | data[2] << 8 | data[3];

   }

   public int readLong() {
     if (tag != cLong) {
        throw new ClassFormatError
          ("This is not a long.");
     }
     return data[0] << 56 | data[1] << 48 | data[2] << 40 |
       data[3] << 32 | data[4] << 24 | data[5] << 16 | data[6] << 8 |
       data[7];

   }
```

(continued)

The PoolEntry class *(continued)*

```
public float readFloat() {
  if (tag != cFloat) {
    throw new ClassFormatError
      ("This is not a float");
  }
  int bits = data[0] << 24 | data[1] << 16 | data[2] << 8 | data[3];
  return Float.intBitsToFloat(bits);

}

public double readDouble() {
  if (tag != cDouble) {
    throw new ClassFormatError
      ("This is not a double");
  }
  long bits = (long) data[0] << 56 | (long) data[1] << 48
   | (long) data[2] << 40 | (long) data[3] << 32 | (long) data[4] << 24
   | (long) data[5] << 16 | (long) data[6] << 8 | (long) data[7];
  return Double.longBitsToDouble(bits);


}

public ClassInfo readClassInfo() {
  if (tag != cClassInfo) {
    throw new ClassFormatError
      ("This is not a ClassInfoStructure");
  }
  return new ClassInfo(tag, data[0] << 8 | data[1]);

}

public RefInfo readFieldRef() {
  if (tag != cFieldRef) {
    throw new ClassFormatError
      ("This is not a FieldRefStructure");
  }
  return new RefInfo(tag, data[0] << 8 | data[1],
  data[2] << 8 | data[3]);

}

public RefInfo readMethodRef() {
  if (tag != cMethodRef) {
    throw new ClassFormatError
      ("This is not a methodRef");
```

(continued)

Listing 4-12
The PoolEntry class *(continued)*

```java
      }
      return new RefInfo(tag, data[0] << 8 | data[1],
      data[2] << 8 | data[3]);

   }

   public RefInfo readInterfaceMethodRef() {
     if (tag != cInterfaceMethodRef) {
       throw new ClassFormatError
         ("This is not an InterfaceMethodRef");
     }
     return new RefInfo(tag, data[0] << 8 | data[1],
     data[2] << 8 | data[3]);

   }

   public NameAndType readNameAndType() {
     if (tag != cNameAndType) {
       throw new ClassFormatError
         ("This is not a Name and Type structure");
     }
     return new NameAndType(tag, data[0] << 8 | data[1],
     data[2] << 8 | data[3]);

   }

   public int readString() {
     if (tag != cString) {

       throw new ClassFormatError
         ("This is not a String");
     }
     return data[0] << 8 | data[1];
   }

   public int tag() {
     return tag;
   }

   public String toString() {

     switch (tag) {
       case cLong:
         return "long            " + String.valueOf(readLong());
       case cDouble:
```

(continued)

The PoolEntry class *(continued)*

```
              return "double        " + String.valueOf(readDouble());
          case cInteger:
              return "int           " + String.valueOf(readInteger());
          case cFloat:
              return "float         " + String.valueOf(readFloat());
          case cFieldRef:
              return "FieldRef      " + String.valueOf(readFieldRef());
          case cMethodRef:
              return "MethodRef     " + String.valueOf(readMethodRef());
          case cNameAndType:
              return "NameAndType   " + String.valueOf(readNameAndType());
          case cInterfaceMethodRef:
              return "InterfaceMethodRef " +
    String.valueOf(readInterfaceMethodRef());
          case cClassInfo:
              return "ClassInfo     " + String.valueOf(readClassInfo());
          case cString:
              return "String        " + String.valueOf(readString());
          case cUTF8:
              return "UTF8          " + readUTF8();
           default:
              throw new ClassFormatError("Unrecognized Constant Type");
      }

  }

  }
```

The PoolEntry class has 11 methods to return values. Each of these methods first checks to make sure that the type requested is in fact the type of this object. If the type doesn't match, then a ClassFormatError is thrown. Once it verifies the type, it converts the data array into a primitive type or object of the appropriate type. In four cases, a new class is required to hold the return type.

The ClassInfo class holds a tag and an index into the constant pool for the name of the class. It appears in Listing 4-13.

Listing 4-13
The ClassInfo class

```
public class ClassInfo {

  int nameIndex;
  int tag;
```

(continued)

Listing 4-13
The ClassInfo class *(continued)*

```
public ClassInfo(int t, int n) {
  tag = t;
  nameIndex = n;
}

public int nameIndex() {
  return nameIndex;
}

}
```

The RefInfo class, shown in Listing 4-14, holds indices for the class and the NameAndType in the constant pool. This is used for method references, field references, and interface method references.

Listing 4-14
The RefInfo class

```
public class RefInfo {

  int classIndex;
  int nameAndTypeIndex;
  int tag;

  public RefInfo(int t, int c, int n) {
    tag = t;
    classIndex = c;
    nameAndTypeIndex = n;
  }

  public int classIndex() {
    return classIndex;
  }

  public int nameAndTypeIndex() {
    return nameAndTypeIndex;
  }

}
```

Finally, the NameAndType class shown in Listing 4-15 holds indices into the constant pool for a name and a descriptor.

Listing 4-15
The NameAndType class

```
public class NameAndType {

    int nameIndex;
    int descriptorIndex;
    int tag;

    public NameAndType(int t, int c, int n) {
        tag = t;
        nameIndex = c;
        descriptorIndex = n;
    }

    public int nameIndex() {
        return nameIndex;
    }

    public int descriptorIndex() {
        return descriptorIndex;
    }

}
```

Access flags

The access flags listed in Table 4-2 are stored in the .class file as a 2-byte bit mask. Bit 15 (the ones bit) is set if the class is public. Bit 11 (the sixteens bit) is set if the class is final. Bit 10 is set if invokespecial needs to treat the class specially. (Don't worry too much about that. I explain what that means in the next chapter.) Bit 6 is set if the class is an interface. Bit 5 is set if the class is abstract. The remaining bits are not yet used.

Table 4-2
Access flags

Bit	Mask	Meaning if set
0	0x8000	Reserved for future use.
1	0x4000	Reserved for future use.
2	0x2000	Reserved for future use.
3	0x1000	Reserved for future use.
4	0x0800	Reserved for future use.
5	0x0400	This is an abstract class or interface.

(continued)

Table 4-2

Access flags *(continued)*

Bit	Mask	*Meaning if set*
6	0x0200	This is an interface.
7	0x0100	Reserved for future use.
8	0x0080	Reserved for future use.
9	0x0040	Reserved for future use.
10	0x0020	This is treated specially by invokespecial.
11	0x0010	This class is final.
12	0x0008	Reserved for future use.
13	0x0004	Reserved for future use.
14	0x0002	Reserved for future use.
15	0x0001	This class or interface is public.

These flags are not independent of each other. If bit 6 is set (this is an interface), then bit 5 must also be set, because all interfaces are abstract. Similarly, a class cannot have both bits 11 and 6 set, because a final class can't be abstract.

The unused bits in the access flags are reserved for future use. For now, you should ignore them when parsing the file. Listing 4-16 provides the filled-out code to read the access flags. Listing 4-16 also introduces several new boolean fields to allow later methods to know the values of these flags.

Listing 4-16

Reading the access flags

```
short access_flags;
boolean isPublic;
boolean isFinal;
boolean isInterface;
boolean isAbstract;
boolean isSpecial;

void readAccessFlags() throws IOException {

  access_flags = theInput.readShort();
  isPublic    = (access_flags & 0x0001) == 0 ? false : true;
  isFinal     = (access_flags & 0x0010) == 0 ? false : true;
  isInterface = (access_flags & 0x0020) == 0 ? false : true;
  isAbstract  = (access_flags & 0x0200) == 0 ? false : true;
  isSpecial   = (access_flags & 0x0400) == 0 ? false : true;
  if (isAbstract && isFinal) {
    throw new ClassFormatError("This class is abstract and final!");
  }
  if (isInterface && !isAbstract) {
```

(continued)

Reading the access flags *(continued)*

```
      throw new ClassFormatError("This interface is not abstract!");
    }
    if (isFinal && isInterface) {
      throw new ClassFormatError("This interface is final!");
    }

  }
```

There are a few things to note about this code. First, it is necessary to make an explicit comparison with == and ?: to zero in order to convert the masked short to a boolean. In a language like C or C++, you would simply take zero to mean false.

The next thing to ask yourself is whether the final if clause is really necessary. Given that this code will throw an error if a class is abstract and final or if a class is an interface and not abstract, can it possibly reach the test for being both final and an interface?

thisClass

Next is a 2-byte unsigned short that is an index into the constant pool. At that index in the constant pool, you should find a ClassInfo structure. This ClassInfo structure represents the current class or interface that you're parsing. Listing 4-17 reads this index and stores the ClassInfo structure it references in a new field: thisClass. Notice how we have to refer back to the constant pool at this point.

Listing 4-17
readClass()

```
    ClassInfo thisClass;

    void readClass() throws IOException {
      int index = theInput.readUnsignedShort();
      thisClass = thePool.readClassInfo(index);
    }
```

Superclass

Immediately following the index of this class, you'll find the index into the constant pool for the ClassInfo structure of this class's superclass (Listing 4-18). Reading this value is almost identical to the previous method.

However, if this class does not have a superclass (that is, if this is java.lang.Object, the only class without a superclass), then the index into the constant pool will be zero. You therefore have to watch out for this special case. If the index is zero, then you should set superclass to null.

Listing 4-18
readSuperclass()

```
ClassInfo superclass;

void readSuperclass() throws IOException {
  int index = theInput.readUnsignedShort();
  if (index == 0) {
    superclass = null;
  }
  else {
    superclass = thePool.readClassInfo(index);
  }
}
```

Interfaces

A single class can implement multiple interfaces. First, an unsigned short tells you how many interfaces that this class implements (possibly zero). There are exactly that many unsigned short indices in the constant pool. Each index points to a ClassInfo structure for the implemented interface. Listing 4-19 is the fleshed-out readInterfaces() method. The interfaces are read, resolved, and stored in a new field array called interfaces.

Listing 4-19
The readInterfaces() method

```
ClassInfo[] interfaces;

void readInterfaces() throws IOException {
  interfaces = new ClassInfo[theInput.readUnsignedShort()];
  for (int i =0; i< interfaces.length; i++) {
    interfaces[i] = thePool.readClassInfo(i);
  }
```

Attributes

The last thing you read from a .class file is the class's attributes. Before you get to a class's attributes, you have to read its fields and methods. However, each field and method also has its own attributes table. Therefore, you should develop the classes needed to read attributes *before* you need them. This class will read the attributes of the fields, the methods, and the class itself.

An attribute table consists of a specified number of attribute_info structures (see Listing 4-20). Each attribute_info structure consists of one unsigned short that is the name index for this attribute. It's an index into the constant pool. Next, there's a 4-byte unsigned int that gives you the length of the attribute's data. Finally, there's an array of data.

Listing 4-20
AttributeInfo

```
import java.io.*;


public class AttributeInfo {

  int nameIndex;
  byte[] data;

  public AttributeInfo(DataInputStream dis) throws IOException {
    nameIndex = dis.readUnsignedShort();
    data = new byte[dis.readInt()];
    int bytesRead = dis.read(data);
    if (bytesRead != data.length) {
      throw new ClassFormatError("Insufficioent bytes in attribute");
    }

  }

}
```

Listing 4-21 is a filled-in readAttributes() method for the Disassembler class. An array of AttributeInfo structures holds the different attributes.

Listing 4-21
readAttributes()

```
AttributeInfo[] attributes;

  void readAttributes() throws IOException {
    attributes = new AttributeInfo[theInput.readUnsignedShort()];
    for (int i = 0; i < attributes.length; i++) {
      attributes[i] = new AttributeInfo(dis);
    }
  }
```

Fields

After you've read the interfaces, you next read the class's fields. Some classes have no fields. For example, the HelloWorld program has only a method. An unsigned short tells you how many fields there are in the class. Then you read that many FieldInfo structures from the file. A FieldInfo structure is composed of five items.

The first unsigned short is the access flags for the field. These tell you whether the field is public, private, protected, static, final, volatile, and/or transient. Table 4-3 lists the bit masks for each of these modifiers. As usual, the bit mask values are chosen so that the bitwise operators can easily pick out individual values. Note that not all of the possible combinations of flags are allowed. For example, a field cannot be both public and private. Each flag is exactly equivalent to a Java keyword, which may modify a field.

Table 4-3
Field access flags

Flag	Bit mask
public	0x0001
private	0x0002
protected	0x0004
static	0x0008
final	0x0010
volatile	0x0040
transient	0x0080

The 2-byte unsigned short immediately following the access flags is the name index—that is, an index into the constant pool that provides the field name's location.

Next comes the descriptor index, another 2-byte unsigned short index into the constant pool. This points to a UTF8 structure, which represents a field descriptor.

Next comes the attributes table for this field. You read this by passing the DataInputStream into the AttributeTable constructor. Listing 4-22 is the full FieldInfo class.

Listing 4-22
The FieldInfo class

```
import java.io.*;


public class FieldInfo {

  int accessflags;
  int nameIndex;
  int descriptorIndex;
  AttributeInfo[] attributes;

  public final static int cPublic = 0x0001;
  public final static int cPrivate = 0x0002;
  public final static int cProtected = 0x0004;
  public final static int cStatic = 0x0008;
  public final static int cFinal = 0x0010;
  public final static int cVolatile = 0x0040;
  public final static int cTransient = 0x0080;

  public FieldInfo( DataInputStream dis) throws IOException {
    accessflags = dis.readUnsignedShort();
    nameIndex = dis.readUnsignedShort();
    descriptorIndex = dis.readUnsignedShort();
    attributes = new AttributeInfo[dis.readUnsignedShort()];
    for (int i = 0; i < attributes.length; i++) {
      attributes[i] = new AttributeInfo(dis);
    }

  }

  public int nameIndex() {
    return nameIndex;
  }

  public int descriptorIndex() {
    return descriptorIndex;
  }

  public boolean isPublic() {
    return (accessflags & cPublic) != 0;
  }

  public boolean isPrivate() {
    return (accessflags & cPrivate) != 0;
  }
```

(continued)

Listing 4-22
The FieldInfo class *(continued)*

```
   public boolean isProtected() {
     return (accessflags & cProtected) != 0;
   }

   public boolean isStatic() {
     return (accessflags & cStatic) != 0;
   }

   public boolean isVolatile() {
     return (accessflags & cVolatile) != 0;
   }

   public boolean isTransient() {
     return (accessflags & cTransient) != 0;
   }

   public boolean isFinal() {
     return (accessflags & cFinal) != 0;
   }

 }
```

Here's the fleshed-out readFields() method for the Disassembler class. It's quite simple, because all the work goes on inside the FieldInfo class.

```
FieldInfo[] fields;

void readFields() throws IOException {
  fields = new FieldInfo[theInput.readUnsignedShort()];
  for (int i = 0; i < fields.length; i++) {
    fields[i] = new FieldInfo[dis];
  }
}
```

Methods

The methods table is similar to the fields table. First, there's an unsigned short to tell you how many methods there are. Then there's an array of method_info structures. As with the FieldInfo structure, this program keeps all the intelligence inside the MethodInfo constructor. Listing 4-23 is the fleshed-out readMethods() method for the Disassembler class.

Listing 4-23
readMethods()

```
MethodInfo[] methods;


void readMethods() throws IOException {
  methods = new MethodInfo[theInput.readUnsignedShort()];
  for (int i = 0; i < methods.length; i++) {
    methods[i] = new MethodInfo[dis];
  }
}
```

The MethodInfo structure is almost identical to a FieldInfo structure. In fact, the only difference is in the permitted values for the access flags and the meaning of the attributes. Listing 4-24 is the MethodInfo class.

Listing 4-24
The MethodInfo class

```
import java.io.*;


public class MethodInfo {

  int accessflags;
  int nameIndex;
  int descriptorIndex;
  AttributeInfo[] attributes;

  public final static int cPublic = 0x0001;
  public final static int cPrivate = 0x0002;
  public final static int cProtected = 0x0004;
  public final static int cStatic = 0x0008;
  public final static int cFinal = 0x0010;
  public final static int cSynchronized = 0x0020;
  public final static int cNative = 0x0100;
  public final static int cAbstract = 0x0400;

  public MethodInfo (DataInputStream dis) throws IOException {
    accessflags = dis.readUnsignedShort();
    nameIndex = dis.readUnsignedShort();
    descriptorIndex = dis.readUnsignedShort();
    attributes = new AttributeInfo[dis.readUnsignedShort()];
    for (int i = 0; i < attributes.length; i++) {
      attributes[i] = new AttributeInfo(dis);
    }
```

(continued)

Listing 4-24
The MethodInfo class *(continued)*

```
    }

    public int nameIndex() {
      return nameIndex;
    }

    public int descriptorIndex() {
      return descriptorIndex;
    }

    public boolean isPublic() {
      return (accessflags & cPublic) != 0;
    }

    public boolean isPrivate() {
      return (accessflags & cPrivate) != 0;
    }

    public boolean isProtected() {
      return (accessflags & cProtected) != 0;
    }

    public boolean isStatic() {
      return (accessflags & cStatic) != 0;
    }

    public boolean isSynchronized() {
      return (accessflags & cSynchronized) != 0;
    }

    public boolean isNative() {
      return (accessflags & cNative) != 0;
    }

    public boolean isAbstract() {
      return (accessflags & cAbstract) != 0;
    }

    public AttributeInfo[] getAttributes() {
      return attributes;
    }

    public String toString() {
      return "NameIndex: " + nameIndex + ";\tDescriptorIndex: " + descriptorIndex;
    }

  }
```

PUTTING IT ALL TOGETHER

Now that the entire .class file has been read into memory and parsed, it can be output as more-or-less-legible source code. You do not need to output items in the order in which they appeared in the .class file. For example, the first thing outputted will be any import statements in the file. Then you'll produce the access specifiers for the class and then the class name itself, followed by any interfaces that the class implements. Next come the fields, and then the methods. Along the way, you'll add in necessary syntax — such as semicolons and keywords — that is normally present in source code but is not included in byte code.

To do this, the Disassembler class needs for eight more methods to be filled out:

```
writeImports();
writeAccess();
writeClassName();
writeInterfaces();
writeFields();
writeMethods();
```

Each of these methods will parse the data structures read in the first part of this chapter to collect the needed information.

Import statements

There's no one place in a .class file where all the import statements are stored. To determine which import statements were in the source code, you have to list all the classes in the constant pool. You might choose to output one import statement for each class, or you might be somewhat more selective. In this example, I have chosen not to produce import statements for the class itself or any classes in java.lang. This makes the disassembled source code more similar to what you actually write in programs. If you wanted to, you could include import statements only for entire packages (for example, import java.util.*) rather than for individual classes. However, I find it convenient to be able to see exactly what classes a particular class references.

To find the classes, you loop through the constant pool and check each entry to see if it's a ClassInfo structure. It's important to remember that the zeroth entry in the constant pool is not included in the .class file. When a ClassInfo structure is found, you use its nameIndex() method to get the class's name as a UTF8 structure from the constant pool. Each name thus retrieved is tested to be sure that it's not the name of this class and that it's not a class from java.lang. Assuming neither of these is the case, an import statement for the class is printed. Listing 4-25 demonstrates the writeImports() method.

Listing 4-25
The writeImports() method

```
public void writeImports() {

  PoolEntry pe = null;
  String thisname =  thePool.readUTF8(thisClass.nameIndex());
  // recall that there's nothing in the zeroth pool entry
  for (int i = 1; i < thePool.howMany(); i++) {
    pe = thePool.read(i);
    if (pe.tag() == PoolEntry.cClassInfo) {
      ClassInfo ci = pe.readClassInfo();
      String name = thePool.readUTF8(ci.nameIndex());
      name = name.replace('/','.');
       postedif (!name.startsWith("java.lang.") && !name.equals(thisname)) {
        theOutput.println("import " + name + ";");
      }
    }
  }

  theOutput.println();

}
```

Access specifiers

The writeAccess() method looks at the access specifiers for the class and prints them in Java form. Listing 4-26 has the code.

Listing 4-26
The writeAccess() method

```
public void writeAccess() {

  if (isPublic) theOutput.print("public ");
  if (isFinal) theOutput.print("final ");
  if (isAbstract) theOutput.print("abstract ");
  if (isInterface) theOutput.print("interface ");
  else theOutput.print("class ");

}
```

Note that if a .class file is not an interface, then it must represent a class. Note also that one access flag, isSpecial, has no equivalent in Java source code. It exists only for the use of the compiler and the virtual machine.

Class and superclass

The next thing you want to know is the name of the class. You can easily retrieve this from the thisClass field, which points to the name of the class in UTF8 format in the constant pool (see Listing 4-27).

Listing 4-27
The writeClassName() method

```
public void writeClassName() {

  String name = thePool.readUTF8(thisClass.nameIndex());
  theOutput.print(name + " ");

}
```

Next, you want to find out which class this class extends (see Listing 4-28). You have to watch out for the special case of java.lang.Object, which has no superclass. Otherwise, this is very similar to the previous method.

Listing 4-28
The writeSuperclass() method

```
public void writeSuperclass() {

 if (superclass.nameIndex() != 0) {
   String name = thePool.readUTF8(superclass.nameIndex());
   theOutput.print("extends " + name + " ");
 }

 }
```

Interfaces

The interfaces are similar except that there may be more than one of them. When you're finished outputting all the interfaces, open the class with an opening brace. The writeInterfaces() method is shown in Listing 4-29.

Listing 4-29

The writeInterfaces() method

```
public void writeInterfaces() {

  if (interfaces.length > 0) {
    String name = thePool.readUTF8(interfaces[0].nameIndex());
    theOutput.print("implements " + name + " ");
    for (int i=1; i < interfaces.length; i++) {
      name =  thePool.readUTF8(interfaces[i].nameIndex());
      theOutput.print(", " + name);
    }
  }
  theOutput.println(" {");

}
```

I've chosen to put the access specifiers, the class name, the class that this extends, all interfaces that this class implements, and the opening brace on a single line of the file. This produces output that looks like:

```
public final class myVector extends java.util.Vector implements
java.io.Serializable {
```

Feel free to adjust this to match your preferences. For example, some people prefer to write each of these on separate lines.

```
public final class myVector
 extends java.util.Vector
 implements java.io.Serializable
 {
```

Both versions produce identical byte code, so when you're working backward from the byte code, there's no way to distinguish the two cases.

Fields

Only two parts of the file are left: the fields and the methods. Let's look at the fields first. It's not at all uncommon for a class to have many fields. You therefore need to loop through all the fields with a for loop. Inside the loop, you check the access specifiers, the name, and the type of each field.

To read the name of the field, you simply read the UTF8 structure in the constant pool at the field's name index. The type of the field requires more effort. Although it is stored as a UTF8 string in the constant pool at the FieldInfo's descriptorIndex, the UTF8 string needs to be decoded first. Primitive types like int or char are encoded as single letters. For example, an int is the capital letter I. Table 4-4 lists the encodings for the primitive types.

Table 4-4
Primitive type encodings

B	byte
C	char
D	double
F	float
I	int
J	long
S	short
Z	boolean

Class types are encoded as the capital letter L, followed by the fully qualified class name, followed by a semicolon. Furthermore, for historical reasons, the periods in the fully qualified class name change to forward slashes. Therefore, inside the constant pool, the String class is written as Ljava/lang/String;, the Object class is written as Ljava/lang/Object;, the Vector class is written Ljava/util/Vector;, and so on. Converting this into the format you expect is easy. Just trim the first and last characters of the string with the substring() method and use the replace() method to change the slashes to periods like this:

```
String s = "Ljava/lang/String;";
String r = d.substring(1, r.length() - 1);
r = r.replace('/', '.');
```

The final type you need to deal with are the array types. These are encoded by prefixing the type of the array with left bracket signs ([), one for each dimension in the array. Thus, a double[] array is encoded as [double. A String[][] array is encoded as [[Ljava/lang/String;. To decode array types, you first count the number of left brackets and then recursively call the decodeDescriptor() method. Listing 4-30 shows the complete decodeDescriptor() method. It takes a single argument — the string to be decoded — and returns the decoded string.

Listing 4-30
The decodeDescriptor() method

```
public String decodeDescriptor(String d) {
    if (d.equals("B")) return "byte";
    else if (d.equals("C")) return "char";
    else if (d.equals("D")) return "double";
    else if (d.equals("F")) return "float";
    else if (d.equals("I")) return "int";
    else if (d.equals("J")) return "long";
    else if (d.equals("S")) return "short";
    else if (d.equals("Z")) return "boolean";
    else if (d.startsWith("L")) {  // object
      String r = d.substring(1, r.length() - 1);
      r = r.replace('/', '.');
      return r;
    }
    else if (d.startsWith("[")) { // array
      int dimensions = d.lastIndexOf('[') + 1;
      String type = decodeDescriptor(d.substring(dimensions));
      for (int i=0; i < dimensions; i++) {
        type += "[]";
      }
      return type;
    }
    else {
      throw new ClassFormatError("Unrecognized Type: " + d);
    }

  }
```

Now that you have a method to decode descriptors, it's easy to finish the writeFields() method. Listing 4-31 demonstrates.

Listing 4-31
The writeFields() method

```
public void writeFields() {

    for (int i = 0; i < fields.length; i++) {
      // indent two spaces
      theOutput.print("  ");

      // print the access specifiers
      if (fields[i].isPublic()) theOutput.print("public ");
      if (fields[i].isPrivate()) theOutput.print("private ");
```

(continued)

The writeFields() method *(continued)*

```
        if (fields[i].isProtected()) theOutput.print("protected ");
        if (fields[i].isStatic()) theOutput.print("static ");
        if (fields[i].isVolatile()) theOutput.print("volatile ");
        if (fields[i].isTransient()) theOutput.print("transient ");
        if (fields[i].isFinal()) theOutput.print("final ");

        //print the type
        String descriptor = thePool.readUTF8(fields[i].descriptorIndex());
        theOutput.print(decodeDescriptor(descriptor) + " ");

        //print the name
        theOutput.print(thePool.readUTF8(fields[i].nameIndex()));

        theOutput.println(";");

    }

}
```

I debated whether to include the code to read a field info structure and convert it into a string in the FieldInfo class or in the Disassembler class. Although it would make somewhat more sense to encapsulate the code in the FieldInfo class, it can be decoded only if each FieldInfo object carries a reference to its constant pool.

Methods

The final piece of the disassembly puzzle is decoding the methods. As with the fields, this will take place inside a loop, because almost all classes have multiple methods. Every method has five parts that you must decode: the access specifiers, the return type, the name, the argument list, the exception list, and the byte codes. Here's a skeleton for the writeMethods() method:

```
public void writeMethods() {

    for (int i = 0; i < methods.length; i++) {

        theOutput.println();
        theOutput.print("  ");
        // access specifiers

        //print the return type
```

```
        //print the name of the method

        //argument list

        //exceptions

        // method body

    }

  }
```

Method access specifiers

The access specifiers are quite simple to read with the methods of the MethodInfo class. Here's the code:

```
if (methods[i].isPublic()) theOutput.print("public ");
if (methods[i].isPrivate()) theOutput.print("private ");
if (methods[i].isProtected()) theOutput.print("protected ");
if (methods[i].isStatic()) theOutput.print("static ");
if (methods[i].isNative()) theOutput.print("native ");
if (methods[i].isSynchronized()) theOutput.print("synchronized ");
if (methods[i].isAbstract()) theOutput.print("abstract ");
```

Method arguments and return type

The arguments and return type are considerably harder to get at. The method descriptor contains a complete list of all of a method's arguments and its return value. These are encoded much like the field type descriptor, except that there can be more than one at a time. The arguments appear in parentheses and the return value follows that. For example, a method with the signature

```
public static void main(String[] args)
```

has the descriptor ([Ljava/lang/String)V. This indicates that the method takes a one-dimensional array of java.lang.String objects and returns void. A method that takes two doubles as arguments and returns a double would have a signature of (DD)D. The disassembler program uses two separate methods to parse the method descriptor. The getReturnType() method gets the return type, and the getArguments() method handles the arguments.

The getReturnType() method (see Listing 4-32) reads the descriptor and passes everything after the closing parenthesis to the decodeDescriptor() method. This is the same decodeDescriptor() method used to get the type of a field. For example, if the method descriptor is (DD)D, then the string "D" is passed to decodeDescriptor(). If the method descriptor is ([Ljava/lang/String)V, then the string "V" is passed to decodeDescriptor().

Listing 4-32
The getReturnType() method

```
public String getReturnType(MethodInfo mi) {
  String descriptor = thePool.readUTF8(mi.descriptorIndex());
  String d = descriptor.substring(descriptor.indexOf(')') + 1);
  return decodeDescriptor(d);
}
```

The getArguments() method is more complex because it needs to parse several arguments at a time. Furthermore, there are no convenient separators between the types. Finally, to make matters even worse, different types can have different sizes in the method descriptor strings. Primitive and void types are always one character wide, but array and object types have undetermined sizes.

Therefore, you must consider the character to decide what to do with it. If the character is one for a primitive data type, then you should pass that character (after converting it to a string) to the decodeDescriptor() method. However, if that character is an L, then you need to read up to the next semicolon and pass that string to decodeDescriptor(). Finally, if a character is a left bracket, then you must read as many brackets as follow and then read a type that may be a single character (that is, a primitive data type) or an object type. In essence, you need to embed the method inside itself to properly handle array types.

Listing 4-33 is the getArguments() method. This uses the variable a to keep track of the number of arguments that have been processed (so that you can tell where commas are needed in the argument list). It uses the variable i to tell which character in the descriptor begins the next type. This method would be much simpler if the descriptor had a constant with format that allowed a and i to be kept in sync.

Listing 4-33
The getArguments() method

```java
public String getArguments(MethodInfo mi) {

    String descriptor = thePool.readUTF8(mi.descriptorIndex());
    String params = descriptor.substring(1,descriptor.indexOf(")"));
    String result = "";
    try {
      int i = 0;
      int a = 0; // number of arguments
      while (i < params.length()) {
        char c = params.charAt(i);
        switch (c) {
          case '[':
            if (a++ != 0) result += ", ";
            int dimensions = 0;
            while (params.charAt(i) == '[') {
              i++;
              dimensions++;
            }
            char t = params.charAt(i);
            String type;
            if (t == 'L') {
                type = decodeDescriptor(params.substring(i, params.indexOf(";",
  i) + 1));
                i = params.indexOf(";", i) + 1;
            }
            else {
              type = decodeDescriptor(String.valueOf(t));
              i++;
            }
            for (int j=0; j < dimensions; j++) {
              type += "[]";
            }
            result += type;
            break;
          case 'L':
            if (a++ != 0) result += ", ";
            String o = params.substring(i+1, params.indexOf(';', i));
            result += o.replace('/', '.');
            i =  params.indexOf(';', i) + 1;
            break;
          case 'B':
          case 'C':
          case 'D':
          case 'F':
          case 'I':
          case 'J':
          case 'S':
```

(continued)

The getArguments() method *(continued)*

```
            case 'Z':
              if (a++ != 0) result += ", ";
              result += decodeDescriptor(String.valueOf(c));
              i++;
              break;
            case 'V':
              i++;
              break;
            default:
              throw new ClassFormatError("Bad Parameter String: " + params + " " +
c);
          }
      }
    }
    catch (StringIndexOutOfBoundsException e) {
    }

    return result;

  }
```

Exceptions thrown by a method

The .class file also tells you which checked exceptions a method can throw. A checked exception is one that you must catch or declare in a throws clause. The exceptions declared in the throws clause of a method are an attribute of the method. The ExceptionsAttribute class, Listing 4-34, holds an array of indices into the constant pool, each of which points to a ClassInfo structure. The ClassInfo structure represents the class of the exception that's thrown.

Listing 4-34
The ExceptionsAttribute class

```
import java.io.*;


public class ExceptionsAttribute {

  int nameIndex;
  int[] exceptions;

  public ExceptionsAttribute(AttributeInfo ai) throws IOException {
    nameIndex = ai.nameIndex();
```

(continued)

Listing 4-34
The ExceptionsAttribute class *(continued)*

```
          ByteArrayInputStream bis = new ByteArrayInputStream(ai.data);
          DataInputStream dis = new DataInputStream(bis);
          exceptions = new int[dis.readUnsignedShort()];
          for (int i = 0; i < exceptions.length; i++) {
            exceptions[i] = dis.readUnsignedShort();
          }
        }

        public int nameIndex() {
          return nameIndex;
        }

        public int howMany() {
          return exceptions.length;
        }

        public int getIndex(int i) {
          return exceptions[i];
        }

        public String toString() {
          return String.valueOf(nameIndex);
        }

      }
```

In the Disassembler class, the getExceptions() method returns a throws clause for a particular method. The exceptions, if any, are stored in an attribute of the method with the name "Exceptions." This attribute does not necessarily exist. Methods that declare no exceptions will not have an Exceptions attribute.

This differs from what appears in the *Java Virtual Machine Specification.* According to that document, "There must be exactly one Exceptions attribute in each method info structure." However, current Java compilers do not write an exceptions attribute in the method _ info structure unless the method actually has a throws clause. Listing 4-35 demonstrates the getExceptions() method.

Listing 4-35

The getExceptions() method

```
public String getExceptions(Method mi) {

    ExceptionsAttribute theExceptions=null;
    String result = "";

    // find the exceptions attribute
    AttributeInfo[] mAttributes = mi.getAttributes();
    for (int i = 0; i < mAttributes.length; i++) {
      String name = thePool.readUTF8(mAttributes[i].nameIndex());
      if (name.equals("Exceptions")) {
        try {
          theExceptions = new ExceptionsAttribute(mAttributes[i]);
        }
        catch (IOException e) {
        }
        break;
      }
    }
    if (theExceptions != null) {
      for (int i = 0; i < theExceptions.howMany(); i++) {
        if (i == 0) result += " throws ";
        else result += ", ";
        ClassInfo ci = thePool.readClassInfo(theExceptions.getIndex(i));
        result += thePool.readUTF8(ci.nameIndex()).replace('/', '.');
      }
    }

    return result;

}
```

The method body

The one piece left is the code inside the methods. This is the one piece of a
Java .class file that you can't easily make to match the source code. That's
because the Java source language in which you write programs is compiled
to the much lower level byte code.

In this chapter, I only show you where the bytes of the byte code are
stored so that you can output them in a disassembly. The next chapter,
however, discusses what those byte codes mean, how you can read and
understand them, and how you can work backward from the byte codes to
Java source code.

The byte codes for each method are stored in a Code attribute for the method. The Code attribute has many different fields, but most of them are used only when interpreting code. In this chapter, you see only the actual byte codes.

The constructor has more information to parse than you need immediately. The toString() method converts the signed bytes in the code array to integers between zero and 255. Listing 4-36 shows this CodeAttribute class.

Listing 4-36
The CodeAttribute class

```java
import java.io.*;


public class CodeAttribute {

    int nameIndex;
    int maxStack;
    int maxLocals;
    byte[] code;
    int startpc;
    int endpc;
    int handlerpc;
    ExceptionTable[] exceptions;
    AttributeInfo[] attributes;

    public  CodeAttribute(AttributeInfo ai) throws IOException {
      nameIndex = ai.nameIndex();
      ByteArrayInputStream bis = new ByteArrayInputStream(ai.data);
      DataInputStream dis = new DataInputStream(bis);
      maxStack = dis.readUnsignedShort();
      maxLocals = dis.readUnsignedShort();
      code = new byte[dis.readInt()];
      dis.read(code);
      exceptions = new ExceptionTable[dis.readUnsignedShort()];
      for (int i = 0; i < exceptions.length; i++) {
        exceptions[i] = new ExceptionTable(dis.readUnsignedShort(),
          dis.readUnsignedShort(), dis.readUnsignedShort(),
          dis.readUnsignedShort());
      }
      attributes = new AttributeInfo[dis.readUnsignedShort()];
      for (int i = 0; i < exceptions.length; i++) {
        attributes[i] = new AttributeInfo(dis);
      }
    }
```

(continued)

The CodeAttribute class *(continued)*

```
public int nameIndex() {
  return nameIndex;
}

// just print the code array
public String toString() {
  String result = "";
  for (int i = 0; i < code.length; i++) {
    int thisByte;
    thisByte = code[i] < 0 ? 256 + code[i] : code[i];
    result += "     " + thisByte + "\n";
  }
  return result;
}

}
```

This class makes reference to another class called ExceptionTable. Listing 4-37 shows this class. It provides information to the virtual machine about where exception handlers begin and end. You won't actually need it until the next chapter. However, this information is included in the .class file, so you have to read it now.

Listing 4-37
The ExceptionTable class

```
public class ExceptionTable {

  int start_pc;
  int end_pc;
  int handler_pc;
  int catch_type;

  public ExceptionTable (int start_pc, int end_pc, int handler_pc, int
catch_type) {

    this.start_pc = start_pc;
    this.end_pc =  end_pc;
    this.handler_pc = handler_pc;
    this.catch_type = catch_type;

  }

}
```

The getCode() method in the Disassembler class is particularly simple. It just needs to find the Code attribute of the method and call its toString() method. Listing 4-38 demonstrates.

Listing 4-38
The getCode() method

```
public String getCode(MethodInfo mi) {

  CodeAttribute theCode = null;

  // find the exceptions attribute
  AttributeInfo[] mAttributes = mi.getAttributes();
  for (int i = 0; i < mAttributes.length; i++) {
    String name = thePool.readUTF8(mAttributes[i].nameIndex());
    if (name.equals("Code")) {
      try{
        theCode = new CodeAttribute(mAttributes[i]);
      }
      catch (IOException e) {

      }
      break;
    }
  }
  if (theCode != null) {
    return theCode.toString();
  }

  return "";

}
```

LEGAL ISSUES

Many software companies want to tell you that it is illegal to disassemble, decompile, or reverse-engineer code. This is flatly wrong. The courts in the United States have decided more than once that this is permissible. (Laws outside the United States may be different. Consult a local attorney if this is a matter of concern.) Because the sort of reverse engineering described here is permitted by law, many companies try to prevent it through copyright, patent, or licensing restrictions.

Copyright protects the expression of an idea, not the idea itself. Copyright does not prevent you from reusing an idea. Thus, if you discover a neat algorithm by investigating the byte codes for SuperDuperApplet.class, just because SuperDuperApplet is copyrighted does not mean you cannot reuse the algorithm in your own programs. Although it is illegal to copy the byte code verbatim and paste it into your own files, it is perfectly legal to rewrite and recompile the algorithm.

A patent is a more serious level of protection. Software patents protect ideas, not merely the expression of ideas. If an organization or individual owns a patent on an algorithm — RSA encryption, for example — then, you are legally required to license the patent from the patent owner before using the algorithm in your own software.

Finally, many companies attempt to protect ideas through licensing. For example, the license for Developer Release 1 of Natural Intelligence's Roaster states that the licensee may not "reverse-engineer, decompile, disassemble, modify, translate, make any attempt to discover the source code of the Software, or create derivative works from the Software." This is fairly standard boilerplate in software licensing agreements. Interestingly, a similar clause is *not* part of the license agreement from Sun for Java 1.0.2. To the best of my knowledge, no one has tested this sort of clause in court, and I cannot offer an educated opinion as to whether it is enforceable. Those aspects of shrink-wrap licenses that people have tested in court tend to relate to matters already covered under copyright law (such as the making of additional copies), so even the validity of shrink-wrap licenses in general is in doubt.

To make matters even more confusing, the laws in 49 of the 50 states are often slightly different from each other. (The laws in Louisiana are wildly different. I am not familiar with laws relating to this in Puerto Rico, Washington, D.C., or other non-state territories in the United States, but I doubt they're as different as Louisiana's.) There is something called the Uniform Commercial Code, UCC for short, which is an effort to get the laws of 49 states to conform to each other. (Louisiana law is really just too different to be included.) As of late 1996, the UCC is being revised. The commercial software industry is trying to have provisions written into the new UCC that would increase the validity and enforceability of shrink-wrap licenses. It remains to be seen what will happen.

One problem with laws like the UCC is that they have a very hard time keeping up with the fast-changing software industry and the Internet. Even if the new UCC does clarify the status of shrink-wrap licenses, it probably will not address the fact that most software downloaded from the Internet does not have shrink-wrap! Some packages like Sun's JDK display a splash screen with the license agreement the first time that a user launches the software with buttons for the user to accept or reject the agreement. To my knowledge, no one has tested such splash screen licenses in court. Even if they are held to be valid, what about splash screens that provide only an "Agree" button and no

"Disagree" button? What if programmer A agrees to the license, but later programmer B starts using that computer and never sees the license? (For that matter, this applies to shrink-wrapped software, too.)

Furthermore, http servers allow .class files to be downloaded from many sites with no license of any sort. My suspicion is that no more than copyright law protects these .class files, but I would not be surprised to see a software company dispute this in court.

As you can see, these issues are quite complex. There are few easy answers. However, on a practical note, nobody is going to know or care if you disassemble a file to satisfy your personal curiosity or expand your knowledge. On rare occasions, companies have gotten perturbed and called out their lawyers when a competitor released a product that could read their file formats. They also tend to be annoyed when a writer publicly reveals information that they'd rather keep private. However, even in these cases there's relatively little they can do besides write threatening letters.

This discussion has been necessarily brief. Table 4-5 lists some more resources on the Internet for investigating these intellectual property matters.

Table 4-5

Some intellectual property resources on the Internet

Resource	Location	Comments
The Oppedahl & Larson Patent Law Web Server	http://www.patents.com/	This law firm has many useful FAQ lists and other information about intellectual property written from a carefully legal perspective.
The Union for the Public Domain	http://www.public-domain.org/	The Union for the Public Domain is fighting the efforts of the copyright industry and the Clinton-Gore administration to allow the copyrighting of facts.
The Yahoo Intellectual Property Page	http://www.yahoo.com/Government/Law/Intellectual_Property/	As usual, Yahoo has a good collection of links to all sorts of resources.
The Electronic Frontier Foundation's "Intellectual Property Online: Patent, Trademark, Copyright" Archive	http://www.eff.org/pub/Intellectual_property/	The Electronic Frontier Organization is primarily concerned with ensuring that freedoms taken for granted in the print world aren't trampled on the Internet.
The League for Programming Freedom	http://www.lpf.org/	The League for Programming Freedom endeavors to make sure programmers aren't unduly burdened by software patents and bad laws.

(continued)

Some intellectual property resources on the Internet *(continued)*

Resource	Location	Comments
The International Federation of Library Associations and Institutions Copyright and Intellectual Property Resources page	http://www.nlc-bnc.ca/ifla/II/cpyright.htm	This page has links to many excellent articles about intellectual property on- and off-line.

ACCESSING CLASS FILES

So far in this chapter I've assumed that you're working with a single .class file. In practice, that's not always true. Sometimes it takes a little work to get a .class file to disassemble. First, you may have to do a little work to retrieve the .class file from a remote Web server. Second, .class files are often distributed as parts of larger zip or jar archives. However, it's not hard to extract the necessary .class file from an archive.

Copying .class files

Most Web browsers play Java applets when they encounter them. They do not save them onto your hard drive in an easily retrievable form. Downloaded .class files may or may not be present in your browser's cache. However, whether or not a browser caches a .class file on disk, you can use the following trick to download a copy of the file you want.

Let's suppose you've seen a cool applet on a Web site at `http://www.idgbooks.com/example.html` and you want to learn how the programmer wrote it. Of course you'll need a copy of the applet's .class files. But how do you get them? This will take a little work, but it's really not hard. Here are the steps.

1. Use your Web browser's View Source command to see the HTML for the Web page. You're looking for the <APPLET> tag like this:

```
<applet code=CoolApplet.class width=200 height=200>
</applet>
```

2. Write a very simple Web page that includes an HREF link to the file you want to look at it. For example,

```
<A HREF="http://www.idgbooks.com/CoolApplet.class">Download Me</a>
```

3. Load the page with the HREF link to the file into your Web browser. Then, use the Save this Link As command in the pop-up menu to save the file on your hard drive, as shown in Figure 4-2. That's it. You should now have a clean copy of the .class file to work with.

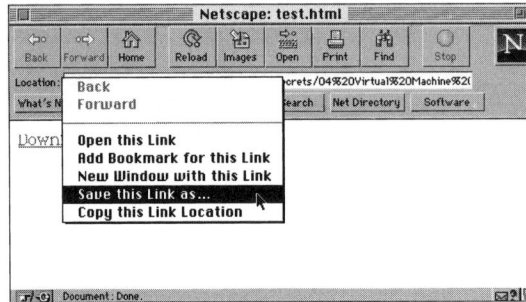

■ **Figure 4-2**
The Save this Link as menu command in the Macintosh version of Netscape.

Zip files

Most VMs include their class libraries in the form of uncompressed zip archives called classes.zip. If you want to poke around in the innards of the class library, the first thing you need to do is unzip this file.

Theoretically, it shouldn't matter whether a package hierarchy is or is not zipped, as long as your CLASSPATH is set up properly. In practice, that's not always true. Before dearchiving someone else's file for experimentation, you should always copy it to a directory that's not in your CLASSPATH. It's best not to work on the original copies.

As soon as the Sysops had installed JDK 1.1 on sunsite.unc.edu, I copied the classes.zip file to a test directory of my home directory and then unzipped it to start poking around. In other words,

```
% mkdir ~/test
% cp /usr/local/java-1.1/lib/classes.zip ~/test
% unzip ~/test/classes.zip
```

There are many tools available for unzipping .zip files. Unzip is the dearchiver of choice for zip files on UNIX. StuffIt Expander works well on the Macintosh. Although PKZip is the original zip program, it cannot handle the long filenames that Java requires. Therefore, on Windows platforms, you should use WinZip instead.

Jar files

Java 1.1 introduced Jar files. Jar is a rough concatenation of "Java archive." Jar files can contain all the .class files, image files, sound files, and other files needed to run an applet. By placing all these different files into a single file, a Web browser can download them with only a single request to the Web server. Depending on the server's load and network conditions, this can save from a few milliseconds to several minutes of time. Furthermore, a Jar file can compress its contents so the savings can be even larger.

Jar files are included on Web pages with applet tags that look like this:

```
<applet code=CoolApplet.class width=200 height=200>
  <param name=archives value="jars/coolapplet.jar">
</applet>
```

You can download a Jar file to your hard drive exactly the same way you'd download a .class file. Once you have the Jar file on your local hard drive, you need to dearchive it to retrieve the individual parts. The java.util.zip package includes classes that can parse and handle Jar files. Sun's JDK 1.1 for Windows and Solaris includes a command line jar program based on this package that you can use to pack and unpack Jar files. An equivalent program will likely be available for the Macintosh by the time this book hits store shelves.

The jar command line syntax (see Table 4-6) is deliberately similar to the classic UNIX tar command. Options are passed as one-character flags that follow the word jar on the command line. Archiving versus dearchiving is chosen through the c (create) or x (extract) flag, not via jar and unjar commands as a PKZip user might expect.

Table 4-6
Command line options for jar

Option	Purpose
c	Creates a new jar archive on System.out.
t	Lists the table of contents of the jar file on System.out.
x	Extracts from System.in.
f	The second argument specifies the jar file to process or create.
v	Produces verbose output on System.err.

For example, to archive all files in the current directory you would type

```
C:\> jar cf allfiles.jar *
```

To archive just some files and directories, specify them by name on the command line like this:

```
C:\> jar cf allfiles.jar CoolApplet.class Helper.class audio images
```

Directories are archived recursively; in other words, their immediate contents and the contents of any sub-directories are archived.

To dearchive the file, you would type the following:

```
C:\> jar xf allfiles.jar
```

Summary

In this chapter, you learn about the format of Java .class files and how to read them. In particular, you learn the following:

- You can view the same program in different formats: pure hexadecimal bytes, ASCII text, disassembled byte code, and Java source code. The first three formats are available in the .class file. The last is the form of the .java source code file.

- How a .class file is organized and how to split it into its component parts.

- How to work backward from the compiled .class byte code file to an approximation of the source that generated it. This task will continue in the next chapter.

- That there are legal issues involved in doing this. Although copyright doesn't prevent reverse engineering any more than it prevents you from reading a book you've bought, it may prevent you from copying what you've learned verbatim. Patents may provide more serious restrictions.

- How to retrieve a .class file, wherever it resides, whether on a Web site, in a zip archive, or in a jar file.

In the next chapter, you learn how to decode and understand method bodies, instead of just printing them as streams of bytes.

JAVA BYTE CODE

*T*he last chapter walked you through the disassembly of a Java .class file. However, I left one crucial part of the file — the bodies of the different methods — in raw bytes rather than converting it back to .java source code. This large topic easily deserves a chapter of its own.

Method bodies are one of the few areas in which it is not always possible to return to the source code format. For one thing, you completely lose all of the information about the identifiers inside a method or in a method's argument list in the compilation phase. There's no way to get it back. Furthermore, .java source code keywords like *for* and *while* don't always map in a one-to-one fashion onto the byte code equivalents. For example, for every for loop, there's an equivalent while loop that produces the same byte code. Given only the byte code, there's no way to tell which one was in the source code. Finally, optimizing compilers essentially rewrite .java source code before turning it into byte code. When you reverse the process, you get back the rewritten source code, not the original.

Although fully accurate decompilation is, in general, not possible, with practice you can learn to understand what the byte codes say. The fundamental problem is that there's often more than one way to say the same thing. However, if you care only about the meaning of what was said, rather than the exact way in which it was expressed, you can extract the meaning from the byte codes. You learn to do this in this chapter.

> **Note** If debugging information is included in the file, then the .class file has a complete copy of the source code, and you can get everything back. However, that is a relatively unchallenging and uninteresting case, so this chapter covers the harder case in which no debugging information is included in the file.

BYTE CODE MNEMONICS

The code in a method body is a linear sequence of bytes. Each byte has an unsigned value between zero and 255. The interpretation of each byte depends on its position. The zeroth byte is always a .java byte code instruction (an opcode, for short). Bytes after that point can be either byte code instructions or arguments for byte code instructions. For example, if the byte at position zero in a method is 16, then the byte at position one is not a byte code, but rather a signed byte to be pushed onto the stack. Data values embedded directly in the code like this are sometimes called *literals*.

The only way to distinguish between opcodes and literals is by starting with the instruction at position zero in the code array and working forward. For example, if the byte zero is 16 and opcode 16 is known to take a one-byte argument, then byte one must be the literal argument for the instruction and byte two must be the next opcode.

Most instructions have a precisely defined number of bytes that should be read as literals following the opcode itself. Opcode 16 always takes exactly one byte as an argument, never zero bytes and never more than one byte. Arguments that by their nature do not take up a fixed number of bytes, such as arrays and strings, are not directly included in the code array. Instead, a 2-byte index into the constant pool is given. Therefore, once you know the possible byte codes and their arguments, you can distinguish between instructions and data. Java enforces the dichotomy between code and data very strictly. This is an essential feature of Java's security.

Human beings aren't very good at remembering the meanings of many small numbers like the 200-plus opcodes. Sun has therefore defined mnemonic strings for these codes. These strings are listed in Table 5-1.

Table 5-1

.java byte codes

Byte Code	Mnemonic	Number of Bytes in the Argument	Meaning
0	nop	0	Do nothing (no operation); skip to the next instruction.
1	aconst_null	0	Push null onto the stack.
2	iconst_m1	0	Push the int -1 onto the stack.
3	iconst_0	0	Push the int 0 onto the stack.
4	iconst_1	0	Push the int 1 onto the stack.
5	iconst_2	0	Push the int 2 onto the stack.
6	iconst_3	0	Push the int 3 onto the stack.
7	iconst_4	0	Push the int 4 onto the stack.
8	iconst_5	0	Push the int 5 onto the stack.
9	lconst_0	0	Push the long 0 onto the stack.
10	lconst_1	0	Push the long 1 onto the stack.
11	fconst_0	0	Push the float 0.0 onto the stack.
12	fconst_1	0	Push the float 1.0 onto the stack.
13	fconst_2	0	Push the float 2.0 onto the stack.
14	dconst_0	0	Push the double 0.0 onto the stack.
15	dconst_1	0	Push the double 1.0 onto the stack.
16	bipush	1	Sign-extend the byte to an int, and push it onto the stack.
17	sipush	2	Combine the bytes into a short, sign-extend it to an int, and push it onto the stack.
18	ldc	1	Push the integer, float, or string at the specified index in the constant pool onto the stack.
19	ldc_w	2	Push the integer, float, or string at the specified index in the constant pool onto the stack.
20	ldc2_w	2	Push the long or double at the specified index in the constant pool onto the stack.
21	iload	1	Push the int local variable at the specified index onto the stack.
22	lload	1	Push the long local variable at the specified index onto the stack.
23	fload	1	Push the float local variable at the specified index onto the stack.
24	dload	1	Push the double local variable at the specified index onto the stack.

(continued)

Table 5-1
.java byte codes *(continued)*

Byte Code	Mnemonic	Number of Bytes in the Argument	Meaning
25	aload	1	Push the reference at the specified index onto the stack.
26	iload_0	0	Push the int variable at the zeroth position in the local frame onto the stack.
27	iload_1	0	Push the int variable at the first position in the local frame onto the stack.
28	iload_2	0	Push the int variable at the second position in the local frame onto the stack.
29	iload_3	0	Push the int variable at the third position in the local frame onto the stack.
30	lload_0	0	Push the long variable at the zeroth position in the local frame onto the stack.
31	lload_1	0	Push the long variable at the first position in the local frame onto the stack.
32	lload_2	0	Push the long variable at the second position in the local frame onto the stack.
33	lload_3	0	Push the long variable at the third position in the local frame onto the stack.
34	fload_0	0	Push the float variable at the zeroth position in the local frame onto the stack.
35	fload_1	0	Push the float variable at the first position in the local frame onto the stack.
36	fload_2	0	Push the float variable at the second position in the local frame onto the stack.
37	fload_3	0	Push the float variable at the third position in the local frame onto the stack.
38	dload_0	0	Push the double variable at the zeroth position in the local frame onto the stack.
39	dload_1	0	Push the double variable at the first position in the local frame onto the stack.
40	dload_2	0	Push the double variable at the second position in the local frame onto the stack.
41	dload_3	0	Push the double variable at the third position in the local frame onto the stack.
42	aload_0	0	Push the reference variable at the zeroth position in the local frame onto the stack.
43	aload_1	0	Push the reference variable at the first position in the local frame onto the stack.

(continued)

.java byte codes *(continued)*

Byte Code	Mnemonic	Number of Bytes in the Argument	Meaning
44	aload_2	0	Push the reference variable at the second position in the local frame onto the stack.
45	aload_3	0	Push the reference variable at the third position in the local frame onto the stack.
46	iaload	0	Push an int from an array onto the stack.
47	laload	0	Push a long from an array onto the stack.
48	faload	0	Push a float from an array onto the stack.
49	daload	0	Push a double from an array onto the stack.
50	aaload	0	Push a reference from an array onto the stack.
51	baload	0	Push a byte or Boolean from an array onto the stack.
52	caload	0	Push a char from an array onto the stack.
53	saload	0	Push a short from an array onto the stack.
54	istore	1	Store an int into the local variable at the specified index.
55	lstore	1	Store a long into the local variable at the specified index.
56	fstore	1	Store a float into the local variable at the specified index.
57	dstore	1	Store a double into the local variable at the specified index.
58	astore	1	Store a reference into the local variable at the specified index.
59	istore_0	0	Pop an int value from the stack, and store it in the local variable at index 0.
60	istore_1	0	Pop an int value from the stack, and store it in the local variable at index 1.
61	istore_2	0	Pop an int value from the stack, and store it in the local variable at index 2.
62	istore_3	0	Pop an int value from the stack, and store it in the local variable at index 3.
63	lstore_0	0	Pop a long value from the stack, and store it in the local variable at index 0.
64	lstore_1	0	Pop a long value from the stack, and store it in the local variable at index 1.
65	lstore_2	0	Pop a long value from the stack, and store it in the local variable at index 2.

(continued)

Table 5-1

.java byte codes *(continued)*

Byte Code	Mnemonic	Number of Bytes in the Argument	Meaning
66	lstore_3	0	Pop a long value from the stack, and store it in the local variable at index 3.
67	fstore_0	0	Pop a float value from the stack, and store it in the local variable at index 0.
68	fstore_1	0	Pop a float value from the stack, and store it in the local variable at index 1.
69	fstore_2	0	Pop a float value from the stack, and store it in the local variable at index 2.
70	fstore_3	0	Pop a float value from the stack, and store it in the local variable at index 3.
71	dstore_0	0	Pop a double value from the stack, and store it in the local variable at index 0.
72	dstore_1	0	Pop a double value from the stack, and store it in the local variable at index 1.
73	dstore_2	0	Pop a double value from the stack, and store it in the local variable at index 2.
74	dstore_3	0	Pop a double value from the stack, and store it in the local variable at index 3.
75	astore_0	0	Pop a reference value from the stack, and store it in the local variable at index 0.
76	astore_1	0	Pop a reference value from the stack, and store it in the local variable at index 1.
77	astore_2	0	Pop a reference value from the stack, and store it in the local variable at index 2.
78	astore_3	0	Pop a reference value from the stack, and store it in the local variable at index 3.
79	iastore	0	Store a value from the stack into an int array.
80	lastore	0	Store a value from the stack into a long array.
81	fastore	0	Store a value from the stack into a float array.
82	dastore	0	Store a value from the stack into a double array.
83	aastore	0	Store a value from the stack into a reference array.
84	bastore	0	Store a value from the stack into a byte or Boolean array.
85	castore	0	Store a value from the stack into a char array.

(continued)

.java byte codes *(continued)*

Byte Code	Mnemonic	Number of Bytes in the Argument	Meaning
86	sastore	0	Store a value from the stack into a short array.
87	pop	0	Pop a word from the stack, and throw it away.
88	pop2	0	Pop two words from the stack, and throw them away.
89	dup	0	Duplicate the top word of the stack onto the top of the stack.
90	dup_x1	0	Duplicate the top word of the stack, and put it two down in the stack.
91	dup_x2	0	Duplicate the top word of the stack, and put it three down in the stack.
92	dup2	0	Duplicate the top two words on the stack onto the top of the stack.
93	dup2_x1	0	Duplicate the top two words of the stack, and put them three down in the stack.
94	dup2_x2	0	Duplicate the top two words of the stack, and put them four down in the stack.
95	swap		Swap the top two words on the stack.
96	iadd	0	Add two ints.
97	ladd	0	Add two longs.
98	fadd	0	Add two floats.
99	dadd	0	Add two doubles.
100	isub	0	Subtract two ints.
101	lsub	0	Subtract two longs.
102	fsub	0	Subtract two floats.
103	dsub	0	Subtract two doubles.
104	imul	0	Multiply two ints.
105	lmul	0	Multiply two longs.
106	fmul	0	Multiply two floats.
107	dmul	0	Multiply two doubles.
108	idiv	0	Divide two ints.
109	ldiv	0	Divide two longs.
110	fdiv	0	Divide two floats.
111	ddiv	0	Divide two doubles.
112	irem	0	Take the remainder of two ints.
113	lrem	0	Take the remainder of two longs.
114	frem	0	Take the remainder of two floats.
115	drem	0	Take the remainder of two doubles.

(continued)

Table 5-1

.java byte codes *(continued)*

Byte Code	Mnemonic	Number of Bytes in the Argument	Meaning
116	ineg	0	Change the sign of the int on the top of the stack.
117	lneg	0	Change the sign of the long on the top of the stack.
118	fneg	0	Change the sign of the float on the top of the stack.
119	dneg	0	Change the sign of the double on the top of the stack.
120	ishl	0	Shift an int left.
121	lshl	0	Shift a long left.
122	ishr	0	Shift an int right with sign extension.
123	lshr	0	Shift a long right with sign extension.
124	iushr	0	Shift an int right without sign extension.
125	lushr	0	Shift a long right without sign extension.
126	iand	0	Bitwise and of the two ints on the top of the stack.
127	land	0	Bitwise and of the two longs on the top of the stack.
128	ior	0	Bitwise or of the two ints on the top of the stack.
129	lor	0	Bitwise or of the two longs on the top of the stack.
130	ixor	0	Bitwise exclusive-or of the two ints on the top of the stack.
131	lxor	0	Bitwise exclusive-or of the two longs on the top of the stack.
132	iinc	2	Increment the local variable at the first argument by the signed byte at the second argument.
133	i2l	0	Convert int to long.
134	i2f	0	Convert int to float.
135	i2d	0	Convert int to double.
136	l2i	0	Convert long to int.
137	l2f	0	Convert long to float.
138	l2d	0	Convert long to double.
139	f2i	0	Convert float to int.
140	f2l	0	Convert float to long.
141	f2d	0	Convert float to double.
142	d2i	0	Convert double to int.

(continued)

.java byte codes *(continued)*

Byte Code	Mnemonic	Number of Bytes in the Argument	Meaning
143	d2l	0	Convert double to long.
144	d2f	0	Convert double to float.
145	i2b	0	Convert int to byte.
146	i2c	0	Convert int to char.
147	i2s	0	Convert int to short.
148	lcmp	0	Compare two longs.
149	fcmpl	0	Compare two floats.
150	fcmpg	0	Compare two floats.
151	dcmpl	0	Compare two doubles.
152	dcmpg	0	Compare two doubles.
153	ifeq	2	Branch if the int on the top of the stack is equal to zero.
154	ifne	2	Branch if the int on the top of the stack is not equal to zero.
155	iflt	2	Branch if the int on the top of the stack is less than zero.
156	ifge	2	Branch if the int on the top of the stack is greater than or equal to zero.
157	ifgt	2	Branch if the int on the top of the stack is greater than zero.
158	ifle	2	Branch if the int on the top of the stack is less than or equal to zero.
159	if_icmpeq	2	Branch if the two ints on the top of the stack are equal.
160	if_icmpne	2	Branch if the two ints on the top of the stack are not equal.
161	if_icmplt	2	Branch if the int second from the top of the stack is less than the int on the top of the stack.
162	if_icmpge	2	Branch if the int second from the top of the stack is greater than or equal to the int on the top of the stack.
163	if_icmpgt	2	Branch if the int second from the top of the stack is greater than the int on the top of the stack.
164	if_icmple	2	Branch if the int second from the top of the stack is less than or equal to the int on the top of the stack.
165	if_acmpeq	2	Branch to the address specified in the argument if the two references on the top of the stack are equal.

(continued)

Table 5-1
.java byte codes *(continued)*

Byte Code	Mnemonic	Number of Bytes in the Argument	Meaning
166	if_acmpne	2	Branch to the address specified in the argument if the two references on the top of the stack are not equal.
167	goto	2	Go to address specified in the arguments.
168	jsr	2	Jump to a subroutine.
169	ret	1	Return from a subroutine.
170	tableswitch	variable	Compare value and branch.
171	lookupswitch	variable	Compare value and branch.
172	ireturn	0	Return an int from a method.
173	lreturn	0	Return a long from a method.
174	freturn	0	Return a float from a method.
175	dreturn	0	Return a double from a method.
176	areturn	0	Return a reference from a method.
177	return	0	Return void from method.
178	getstatic	2	Get a static field from a class.
179	putstatic	2	Sets a static field in a class.
180	getfield	2	Get a field from an object.
181	putfield	2	Set a field in an object.
182	invokevirtual	2	Call an instance method.
183	invokespecial	2	Call a constructor in special circumstances.
184	invokestatic	2	Call a static method.
185	invokeinterface	4	Call an interface method.
186			Not used in Java 1.0.2.
187	new	2	Create a new object.
188	newarray	1	Create a new array of primitive types.
189	anewarray	2	Create a new array of references.
190	arraylength	0	Get the length of an array.
191	athrow	0	Throw exception or error.
192	checkcast	2	Check casts between object types.
193	instanceof	2	Determine if an object has a given type.
194	monitorenter	0	Allow a thread to take ownership of the monitor associated with an object.
195	monitorexit	0	Allow a thread to give up ownership of the monitor associated with an object.
196	wide	4 or 6	Extend the local variable index used by the iload, aload, fload, dload, istore, astore, fstore, dstore, ret, and iinc instructions.

(continued)

.java byte codes *(continued)*

Byte Code	Mnemonic	Number of Bytes in the Argument	Meaning
197	multianewarray	3	Create a new multidimensional array.
198	ifnull	2	Branch to the address specified in the arguments if the reference popped from the top of the stack is null.
199	ifnonnull	2	Branch to the address specified in the arguments if the reference popped from the top of the stack is not null.
200	goto_w	4	Branch to the address specified in the arguments.
201	jsr_w	4	Jump to the subroutine at the address specified in the arguments.

Although these mnemonics may seem just as cryptic as the raw bytes at first glance, they do have a logic to them. For example, opcodes that begin with the letter i commonly operate on int types. Instructions that begin with the letter l operate on longs. Instructions that begin with f operate on floats, and instructions that begin with d operate on doubles. Instructions that begin with a operate on references. Opcodes that contain the word *add* generally add things. Opcodes that contain the word *sub* generally subtract things. You get the idea. The rest of this chapter looks at what these instructions do. By the time you finish this chapter, these mnemonics will make perfect sense to you.

USING MNEMONICS IN THE DISASSEMBLER

In Chapter 4, you saw method bodies printed as raw bytes. Although it's possible to use Table 5-1 and a good memory to understand what those bytes mean, I certainly wouldn't recommend it. Instead, I expand the CodeAttribute class so that it uses mnemonics instead of raw bytes. This is shown in Listing 5-1.

Although Listing 5-1 looks frighteningly long, it is mostly one big switch statement that reads the next opcode and its arguments and returns a string. Because there are more than 200 opcodes, the readCode() method has to be quite long. However, most of the cases in the switch statement are very simple. Over half of them merely return an opcode. Most of the rest return an opcode and some literal data.

The three exceptions are the cases for the lookupswitch, tableswitch, and wide instructions. These are special because they have variable-length data encoded in the code array. I discuss them in more detail later in this chapter, when I discuss the meaning of those instructions.

Listing 5-1
The CodeAttribute class

```
import java.io.*;


public class CodeAttribute {

  int nameIndex;
  int maxStack;
  int maxLocals;
  byte[] code;
  ExceptionTable[] exceptions;
  AttributeInfo[] attributes;
  public CodeAttribute(AttributeInfo ai) throws IOException {
    nameIndex = ai.nameIndex();
    ByteArrayInputStream bis = new ByteArrayInputStream(ai.data);
    DataInputStream dis = new DataInputStream(bis);
    maxStack = dis.readUnsignedShort();
    maxLocals = dis.readUnsignedShort();
    code = new byte[dis.readInt()];
    dis.read(code);
    exceptions = new ExceptionTable[dis.readUnsignedShort()];
    for (int i = 0; i < exceptions.length; i++) {
      exceptions[i] = new ExceptionTable(dis.readUnsignedShort(),
        dis.readUnsignedShort(), dis.readUnsignedShort(),
        dis.readUnsignedShort());
    }
    attributes = new AttributeInfo[dis.readUnsignedShort()];
    for (int i = 0; i < exceptions.length; i++) {
      attributes[i] = new AttributeInfo(dis);
    }
  }

  public int nameIndex() {
    return nameIndex;
  }

  // just print the code array
  public String toString() {

    ByteArrayInputStream bis = new ByteArrayInputStream(code);
    DataInputStream dis = new DataInputStream(bis);
    StringBuffer result = new StringBuffer(4*code.length);
```

(continued)

The CodeAttribute class *(continued)*

```
        try {
          while (bis.available() > 0) {
            result.append(readCode(dis));
            result.append('\n');
          }
        } // end try
        catch (IOException e) {

        }
        return result.toString();

      }

      String readCode(DataInputStream dis) throws IOException {

        int pad, defaultByte;
        int position = code.length - dis.available();
        int opcode = dis.readUnsignedByte();
        String result;


        switch (opcode) {
          case 0: return position + "    nop";
          case 1: return position + "    aconst_null";
          case 2: return position + "    iconst_m1";
          case 3: return position + "    iconst_0";
          case 4: return position + "    iconst_1";
          case 5: return position + "    iconst_2";
          case 6: return position + "    iconst_3";
          case 7: return position + "    iconst_4";
          case 8: return position + "    iconst_5";
          case 9: return position + "    lconst_0";
          case 10: return position + "    lconst_1";
          case 11: return position + "    fconst_0";
          case 12: return position + "    fconst_1";
          case 13: return position + "    fconst_2";
          case 14: return position + "    dconst_0";
          case 15: return position + "    dconst_1";
          case 16: return position + "    bipush " + dis.readByte();
          case 17: return position + "    sipush " + dis.readShort();
          case 18: return position + "    ldc " + dis.readUnsignedByte();
          case 19: return position + "    ldc_w " + dis.readUnsignedShort();
          case 20: return position + "    ldc2_w " + dis.readUnsignedShort();
          case 21: return position + "    iload " + dis.readUnsignedByte();
          case 22: return position + "    lload " + dis.readUnsignedByte();
```

(continued)

Listing 5-1
The CodeAttribute class *(continued)*

```
case 23: return position + "    fload " + dis.readUnsignedByte();
case 24: return position + "    dload " + dis.readUnsignedByte();
case 25: return position + "    aload " + dis.readUnsignedByte();
case 26: return position + "    iload_0";
case 27: return position + "    iload_1";
case 28: return position + "    iload_2";
case 29: return position + "    iload_3";
case 30: return position + "    lload_0";
case 31: return position + "    lload_1";
case 32: return position + "    lload_2";
case 33: return position + "    lload_3";
case 34: return position + "    fload_0";
case 35: return position + "    fload_1";
case 36: return position + "    fload_2";
case 37: return position + "    fload_3";
case 38: return position + "    dload_0";
case 39: return position + "    dload_1";
case 40: return position + "    dload_2";
case 41: return position + "    dload_3";
case 42: return position + "    aload_0";
case 43: return position + "    aload_1";
case 44: return position + "    aload_2";
case 45: return position + "    aload_3";
case 46: return position + "    iaload";
case 47: return position + "    laload";
case 48: return position + "    faload";
case 49: return position + "    daload";
case 50: return position + "    aaload";
case 51: return position + "    baload";
case 52: return position + "    caload";
case 53: return position + "    saload";
case 54: return position + "    istore " + dis.readUnsignedByte();
case 55: return position + "    lstore " + dis.readUnsignedByte();
case 56: return position + "    fstore " + dis.readUnsignedByte();
case 57: return position + "    dstore " + dis.readUnsignedByte();
case 58: return position + "    astore " + dis.readUnsignedByte();
case 59: return position + "    istore_0";
case 60: return position + "    istore_1";
case 61: return position + "    istore_2";
case 62: return position + "    istore_3";
case 63: return position + "    lstore_0";
case 64: return position + "    lstore_1";
case 65: return position + "    lstore_2";
case 66: return position + "    lstore_3";
case 67: return position + "    fstore_0";
case 68: return position + "    fstore_1";
```

(continued)

The CodeAttribute class *(continued)*

```
case 69: return position + "    fstore_2";
case 70: return position + "    fstore_3";
case 71: return position + "    dstore_0";
case 72: return position + "    dstore_1";
case 73: return position + "    dstore_2";
case 74: return position + "    dstore_3";
case 75: return position + "    astore_0";
case 76: return position + "    astore_1";
case 77: return position + "    astore_2";
case 78: return position + "    astore_3";
case 79: return position + "    iastore";
case 80: return position + "    lastore";
case 81: return position + "    fastore";
case 82: return position + "    dastore";
case 83: return position + "    aastore";
case 84: return position + "    bastore";
case 85: return position + "    castore";
case 86: return position + "    sastore";
case 87: return position + "    pop";
case 88: return position + "    pop2";
case 89: return position + "    dup";
case 90: return position + "    dup_x1";
case 91: return position + "    dup_x2";
case 92: return position + "    dup2";
case 93: return position + "    dup2_x1";
case 94: return position + "    dup2_x2";
case 95: return position + "    swap";
case 96: return position + "    iadd";
case 97: return position + "    ladd";
case 98: return position + "    fadd";
case 99: return position + "    dadd";
case 100: return position + "    isub";
case 101: return position + "    lsub";
case 102: return position + "    fsub";
case 103: return position + "    dsub";
case 104: return position + "    imul";
case 105: return position + "    lmul";
case 106: return position + "    fmul";
case 107: return position + "    dmul";
case 108: return position + "    idiv";
case 109: return position + "    ldiv";
case 110: return position + "    fdiv";
case 111: return position + "    ddiv";
case 112: return position + "    irem";
case 113: return position + "    lrem";
case 114: return position + "    frem";
case 115: return position + "    drem";
```

(continued)

Listing 5-1
The CodeAttribute class *(continued)*

```
case 116: return position + "    ineg";
case 117: return position + "    lneg";
case 118: return position + "    fneg";
case 119: return position + "    dneg";
case 120: return position + "    ishl";
case 121: return position + "    lshl";
case 122: return position + "    ishr";
case 123: return position + "    lshr";
case 124: return position + "    iushr";
case 125: return position + "    lushr";
case 126: return position + "    iand";
case 127: return position + "    land";
case 128: return position + "    ior";
case 129: return position + "    lor";
case 130: return position + "    ixor";
case 131: return position + "    lxor";
case 132: return position + "    iinc "
    + dis.readUnsignedByte() + " " + dis.readUnsignedByte() ;
case 133: return position + "    i2l";
case 134: return position + "    i2f";
case 135: return position + "    i2d";
case 136: return position + "    l2i";
case 137: return position + "    l2f";
case 138: return position + "    l2d";
case 139: return position + "    f2i";
case 140: return position + "    f2l";
case 141: return position + "    f2d";
case 142: return position + "    d2i";
case 143: return position + "    d2l";
case 144: return position + "    d2f";
case 145: return position + "    i2b";
case 146: return position + "    i2c";
case 147: return position + "    i2s";
case 148: return position + "    lcmp";
case 149: return position + "    fcmpl";
case 150: return position + "    fcmpg";
case 151: return position + "    dcmpl";
case 152: return position + "    dcmpg";
case 153: return position + "    ifeq " + dis.readShort();
case 154: return position + "    ifne " + dis.readShort();
case 155: return position + "    iflt " + dis.readShort();
case 156: return position + "    ifge " + dis.readShort();
case 157: return position + "    ifgt " + dis.readShort();
case 158: return position + "    ifle " + dis.readShort();
case 159: return position + "    if_icmpeq " + dis.readShort();
case 160: return position + "    if_icmpne " + dis.readShort();
```

(continued)

The CodeAttribute class *(continued)*

```
        case 161: return position + "    if_icmplt " + dis.readShort();
        case 162: return position + "    if_icmpge " + dis.readShort();
        case 163: return position + "    if_icmpgt " + dis.readShort();
        case 164: return position + "    if_icmple " + dis.readShort();
        case 165: return position + "    if_acmpeq " + dis.readShort();
        case 166: return position + "    if_acmpne " + dis.readShort();
        case 167: return position + "    goto " + dis.readShort();
        case 168: return position + "    jsr " + dis.readShort();
        case 169: return position + "    ret " + dis.readUnsignedByte();
        case 170:  // tableswitch
          pad = 3 - (position % 4);
          dis.skip(pad);
          defaultByte = dis.readInt();
          int low = dis.readInt();
          int high = dis.readInt();
          result = position + "    tableswitch "
           + defaultByte + " " + low + " " + high;
          for (int i = low; i < high; i++) {
            int newPosition = position + pad + 12 + (i-low)*4;
            result += "\n" + newPosition + "    " + dis.readInt();
          }
          return result;
        case 171: // lookupswitch
          pad = 3 - (position % 4);
          dis.skip(pad);
          defaultByte = dis.readInt();
          int npairs = dis.readInt();
          result = position + "    lookupswitch " + defaultByte + " " + npairs;
          for (int i = 0; i < npairs; i++) {
            int newPosition = position + pad + 12 + i*8;
            result += "\n" + newPosition + "    "
             + dis.readInt() + " " + dis.readInt();
          }
          return result;
        case 172: return position + "    ireturn";
        case 173: return position + "    lreturn";
        case 174: return position + "    freturn";
        case 175: return position + "    dreturn";
        case 176: return position + "    areturn";
        case 177: return position + "    return";
        case 178: return position + "    getstatic " + dis.readUnsignedShort();
        case 179: return position + "    putstatic " + dis.readUnsignedShort();
        case 180: return position + "    getfield " + dis.readUnsignedShort();
        case 181: return position + "    putfield " + dis.readUnsignedShort();
        case 182: return position + "    invokevirtual " +
dis.readUnsignedShort();
```

(continued)

Listing 5-1
The CodeAttribute class *(continued)*

```
      case 183: return position + "    invokespecial " +
dis.readUnsignedShort();
      case 184: return position + "    invokestatic " + dis.readUnsignedShort();
      case 185:
        return "invokeinterface " + dis.readUnsignedShort() + " "
         + dis.readUnsignedByte();
      // 186 is unimplemented in Java 1.0.2
      case 187: return position + "    new " + dis.readUnsignedShort();
      case 188: return position + "    newarray " + dis.readByte();
      case 189: return position + "    anewarray " + dis.readUnsignedShort();
      case 190: return position + "    arraylength";
      case 191: return position + "    athrow";
      case 192: return position + "    checkcast " + dis.readUnsignedShort();
      case 193: return position + "    instanceof " + dis.readUnsignedShort();
      case 194: return position + "    monitorenter";
      case 195: return position + "    monitorexit";
      case 196:
        int nextCode = dis.readUnsignedByte();
        switch(nextCode) {
          case 132: // iinc
          return "wide\n" + (position+1) + "    iinc" + dis.readUnsignedShort()
           + " " + dis.readUnsignedShort();
          case 21:
            return "wide\n" + (position+1) + "    iload" +
dis.readUnsignedShort();
          case 22:
            return "wide\n" + (position+1) + "    lload" +
dis.readUnsignedShort();
          case 23:
            return "wide\n" + (position+1) + "    fload" +
dis.readUnsignedShort();
          case 24:
            return "wide\n" + (position+1) + "    dload" +
dis.readUnsignedShort();
          case 25:
            return "wide\n" + (position+1) + "    aload" +
dis.readUnsignedShort();
          case 54:
            return "wide\n" + (position+1) + "    istore" +
dis.readUnsignedShort();
          case 55:
            return "wide\n" + (position+1) + "    lstore" +
dis.readUnsignedShort();
          case 56:
            return "wide\n" + (position+1) + "    fstore" +
dis.readUnsignedShort();
```

(continued)

The CodeAttribute class *(continued)*

```
        case 57:
            return "wide\n" + (position+1) + "    dstore" +
dis.readUnsignedShort();
        case 58:
            return "wide\n" + (position+1) + "    astore" +
dis.readUnsignedShort();
        } // end switch
    case 197:
        return "multianewarray " + dis.readUnsignedShort() + " " +
dis.readUnsignedByte();
    case 198: return position + "    ifnull " + dis.readShort();
    case 199: return position + "    ifnonnull " + dis.readShort();
    case 200: return position + "    goto_w " + dis.readInt();
    default: return position + "    unknown_opcode " + opcode;
    } // end switch

  }

}
```

The nameIndex() and CodeAttribute() methods are the same ones that you saw in the preceding chapter. The readCode() method is a big lookup table that returns the next opcode mnemonic and its arguments from the code array. Some instructions take one or more of their arguments from the bytes that follow them in the code array. Therefore, you can't just blindly convert each byte to a mnemonic. Some bytes must remain bytes. Opcodes 170, 171, and 196 (tableswitch, lookupswitch, and wide) can take a varying number of arguments, so extra logic is required to handle them. I describe this logic later in this chapter, when I discuss those instructions.

Armed with this information, you should now have a better idea of what's going on inside the methods when you disassemble a program. For example, disassembling HelloWorld, you get the output shown in Listing 5-2.

Listing 5-2
HelloWorld disassembled into byte code mnemonics

```
import java.io.PrintStream;

class HelloWorld extends java.lang.Object  {

  public static void main() {

0    getstatic 7
```

(continued)

Listing 5-2
HelloWorld disassembled into byte code mnemonics *(continued)*

```
3    ldc 1
5    invokevirtual 8
8    return

  }


  void <init>() {

0    aload_0
1    invokespecial 6
4    return

  }

}

/*
1:   String            18
2:   ClassInfo         19
3:   ClassInfo         25
4:   ClassInfo         26
5:   ClassInfo         27
6:   MethodRef         ClassIndex: 4;    NameAndTypeIndex: 9
7:   FieldRef          ClassIndex: 5;    NameAndTypeIndex: 10
8:   MethodRef         ClassIndex: 3;    NameAndTypeIndex: 11
9:   NameAndType       NameIndex: 14;    DescriptorIndex: 12
10:  NameAndType       NameIndex: 29;    DescriptorIndex: 22
11:  NameAndType       NameIndex: 30;    DescriptorIndex: 13
12:  UTF8              ()V
13:  UTF8              (Ljava/lang/String;)V
14:  UTF8              <init>
15:  UTF8              Code
16:  UTF8              ConstantValue
17:  UTF8              Exceptions
18:  UTF8              Hello World
19:  UTF8              HelloWorld
20:  UTF8              HelloWorld.java
21:  UTF8              LineNumberTable
22:  UTF8              Ljava/io/PrintStream;
23:  UTF8              LocalVariables
24:  UTF8              SourceFile
25:  UTF8              java/io/PrintStream
26:  UTF8              java/lang/Object
27:  UTF8              java/lang/System
28:  UTF8              main
```

(continued)

HelloWorld disassembled into byte code mnemonics *(continued)*

```
29:   UTF8              out
30:   UTF8              print

*/
```

Listing 5-2 is the most intelligible disassembly yet. The rest of this chapter describes the various opcodes, so you can really understand what's going on inside the file.

STACKS, FRAMES, AND POOLS

Instructions require data on which to operate. You can take this data from five places: the method stack, the heap, the constant pool, the local variable array, and the byte code itself. The method stack, the local variable array, and the byte code are specific to the method. The constant pool and the heap are shared by all other threads and methods executing in the same virtual machine.

All of the operations in a method such as addition or subtraction take place on the stack. For example, to add two integers, the integers are first pushed onto the stack, then they're popped off of the stack, and then their sum is pushed back onto the stack.

The local variable array is a temporary holding area for local variables declared in the method and arguments passed to the method. You have to copy those local variables onto the stack before you can do anything with them.

Instructions that access the heap get references to items in the heap from the stack. You learned about the constant pool in the last chapter. Operations that access the constant pool also use indices into the pool placed on the heap.

When the Java virtual machine is running, each thread has a stack of frames. (This is related neither to HTML frames nor to the java.util.Stack class.) A frame holds the local variables and arguments for a method and a working area for the method called the *operand stack*. When a method is called, the virtual machine creates a new frame for the method with space for its local variables and its local stack. This frame is placed on top of the thread's stack. When the method completes, this frame is popped from the thread's stack, and the method's return value (if any) is pushed onto the top of the calling method's stack.

Each method operates on the values contained in its local variable array and on its method stack. You can think of the local variable array as an array of 32-bit words, and the method stack as a stack of 32-bit words.

Let's look at a simple example. Consider the following method, which adds two to four and returns the sum:

```
public int six() {

    int a = 4;
    int b = 2;
    int c = a + b;
    return c;

}
```

Here's the same method as disassembled byte code:

```
public int six() {

0   iconst_4
1   istore_1
2   iconst_2
3   istore_2
4   iload_1
5   iload_2
6   iadd
7   istore_3
8   iload_3
9   ireturn

}
```

Let's investigate this byte code instruction by instruction, to see what effect each one has on the array of local variables and the stack.

You first need to look at the number of different locations referenced by load and store instructions to determine how many local variables are used.

Instruction 0 pushes the constant 4 onto the stack. That doesn't affect the local variable array at all.

Instruction 1 stores a value into position 1 in the local variable array. The local variable array therefore must have at least one entry.

Instruction 2 pushes the constant value 2 onto the method stack. Again, this has no effect on the local variable array.

Instruction 3 stores a variable into position 2 in the local variable array. Therefore, there are at least positions 1 and 2 in the local variable array, so that array has to be at least 2 entries long.

Instructions 4 and 5 move values from the local variable array at positions 1 and 2 onto the stack. However, you've already seen variables 1 and 2, so that's nothing new. Instruction 6 adds the two variables onto the top of the stack and puts the result back on the stack. Again, the local variable array is not changed.

Instructions 7 and 8 store something into the third position in the local variable array and then load it onto the stack. So there now have to be at least 3 entries in the local variable array.

Finally, instruction 9 returns and completes the method.

So far, we've counted three local variables in positions 1 through 3. However, in a non-static method, the zeroth position always holds a reference to the current object. Therefore, there are four total local variables in positions 0 through 3.

Note

You can also get this information from the maxLocals field of the CodeAttribute class.

In this example, the source code contains three local variables — a, b, and c—and the byte code contains four local variables. The number of local variables in the .java source code is not necessarily the same as the number of local variables used by the byte code. The byte code may have more local variables if it needs temporary storage, or it may have fewer if some variables can be reused. The other thing to note is that the names of the local variables are completely lost in compilation; only their types are known.

When the method is first called, an array of four words is allocated to hold the local variables. The zeroth element of the array is a reference to this object. The first element of the array corresponds to the int variable a; the second element of the array correspondents to the int variable b; and the third element of the array correspondents to the int variable c. The stack is initially empty. Figure 5-1 demonstrates.

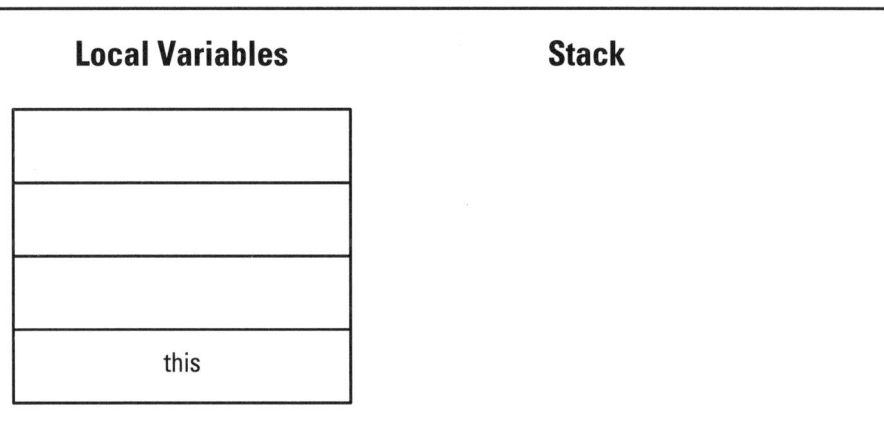

Local Variables   **Stack**

this

Figure 5-1
The local variable array and the stack when the method is loaded.

The zeroth instruction is iconst _ 4. The const family of instructions push values onto the operand stack. This instruction begins with the letter i, so it pushes an int value. It ends with _ 4, so the value pushed is four. Thus, after this instruction has executed, the operand stack is one word high, and the int 4 is on the top of the stack. Figure 5-2 shows the state of the local variable array and the operand stack after this instruction is executed.

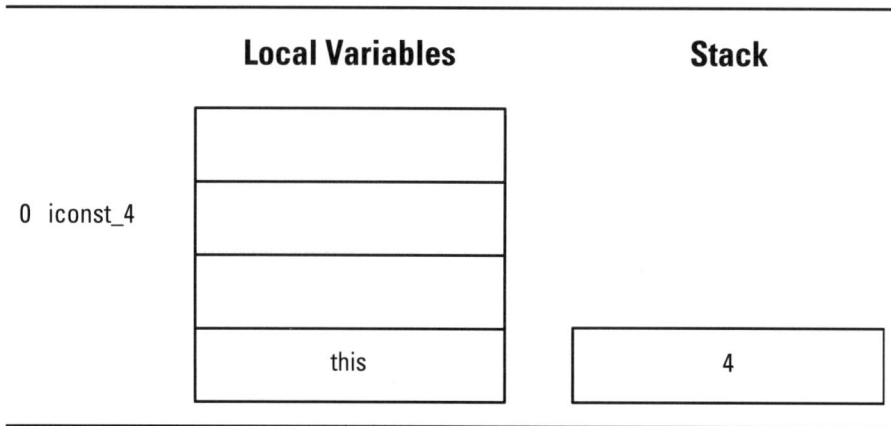

Local Variables   **Stack**

0 iconst_4

this   4

Figure 5-2
The local variable array and the stack after instruction 0.

The first instruction is istore _ 1. The store family of instructions pop values from the operand stack and store them in the local variable array. This instruction begins with the letter i, so it stores an int value. It ends with _ 1, so the value is stored in local variable 1. Therefore, 4 is popped off the stack and stored in local variable 1. After this instruction has executed, the operand stack is empty. Figure 5-3 shows the state of the local variable array and the operand stack after this instruction is executed.

The second instruction is iconst _ 2. This pushes the int 2 onto the stack. Figure 5-4 shows the state of the local variable array and the operand stack after this instruction is executed.

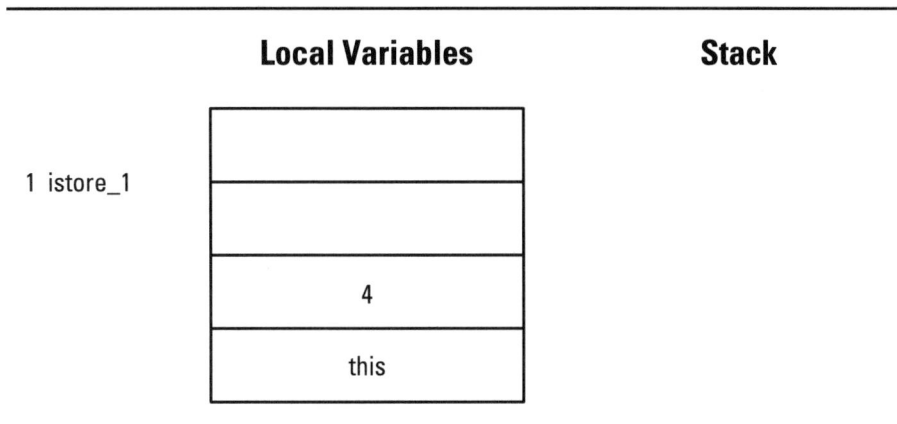

Local Variables   **Stack**

1 istore_1

4
this

Figure 5-3
The local variable array and the stack after instruction 1.

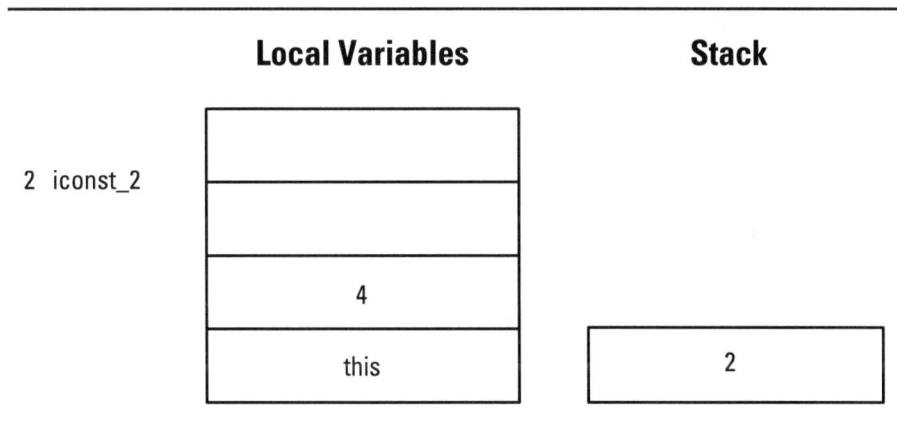

Local Variables   **Stack**

2 iconst_2

4
this

2

Figure 5-4
The local variable array and the stack after instruction 2.

The third instruction is istore _ 2. It pops the top of the stack and stores it in local variable 2. After this instruction has executed, the operand stack is empty. Figure 5-5 shows the state of the local variable array and the operand stack.

The fourth instruction is iload _ 4. The load family of instructions pushes values from the local variable array onto the operand stack. This instruction begins with the letter i and ends with _ 4, so it pushes the int 4.

Local Variables   **Stack**

3 istore_2

2
4
this

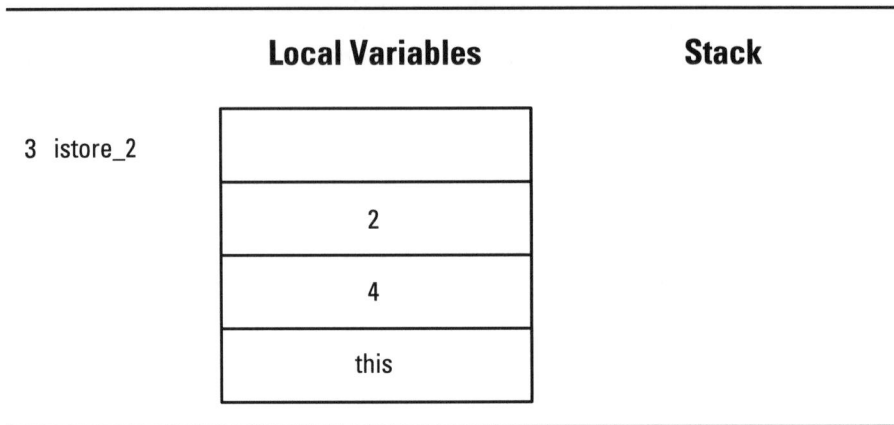

Figure 5-5
The local variable array and the stack after instruction 3.

Unlike popping a value from the stack, loading a value from the local variable array does not remove it from the array. Local variable 1 still has the value 4 after this instruction is executed. Figure 5-6 shows the state of the local variable array and the operand stack.

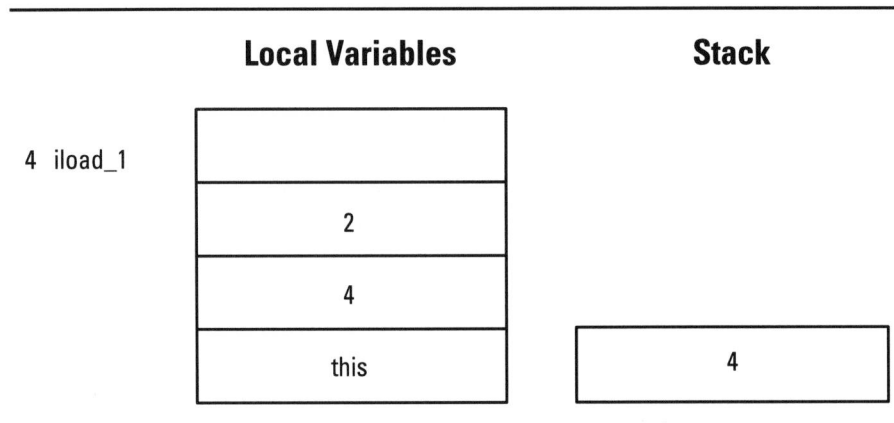

Local Variables   **Stack**

4 iload_1

2
4
this

4

▮ **Figure 5-6**
The local variable array and the stack after instruction 4.

The fifth instruction is iload _ 2. This pushes the second local variable onto the stack. After this instruction has executed, the operand stack is two words high, and the int 2 is on the top of the stack. Figure 5-7 shows the state of the local variable array and the operand stack.

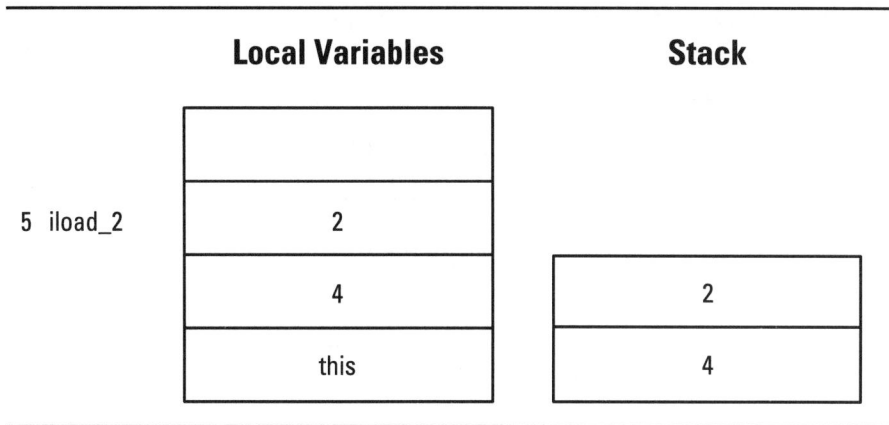

Local Variables   Stack

5 iload_2

2
4
this

Stack
2
4

Figure 5-7
The local variable array and the stack after instruction 5.

The sixth instruction is iadd. The add family of instructions pops two values from the operand stack, adds them, and pushes the result back onto the stack. This instruction begins with the letter i, so it adds ints. After this instruction has executed, the operand stack is one word high, and the int 6 is on the top of the stack. Figure 5-8 shows the state of the local variable array and the operand stack.

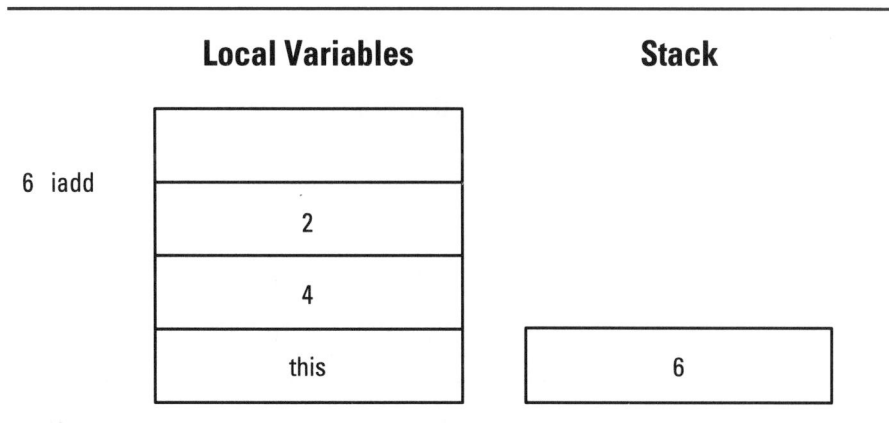

Local Variables   Stack

6 iadd

2
4
this

Stack
6

Figure 5-8
The local variable array and the stack after instruction 6.

The seventh instruction is istore_ 3. This pops the top of the stack and stores it in local variable 3. After this instruction has executed, the operand stack is empty. Figure 5-9 shows the state of the local variable array and the operand stack.

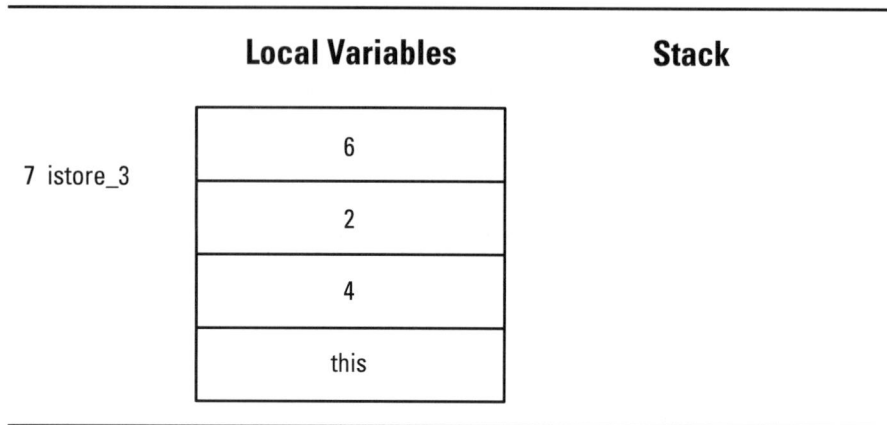

Local Variables   **Stack**

7 istore_3

6
2
4
this

Figure 5-9
The local variable array and the stack after instruction 7.

The eighth instruction is iload_ 3. This pushes the value 6 from local variable 3 onto the top of the stack. After this instruction has executed, the operand stack is one word high, and the int 6 is on the top of the stack. Figure 5-10 shows the state of the local variable array and the operand stack.

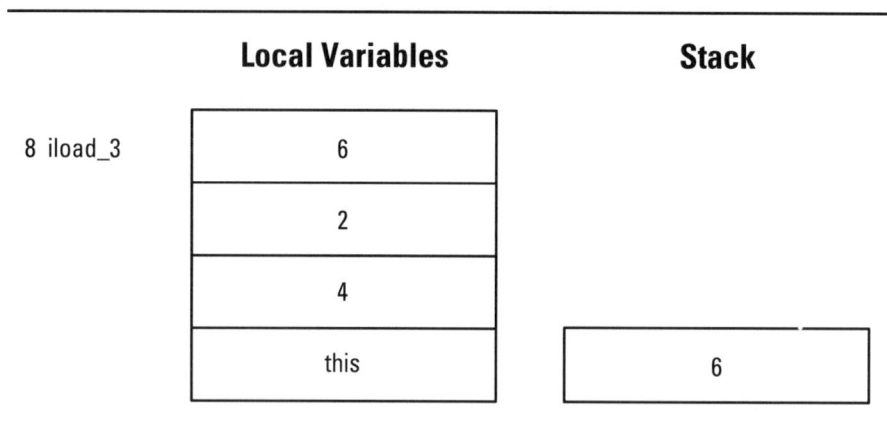

Local Variables   **Stack**

8 iload_3

6
2
4
this

6

Figure 5-10
The local variable array and the stack after instruction 8.

The ninth and final instruction in this method is ireturn. This instruction pops the int from the top of the stack and returns it to the method that calls this method. There's no picture here because this instruction destroys the frame, so there are no more local variables or stack words after this instruction is executed.

You may have noted that the seventh and eighth instructions weren't strictly necessary. The value 6 was on the top of the stack after instruction 6 and could have been returned then. This would be equivalent to rewriting the .java source code without the intermediate variable c, like this:

```
public int six() {

    int a = 4;
    int b = 2;
    return a+b;

}
```

An optimizing compiler might have noticed this and omitted the seventh and eighth instructions. A very good optimizing compiler could have noticed that this method uses only constants and always returns 6. It would have thus rewritten the source code like this:

```
public int six() {

    return 6;

}
```

In fact, this is exactly what javac -O does. The following is the byte code emitted by javac with the -O flag to indicate that it should perform optimization.

```
public int six() {

0    bipush
1    6
2    ireturn

}
```

The bipush instruction sign-extends the next byte in the code array to an int and pushes it onto the stack. The ireturn instruction in byte 2 then returns that int from the top of the stack. By using the optimizer, you've reduced nine instructions to three, a saving of 66 percent in both time and space. This is one reason why the names of the local variables are not stored in the byte code. By the time an optimizer is through with the code, there may not be any variables left.

THE OPCODES

There are more than 200 different opcodes in the Java virtual machine. You certainly don't need to memorize all of them. I suggest that you skim over this section to get a feel for how the different classes of opcodes behave. Then return here for reference when you need more details about a particular opcode that you've encountered in a disassembly.

Nop

Nop is short for "no operation." When the virtual machine encounters a nop instruction, it does nothing and moves to the next instruction. Neither the stack nor the local variable array is affected.

I've never actually seen a nop instruction appear in .java byte code. It is probably a holdover from other architectures in which nop instructions were used to ensure code alignment.

Pushing values onto the stack

The instructions in this section push values onto the stack. This usually precedes some other instruction that uses these values as arguments.

The const codes

The 15 const instructions push frequently occurring constants onto the operand stack. The mnemonics for these instructions all take the form

```
typeconst _ value
```

where *type* is one of a, i, l, or f and *value* is the value pushed onto the stack. Thus, iconst _ 2 pushes the int 2 onto the stack, and fconst _ 1 pushes the float 1.0 onto the stack. iconst_m1 pushes -1 onto the stack, and aconst_null pushes the null reference onto the stack.

bipush and sipush

The bipush instruction pushes a signed byte constant onto the stack. It operates on the byte in the code array immediately following itself. It sign-extends the byte to an int and pushes it onto the stack.

The sipush instruction pushes a signed short constant onto the stack. It takes the short from the two bytes of the code array immediately following itself. As with everything else in Java, these bytes are in Big-Endian order. The instruction sign-extends the short to an int and pushes it onto the stack.

The ldc codes

The abbreviation ldc stands for "load constant." The three ldc codes copy values from the constant pool onto the stack.

The ldc instruction interprets the byte that follows it in the code array as an unsigned index into the constant pool. If that entry in the constant pool is a float or an int, then that value is copied onto the stack. However, if that entry in the constant pool is a string (that is, if it is an index to a UTF8 structure), then a new String object is constructed and initialized to the value of the UTF8 structure. Then a reference to this new String object is placed on the stack.

The ldc_w instruction is the same, except that it uses a 2-byte unsigned index into the constant pool. The ldc instruction is used when the desired constant is somewhere between index 0 and index 255. Larger indices require the ldc_w instruction. You can think of ldc_w as an abbreviation for "load constant wide."

The ldc2_w instruction copies an 8-byte long or double value from the constant pool into the top two words of the stack. The two bytes of the code array immediately following the ldc2_w instruction are interpreted as an unsigned short index into the constant pool.

Stack manipulation

Several instructions operate directly on the words on the stack, without concerning themselves with what those words mean.

The pop and pop2

The pop instruction removes or "pops" the top word from the stack and does nothing with it. The word is completely lost. This instruction can be used only when a word length quantity like an int or a reference is on the stack. You can't use it when there's a two-word type like a double or a long on the stack. For those types, you must use the pop2 instruction, which pops two words from the stack and discards them. You can also use the pop2 instruction to remove two words that contain ints or floats or references from the stack. However, the Java virtual machine does not allow this (or any other) instruction to split the two words of a long or a double.

The dup codes

The three dup instructions duplicate a word from the stack and put the copy back in the stack. They differ as to where in the stack they put the copy. The three dup2 instructions duplicate the two words on the top of the stack and put those words back in the stack. They, too, differ as to where exactly they put the words back in the stack. These are the only instructions in the virtual machine that put words somewhere other than on the top of the stack. All of these instructions enforce the integrity of longs and doubles. That is, they do not allow you to move half of a two-word quantity or to move a word between the two words in a long or a double.

The dup instruction copies the top word on the stack and puts the copy on the top of the stack. Figure 5-11 shows one possible stack before and after the dup instruction.

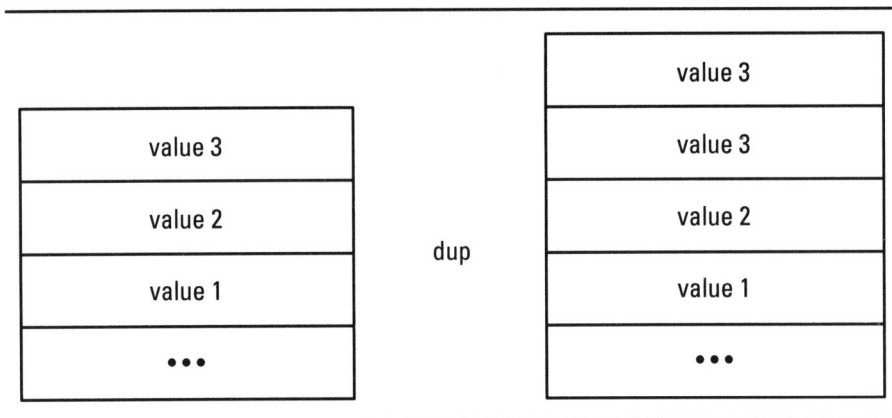

Figure 5-11
The stack, before and after the dup instruction.

The dup_x1 instruction copies the top word on the stack and puts the copy two words down in the stack. This forces the two words that were on the top of the stack to each move up one place. If the stack is as shown on the left side of Figure 5-12, then after the dup_x1 instruction has been executed, the stack will be in the state shown on the right of Figure 5-12.

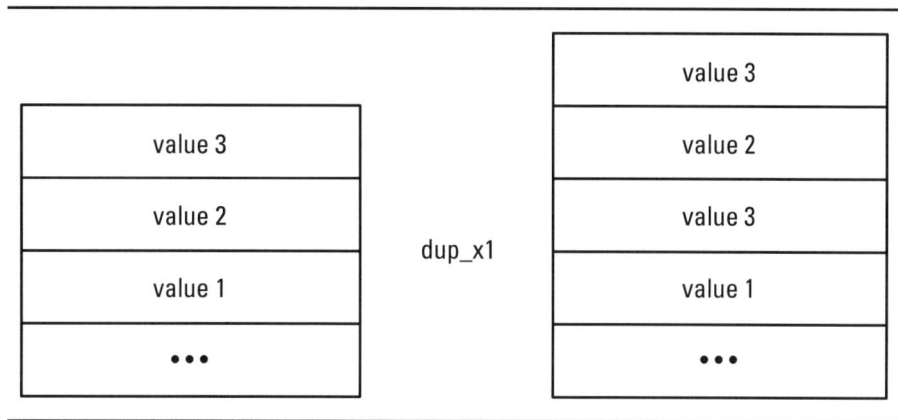

Figure 5-12
The stack, before and after the dup_x1 instruction.

The dup_x2 instruction copies the top word on the stack and puts the copy three words down in the stack. This forces the three words on the top of the stack to each move up one. If the stack is as shown on the left side of Figure 5-13, then after the dup_x2 instruction has been executed, the stack will be in the state shown on the right of Figure 5-13.

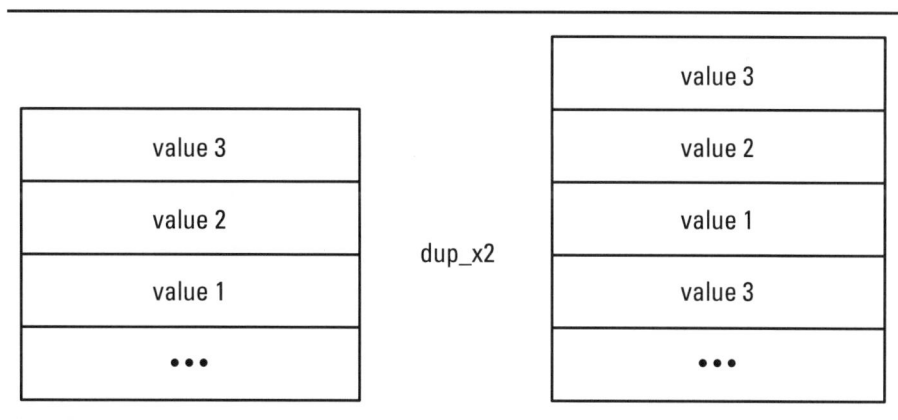

Figure 5-13
The stack, before and after the dup_x2 instruction.

The dup2 instruction copies the top two words on the stack and puts the copies on the top of the stack. Figure 5-14 illustrates this.

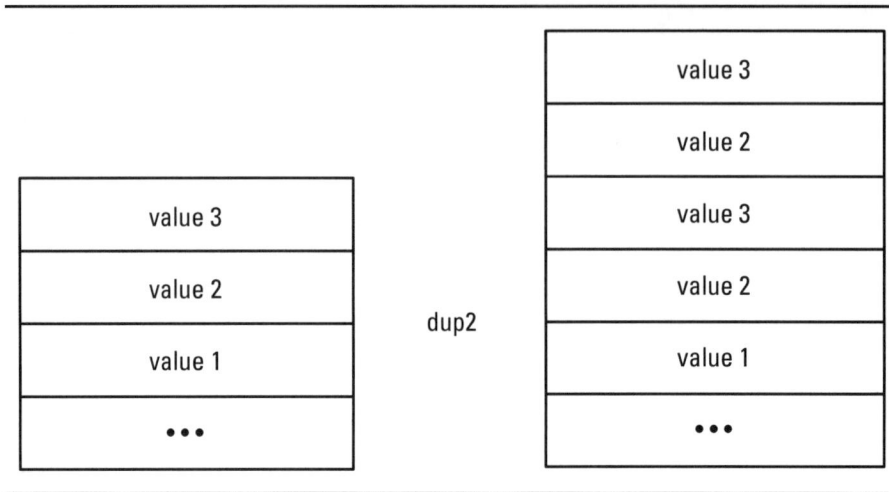

Figure 5-14
The stack, before and after the dup2 instruction.

The dup2_x1 instruction copies the top words on the stack and puts the copies three words down in the stack. Figure 5-15 demonstrates.

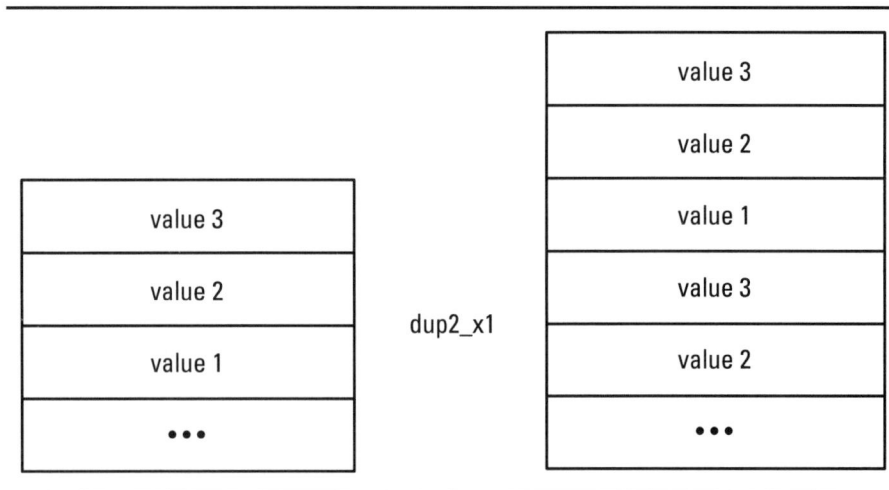

Figure 5-15
The stack, before and after the dup2_x1 instruction.

Finally, the dup2_x2 instruction copies the top words on the stack and puts the copies four words down in the stack. Figure 5-16 demonstrates.

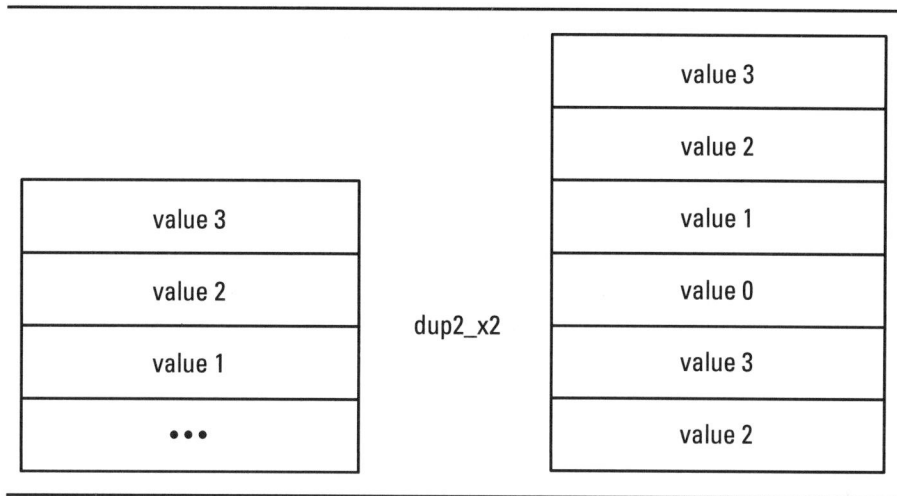

	value 3
	value 2
value 3	value 1
value 2	value 0
value 1	value 3
•••	value 2

dup2_x2

Figure 5-16
The stack, before and after the dup2_x2 instruction.

swap

The swap instruction swaps the two words on the top of the stack. That is, the word on the top of the stack moves down one and the word immediately below the top of the stack moves up one, to the top. The size of the stack does not change. Figure 5-17 illustrates this. As always, the swap instruction cannot be used to split or reverse the two words in a long or a double.

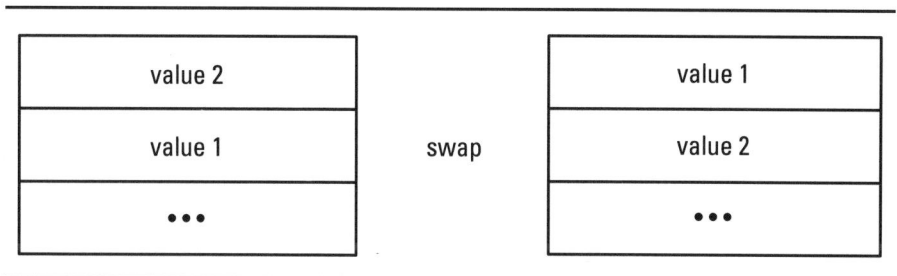

value 2	value 1
value 1	value 2
•••	•••

swap

Figure 5-17
A stack, before and after the swap instruction.

The local variable array

By far, the largest number of byte codes are the load and store instructions. There are more than 60 of these. The load instructions load a variable onto the stack from the local variable array. The store instructions pop a value from the stack and stores it into the local variable array.

Although there are more than 60 of these instructions, they're quite easy to understand. All of the load instructions act very much alike. They differ primarily in the type of value that each one loads and secondarily in how they determine the local variable to load. Similarly, all the store instructions act the same. They also differ in the type of value that each one stores and in how they determine the local variable into which to store values.

Each of these instructions begins with a letter that indicates the type of value on which it operates. For example, instructions that begin with the letter l operate on longs, and instructions that begin with f operate on floats. Table 5-2 lists these mappings between first letters and types.

Table 5-2
Type abbreviations

Letter	Type
a	reference
b	byte or boolean
c	char
d	double
f	float
i	int
l	long
s	short

Furthermore, instructions that begin with one of these letters followed by the letter a operate on arrays of the type. Thus, iload loads an int value from the local variable array onto the stack, but iaload loads a value from an array of ints onto the stack. (I discuss arrays in more detail later.)

Instructions that end with an underscore (_) followed by a small integer (0, 1, 2, or 3) operate on the local variable at that point in the local variable array. Otherwise, the next byte in the code array is used as an unsigned index into the local variable array. Thus, istore_2 pops a value from the stack and stores it in local variable 2. However, istore first reads another byte from the code array to determine which local variable it should use to store the value that it pops from the top of the stack.

There are 12 basic instructions that work with the local variable array: aload, iload, fload, lload, dload, istore, fstore, astore, lstore, dstore, ret, and iinc. Each of these instructions is followed by a single, unsigned byte. This byte determines which local variable is used. The use of a single byte is very space-efficient. However, it does place an upper limit of 256 local variables, fewer if some of them are longs or doubles. Sometimes this isn't quite enough.

The wide instruction allows access to many more local variables — up to 65,536. When wide precedes any of the first 11 of these instructions (that is, any except ret), the instruction uses the next two bytes in the code array, rather than only one byte, as an index into the local variable array.

For example, istore 2 normally means to pop an int from the stack and store it in local variable 2. However, if the instruction before istore is wide, then you have to read an extra byte. Thus, wide istore 2 8 means to pop an int from the stack and store it in local variable 520. Figure 5-18 demonstrates.

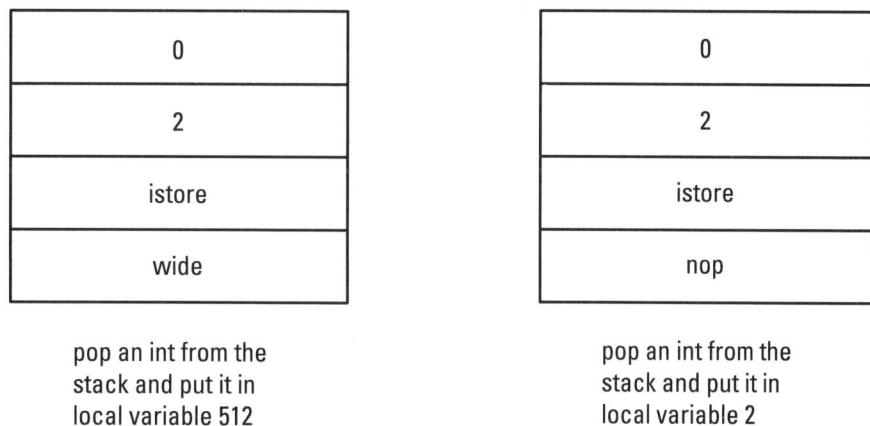

0
2
istore
wide

pop an int from the
stack and put it in
local variable 512

0
2
istore
nop

pop an int from the
stack and put it in
local variable 2

Figure 5-18
The effect of the wide instruction.

The wide instruction has an even larger effect on the iinc instruction. Recall that normally the iinc instruction is followed in the code array by two bytes, an index into the local variable array and the constant increment. When preceded by wide, both of these are widened to 2-byte shorts, the first unsigned and the second signed. Thus, wide iinc 0 2 2 0 means "increment local variable 2 by 512."

Arithmetic

Arithmetic byte codes come in two groups: the binary operators and the unary operators. Most of the common operators that you're familiar with, such as + and *, are binary operators. This means that they take two arguments. For example, you always add numbers two at a time. There's no way to add just a single number, even when you write something like this:

```
int a = 3 + 7 + c;
```

Java first adds the 3 and the 7. Then it adds c to their sum. That is, it splits the calculation into two parts, like this:

```
int temp = 3 + 7;
int a = temp + c;
```

In fact, you do this sort of splitting implicitly when you add a series of numbers yourself by hand.

The only unary arithmetic operator in Java is the minus sign (-). This operator changes the sign of a variable. Thus, if the int variable a is 7, then -a is -7. This can be a little confusing, because the - character serves two other purposes in Java. It is also the binary subtraction operator in expressions like 3 - 7 and can be a part of numeric literals like -7 or -98.6. Although these appear to be the same thing in .java source code, they are three different things in .java byte code.

All byte code binary arithmetic instructions operate on two values of the same type. In other words, ints can be added only to other ints, floats to other floats, and so on. You can't add an int and a double or multiply a float times a long. If you need to combine two types in one expression, you must first use one of the type conversion operators that we discuss later.

The add codes

There are four addition instructions: iadd, ladd, fadd, and dadd. These add ints, longs, floats, and doubles respectively.

The instructions iadd and fadd pop two words off the stack, add them, and push the sum back onto the stack. After the instruction has executed, the stack is one word shorter. Figure 5-19 shows the addition of two ints — 4 and 2 — to get 6.

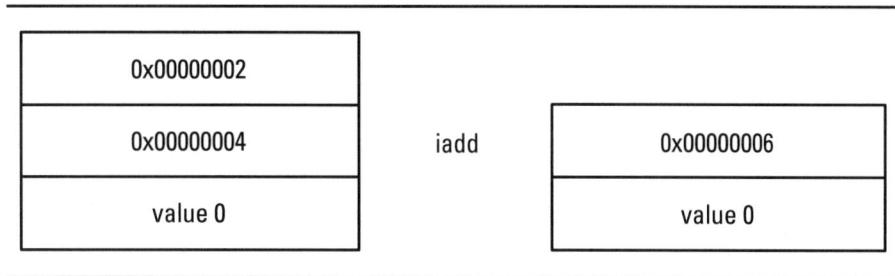

0x00000002		
0x00000004	iadd	0x00000006
value 0		value 0

Figure 5-19
Adding 4 to 2 to get 6.

The instructions ladd and dadd pop four words from the stack, add them, and push a two-word result back onto the stack. After the instruction has executed, the stack is two words shorter. Figure 5-20 shows the addition of the long values 4L and 2L to get 6L.

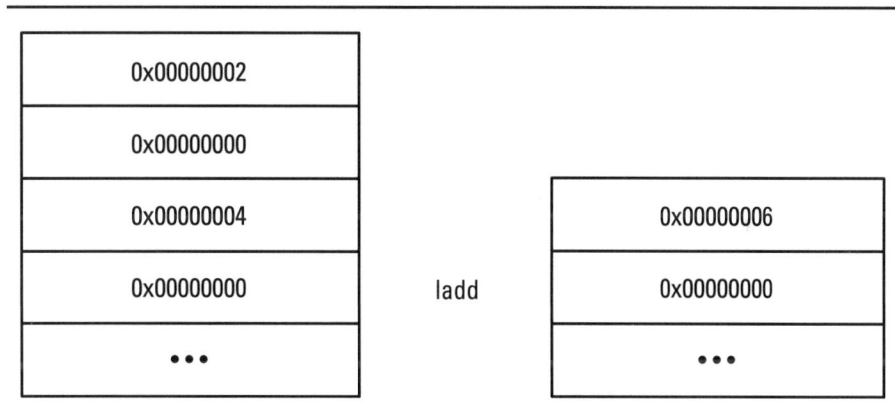

0x00000002		
0x00000000		
0x00000004		0x00000006
0x00000000	ladd	0x00000000
•••		•••

Figure 5-20
Adding 4L to 2L to get 6L.

The sub codes

Subtraction is similar to addition. There are four subtraction operators —
isub, lsub, fsub, and dsub — one each for ints, longs, floats, and doubles.
Unlike addition, subtraction is not commutative; that is, a - b is not, in
general, the same as b - a. Therefore, it's important to note that the value on
the top of the stack is subtracted from the value immediately below it, and
not the other way around. Figure 5-21 and Figure 5-22 demonstrate this.

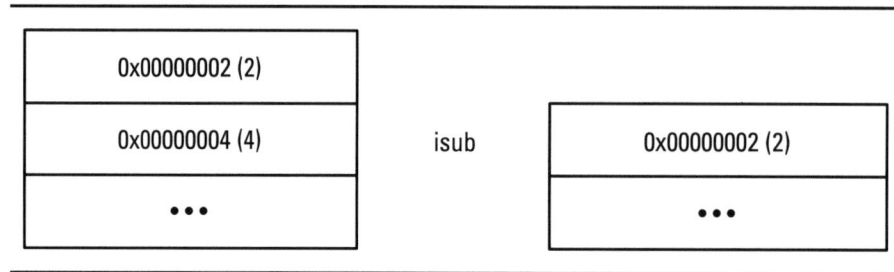

0x00000002 (2)		
0x00000004 (4)	isub	0x00000002 (2)
•••		•••

Figure 5-21
4 - 2 = 2.

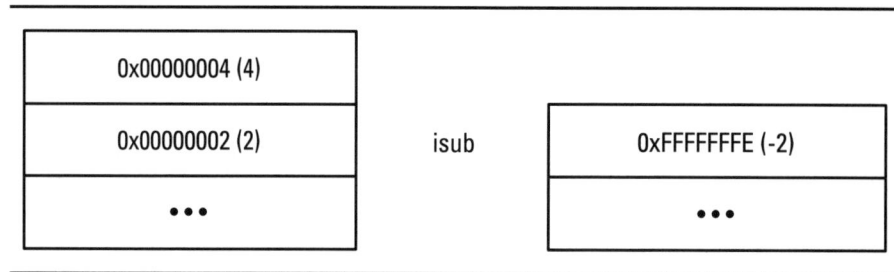

0x00000004 (4)		
0x00000002 (2)	isub	0xFFFFFFFE (-2)
•••		•••

Figure 5-22
2 - 4 = -2.

Floats are subtracted exactly the same way. Longs and doubles are too,
except that each number requires two words. Figure 5-23 shows what
happens on the stack when you subtract 2L from 4L.

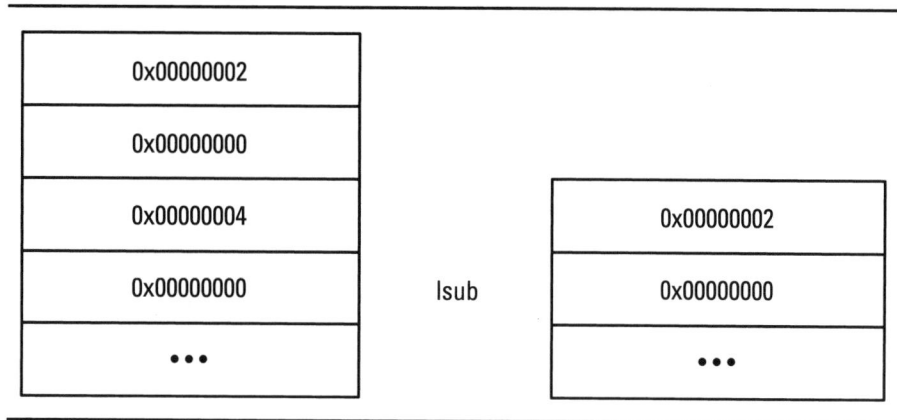

Figure 5-23
4L - 2L.

The mul codes

There are four multiplication instructions: imul, lmul, fmul, and dmul. These multiply ints, longs, floats, and doubles, respectively. The instructions imul and fmul pop two words off the stack, multiply them, and push the product back onto the stack. After the instruction has executed, the stack is one word shorter. Figure 5-24 shows the multiplication of two ints — 4 and 2 — to get 8.

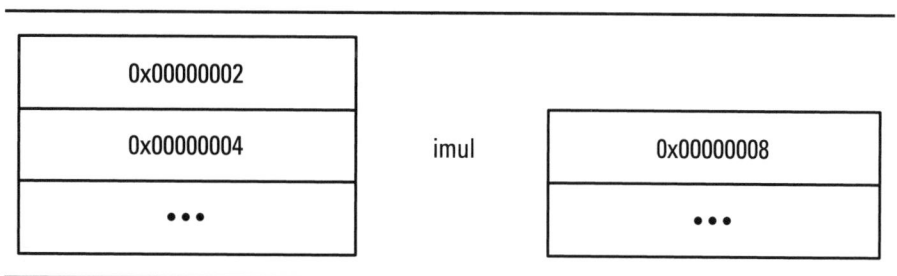

Figure 5-24
Multiplying 4 by 2 to get 8.

The instructions lmul and dmul pop two two-word values from the stack (a total of four words), multiply them, and push a two-word result back onto the stack. After the instruction has executed, the stack is two words shorter. Figure 5-25 shows the multiplication of the long values 4L and 2L to get 8L.

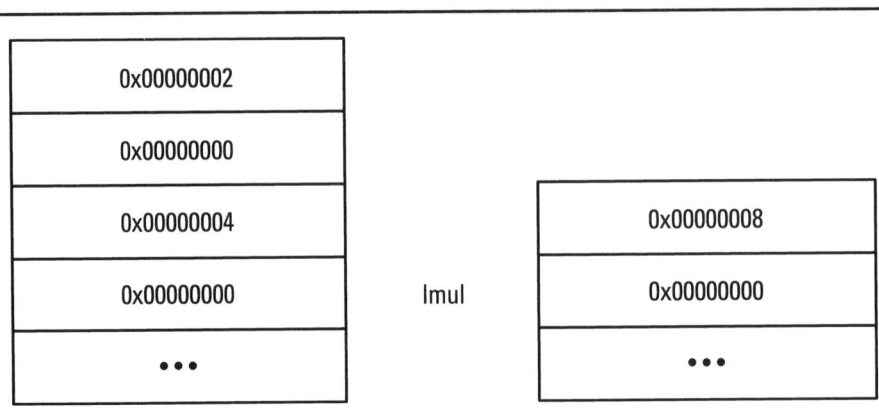

Figure 5-25
Multiplying 4L by 2L to get 8L.

The div codes

By now, this process should seem familiar. You can probably guess that there are four division instructions, that they are idiv, ldiv, fdiv, and ddiv, and that they divide ints, longs, floats, and doubles, respectively.

Division, like subtraction, is not commutative. Ten divided by five is two, but five divided by ten is one half. (In Java, 5 / 10 is actually 0, because integer division truncates toward zero.) The first value popped from the stack is divided into the second number popped from the stack. In other words, the first number popped from the stack is the dividend, and the second number popped from the stack is the divisor. Figures 5-26 and 5-27 demonstrate this.

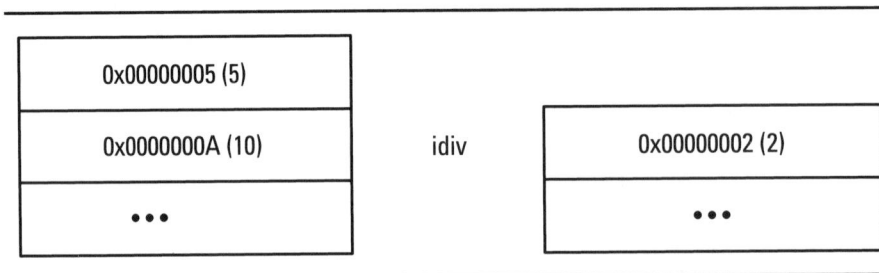

Figure 5-26
5 / 10 = 0.

0x00000005 (5)	
0x0000000A (10)	idiv
•••	

0x00000002 (2)
•••

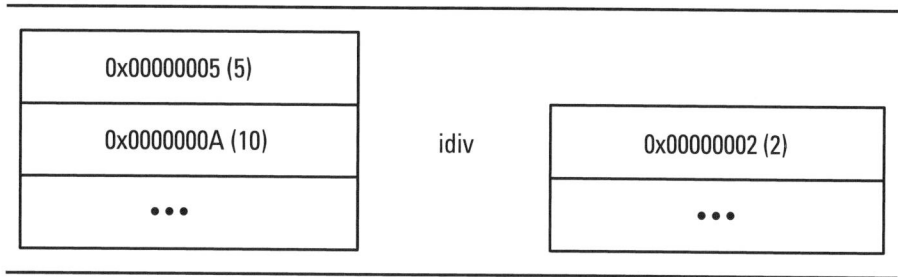

Figure 5-27
10 / 5 = 2.

Floats are divided exactly the same way, except that no truncation towards zero is necessary. Longs and doubles are also, except that each number requires two words. Figure 5-28 shows what happens when you divide 10L by 5L.

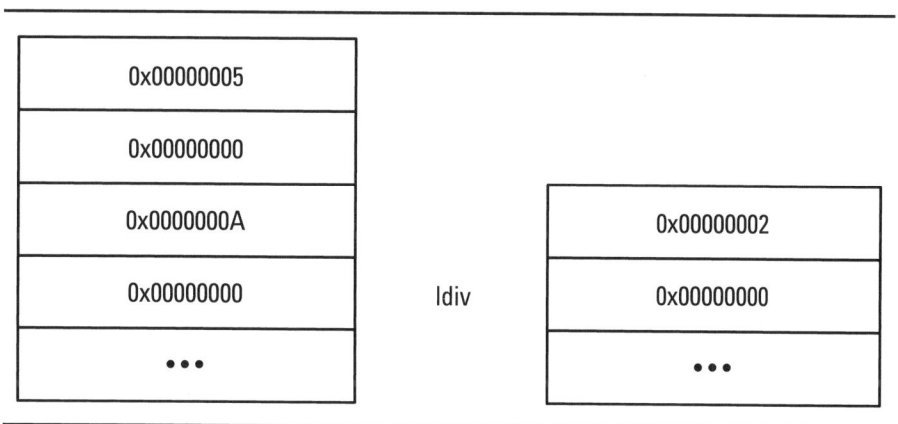

0x00000005
0x00000000
0x0000000A
0x00000000
•••

ldiv

0x00000002
0x00000000
•••

Figure 5-28
10L / 5L = 2L.

The rem codes

The rem codes are used for the Java remainder operator, %. As usual, there are four of them — irem, lrem, frem, and drem — one each for ints, longs, floats, and doubles. Like division, taking the remainder is not commutative. 10 % 2 is 0, but 2 % 10 is 2. The first value popped from the stack is divided into the second number popped from the stack, and the remainder is pushed onto the stack. Figures 5-29 and 5-30 demonstrate.

0x0000000A (10)		
0x00000002 (2)	irem	0x00000002 (2)
•••		•••

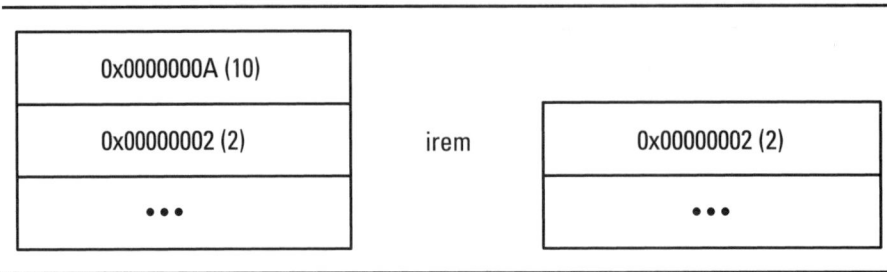

Figure 5-29
2 % 10= 0.

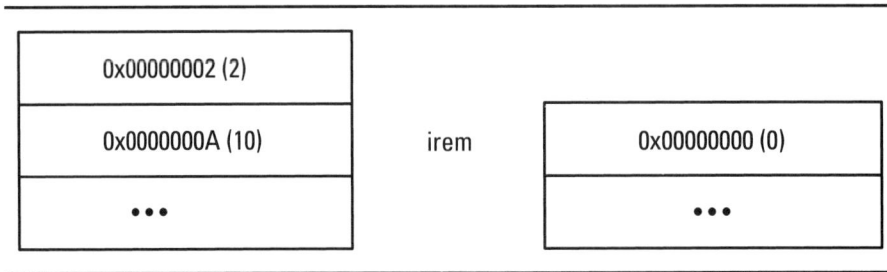

0x00000002 (2)		
0x0000000A (10)	irem	0x00000000 (0)
•••		•••

Figure 5-30
10 % 2 = 5.

Floats are handled exactly the same way. Longs and doubles are too, except that each number requires two words. Figure 5-31 shows what happens when you take the remainder of 10L by 2L.

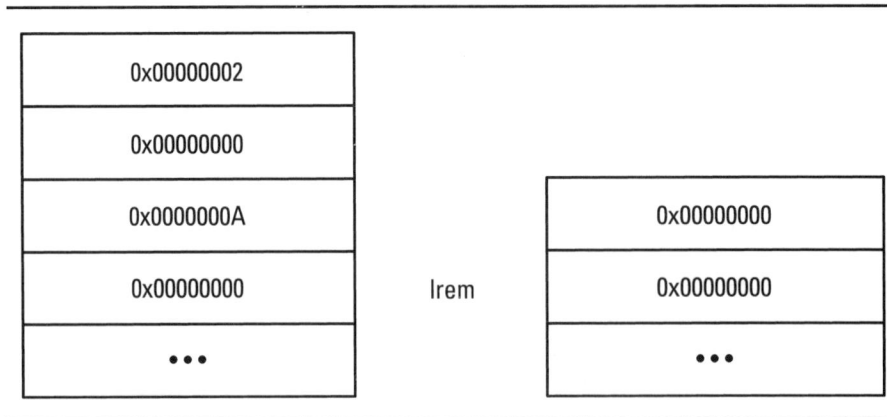

0x00000002		
0x00000000		
0x0000000A	lrem	0x00000000
0x00000000		0x00000000
•••		•••

Figure 5-31
10L % 5L = 0L.

The neg codes

The final group of arithmetic instructions is different. These are the neg instructions — ineg, lneg, fneg, and dneg — for ints, longs, floats, and doubles, respectively. Each of these pops only one value from the stack, not two. The instructions ineg and fneg pop one 32-bit word. The instructions lneg and dneg pop two 32-bit words. In either case, the value is negated; that is, its sign is changed, and the result is pushed back onto the stack. This is semantically equivalent to multiplying by -1, although in general, using the negation operator will be faster. The size of the stack does not change. Figure 5-32 shows the negation of the int value 255. Figure 5-33 shows the negation of the long value -32.

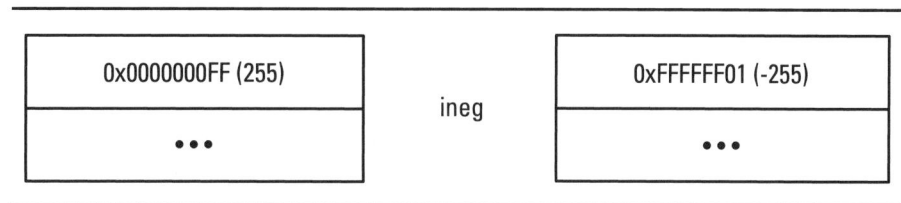

0x0000000FF (255)		0xFFFFFF01 (-255)
•••	ineg	•••

Figure 5-32
Negating 255 (0x000000FF) to get -255 (0xFFFFFF01).

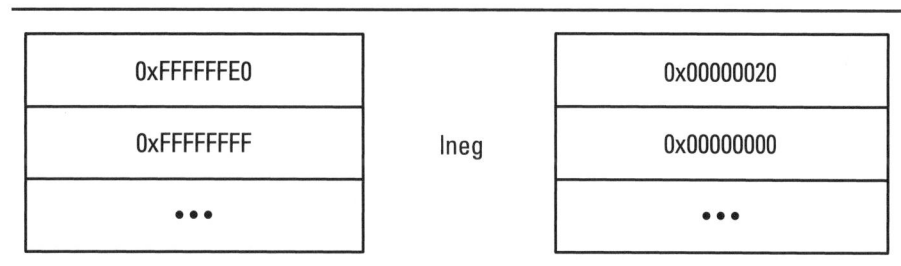

0xFFFFFFE0		0x00000020
0xFFFFFFFF	lneg	0x00000000
•••		•••

Figure 5-33
Negating -32L (0xFFFFFFFFFFFFFFE0) to get 32L (0x0000000000000020).

Bit manipulation

The bit-level byte code instructions map very closely to the bit-level operators. For each bit-level operator like << or ~, there are exactly two instructions, one for ints and one for longs. (Remember that you can't use bit-level operators on floats, doubles, or references.)

Shift operators

There are six shift operators: ishl, lshl, ishr, lshr, iushr, and lushr. Each pops two operands from the stack and returns the result to the stack. The instructions beginning with i operate on ints, and the instructions beginning with l operate on longs.

Shift left

The ishl and lshl instructions correspond to the << operator. They're also used by the <<= operator. The first value popped from the stack is the number of bits to shift left. The second value popped from the stack is the value that will be shifted. The vacated bits are filled with zeroes. When an ishl instruction has completed, the stack is one word shorter. When an lshl instruction has completed, the stack is two words shorter. Figure 5-34 shows the int value 255 being left-shifted eight places. Figure 5-35 shows the long value -32L being left-shifted eight places.

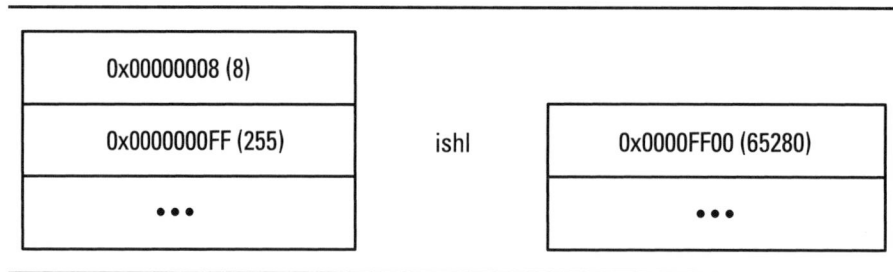

0x00000008 (8)		
0x0000000FF (255)	ishl	0x0000FF00 (65280)
•••		•••

Figure 5-34
255 << 8.

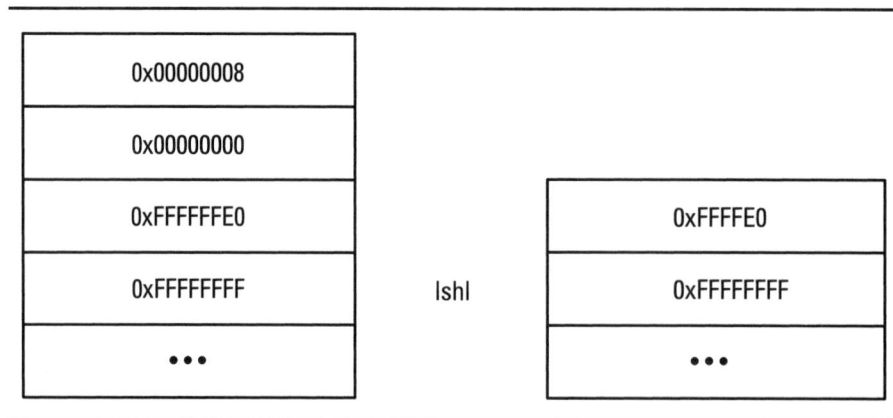

0x00000008		
0x00000000		
0xFFFFFFE0	lshl	0xFFFFE0
0xFFFFFFFF		0xFFFFFFFF
•••		•••

Figure 5-35
-32l << 8.

Shift right

The ishr and lshr instructions correspond to the >> and >>= operators. The first value popped from the stack is the number of bits to shift right. The second value popped from the stack is the value that will be shifted. The vacated bits are filled with the sign bit — 0 for positive numbers and 0 or 1 for negative numbers. When an ishr instruction has completed, the stack is one word shorter. When an lshr instruction has completed, the stack is two words shorter. Figure 5-36 shows the int value 255 being right-shifted four places. Figure 5-37 shows the long value -32L being right-shifted eight places.

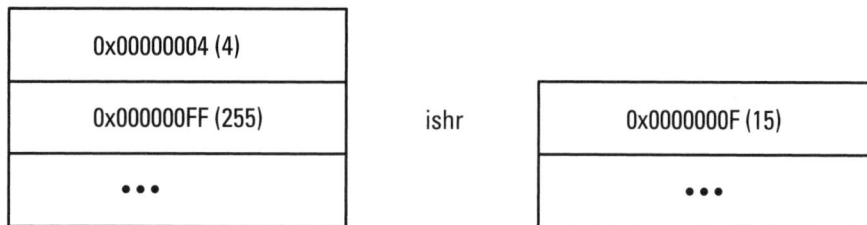

Figure 5-36
255 >> 4.

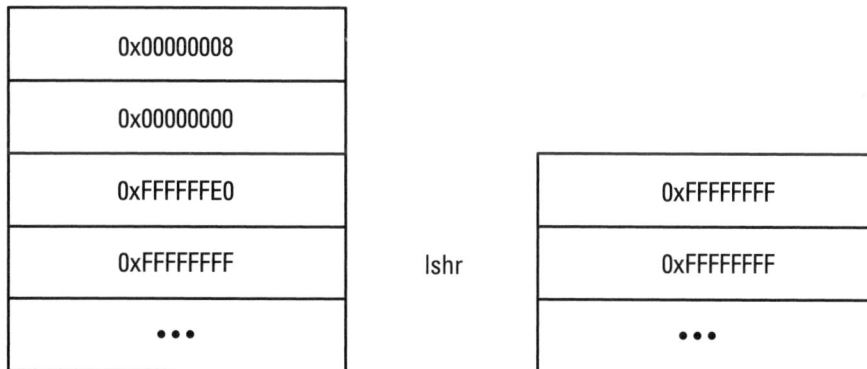

Figure 5-37
-32l >>> 8.

Unsigned shift right

The iushr and lushr instructions correspond to the >> and >>= operators. The first value popped from the stack is the number of bits to shift right. The second value popped from the stack is the value that will be shifted. The vacated bits are filled with zeroes, regardless of the sign of the number. When an iushr instruction has completed, the stack is one word shorter. When a lushr instruction has completed, the stack is two words shorter. Figure 5-38 shows the int value -32 being unsigned-right-shifted eight places.

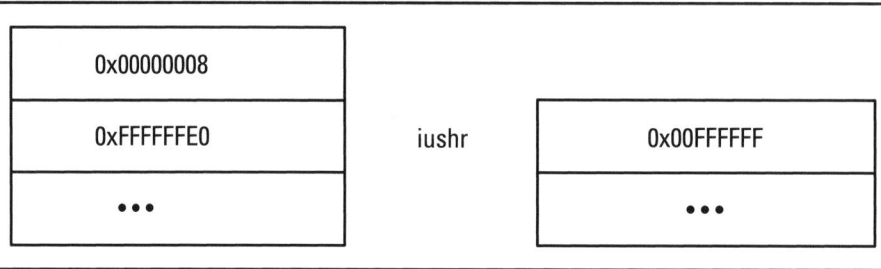

Figure 5-38
-32 >> 8.

Combination

The bitwise operators &, |, and ^ each have two corresponding byte code instructions, one each for ints and longs. These are iand, land, ior, lor, ixor, and lxor. Each behaves exactly as you would expect. The int instructions pop two words off the operand stack, combine them with the appropriate operator, and push the result back onto the stack. The long instructions pop four words off the operand stack, combine them with the appropriate operator, and push two words back onto the stack. Figure 5-39 shows the conjunction of the ints -32 and 8. Figure 5-40 shows the disjunction of the ints -32 and 8. Figure 5-41 shows the xor of the longs -32 and 255.

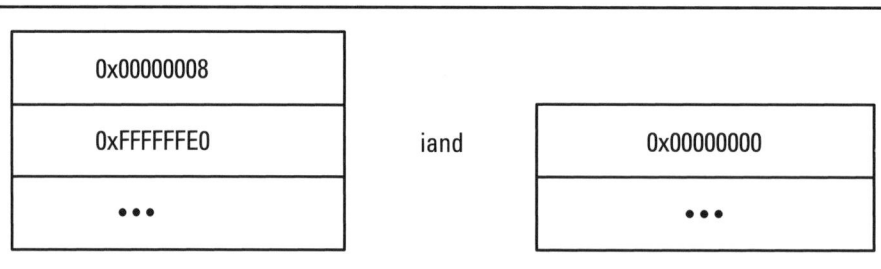

Figure 5-39
-32 & 8.

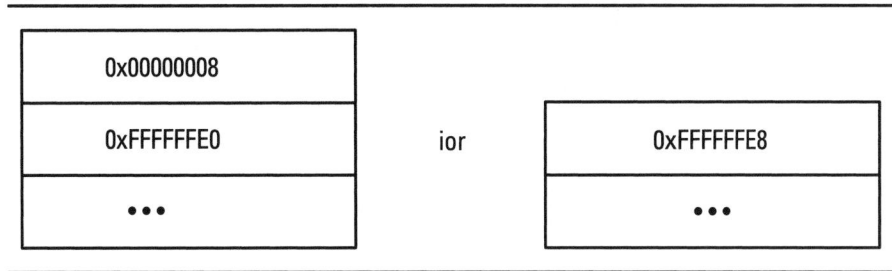

Figure 5-40
-32 | 8.

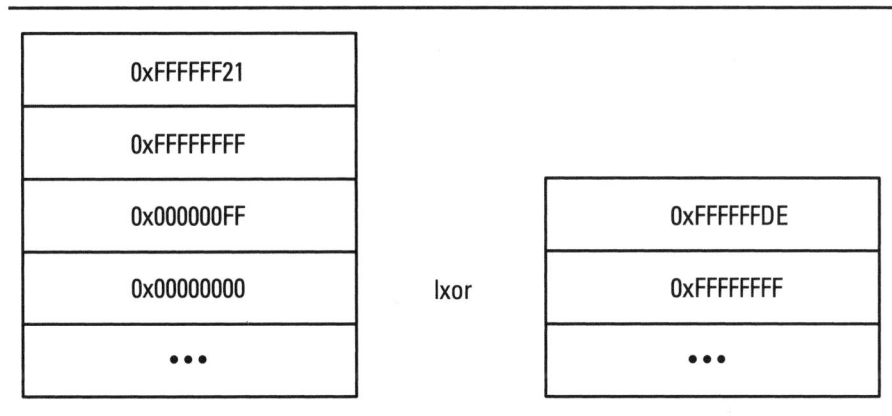

Figure 5-41
-32L ^ 255L.

The iinc instruction

The iinc instruction isn't absolutely necessary. There aren't any Java source files that cannot be compiled without it. However, it does allow loops to run much more quickly. The byte immediately after the iinc instruction in the code array is an unsigned index into the local variable array. The byte after that is a signed byte by which the local variable will be incremented. The iinc instruction is most commonly used to compile the ++, --, += and -= operators, especially in loops. The iinc instruction is the only one that operates directly on a value in the local variable array without moving the value onto the stack first.

For example, consider this for loop:

```
public void loop() {

    for (int i = 0; i < 20; i += 2) {

    }

}
```

With no optimization, Sun's javac 1.0.2 compiler compiles this to

```
public void loop() {

0    iconst_0
1    istore_1
2    goto
3    0
4    6
5    iinc
6    1
7    2
8    iload_1
9    bipush
10   20
11    if_icmplt
12   -1
13   -6
14    return

}
```

The zeroth instruction, iconst_0, pushes the int 0 onto the operand stack. The second instruction, istore_1, moves the int onto the top of the stack into local variable 1. Therefore, local variable 1 is now 0. The second instruction, goto, reads the next two bytes as a signed short telling how many bytes to jump over. Here, the value of the short is 6, so the goto jumps to instruction 8, iload_1. This instruction pushes the int in local variable 1 onto the stack. Next, instruction 9, bipush, pushes the value 20 onto the stack. Instruction 11 pops the top two values from the stack and checks to see whether the second value popped (the int that was one down in the stack) is less than the second value popped (the int that was on top of the stack). If it is, then the next two bytes are read as the signed short address of the instruction to which control should jump. In this case, control jumps back six bytes, that is, to instruction 11 - 6, which is instruction 5, iinc. The first byte after iinc is 1, and the second byte is 2, so

2 is added to local variable 1. Because local variable 1 was 0, it's now 2. Now we're back at instruction 7. Again, local variable 1 is pushed onto the stack, and the int constant 20 is pushed onto the stack. Once again they're compared, and control jumps back to instruction 5. Once again, local variable 1 is incremented by 2. It's now 4. This continues until local variable 1 reaches the value 20. At that point, the comparison fails, and control moves to statement 14, return.

The alternative way to compile this code, without the iinc instruction, takes many more instructions. You have to push extra values onto the stack, add them there, and then store the result back in local variable 1, like this:

```
    public void loop() {

    0    iconst_0
    1    istore_1
    2    goto 6
    5    iload_1
    6    iconst_2
    7    iadd
    8    istore_1
    9    iload_1
    10   bipush 20
    12    if_icmplt
    13   -1
    14   -7
    15    return


    }
```

With the iinc instruction, the for loop is one byte and three instructions shorter than it would be otherwise.

Conversion codes

You may have noticed that all the instructions discussed so far operate only on values of the same type. For example, there are instructions to add two ints, to add two floats, to add two longs, and to add two doubles. However, there is no instruction that adds an int to a double, a float to a double, a float to a long, or any other combination of primitive data types. At the level of the virtual machine, only values of the same type may be operated on or compared. Before a statement like "float f = 7.5 + 6;" can be compiled, the int value 6 must be promoted to a float.

There are 14 conversion instructions. They all look like i2l or f2d. The first letter is the type from which you convert. The last letter is the type to which you convert. Thus, i2l converts an int to a long, and f2d converts a float to a double. All conversions take place as specified in the *Java Language Specification* and in Chapter 2 of this book.

Each of these instructions pops the appropriate number of words from the stack (one for an int or a float and two for a long or a double) and pushes the converted value back onto the stack. The instructions are as follows:

i2l	int to long
i2f	int to float
i2d	int to double
l2i	long to int
l2f	long to float
l2d	long to double
f2i	float to int
f2l	float to long
f2d	float to double
d2i	double to int
d2l	double to long
d2f	double to float
i2b	int to byte
i2c	int to char
i2s	int to short

For example, the method here is compiled to the byte codes that follow:

```
public double convert() {

    int i = 6;
    double d = i;
    return d;

}
```

Note in particular instruction 6, where the int value 6 on top of the stack is promoted to the double value 6.0 before being stored in the local variable array. The other conversion instructions are used in exactly the same way.

```
public double convert() {

0    bipush 6
2    istore_1
3    iload_1
4    i2d
```

```
5    dstore_2
6    dload_2
7    dreturn

}
```

Comparison instructions

There are 17 comparison instructions. Java has the most direct support for comparisons on ints. There are five instructions that compare the int on the top of the stack to zero and branch accordingly. There are five more instructions that compare the top two ints on the stack and branch accordingly. There are five comparison instructions that compare the top two longs, floats, or doubles on the stack and push a 1 or 0 onto the stack, depending on the result. Finally, there are two instructions that compare references for equality and branch depending on the result.

In all cases where the result of a comparison is a branch, the two bytes immediately following the comparison instruction are a signed short giving the relative position in the code array to which it should branch. Positive values mean a jump forward. Negative values mean a jump backward. For example, consider this instruction:

```
12   if_icmplt
13   -1
14   -7
```

Here the top two ints on the stack are popped and compared. If the second word popped is less than the first word popped, then control branches back seven bytes before byte 12. If the second int popped is not less than the first int popped, then control moves forward to byte 15, the next instruction after if_icmplt.

Compare int to zero

Six instructions compare the int on the top of the stack to 0:

ifeq	branch if equal to zero
ifne	branch if not equal to zero
iflt	branch if less than 0
ifge	branch if greater than or equal to zero
ifgt	branch if greater than 0
ifle	branch if less than or equal to 0

The first two, ifeq and ifne, are used primarily to add a branch after a comparison between two longs, floats, or doubles. For example, consider the following method and its byte code equivalent:

```
public int compare() {

   double d1 = 5.6;
   double d2 = 7.8;
   if (d1 > d2) {
      return 3;
   }
    else {
      return 5;
    }


}

   public int compare() {

0    ldc2_w
1    0
2    6
3    dstore_1
4    ldc2_w
5    0
6    9
7    dstore_3
8    dload_1
9    dload_3
10   dcmpl
11   ifle
12   0
13   5
14   iconst_3
15   ireturn
16   iconst_5
17   ireturn

    }
```

The two doubles, 5.6 and 7.8, are compared with the dcmpl instruction in line 10. The result of that comparison, a 0 or a 1, is pushed onto the stack. Then instruction 11, ifle, pops the result off the stack. If it's less than or equal to zero, execution branches ahead five bytes to byte 16, and 5 is returned. Otherwise, control continues with instruction 14, and 3 is returned.

Comparing two values

Suppose that the top of the stack holds two int values, as shown in Figure 5-42. There are six instructions that pop these two ints and branch depending on how they compare.

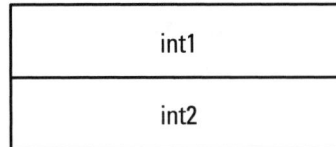

int1
int2

Figure 5-42
A stack with two int values.

if_icmpeq	branch if int1 equals int2
if_icmpne	branch if int1 does not equal int2
if_icmplt	branch if int2 is less than int1
if_icmpge	branch if int2 is greater than or equal to int1
if_icmpgt	branch if int2 greater than int1
if_icmple	branch if int2 less than or equal to int1

Comparisons between non-int data types aren't as common, so there are fewer instructions to handle all the different cases. Therefore, comparisons between non-int data types often take longer and result in larger code sizes.

There is exactly one instruction to compare two longs: lcmpl. It pops two longs from the stack. If the two longs are equal, lcmpl pushes zero back onto the stack. If they're not equal and the first long is greater than the second long popped, then -1 is pushed onto the stack. Finally, if the second long popped is greater than the first long popped, 1 is pushed onto the stack. Depending on the actual comparison that was made in the source code, one of the ifeq, ifne, ifgt, ifge, iflt, or ifle instructions would normally be used to test this value and decide whether to branch.

The fcmpl, fcmpg, dcmpl, and dcmpg instructions behave almost exactly the same as lcmpl except that they operate on floats and doubles. Each of these four instructions pops the top two values from the stack. If they're not equal and the first value popped is greater than the second value popped, then -1 is pushed onto the stack. Finally, if the second value popped is greater than the first value popped, 1 is pushed onto the stack.

However, they differ in what they do with NaN values. Recall that NaN is unordered. Any comparison with NaN must return false. If either value popped is NaN, then fcmpg and dcmpg push 1 onto the stack, and fcmpl and dcmpl push -1 onto the stack. These two variations are needed to handle NaN comparisons properly.

Reference comparisons

There are four comparison instructions that are used with reference data types. Greater than and less than comparisons make no sense for references, but you can compare references for equality. The if_acmpeq instruction branches if the two references on the top of the stack are equal. The if_acmpne instruction branches if they're not equal. The ifnull instruction branches if the reference popped from the top of the stack is null. The ifnonnull instruction branches if the reference popped from the top of the stack is not null. All four of these instructions read the next two bytes after the instruction as a signed short giving the relative offset to which they should branch.

Unconditional branching

There are five instructions that branch unconditionally. The instructions goto and goto_w are commonly used to compile while, for, and do-while loops. The instructions jsr, jsr_w, and ret are used to compile finally clauses. The goto and jsr instructions read the next two bytes in the code array as a signed short specifying the location to which it should branch. The goto_w and jsr_w use the next four bytes as a signed int specifying the locations to which they should branch. The jnr, jsr_w, and ret instructions are covered in the section on Exceptions later in this chapter.

Switching

Although a switch statement is logically equivalent to a sequence of if-else if-else if-...-else statements, Java provides special support to allow it to be executed more efficiently. The tableswitch instruction is used when the cases mostly cover a range of integers. For example:

```
switch (j) {
  case 0:
  case 1:
  case 2:
  case 3:
```

```
      case 5:
      default:
    }
```

The lookupswitch instruction is used when the cases are further apart. For example:

```
switch (j) {
  case 0:
  case -121:
  case 236:
  case 342:
  case 5:
  default:
}
```

Both the tableswitch and lookupswitch instructions are variable-length instructions. They are the only such instructions in the Java virtual machine. Each of these instructions is followed in the code array by some padding and a table of locations of instructions to which they should branch. This table is called a *jump table*. The two instructions differ in how the jump table is stored.

Each of these instructions requires that its table be aligned on a 4-byte boundary in the code array. In other words, the jump table always starts on byte 4, 8, 12, 16, 20, or some other multiple of four. Between zero and three null bytes are added as padding immediately following the switch instruction, to ensure that the jump table is 4-byte aligned.

tableswitch

Following the tableswitch instruction and the zero-to-three padding bytes are three 4-byte, signed int values. The first is called default; the second is called low; and the third is called high. After these three ints, there's a jump table of relative offsets. Each entry in the jump table is a signed, 4-byte int that is an address of an instruction to jump to relative to the tableswitch instruction. For example, if a jump table entry is 72 and the tableswitch is at instruction 17, then when that jump table entry is chosen, control jumps to instruction 72+17, which is instruction 89. There are always exactly high - low + 1 entries in the jump table. Because each jump table entry takes four bytes, the jump table is 4 * (high - low +1) bytes long.

The index of the jump table entry to jump to is popped from the stack. If this number is between low and high inclusive, then the appropriate jump table entry is read, and control moves to the instruction indicated by that jump table entry. Otherwise, the default value is added to the address of the tableswitch instruction, and control jumps to that location. For example, consider the tswitch method:

```
public int tswitch(int i) {

  int result = 0;

  switch (i) {
    case 0:
      result += 2;
    case 1:
      result += 3;
    case 2:
      result += 4;
    case 3:
      result += 6;
    case 5:
      result += 7;
    default:
  }

  return result;

}
```

Without optimization, tswitch() is compiled to the byte codes shown in Listing 5-3. The tableswitch instruction is byte 3. The next byte is byte 4, so no padding bytes are needed. Bytes 4 through 7 are the default value, in this case 52. Bytes 8 through 11 are the low value in the jump table, here 0. Bytes 12 through 15 are the high value in the jump table, here 5. Remember that the lowest value in the switch statement was 0 and the highest was 5. Therefore, there will be six entries in this jump table, entries 0 through 5.

The jump table itself is stored in bytes 16 through 39. This is not a large method or a large switch statement, so it's easy to read the different ints by just looking at the last byte in each 4-byte set. The jump table entries are 37, 40, 43, 46, 52, and 49 — in that order. Thus, if the int value 0 is popped from the stack, control jumps to 37+3, that is instruction 40, iinc. If the int value 1 is popped from the stack, control jumps to instruction 40+3 or 43, a different iinc instruction.

You may have noticed that the instructions for each jump are not disjointed. Once a jump takes place, all subsequent instructions are executed. That's because I left break statements out of the cases to simplify the code. If 0 is passed into this version of tswitch(), 2+3+4+6+7=22 is returned. I add break statements in the next section.

Listing 5-3

The compiled tswitch instruction

```
    public int tswitch(int) {

0    iconst_0
1    istore_2
2    iload_1
3    tableswitch
4    0
5    0
6    0
7    52
8    0
9    0
10   0
11   0
12   0
13   0
14   0
15   5
16   0
17   0
18   0
19   37
20   0
21   0
22   0
23   40
24   0
25   0
26   0
27   43
28   0
29   0
30   0
31   46
32   0
33   0
34   0
35   52
36   0
37   0
38   0
39   49
40   iinc
41   2
42   2
43   iinc
```

(continued)

Listing 5-3

The compiled tswitch instruction *(continued)*

```
44   2
45   3
46     iinc
47   2
48   4
49     iinc
50   2
51   6
52     iinc
53   2
54   7
55     iload_2
56     ireturn


     }
```

Control should never jump out of the current method, nor should the index that you use fall outside the jump table. Similarly, control should only jump to actual instructions, like iinc, not to data values like the 2 in byte 41. In general, the compiler should prevent this. If it does not, the classfile verifier should detect the problem and refuse to run the program.

lookupswitch

A tableswitch jump table can use a lot of extra space needlessly. Consider the lswitch() method:

```
public int lswitch(int i) {

  int j = 0;
  switch (i) {
    case 0:
       j+= 8;
    case -121:
       j -= 78;
    case 236:
       j /= 2;
    case 342:
       j *= 87;
    case 5:
       j -= 5;
    default:
  }
```

```
        return j;


    }
```

Because the lowest value is -121 and the highest value is 342, compiling this with tableswitch would produce a jump table (342 - -121 + 1)*4 or 1856 bytes long for only five cases. This clearly is inefficient. Instead, a match-offset table is used. Here's how it's set up.

Immediately following the padding bytes are four bytes that make up a signed int called default. This has the same meaning as it does for tableswitch; that is, if the value popped from the stack does not match any of the cases, then it should add this int to the address of the lookupswitch instruction and jump to the resulting address.

The four bytes after default are a signed int called npairs. This is the number of cases stored in the match-offset table and should be a positive number.

Each entry in the match-offset table is composed of two 4-byte ints. The first int is the value to be matched; the second int is the offset from the lookupswitch instruction to jump to. Thus, if npairs is 5, as in the above example, then there are 5*4*2=40 bytes in the match offset table. This saves 1,816 bytes compared with using a jump table, quite a substantial savings. The entries in the match-offset table are sorted by the values to match. They are not necessarily in the order in which they appear in the source code. The lswitch() method listed earlier compiles into the byte codes in Listing 5-4.

The lookup switch instruction falls on byte 3. Again, no padding is needed. The default value is in bytes 4 through 7 and is equal to 67. Therefore, when the default case is selected, control jumps to byte 70. Bytes 8 through 11 are the number of pairs, in this example 5-. The match-offset pairs themselves are in bytes 12 through 51. Notice that the first pair matches the value -121 (bytes 12 through 15) and jumps to instruction 55, 52 bytes after instruction 3 (bytes 16 through 19). The other four pairs are similar.

Notice also that the matches in the byte code have been ordered as -121, 0, 5, 236, 342, even though the source code placed them out of order as 0, -121, 236, 342, 5-. On the other hand, the actions they take are in the same order in which they appeared in the source code.

Listing 5-4
The lookupswitch

```
    public int lswitch(int) {

0    iconst_0
1    istore_2
```

(continued)

Listing 5-4
The lookupswitch *(continued)*

```
 2   iload_1
 3   lookupswitch
 4   0
 5   0
 6   0
 7   67
 8   0
 9   0
10   0
11   5
12   -1
13   -1
14   -1
15   -121
16   0
17   0
18   0
19   52
20   0
21   0
22   0
23   0
24   0
25   0
26   0
27   49
28   0
29   0
30   0
31   5
32   0
33   0
34   0
35   64
36   0
37   0
38   0
39   -20
40   0
41   0
42   0
43   55
44   0
45   0
46   1
```

(continued)

The lookupswitch *(continued)*

```
47  86
48  0
49  0
50  0
51  59
52   iinc
53  2
54  8
55   iinc
56  2
57  -78
58   iload_2
59   iconst_2
60   idiv
61   istore_2
62   iload_2
63   bipush
64  87
65   imul
66   istore_2
67   iinc
68  2
69  -5
70   iload_2
71   ireturn

    }
```

Objects

Until now, this chapter has considered methods as self-contained entities. However, in real programs, methods call other methods. They use fields in the object to which they belong and in other objects to which they possess references. They can create new objects and access the methods and fields of those objects. All of this can be accomplished with only nine new instructions.

In general, all of these instructions operate on or return a reference value. Recall that a reference is a 32-bit object identifier for an object.

All instance methods have a reference to the object to which they belong stored in the zeroth position of the local variable array. This enables them to call other methods and to refer to fields in their own object. Static methods do not belong to a particular object, so they do not have such a reference in their local variable array.

These instructions make frequent use of items in the constant pool. Keep in mind that items in the constant pool may themselves refer to other items in the constant pool.

Fields

The getfield instruction pops a reference from the stack. This reference is used as an index into the constant pool to get a FieldRef out of the pool. The FieldRef is used by the virtual machine to find the appropriate field and put its value on the stack.

For example, consider the simple class in Listing 5-5. It compiles to the byte codes shown in Listing 5-6.

Listing 5-5
FieldExample

```
public class FieldExample {

  int i;

  public int getField() {

    return i;

  }

  public void setField(int i) {

    this.i = i;

  }

}
```

Listing 5-6
FieldExample in byte code

```
public class FieldExample extends java.lang.Object  {

  int i;

  public int getField() {

0    aload_0
1    getfield
2    0
```

(continued)

FieldExample in byte code *(continued)*

```
3    4
4    ireturn

    }


    public void setField(int) {

0    aload_0
1    iload_1
2    putfield
3    0
4    4
5    return

    }


    public void <init>() {

0    aload_0
1    invokespecial
2    0
3    3
4    return

    }

}
```

The first instruction in both the getField() and setField() methods is
aload_0. This loads the reference from the zeroth local variable onto the
stack. In a non-static method, this is always a reference to the current object.

The next instruction in the getField() method is getfield. This pushes the
value of the fourth entry in the constant pool onto the stack. There's not
enough information here yet to tell what that entry is. I'll soon revise the
Disassembler class to make it more obvious exactly what that entry is. Then
the value is returned.

The setField() method also begins by pushing a reference to the current
object onto the stack with aload_0. Then the first argument to the method,
local variable 1, is pushed onto the stack. The putfield instruction pops this
value from the stack and puts it in the field referred to by constant pool
entry 4. Again, you don't know exactly what that field is from the byte code
alone. You also need to look at the constant pool.

Note

There's a third method in the byte code for the FieldExample class: public void <init>(). It's more than a little disconcerting because there was no <init> method in the source code. In fact, <init> isn't even a legal Java identifier because of the angle brackets.

<init> is a constructor. In .java byte code, all constructors are named <init> rather than the name of the class as in .java source code. Furthermore, all classes have at least one constructor, by default a constructor with no arguments, even if the source code does not. Constructors are discussed in more detail later in this chapter.

Static fields are similar except that the getstatic and putstatic instructions are used instead of getfield and putfield. The two bytes following the instruction are an index into the constant pool. That entry in the constant pool should contain a FieldRef structure. With getstatic, the value of that field is pushed onto the static. With putstatic, a value is popped from the stack and stored in that field.

Methods

There are four instructions in Java to call methods: invokevirtual, invokespecial, invokeinterface, and invokestatic. Invokevirtual is used for normal method calls. The invokeinterface instruction is used to call methods defined in interfaces. The invokestatic instruction is used to call static methods. Finally, the invokespecial instruction is used to call methods in the superclasses of the current object.

Although these instructions differ in the kinds of methods they invoke, they all behave similarly. Each reads the next two bytes in the code array as an index into the constant pool. That pool entry is a Methodref. The Methodref is inspected to find out what arguments the method takes. These are popped from the stack and placed in the local variable array of the invoked method. Then control moves to the invoked method. If the invoked method returns a value, that value is pushed onto the stack of the current method.

For example, consider the disassembly of the HelloWorld program in Listing 5-7. The main() method first gets the seventh static field from the constant pool. The seventh static field in the constant pool is another index into the constant pool, 4. The fourth entry in the constant pool is still another index into the constant pool, 28. Finally, the 28th entry in the constant pool is the static field you want, java.lang.System. A reference to this static object is placed on the operand stack.

Next, the ldc instruction pushes the first item in the constant pool onto the stack. The first item in the pool is a string, the UTF8 value of which is stored at position 29. Therefore, a new string object is created with the value at position 29 in the pool "Hello World!" A reference to this string is pushed onto the stack.

Now the invokevirtual instruction calls the method referenced by entry 6 in the constant pool. Entry 6 in the constant pool has ClassIndex 3 and NameAndTypeIndex 9. These are other entries in the constant pool. Entry 3 points to the UTF8 at entry 14, which is java/io/PrintStream. This tells you that a method of a java.io.PrintStream object is to be invoked. The NameAndTypeIndex points to entry 9. There you see a NameAndType entry with a NameIndex of 12 and a DescriptorIndex of 21. Entry 12 is println so the specific method being called is println(). Entry 21 is (Ljava/lang/String;)V, which tells you that the method takes a single string as an argument and returns void.

Listing 5-7
HelloWorld disassembled

```
import java.io.PrintStream;

class HelloWorld extends java.lang.Object  {

   public static void main(java.lang.String[]) {

0    getstatic
1    0
2    7
3    ldc
4    1
5    invokevirtual
6    0
7    6
8    return

   }


   public void <init>() {

0    aload_0
1    invokespecial
2    0
3    8
4    return

   }
```

(continued)

Listing 5-7
HelloWorld disassembled *(continued)*

```
    }

    /*
    1:   String              29
    2:   ClassInfo           30
    3:   ClassInfo           14
    4:   ClassInfo           28
    5:   ClassInfo           22
    6:   MethodRef           ClassIndex: 3;    NameAndTypeIndex: 9
    7:   FieldRef            ClassIndex: 4;    NameAndTypeIndex: 10
    8:   MethodRef           ClassIndex: 5;    NameAndTypeIndex: 11
    9:   NameAndType         NameIndex: 12;    DescriptorIndex: 21
    10:  NameAndType         NameIndex: 20;    DescriptorIndex: 27
    11:  NameAndType         NameIndex: 26;    DescriptorIndex: 31
    12:  UTF8                println
    13:  UTF8                ConstantValue
    14:  UTF8                java/io/PrintStream
    15:  UTF8                Exceptions
    16:  UTF8                LineNumberTable
    17:  UTF8                SourceFile
    18:  UTF8                LocalVariables
    19:  UTF8                Code
    20:  UTF8                out
    21:  UTF8                (Ljava/lang/String;)V
    22:  UTF8                java/lang/Object
    23:  UTF8                main
    24:  UTF8                HelloWorld.java
    25:  UTF8                ([Ljava/lang/String;)V
    26:  UTF8                <init>
    27:  UTF8                Ljava/io/PrintStream;
    28:  UTF8                java/lang/System
    29:  UTF8                Hello World!
    30:  UTF8                HelloWorld
    31:  UTF8                ()V

    */
```

The init method also uses an invoke instruction:, invokespecial. This invokes the method described by entry 8 in the constant pool. Entry 8 has a ClassIndex of five and a NameAndTypeIndex of 11. Looking at entry 5, you are referred to the UTF8 at entry 22, java/lang/Object. You are therefore invoking a method in java.lang.Object. Looking at entry 11, you're referred to the NameIndex at entry 26 and the DescriptorIndex at entry 31. Entry 26 is <init> and entry 31 is ()V. Therefore, the invokespecial instruction is invoking the noargs constructor from java.lang.Object. Remember that the first action of every constructor is to invoke a constructor for the superclass.

The invokestatic and invokeinterface instructions behave exactly the same way. The only difference is that invokestatic invokes static methods and invokeinterface invokes methods from interfaces.

Returning values from methods

Returning values from methods is straightforward. You can return an int, a float, a long, a double, a reference, or nothing at all. In byte code, the last line of each method will be one of the six return instructions. A value of the appropriate type is popped from the stack and pushed onto the top of the stack of the calling method. After that, all data for this method call is disposed of. The six return instructions are

ireturn	pop an int from the stack and return it
lreturn	pop a long from the stack and return it
freturn	pop a float from the stack and return it
dreturn	pop a double from the stack and return it
areturn	pop a reference from the stack and return it
return	return to the calling method but do not put any value on the stack

You've seen examples of these instructions at the end of every complete disassembled method in this chapter. Even if there's no return statement in the source code, the compiler inserts a generic return statement at the end of each method.

Creating new objects

Now that you know how to work with fields and methods in Java byte code, the only object instruction left is the creation of new objects. There is a single instruction to create new objects, the appropriately named new instruction. Listing 5-8 is a very simple class that does one thing: create a new java.lang.Integer object with the value 7.

Listing 5-8
Create a new object

```
class newTest {

    public void makeInteger() {
```

(continued)

Listing 5-8
Create a new object *(continued)*

```
    Integer i = new Integer(7);


    }


}
```

Listing 5-9 shows the byte code for this example. Notice the new instruction at byte 0 of the makeInteger() method. This is followed by the two bytes of a signed short with the value 3. If you guessed that this 3 is an index into the constant pool, you are correct.

Entry 3 in the constant pool is a ClassInfo structure that points to the UTF8 structure in entry 19 of the constant pool. That entry is java/lang/Integer, and it tells the new instruction to create a new object of type java.lang.Integer.

The new instruction only allocates space for the object in the virtual machine. It does not initialize it. The constructor still needs to be called. Bytes 3 and 4 push the argument for the constructor onto the stack. Bytes 5 through 7 invoke the constructor with the invokespecial instruction. Finally, byte 8 returns void.

Listing 5-9
Byte code for the new operator

```
class newTest extends java.lang.Object  {


    public void makeInteger() {

0    new
1    0
2    3
3    bipush
4    7
5    invokespecial
6    0
7    5
8    return


    }


    void <init>() {

0    aload_0
1    invokespecial
```

(continued)

Byte code for the new operator *(continued)*

```
2    0
3    4
4    return

    }

}

/*
1:   ClassInfo         20
2:   ClassInfo         22
3:   ClassInfo         19
4:   MethodRef         ClassIndex: 1;   NameAndTypeIndex: 7
5:   MethodRef         ClassIndex: 3;   NameAndTypeIndex: 6
6:   NameAndType       NameIndex: 21;   DescriptorIndex: 9
7:   NameAndType       NameIndex: 21;   DescriptorIndex: 24
8:   UTF8              this
9:   UTF8              (I)V
10:  UTF8              newTest.java
11:  UTF8              ConstantValue
12:  UTF8              LocalVariableTable
13:  UTF8              Exceptions
14:  UTF8              LineNumberTable
15:  UTF8              SourceFile
16:  UTF8              LocalVariables
17:  UTF8              Code
18:  UTF8              makeInteger
19:  UTF8              java/lang/Integer
20:  UTF8              java/lang/Object
21:  UTF8              <init>
22:  UTF8              newTest
23:  UTF8              LnewTest;
24:  UTF8              ()V

*/
```

Arrays

In Java, arrays are objects and array variables are references. However, there are four byte codes that operate specifically on arrays. The newarray instruction allocates new arrays of primitive types such as int and double. The anewarray instruction allocates new arrays of references. The multianewarray instruction allocates multidimensional arrays of any type.

The arraylength instruction returns the length of an array. The iaload, laload, faload, daload, aaload, baload, caload, and saload instructions copy values from an array onto a stack. The iastore, lastore, fastore, dastore, aastore, bastore, castore, and satore instructions pop values from the stack and put them in an array.

Creating arrays

When you write a statement like

```
int[] e = new int[7];
```

Java must allocate the right amount of space in the heap for an array of seven ints. To do this, it first pushes the value 7 onto the stack. Then it uses the newarray instruction to actually allocate the space. The number of ints to allocate is popped from the stack. The type of the array to allocate is read from the next byte in the code array. An int array is type 11. A reference to the array is pushed onto the stack. This reference is then popped from the stack and copied into whichever position e occupies in the local variable array. Thus, the byte code would look something like this:

```
bipush
7
newarray
11
astore_1
```

The newarray instruction knows the sizes of the different types it can hold and allocates the appropriate amount of space.

Table 5-3

Type codes for arrays

Code	Type
4	boolean
5	char
6	float
7	double
8	byte
9	short
10	int
11	long

Arrays are one of the few areas in Java in which all primitive data types are supported equally. Short arrays really are arrays of shorts and not just a subset of ints. Although the difference in storage requirements between a single short variable and a single int variable is trivial on modern computers, the difference between a large array of shorts and a large array of ints can still be significant.

anewarray

Arrays of objects are really arrays of references. The type of such an array is given as a 2-byte index into the constant pool that follows the anewarray instruction. Like the newarray instruction, the length of the array is popped from the stack, and a reference to the new array is pushed onto the stack. Thus,

```
Integer[] e = new Integer[7];
```

might compile to something like this:

```
0    bipush
1    7
2    anewarray
3    0
4    3
5    astore_1
...
/* Constant Pool
1:   ClassInfo         21
2:   ClassInfo         23
3:   ClassInfo         20
...
20:  UTF8              java/lang/Integer
...
```

The difference between newarray and anewarray is that newarray encodes the type of the data directly into the code array, whereas anewarray needs to refer to the constant pool.

multianewarray

The multianewarray instruction creates multidimensional arrays of both primitive and reference types. The multianewarray instruction is similar to the anewarray instruction. The type of the array is read from the constant pool. The index into the constant pool is a 2-byte short that immediately follows the multianewarray instruction. Following this is an unsigned byte that contains the number of dimensions in the array.

Multidimensional arrays of primitive types such as int or double are listed in the constant pool as a series of left brackets, one for each dimension, followed by a letter for the type. Thus, a two-dimensional array of ints (int[][]) is listed as [[I, and a three-dimensional array of doubles (double[][][]) is listed as [[[D. Table 5-4 lists the abbreviations for the different primitive data types.

Table 5-4
Abbreviations for the primitive data types used in the constant pool

Abbreviation	Type
B	byte
C	char
D	double
F	float
I	int
J	long
S	short
Z	boolean

A line of code like this

```
int[][] i = new int[7][6];
```

might be compiled like this:

```
...
0   bipush
1   7
2   bipush
3   6
4   multianewarray
5   0
6   3
7   2
8   astore_1
...
/* Constant Pool
1:  ClassInfo        16
2:  ClassInfo        19
3:  ClassInfo        17
...
17:  UTF8            [[I
...
```

Accessing components of arrays

It's not enough just to create arrays. You also have to be able to put values in the arrays (storing) and get values out of the arrays (loading).

Loading

There are eight instructions to copy values from an array onto the operand stack, one for each primitive data type except boolean and one for reference types. These instructions operate purely on the stack. Each pops the index of the component to load from the array and a reference to the array from the stack. Then, the component at that index in the array is pushed onto the stack. Figure 5-43 demonstrates with the iaload instruction:

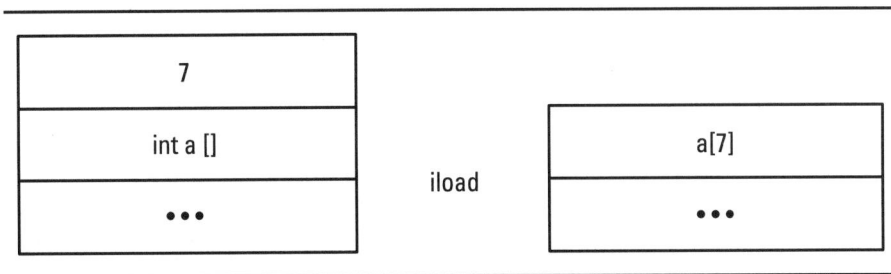

Figure 5-43
The stack before and after an iaload instruction.

The aaload, saload, caload, and faload instructions behave identically, except that they operate on arrays of type reference, short, char, and float, respectively, and push those types onto the stack. As usual, shorts and chars are zero-extended to ints before being pushed onto the stack. The baload instruction does double duty for loading both bytes and booleans. The result is sign-extended to an int. Otherwise, baload behaves exactly like iaload.

The daload and laload instructions copy doubles and longs from an array onto the stack. Of course, each requires two words on the stack for the result. Figure 5-44 demonstrates with the daload instruction.

Storing

There are eight instructions to pop values from the operand stack and store them in an array, one for each primitive data type except boolean and one for reference types. These instructions operate purely on the stack. Each pops three values from the stack, the value to be placed in the array, the index at which to place it, and a reference to the array in that order. Nothing is pushed back onto the stack. Then the value is stored in at that index in the array. Figure 5-45 demonstrates with the iastore instruction.

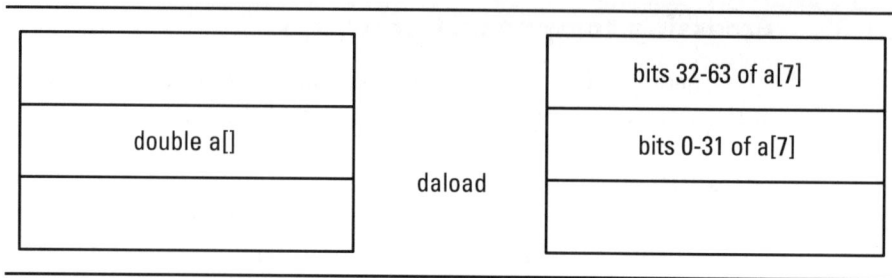

		bits 32-63 of a[7]
double a[]	daload	bits 0-31 of a[7]

Figure 5-44
The stack before and after a daload instruction.

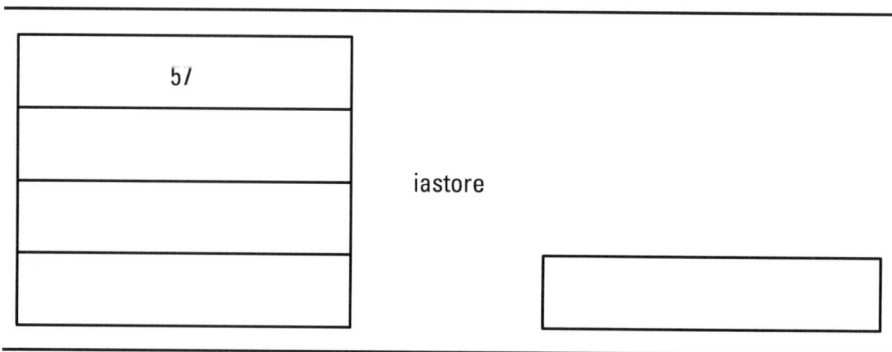

57
iastore

Figure 5-45
a[7] = 57.

The aastore and fastore instructions behave identically, except that they operate on arrays of type reference and float respectively and pop those types onto the stack.

The sastore and castore instructions pop a 4-byte int from the stack, lop off the high-order two bytes, and store the result in the referenced array. As long as the value actually fits in a short or a char, this is transparent and works exactly as does the iastore instruction. However, as discussed in Chapter 2, you encounter problems with int values above 32,767 or below -32,768.

The bastore instruction stores both bytes and booleans. It pops a 4-byte int, an index, and a reference to an array from the stack, truncates the int to 1-byte, and stores the truncated result at the indexed position in the referenced array.

The dastore and lastore pop doubles and longs from the stack and store them in an array. These instructions pop four words from the stack: the low-order four bytes of the value, the high-order four bytes of the value, the index into the array, and a reference to an array. Figure 5-46 demonstrates with the lastore instruction.

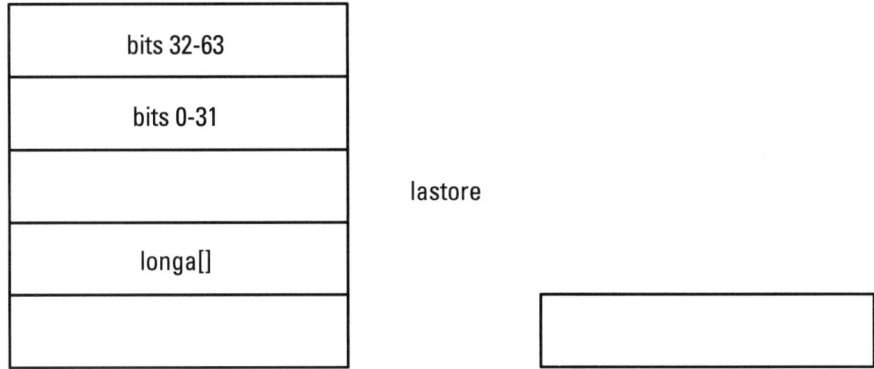

| bits 32-63 |
| bits 0-31 |
| |
| longa[] |
| |

lastore

Figure 5-46
The stack before and after a lastore instruction.

arraylength

The arraylength instruction pops a reference to an array from the stack, checks the length of the array, and pushes the result back onto the stack. This instruction is used when you access the length "member" of an array. For example, it's common to loop through all the command line arguments to main like this:

```
public static void main(String[] args) {

    for (int j = 0; j < args.length; j++) {
      // do something with each argument
    }
}
```

The length of the args array is taken by pushing a reference to args onto the stack, executing the arraylength instruction, and then popping the result. Here's the byte code:

```
public static void main(java.lang.String[]) {

0   iconst_0
1   istore_1
2   goto
```

```
3    0
4    6
5    iinc
6    1
7    1
8    iload_1
9    aload_0
10   arraylength
11   if_icmplt
12   -1
13   -6
14   return


     }
```

Because main() is a static method, the zeroth component of the local variable array is the first argument to the method, not a reference to the current object. In other words, it's a reference to the args array. Thus, byte 9 — aload_0 — pushes a reference to args onto the operand stack. Byte 10 — arraylength — pops that reference from the stack and pushes the length of the array onto the stack.

Exceptions

Exceptions are implemented mostly through the opcodes that you've already encountered, such as new, astore, and goto. The one new opcode that you need to throw exceptions is athrow. The opcode athrow pops a reference to a Throwable object (an instance of a subclass of java.lang.Error or java.lang.Exception) from the stack and then searches the current frame for the nearest catch clause that catches that type of Throwable.

If a catch clause is found that catches this exception, then control moves into the catch clause and program execution resumes there. If, on the other hand, no catch clause is found that can handle this type of exception or error, then the current thread terminates.

Catch clauses do not require any special opcodes. They are just different areas of the byte code for a method. The ExceptionsTable attribute for a method stores the addresses of the catch clauses that handle different classes of exceptions.

The finally clauses do require some extra instructions, however. The jsr and jsr_w instructions move flow control from one place in the byte code into the finally clause. The finally clause is terminated with a ret instruction that moves flow control back. Thus, multiple try and catch clauses can all share one finally clause, and the code does not need to be duplicated.

Consider Listing 5-10. This program exercises nearly all of Java's exception mechanisms. In the catchException() method, a runtime exception is thrown and caught without an explicit throw statement. In throwRuntimeException, a RuntimeException is constructed and thrown with a throw statement. In throwCheckedException(), a checked exception is declared in a throws clause and thrown by a throw statement. Last, finallyTest() catches the exception thrown by throwCheckedException() and uses a finally clause. Look at how these compile to byte codes.

Listing 5-10
The ExceptionTest program

```
class ExceptionTest {

  public static void main(String[] args) {

    ExceptionTest et = new ExceptionTest();
    et.catchException();
    et.finallyTest();

  }

  void catchException() {

    int[] a = new int[5];
    try {
      a[5] = 7;
    }
    catch (ArrayIndexOutOfBoundsException e) {
      System.err.println(e);
    }

  }


  void throwRuntimeException() {

    throw new NullPointerException("This is a test");

  }

  void throwCheckedException() throws InterruptedException {

    throw new InterruptedException("This is a test");

  }
```

(continued)

Listing 5-10
The ExceptionTest program *(continued)*

```
The ExceptionTest program

  void finallyTest() {

    try {
      throwCheckedException();
    }
    catch (Exception e) {
      System.err.println(e);
    }
    finally {
      System.out.println("All done!");
    }

  }

}
```

Listing 5-11 has the compiled (but disassembled) byte code form of this program.

Listing 5-11
ExceptionTest disassembled

```
import java.io.PrintStream;

class ExceptionTest extends java.lang.Object  {


  public static void main(java.lang.String[]) {

0     new 10
3     dup
4     invokespecial 12
7     astore_1
8     aload_1
9     invokevirtual 16
12    aload_1
13    invokevirtual 15
16    return

  }


  void catchException() {
```

(continued)

ExceptionTest disassembled *(continued)*

```
0     iconst_5
1     newarray 10
3     astore_1
4     aload_1
5     iconst_5
6     bipush 7
8     iastore
9     return
10    astore_2
11    getstatic 17
14    aload_2
15    invokevirtual 20
18    return

    }


   void throwRuntimeException() {

0     new 5
3     dup
4     ldc 1
6     invokespecial 21
9     athrow

    }


   void throwCheckedException() throws java.lang.InterruptedException {

0     new 7
3     dup
4     ldc 1
6     invokespecial 14
9     athrow

    }

   void finallyTest() {

0     aload_0
1     invokevirtual 13
4     goto 14
7     astore_3
8     getstatic 17
11    aload_3
```

(continued)

Listing 5-11
ExceptionTest disassembled *(continued)*

```
12    invokevirtual 20
15    goto 3
18    jsr 10
21    return
22    astore_1
23    jsr 5
26    aload_1
27    athrow
28    astore_2
29    getstatic 18
32    ldc 2
34    invokevirtual 19
37    ret 2

    }


    void <init>() {

0     aload_0
1     invokespecial 11
4     return


    }


}


/*
1:   String          37
2:   String          63
3:   ClassInfo       67
4:   ClassInfo       58
5:   ClassInfo       42
6:   ClassInfo       43
7:   ClassInfo       66
8:   ClassInfo       62
9:   ClassInfo       52
10:  ClassInfo       57
11:  MethodRef       ClassIndex: 9;  NameAndTypeIndex: 28
12:  MethodRef       ClassIndex: 10; NameAndTypeIndex: 28
13:  MethodRef       ClassIndex: 10; NameAndTypeIndex: 26
14:  MethodRef       ClassIndex: 7;  NameAndTypeIndex: 23
15:  MethodRef       ClassIndex: 10; NameAndTypeIndex: 22
16:  MethodRef       ClassIndex: 10; NameAndTypeIndex: 27
17:  FieldRef        ClassIndex: 8;  NameAndTypeIndex: 30
18:  FieldRef        ClassIndex: 8;  NameAndTypeIndex: 29
```

(continued)

ExceptionTest disassembled *(continued)*

19:	MethodRef	ClassIndex: 6;	NameAndTypeIndex: 25
20:	MethodRef	ClassIndex: 6;	NameAndTypeIndex: 24
21:	MethodRef	ClassIndex: 5;	NameAndTypeIndex: 23
22:	NameAndType	NameIndex: 36;	DescriptorIndex: 69
23:	NameAndType	NameIndex: 60;	DescriptorIndex: 51
24:	NameAndType	NameIndex: 31;	DescriptorIndex: 38
25:	NameAndType	NameIndex: 31;	DescriptorIndex: 51
26:	NameAndType	NameIndex: 33;	DescriptorIndex: 69
27:	NameAndType	NameIndex: 53;	DescriptorIndex: 69
28:	NameAndType	NameIndex: 60;	DescriptorIndex: 69
29:	NameAndType	NameIndex: 50;	DescriptorIndex: 61
30:	NameAndType	NameIndex: 39;	DescriptorIndex: 61
31:	UTF8	println	
32:	UTF8	this	
33:	UTF8	throwCheckedException	
34:	UTF8	Ljava/lang/ArrayIndexOutOfBoundsException;	
35:	UTF8	a	
36:	UTF8	finallyTest	
37:	UTF8	This is a test	
38:	UTF8	(Ljava/lang/Object;)V	
39:	UTF8	err	
40:	UTF8	ConstantValue	
41:	UTF8	LocalVariableTable	
42:	UTF8	java/lang/NullPointerException	
43:	UTF8	java/io/PrintStream	
44:	UTF8	Exceptions	
45:	UTF8	LineNumberTable	
46:	UTF8	SourceFile	
47:	UTF8	LocalVariables	
48:	UTF8	Code	
49:	UTF8	throwRuntimeException	
50:	UTF8	out	
51:	UTF8	(Ljava/lang/String;)V	
52:	UTF8	java/lang/Object	
53:	UTF8	catchException	
54:	UTF8	ExceptionTest.java	
55:	UTF8	main	
56:	UTF8	Ljava/lang/Exception;	
57:	UTF8	ExceptionTest	
58:	UTF8	java/lang/ArrayIndexOutOfBoundsException	
59:	UTF8	([Ljava/lang/String;)V	
60:	UTF8	<init>	
61:	UTF8	Ljava/io/PrintStream;	
62:	UTF8	java/lang/System	
63:	UTF8	All done!	
64:	UTF8	et	

(continued)

Listing 5-11
ExceptionTest disassembled *(continued)*

```
65:   UTF8              LExceptionTest;
66:   UTF8              java/lang/InterruptedException
67:   UTF8              java/lang/Exception
68:   UTF8              [I
69:   UTF8              ()V
70:   UTF8              args
71:   UTF8              [Ljava/lang/String;
72:   UTF8              e


*/
```

There's only one new opcode in any of these: athrow. Exception handling is implemented mostly with a series of goto instructions. For example, look at the catchException() method:

```
        void catchException() {

    0   iconst_5
    1   newarray 10
    3   astore_1
    4   aload_1
    5   iconst_5
    6   bipush 7
    8   iastore
    9   return
    10  astore_2
    11  getstatic 17
    14  aload_2
    15  invokevirtual 20
    18  return


        }
```

The catch clause is not actually included in the byte code as such. One block of code from instruction 0 through instruction 9 handles the normal form of execution. It's terminated with the return opcode in instruction 9. Then the catch clause is included in instruction 10 through instruction 15. The ExceptionsTable for a method tells the virtual machine which sets of instructions handle which exceptions.

The throwCheckedException() and throwRuntimeException() methods are very similar and quite simple. In essence, each just creates a new Exception object on the stack using standard constructors. Then, when the exception is on top of the stack, ready to go, the athrow instruction actually throws it. When the program runs, the virtual machine will see this exception and will work its way up the call chain looking for the nearest catch clause that can handle the exception. If it doesn't find one, it shuts down the thread that threw the exception.

```
    void finallyTest() {

0     aload_0
1     invokevirtual 13
4     goto 14
7     astore_3
8     getstatic 17
11    aload_3
12    invokevirtual 20
15    goto 3
18    jsr 10
21    return
22    astore_1
23    jsr 5
26    aload_1
27    athrow
28    astore_2
29    getstatic 18
32    ldc 2
34    invokevirtual 19
37    ret 2


    }
```

The finallyTest() method demonstrates one more instruction, jsr. The jsr opcode ensures that the code in a finally clause is executed. You should notice that there are two jsr instructions: one in line 18 and one in line 23. The jsr at line 18 jumps 10 places ahead to line 28. The jsr at line 23 jumps five places ahead, also to line 28. They're both executing the same finally clause, one from inside the main body of the code and one from inside the catch clause. The ret instruction in line 37 causes control to return to the point in the method where it started. It is *not* the same as the return instruction that exits the method.

Type checking

Two opcodes check the types of values operated on. The opcode instanceof implements the instanceof operator and compares the types of two references on the stack, whereas checkcast checks to see whether a cast between two types is permitted.

instanceof

The instanceof instruction is used to compile the instanceof operator. It determines whether a particular object is an instance of a specified class. A reference to the object is popped from the stack. The two bytes after the instanceof instruction in the code array are an index into the constant pool where a ClassInfo structure will be found. If the object is a non-null instance of the class, then the int value 1 is pushed onto the stack. Otherwise, 0 is pushed onto the stack. Whether an object is an instance of a class is determined exactly as it is for the instanceof operator in .java source code.

checkcast

The checkcast instruction pops a reference from the stack and compares that object to a ClassInfo structure in the constant pool. The index to the ClassInfo structure in the constant pool is read from the two bytes in the code array immediately following the checkcast instruction. If the object can be cast to the given type, then the reference to it is pushed back onto the stack. There is thus no net change in the stack. However, if the object may not be cast to the specified type, then a ClassCastException is thrown. The rules for determining whether to push back the reference or throw an exception are the same as the rules given in the *Java Language Specification* for determining whether a cast is permitted.

The checkcast instruction behaves very much like the instanceof instruction. The two differences are what each instruction does to the stack and the treatment of null. Instanceof puts an int onto the stack. Checkcast puts a reference onto the stack or throws a ClassCastException. Null is not an instance of any type, but it may be cast to any type.

Threads: monitorenter and monitorexit

Most of Java's thread support is either in the class libraries or in other parts of the virtual machine. The only part that requires direct byte code support is synchronization. There are two instructions that allow a thread to place and release locks on objects. These are monitorenter and monitorexit.

Each object is associated with a unique monitor. When a thread executes the monitorenter instruction, it pops a reference to an object from the stack and tries to take possession of the monitor for that object. If some other thread already possesses that monitor, then this thread stops and waits for the monitor to be released. To release a monitor, a thread uses the monitorexit instruction. A reference to the object whose monitor is to be released is popped from the stack.

DECOMPILERS AND OTHER TOOLS

With the tools developed in the last few chapters, you should be able to make sense out of almost any Java .class file you come across. This is an immensely useful debugging skill, especially when you're using third-party software for which you do not have source code. If you're uncertain whether a bug is in your code, in the vendor's code, or in your understanding of what the vendor's library does, you can disassemble the relevant files and find out. However, some readers may wonder if it's possible to go one step further. Can you move from a .class file to actual .java source code?

In general the answer is no, you cannot. Some information that is contained in .java source files, notably the names of local variables and comments, is simply not present anywhere in a .class file. Nonetheless, it's often possible to fill in the blanks and recognize certain common patterns. Throughout this chapter, you've seen how different constructs tend to compile. For example, when you see a tableswitch or lookupswitch statement in disassembled byte code, you know that there's a switch statement in the source code. With experience and practice, it's not very hard to manually rewrite disassembled byte code as .java source code. If you don't understand a particular method, it's often helpful to start rewriting it as .java source code. What the method is doing will often become apparent as you translate it.

Algorithmically converting byte codes to source code is more difficult. There is at least one free tool to help you though. HanPeter van Vliet's Mocha is a free decompiler for Java. It can normally back out .java source code from most .class files. At least in the version that was available at the time I was writing this, Mocha does choke on some files. In those cases, you have to drop back to disassembly.

Unfortunately, as this book was going to press, the Mocha Web page disappeared from the Net. Unconfirmed Usenet gossip has it that HanPeter van Vliet died of cancer in late 1996. At this point, the future of Mocha is uncertain, but more unconfirmed Usenet gossip says that it may reappear as part of an unreleased Borland product. Several other people have placed Mocha on their Web sites, but I'm hesitant to include URLs that seem to change monthly in a book that takes longer than that just to get from warehouse to bookstore. I suggest doing a search on "Mocha" and "HanPeter van Vliet" at your favorite Web search engine to try to track it down.

Mocha is quite simple to use. Just type **java Mocha.decompiler** *filename*.**class** on the command line. Mocha then analyzes the file and puts its best guess as to the source code in a file called *filename*.mocha. For example:

```
% java mocha.Decompiler HelloWorld.class
```

Here's the result when Mocha was used to decompile the HelloWorld program:

```
/* Decompiled by Mocha from HelloWorld.class */
/* Originally compiled from HelloWorld.java */

import java.io.PrintStream;

class HelloWorld
{
    public static void main(String astring[])
    {
        System.out.println("Hello World!");
    }

    public HelloWorld()
    {
    }
}
%
```

There are several differences between the original .java source code and the decompiled version:

- The HelloWorld() constructor is included in the decompiled program because it was in the byte code. It wasn't in the original source code.

- Mocha did not find the name of the String array that was passed into the main method. It was args[] in the source code but simply astring[] here.

- The white space is different. In fact, Mocha often does a better job of uniformly and consistently inserting white space than manual placement or many fancy source code editors. More than one programmer has been surprised to see that Mocha outputs cleaner code than he or she originally wrote!

Although Mocha was the first Java decompiler and is still the best known, several other companies have developed Java decompilers of varying degrees of usefulness. A research scientist at IBM published a technical report on decompiling Java, and he may have developed a working decompiler. However, IBM reclassified the report before I was able to get a copy of it.

Wingsoft, `http://www.wingsoft.com/`, is a startup company that released a payware Java decompiler called WingDis as this book was going to press. Initial testing indicates that WingDis is about as reliable as Mocha. However, both Mocha and WingDis have problems with switch statements, complicated loops, and try-catch-finally blocks. WingDis is included on the CD.

SUMMARY

This rather long chapter explore the meaning of more than 200 different opcodes in Java. It also completed the disassembly project that began in Chapter 4. Among other things you learn:

- Opcodes, also known as byte codes, each have exactly one mnemonic constant to represent them. However, these mnemonic constants are conveniences for disassemblers. Java uses only the raw numbers.

- Most opcodes come in multiple flavors that handle different data types. Thus, although there are a little over 200 opcodes, many of them are simple variations of each other. Therefore, you really need to know only about 60 of them.

- With a few exceptions, opcodes take values from the byte codes following the opcode in the file and/or from the stack. All values are returned to the stack. The byte codes never change while a program is running.

- The load opcodes move values from the local variable array to the stack. The store opcodes move values from the stack to the local variable array.

In the next chapter, I back off from this extremely low-level approach and start to investigate threading and garbage collection. You learn about the different ways that these technologies can be implemented, learn how to determine in which fashion they are implemented on a particular platform, and learn how to test new platforms.

The Sun Classes

THREADS AND GARBAGE COLLECTION

6

*J*ava specifies more details about its environment than most programming languages do. For example, the lengths of all numeric data types are precisely defined. A floating-point addition cannot round up on one platform and down on another. Most of the time, you can assume that a Java program with no deliberately random elements will produce the same output given the same input on two different virtual machines on two different platforms. When that is not the case, it normally indicates a bug in one or both of the runtime environments.

There are three major exceptions to this rule. The first is that the AWT.GUI interfaces produced by Java are intentionally different on different platforms. Java programs are supposed to take on the look-and-feel of the native system rather than providing a unique Java look-and-feel. In a higher sense, Java programs have a meta-consistency in that every program has the look of its native host. This will not concern us here.

The other two areas where differences in Java runtimes can produce different results depending on implementation are thread models and garbage collection. Although the *Java Language Specification* and the *Java Virtual Machine* Specification between them leave little unspecified, they do not explicitly specify many important characteristics of the threading model and the garbage collection algorithm. Any algorithms that adhere to Java's defined semantics and syntax are permissible. Indeed, different virtual machines have made different choices for some of these possible algorithms. This chapter explores those choices.

THREADS

When writing a virtual machine, there are a number of decisions that you must make based on the capabilities of both the host platform and the programmer writing the VM. Some operating systems, such as Solaris, Windows NT, and the BeOS, provide native support for multithreading. Other platforms, like the Mac, offer it as an optional add-on. Still others, such as Windows 3.1, do not support any form of threading.

The first decision that an implementer must make is whether to use native threads, if available, or to create his or her own thread model. Native threads have the advantage of speed and scaling across multiple processors on a multiprocessing machine. However, a non-native thread package has the advantage of portability, applicability to platforms like Windows 3.1 that do not support threads at all, and, perhaps surprisingly, being easier to code.

The second decision that an implementer must make about the thread model is whether to use cooperative or preemptive threading for threads of equal priority. In cooperative models, once a thread gets control, it continues to run until it explicitly relinquishes control or it blocks. In a preemptive model, the virtual machine can step in and hand control from one thread to another at any time. Both models have their advantages and disadvantages.

Java threads are always preemptive between priorities. A higher priority thread always takes precedence over a lower priority thread. If a higher priority thread goes to sleep or blocks, then a lower priority thread can run. However, as soon as the higher priority thread wakes up or unblocks, it interrupts the lower priority thread and runs until it finishes, until it blocks again, or until it is preempted by an even higher priority thread. This is how all conforming implementations of Java must behave.

However, nothing in the Java Language Specification specifies what is supposed to happen with equal priority threads. On some systems, these threads are time-sliced, and the runtime allots a certain amount of time to a thread. When that time is up, the runtime preempts the running thread and switches to the next thread with the same priority. On other systems, a running thread is not preempted in favor of a thread with the same priority. It continues to run until it blocks, explicitly yields control, or is preempted by a higher priority thread.

These two decisions are not independent. For example, if you choose to implement native threads on the PowerMac, the threads must be cooperative because that's what threads are on the PowerMac. On the other hand, native threads on the 680X0 Macs are preemptive, so Java threads implemented through the Mac's ThreadManager on 680X0 Macs must be preemptive, too.

Cooperative versus preemptive threads

Consider Listing 6-1. This program starts two threads, each of which counts to two billion using the instance variable myCounter. Both threads have the default priority (Thread.NORM_PRIORITY, 5). The ThreadTest class also has a static variable called classCounter that stays in lockstep with myCounter as long as only a single thread is running. However, if multiple ThreadTest objects both try to change that variable, it will get out of sync with at least one of them.

The run() method never explicitly yields control to any other threads. On a cooperative system, it runs until completion. Therefore, desynchronization between classCounter and myCounter can occur only on a preemptive system. The run() method checks for desynchronization and, if it finds it, sets the class variable preemptive to true, prints a message to that effect, and returns. On the other hand, if the run() method completes two billion iterations without being preempted, it assumes that the threading is cooperative and prints a message to that effect on System.out.

Listing 6-1
The ThreadTest class

```
public class ThreadTest extends Thread {

  int myCounter = 0 ;
  static int classCounter = 0;
  static boolean preemptive = false;

  public static void main(String[] args) {

    ThreadTest t1 = new ThreadTest();
    ThreadTest t2 = new ThreadTest();
    t1.start();
    t2.start();

  }
```

(continued)

Listing 6-1
The ThreadTest class *(continued)*

```
public void run() {

  classCounter = myCounter;
  while (myCounter < 2000000) {
    if (classCounter != myCounter) {
      preemptive = true;
      System.out.println("Threads are preemptive\n" +
        "classCounter: " + classCounter + "\n" +
        "myCounter: " + myCounter);
      return;
    }
    classCounter = ++myCounter;
  }
  if (!preemptive) System.out.println("Threads are cooperative");

  }

}
```

I ran this program on a number of different virtual machines. The results appear in Table 6-1.

Table 6-1
Threading model in different virtual machines

Secret

Virtual machine	Thread model
Roaster DR 2.3	preemptive
Sun Mac JDK 1.0.2	preemptive
Metrowerks Code Warrior 9-11	preemptive
Microsoft Internet Explorer Mac	preemptive
Netscape Navigator 3.0 Mac	preemptive
Sun Solaris JDK 1.0.2	cooperative
Sun Solaris JDK 1.1	cooperative
Sun Windows95/NT JDK 1.0.2	preemptive
Sun Windows95/NT JDK 1.1	preemptive
Macintosh Runtime for Java	preemptive

Cooperating

Because you cannot be sure whether you will be working with a cooperative or preemptive model, it is important not to assume that preemption is available. CPU-intensive threads should yield control at periodic intervals. There are four different ways that a thread can give up control and allow other threads to run. The thread can

- block
- call Thread.yield()
- go to sleep
- be suspended

Blocking occurs when a thread has to wait for an operation to complete. Most commonly, this is an I/O operation, particularly one involving a network connection. It is also possible for a call to block while waiting for user input. Placing I/O and user input in separate, high priority threads is often a good idea because it allows the program to use the computer more efficiently. Other CPU-intensive threads can get a lot of work done while waiting for data to come in over the network or for the user to type a character or two.

When a program calls Thread.yield(), it is signifying that the current thread, the one that called Thread.yield(), is willing to step aside in favor of another thread. The VM looks to see if any other threads of the same priority are ready to run. If any are the same priority, it pauses the currently executing thread and passes control to the next thread in line. If no other threads of the same or higher priority are ready to run, control returns to the thread that yielded. Thus, Thread.yield() only signals a willingness to give up control. It does not guarantee that the thread will actually stop. That depends completely on what other threads exist and what their statuses are.

```
public static void yield()
```

If a thread definitely wants to give up control for a period of time, whether or not there are any other threads of equal or higher priority ready to run, then it can call sleep(). The sleep() methods put a thread to sleep for a certain amount of time, during which even lower priority threads have an opportunity to run.

```
public static void sleep(long milliseconds) throws InterruptedException
public static void sleep(long milliseconds, int nanoseconds) throws
InterruptedException
```

Finally, a thread can be suspended. When a thread calls suspend() or more commonly, when a different thread invokes the thread's suspend() method, it is paused indefinitely until some other thread starts it running again by invoking its resume() method:

```
public final void suspend()
public final void resume()
```

Forcing preemption

It is possible to build your own preemptive thread scheduler that works in all virtual machines. Recall that threads of different priorities are scheduled preemptively. A higher priority thread will always preempt a lower priority thread. Only the behavior of threads of equal priorities is uncertain. Therefore, it is possible to write a higher priority thread scheduler that slices time for lower priority threads.

This is simpler than it sounds. The higher priority thread scheduler does not need to explicitly track or communicate with lower priority threads to allot them time. When faced with a choice of which thread to run, Java selects the highest priority, non-blocked, non-sleeping thread that has not run for the longest time. For example, suppose you have three threads with normal priority, n1, n2, and n3. Then suppose there is a thread scheduler thread with higher priority, ts. Now suppose they're started in this order with these priorities:

```
ts.setPriority(6);
n1.setPriority(5);
n2.setPriority(5);
n3.setPriority(5);
ts.start();
n1.start();
n2.start();
n3.start();
```

The thread ts starts and almost immediately goes to sleep. By sleeping, it explicitly yields control. The runtime then looks for the next highest priority thread to run. There are three from which to choose: n1, n2, and n3. Which one the runtime chooses is unpredictable. It may be n1, but it may be n2 or n3. Without loss of generality, suppose n1 is the first one to start. On a cooperative system, it is going to run until it finishes, it blocks, it yields control, or it is preempted. Threads n2 and n3 cannot preempt n1 on a cooperative system. Their priorities are the same. However, the ts thread can preempt n1 because it has a higher priority: 6 instead of 5.

Assume that while n1 is running, ts wakes up. Because ts has a higher priority than n1, the VM hands control to ts. Now suppose ts goes right back to sleep. The VM again has to choose between the available threads of lower priority. However, the VM knows that n1 has already had some time, so it will not pick n1. Instead, it will pick n2 or n3. Again the choice is unpredictable, but assume, without loss of generality, that it picks n2. Now n2 runs until it is preempted. Threads n1 and n3 cannot preempt it, but ts can. Thus when ts wakes up again, it gets control. Now assume that ts goes right back to sleep. Again, the VM has to pick one of the priority 5 threads to run. This time, both n1 and n2 have already run, so it will pick n3.

Thread n3 runs until ts wakes up again. Then ts takes control briefly and then goes back to sleep. The VM again must pick between the three available threads. This time, all three have already run, but n3 just ran, and n2 ran just before that, so n1 has been waiting to run for the longest time. The VM therefore starts running n1.

From this point on, the order is completely predictable. Every time the ts thread wakes up, it preempts the running n thread. Every time it goes back to sleep, the n thread that has been preempted the longest starts running again. Thus, from here on out, the n threads run in the order n1, n2, n3, n1, n2, n3, n1, n2, n3, n1, n2, and so on. If the initial unpredictable choices of order had been made differently, then the cycle might be different (for example, n2, n1, n3, instead of n1, n2, n3), but the larger repetitive structure would be the same. (for example, n2, n1, n3, n2, n1, n3, n2, n1, n3,...).

The sleep interval of ts determines how long a time slice each thread gets when it does run. For example, ts can dole out time slices of 5 milliseconds by sleeping for 5 milliseconds, time slices of 50 milliseconds by sleeping for 50 milliseconds, time slices of 500 milliseconds by sleeping for 500 milliseconds, and so on.

Listing 6-2 is a simple TimeSlicer class that implements the described behavior. You construct it, start it, and forget about it. Thereafter, all equal priority threads are guaranteed to be time-sliced. You can set the length of the time slice and the priority of the thread when you construct it. The defaults are 100 milliseconds for the time slice and a priority of

Thread.NORM_PRIORITY+1. This object will only slice time for threads with priorities less than its own. By running this thread inside your program, you guarantee that one CPU-intensive thread will not starve other threads with the same priority.

Listing 6-2
The TimeSlicer class

```
public class TimeSlicer extends Thread {

  int sleeptime;

  public TimeSlicer() {

    this(100, Thread.NORM_PRIORITY+1);

  }

  public TimeSlicer(int sleeptime) {

    this(sleeptime, Thread.NORM_PRIORITY+1);

  }


  public TimeSlicer(int sleeptime, int priority) {

    super("TimeSlicer");
    this.sleeptime = sleeptime;
    if (priority < Thread.MIN_PRIORITY) priority = Thread.MIN_PRIORITY;
    if (priority > Thread.MAX_PRIORITY) priority = Thread.MAX_PRIORITY;
    setPriority(priority);
    // If this is the only thread left, the VM should exit
    setDaemon(true);

  }

  public void run() {

    while (true) {
      try {
        sleep(sleeptime);
      }
      catch (InterruptedException e) {
      }
    }
```

(continued)

The TimeSlicer class *(continued)*

```
    }


  }
```

You may wonder what this TimeSlicer program is going to do on a fully preemptive system, one that already time slices equal priority threads. On these systems, it just wastes a small and probably insignificant number of CPU cycles. It certainly doesn't cause any problems as long as you don't set the time slice too small. One hundred milliseconds is often a good value.

Native versus emulated threads

Many modern operating systems, including Solaris, MacOS, BeOS, and Windows NT, support multithreading of native code. This is especially important on systems with multiple CPUs, as it allows computationally-intensive tasks to be split across different processors.

Java is also multithreaded. However, until relatively recently, Java virtual machines have not taken advantage of native multiprocessing. The Java virtual machine itself runs on only one processor, and thus all Java threads use at most one processor.

Note It is possible, if multiple virtual machines are running simultaneously, that they are running on different processors.

At the time of this writing, this is beginning to change. Sun has released an experimental version of the 1.0.2 virtual machine for Solaris 2.6 (X86 or Sparc) that uses native, preemptive threads that can be split across multiple processors. Microsoft's Win32 virtual machine used in Visual J++ and Internet Explorer also uses native threads. Presumably, these can run on multiple processors, though I don't have a multiprocessor X86 box available for testing to confirm this. Table 6-2 lists the different Java virtual machines for which I was able to determine underlying thread support.

Table 6-2
Native or emulated threads

Virtual machine	*Thread model*
Roaster DR 2.3	emulated
Sun Mac JDK 1.0.2	emulated
Metrowerks Code Warrior 9-11	emulated

(continued)

Table 6-2

Native or emulated threads *(continued)*

Virtual machine	Thread model
Microsoft Internet Explorer Mac	emulated
Microsoft Internet Explorer Windows 95/NT Visual J++	native
Netscape Navigator 3.0 Mac	emulated
Sun Solaris JDK 1.0.2	emulated
Sun Solaris JDK 1.1	native by default, optionally emulated, an add-on package is required to use more than one processor even with native threads
Sun Windows95/NT JDK 1.0.2	emulated
Sun Windows95/NT JDK 1.1	emulated
Macintosh Runtime for Java	emulated

As you can see, at this point most virtual machines implement their own thread models. They do not use the native threading package. When Java was first invented, it was intended for small, cheap consumer electronics-like set-top boxes. It was not planned to run on top of a powerful, modern operating system like Solaris or Windows NT. In fact, in many ways Java was going to be the operating system. Therefore, Sun's initial versions of Java included their own threading engines in the virtual machine. Most later ports of the virtual machine were based on Sun's early work, so programmers merely ported the same threading engine rather than rewriting the virtual machine from scratch to use native threads.

Now, a couple of years after the first public release of Java, we're just beginning to see the first VMs that are independent enough from Sun's original that they can use the native threads. Microsoft's Win32 VM uses native threads, as does an experimental version of Sun's more recent Java 1.0.2 VM. As time passes, more vendors are likely to rewrite their virtual machines to take advantage of native threads, especially as powerful multiprocessing desktop machines become more common and affordable.

GARBAGE COLLECTION

Garbage collection isn't quite as obvious a source of differences between programs running on different platforms. Different choices in garbage collection algorithms are unlikely to produce different outputs. However, garbage collection does have a significant impact on performance. A poor garbage collection algorithm can really kill the performance of a program, whereas a good one should be unnoticeable. As you'll see, the garbage collection algorithms used in early and current virtual machines are mediocre at best. Improved garbage collection would be a significant optimization for Java.

Reference counting

The most obvious garbage collection algorithm, and the one with which most people are familiar, is called *reference counting*. Reference counting is not only the simplest, most familiar garbage collection algorithm, but also one of the worst. Many early criticisms of Java were based on the misconception that Java used reference counting. No Java virtual machines use reference counting; no virtual machines have ever used reference counting in the past; and none are likely to in the future. Nonetheless, because reference counting is easy to understand and forms a basis for a performance comparison with other algorithms, I will discuss it briefly here.

In reference counting garbage collectors, every object that's created is associated with an integer called its *reference count*. Each time the object is assigned to a reference variable, its reference count is incremented by one. Each time that a reference variable goes out of scope or is assigned to a different object, the reference count of the object previously referred to is decremented by one. For example, the following code fragment creates two objects: an Integer with the value 17 and an Integer with the value 32.

```
public void refTest() {

    Integer myInt = new Integer(17); // reference count 1 for Integer(17)
    Integer anotherInt = myInt; // reference count 2 for Integer(17)
    myInt = new Integer(32); // reference count 1 for Integer(17), reference
count 1 for Integer(32)
    myInt = null; //  reference count 1 for Integer(17), reference count 0
for Integer(32)

    return; // reference count 0 for both Integers

}
```

When the reference count for any object reaches zero, it's garbage-collected. Furthermore, any objects to which it holds references then have their reference counts decremented by one. This collection can be synchronous — that is, the object is deleted as soon as its reference count reaches zero — or it can be asynchronous — that is, the object is merely added to a list of objects to be freed the next time the garbage collector runs.

In practice, garbage collection can be much more complex. Of course, this should come as no surprise. The difficulty of choosing when to free memory is responsible for many of the bugs in non-garbage collected languages like C++. It's better to let the compiler and runtime count your references for you rather than keeping them all in your head. In fact, it's not uncommon for programmers trying to find memory leaks to build a form of reference counting into their programs just to see where the memory is leaking. There are even a number of C and C++ tools that add reference counting to existing C and C++ code, precisely to help programmers find memory leaks.

The real complexity in reference counting comes when fields in different objects and even in different threads refer to the same object. For example,

```
public Vector makeInts() {

    Vector v = new Vector();
    Integer myInt;
    for (int i = 0; i < 100; i++) {
      v.addElement(new Integer(i));
    }

    return v;

}
```

This method 100 objects, stuffs each one in a Vector, and then returns the Vector. Presumably, some other method now possesses a reference to the Vector and from there can get a reference to each Integer object in the Vector so that they can't be garbage-collected when the method returns.

This actually isn't so bad. A good reference counting implementation handles this case with ease. The real problem comes with circular references like the one in Listing 6-3:

Listing 6-3
A Point class that produces circular references

```
public class  Point {

    int x;
    int y;
    Point next;
```

(continued)

A Point class that produces circular references *(continued)*

```
public Point(x, y) {

    this.x = x;
    this.y = y;

}

public static void circle() {

    Point p1 = new Point(3, 2);
    Point p2 = new Point(1, 2);
    p2.next = p1;
    p1.next = p2;

}

}
```

Consider what happens as soon as some piece of code invokes Point.circle(). Two new Point objects are created. The first object contains a reference to the second object, and the second object contains a reference to the first. If a reference count is being kept, then each of these objects has a reference count of at least one. Neither object can ever be freed by the garbage collector. Even if there's no way for the running program to get at either of these points any more, they still can't be freed because they refer to each other.

This is not a particularly artificial example. A circular, linked list is a relatively common data structure that would never allow itself to be garbage-collected by a pure reference counting garbage collector. Many callback patterns require each component in a container to have a reference to its parent as well as requiring the parent container to have references to each of its children. Furthermore, although these examples have fairly explicit cycles, less obvious ones often occur, purely by accident.

Reference counting in isolation is not an adequate garbage collection algorithm. By itself, it leads to too many memory leaks. You need to supplement it or replace it with a different algorithm that can recognize cycles of otherwise unreferenced objects as garbage.

Mark and sweep

The garbage collection algorithm chosen by Sun and used by most Java virtual machines is called *mark and sweep*. Mark and sweep garbage collection is divided into two phases: the marking of all references and the sweeping away of all unreferenced objects. It has the advantage of eliminating cyclical garbage. It has the disadvantage of bringing most other operations to a halt for a non-trivial amount of time.

The garbage collector runs in a separate thread that's started when the virtual machine is initialized. In fact, this thread has a low priority, Thread.MIN_ PRIORITY, so it runs only when nothing else is running. This thread scans Java's memory for anything that looks like it might be a reference to an object. Each object whose address appears in something that looks like a reference is *marked*. When the marking is complete, any objects in the heap that remain unmarked are freed — that is, they are deleted and the memory they occupied is opened up to other objects.

Java's garbage collection algorithm is *conservative*. This means that it will occasionally find something that looks like a reference but isn't. If it does, it will mark the referred block of memory and not garbage-collect it. In short, Java thinks it is more important not to free memory that might be actually in use than it is to free *everything* that isn't used. This is also a performance optimization because the garbage collector does not have to do as much work to determine whether something really is a reference to an object or not. However, this approach can cause small memory leaks. Generally, memory leaks caused by the garbage collector's conservatism are small enough that they're not a problem.

Most of the time, the garbage collector runs in a low priority thread in the background that won't interfere with the rest of your program. In fact, it should do nothing at all as long as your program is doing something and not just twiddling its thumbs. However, if the Java runtime runs out of memory, the garbage collector takes over at a high priority to try to free up some more memory. This can cause noticeable but unpredictable pauses in your programs.

The efficiency of garbage collection versus manual memory management is a common source of language bigot flame wars. One of the touchstones is whether or not garbage collector induced pauses are inherent to garbage collection. Although it's likely that a garbage collector could be devised for

Java that did not lead to unexpected pauses, the fact is that current Java garbage collectors do in fact produce unexpected pauses at inopportune moments.

You can explicitly request that garbage be collected by calling System.gc(). However, this does not guarantee that garbage collection will happen immediately, only that it will take place at the next idle point in your program.

Generational garbage collection

Generational garbage collection takes advantage of the fact that most objects don't live very long. In fact, they often don't live past the method that created them. Take another look at the refTest example:

```
public void refTest() {

    Integer myInt = new Integer(17); // reference count 1 for Integer(17)
    Integer anotherInt = myInt; // reference count 2 for Integer(17)
    myInt = new Integer(32); // reference count 1 for Integer(17), reference
count 1 for Integer(32)
    myInt = null; // reference count 1 for Integer(17), reference count 0
for Integer(32)

    return; // reference count 0 for both Integers

}
```

This method creates two objects, neither of which is referred to after the method returns. It would be nice to collect these objects immediately without checking every other object in the heap. A generational scheme is not a replacement for mark and sweep garbage collection, but rather a supplement to it. With generational garbage collection, a full pass though the heap looking for garbage needs to be run less often.

Furthermore, those few objects that do live past their initial scope may very well live until the program terminates. A generational garbage collector frequently checks recently created objects to see if they're still in scope and ignores most other objects most of the time. It can check the entire heap on a much less frequent basis. The performance improvement from a generational scheme is truly stunning and often brings garbage collection up to the speed of manual memory managers.

Regrettably, no current Java virtual machines implement generational garbage collection. However, it is likely that some VMs will begin to do this in 1997 or 1998.

SUMMARY

In this chapter, you learn the following:

- In cooperative threading environments, a thread must explicitly yield control before other threads of the same priority can take over. In preemptive environments, the virtual machine can forcibly pause a thread and offer time to other threads.

- Many Java virtual machines do not use the host's native thread environment.

- Not all garbage collection algorithms are created equal. Java virtual machines are likely to improve in the future by using faster garbage collectors.

CONTROLLING APPLETS

7

*A*lmost every Java book on the market tells you how to write applets and embed them on Web pages. This chapter takes a different tack. I'm going to explain how to write an applet viewer — that is, a program that lets you load and run applets. This may be a Web browser, or it may even be another applet itself. To do this, you need to delve fairly deeply into what really happens when a Web browser loads and plays an applet.

In this chapter, you learn how to use applets as components as well as containers, how to write and set applet contexts and applet stubs, how to define and use a ClassLoader, and how to program and install a SecurityManager. When you're through with this chapter, you'll know just about everything that you need to know to let your own applications play applets.

WHAT IS AN APPLET?

The word *applet* has several different meanings. Many people incorrectly use it to mean a small application. Others consider an applet to be a secure program that can be embedded in a Web page. In this chapter, I use the word applet very precisely. In this chapter, when I write *applet,* I mean an object that is an instance of the java.applet.Applet class or one of its subclasses, and nothing else.

With this definition, it's easy to say what an applet is. The java.applet. Applet class is a subclass of java.awt.Panel, so applets are panels. The java. awt.Panel class extends java.awt.Container, so applets are containers. The java.awt.Container class extends java.awt.Component, so applets are components. Finally, java.awt.Component extends java.lang.Object, so applets are objects.

The Applet class does not override many methods in its superclasses. In fact, it overrides only two, and both are variants of resize() from java.awt. Component:

```
public void resize(int width, int height)
public void resize(Dimension d)
```

Both of these methods are deprecated in Java 1.1 in favor of setSize(). A little surprisingly, java.applet.Applet does not override setSize().

The Applet class, therefore, inherits many methods from its superclasses, some more useful than others. From the java.lang.Object class, java.applet. Applet inherits equals(), finalize(), getClass(), hashCode(), notify(), notifyAll(), and wait(). It also inherits clone(), but java.applet.Applet does not implement Cloneable. If you want to clone an applet, you must declare that your subclass implements Cloneable. Depending on your application, you may or may not want to override equals(), hashCode(), and finalize() in your subclass.

Moving further down the hierarchy, applets are components. This means that applets can process events and that applets can be added to containers. Novice Java programmers often wonder where common applet methods, like update(), setSize(), repaint(), and processMouseEvent(), come from, because they're not documented in the API documentation for java.applet.Applet. These methods (and many more) are all inherited from java.awt.Component. The only methods in the Component class that Applet overrides are the two polymorphic resize() methods. In Java 1.1, these are deprecated and replaced by setSize(), which is not overridden in java.applet.Applet.

Moving one step further down the hierarchy, applets are instances of java.awt.Container. Because an applet is a container, it can hold other components. Typical methods inherited from the Container class include add(), doLayout(), deliverEvent(), list(), and several more. The Applet class does not override any methods in this class, although the Panel class that extends Container and that Applet extends does override addNotify(). Generally, this will be unimportant.

Containers are supposed to have LayoutManagers, and applets are no exception. The LayoutManager for an applet is normally taken from the next class in the inheritance hierarchy, java.awt.Panel. The Panel class has only three methods — Panel(), Panel(LayoutManager lm), and addNotify() — each of which the Applet class inherits. You can't override the constructors, and it's uncommon to override addNotify(). The main thing you need to know is that if a LayoutManager isn't passed to the Panel() constructor, Java uses a FlowLayout as the default. Thus, applets use FlowLayouts unless you explicitly request a different LayoutManager with setLayout().

The final class in the hierarchy is java.applet.Applet, which is an immediate subclass of java.awt.Panel. It has one private field and 21 public methods:

```
private AppletStub stub;
public final void setStub(AppletStub stub)
public boolean isActive()
public URL getDocumentBase()
public URL getCodeBase()
public String getParameter(String name)
public AppletContext getAppletContext()
public void showStatus(String msg)
public Image getImage(URL url)
public Image getImage(URL url, String name)
public AudioClip getAudioClip(URL url)
public AudioClip getAudioClip(URL url, String name)
public void play(URL url)
public void play(URL url, String name)
public String getAppletInfo()
public String[][] getParameterInfo()
public void init()
public void start()
public void stop()
public void destroy()
public void resize(int width, int height)
public void resize(Dimension d)
```

Except for resize(), mentioned earlier, the methods of the Applet class are unique. They do not override any of their parents' methods. Your applets will inherit from this class and perhaps override some of these methods. The first six methods are thin veneers over the equivalent methods of the AppletStub interface, which the stub field implements (more about that later in this chapter). The next seven methods are thin veneers over the equivalent methods in the java.applet.AppletContext interface (more about those later too). The next six methods do nothing in their default implementations. They exist to be overridden in your subclasses. If Applet were an abstract class, these methods might well be abstract. In fact, the only methods of the Applet class fully implemented inside the class are the deprecated resize() methods!

APPLETS ARE COMPONENTS TOO

Most of the time, when programming with applets in Java, you write subclasses of java.applet.Applet. These classes generally override some subset of the getAppletInfo(), getParameterInfo(), init(), start(), stop(), and destroy() methods. The compiled applet is loaded into an applet viewer or Web browser program, where — from the programmer's point of view — the applet controls the execution of the entire program. This use of applets is more than adequately covered in dozens of books, including my own *The Java Developer's Resource* (Prentice Hall, 1997). I won't repeat that discussion here.

What I want to talk about is something a little less common: how to embed applets into other programs — that is, how to use applets as components as well as containers. You'll need this knowledge if you want to write your own stand-alone application that supports applets. There's no reason why applets have to be limited to being just part of Web pages. There are many other applications where it's useful to be able to plug in external objects, and there's a large library of applets available to be plugged in.

main() methods for applets

Because applets are components, they can be embedded in containers. This is most commonly used to make applets that work as both applets and applications. The trick is to instantiate the applet in the main() method, create a new Frame for the applet, add the applet to the Frame, and then call the applet's init() and start() methods. Listing 7-1 demonstrates with a simple HelloWorld applet.

Listing 7-1
This program is both an applet and a stand-alone application.

```
import java.applet.Applet;
import java.awt.*;


public class HelloWorldApplet extends Applet {

  public static void main(String[] args) {

    Frame f = new Frame("Hello World!");
    HelloWorldApplet h = new HelloWorldApplet();
    h.init();
    h.start();
    f.add("Center", h);
    f.pack();
    f.show();

  }

  public void init() {

    add(new Label("Hello World!"));

  }

}
```

Figure 7-1 shows this applet running as a stand-alone application. Figure 7-2 shows it running in a Web browser.

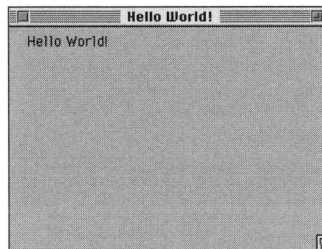

Figure 7-1
HelloWorld as an application.

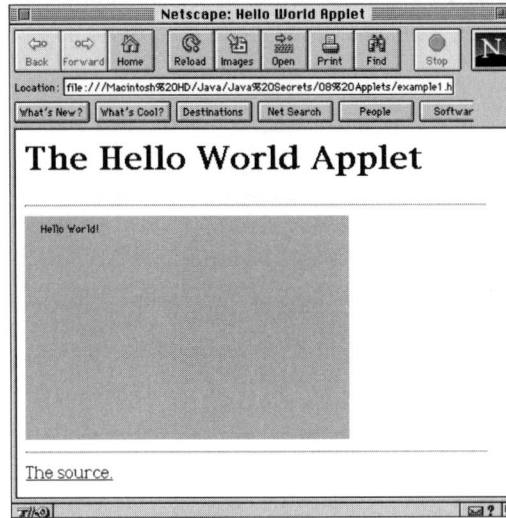

■ **Figure 7-2**
■ *HelloWorld as an applet.*

Including applets in non-applets

Because applets are components, you can add them to other programs. And you can add more than one to a single application. Listing 7-2 creates a Frame and places the applet from Listing 7-1 into the north and south sections. Figure 7-3 shows this program running.

Listing 7-2
The MultiApplet class

```
import java.applet.Applet;
import java.awt.*;


public class MultiApplet extends Frame {

  public static void main(String[] args) {

    MultiApplet ma = new MultiApplet("MultiApplet");
    ma.resize(200,200);
```

(continued)

The MultiApplet class *(continued)*

```
        ma.setLayout(new GridLayout(2, 1));
        ma.launchApplet();
        ma.launchApplet();
        ma.show();

    }

    public MultiApplet(String s) {
      super(s);
    }

    void launchApplet() {

      Applet theApplet = new HelloWorldApplet();
      add(theApplet);
      theApplet.init();
      theApplet.start();

    }
  }
```

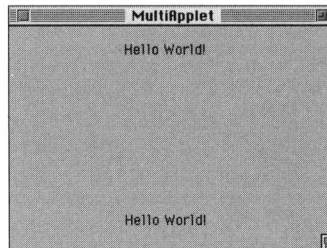

■ **Figure 7-3**
Two copies of the HelloWorldApplet loaded into one Frame.

The point here is that you don't always need to think of an applet as the main driver for your program. Other classes can load, install, and run applets as necessary. If you think about it, you should realize that HotJava is just a big Java program that occasionally adds applets to itself. There's no reason why your programs can't do this, too.

Dynamically loading applets

Listing 7-2 separates the applet from the class that loads it. Logically, the next question to ask is whether you can dynamically choose the applet to be loaded into a program rather than hardwiring it into the source code. The answer is yes. After all, that's exactly what an applet viewer or HotJava does.

The key is to use the Class.forName() method to load the applet's .class file, then use the Class.newInstance() method to instantiate it. This works only for classes that have a noargs constructor, but because that covers pretty much all applets, you're home free.

Conversely, this explains why it's not a good idea to give your applets constructors. If your applet has a constructor that takes arguments but does not also have a noargs constructor, then neither a Web browser nor the applet viewer will be able to instantiate it.

Listing 7-3 is a very simple applet viewer. The user enters the name of the applet in the TextField and presses Return or clicks the Reload button to reload the applet. This simple viewer assumes that the applet lives in the user's CLASSPATH. Figure 7-4 shows this applet running with the Clock2 applet loaded. (This is one of Sun's standard demo applets included with the JDK.)

Listing 7-3
A simple applet viewer

```
import java.applet.*;
import java.awt.*;


public class SimpleAppletViewer extends Frame {

  Applet theApplet = null;
  Panel appletPanel = new Panel();
  TextField appletName = new TextField(32);
  Button reloadButton = new Button("Reload");
  Button restartButton = new Button("Restart");

  public static void main(String[] args) {

    SimpleAppletViewer sav = new SimpleAppletViewer();
    sav.show();

  }
```

(continued)

A simple applet viewer *(continued)*

```
public SimpleAppletViewer() {

  super("Simple Applet Viewer");
  init();
  resize(400, 200);

}

protected void init() {

  Panel p1 = new Panel();
  p1.setLayout(new GridLayout(2, 1));
  p1.add(appletName);
  Panel p2 = new Panel();
  p2.add(reloadButton);
  p2.add(restartButton);
  p1.add(p2);
  add("South", p1);
  appletPanel.setLayout(new BorderLayout());
  add("Center", appletPanel);

}

public void loadApplet(String name) {

  removeApplet();
  if (name != null && !name.equals("")) {
    try {
      Class c = Class.forName(name);
      theApplet = (Applet) c.newInstance();
      appletPanel.add("Center", theApplet);
      theApplet.init();
      theApplet.start();
      validate();
    }
    catch (ClassNotFoundException e) {
      System.err.println(e);
    }
    catch (InstantiationException e) {
      System.err.println(e);
    }
    catch (IllegalAccessException e) {
      System.err.println(e);
    }
```

(continued)

Listing 7-3
A simple applet viewer *(continued)*

```
      }

   }

   public void removeApplet() {

      if (theApplet != null) {
         theApplet.stop();
         theApplet.destroy();
         appletPanel.remove(theApplet);
         theApplet = null;
      }

   }

   public void reload() {

      String name = appletName.getText();

      if (theApplet != null) {
         Class c = theApplet.getClass();
         name = c.getName();
         removeApplet();
      }

      loadApplet(name);

   }

   public void restart() {
      if (theApplet != null) {
         theApplet.stop();
         theApplet.start();
      }
      else loadApplet(appletName.getText());
   }

   public boolean action(Event e, Object what) {

      if (e.target == restartButton) {
         restart();
         return true;
      }
      else if (e.target == reloadButton) {
         reload();
         return true;
```

(continued)

A simple applet viewer *(continued)*

```
        }
    else if (e.target == appletName) {
      loadApplet(appletName.getText());
      return true;
    }

    return super.handleEvent(e);

  }

}
```

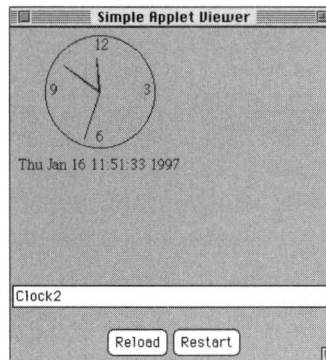

Figure 7-4
The SimpleAppletViewer with the Clock2 applet loaded.

The SimpleAppletViewer, although functional, is missing several important parts. First of all, it relies on the applet .class file to be in the CLASSPATH. This is enough for a first attempt, but in the long term, you want a means for the applet viewer to load classes from any file on the hard drive, and perhaps even from the network. So this applet viewer needs a ClassLoader to read byte code files.

Second, this applet viewer provides only the most minimal level of security. There's absolutely nothing to stop an applet it loads from connecting to a network server, downloading a file full of native code to your computer, and launching it; of course, the native code can then do pretty much anything it wants with your system. So this applet viewer needs a SecurityManager to prevent this and other attacks.

Third, you may have noticed that many applets don't run in this applet viewer. In fact, some force it to quit with a NullPointerException. In particular, you have problems with any applet that calls one or more of the following methods:

```
public boolean isActive()
public URL getDocumentBase()
public URL getCodeBase()
public String getParameter(String name)
public AppletContext getAppletContext()
public void showStatus(String msg)
public Image getImage(URL url)
public Image getImage(URL url, String name)
public AudioClip getAudioClip(URL url)
public AudioClip getAudioClip(URL url, String name)
public void play(URL url)
public void play(URL url, String name)
```

That's a lot of methods. The reason that these methods fail in SimpleAppletViewer is that each implicitly relies on the applet's stub or the applet's context. So to make this viewer fully functional, you also need to provide each applet with an AppletStub object and an AppletContext object.

Summing up, there are four things this applet viewer (or any other program that loads applets) needs:

- An AppletStub
- An AppletContext
- A ClassLoader
- A SecurityManager

I show you how to write classes for each of these in the next three sections.

STUBS AND CONTEXT

The applet's stub is an object that implements the java.applet.AppletStub interface. If you look at the documentation for the java.applet.AppletStub interface, you'll see that it declares six methods:

```
boolean isActive();
URL getDocumentBase();
URL getCodeBase();
String getParameter(String name);
AppletContext getAppletContext();
void appletResize(int width, int height);
```

It's no coincidence that the first five of these are the first five methods that cause problems in the SimpleAppletViewer. The java.applet.Applet class has a private AppletStub field called, simply enough, stub. When the five methods of the same name in the Applet class are invoked, all they do is call the corresponding method of the stub object. For example, getCodeBase() just returns stub.getCodeBase().

Note

The sixth method in the AppletStub interface, appletResize(), is also called by the corresponding method in java.applet.Applet. However, unlike the other five methods, the Applet class's resize() method does not *just* call stub.appletResize(). It also performs some independent calculations and checks to see whether stub is null before calling its appletResize() method. If stub is null, then Applet.resize() will not call stub.appletResize().

The applet's context is an object that represents the Web browser or the applet viewer. Abilities that are normally present in a Web browser, such as downloading an image from a URL, are passed off to the Web browser via the AppletContext interface.

Unlike the stub, an applet's AppletContext is not stored in a private field in the applet. Instead, it is retrieved with the getAppletContext() method (which calls stub.getAppletContext()) whenever it's needed.

The AppletContext interface declares seven methods:

```
Image getImage(URL u)
AudioClip getAudioClip(URL u)
Applet getApplet(String name)
Enumeration getApplets()
void showDocument(URL u)
public void showDocument(URL u, String target)
void showStatus(String status)
```

Three of these methods, getAudioClip(), getImage(), and showStatus(), are used to implement the similarly named methods in java.applet.Applet. The getAudioClip() method is also used indirectly by the play() methods of java.applet.Applet. If an applet does not have a context, then getApplet-Context() returns null. Thus, if there isn't a context, calling any of these methods throws a NullPointerException. If an applet has a context but does not have a stub, then getAppletContext() throws a NullPointerException, so these methods still throw NullPointerExceptions.

To make the applet viewer more robust, you need to provide a stub and a context for the applet. There are two ways you can do this. You can use the sun.applet.AppletPanel and sun.applet.AppletViewer classes, which implement AppletStub and AppletContext respectively, or you can write your own. The AppletPanel and AppletViewer classes are covered in Chapter 9. In this chapter, you learn how to write your own.

Writing applet contexts

The AppletContext interface represents the Web browser or applet viewer itself. Therefore, the most logical place to implement it is in the primary AppletViewer class. This class will need to have seven methods:

```
AudioClip getAudioClip(URL u)
Image getImage(URL u)
Applet getApplet(String name)
Enumeration getApplets()
void showDocument(URL u)
public void showDocument(URL u, String target)
void showStatus(String status)
```

getImage()

The getImage() method is the simplest of the seven to implement because you can fall back on the similarly named method in the java.awt.Toolkit class, like this:

```
public Image getImage(URL u) {
  return Toolkit.getDefaultToolkit().getImage(u);
}
```

This is fully documented in the java classes, so it's fairly reliable. A problem occurs only if the default toolkit can't be found for some reason. Then, an AWTError is thrown, which is a subclass of java.lang.Error. This is likely to happen only if you're trying to run the applet in a purely character mode environment.

getAudioClip()

The getAudioClip() method is probably the most difficult of the seven methods to implement without resorting to the sun classes, mainly because there are no documented classes that implement the AudioClip or any other sound interface. You have to use the sun classes or native methods to play sound. In Java 1.1 there is simply no other way.

The best that you can do for now is to create do-nothing methods that don't actually play sounds or download audio files, but don't throw exceptions either. Listing 7-4 is such a NullAudioClip class. In Chapter 11, I revisit this topic and show you how to use the sun classes to actually play audio.

Listing 7-4
The NullAudioClip class

```
import java.applet.AudioClip;


public class NullAudioClip implements AudioClip {

  public void play() {};
  public void loop() {};
  public void stop() {};


}
```

To use this class, your applet context needs the following getAudioClip() method:

```
public AudioClip getAudioClip(URL u) {
  return new NullAudioClip();
}
```

getApplet()

The getApplet() method is supposed to return a particular named applet in the context. It is allowed to return null if the named applet is not present in the context. Names are set by using the NAME parameter to the APPLET tag in an HTML file like this:

```
<applet code="Clock2" width=100 height=100 name="The Clock">
```

This applet viewer does not yet load applets from HTML files, so applets don't have names. Thus, for now, just return null. Later, when I add the ability to read HTML files, I also expand this method to allow retrieving a reference to an applet by name.

```
public Applet getApplet(String s) {
  return null;
}
```

getApplets()

The getApplets() method is a little less empty. It is supposed to return an Enumeration (that is, an object such as Vector that implements the java.util.Enumeration interface) of all the applets currently loaded in the AppletContext. It's easy to add a Vector field called theApplets that tracks all currently loaded applets. Applets are added to theApplets in the loadApplet() method and removed from them in the removeApplet() method. This requires some simple changes to loadApplet() and removeApplet() as well.

```
Vector theApplets = new Vector();

public void loadApplet(String name) {

  removeApplet();
  if (name != null && !name.equals("")) {
    try {
      Class c = Class.forName(name);
      Applet theApplet = (Applet) c.newInstance();
      appletPanel.add(theApplet);
      add("Center", appletPanel);
      theApplets.addElement(theApplet);
      theApplet.init();
      theApplet.start();
      validate();
    }
    catch (ClassNotFoundException e) {
      System.err.println(e);
    }
    catch (InstantiationException e) {
      System.err.println(e);
    }
    catch (IllegalAccessException e) {
```

```
        System.err.println(e);
      }

    }

  }

  public void removeApplet() {
    if (theApplet != null) {
      theApplet.stop();
      theApplet.destroy();
      theApplets.removeElement(theApplet);
      remove(appletPanel);
      theApplet = null;
      appletPanel = new Panel();
      add("Center", appletPanel);
      validate();
    }
  }

  public Enumeration getApplets() {
    return (Enumeration) theApplets;
  }
```

This method isn't very significant now, but it will be when the applet viewer is allowed to run more than one applet at a time.

showDocument()

Sun's documentation states that the AppletContext is permitted to ignore calls to showDocument(). In fact, Sun's applet viewer does exactly that. Therefore, I'll initially use two do-nothing showDocument() methods. However, once a full class loader is implemented, I'll revisit these methods and expand on them.

```
        public void showDocument(URL url) {};
        public void showDocument(URL url, String target) {};
```

showStatus()

The final method that the AppletContext needs is showStatus(). This isn't hard to implement. You just add a TextField to the applet viewer to display a status line. This also requires minor changes to the init() method to add the status field to the Frame, as shown in the following.

```
TextField status = new TextField(32);

public void init() {

  Panel p1 = new Panel();
  p1.setLayout(new GridLayout(3, 1));
  Panel p0 = new Panel();
  p0.setLayout(new FlowLayout(FlowLayout.LEFT));
  p0.add(new Label("Applet: "));
  p0.add(appletName);
  p1.add(p0);
  Panel p2 = new Panel();
  p2.add(loadButton);
  p2.add(removeButton);
  p2.add(reloadButton);
  p2.add(restartButton);
  p1.add(p2);
  Panel p4 = new Panel();
  p4.setLayout(new FlowLayout(FlowLayout.LEFT));
  p4.add(new Label("Status: "));
  status.setEditable(false);
  p4.add(status);
  p1.add(p4);
  add("South", p1);
  appletPanel.setLayout(new BorderLayout());
  add("Center", appletPanel);

}


public void showStatus(String s) {
  status.setText(s);
}
```

An applet viewer with context

Listing 7-5 contains the complete ContextAppletViewer class. It uses all the methods discussed above as well as a few additional modifications to provide an AppletContext for the applet.

Listing 7-5
TheContextAppletViewer

```
import java.applet.*;
import java.awt.*;
```

(continued)

TheContextAppletViewer *(continued)*

```
import java.util.*;
import java.net.URL;


public class ContextAppletViewer extends Frame implements AppletContext {

  Applet theApplet = null;
  Panel appletPanel = new Panel();
  TextField appletName = new TextField(32);
  Button loadButton = new Button("Load");
  Button removeButton = new Button("Remove");
  Button reloadButton = new Button("Reload");
  Button restartButton = new Button("Restart");
  Vector theApplets = new Vector();
  TextField status = new TextField(32);

  public static void main(String[] args) {

    ContextAppletViewer cav = new ContextAppletViewer("Context Applet Viewer");
    cav.show();

  }

  public void init() {

    Panel p1 = new Panel();
    p1.setLayout(new GridLayout(3, 1));
    Panel p0 = new Panel();
    p0.setLayout(new FlowLayout(FlowLayout.LEFT));
    p0.add(new Label("Applet: "));
    p0.add(appletName);
    p1.add(p0);
    Panel p2 = new Panel();
    p2.add(loadButton);
    p2.add(removeButton);
    p2.add(reloadButton);
    p2.add(restartButton);
    p1.add(p2);
    Panel p4 = new Panel();
    p4.setLayout(new FlowLayout(FlowLayout.LEFT));
    p4.add(new Label("Status: "));
    status.setEditable(false);
    p4.add(status);
    p1.add(p4);
    add("South", p1);
    appletPanel.setLayout(new BorderLayout());
```

(continued)

Listing 7-5
TheContextAppletViewer *(continued)*

```
     add("Center", appletPanel);

}

public ContextAppletViewer(String s) {

  super("Context Applet Viewer");
  init();
  resize(350, 250);

}

public void loadApplet(String name) {

  removeApplet();
  if (name != null && !name.equals("")) {
    try {
      Class c = Class.forName(name);
      theApplet = (Applet) c.newInstance();
      appletPanel.add("Center", theApplet);
      theApplets.addElement(theApplet);
      theApplet.init();
      theApplet.start();
      validate();
    }
    catch (ClassNotFoundException e) {
      showStatus(e.toString());
    }
    catch (InstantiationException e) {
      showStatus(e.toString());
    }
    catch (IllegalAccessException e) {
      showStatus(e.toString());
    }

  }

}

public void removeApplet() {

  if (theApplet != null) {
    theApplet.stop();
    theApplet.destroy();
```

(continued)

TheContextAppletViewer *(continued)*

```
        theApplets.removeElement(theApplet);
        appletPanel.remove(theApplet);
        theApplet = null;
        validate();
        repaint();
     }

  }

  public void reload() {

     if (theApplet != null) {
        Class c = theApplet.getClass();
        String name = c.getName();
        removeApplet();
        loadApplet(name);
     }

  }

  public void restart() {

    if (theApplet != null) {
        theApplet.stop();
        theApplet.start();
     }

  }

  public boolean action(Event e, Object what) {

     if (e.target == restartButton) {
        restart();
        return true;
     }
     else if (e.target == reloadButton) {
        reload();
        return true;
     }
     else if (e.target == loadButton) {
        loadApplet(appletName.getText());
        return true;
     }
     else if (e.target == removeButton) {
        removeApplet();
```

(continued)

Listing 7-5
TheContextAppletViewer *(continued)*

```
        return true;
    }
    else if (e.target == appletName) {
      loadApplet(appletName.getText());
      return true;
    }

    return false;

}

public Image getImage(URL u) {
  return Toolkit.getDefaultToolkit().getImage(u);
}

public AudioClip getAudioClip(URL u) {
  return new NullAudioClip();
}

public Applet getApplet(String s) {
  return null;
}

public Enumeration getApplets() {
  return (Enumeration) theApplets;
}

public void showDocument(URL url) {};

public void showDocument(URL url, String target) {};

public void showStatus(String s) {
  status.setText(s);
}

}
```

To sum up, the AppletContext described here can show status methods, load images, and return an Enumeration of the loaded applets. That is, it fully handles

```
Image getImage(URL u)
Enumeration getApplets()
void showStatus(String status)
```

However, it fudges audio clips, documents, and requests for a named applet. The following four methods still need more work:

```
AudioClip getAudioClip(URL u)
Applet getApplet(String name)
void showDocument(URL u)
public void showDocument(URL u, String target)
```

However, at least they no longer lead to applets crashing with NullPointerExceptions.

Writing applet stubs

An applet's stub is as essential to its functioning as the applet's context. However, although applet programmers will occasionally refer directly to the methods of AppletContext, AppletStub exists almost entirely behind the scenes. The stub field of the Applet class is private and set automatically by the system, so there's no easy way for most applets to even get a reference to their own stubs. None of this makes the proper functioning of the stub any less important.

To write a stub, you create a class that implements the AppletStub interface — I'll call this one SimpleAppletStub — and pass it to the Applet's setStub() method immediately after constructing the applet like this:

```
HelloWorldApplet h = new HelloWorldApplet();
h.setStub(new SimpleAppletStub());
```

The AppletStub must implement six methods:

```
public abstract boolean isActive()
public abstract URL getDocumentBase()
public abstract URL getCodeBase()
public abstract String getParameter(String name)
public abstract AppletContext getAppletContext()
public abstract void appletResize(int width, int height)
```

Listing 7-6 is a class called SimpleAppletStub that implements all six of these. The appletResize() method is a simple do-nothing method. The getAppletContext() method returns a reference to the AppletContext that created the stub. The getCodeBase(), getDocumentBase(), and getParameter() methods all return null because the applet viewer hasn't actually read any HTML files to get these items yet. This will be fixed shortly. Finally, the isActive() method returns true once the applet is started and false once the applet has stopped.

Listing 7-6

The SimpleAppletStub class

```
import java.applet.*;
import java.net.URL;


public class SimpleAppletStub implements AppletStub {

  AppletContext ac;
  boolean isActive = false;

  public SimpleAppletStub(AppletContext ac) {
    this.ac = ac;
  }

  public void activate() {
    isActive = true;
  }

  public void deactivate() {
    isActive = false;
  }

  public  boolean isActive() {
    return isActive;
  }

  public URL getDocumentBase() {
    return null;
  }

  public URL getCodeBase() {
    return null;
  }

  public String getParameter(String name) {
    return null;
  }

  public AppletContext getAppletContext() {
    return ac;
  }

  public void appletResize(int width, int height) {

  }

}
```

The activate() and deactivate() methods are for the benefit of the AppletContext so that it can tell the stub that it's active when it calls the applet's start() method and tell the stub it's inactive when it calls the applet's stop() method. This relies on only the AppletContext calling start() and stop(). If the applet stops or starts itself, isActive() can get confused. This problem is shared by Sun's own applet viewer and is one reason why it's not a good idea to call start() and stop() from inside your own applet.

Note The most common reason for calling start() inside an applet is because you're instantiating it inside main(). This use is fine. The main() method is called only if the applet is running on its own, not inside a Web browser or applet viewer, so there's no AppletStub to confuse things.

Better main() methods for applets

Traditional applet/applications can't use the full power of the Applet class because too much of that class relies on the AppletStub and the Applet-Context, objects that an applet instantiated in main() normally doesn't have. However, with what you've seen in the last two sections, it's not hard to provide a simple stub and context for all your applet/applications.

These applet/applications don't require a full-blown applet viewer. Instead, you can use the SimpleAppletContext class in Listing 7-7.

Listing 7-7
The SimpleAppletContext class

```
import java.applet.*;
import java.awt.*;
import java.net.*;
import java.util.*;


public class SimpleAppletContext implements AppletContext {

  Vector theApplets = new Vector();

  public void addApplet(Applet a) {
    theApplets.addElement(a);
  }

  public void removeApplet(Applet a) {
    try {
      theApplets.removeElement(a);
```

(continued)

Listing 7-7
The SimpleAppletContext class *(continued)*

```
    }
    catch (NoSuchElementException e) {
    }
  }

  public Image getImage(URL u) {
    return Toolkit.getDefaultToolkit().getImage(u);
  }

  public AudioClip getAudioClip(URL u) {
    return new NullAudioClip();
  }

  public Applet getApplet(String s) {
    return null;
  }

  public Enumeration getApplets() {
    return (Enumeration) theApplets;
  }

  public void showDocument(URL url) {};

  public void showDocument(URL url, String target) {};

  public void showStatus(String s) {
    System.out.println(s);
  }

}
```

The big additions to this class are the addApplet() and removeApplet() methods. These allow other classes to tell the SimpleAppletContext object that it's providing services for an applet or that it's no longer providing such services, thus keeping the Vector theApplets properly filled. Normally, you don't need to do this because you presume that the AppletContext itself loads the applets. However, in this special case, the applets are loaded by the Java runtime and have to let the AppletContext know about their existence after the fact.

To use this AppletContext in conjunction with the SimpleAppletStub class of Listing 7-6, just pass it to the SimpleAppletStub() constructor and then call the applet's setStub() method in your main() method immediately after constructing the applet. Listing 7-8 demonstrates with a revised

HelloWorld applet. Of course, HelloWorld doesn't really need a context or a stub, but the procedure is identical for far more complicated applets that do.

Listing 7-8
The HelloWorldApplet with an AppletContext and an AppletStub

```
import java.applet.Applet;
import java.awt.*;


public class HelloWorldApplet extends Applet {

  public static void main(String[] args) {

    Frame f = new Frame("Hello World!");
    HelloWorldApplet h = new HelloWorldApplet();
    SimpleAppletContext sac = new SimpleAppletContext();
    sac.addApplet(h);
    SimpleAppletStub sas = new SimpleAppletStub(sac);
    h.setStub(sas);
    f.resize(300, 200);
    f.add("Center", h);
    f.show();
    h.init();
    h.start();

  }

  public void init() {

    add(new Label("Hello World!"));

  }

}
```

The SimpleAppletStub class of Listing 7-6 is normally sufficient for a stub, although you may want to extend it with a better getParameter() method.

LOADING CLASSES

What everyone notices about applets is that they are played on Web pages by Web browsers. So far, our applet viewer can't handle that. It can load applets only from the local CLASSPATH. To allow applets and other classes to be loaded from anywhere on the Internet or on the local file system, you include ClassLoader.

A ClassLoader is a subclass of java.lang.ClassLoader that knows how to read a stream of bytes from some source and convert that stream of bytes into a java.lang.Class object. This section develops a simple ClassLoader that loads classes from a URL. It does not understand ZIP or JAR archives, though that support would not be difficult to add if you cared to.

Not all classes are loaded by a ClassLoader. In fact, when an application starts up, no ClassLoader is installed. When no ClassLoader is installed, classes are loaded from the CLASSPATH. The main purpose of a ClassLoader is to expand the locations from which classes can be loaded, allowing them to come from somewhere other than the local CLASSPATH.

java.lang.Classloader is an abstract class. The single abstract method is loadClass(). Most of the remaining methods are declared final for security reasons. To create a new ClassLoader, you subclass java.lang.ClassLoader and override loadClass():

```
public Class loadClass(String name) throws ClassNotFoundException
```

Your loadClass() method will be called when you explicitly ask the ClassLoader to load a class. It will also be called when any object in a class loaded by this ClassLoader tries to instantiate an object of a class not in the local CLASSPATH. However, this method should not automatically try to load the classes from the network. It should first check to see if the class was previously loaded. If so, it should retrieve the class from a cache and not reload it. Second, it should try to find the requested class in the CLASSPATH. This is extremely important for security. Otherwise, network classes could replace the standard Java classes. Only if the class has not been previously loaded and is not available in the CLASSPATH should it be loaded from the network.

If loadClass() does decide to load the class from the network, it should read all the bytes of the .class file. Then it should pass them in a byte array to the defineClass() method to convert them into a java.lang.Class object.

```
protected final Class defineClass(byte data[], int offset, int length)
protected final Class defineClass(String name, byte data[], int offset, int
length)
```

Listing 7-9 is a simple URLClassLoader class that loads classes from a specified URL. The constructor merely strips the filename, if any, off the URL so that a directory URL (that is, one that ends in a /) is left. The loadClass method is called to actually load classes. The private downloadClass() method

retrieves the byte codes from the server and creates a new Class object with
them by calling the defineClass() method.

Listing 7-9
The URLClassLoader class

```
import java.util.*;
import java.io.*;
import java.net.*;


public class URLClassLoader extends ClassLoader {

  Hashtable cache = new Hashtable();
  URL theURL;

  public URLClassLoader(URL u) {

    // convert to a directory URL
    String file = u.getFile();
    int i = file.lastIndexOf('/');
    if ((i > 0) && (i < file.length()-1)) {
      try {
            u = new URL(u, file.substring(0, i+1));
      }
        catch (MalformedURLException e) {
      }
    }

    theURL = u;

  }

  public URL getURL() {
    return theURL;
  }

  private Class downloadClass(String name) throws IOException {

    if (!name.toLowerCase().endsWith(".class")) name += ".class";
    URL u = new URL(theURL, name);

    InputStream is = null;
    try {
      try {
        URLConnection uc = u.openConnection();
```

(continued)

Listing 7-9
The URLClassLoader class *(continued)*

```
            uc.setAllowUserInteraction(false);
            is = uc.getInputStream();
            int cl = uc.getContentLength();
            int buffersize;

            // Many servers don't return content length headers
            // If so, we'll guess that 2048 is long enough
            // and expand the array as we need to.
            if (cl <= 0) buffersize = 2048;
            else buffersize = cl;
            byte dotclass[] = new byte[buffersize];

            int totalRead = 0;
            int bytesRead = 0;
            while ((bytesRead = is.read(dotclass, totalRead, dotclass.length -
totalRead))
                >= 0) {
              totalRead += bytesRead;
              if (totalRead == dotclass.length) {
                if (cl < 0) {
                  // We don't know the content-length so we
                  // keep reading until there aren't any bytes left
                  byte temp[] = new byte[2*totalRead];
                  System.arraycopy(dotclass, 0, temp, 0, totalRead);
                  dotclass = temp;
                }
                else {
                  break;
                }
              }
            }
            return defineClass(dotclass, 0, totalRead);
          }
          finally {
            if (is != null) is.close();
          }
        }
        catch (IOException e) {
          throw e;
        }
        catch (Throwable t) {
          throw new IOException(u + " did not load");
        }

      }
```

(continued)

The URLClassLoader class *(continued)*

```java
public Class loadClass(String name) throws ClassNotFoundException {

    return loadClass(name, true);

}


    public Class loadClass(String name, boolean resolve) throws
ClassNotFoundException {

    Class c = null;

    // try to get it from the cache;
    c = (Class) cache.get(name);
    if (c == null) {   // not in the cache
      try {
            return findSystemClass(name);
      }
       catch (Throwable t) {
       }
       // not a system class
       try {
         c = downloadClass(name);
       }
       catch(IOException e) {
         System.err.println(e);
         // download failed
       }
    }

    if (c == null) {
      throw new ClassNotFoundException(name);
    }

    if (resolve) {
      resolveClass(c);
    }
     cache.put(name, c);

    return c;

  }

 }
```

For this class to be available to the applet viewer, the applet viewer must instantiate it and then call its loadClass() method to get a Class object instead of relying on Class.forName(). Listing 7-10 is a URLAppletViewer that does exactly this. It first reads the name of the applet from a TextField and then it tries to parse that as a URL. If it succeeds, it loads the applet from the URL. If it fails, it tries to load the applet from the CLASSPATH as before.

Listing 7-10

The URLAppletViewer

```
import java.applet.*;
import java.awt.*;
import java.net.*;
import java.util.*;


public class URLAppletViewer extends Frame implements AppletContext {

  Applet theApplet = null;
  SimpleAppletStub theStub = null;
  Panel appletPanel = new Panel();
  TextField appletName = new TextField(35);
  Button loadButton = new Button("Load");
  Button removeButton = new Button("Remove");
  Button reloadButton = new Button("Reload");
  Button restartButton = new Button("Restart");
  Vector theApplets = new Vector();
  TextField status = new TextField(33);

  public static void main(String[] args) {

    URLAppletViewer uav = new URLAppletViewer();
    uav.show();
//    System.setSecurityManager(new SimpleSecurityManager());

  }

  public URLAppletViewer() {

    super("URL Applet Viewer");
    init();
    resize(400, 250);

  }

  protected void init() {
```

(continued)

The URLAppletViewer *(continued)*

```
        Panel p1 = new Panel();
        p1.setLayout(new GridLayout(3, 1));
        Panel p0 = new Panel();
        p0.setLayout(new FlowLayout(FlowLayout.LEFT));
        p0.add(new Label("URL: "));
        p0.add(appletName);
        p1.add(p0);
        Panel p2 = new Panel();
        p2.add(loadButton);
        p2.add(removeButton);
        p2.add(reloadButton);
        p2.add(restartButton);
        p1.add(p2);
        Panel p4 = new Panel();
        p4.setLayout(new FlowLayout(FlowLayout.LEFT));
        p4.add(new Label("Status: "));
        status.setEditable(false);
        p4.add(status);
        p1.add(p4);
        add("South", p1);
        appletPanel.setLayout(new BorderLayout());
        add("Center", appletPanel);

    }


    public void loadApplet(String name) {

      removeApplet();
      // is the name a URL?
      try {
        URL u = new URL(name);
        loadApplet(u);
        return;
      }
      catch(MalformedURLException e) {
      }

      removeApplet();
      if (name != null && !name.equals("")) {
        try {
          Class c = Class.forName(name);
          theApplet = (Applet) c.newInstance();
          appletPanel.add("Center", theApplet);
          theApplets.addElement(theApplet);
```

(continued)

Listing 7-10
The URLAppletViewer *(continued)*

```
            theApplet.init();
            theApplet.start();
            validate();
        }
        catch (Exception e) {
          showStatus(e.toString());
        }
    }


  }

  public void loadApplet(URL u) {

    Class c = null;
    removeApplet();

    try {
      URLClassLoader ucl = new URLClassLoader(u);
      String appletname = u.getFile();
      appletname = appletname.substring(appletname.lastIndexOf('/')+1);
      showStatus("Loading " + appletname);
      c = ucl.loadClass(appletname);
      theApplet = (Applet) c.newInstance();
      theStub = new SimpleAppletStub(this);
      theApplet.setStub(theStub);
      appletPanel.add("Center", theApplet);
      theApplets.addElement(theApplet);
      theApplet.init();
      theStub.activate();
      theApplet.start();
      validate();
      repaint();
    }
    catch (Exception e) {
      showStatus(e.toString());
    }

  }


  public void removeApplet() {

    if (theApplet != null) {
      theApplet.stop();
      theApplet.destroy();
```

(continued)

The URLAppletViewer *(continued)*

```
      theApplets.removeElement(theApplet);
      appletPanel.remove(theApplet);
      theApplet = null;
      validate();
      repaint();
    }

  }


  public void reload() {

    String name = appletName.getText();

    if (theApplet != null) {
      Class c = theApplet.getClass();
      name = c.getName();
      removeApplet();
      loadApplet(name);
    }

  }


  public void restart() {
   if (theApplet != null) {
      theApplet.stop();
      theApplet.start();
    }
    else loadApplet(appletName.getText());
  }

  public boolean action(Event e, Object what) {

    if (e.target == restartButton) {
      restart();
      return true;
    }
    else if (e.target == reloadButton) {
      reload();
      return true;
    }
    else if (e.target == loadButton) {
      loadApplet(appletName.getText());
      return true;
    }
    else if (e.target == removeButton) {
```

(continued)

Listing 7-10
The URLAppletViewer *(continued)*

```
      removeApplet();
      return true;
    }
    else if (e.target == appletName) {
      loadApplet(appletName.getText());
      return true;
    }

    return false;

  }


  public Image getImage(URL u) {
    return Toolkit.getDefaultToolkit().getImage(u);
  }

  public AudioClip getAudioClip(URL u) {
    return new NullAudioClip();
  }

  public Applet getApplet(String s) {
    return null;
  }

  public Enumeration getApplets() {
    return (Enumeration) theApplets;
  }

  public void showDocument(URL url) {};

  public void showDocument(URL url, String target) {};

  public void showStatus(String s) {
    status.setText(s);
  }

}
```

The URLAppletViewer still differs from Sun's applet viewer in that it needs a URL to the actual applet .class file, not to an HTML file containing an <APPLET> tag. I remove that final restriction soon. But first, I investigate what can be done to make the applet viewer more secure.

SETTING SECURITY POLICIES

If your program might load potentially hostile applets, it needs a
SecurityManager. SecurityManagers are quite easy to code. You just need to
make about 18 decisions about what will and will not be allowed.

Each action that might conceivably cause a security problem, such as
reading a file, opening a network connection, or loading a native code
library, is matched to one method in the java.lang.SecurityManager class.
Table 7-1 lists the different methods and what they check.

Table 7-1
The check methods of java.lang.SecurityManager

Method	Checks for
checkConnect(String host, int port)	Is an outgoing connection to the specified host and port allowed?
checkConnect(String host, int port, Object o)	Is an outgoing connection to the specified host and port allowed, given the execution context o?
checkAccept(String host, int port)	Is an incoming socket connection from hostname on the specified port permitted?
checkMulticast(InetAddress ia)	May the client use IP multicast to the address ia?
checkMulticast(InetAddress ia, byte ttl)	May the client use IP multicast with the specified Time-To-Live value?
checkListen(int port)	May a ServerSocket be opened to listen for incoming connections on this port?
checkSetFactory()	May the client set a networking-related factory such as URLConnectionFactory?
checkAccess(Thread t)	May the calling thread (Thread.currentThread()) modify the Thread object t ?
checkAccess(ThreadGroup tg)	May the calling thread modify the ThreadGroup tg?
checkAwtEventQueueAccess()	May a client get access to the main event queue?
checkCreateClassLoader()	May a new ClassLoader be created?
checkExec(String cmd)	May the system command cmd be executed?
checkExit(int code)	May the virtual machine be forced to exit with this exit code?
checkLink(String libname)	Is the named native library accessible?
checkMemberAccess(Class c, int n)	May a client use java.lang.reflect to access the nth member of the class c?
checkPackageAccess(String pkg)	May the client access the package named pkg?

(continued)

Table 7-1

The check methods of java.lang.SecurityManager *(continued)*

Method	Checks for
checkPackageDefinition(String pkg)	May the client add a class to the package named pkg?
checkPropertyAccess(String pname)	May the client read the specific system property named pname?
checkPropertiesAccess()	May the client read the entire list of system properties?
checkSecurityAccess(String provider)	May this provider do this?
checkSystemClipboardAccess()	May the client read and write the System clipboard?
checkTopLevelWindow(Object o)	May the caller create a top-level window, that is a new Frame, Window, or Dialog, given the execution context o?
checkPrintJobAccess()	May the client start printing?
checkDelete(String filename)	May the file with the given name be deleted?
checkRead(FileDescriptor fd)	May the client read from the file with FileDescriptor fd?
checkRead(String filename)	May the client read from the file with name filename?
checkRead(String filename, Object o)	May the client read from the file named filename given the execution context o?
checkWrite(FileDescriptor fd)	May the client create an output file with the specified file descriptor?
checkWrite(String filename)	May a file with the specified filename be created for output?

When the Java runtime wants to perform one of these potentially dangerous actions, it checks with the installed SecurityManager to see if the action is allowed. If it is allowed, the method returns normally, and program execution continues. However, if the action is disallowed, the check method throws a SecurityException.

By default, all of these actions are disallowed. If you want to allow any of these actions, then you must override the appropriate method so that it does not throw a SecurityException. This does not need to be a universal decision. You can check a number of conditions such as the host from which the code came to determine whether or not to allow the action.

Not all security features of Java are built into the SecurityManager class. Many of the lower-level features, like not allowing an int to be treated as a pointer, are built into the virtual machine at a much lower level than this. You cannot turn these off no matter how lenient you make your SecurityManager.

Secret

The most common thing that you should check before deciding whether or not to allow an action is where the class that asked for the action came from. In general, classes that were loaded from the CLASSPATH are assumed to be non-malicious and are therefore allowed a much greater degree of access to the system. You can use the classLoaderDepth() method to determine how deep in the method stack a ClassLoader appears. A class loader depth of 1 means that this method is being called by the ClassLoader object itself, which is generally fine, assuming you've installed a ClassLoader and forbidden other classes to do so. A class loader depth of more than one means that ultimately one of the classes on the stack was loaded by a class loader and not from the presumably trusted segment of the local file system. So, as a rule of thumb, if the int returned by SecurityManager.classLoaderDepth() is not equal to two, then you're dealing with code from an untrusted source, and you should be more careful.

For an applet viewer, you need to allow at least some network access so that .class files can be downloaded. You also need to allow new classes to be defined on the fly. File reading also needs to be enabled when the applet is loaded from the local file system. However, reading of files should be disabled when the applet does not come from the local file system, and writing and deleting of files can be completely disallowed. Similarly, multicast sockets, linking to native libraries, executing system commands, and exiting the virtual machine should all be disallowed. Listing 7-11 is a SecurityManager class that implements this policy.

Listing 7-11
The SimpleSecurityManager class

```
import java.io.*;
import java.net.*;
import java.util.*;


public class SimpleSecurityManager extends SecurityManager {


  /**
   * This method returns true if invoked indirectly from an applet.
   * The assumption is that there are no class loaders except those
   * used to load the applet.
   */
```

(continued)

Listing 7-11
The SimpleSecurityManager class *(continued)*

```
boolean inApplet() {
  return inClassLoader();
}


/**
 * Applets may not create new class loaders.
 */
public synchronized void checkCreateClassLoader() {
 if (classLoaderDepth() == 2) {
   throw new SecurityException("Applets may not create new class loaders");
 }
}


/**
 * Applets may not manipulate threads outside their own thread group.
 * This is actually a stronger restriction than imposed by Java 1.0
 * in which threads are allowed to manipulate any applet thread group.
 */
public synchronized void checkAccess(Thread t) {
 if (classLoaderDepth()==2) {
   ThreadGroup ctg = Thread.currentThread().getThreadGroup();
   if (t.getThreadGroup() != ctg) {
    throw new SecurityException("Applets may not manipulate threads outside
their own thread group");
   }
 }
}


/**
 * Applets may only manipulate their own thread group
 */
public synchronized void checkAccess(ThreadGroup tg) {
  if (classLoaderDepth()==4 && (tg !=
Thread.currentThread().getThreadGroup())) {
   throw new SecurityException("Applets may only manipulate their own thread
group");
  }
}


/**
 * Applets may not call System.exit().
 */
public synchronized void checkExit(int status) {
  if (inApplet()) {
   throw new SecurityException("Applets may not exit the VM");
```

(continued)

The SimpleSecurityManager class *(continued)*

```
    }
  }

  /**
   * Applets may not call System.exec()
   */
  public synchronized void checkExec(String cmd){
    if (inApplet()) {
      throw new SecurityException("Applets may not call system commands");
    }
  }

  /**
   * Applets may not link to native libraries.
   */
  public synchronized void checkLink(String lib){
    if (classLoaderDepth() == 3) {
        throw new SecurityException("Applets may not link to native
libraries.");
    }
  }

  /**
   * Applets may not read the entire system properties list
   */
  public synchronized void checkPropertiesAccess() {
    if (classLoaderDepth() == 2) {
      throw new SecurityException("Applets may not read the entire system
properties list");
    }
  }

  /**
   * Applets may only read the system property <i>foo</i>
   * if the system property <i>foo.applet</i> exists and has
   * the String value "true".
   */
  public synchronized void checkPropertyAccess(String name) {
    if (classLoaderDepth() == 2) {
      if (!((System.getProperty(name + ".applet").equalsIgnoreCase("true")))) {
        throw new SecurityException("Cannot read system property " + name);
      }
    }
  }
```

(continued)

Listing 7-11
The SimpleSecurityManager class *(continued)*

```java
/**
 * Applets may not read files unless they're loaded from a file URL.
 */
public synchronized void checkRead(String file) {

    URLClassLoader loader = (URLClassLoader) currentClassLoader();
    if (loader == null) return;
    if (loader.getURL().getProtocol().equalsIgnoreCase("file")) return;
    throw new SecurityException("Applets cannot read files");

}

public void checkRead(String file, Object context) {

  if (context != null) {
    URL u = (URL) context;
    if (!(u.getProtocol().equalsIgnoreCase("file"))) {
      throw new SecurityException("Applets cannot read files");
    }
  }

}

/**
 * Applets may not write files.
 */
public synchronized void checkWrite(String file) {
  throw new SecurityException("Applets may not write files.");
}

/**
 * Applets may not read from non-socket file descriptors
 */
public synchronized void checkRead(FileDescriptor fd) {
  if ((inApplet() && !inClass("java.net.SocketInputStream")) || (!fd.valid()) )
{
    throw new SecurityException("Applets cannot open file descriptors");
  }
}

/**
 * Applets may not write to non-socket file descriptors
 */
public synchronized void checkWrite(FileDescriptor fd) {
  if ((inApplet() && !inClass("java.net.SocketInputStream")) || (!fd.valid()) )
```

(continued)

The SimpleSecurityManager class *(continued)*

```
  {
      throw new SecurityException("Applets cannot open file descriptors");
    }
  }

  /**
   * Applets may not open server sockets
   */
  public synchronized void checkListen(int port) {
    if (inApplet()) {
      throw new SecurityException("Applets may not open server sockets");
    }
  }

  /**
   * Applets may not open server sockets.
   */
  public synchronized void checkAccept(String host, int port) {
    throw new SecurityException("Applets may not open server sockets");
  }

  /**
   * Check if an applet can connect to the given host:port.
   */
  public synchronized void checkConnect(String remoteHost, int port) {

    URLClassLoader loader = (URLClassLoader) currentClassLoader();
    if (loader == null) {
      return;
    }

    String localHost = loader.getURL().getHost();
    if (remoteHost.equals(localHost)) return;

    try {
      inCheck = true;
      if
(InetAddress.getByName(localHost).equals(InetAddress.getByName(remoteHost))) {
        return;
      }
    }
    catch (UnknownHostException e) {
    }
    finally {
      inCheck = false;
    }
```

(continued)

Listing 7-11
The SimpleSecurityManager class *(continued)*

```
    throw new SecurityException("Cannot open a socket to " + remoteHost);

}

public void checkConnect(String host, int port, Object context) {

  checkConnect(host, port);

}

/**
 * Applets may not create top-level windows
 */
public synchronized boolean checkTopLevelWindow(Object window) {

 if (inClassLoader()) return false;
 return true;
}

/**
 * Allow applets unrestricted package access.
 */
public synchronized void checkPackageAccess(String pkg) {


}

/**
 *  Allow applets to define packages
 */
public synchronized void checkPackageDefinition(String pkg) {

}

/**
 * Applets may not set a networking-related object factory.
 */
public synchronized void checkSetFactory() {

  throw new SecurityException("Applets cannot set network factories");

}
```

(continued)

The SimpleSecurityManager class *(continued)*

```
// New methods in 1.1

/**
 * Applets may not access the AWT event queue
 */
public synchronized void checkAwtEventQueueAccess() {

   if (inClassLoader()) {
      throw new SecurityException("Applets may not access the AWT event queue
directly");
   }

}

/**
 * Applets may not multicast
 */
public synchronized  void checkMulticast(InetAddress maddr) {

   throw new SecurityException("Applets may not multicast");

}

/**
 * Applets may not multicast
 */
public synchronized void checkMulticast(InetAddress maddr, byte ttl) {

   throw new SecurityException("Applets may not multicast");

}

/**
 * Applets may not print
 */
public synchronized void checkPrintJobAccess() {

   if (inClassLoader()) {
      throw new SecurityException("Applets may not print");
   }

}

/**
 * Applets may not access the System clipboard directly
 */
```

(continued)

Listing 7-11
The SimpleSecurityManager class *(continued)*

```
public synchronized void checkSystemClipboardAccess() {

    if (inClassLoader()) {
        throw new SecurityException("Applets may not access the System
clipboard");
    }

}



/**
 * Applets may only access the public members or a class through reflection
 */
public synchronized void checkMemberAccess(Class c, int type) {

    if (type != 0) {
        throw new SecurityException("Applets may not access declared members");
    }

}



/**
 * For now, do not restrict access based on the provider
 */
public synchronized void checkSecurityAccess(String provider) {

}

}
```

Mostly, this security policy mimics Sun's. It's a little more restrictive in some ways, primarily in not allowing applets access to threads in different thread groups. It's a little less restrictive in others, particularly in allowing applets to define new classes in any package. It's also considerably less configurable. Sun's AppletSecurity SecurityManager class, which you encounter in Chapter 9, permits the network security levels to be adjusted and allows access control lists to permit some access to the file system.

When an application starts up, no SecurityManager is in place and everything is permitted. However, a SecurityManager can be installed into an application by using the System.setSecurityManager() method like this:

```
System.setSecurityManager(new mySecurityManager());
```

The SecurityManager can be set only once in the lifetime of a Java application. This is a security feature to prevent rogue applets from slipping out of their sandboxes by changing the SecurityManager to something more lenient. Additional attempts to set the SecurityManager throw Security-Exceptions.

You can add the SimpleSecurityManager to the URLAppletViewer with a one-line addition to the main() method. The new main() method looks like this:

```
public static void main(String[] args) {

  URLAppletViewer uav = new URLAppletViewer();
  uav.show();
  System.setSecurityManager(new SimpleSecurityManager());

}
```

You won't need to call the methods of the SecurityManager class directly unless you want to check whether a particular operation is allowed before attempting it.

LOADING APPLETS FROM WEB PAGES

Until now, this chapter has shown how to load applets directly from .class files. Of course, in real world programming, the purpose of applets is to be embedded in Web pages. There are no special tricks to loading an applet from a Web page. This just adds an extra step. First, you must download the HTML file from a URL or other source. Then you have to parse it to find applet tags, and then download the .class file for the applet from the location specified in the CODE and CODEBASE parameters of the <APPLET> tag.

I am not going to create a generic HTML parser here. Instead, I write a method that scans an InputStream for the first <APPLET> tag it finds. This tag and everything between it and the closing </APPLET> tag will be passed to the constructor of a new class, AppletTag, which parses the tag. A better implementation might handle multiple <APPLET> tags and special cases like missing </APPLET> tags.

Listing 7-12 shows this class. This AppletTag object is returned and can be further queried for the values of specific parameters such as height, width, and name. Thus, the problem is split into two parts: finding the <APPLET> tag itself and parsing the <APPLET> tag.

Listing 7-12
The AppletTag class

```
import java.util.Hashtable;
import java.net.*;


public class AppletTag {

  String code;
  URL codebase;
  int width;
  int height;
  String name = null;
  Hashtable params;
  String alt = "";

  public AppletTag(String s) {

    String at = s.substring(0, s.indexOf('>'));
    code = readParameter(at, "code");
    try {
      codebase = new URL(readParameter(at, "codebase"));
    }
    catch (MalformedURLException e) {
      codebase = null;
    }
    name = readParameter(at, "name");
    alt = readParameter(at, "alt");
    width = Integer.parseInt(readParameter(at, "width"));
    height = Integer.parseInt(readParameter(at, "height"));

    int nextParam = -1;
    String ucs = s.toUpperCase();
    while ((nextParam = ucs.indexOf("<PARAM ", nextParam+1)) != -1) {
      String name = readParameter(s.substring(nextParam, s.indexOf("\\>")),
"name");
      String value = readParameter(s.substring(nextParam, s.indexOf("\\>")),
"value");
      params.put(name, value);
    }

  }

  String readParameter(String tag, String key) {

    key = key.toLowerCase();
    String ltag = tag.toLowerCase();
```

(continued)

The AppletTag class *(continued)*

```
    int e1;
    int k1 = ltag.indexOf(key + '=');
    if (k1 == -1) {
      k1 = ltag.indexOf(key + ' ');
      int k2 = ltag.indexOf(' ', k1);
      while (ltag.charAt(k2) == ' ') k2++;
      if (ltag.charAt(k2) != '=') return null;
      e1 = k2;
    }
    else {
      e1=ltag.indexOf('=', k1);
    }

    // e1 is now positioned on the equals sign
    // skip spaces, if any
    int v1 = e1+1;
    while (tag.charAt(v1) == ' ') v1++;

    try {
      char c = tag.charAt(v1);
      if (c == '"') {
        return tag.substring(v1+1, tag.indexOf('"', v1+1));
      }
      else {
        return tag.substring(v1, tag.indexOf(' ', v1));
      }
    }
    catch (StringIndexOutOfBoundsException e) {
      System.err.println(e);
      return null;
    }

  }


  public URL codebase() {
    return codebase;
  }

  public String code() {
    return code;
  }

  public int width() {
    return width;
  }
```

(continued)

Listing 7-12
The AppletTag class *(continued)*

```
public int height() {
  return height;
}

public String name() {
  return name;
}

public String alt() {
  return alt;
}

public Hashtable params() {
  return params;
}

}
```

Perhaps surprisingly, I found this task to be one of the hardest in this chapter. Although the other programs offered here required fairly deep understanding of how Java operates, the principles here are obvious. On the other hand, the algorithms required to implement these principles are relatively complex, whereas the algorithms needed to implement the earlier programs were quite simple. The biggest problem is the flexibility of HTML tags. Tag keywords may or may not be in uppercase. They may or may not contain embedded spaces. They may or may not be surrounded in double quotation marks if they don't contain embedded spaces. Compared to most of what's done in this chapter, HTML parsing is a hard problem, even if you're just looking for a couple of tags and ignoring everything else.

You also need to modify the applet viewer so that it knows it's reading an HTML file and not a .class file. This is done in Listing 7-13, the HTMLAppletViewer class. Finally, because you're now reading from HTML instead of directly from a .class file, parameters can be passed to applets. This requires a modified AppletStub class, in this case, the ParamAppletStub class of Listing 7-14.

Listing 7-13
The HTMLAppletViewer

```
import java.applet
import java.awt.*;
import java.net.*;
import java.io.*;
import java.util.*;


public class HTMLAppletViewer extends Frame implements AppletContext {

  Applet theApplet = null;
  AppletTag theTag = null;
  ParamAppletStub theStub = null;
  Panel appletPanel = new Panel();
  TextField thePage = new TextField(40);
  Button loadButton = new Button("Load");
  Button removeButton = new Button("Remove");
  Button reloadButton = new Button("Reload");
  Button restartButton = new Button("Restart");
  Vector theApplets = new Vector();
  TextField status = new TextField(33);
  URL documentBase = null;

  public static void main(String[] args) {

    HTMLAppletViewer hav = new HTMLAppletViewer();
    System.setSecurityManager(new SimpleSecurityManager());
    hav.show();

  }

  public HTMLAppletViewer() {

    super("HTML Applet Viewer");
    init();

  }

  public void init() {

    Panel p1 = new Panel();
    p1.setLayout(new GridLayout(3, 1));
    Panel p0 = new Panel();
    p0.setLayout(new FlowLayout(FlowLayout.LEFT));
    p0.add(new Label("URL: "));
    p0.add(thePage);
    p1.add(p0);
```

(continued)

Listing 7-13
The HTMLAppletViewer *(continued)*

```
        Panel p2 = new Panel();
        p2.add(loadButton);
        p2.add(removeButton);
        p2.add(reloadButton);
        p2.add(restartButton);
        p1.add(p2);
        Panel p4 = new Panel();
        p4.setLayout(new FlowLayout(FlowLayout.LEFT));
        p4.add(new Label("Status: "));
        status.setEditable(false);
        p4.add(status);
        p1.add(p4);
        add("South", p1);
        add("Center", appletPanel);
        resize(400, 250);

    }

    public void readPage(String s) {

        // is the name a URL?
        try {
            documentBase = new URL(s);
            theTag = parsePage(documentBase.openStream());
            if (theTag != null) {
                System.out.println(theTag);
                loadApplet();
            }
        }
        catch(MalformedURLException e) {
        }
        catch(IOException e) {
        }


    }

    public AppletTag parsePage(InputStream in) throws IOException {

        String at = null;
        int c;
        while ((c = in.read()) != -1) {
            if (c != '<') continue;
            c = in.read();
            if (c == ' ') continue; // just a < sign
            String tag = scanTag(c, in);
```

(continued)

The HTMLAppletViewer (continued)

```
      if (tag.toUpperCase().startsWith("<APPLET ")) at = tag;
      if (tag.toUpperCase().startsWith("<PARAM ") && at != null) at += tag;
      if (tag.toUpperCase().startsWith("</APPLET") && at != null) {
        at += tag;
        break;
      }
    }
    return new AppletTag(at);

  }

  String scanTag(int c, InputStream in) throws IOException {

    StringBuffer sb = new StringBuffer("<" + (char) c);
    while ((c = in.read()) != -1) {
      sb.append((char) c);
      if (c == '>') break;
    }

    return sb.toString();

  }


  public void loadApplet() {

    Class c = null;
    removeApplet();
    URLClassLoader ucl;

    if (theTag != null) {
      try {
        if (theTag.codebase() != null) ucl = new
URLClassLoader(theTag.codebase());
        else ucl = new URLClassLoader(documentBase);
        c = ucl.loadClass(theTag.code());
        theApplet = (Applet) c.newInstance();
        theStub = new ParamAppletStub(this, theTag.params(), documentBase,
theTag.codebase());
        theApplet.setStub(theStub);
        theApplet.resize(theTag.height(), theTag.width());
        appletPanel.add(theApplet);
        theApplets.addElement(theApplet);
        theApplet.init();
        theStub.activate();
```

(continued)

Listing 7-13
The HTMLAppletViewer *(continued)*

```
          theApplet.start();
          validate();
        }
        catch (Exception e) {
          showStatus(e.toString());
        }

    }
  }


  public void removeApplet() {

    if (theApplet != null) {
      theApplet.stop();
      theStub.deactivate();
      theApplet.destroy();
      theApplets.removeElement(theApplet);
      appletPanel.remove(theApplet);
      theApplet = null;
      validate();
      repaint();
    }
  }

  public void reload() {

    if (theTag != null) {
      loadApplet();
    }

  }

  public void restart() {

   if (theApplet != null) {
      theApplet.stop();
      theApplet.start();
    }

  }

  public boolean action(Event e, Object what) {

    if (e.target == restartButton) {
      restart();
```

(continued)

The HTMLAppletViewer *(continued)*

```
      return true;
    }
    else if (e.target == reloadButton) {
      reload();
      return true;
    }
    else if (e.target == loadButton) {
      loadApplet();
      return true;
    }
    else if (e.target == removeButton) {
      removeApplet();
      return true;
    }
    else if (e.target == thePage) {
      loadApplet();
      return true;
    }

    return false;

  }

  public Image getImage(URL u) {
    return Toolkit.getDefaultToolkit().getImage(u);
  }

  public AudioClip getAudioClip(URL u) {
    return new NullAudioClip();
  }

  public Applet getApplet(String s) {
    return null;
  }

  public Enumeration getApplets() {
    return (Enumeration) theApplets;
  }

  public void showDocument(URL url) {};

  public void showDocument(URL url, String target) {};

  public void showStatus(String s) {
    status.setText(s);
  }

}
```

Listing 7-14
The ParamAppletStub class

```java
import java.applet.*;
import java.net.URL;
import java.util.Hashtable;


public class ParamAppletStub implements AppletStub {

  AppletContext ac;
  boolean isActive = false;
  Hashtable params;

  public ParamAppletStub(AppletContext ac, Hashtable params) {
    this.ac = ac;
    this.params = params;
  }

  public void activate() {
    isActive = true;
  }

  public void deactivate() {
    isActive = false;
  }

  public  boolean isActive() {
    return isActive;
  }

  public URL getDocumentBase() {
    return null;
  }

  public URL getCodeBase() {
    return null;
  }

  public String getParameter(String name) {
    return (String) params.get(name);
  }

  public AppletContext getAppletContext() {
    return ac;
  }
```

(continued)

The ParamAppletStub class *(continued)*

```
public void appletResize(int width, int height) {

}

}
```

SUMMARY

In this chapter, you learn the following:

- An applet is an instance of java.applet.Applet or one of its subclasses. It inherits from java.lang.Object, java.awt.Component, java.awt. Container, and java.awt.Panel.

- Every applet should have a stub, which is an object that implements the AppletStub interface. One possible such object is an instance of sun.applet.AppletPanel. An applet's stub is set with the setStub() method.

- The context of an applet is an object that implements java.applet.AppletContext. This represents the Web browser or applet viewer and encapsulates functionality provided by a Web browser. You get a reference to an object's context with the getAppletContext() method.

- Every program that loads applets needs a ClassLoader object that understands how to locate and download the .class files for that applet.

- Every program that plays applets loaded from untrusted sources should install a SecurityManager to make sure that the applets don't get out of hand.

INTRODUCING THE SUN CLASSES

8

*T*his chapter begins your initiation into the mysteries of the sun classes, several packages of undocumented classes that add considerable power to Java programs. The following are just a few of the things you can do with the undocumented classes covered in the next ten chapters:

- Communicating with FTP, mail, and news servers
- Encoding and decoding data
- Converting between character sets
- Playing audio files

As you can see, Sun has hidden a great deal of functionality inside the sun classes. This book reveals it.

A little knowledge is a dangerous thing. Blindly using these classes without taking appropriate precautions is a recipe for disaster. Some of these classes may not be present in future releases of Java. They may not even be present in Java implementations not written by Sun. If they are present, their methods may not have the same signatures. Nonetheless, they provide too much additional power to be ignored, and there are some very simple techniques that enable you to use these packages safely in even non-conforming implementations. In this chapter, I show you how to use these classes without abusing them.

WHAT THE SUN CLASSES ARE

Secret

The sun classes are divided into 11 packages with a hierarchy that loosely mirrors the hierarchy of the java packages. These packages are, in no particular order:

- sun.applet
- sun.awt
- sun.io
- sun.net
- sun.rmi
- sun.security
- sun.beans
- sun.audio
- sun.jdbc
- sun.misc
- sun.tools

In most implementations, these packages are part of the basic class hierarchy stored in the main classes.zip file. If you unzip this file, you'll find all these packages.

Some of these packages are broken up into subpackages. For example, in addition to nine classes and exceptions of its own, sun.net contains four subpackages: sun.net.smtp, sun.net.www, sun.net.ftp, and sun.net.nntp.

The first seven packages listed here mostly provide low-level support for the equivalent java packages.

The sun.applet package is composed of concrete implementations of abstract classes and interfaces, as well as some helper classes for applet functions. In particular, this is where you find actual implementations of the AppletContext, AppletStub, and AudioClip interfaces. Most of these are used only by the applet viewer. Most browsers provide their own equivalents for these classes rather than using the ones from Sun's JDK. These are covered in Chapter 9.

The sun.awt package includes several additional LayoutManagers and components as well as some platform specific features and classes that work behind the scenes to load, decompress, and display images. These are discussed in Chapter 10

The sun.io package has several dozen classes that are concrete subclasses of the abstract java.io.CharToByteConverter and java.io.ByteToChar Converter classes. These classes handle conversions between Unicode and different character sets like Big 5 Chinese, Macintosh Turkish, and UTF-8. These are discussed in detail in Chapter 18.

The sun.net package probably includes more immediately useful classes than any of the other sun packages. This package has classes and sub-packages that handle SMTP, NNTP, FTP, and HTTP; generic classes for other kinds of network clients and servers; and much of the infrastructure needed to support content handlers, protocol handlers, and URLs. This is the richest sun package, and it will occupy a relatively large portion of this book. Chapters 13 through 17 investigate the different sun.net classes.

The sun.rmi package contains four subpackages that provide the infrastructure needed for remote method invocation (RMI). When you're writing remote object clients and servers, you have to use the java.rmi packages only because a lot of the details of the protocol are hidden in the subpackages of sun.rmi. The sun.rmi.registry package handles the naming and binding of names to remote objects. The sun.rmi.rmic package provides the tools needed to generate stubs and skeletons for your remote objects. The sun.rmi.server and sun.rmi.transport packages handle marshaling and unmarshaling of arguments, remote references, and the specific protocols used to make remote method calls.

The sun.security package is split into four subpackages that support the java.security package. These provide code signing and authentication. The sun.security package has specific implementations of the following:

- The Certificate, Key, PrivateKey, PublicKey, and Principal interfaces from the java.security package.

- The Acl, AclEntry, Group, Owner, and Permission interfaces from java.security.acl package.

- The DSAKey, DSAPublicKey, DSAPrivateKey, DSAKeyPairGenerator, and DSAParams interfaces from the java.security.interfaces package.

The sun.beans package provides much of the infrastructure for the Java Beans component architecture. It's a relatively late addition to the main Java API, making its first appearance in JDK 1.1b3. It was originally scheduled to be an optional add-on to Java 1.1 and to be integrated in Java 1.2. Much of the Beans API is still relatively raw, and many parts remain to be fleshed out, such as a compound document model and interaction with other component models like ActiveX and OpenDoc. Therefore, the sun.beans package is particularly likely to change. At this point, I'd recommend staying away from it.

The sun.audio package provides the infrastructure for reading a stream of audio data and playing it. It's mainly called by the sun.applet.AudioClip class, which implements the java.applet.AudioClip interface. You can use sun.audio to play audio files in non-applets. This is covered in Chapter 11.

JDBC stands for "Java DataBase Connectivity." The sun.jdbc package provides the infrastructure for the java.sql package in the core API.

The sun.misc package includes a few necessary classes that didn't quite fit in anywhere else. This includes classes to encode and decode data in a variety of formats, including Base 64 and uuencode. There are also classes to time events, work with the cache, process regular expressions, and manipulate threads in the virtual machine. Chapter 12 discusses some of these classes.

The sun.tools package includes the building blocks for many development tools with which you're probably familiar. The sun.tools.asm package contains the building blocks for a Java byte code assembler. The sun.tools.debug package is used by Sun's minimal debugger, jdb. The sun.tools.jar package supports the creation of Jar files via the java.util.zip package. The sun.tools.java package includes some (though not all) of the pieces needed by the Java byte code interpreter. The sun.tools.javac package is used to build the javac compiler. The sun.tools.javadoc package is used to build the javadoc documentation tool. The sun.tools.native2ascii package includes a single class, Main, which converts a file written in a local character set to ISO-Latin 1 with Unicode escapes, or vice versa. The sun.tools.serialver Class is the basis for the serialver command, which returns a version ID for a class. The sun.tools.tree package assists in byte code verification of class files. Finally, the sun.tools.ttydebug package is the basis for a remote debugger that runs in one virtual machine while debugging a program running in another virtual machine.

WHY THE SUN CLASSES EXIST

Given that the sun classes are so useful, you're probably wondering why they aren't documented. Why not just put everything into the java packages and leave it at that? There are several reasons.

First of all, many of the classes in the sun packages are relatively implementation-specific. For example, the java.applet.AppletContext interface is supposed to represent the Web browser or applet viewer. Thus, every Web browser and applet viewer will have a different class to represent them. All of these objects implement the methods of the AppletContext interface, but otherwise they are different. In Sun's JDK, this class is sun.applet.AppletViewer. In Netscape, the AppletContext interface is implemented by the MozillaAppletContext class instead.

Other classes in the sun packages are tools and utilities needed by Java developers, but not by people merely running applets. For example, there's an entire package called sun.javac that contains all the classes you need to build a working Java compiler. There's no reason for these classes to be included in a browser's class library because browsers only run applets; they don't compile them. However, if you're writing development tools, then these classes can be very helpful.

Netscape 2.0's class library was not as heavily customized as the one in Versions 3.0 and later. On platforms where it ran, the Netscape 2.0 VM actually did contain the right classes to allow javac to run. Indeed, many programmers who worked on platforms that Netscape supported but Sun did not (like SunOS 4.1) took advantage of this to compile Java code. However, more recent versions of Netscape have stingier class libraries and can no longer compile Java code.

Some parts of the sun packages isolate platform dependencies. For example, the Solaris distribution of the JDK includes a sun.awt.motif package with classes like CharToByteX11Dingbats and X11Image that simply aren't relevant to other platforms. The Mac JDK includes sun.awt.macos with a MacFontMetrics class and a MacGraphics class, among others. Many peer components that produce GUI widgets with the native look-and-feel are also included in these packages. This fits in with Java's philosophy that the public Java API should be completely cross-platform. All platform dependencies should be hidden.

The most interesting parts of the sun packages are the ones that Javasoft simply never finished. Many of these were quick hacks that were needed for a particular program, most commonly HotJava. These classes may move into the java packages in the future, just as soon as Javasoft gets around to completing and documenting them. For example, the MulticastSocket class was in the sun.net package in Java 1.0 but moved into the java.net package in Java 1.1. Most of the Sun classes discuss in this book fall into this last category.

USING THE SUN CLASSES SAFELY

As you'll see in the next several chapters, the sun classes are extremely useful. If you're writing quick hacks for your own use, there's no reason at all not to use them. For example, why should you waste your time coding quicksort for the 1,017th time in your life when there's a perfectly good quicksort() method in the sun.misc.Sort class? The case is even more clear when you consider some of the more complicated classes like sun.net.ftp. FtpClient. Providing similar functionality from scratch would require many hours of studying the FTP protocol RFCs, testing the responses of different servers, and hunting down bugs in input streams that block unexpectedly. If all you need is a simple mirror program for your personal use, then you can write it much more quickly by using the sun.net.ftp.FtpClient class.

However, matters are somewhat trickier when your application will be run by more than one person. The more people who are going to run it, the trickier it gets. If it's just going to be other people in your work group or lab, then you can probably safely assume that they have the same Java environment that you do and can run the same programs that you can. If they can't, then they can always come find you to fix it. The real problem arises if, at a later point, the environment changes in an incompatible fashion that breaks your program. This can be a problem, but it may be possible to fix the problem at that point. Alternatively, you may be able to use the sun classes as part of a quick prototype and code it correctly later.

The problems get worse when you're distributing an application outside of your immediate environment. The sun classes are not much help if your audience doesn't have access to them. Most people will have some of the sun classes available in their CLASSPATH, but different people will have different classes available. People writing Java code may have all of the sun classes available. Users running HotJava probably will, too. However, people using Netscape may have only a few of the sun classes, and which ones they have will vary from version to version and platform to platform. However, there are a few simple steps you can take to make sure the classes are available to your users.

Put the classes you use on your Web server

If you're writing applets that will be served from Web servers and run in Web browsers, the best solution is to make the Sun classes you need (or even the entire Sun hierarchy) available from your CODEBASE.

Suppose that an applet that lives at `http://sunsite.unc.edu/javafaq/secrets/MyApplet.class` tries to instantiate a sun.awt.VerticalBagLayout object. If there is a sun.awt.VerticalBagLayout class somewhere in the browser's CLASSPATH, then it will be found and the object will be created with no further fuss. On the other hand, suppose that the VerticalBagLayout class isn't found. Then the browser asks the Web server for it. Specifically, it requests the following URL:

`http://sunsite.unc.edu/javafaq/secrets/sun/awt/VerticalBagLayout.class.`

Therefore, if you put this directory structure in place at `http://sunsite.unc.edu/javafaq/secrets/`, the applet will be able to run whether or not the user has that file installed.

You may need to unzip the JDK's classes.zip file to find the classes you need, but this is generally not a big problem.

A much more serious issue is that, for this to work, the class must be self-contained. In particular, it must not invoke any package methods in other classes in the package. Attempting to do so will throw a Security-Exception. You see, classes downloaded from your Web page aren't really in the sun packages at all.

The class loader ensures that there's a unique namespace for each network source that is different from the name space used for system classes loaded from a local file system. It's as if a class that came from `http://sunsite.unc.edu/javafaq/secrets/sun/awt/VerticalBagLayout.class` wasn't sun.awt. VerticalBagLayout, but rather edu.unc.sunsite.sun. awt.VerticalBagLayout. (That's not really the exact name that would be used, but you get the idea.) In essence, classes downloaded from the network can never be in the same packages as classes loaded from the local file system.

Sometimes this is acceptable. The sun.awt.VerticalBagLayout class does not refer to any other classes in the sun.awt package. It can stand on its own, so it doesn't really matter whether it's sun.awt.VerticalBagLayout or edu.unc.sunsite.sun.awt.VerticalBagLayout.

On the other hand, some classes work only in conjunction with the package access methods of other classes. For example, sun.misc.Queue is totally dependent on the sun.misc.QueueElement Class. QueueElement is a non-public class whose constructor has package access. The fields in the QueueElement class also have only package access. In fact, the only public method is toString().

```
QueueElement next
QueueElement prev
Object obj
QueueElement(Object obj)
public String toString()
```

The Queue Class needs to access all of these package methods to do its job, so it runs into a problem if the sun.misc.Queue class isn't there.

Of course, in many situations like this, the reasons that the necessary methods have package access is that the classes are tied together very closely. If the sun.misc.Queue class isn't present in the CLASSPATH, then chances are good that the sun.misc.QueueElement class isn't either. Therefore, you can just put both in the appropriate locations on your Web server.

In fact, if you don't feel like disassembling the classes to see what a given class depends on, you can just go ahead and put the entire Sun hierarchy on your web site and let the ClassLoader decide what it needs to download and when. Classes should be loaded from the local CLASSPATH first, and only if the classes aren't there will your Web site be searched.

There's still a possible problem if a class from your Web site invokes a package access method or accesses a package access field in a class that does exist in the local CLASSPATH, but this is relatively unlikely.

Distribute the classes with your application

Stand-alone applications will generally not connect to a Web server to download a class file. However, if you're writing a stand-alone application, you have a few other options. The best option is to distribute the necessary class with your application. This is the simplest and most effective solution.

The second option is to request that users download and install the necessary files in their CLASSPATH themselves. This isn't the easiest thing in the world to get users to do, much less do properly. You could probably write an installer program in Java that would download the necessary files from ftp.javasoft.com, unzip them, and move them into the right directories in your application folder.

Write an equivalent class

A third option is to rewrite the necessary class yourself using Sun's class as a guide. This will be much easier if you have access to the source code for the sun classes, even in an earlier version. If so, you may be able to just copy the code into a new file, change the package statement, and recompile it — for example, com.idgbooks.misc.BASE64Encoder.class instead of sun.misc. BASE64Encoder.class. This may require no more than changing the single package statement at the top of the source code. In more complex classes, you may also need to change and recompile superclasses and other sun classes to which the class you're interested in refers.

Legal issues

In general, none of these three options — putting classes on your Web server, distributing the classes with your application, or writing equivalent classes — should be a problem for non-commercial applications. Sun's copyright notice in the various source code files reads:

> Copyright (c) 1994 Sun Microsystems, Inc. All Rights Reserved.
>
> Permission to use, copy, modify, and distribute this software and its documentation for NON-COMMERCIAL purposes and without fee is hereby granted provided that this copyright notice appears in all copies. Please refer to the file "copyright.html" for further important copyright and licensing information.

This is taken from Version 1.0.1 of the Java source code for Solaris. Source code for the sun packages of Java 1.1 had not yet been released at the time I was writing this book. The copyright language may be tightened up somewhat in that version.

Other license agreements are less clear. For example, the installation procedure for Java 1.1 beta 2 says this:

> The Software is copyrighted and title to all copies is retained by Sun and/or its licensers. Licensee shall not make copies of Software, other than a single copy of Software in machine-readable format for backup or archival purposes and, if applicable, Licensee may print one copy of online documentation, in which event all proprietary rights notices on Software and online documentation shall be reproduced and applied to all copies. Licensee shall not modify, decompile, disassemble, decrypt, extract, or otherwise reverse-engineer Software.

It is unclear at the time of this writing what the final resolution will be. It is even less clear what is and is not legally valid in these license agreements, as discussed in Chapter 4. As a practical matter, I wouldn't worry about this too much if you're not shipping shrink-wrapped payware. If you are shipping shrink-wrapped payware, it's not too difficult to negotiate a redistribution license for the JDK from Sun. Just be sure you're allowed to ship it in parts, rather than as one large installer file.

Checking for the presence of the sun classes

Java makes it relatively easy to determine whether a particular class or method exists at runtime. Most of the time, you just assume that the classes that you need will be present. However, when using undocumented classes, you can't afford to be that careless. The basic trick is to catch a NoClass DefFoundError when you first try to construct an instance of a sun class. This is a good way to check for the presence of the few classes that may not be present at runtime.

Note There's also a java.lang.ClassNotFoundException. This is a checked exception that's useful primarily when working directly with ClassLoaders. It is not the same thing as NoClassDefFoundError. Most of the time, you are quite conscious of when a ClassNotFoundException can be thrown, whereas a NoClassDefFoundError comes as a complete surprise. However, when you're using the sun classes, you're already in a very strange place, so normal rules about what's expected and what's not don't apply.

For example, in Chapter 11 you'll see a SoundPlayer program that uses the sun.audio classes. Here's the open() method from that class:

```
public void open() {
  FileDialog fd = new FileDialog(this, "Please select a .au file:");
  fd.setFilenameFilter(this);
  fd.show();
  try {
    theFile = new File(fd.getDirectory() + "/" + fd.getFile());
    if (theFile != null) {
      filename.setText(theFile.getName());
      FileInputStream fis = new FileInputStream(theFile);
      AudioStream as = new AudioStream(fis);
      theData = as.getData();
    }
  }
  catch (IOException e) {
    System.err.println(e);
  }
}
```

The sun.audio.AudioStream class is used to read the data. If you think that class might not be available, wrap it in a try-catch block like this:

```
public void open() {
  FileDialog fd = new FileDialog(this, "Please select a .au file:");
  fd.setFilenameFilter(this);
  fd.show();
  try {
    theFile = new File(fd.getDirectory() + "/" + fd.getFile());
    if (theFile != null) {
      filename.setText(theFile.getName());
      FileInputStream fis = new FileInputStream(theFile);
      try {
        AudioStream as = new AudioStream(fis);
        theData = as.getData();
      }
      catch (NoClassDefFoundError e) {
        theData = null;
      }
    }
  }
  catch (IOException e) {
    System.err.println(e);
  }
}
```

Here, if the class isn't present, then the audio file simply isn't played. In some applications, this would be acceptable if the audio were not crucial to the application. I'm sure you can think of other things you can do once you catch the exception as well. For example, you may want to print an error message and ask the user to install the required classes.

Listing 8-1 demonstrates another approach to the problem. Suppose that you want to use the sun.awt.VerticalBagLayout LayoutManager described in Chapter 10. You can wrap it inside a class of your own devising. Your own MyVerticalLayout class implements the LayoutManager interface and thus can be used wherever you'd use a VerticalBagLayout. It has a LayoutManager field called sub that does all the work. Each of the LayoutManager methods just calls the equivalent method in sub.

The constructor tries to set sub to a VerticalBagLayout. However, if it fails-that is, if a NoClassDefFoundError is thrown-then it falls back to a simple FlowLayout.

The fallback position can be adjusted depending on your needs. You might prefer to use a GridLayout with one column and a certain number of rows. In some cases, you may want to write your own class that provides some of the functionality normally provided by the sun class. In Listing 8-1, I was lucky in that it was really the interface that was needed and not the class. You must decide which fallback position to choose on a case-by-case basis.

Listing 8-1
A LayoutManager that tries to use a sun.awt.VerticalBagLayout but falls back to a FlowLayout if necessary

```java
import java.awt.*;


public class MyVerticalLayout implements LayoutManager {

  LayoutManager sub;

  public MyVerticalLayout() {
    this(0);
  }

  public MyVerticalLayout(int vgap) {

    try {
      sub = (LayoutManager) new sun.awt.VerticalBagLayout(vgap);
    }
    catch (SecurityException e) {
      sub = (LayoutManager) new FlowLayout(FlowLayout.LEFT, vgap, vgap);
    }
    catch (NoClassDefFoundError e) {
      sub = (LayoutManager) new FlowLayout(FlowLayout.LEFT, vgap, vgap);
    }
  }
  public void addLayoutComponent(String name, Component comp) {
    sub.addLayoutComponent(name, comp);
  }

  public void removeLayoutComponent(Component comp) {
    sub.removeLayoutComponent(comp);
  }

  public Dimension minimumLayoutSize(Container target) {
    return sub.minimumLayoutSize(target);
  }

  public Dimension preferredLayoutSize(Container target) {
    return sub.preferredLayoutSize(target);
  }
```

(continued)

A LayoutManager that tries to use a sun.awt.VerticalBagLayout but falls back to a FlowLayout if necessary *(continued)*

```
public void layoutContainer(Container target) {
  sub.layoutContainer(target);
}

public String toString() {
 return sub.toString();
 }


 }
```

Checking for methods and fields

The biggest problem when using the sun classes is certainly their very existence. Most of the time, if a class is present in the user's CLASSPATH at all, then it can be used safely. However, there is a small chance that classes may change in incompatible ways between platforms and versions. You can always check the system properties java.version and os.arch to see if you're running on a platform that you've tested and verified before calling the sun classes. However, most of us don't have the resources to test the dozens of different Java environments already on the market, and the problems are only going to get worse as time goes on and more vendors release their own virtual machines.

Therefore, if you're worried that a class may change its public contract between versions, you can also check for the presence of individual fields and methods before using them. If a class is found but a method isn't, then a NoSuchMethodError is thrown. If a class is found but a field isn't, then a NoSuchFieldError is thrown. Both extend java.lang.IncompatibleClass ChangeError. Normally these errors are caught at compile-time, but again we're in a weird space here.

Note: The java.lang package also includes the NoSuchMethodException checked exception. This is obsolete and is no longer thrown in Java 1.1. It is included for backward compatibility only.

For example, suppose you were using the sun.misc.Sort class. In Sun's Solaris JDK, sun.misc.Sort has the following public methods:

```
public static void quicksort(Object[] items, int start, int end, Compare c)
public static void quicksort(Object[] items, Compare c)
```

This class sorts lists of objects using an object that implements the sun.misc.Compare interface. The first argument to each quicksort method is an array of objects to be sorted. The final argument is an object that implements the sun.misc.Compare interface. The first variant also specifies the starting and ending indexes in the array between which to sort. This method can be called recursively to sort the entire array, and indeed that's what the second method does.

The Compare interface declares a single method, doCompare():

```
public abstract int doCompare(Object o1, Object o2)
```

Implementations of Compare are specialized to handle different types of objects. They should return 1 if the first object is greater than the second object, 0 if they're equal, and -1 if the first object is less than the second object. Listing 8-2 demonstrates an IntegerCompare class.

Note

Actually, any positive number can replace 1, and any negative number can replace -1.

Listing 8-2
The IntegerCompare class

```
public class IntegerCompare implements sun.misc.Compare {

   public int doCompare(Object o1, Object o2) {     Integer I1 = (Integer) o1;
     Integer I2 = (Integer) o2;

     int i1 = I1.intValue();
     int i2 = I2.intValue();
     if (i1 > i2) return 1;
     else if (i1 == i2) return 0;
     else return -1;

   }

}
```

There's also a StringCompare class in the sun.net.www.protocol.file package. You'll see it in Chapter 17 in a discussion of the file protocol handler of which it's a part.

The point of this chapter is that there's nothing much to stop Sun from changing the public methods in the Sort class. It's not really a problem if they add methods, but it could be a problem if they change a method's name or make a previously public method private. To avoid this, you can catch NoSuchMethodErrors. For example, Listing 8-3 tries to use quicksort, but falls back to a user-written bubblesort if the quicksort method isn't found.

Listing 8-3
An example of checking for methods

```
public class Sorter {

  public static void sort(Object[] items, int start, int end, Compare c) {

    try {
      sun.misc.Sort.quicksort(items, start, end, c);
    }
    catch (NoSuchMethodError e) {
      bubblesort(items, start, end, c);
    }
    catch (NoClassDefFoundError e) {
      bubblesort(items, start, end, c);
    }

  }

  public static void sort(Object[] items, Compare c) {
    sort(items, 0, items.length-1, c);  }

  static void bubblesort(Object[] items, int start, int end, Compare c) {

    boolean done = false;

    while (!done) {
      done = true;
      for (int i = start; i < end-1; i++) {

        if (c.doCompare(items[i],items[i+1]) > 0) {
          done = false;
          Object temp = items[i];
          items[i] = items[i+1];
          items[i+1] = temp;
        }
      }
    }

  }

}
```

SUMMARY

In this chapter, you learn the following:

- The sun packages include useful classes for many things, including sending e-mail, uuencoding files, compiling Java programs, laying out components, and a great deal more.

- Some of the Sun classes are incomplete or buggy, so be careful when using them. Test your programs thoroughly on multiple platforms before releasing them.

- Do not assume that everyone will have the necessary classes installed. Make sure you can distribute the classes that you need with your applet or application. If you can't do this, catch NoClassDefFoundErrors and NoSuchMethodErrors, and provide alternative solutions.

Using the sun. applet Classes to View Applets

## 9

*C*hapter 7 should have convinced you that it's no trivial thing to program an applet viewer. Programming a Web browser that can play applets is still more difficult. Of course, Sun does all these things through their applet viewer and HotJava. Therefore, these problems must have been solved already, and it's not absolutely necessary that you solve them all again yourself. However, the classes that solve these problems are not exposed to the programmer as part of the public API. Instead, they're hiding in the sun classes.

As you saw in Chapter 7, there are four fundamental things your program needs to play applets:

- An AppletContext
- An AppletStub
- A ClassLoader
- A SecurityManager

The sun.applet package includes all four of these, as well as several more support classes. Instead of writing your own variants of these, as you did in Chapter 7, you can use the sun.applet classes instead. However, if you choose this option, you should be aware that these classes make large assumptions about other classes in the package. For example, the checkAccess() methods of the AppletSecurity class rely on the inner workings of both the AppletThreadGroup class and the AppletViewer class. It is generally not possible to use just one of these classes without using all of them. Similarly, it is difficult to replace just one of these classes without replacing all of them. If you do, you'll almost certainly need access to the source code for these classes so that you can fully understand the undocumented contracts between these classes.

THE SUN.APPLET PACKAGE

The driving program in this package is sun.applet.AppletViewer. This class has a main() method that is invoked when you execute the appletviewer program from the command line:

```
% appletviewer http://sunsite.unc.edu/javafaq/HelloWorld.html
```

Secret

The appletviewer program actually points to a shell script or .exe file which, after performing a few manipulations with the CLASSPATH, invokes the Java interpreter to launch the appletviewer like this:

```
% java sun.applet.AppletViewer http://sunsite.unc.edu/javafaq/
HelloWorld. html
```

The AppletViewer main() method reads the files or URLs specified on the command line looking for <APPLET> tags. It creates a new AppletViewer object for each <APPLET> tag that it finds. The AppletViewer class implements the AppletContext interface, and this AppletViewer object also provides a context for the applet. The AppletViewer class also manages the menus and menu bars and installs an AppletSecurity object as the security manager.

An AppletPanel is placed inside the AppletViewer. The AppletPanel class is a subclass of java.awt.Panel, which implements the AppletStub interface. This panel controls the applet while it's being loaded. In particular, it creates a new thread to process load, start, stop, init, and destroy events directed to the applet. This thread belongs to a ThreadGroup, which is an instance of the AppletThreadGroup class. This allows the runtime to distinguish between threads that belong to the applet and threads that belong to the runtime.

Once the applet panel is created, the AppletViewer object sends load, init, and start events to it in rapid succession. Not surprisingly, this causes the AppletPanel to load, initialize, and start the applet. The AppletPanel loads classes using an AppletClassLoader object. The AppletClassLoader class is quite similar in function to the URLClassLoader that you saw in Chapter 7. A different AppletClassLoader object is used for each different CODEBASE from which applets are loaded.

Assuming no errors occur in the loading and initializing of the class (for example, not being able to connect to the remote host to read the byte codes), control from that point on mostly passes to the applet itself. However, events directed at the AppletViewer, such as selecting File/Quit from the AppletViewer menu, are handled inside the AppletViewer class. Furthermore, any calls to the applet's context, either direct or indirect, are handled by the applet viewer; and any calls to the applet's stub, either direct or indirect, are handled by the applet panel.

Although these are the main classes of the sun.applet package, there are about a dozen more support classes. AppletCopyright, AppletProps, and TextFrame are informational dialog boxes. AppletAudioClip implements the AudioClip interface and is returned by the various getAudioClip() methods of AppletContext. AppletImageRef is used to help download images.

There are also three exceptions indicating various problems: Applet IllegalArgumentException, AppletIOException, and AppletSecurity Exception. Each of these is a subclass of the normal, non-applet equivalent, which is what you'll mostly catch.

THE APPLETVIEWER CLASS

The sun.applet.AppletViewer class is one of the few classes in the sun package with a main() method. Thus, it's one of the few you can launch directly from the command line. The main() method reads the command line arguments, interprets them as either URLs or files (by seeing whether or not they contain colons), parses those files and URLs looking for <APPLET> tags, and constructs an AppletViewer object for each <APPLET> tag that it finds. The applets are then loaded and played.

The constructor

The AppletViewer class itself is a subclass of java.awt.Frame. Therefore, one simple way to add applet support to your applications is to load applets into a new AppletViewer by using this constructor:

```
public AppletViewer(int x, int y, URL u, Hashtable atts)
```

Note

In some earlier versions of Java, this constructor wasn't public, but it is public in Java 1.1.

Here, x and y are the coordinates of the upper-left corner of the Applet-Viewer window; u is the URL of the HTML page in which the applet is embedded; and atts is a Hashtable that should contain the parameters to the <APPLET> tag and the name-value pairs given in <PARAM> tags. For example, suppose this is your <APPLET> tag set:

```
<applet codebase="http://java.sun.com/applets/applets/NervousText"
code="NervousText.class" width=300 height=125>
<param name="text" value="This is cool!">
This is cool!
</applet>
```

The atts Hashtable would have these name-value pairs:

"codebase"	"http://java.sun.com/applets/applets/NervousText"
"code"	"NervousText.class"
"alt"	"alt"
"width"	"300"
"height"	"125"
"align"	"align"
"vspace"	"vspace"
"hspace"	"hspace"
"name"	"name"
"archives"	"archives"
"text"	"This is cool!"
"object"	"object"

Each key and value in this Hashtable must be a String object. If a possible parameter to the <APPLET> tag is not included in the tag set, then you should add it anyway; just use the key name as the value. However, at a minimum, your Hashtable must contain values for the keys "code," "width," and "height."

Other methods

Once the AppletViewer object has been constructed, there's relatively little you do directly with this class. You can use the methods of the superclass, java.awt.Frame, to manipulate the AppletViewer window. You can also call your applet's AppletContext, directly or indirectly, which results in calls to the equivalent methods of AppletViewer. I discuss these in the next section. Other than the constructor and the AppletContext methods, there are only five public methods in sun.applet.AppletViewer. These are as follows:

```
public static void main(String[] args)
public static void init()
public boolean handleEvent(Event evt)
public void updateAtts()
public static synchronized void networkProperties()
```

public static void main(String[] args)

The main() method is used when AppletViewer is invoked from the command line. You'll rarely call it directly. The args[] array is a list of URLs and filenames from which applets are to be loaded.

Of course, just because the main method is usually invoked only by the runtime doesn't mean you can't call it. If you like, you can start an AppletViewer to read a series of URLs, like this:

```
String[] args = {"http://sunsite.unc.edu/javafaq/HelloWorld.html",
  "http://sunsite.unc.edu/javafaq/examples/10/10.2.html"};
AppletViewer.main(args);
```

This will use the normal ClassLoader, SecurityManager, and other support classes. You might do this if you were writing an Integrated Development Environment (IDE), for example.

public static void init()

The main() method invokes the init() method when AppletViewer is called from main(). It installs a new AppletSecurity object as the SecurityManager and sets a number of System properties to their default values. The properties and their defaults are listed in Listing 9-1.

Listing 9-1
The Sun AppletViewer default properties in Java 1.1b3

```
acl.read=+
acl.read.default=
acl.write=+
acl.write.default=
browser=sun.applet.AppletViewer
browser.version=1.06
```

(continued)

Listing 9-1

The Sun AppletViewer default properties in Java 1.1b3 *(continued)*

```
browser.vendor=Sun Microsystems Inc.
http.agent=JDK/1.1
firewallSet=true
firewallHost=sunweb.ebay
firewallPort=80
package.restrict.access.sun=true
package.restrict.access.netscape=true
package.restrict.definition.java=true
package.restrict.definition.sun=true
package.restrict.definition.netscape=true
java.version.applet=true
java.vendor.applet=true
java.vendor.url.applet=true
java.class.version.applet=true
os.name.applet=true
os.version.applet=true
os.arch.applet=true
file.separator.applet=true
path.separator.applet=true
line.separator.applet=true
```

The acronym acl stands for "access control list." The acl properties are used by the AppletSecurity SecurityManager to determine which files may and may not be read and written. By default, no files are included in the access control list.

The browser and http properties identify the Web browser or, in this case, the appletviewer. Of course, the exact values vary from version to version. The firewall properties are set by default, but will be used only if a SocketFactory requests them. At the time of this writing, that's not the case.

The package properties determine whether applets are allowed to access or define classes in a given package. According to these defaults, an applet may not use classes in the sun or netscape packages and may not define classes in the sun, netscape, or java packages. It's up to the SecurityManager to enforce this. If a package is not listed, then applets may both use classes in the package and add new classes to the package.

The last ten properties are probably not what you expect. They define whether the AppletSecurity SecurityManager is able to read the corresponding property, not whether the property is actually true or false. For example, if the property java.version.applet is true, as it is here, then an applet is allowed to read the value of the property java.version. However, if the property java.version.applet is false or does not exist, then applets may not read the property java.version. In general, applets are allowed to read properties that reveal information about the environment, such as java.version or os.version (the operating system version). However, applets are not allowed to read properties that reveal information about the user, such as user.name.

Any or all of these may be overridden by the .hotjava/properties file. This file contains a list of properties in the same format. A line beginning with a # is a comment. Other lines contain the names of specific properties, followed by an = sign, followed by the String value of the property. Generally, you do not edit this file directly. Instead, you edit it by selecting Properties from the File menu. Then an AppletProps frame is constructed to allow the user to modify the properties.

If you do not call AppletViewer.main(), then you have a choice of whether or not to call AppletViewer.init(). If you like these defaults, you should call AppletViewer.init(). If you don't, you should replace them in a method of your own. The biggest question to ask yourself is whether you're happy with the AppletSecurity SecurityManager. AppletViewer.init() sets the system SecurityManager to a new AppletSecurity object, and once set, it can't be changed. You can always change a few System properties later, but you will have to stick with the decision you make about SecurityManager.

public boolean handleEvent(Event evt)

The handleEvent() method is called by the runtime. You should not call it directly. If you want to send an event, pass it to sendEvent() instead.

The AppletViewer class handles APPLET_RESIZE, WINDOW_ICONIFY, WINDOW_DEICONIFY, WINDOW_DESTROY, and ACTION_EVENT events. All other events are passed to the superclass (java.awt.Frame) for handling. Table 9-1 explains the meaning of these events.

Table 9-1

Events handled by the AppletViewer class

Event	*Result*
AppletPanel.APPLET_RESIZE	Resizes the AppletViewer to its preferred size and validates it.
Event.WINDOW_ICONIFY	Hides the applet and stops it.
Event.WINDOW_DEICONIFY	Shows the applet and starts it.
Event.WINDOW_DESTROY	Stops the applet, destroys the applet, and then exits the virtual machine.
Event.ACTION_EVENT	Checks the string in the event's argument field, and calls the appropriate method. This handles menu selections.

public void updateAtts()

Because an applet running in an AppletViewer can change size, the updateAtts() method checks the current size of the applet and updates the width and height entries in the attributes table. Recall that this was passed into the AppletViewer() constructor in the form of a Hashtable and that width and height are normally read from the WIDTH and HEIGHT parameters of the <APPLET> tag.

The AppletViewer calls this method whenever the AppletViewer is cloned or when the applet tag is shown; that is, whenever the user selects Clone or Tag from the Applet menu. You may also want to call this method if you're going to do something that relies on having an up-to-date height and width for the AppletViewer, but 99 times out of 100, you'll really want to know the applet's height and width instead, and you can always get that by calling Applet.getSize().

public static synchronized void networkProperties()

The networkProperties() method just shows the AppletProps window so the user can change his or her network properties, such as the firewall and the level of network access allowed. This method is invoked when the user selects Properties from the AppletViewer's File menu.

This method had only package access in Java 1.0. It's unclear why it suddenly became public in Java 1.1. However, it *is* public, so if you feel a need to ask the user to change or verify the network properties, you can.

The AppletContext methods

The AppletViewer class implements all seven methods of the AppletContext interface. These are as follows:

```
public AudioClip getAudioClip(URL u)
public Image getImage(URL u)
public Applet getApplet(String name)
public Enumeration getApplets()
public void showDocument(URL u)
public void showDocument(URL u, String target)
public void showStatus(String status)
```

The getAudioClip() method downloads an .au file from the URL u and stores it in a sun.applet.AppletAudioClip object. It does keep a cache of previously loaded AudioClips, and if you ask for the same clip twice, it will be retrieved from the cache the second time. AudioClips are discussed in detail in Chapter 11.

The getImage() method downloads an image file from the URL u and returns a reference to the data as a java.awt.Image object. The AppletViewer class also maintains a cache of previously loaded images, and if you ask for the same image twice, it will be retrieved from the cache the second time. The actual code to download the images comes from the java.awt.Toolkit class, and aside from the cache, this method is equivalent to Toolkit.get DefaultToolkit().getImage().

The getApplet() method loops through all the applets currently loaded into AppletViewers in this Java runtime, looking for an applet with the specified name. It returns the first such applet that it finds. If it finds none with the right name, it returns null.

The getApplets() method returns an Enumeration (more specifically a Vector) of all the applets currently running inside AppletViewers in this Java runtime.

The two polymorphic showDocument() methods do absolutely nothing in the AppletViewer. (In Web browsers, they tend to change the page that the browser is displaying.)

Finally, the showStatus() method displays a short text message in the status Label of the AppletViewer.

THE APPLETPANEL AND APPLETVIEWERPANEL CLASSES

The AppletPanel class is an abstract subclass of java.awt.Panel that implements java.applet.AppletStub and java.lang.Runnable. Because AppletPanel is abstract, it can never be instantiated. Instead, its concrete subclass, AppletViewerPanel, is instantiated. The AppletViewer embeds each applet in an AppletViewerPanel and then adds the AppletViewerPanel to itself. (Recall that AppletViewer is a Frame.)

The AppletViewerPanel class has a constructor and four other public methods:

```
AppletViewerPanel(URL documentURL, Hashtable atts)
public String getParameter(String name)
public URL getDocumentBase()
public URL getCodeBase()
public AppletContext getAppletContext()
```

The constructor is not public. The only simple way to get a reference to an instance of this class is to load an applet into the AppletViewer and then call getContainer() and cast the resulting object to sun.applet.AppletViewerPanel.

The other four methods implement four of the six methods in the AppletStub interface. Thus, any method that calls an AppletStub method for an applet playing in an AppletViewer will indirectly invoke these methods. The other two methods of the AppletStub interface are implemented in the AppletPanel class. These are as follows:

```
public abstract boolean isActive()
public abstract void appletResize(int width, int height)
```

The AppletViewer() constructor creates a new AppletViewerPanel for the applet it's loading. This AppletViewerPanel will be the stub for the applet. The AppletViewer adds the panel to its center. (Remember that AppletViewer is a subclass of java.awt.Frame whose default Layout-Manager is BorderLayout.) Then AppletViewer calls the panel's init() method and sends the panel APPLET_LOAD, APPLET_INIT and APPLET_START messages, in that order.

The AppletPanel's init() method creates a new thread using itself as the seed because it implements Runnable. This thread is just a large event loop that waits for messages to come in via the sendEvent() method. An AppletPanel knows how to respond to seven events, all of which are public final static int constants:

```
AppletPanel.APPLET_DISPOSE = 0;
AppletPanel.APPLET_LOAD = 1;
AppletPanel.APPLET_INIT = 2;
AppletPanel.APPLET_START = 3;
AppletPanel.APPLET_STOP = 4;
AppletPanel.APPLET_DESTROY = 5;
AppletPanel.APPLET_QUIT = 6;
```

These events are *not* the same as the events handled by handleEvent(). AppletPanel also has a completely separate handleEvent() method inherited from its superclasses that handles the usual collection of events like Event.MOUSE_DOWN. The run() method sees only the AppletPanel events, and handleEvent()sees only the java.awt.Event events. There are two different but parallel mechanisms for event handling in AppletPanels. The new one, and the one I'm writing about here, handles only the eight events listed earlier.

The AppletViewer tells the AppletPanel what to do by passing one of the previously-named constants to the AppletPanel's public sendEvent() method:

```
public void sendEvent(int id)
```

As I said, after calling the AppletPanel's init() method to start the panel's event loop running, the AppletViewer sends the panel the AppletPanel. APPLET_LOAD, AppletPanel.APPLET_INIT, and AppletPanel.APPLET_ START messages, in that order.

The AppletPanel responds to the APPLET_LOAD message by loading the applet. To do this, it first looks for an AppletClassLoader for the codebase. If one hasn't already been created, it constructs a new one. Then this ClassLoader loads the byte codes for the class over a URLConnection. Next, the AppletPanel instantiates the class with the Class.newInstance() method. Assuming that the applet is loaded and instantiated successfully, the AppletPanel then sets the applet's stub to the AppletPanel itself and places the applet in its center. The container hierarchy is shown in Figure 9-1. Of course, the applet itself may contain other panels and components.

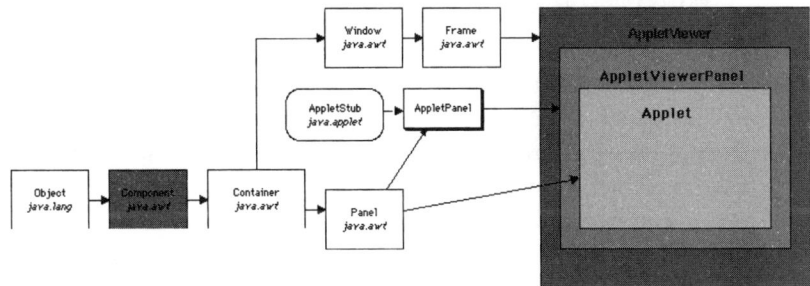

Figure 9-1

An Applet, a subclass of java.awt.Panel, is contained in an AppletViewerPanel, a subclass of sun.applet.AppletPanel, which is itself contained in an AppletViewer, a subclass of java.awt.Frame.

Next, the AppletPanel must respond to the APPLET_INIT method sent by the AppletViewer. This is relatively straightforward. The AppletPanel responds by calling the applet's init() method and performing a few simple housekeeping tasks.

The next event in the queue is APPLET_START, again put there by the AppletViewer. This too is easy to respond to: Just call the applet's start() method, resize it, show it, and validate it.

At this point, the AppletPanel waits. The next event can be some time in coming. However, eventually the AppletPanel should see APPLET_STOP, APPLET_DESTROY, and APPLET_DISPOSE methods, all sent by the AppletViewer in response to user actions like closing a window or choosing the Quit Menu Item from the File menu.

The AppletPanel responds to the APPLET_STOP message by calling the applet's stop() method and hiding it. At this point, APPLET_START may still be called to restart the applet. Alternately, if the APPLET_STOP message is followed by an APPLET_DESTROY message, then the applet's destroy() method is called. Generally, this is immediately followed by an APPLET_DISPOSE message, which causes the applet to be removed from the AppletPanel.

The AppletPanel class overrides two public methods from java.awt. Component, specifically:

```
public Dimension minimumSize()
public Dimension preferredSize()
```

Each AppletPanel has a Dimension field called appletSize that is initially set to height 100 and width 100. However, this is changed inside the init() method to whatever values are specified in the HEIGHT and WIDTH parameters to the <APPLET> tag. The minimumSize() and preferredSize() methods both return this Dimension field. Its value can be adjusted after the AppletPanel is inited via the appletResize() method that follows.

The AppletPanel class has two public methods that are used when it acts in the capacity of an AppletStub. These are as follows:

```
public boolean isActive()
public void appletResize(int width, int height)
```

The isActive() method is called to determine whether the applet is currently active. *Active* is defined as having been started and not yet stopped. In other words, the applet is inactive when it's created, active after it's processes the APPLET_START message, and inactive again once it processes the APPLET_STOP message. The applet may become active again if the APPLET_START message is sent a second time.

Secret

This is a little on the kludgy side because it's possible for objects other than the applet panel to call the applet's start() and stop() methods, in which case the true activity state of the applet can be out of sync with what the AppletPanel expects. This is a good reason not to call start() and stop() from methods that may be used by an AppletViewer or a Web browser yourself. However, if the applet needs to run as a stand-alone application from main(), you must call start() and stop() yourself. This is generally not a problem because when main() is called, the applet won't be running inside a Web browser or appletviewer.

The appletResize() method is simpler. It resizes the AppletPanel to the specified width and height.

The other four methods of AppletStub are not implemented in this class. They are implemented in AppletViewerPanel and should be implemented in any concrete subclass of AppletPanel you code yourself.

AppletPanel also has several protected methods that you may need to call or override if you subclass AppletPanel yourself. These are as follows:

```
protected void showAppletStatus(String status)
protected void showAppletLog(String str)
protected void showAppletException(Throwable t)
protected synchronized void sendEvent(Event evt)
```

The showAppletStatus() method is used by the AppletPanel to display the current status of the applet, such as `applet loaded`, `applet not loaded`, `applet started`, and so on. The message is displayed in the status area of the appletviewer, as if put there by the showStatus() method.

The showAppletLog() method is used to send error messages when there's an anticipated Exception in the event loop. The error message passed in the str argument is printed on System.out.

The showAppletException() method is called when the event loop in the run() method encounters certain kinds of Exceptions. This method just prints the stack trace on System.err by calling t.printStackTrace().

This sendEvent() method differs from the public sendEvent() method in the argument list. This one accepts a java.awt.Event object rather than a numeric ID. The earlier public sendEvent() method creates a new Event object with the specified ID and then passes it on to this method to actually place the event in the queue.

THE APPLETCLASSLOADER CLASS

AppletClassLoader is a subclass of java.lang.ClassLoader that understands codebases and URLConnections. Because it uses a URLConnection to download class data, it's unreliable in a few VMs, particularly early Mac VMs, where the URLConnection class was more than a little buggy.

Each AppletClassLoader object is associated with a single URL called its *base*. This corresponds to the CODEBASE parameter of the <APPLET> tag. It defines the location from which classes will be downloaded. The base is set when the object is constructed and cannot be changed. Of course, AppletClassLoader looks for classes in the local CLASSPATH first, and then in the cache of previously loaded classes and then finally out on the network.

For example, if an AppletClassLoader had a base of `http://sunsite.unc.edu/javafaq/classes/` and is asked to load a new class called Foo that is not in the cache or the CLASSPATH, it will look for it at the URL `http://sunsite.unc.edu/javafaq/classes/Foo.class`. If the same class loader is asked to load the class edu.unc.sunsite.database.Record, it will try to retrieve the file `http://sunsite.unc.edu/javafaq/classes/edu/unc/sunsite/database/Record.class`.

The constructor, AppletClassLoader(URL base), is package access only, so you're unlikely to use it in your own programs. However, an applet may be able to get a reference to an instance of this class by calling getClass().getClassLoader() to find out who loaded it. If you do this, you'll have access to the single public method, loadClass():

```
public Class loadClass(String name) throws ClassNotFoundException
```

This allows you to ask the ClassLoader to load a particular class by name from the local CLASSPATH, its cache, or the base URL, in that order. I really can't imagine why you might want to do this because all the classes you need will be loaded automatically when you refer to them. I suppose this might allow you to start loading the classes that you know you'll need later in a low priority thread when your applet starts up, so it can play more smoothly later on; however, this is probably not necessary.

THE APPLETSECURITY CLASS

The AppletSecurity class is a subclass of java.lang.SecurityManager that implements a security protocol suitable for untrusted applets. It overrides most public methods in the SecurityManager class.

If one of these methods encounters a security violation, it throws a new sun.applet.AppletSecurityException. This is a subclass of java.lang.Security-Exception, and it has only two constructors:

```
public AppletSecurityException(String name)
public AppletSecurityException(String name, String arg)
```

It's used just like a regular SecurityException, but tags the exception as having been thrown by the AppletSecurity SecurityManager. AppletSecurity-Exceptions are used inconsistently. On occasion, a raw SecurityException is thrown instead.

Network security

These methods check whether an applet is allowed to communicate in a certain way with a particular host. Many of the methods in the java.net classes call these methods before making a connection.

checkConnect()

There are three checkConnect() methods to determine whether network connections to specified hosts and ports are allowed. These are as follows:

```
public void checkConnect(String host, int port)
public void checkConnect(String host, int port, Object o)
public synchronized void checkConnect(String fromHost, String toHost)
```

The third method is unique to this class and does not override any method in the superclass. If a URL is passed as the third argument to checkConnect(), then an AppletSecurityException is thrown, unless connections are allowed to both the host in the host argument and the host in the URL argument.

However, despite the different signatures, all three methods check essentially the same thing. First, the runtime looks at the value of the system property appletviewer.security.mode. This can be set manually in the .hotjava/properties file or via the AppletProps Frame discussed earlier. This should have one of three string values: "none," "host," or "unrestricted." The default is "host."

In "unrestricted" mode, checkConnect() never throws an exception. All connections are permitted. In "none" mode, connections made by the runtime or by sun.net.www.http.HttpClient are allowed. However, all other connections attempted by the applet or any class loaded by the applet will fail.

Of course, the default mode is "host," which is the most complicated of all. Connections by the runtime and sun.net.www.http.HttpClient are still allowed unconditionally. However, connections by the applet or classes loaded, invoked directly or indirectly by the applet, are allowed if and only if they are connections back to the host from which the applet came.

The AppletSecurity class never checks the port, although that is passed as an argument in the first two checkConnect() methods. If a connection is allowed to a given host, a connection is allowed to any port on that host.

checkMulticast()

The checkMulticast() methods determine whether an applet is allowed to broadcast to or receive from multicast sockets.

```
public void checkMulticast(InetAddress ia)
public void checkMulticast(InetAddress ia, byte ttl)
```

Applets are not allowed to send or receive multicast data under any circumstances, regardless of the network security settings, the host and port, or the Time-To-Live value. These methods always throw an AppletSecurity-Exception when called from inside an applet.

checkAccept()

The checkAccept() method determines whether a ServerSocket may accept a connection from the specified host and port:

```
public void checkAccept(String host, int port)
```

Applets are not allowed to accept connections under any circumstances, regardless of the network security settings or the host and port. This method always throws an AppletSecurityException when called from inside an applet.

checkListen()

The checkListen() method determines whether an applet may create a ServerSocket that listens for connections on the specified port:

```
public void checkListen(int port)
```

Currently, applets are not allowed to create server sockets, regardless of the network security settings or the host and port. Therefore, this method always throws an AppletSecurityException when called from inside an applet.

checkSetFactory()

This method is called to determine whether an applet is allowed to set a networking-related factory like java.net.SocketImplFactory.

```
public void checkSetFactory()
```

Applets are never allowed to set factories. This method always throws a SecurityException.

Host security

These methods are used to determine how much access the applet has to the native operating system. In general, they're quite restrictive because any significant access to the host system would allow the applet to bypass pretty much all other security checks. These methods are mostly called by the classes in java.lang.

checkExec()

Applets are never allowed to execute system commands. Therefore, this method always throws an AppletSecurityException.

```
public void checkExec(String cmd)
```

checkExit()

Applets are never allowed to cause the virtual machine to exit. Therefore, this method always throws an AppletSecurityException.

```
public void checkExit(int code)
```

checkLink()

Applets are not allowed to link new dynamic libraries of native code. Therefore, this method always throws an AppletSecurityException.

```
public void checkLink(String libname)
```

checkPropertiesAccess()

Applets are not allowed to read the entire list of system properties. Therefore, this method always throws an AppletSecurityException.

```
public void checkPropertiesAccess()
```

checkPropertyAccess(String pname)

Applets are allowed to read the values of some system properties. Generally, they can read properties that reveal information about the Java or host environment, such as the version of the virtual machine or the operating system name, but they're not allowed to read properties which might reveal personal information about the user, like the user's e-mail address.

```
public void checkPropertyAccess(String pname)
```

To control this, the checkPropertyAccess() method looks to see if there is a corresponding property to pname called pname.applet. If the property pname.applet exists and has the string value "true," then the applet is allowed to read the property pname. Otherwise, an AppletSecurityException is thrown.

checkSystemClipboardAccess()

The system clipboard is where data that is cut or copied is stored. The system clipboard can contain a variety of information from any application running on the host. Revealing this data could lead to major privacy violations. Therefore, applets are not allowed to read from the clipboard. This method always throws an AppletSecurityException.

```
public void checkSystemClipboardAccess()
```

checkPrintJobAccess()

Although it's not hard to think of reasons why an applet might want to print, just like you can think of reasons why an applet might want to read from or write to the file system, allowing applets access to printers does open a number of security holes. There's no good way unambiguously to separate the proper uses of the printer from improper uses. Therefore, when called from inside an applet, this method throws a SecurityException.

```
public void checkPrintJobAccess()
```

This does not mean that the AppletViewer, the Web browser, or other programs cannot print. It just means the applet itself can't initiate a print job.

This method is invoked primarily by the printing-related classes of java.awt.

Runtime security

These methods are used to determine how much control over the Java runtime an applet is allowed. For the most part, these methods are quite restrictive because an applet should live inside the runtime, not control it.

checkAccess()

This method checks whether the current thread is allowed to modify the specified Thread or ThreadGroup; for example by raising or lowering its priority.

```
public void checkAccess(Thread t)
public void checkAccess(ThreadGroup tg)
```

In Java 1.0, applets are allowed to modify any thread that is a member of an AppletThreadGroup. This allows applets to control other applets and to spawn different thread groups for different purposes. However, it does open some denial of service attacks. Therefore, this has been tightened up in Java 1.1 so that a thread is allowed to modify only other threads in the same ThreadGroup as itself, whether or not they're in an AppletThreadGroup.

checkAwtEventQueueAccess()

The checkAwtEventQueueAccess() method is new in Java 1.1. It checks to see if the applet client can get direct access to the AWT event queue:

```
public void checkAwtEventQueueAccess()
```

Applets are not allowed direct access to the AWT event queue, so this method throws an AppletSecurityException when called from inside an applet.

checkTopLevelWindow(Object o)

This method is slightly misnamed. A top-level window is a native window in the native GUI. Applets are allowed to create top-level windows. However, to avoid impersonating other non-applet windows, a top-level window created by an applet has an extra tag that identifies the window as belonging to an applet:

```
public synchronized boolean checkTopLevelWindow(Object o)
```

Before creating a new Frame or Dialog, the Frame and Dialog classes call checkTopLevelWindow() to find out whether or not they need to include this warning string. If the call was directly or indirectly invoked via a class that was loaded from a ClassLoader, this method returns false. This means that unmarked top-level windows are not allowed, and a window with a warning message should be displayed instead. Otherwise, this method returns true.

This is the only method in the SecurityManager class that does not return void. It's also the only method that does not throw a SecurityException.

Class system security

Much effort has been spent ensuring that the type safety of Java can't be subverted. This is especially important in Java 1.1 with the addition of the Reflection API. Applets should not be allowed to replace system classes, use their own class loaders, or otherwise subvert the type system.

checkMemberAccess()

The checkMemberAccess() method is used by the java.lang.reflect package to determine whether the applet is allowed to access the public or declared members (field and methods) of the Class object c. Otherwise, access protection would be easy to violate:

```
public void checkMemberAccess(Class c, int n)
```

The int argument n should be one of the two mnemonic constants Member.PUBLIC and Member.DECLARED. Member.PUBLIC asks whether the applet is allowed to reflect on the public members of the class, including inherited members. Member.DECLARED asks whether the applet is allowed to reflect on all members of the class, including only those members actually declared in the class, not inherited members.

Applets are allowed to reflect on the public members of the class. If an applet tries to reflect on the declared members of a class, then an Applet-SecurityException is thrown.

checkPackageAccess()

Applets are not necessarily allowed access to all classes present on the host system. This method checks whether classes and methods from the package name pkg may be invoked:

```
public void checkPackageAccess(String package_name)
```

This method is fairly coarse. It just looks at the first part of the package. For example, if you ask it to check whether you can access java.lang.reflect, it just checks whether it can access everything in the java packages.

To determine whether access is allowed to a given package, this method tests whether the system property package.restrict.access.pkg where pkg is the outermost package. For example, to determine whether an applet can access sun.net.nntp, checkPackageAccess() tests whether the system property package.restrict.access.sun exists and equals "true." If this is the case, checkPackageAccess() throws an AppletSecurityException. Otherwise, access is allowed.

By default, no package.restrict.access properties are set, so applets have access to all public classes in all packages.

checkPackageDefinition()

This method checks whether an applet is allowed to define new packages in the package package_name.

```
public void checkPackageDefinition(String package_name)
```

Once again, only a very coarse-grained check is made for the outermost package. Access must be set at the level of the java or sun or netscape packages, not at lower levels like sun.net or java.util.

The system property package.restrict.definition.pkg (where pkg is the outermost package) determines whether new classes can be defined in the package pkg. For example, to determine whether an applet can define a new class in sun.net.nntp, checkPackageDefinition() tests whether the system property package.restrict.definition.sun exists and equals "true." If this is the case, checkPackageDefinition() throws an AppletSecurityException. Otherwise, access is allowed.

checkCreateClassLoader()

Applets are not allowed to create class loaders. Doing so would enable them to bypass a number of important checks on classes. Therefore, this method always throws an AppletSecurityException when called from inside an applet:

```
public void checkCreateClassLoader()
```

checkSecurityAccess(String provider)

In the future, this method may be used to restrict certain operations to a particular provider. However, currently (in Java 1.1), this method always throws an AppletSecurityException when called from inside an applet:

```
public void checkSecurityAccess(String provider)
```

File system security

These six methods determine whether Java is allowed to read, write, or delete particular files. Although it's often stated that applets can't do any of these things, the reality is considerably more complex, especially for reading. Applets loaded from file URLs must be able to read media and class files from the document base. Access control lists do permit the granting of additional privileges to file access in some directories. Finally, on many operating systems, network sockets appear to be just another file, so the checkRead() and checkWrite() methods must distinguish between disk access and network connections, even when the operating system is trying to eliminate that distinction.

checkDelete()

The checkDelete() method is the only check method in java.lang.
SecurityManager that is not overridden in the AppletSecurity class.

```
public void checkDelete(String filename)
```

The base method that AppletSecurity inherits simply throws a
SecurityException. Therefore, once an AppletSecurity SecurityManager is
installed, no files may be deleted under any circumstances by any Java class.

checkWrite()

There are two polymorphic checkWrite() methods. The first checks to see if
writing to a file with a particular filename is allowed; the second checks to
see if writing to a file with a particular file descriptor is allowed:

```
public void checkWrite(String filename)
public void checkWrite(FileDescriptor fd)
```

The checkWrite(String filename) compares the filename to the names in
the access control list. The access control list is an array of strings, mostly
representing directory names, where applets are allowed to write files. For
example, if the access control list contains the string "/usr/tmp," then
applets could write files in the directory "/usr/tmp." It is not at all unusual
for the access control list to be empty. In fact, that's the more common case.
If the file does not begin with a string in the access control list, then an
AppletSecurityException is thrown.

The checkWrite(FileDescriptor fd) method does not concern itself with
access control lists. Instead, it checks to see whether the write is going to a
socket. More specifically, it checks whether the stream being written to is an
instance of java.net.SocketOutputStream. If it is, the write is allowed to
happen. Otherwise, an AppletSecurityException is thrown.

checkRead()

There are four polymorphic checkRead() methods in the AppletSecurity
class, although there are only three in java.lang.SecurityManager. The first
variant checks whether reading a particular file is allowed. The second
checks whether reading from a particular file descriptor is allowed. The
third checks whether reading from a particular file given a particular
context is allowed, and the fourth checks whether reading a particular file is
allowed, given that the applet was downloaded from a particular URL.

```
public synchronized void checkRead(String filename)
public void checkRead(FileDescriptor fd)
public void checkRead(String filename, Object context)
public synchronized void checkRead(String file, URL base)
```

The checkRead(String filename) method allows files whose names start with strings in the access control list to be read. If the applet was loaded from a file URL, files in the document base directory or its subdirectories may also be read. If neither condition is true, an AppletSecurityException is thrown.

The checkRead(FileDescriptor fd) method checks to see whether the read is coming from a socket. More specifically, it checks whether the stream being read is an instance of java.net.SocketInputStream. If it is, the read is allowed. Otherwise, an AppletSecurityException is thrown.

The checkRead(String filename, URL base) method allows the file to be read if the filename starts with one of the strings in the access control list. It also allows the file to be read if the base argument is a file URL and the filename is in the same directory as the base or one of its subdirectories. Otherwise, an AppletSecurityException is thrown. The checkRead(String filename) method essentially calls checkRead(filename, getDocumentBase()), which is why these two methods sound the same.

Finally, the checkRead(String filename, Object context) does a twofold check. First, it checks to see whether the name filename is in the access control list or in a directory or subdirectory of the document base. If that test is passed and the context is non-null, then checkRead() casts the context to a URL object u and calls checkRead(filename, u).

In short, reads are allowed on a file if the file is really a socket, if the filename starts with one of the strings in the access control list, or if the applet was loaded from a file URL and the file being read is in the same directory as the file URL or one of its subdirectories. Otherwise, an AppletSecurityException is thrown.

SUPPORT CLASSES

Although the preceding four sections elaborated on the main classes that drive the AppletViewer program, there are a few more classes in the sun.applet package that are used in support of these. As a general rule, you won't call any of them directly; several of them aren't even public. However, you may need to know a little more about them to understand fully how the appletviewer works. These classes include AppletAudioClip, AppletThreadGroup, AppletCopyright, AppletProps, and TextFrame.

AppletAudioClip

The AppletAudioClip class uses the sun.audio package to implement the java.applet.AudioClip interface. This class is explored in detail in Chapter 11. In brief, the AppletAudioClip has one constructor and four other methods (all public) that allow you to download and play audio files in Sun's .au format.

```
public AppletAudioClip(URL u)
public synchronized void loop()
public synchronized void play()
public synchronized void stop()
public String toString()
```

You create a new AppletAudioClip object by passing the URL of the .au file to the AppletAudioClip constructor or, more commonly, by passing the URL to the getAudioClip() method of java.applet.Applet. You can then play the clip by calling its play() method, play it continuously by calling its loop() method, or stop it by calling stop(). For example:

```
AppletAudioClip spacemusic = new AppletAudioClip(new URL("http://www.
idgbooks.com/spacemusic.au"));
    spacemusic.play();
```

You learn a lot more about what's going on behind the scenes in this class in Chapter 11.

AppletThreadGroup

The AppletThreadGroup class is a simple extension of java.lang.ThreadGroup with a single method, the constructor:

```
AppletThreadGroup(String name)
```

The constructor sets the maximum priority for applet threads to one more than Thread.NORM_PRIORITY (that is, six). However, the main purpose of the group is to identify applet-spawned threads as separate from other threads for the AppletSecurity.checkAccess() method. Applets are allowed to manipulate threads in AppletThreadGroups. They are not allowed to manipulate threads outside applet thread groups.

AppletCopyright

The AppletCopyright class is a non-public class that extends Frame. It puts up the message box shown in Figure 9-2 and waits for the user to accept or reject the agreement. The text in the Frame comes from the COPYRIGHT file in the java.home directory. If the user accepts the agreement, then Java makes a note of this in the user's .hotjava properties file so the message will not need to be shown again. If the user rejects the agreement, the virtual machine exits.

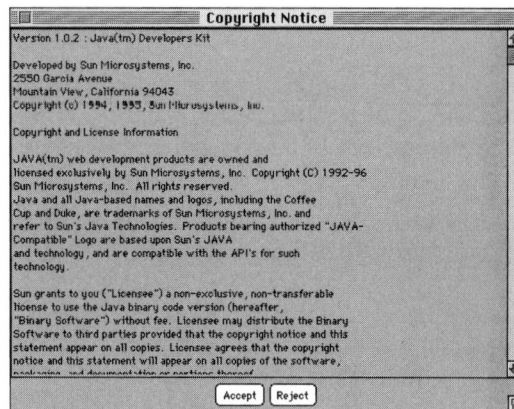

Figure 9-2
The AppletCopyright Frame.

I can think of little reason to use this class unless perhaps you're a Sun licensee and they require it of you. Although you might need to display license boxes of your own, this class is non-public and provides no easy means to adjust the text displayed. It would be quite simple to duplicate this functionality in a class of your own, though.

AppletProps

The AppletProps class extends java.awt.Frame, but it's really a dialog box for setting preferences. The dialog box is shown in Figure 9-3. As you can see, it lets you set your http proxy server and port, your firewall server and port, and the level of network and class access you allow applets to have. These are all stored in the system properties list.

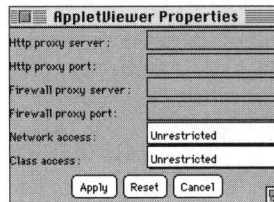

Figure 9-3

The AppletProps Frame.

This class itself is package access, and the only public method is action(). Therefore, there's little call to use it directly. A new AppletProps Frame is constructed and shown by the AppletViewer class when the user chooses the menu option File⇨Properties.

TextFrame

The TextFrame class is yet another package access subclass of Frame that acts as a simple message box. This class is used to produce the message box you see when you select Tag or Info from the Applet Viewer Tag or Info menu, as shown in Figures 9-4 and 9-5 respectively.

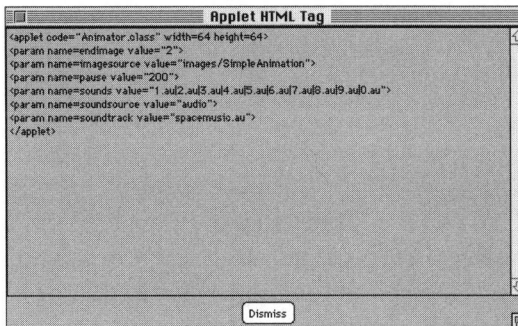

Figure 9-4

The AppletTag TextFrame.

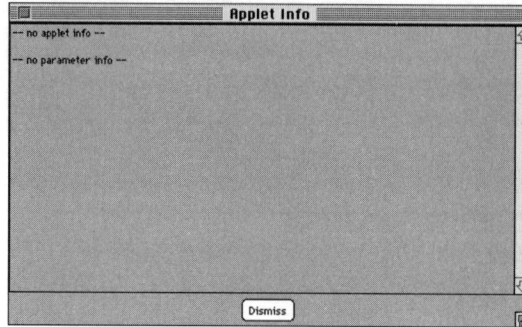

Figure 9-5
The Apple Info TextFrame.

The AppletViewer creates the text and the title, then passes them to the TextFrame() constructor:

```
TextFrame(int x, int y, String title, String text)
```

The only other method is handleEvent(), which just waits for the user to dismiss the Frame. Because neither the class itself nor the constructor is public, you're unlikely to use it directly, but you may want to create something similar for your own use.

SUMMARY

In this chapter, you learn the following:

- When you type appletviewer example1.html on the command line, you're really invoking a shell script or executable file that invokes the main() method of the AppletViewer class. This is a subclass of java.awt.Frame that implements java.applet.AppletContext.

- The AppletViewer class parses the files and URLs referenced on the command line looking for <APPLET> tags. Each <APPLET> tag leads to the creation of a new AppletViewer object.

- The AppletViewer object creates an AppletViewerPanel. The Applet-ViewerPanel uses an AppletClassLoader object to load the byte codes for the applet and instantiate it inside the AppletViewerPanel. The AppletViewerPanel is then added to the center of the AppletViewer Frame.

- The AppletViewerPanel has an event loop of its own that the AppletViewer talks to by invoking its sendEvent() method.

- The AppletViewer sets an AppletSecurity object to be the system Security Manager.

CONTROLLING AUDIO PLAYBACK WITH SUN.AUDIO

10

*J*ava audio is quite limited. Only 8-bit, 8-kilohertz (kHz), mono, μlaw-encoded files are supported. This format is a subset of both Sun's .au sound file format and the Windows .wav sound format. Sound is digitized, and no compression is used, so these files tend to be rather large.

You access sound data mostly through the java.applet. AudioClip interface. This interface has three methods that allow you to play, loop, and stop an audio clip. These eponymous methods are as follows:

```
public abstract void play()
public abstract void loop()
public abstract void stop()
```

The java.applet.Applet class has two polymorphic methods that retrieve AudioClip objects from a URL and two polymorphic methods that just play audio files located at a URL without saving it. These are as follows:

```
public AudioClip getAudioClip(URL url)
public AudioClip getAudioClip(URL url, String filename)
public void play(URL u)
public void play(URL u, String filename)
```

All four of these methods download AudioClip objects by using the getAudioClip() method of the AppletContext interface.

```
public abstract AudioClip getAudioClip(URL u)
```

That pretty much covers everything there is to say about the documented audio classes in the core of Java 1.0 and 1.1. If that was all there was to it, this would be a very short chapter. Fortunately, there's a lot more going on in the undocumented sun.audio classes, and that's what this chapter covers.

APPLETAUDIOCLIP

Because both AudioClip and AppletContext are interfaces, there are two questions that should immediately come to mind. The first question is, what classes actually implement AudioClip? The second question is, what do the classes that implement AppletContext do in the getAudioClip() method?

Secret

In Java 1.1 and earlier, there is exactly one class that implements the AudioClip interface: sun.applet.AppletAudioClip. More may be added in the future, especially once the Java Media API is released. The AppletAudioClip class has three fields, one public constructor, and four public methods:

```
URL url;
AudioData data;
InputStream stream;
public AppletAudioClip(URL u)
public synchronized void play()
public synchronized void loop()
public synchronized void stop()
public String toString()
```

The url field is just the URL from which the AudioClip is downloaded. The data field is a sun.audio.AudioData object that contains the bytes of data for the sound. The stream field is used to synchronize between the play(), loop(), and stop() methods.

The constructor is used to create a new AudioClip object. When an AudioClip is constructed, the runtime opens a URLConnection to the URL u. Then the data — that is, the raw bytes of the audio file — are read into the AudioData object data. Once the bytes are read in, the sound can be played once or repeatedly.

The AppletAudioClip's play() method constructs a new AudioDataStream from its AudioData field, data. It passes this AudioDataStream to the

AudioPlayer.player object to be played. The loop() method does almost exactly the same thing, except that it constructs a ContinuousAudioDataStream from the data field. The stop() method stops playing the stream, then closes the stream.

Finally, toString() provides a string representation of this object that includes the class name and the URL from which the data came.

AudioData

Secret

The sun.audio.AudioData class is a wrapper for a byte array called buffer that stores the bytes of an audio clip. There is only one method, the public constructor AudioData():

```
byte[] buffer
public AudioData(byte[] data)
```

This constructor just sets the buffer field equal to the data argument. The data itself is not copied from data[] to buffer[]; only a reference is copied.

This class is primarily a convenient way to hold binary audio data. Instances of the class are normally created by the sun.applet.AudioClip class.

AudioPlayer

Secret

The AudioPlayer class is a subclass of java.lang.Thread, which plays audio streams. There is never more than one instance of this class in existence at a time. This single instance manages competing requests for the audio capabilities of the physical hardware. How it does this is an interesting trick.

The AudioPlayer class has a single private noargs constructor; that is

```
private AudioPlayer()
```

Therefore, this class cannot be instantiated by any class other than itself, nor can it be subclassed. That's because subclass constructors implicitly call the superclass constructor, which in this case is private, and thus they cannot be invoked by subclasses. However, the AudioPlayer class contains a public, final, static instance of itself called player; that is

```
public static final AudioPlayer player = new AudioPlayer();
```

As soon as the AudioPlayer class is loaded, this class variable is initialized. Because player is static and final, it will never be reinitialized or changed during the life of the current program. There are no other class variables or methods in AudioPlayer, so no other instances of the class will be created. This is the only one you get.

This class has three public methods that are used to control the playing of a stream of audio data. These are

```
public synchronized void start(InputStream in)
public synchronized void stop(InputStream in)
public void run()
```

The run() method is called automatically by the thread superclass once the thread is started. The thread is started by the constructor, so you don't need to start it manually. The remaining two methods control audio playing. These must always be called via the class variable player, so you use them like this:

```
AudioPlayer.player.start(audioStream)
AudioPlayer.player.stop(audioStream)
```

In theory, the InputStream you pass to the start() method can be any InputStream at all. In practice, you should pass some form of audio stream, preferably either an AudioDataStream or a ContinuousAudioDataStream.

THE AUDIO STREAMS

Secret

There are six different audio stream classes defined in the sun.audio package: AudioStream, NativeAudioStream, AudioTranslatorStream, AudioSequenceStream, AudioDataStream, and ContinuousAudioDataStream. All are indirect subclasses of java.io.InputStream.

To understand these streams, you first have to realize that Java understands only one audio format: Sun's .au format. This is a fairly simple format that includes a header followed by the binary data. This is shown in Figure 10-1. Java doesn't even understand all variants of this format. Java sound data must be 8-bit, 8-kHz, mono, µlaw encoded.

In Java, as soon as any sort of audio stream is created, the header is immediately read — generally by the NativeAudioStream() constructor. If any problems are encountered — in particular if this is not an 8-bit, µlaw encoded, mono, 8-kHz sound — then a sun.audio.InvalidAudioFormatException, a subclass of java.io.IOException, is thrown. If no problems are encountered, then the stream marker is positioned between the header and the data. The data is then generally read into and stored in an AudioData object.

Magic Number	A 4 byte signed integer to identify the file. This should be either 0x2E736E64 or 0x2E736400
Header Size	A 4 byte signed integer that specifies the number of bytes in the header. This should be at least 24.
data length	A 4 byte signed integer that specifies the number of bytes in the data part of this file.
Encoding	A 4 byte signed integer that specifies the type of encoding used. The value 1 means ulaw encoding, the only kind currently supported.
Sample Rate	A 4 byte signed integer that specifies the sample frequency of the data. Java only officially understands 8 kHz (8000 Hz) sampling, but a little leeway is allowed on the higher side. Java will actually work with files between 8000 and 8999 Hz.
Number of Channels	a 4 byte signed integer specifying the number of channels in this audio file. 1 is mono. 2 is stereo. Java can only play mono sound.
Additional Header Bytes	Any additional header data Java doesn't parse, calculated by subtracting 24 (the number of bytes in the six previous fields) from the value of the header size field
Data	The actual binary audio data. The number of bytes here is given by the data length field in the header.

Figure 10-1
The .au header format.

The audio stream classes are divided into two types that are not reflected by the class hierarchy. AudioStream, NativeAudioStream, AudioTranslatorStream, and AudioSequenceStream are *reader* streams. They are used to read audio data from a source like a network connection or a file.

AudioDataStream and ContinuousAudioDataStream are *player* streams. They are used to play sounds through AudioPlayer.player.play() method. You can play a reader stream if you want to, but you'll lose it if you do, for good for reasons that I explain now.

Sound data comes from somewhere, perhaps a file, perhaps a network connection, perhaps somewhere else. This is presented as an input stream. The constructors for the AudioStream, NativeAudioStream, and AudioTranslatorStream classes chain the objects that they create to the originating stream. Then they read the header from the stream. They do not read the data. Thus, the first time you call read() on one of these streams, you get the first byte of audio data. You can read fully from these streams only once. After that, the stream is closed, and the data is lost unless you saved it somewhere.

Sound files are big, and downloading them is an expensive operation. More often than not you want to reuse a sound; you therefore need somewhere to save the sound. It follows, then, that you should never play an AudioStream, NativeAudioStream, AudioSequenceStream, or AudioTranslatorStream directly. You could, but you'd get to play it only once. After that, the bytes would be gone.

Therefore, instead of playing the sound, you use the data bytes of the AudioStream object to construct a new AudioData object. The AudioData object stores the bytes of the sound. Whenever you need to play the sound, you can use the AudioData object to create an AudioDataStream or ContinuousAudioDataStream. You can use a single AudioData object to create multiple AudioDataStreams. Thus, you can use the sound without *using up* the sound.

AudioStream

The AudioStream class is a subclass of java.io.FilterInputStream that converts a InputStream to an AudioStream. The main filtering that it does involves reading the header. There is one constructor in this class:

```
public AudioStream(InputStream in) throws IOException
```

The specific IOException likely to be thrown by this constructor is a sun.audio.InvalidAudioFormatException. This IOException means that Java was unable to translate the data into some format it understands (currently 8-bit μlaw single channel 8-kHz).

AudioStream overrides one method in its superclass. This is:

```
public int read(byte buf[], int pos, int len) throws IOException
```

The main difference between this read() method and the read() method with the same signature in FilterInputStream is that this one calls Thread. currentThread().yield() to yield some time to other processes. This is important, because digital audio files are quite large and may take quite a while to load when downloaded from the Internet.

The AudioStream class also has two new public methods not present in its superclass. These are as follows:

```
public AudioData getData() throws IOException
public int getLength()
```

The getData() method reads all the data from the AudioStream and returns an AudioData object containing that data. The getLength() method returns the number of bytes in the data part of the .au file. The length of the header is not included in this calculation.

NativeAudioStream

The NativeAudioStream class is a subclass of java.io.FilterInputStream that is customized for the native audio format on the host platform. It is one of the few parts of Java written in Java that differs from platform to platform. (Most platform dependencies are isolated in native code.)

On Solaris and Windows, the NativeAudioStream constructor just reads various header information out of the stream and positions the stream at the beginning of the data. If any of the header information indicates that this is not an audio format that Java can handle — that is, it is not 8-bit, μlaw-encoded, single-channel, 8-kHz data — then an InvalidAudioFormatException is thrown:

```
public NativeAudioStream(InputStream in) throws IOException
```

The constructor mostly just tests the header to make sure the file is 8-bit, μlaw-encoded, single-channel, 8-kHz data; however, it does store the length of the data in a package-access field called length. You can retrieve the value of this field with the public getLength() method:

```
public int getLength()
```

This merely returns the number of bytes in the data part of the file. This will be a little less than the length of the file itself because the bytes in the headers are not included.

AudioTranslatorStream

The AudioTranslatorStream class is a subclass of sun.audio.AudioStream. As of Java 1.0 and 1.1, it's just a placeholder that adds nothing to its superclass, AudioStream. Presumably at some point in the future, it will translate different formats into formats understood by the runtime environment. However, this is not yet the case.

AudioDataStream

Secret

The AudioDataStream class is a subclass of java.io.ByteArrayInputStream that is used to convert the data in an AudioData object's buffer[] into a ByteArrayInputStream. It has a public constructor and nothing more. That constructor is

```
public AudioDataStream(AudioData ad)
```

This constructor itself is quite simple. It just calls the superclass constructor with ad's data buffer — that is, super(ad.buffer).

It's not clear why this has been split into a separate class. It would have been just as easy to give AudioData a getInputStream() method like this:

```
public InputStream getInputStream() {
  return new ByteArrayInputStream(buffer);
}
```

Nonetheless, that is the way it is.

AudioDataStream objects are mostly used as input for the play() and stop() methods of the AudioPlayer.player object.

ContinuousAudioDataStream

Secret

ContinuousAudioDataStream is a subclass of sun.audio.AudioDataStream that is used for looping audio. Looping audio is audio that starts over at the beginning as soon as it reaches the end. This class has one constructor and three methods, all public:

```
public ContinuousAudioDataStream(AudioData data)
public int read()
public int read(byte buf[], int pos, int len)
```

The constructor just calls the superclass's constructor and passes it the data object. The difference between an AudioDataStream and a ContinuousAudioDataStream is in the read() methods. The two read() methods of this class wrap around to the beginning of their byte array once they run out of data. This provides the looping effect used by AudioClip.loop(). The AudioPlayer class used by AudioClip.loop() does not have a loop() method, but by passing a ContinuousAudioDataStream object to AudioPlayer.play(), you get continuous looping.

Secret

The Catch

There's a problem with this scheme. The Enumeration lets you specify which streams will be connected in this stream, but it does not specify in which order they will be connected. In other words, there's no guarantee that the AudioStream with the Hello message will be played before the AudioStream with the Goodbye message.

To understand what's going on, you have to look at the undocumented and non-guaranteed internals of the object you pass that implements the Enumeration interface. The elements() method of the java.util.Vector class returns a java.util. VectorEnumerator object. VectorEnumerator is a non-public class. This just returns successive elements in the Vector in order. Thus, a VectorEnumerator will return the first element in the Vector before the second. On the other hand, the elements() and keys() methods of the java.util. Hashtable class return a java.util. HashtableEnumerator object. Because of the nature of the Hashtable, there's no guarantee at all about the order in which elements will be returned.

The bottom line is that a Vector is a relatively good thing to enumerate to create an AudioStreamSequence. Just add the elements to the Vector in the order you want the clips played. A Hashtable is a relatively bad thing to enumerate to create an AudioStreamSequence because there's no guarantee what order you'll get when you enumerate it. If you use another class that implements Enumeration, be sure to test its ordering properties first.

AudioStreamSequence

Secret

The AudioStreamSequence class is a subclass of java.io.SequenceInputStream that can combine multiple audio streams into a single stream. Suppose that you have ten .au files, each of which contains one song from a CD. You could load each of those .au files into an AudioStream and then connect those ten separate streams with an AudioStreamSequence. AudioStreamSequence is like splicer tape for digital audio.

The primary method of the AudioStreamSequence class is the constructor:

```
public AudioStreamSequence(Enumeration e)
```

The Enumeration object passed as the constructor's argument must contain the AudioStream objects you wish to connect.

For example, suppose track1 through track8 are all AudioStream objects, each containing a song followed by a few seconds of silence (to separate the songs). You would play a "CD" containing those songs like this:

```
Vector v = new Vector();
v.addElement(track1);
v.addElement(track1);
```

```
v.addElement(track2);
v.addElement(track3);
v.addElement(track4);
v.addElement(track5);
v.addElement(track6);
v.addElement(track7);
v.addElement(track8);
AudioStreamSequence cd = new AudioStreamSequence(v.elements());
AudioData ad = new AudioData(cd);
AudioPlayer.player.start(new AudioDataStream(ad));
```

Note

You may be wondering why you can't just play the tracks in sequence like this without using an AudioStreamSequence at all:

```
AudioPlayer.player.start(track1);
AudioPlayer.player.start(track2);
AudioPlayer.player.start(track3);
AudioPlayer.player.start(track4);
AudioPlayer.player.start(track5);
AudioPlayer.player.start(track6);
AudioPlayer.player.start(track7);
AudioPlayer.player.start(track8);
```

As you'll see in the next section, if you try this, you get a cacophonous babel of eight tracks playing at the same time, not eight tracks playing one after the other.

In addition to the constructor, the AudioStreamSequence class overrides two read() methods:

```
public int read() throws IOException
public int read(byte buf[], int pos, int len) throws IOException
```

The differences between these methods and those in the superclass are all internal to the AudioSequenceStream class. As a programmer, you don't need to worry about them. The main thing they do is recognize when they have to switch from one of the streams in the enumeration to another.

AUDIODEVICE

Secret

The sun.audio.AudioDevice class represents the actual hardware that plays audio files. It is the only audio-related class that resorts to native methods. If you're porting Java to a new platform, this is probably the only file you'll need to rewrite to make audio work.

Because most computers only have a single audio output device, the AudioDevice class uses the same trick used by the AudioPlayer class to make sure there's only one instance of itself in existence; that is, it declares its one constructor private, but instantiates a public final static AudioDevice field called device inside itself. This is instantiated the first time the class is loaded. You can access this public field as AudioDevice.device if you want to use the device directly.

The AudioPlayer class has a field that contains a reference to this single instance of AudioPlayer. It uses this field to actually play audio files.

Although most normal workstations and microcomputers only have a single audio output device, the AudioDevice class can play multiple audio clips at one time by mixing the audio streams.

The open() method opens the audio device for playing a sound. The close() method closes it. Here, *open* and *close* have meanings inherited from the UNIX world, where everything is treated as a file, even decidedly non-file-like hardware like the speaker or audio-synthesizer. You do not need to call these methods explicitly. They will be invoked automatically as necessary:

```
public synchronized void open()
public synchronized void close()
```

To actually play the audio data, you pass an InputStream containing the data, generally an AudioDataStream or ContinuousAudioDataStream, to the openChannel() method:

```
public synchronized void openChannel(InputStream in)
```

This does not play the audio data directly. Instead, the InputStream is inserted into the list of streams to be played. To stop playing a sound, you pass the same stream object to the closeChannel() method:

```
public synchronized void closeChannel(InputStream in)
```

Nothing happens if it is not actually in the queue of streams to be played.

To start playing all the InputStreams that have been queued, mixed together, you call the play() method:

```
public void play()
```

This plays as long as any of the InputStreams currently in the queue have data left to be played. Note that the streams are played in parallel, not in series. If seven three-second audio clips are placed in the queue and then play() is called, it only takes three seconds to play them all, not 21 seconds.

To close all the InputStreams fed to the AudioDevice at once, use the closeStreams() method:

```
public synchronized void closeStreams()
```

Finally, if for some reason you need to know how many clips are currently loaded into the queue, you can find out with the openChannels() method:

```
public int openChannels()
```

THE PROCESS

That was a fairly large number of classes for you to absorb. In this section, you get to see the steps that happen when you download an audio clip using an applet's play() method:

Secret

1. The applet's play() method is invoked with a URL object u, which for the sake of argument points to `http://www.myhost.com/mysound.au`.

2. Applet.play() calls getAppletContext().getAudioClip(u)

3. The AppletContext object checks to see if it already has the requested AudioClip in its cache. If it does, it returns the object in the cache, and jumps ahead to Step 13. Otherwise, it instantiates a new AppletAudioClip object with the URL object u.

4. The AppletAudioClip constructor calls u.openConnection() to open a URLConnection uc to `http://www.myhost.com/mysound.au`.

5. The AppletAudioClip constructor calls URLConnection.getInputStream() to get an InputStream in from the URL.

6. The AppletAudioClip() constructor passes the URLConnection's InputStream in to the AudioStream constructor.

7. The AudioStream constructor passes the InputStream constructor to the NativeAudioStream constructor.

8. The NativeAudioStream constructor assumes the stream is an 8-bit, μlaw encoded, mono, 8-kHz .au file. It tries to read the header under this assumption. If it fails, it throws an InvalidAudioFormatException.

9. Assuming that the NativeAudioStream constructor succeeds, the AppletAudioClip object now has an object of type NativeAudioStream. It calls this object's getData() method to get an AudioData object for this stream.

10. The AudioStream.getData() method reads all the data it can from the underlying stream and stores it in a byte array.

11. Next, AudioStream.getData() passes this byte array to the AudioData() constructor.

12. Finally, AudioStream.getData() returns a reference to the AudioData object to the AppletAudioClip object, which places the reference in its data field. The AppletAudioClip() constructor is now finished, so control returns to the AppletContext object's getAudioClip() method.

13. The AppletContext.getAudioClip() method returns the AppletAudioClip object to the Applet.play() method.

14. The applet now calls AppletAudioClip.play().

15. The AppletAudioClip passes its data field to the AudioDataStream() constructor to create a new AudioDataStream object.

16. The AppletAudioClip passes this AudioDataStream object to AudioPlayer.player.start(stream).

17. The player object passes the AudioDataStream object to the AudioDevice.device.openChannel() method to add it to the list of streams being played.

At this point, the thread is finished with the sound. A separate thread notices that there's now another sound in the AudioDevice.device object's queue and begins playing it by using AudioDevice.play() and various native methods of the AudioDevice class.

This procedure is only trivially different if Applet.getAudioClip() is called instead.

PUTTING IT ALL TOGETHER

It's more than a little surprising that there is so little support for sound in most of Java. It's not just that the available sound formats are so limited. Adding support for more formats would have been quite a lot of work, after all. It's that sound is really supported only in applets that run on Web pages. Even applets that run as applications by being instantiated in main() don't have the AppletContext that's necessary to play audio clips.

Listing 10-1 demonstrates how you can use the sun.audio classes to add sound to applications that aren't applets. This is a SoundPlayer class. It has a simple interface shown in Figure 10-2. A label gives the name of the sound file that's currently loaded. Four buttons let the user open, play, loop, and stop sound files.

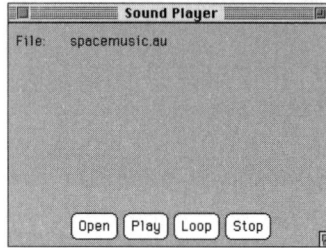

Figure 10-2
The SoundPlayer class.

Each button corresponds to a method. The open button leads to the open() method (via the action() method), which uses a FileDialog to let the user select a file to be played. The SoundPlayer class implements the FilenameFilter interface, so files that can be picked are limited to .au and .wav files. Regrettably, there's no easy way to limit the user's choice to that subset of .au and .wav files that can actually be played by Java. The file is opened, and its contents are used to construct a new AudioData object called theData.

The theData field is used by both the play() and the loop() methods. When either the play or the loop button is pressed, first any track that is now playing is stopped by passing it to AudioPlayer.player.stop(). Next, a check is made to see if theData is null. If it is, the user is asked to select a file for playing. If the user selects a file or theData is not null, then theData is used to construct an AudioDataStream for playing or ContinuousAudioDataStream for looping. This is then passed to AudioPlayer.player.start() and then stored in the nowPlaying field so the user can stop it later if he or she wants to.

The remainder of the SoundPlayer class is straightforward AWT material. The SoundPlayer constructor lays out the GUI for the program. The main() method creates a nem instance of SoundPlayer and shows it. The action() method tests to see whether the action was a hit on one of the four buttons. If it was, it passes it to the corresponding method and returns true. Otherwise, it returns false.

Listing 10-1
The SoundPlayer class

```
import sun.audio.*;
import java.awt.*;
import java.io.*;

public class SoundPlayer extends Frame implements FilenameFilter {

  Button openButton = new Button("Open");
  Button playButton = new Button("Play");
  Button loopButton = new Button("Loop");
  Button stopButton = new Button("Stop");
  Label filename = new Label("                ");
  File theFile = null;
  AudioData theData = null;
  InputStream nowPlaying = null;

  public SoundPlayer() {
    super("Sound Player");
    resize(300, 200);
    Panel north = new Panel();
    north.setLayout(new FlowLayout(FlowLayout.LEFT));
    north.add(new Label("File: "));
    north.add("North", filename);
    add("North", north);
    Panel south = new Panel();
    south.add(openButton);
    south.add(playButton);
    south.add(loopButton);
    south.add(stopButton);
    add("South", south);
  }

  public static void main(String[] args) {
    SoundPlayer sp = new SoundPlayer();
    sp.show();
  }

  public void open() {
    FileDialog fd = new FileDialog(this, "Please select a .au file:");
    fd.setFilenameFilter(this);
    fd.show();
    try {
      theFile = new File(fd.getDirectory() + "/" + fd.getFile());
      if (theFile != null) {
        filename.setText(theFile.getName());
        FileInputStream fis = new FileInputStream(theFile);
        AudioStream as = new AudioStream(fis);
        theData = as.getData();
```

(continued)

Listing 10-1
The SoundPlayer class *(continued)*

```
        }
      }
      catch (IOException e) {
        System.err.println(e);
      }
    }

    public void play() {
      stop();
      if (theData == null) open();
      if (theData != null) {
        AudioDataStream ads = new AudioDataStream(theData);
        AudioPlayer.player.start(ads);
        nowPlaying = ads;
      }
    }

    public void stop() {
      if (nowPlaying != null) {
        AudioPlayer.player.stop(nowPlaying);
        nowPlaying = null;
      }
    }

    public void loop() {
      stop();
      if (theData == null) open();
      if (theData != null) {
        ContinuousAudioDataStream cads = new ContinuousAudioDataStream(theData);
        AudioPlayer.player.start(cads);
        nowPlaying = cads;
      }
    }

    public boolean action(Event e, Object what) {

      if (e.target == playButton) {
        play();
        return true;
      }
      else if (e.target == openButton) {
        open();
        return true;
      }
      else if (e.target == loopButton) {
        loop();
        return true;
```

(continued)

The SoundPlayer class *(continued)*

```
      }
    else if (e.target == stopButton) {
      stop();
      return true;
    }

    return false;

  }

  public boolean accept(File dir, String name) {

    name = name.toLowerCase();
    if (name.endsWith(".au")) return true;
    if (name.endsWith(".wav")) return true;
    return false;

  }

}
```

SUMMARY

In this chapter, you learn the following:

- The java.applet.AudioClip interface is implemented by objects that represent sounds. Classes that implement this interface must have play(), loop(), and stop() methods.

- In Java 1.1 and earlier, the only class that implements the AudioClip interface is sun.applet.AppletAudioClip. More are likely to be added with the release of the Java Media API.

- In Java 1.1 and earlier, only 8-bit, 8-kHz, mono, μlaw encoded sound files are supported. More are likely to be added with the release of the Java Media API.

- Most of the time, you load an AudioClip from a URL with the getAudioClip() or play() methods of java.applet.Applet.

- Data for an AppletAudioClip is stored in an AudioData object.

- The AudioStream, NativeAudioStream, and AudioTranslatorStream classes are used to parse the headers of audio files. Once the header is completely parsed the remaining data may be played, but is generally stored in an AudioData object instead.

- The AudioPlayer.player object is used to play audio streams, generally AudioDataStreams or ContinuousAudioDataStreams. An AudioDataStream is constructed from an AudioDataObject

- The AudioDevice class uses private, native methods to interface with the audio hardware on a platform. The AudioPlayer.player object calls its public methods to add audio streams to the list of sounds being played.

CONTROLLING THE AWT WITH THE SUN.AWT PACKAGE

## 11

*T*he sun.awt package contains a number of classes for various AWT details. There are several new LayoutManager classes. There's also a new component, FocusingTextField, and some support classes for the runtime and the public parts of the AWT.

ALIGNING OBJECTS WITH THE SUN.AWT LAYOUTMANAGERS

The sun.awt package contains four additional Layout Managers: HorizBagLayout, VerticalBagLayout, Variable GridLayout, and OrientableFlowLayout. It's unclear why these are in the sun packages instead of the java packages. Perhaps the designers weren't completely happy with the results and wanted more time to think about and tinker with the classes before releasing them to the world. Three of these four classes don't handle overstuffed containers very well — that is, containers that have more components than they have space for. The fourth class, OrientableFlowLayout, is useful in simple situations but often produces unattractive results in complex, multicolumn layouts. The class authors may intend to fix some of these details and have just not gotten around to doing it yet.

HorizBagLayout

Secret

This LayoutManager implements a *horizontal bag layout*. This means that components are tossed into the bag in a horizontal line from left to right. This is very similar to java.awt.FlowLayout. The main difference is that the HorizBagLayout will not wrap components onto the next line if necessary. Instead, the components just march off the right side of the window. This guarantees that all components fit on one line, but you will not normally want this behavior. Although you may want your interface elements on one line, if they simply can't fit, you almost always want them to wrap around rather than simply disappear.

With a HorizBagLayout, components may be cut off or lost completely, as the top of Figure 11-1 shows. How many buttons are there really in this applet? five? six? seven? ten? eighty-two? You don't know, and in general the user isn't going to know either. Figure 11-1 shows a HorizBagLayout in the applet viewer, but the situation's even worse when the applet runs in a Web browser. A user can resize the applet viewer window. A user cannot resize an applet's space on a Web page.

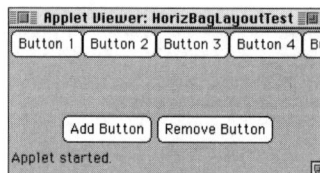

Figure 11-1
HorizBagLayouts have a tendency to cut off the edges of a component or even completely obscure them.

Listing 11-1 is a simple applet that demonstrates the use of the HorizBagLayout class. There are two panels: one in the north of the applet and one in the south. The north panel is laid out with a HorizBagLayout; the south panel with the default FlowLayout. The south panel contains two buttons: addButton and removeButton. Whenever the user presses addButton, it adds a new Button to the north panel. When the user presses removeButton, it removes a button from the north panel. This way, you can test the HorizBagLayout with different numbers of buttons. References to the buttons currently located in the north panel are stored in a Vector called buttons to simplify the removing of buttons.

Listing 11-1
The HorizBagLayoutTest applet

```
import java.awt.*;
import sun.awt.HorizBagLayout;
import java.applet.Applet;
import java.util.*;

public class HorizBagLayoutTest extends Applet {

  Panel north = new Panel();
  Panel south = new Panel();
  Button addButton = new Button("Add Button");
  Button removeButton = new Button("Remove Button");
  Vector buttons = new Vector();

  public void init() {

    setLayout(new BorderLayout());
    south.add(addButton);
    south.add(removeButton);
    Button b = new Button("Button 1");
    buttons.addElement(b);
    north.add(b);
    north.setLayout(new HorizBagLayout());
    add("South", south);
    add("North", north);

  }

  public boolean action(Event e, Object what) {

    if (e.target == addButton) {
      Button b = new Button("Button " + (buttons.size() + 1));
      buttons.addElement(b);
      north.add(b);
      validate();
      return true;
    }
```

(continued)

Listing 11-1
The HorizBagLayoutTest applet *(continued)*

```
else if (e.target == removeButton) {
  try {
    Button b = (Button) buttons.lastElement();
    north.remove(b);
    buttons.removeElementAt(buttons.size() - 1);
  }
  catch (NoSuchElementException nse) {
  }

  return true;
}
return false;

}

}
```

Figure 11-1 was created with this program and shows six buttons (or would, if the fifth and sixth ones were not cut off). Figures 11-2 and 11-3 show one button and three buttons respectively.

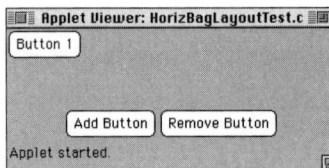

Figure 11-2
The north panel with one button laid out with a HorizBagLayout.

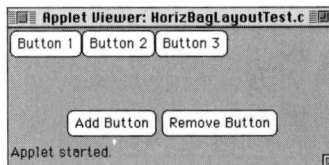

Figure 11-3
The north panel with three buttons laid out with a HorizBagLayout.

The main thing to note about this program is how little effort it takes to use the HorizBagLayout. As with most other LayoutManagers, you just set it and forget it with the following line:

```
north.setLayout(new HorizBagLayout());
```

Once the Layout has been set, just add components to the panel as you usually do. The HorizBagLayout works mostly behind the scenes.

If you want to, you can specify a horizontal gap between the components by passing an int representing the number of pixels in the gap to the constructor. For example, to request a gap of five pixels between components you would write instead

```
north.setLayout(new HorizBagLayout(5));
```

The default is no gap (zero pixels).

The HorizBagLayout class implements all the methods of the LayoutManager interface, specifically

```
public abstract void addLayoutComponent(String  name, Component  comp)
public abstract void layoutContainer(Container  parent)
public abstract Dimension minimumLayoutSize(Container  parent)
public abstract Dimension  preferredLayoutSize(Container  parent)
public abstract void removeLayoutComponent(Component  comp)
```

These all do the same things they do in the other LayoutManager classes with which you're familiar. As with the usual LayoutManagers, you do not need to call these methods directly. Their containers will call them when those containers are validated.

HorizBagLayout also has a toString() method that returns strings that look like "HorizBagLayout[hgap=5]" where the integer is, of course, the horizontal gap between components. As with the other methods of this class, you would rarely call this method directly.

VerticalBagLayout

The VerticalBagLayout is very much like HorizBagLayout, except that it lays out components from top to bottom instead of from left to right. Components that don't fit in a single column run off the bottom.

Secret

The VerticalBagLayout is slightly more useful than the HorizBagLayout because there's no other LayoutManager that draws components from top to bottom. The GridLayout will do this, but it resizes the components to fit the grid boxes rather than the other way around. VerticalBagLayout is sufficient for quick hacks, but if you really need something like this in a serious application, then I recommend writing a custom LayoutManager that places components from top to bottom and then moves to the next column (like Chinese text).

As with other LayoutManagers, the only two methods that you're likely to call are the following two constructors:

```
public VerticalBagLayout()
public VerticalBagLayout(int vgap)
```

The first creates a new VerticalBagLayout with no gap between components; the second inserts vgap pixels of vertical space between each pair of components.

The constructors are normally the only methods of this class that you call. However, there are six more: the methods declared by the LayoutManager interface and toString()—specifically,

```
public abstract void addLayoutComponent(String  name, Component  comp)
public abstract void layoutContainer(Container  parent)
public abstract Dimension minimumLayoutSize(Container  parent)
public abstract Dimension  preferredLayoutSize(Container  parent)
public abstract void removeLayoutComponent(Component  comp)
public void toString()
```

The first five all do the same things that they do in the other LayoutManager classes with which you're familiar. As with the usual LayoutManagers, you don't need to call these methods directly. Their containers will call them when those containers are validated.

The toString() method returns strings that look like "VerticalBagLayout [vgap=5]," where the integer is, of course, the vertical gap between components.

Listing 11-2 is a simple applet that demonstrates the VerticalBagLayout. The VerticalBagLayout panel is placed in the east of the applet, and the addButton and removeButton buttons are placed in the west. Otherwise, this is much the same as Listing 11-1. Figures 11-4, 11-5, and 11-6 show this applet with one, three, and six buttons in the east panel respectively.

Listing 11-2
The VerticalBagLayoutTest applet

```
import java.awt.*;
import sun.awt.VerticalBagLayout;
import java.applet.Applet;
import java.util.*;

public class VerticalBagLayoutTest extends Applet {

  Panel east = new Panel();
  Panel west = new Panel();
  Button addButton = new Button("Add Button");
  Button removeButton = new Button("Remove Button");
  Vector buttons = new Vector();

  public void init() {

    setLayout(new BorderLayout());
    west.add(addButton);
    west.add(removeButton);
    Button b = new Button("Button 1");
    buttons.addElement(b);
    east.add(b);
    east.setLayout(new VerticalBagLayout());
    add("West", west);
    add("East", east);

  }

  public boolean action(Event e, Object what) {

    if (e.target == addButton) {
      Button b = new Button("Button " + (buttons.size() + 1));
      buttons.addElement(b);
      east.add(b);
      validate();
      return true;
    }
    else if (e.target == removeButton) {
      try {
        Button b = (Button) buttons.lastElement();
        east.remove(b);
        buttons.removeElementAt(buttons.size() - 1);
      }
      catch (NoSuchElementException nse) {
```

(continued)

Listing 11-2
The VerticalBagLayoutTest applet *(continued)*

```
        }

        return true;
    }
    return false;

  }

}
```

Figure 11-4
The east panel with one button laid out with a VerticalBagLayout.

Figure 11-5
The east panel with three buttons laid out with a VerticalBagLayout.

Figure 11-6
The east panel with six buttons laid out with a VerticalBagLayout. The sixth button is partially cut off.

Note

This applet is evidence of the danger of relying too much on the sun classes. Did you notice that the applet viewer looks different in Figures 11-1 through 11-3 than the applet viewer in Figures 11-4 through 11-6? It is different. The first set of pictures were taken with Natural Intelligence's Roaster VM, the second set with Sun's JDK for the Mac. Listing 11-1 compiled and ran fine with Roaster DR2.3. Listing 11-2 compiled but failed to run. It also failed to run with Metrowerks Code Warrior 10 VM, which is used by Internet Explorer for the Mac. However, Sun's Mac VM was able to run the program. All these VMs include the sun.awt.VerticalBagLayout class, but here and elsewhere you'll find that the sun classes often aren't as well tested and debugged as the java classes are.

VariableGridLayout

Secret

The GridLayout class is easy to understand but suffers the severe disadvantage that all components placed in it are resized to the size of a grid cell. GridbagLayout is more flexible but much more difficult to understand and use. VariableGridLayout is a subclass of GridLayout that combines the ease of use of a GridLayout with the flexibility of a GridbagLayout.

A VariableGridLayout allows the programmer to adjust the relative sizes of the different rows and columns.

A new VariableGridLayout is created with one of two constructors that mirrors the GridLayout constructors:

```
public VariableGridLayout(int num_rows, int num_cols)
public VariableGridLayout(int num_rows, int num_cols, int hgap, int vgap)
```

The first constructor creates a grid with num_rows rows and num_cols columns for a total of num_rows times num_columns grid cells. The second constructor also specifies horizontal and vertical space between the cells in pixels. These constructors behave exactly like the matching superclass constructors GridLayout().

The difference comes with four new methods that set and get the relative amount of space taken up by the different rows and columns. These are

```
public void setRowFraction(int rowNum, double fraction)
public void setColFraction(int colNum, double fraction)
public double getRowFraction(int rowNum)
public double getColFraction(int colNum)
```

The fraction argument to the setRowFraction() method determines the part of the available horizontal space that will be allocated to row rowNum. Row numbers range from zero to one less than the number of rows. Setting a row fraction for a row outside this range throws an ArrayIndexOutOfBoundsException.

The fraction argument to the setColFraction() method determines the part of the available vertical space that will be allocated to column colNum. Column numbers range from zero to one less than the number of columns. Setting a column fraction for a column outside this range throws an ArrayIndexOutOfBoundsException.

Note

There's really no reason why these ArrayIndexOutOfBoundsExceptions couldn't be caught and handled inside the VariableGridLayout class. This is another example that less care and thought has been taken with the sun classes than with the java classes.

The getRowFraction() and getColFraction() methods return the fraction for the requested row and column. However, these methods are less commonly needed. Normally, you'll set up the row and column fractions once, immediately after you create the VariableGridLayout object, and then not concern yourself with them again.

The sum of the row fractions or the sum of the column fractions can add up to more or less than 1.0 (100%). If the fractions add to less than 100%, the remaining space is evenly allocated among the rows or columns which were not explicitly set, as shown in Figure 11-7. If all columns or rows are explicitly allocated and there's still leftover space, that space is left empty, and the components are scrunched in the upper-left corner of the container, as shown in Figure 11-8. If the explicitly allocated columns and rows take up more than 100% of the space, then some of them slide off the bottom or the right of the container, and the unset rows or columns disappear, as shown in Figure 11-9.

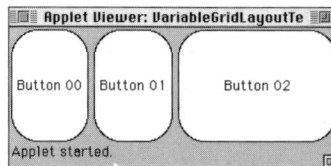

Figure 11-7

Three buttons arranged in a one-row, three-column VariableGridLayout. The first two columns each take up 0.25 (25%) of the space. The third column is not specified but takes up the remaining 0.5 (50%) of the space.

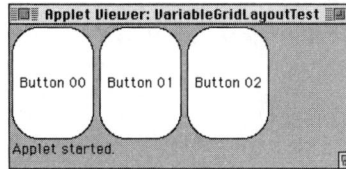

Figure 11-8
Three buttons arranged in a one-row, three-column VariableGridLayout. Each button takes up 0.25 (25%) of the space. The remaining 0.25 (25%) of the space is empty.

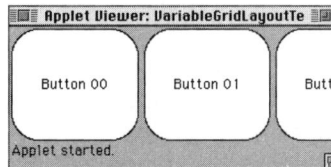

Figure 11-9
Three buttons arranged in a one-row, three-column VariableGridLayout. Each button takes up 0.4 (40%) of the space. The last button is cut off.

All three figures were produced with Listing 11-3, VariableGridLayoutTest. This applet reads a series of PARAM tags to determine how many rows and columns to allot itself and how to space them. Then it places a button in each grid cell.

Listing 11-3
VariableGridLayoutTest

```
import sun.awt.VariableGridLayout;
import java.awt.*;
import java.applet.Applet;

public class VariableGridLayoutTest extends Applet {

  int num_rows;
  int num_cols;
  int hgap;
  int vgap;
```

(continued)

Listing 11-3

VariableGridLayoutTest *(continued)*

```java
public void init() {

    num_rows = readIntegerParameter("num_rows", 3);
    num_cols = readIntegerParameter("num_cols", 3);
    hgap = readIntegerParameter("hgap", 0);
    vgap = readIntegerParameter("vgap", 0);

    VariableGridLayout vgl = new VariableGridLayout(num_rows, num_cols, hgap,
vgap);

    for (int i = 0; i < num_rows; i++) {
      try {
        String s = getParameter("row" + i);
        double d = Double.valueOf(s).doubleValue();
        vgl.setRowFraction(i, d);
      } // end try
      catch (Exception e) {
      }
    } // end for

    for (int i = 0; i < num_cols; i++) {
      try {
        String s = getParameter("col" + i);
        double d = Double.valueOf(s).doubleValue();
        vgl.setColFraction(i, d);
      } // end try
      catch (Exception e) {
      }
    } // end for

    setLayout(vgl);

    for (int i = 0; i < num_rows; i++) {
      for (int j = 0; j < num_cols; j++) {
        add(new Button("Button " + i + j));
      } // end j for
    } // end i for

  } // end init()


  int readIntegerParameter(String name, int dflt) {
```

(continued)

VariableGridLayoutTest *(continued)*

```
      try {
        String s = getParameter(name);
        int i = Integer.parseInt(s);
        return i;
      }
      catch (Exception e) {
        return dflt;
      }

    }

  }
```

Finally, note that VariableGridLayout has all the usual LayoutManager methods like addLayoutComponent() and layoutContainer(), though it's unusual to call them directly. It also has a toString() method that lists the number of rows, the number of columns, the sizes of the horizontal and vertical gaps, and the fractions of each row and column.

OrientableFlowLayout

Secret

Did you ever think that it might be nice to have a FlowLayout that flowed from top to bottom instead of left to right? This might be useful if you were designing an applet for a Taiwanese audience whose eyes are accustomed to moving from the top of a page to the bottom.

The sun.awt.OrientableFlowLayout class is a subclass of java.awt. FlowLayout for which you can choose the direction of flow — that is, right to left or top to bottom. This is especially useful when you don't draw all your components at once, but gradually add them over time in response to user actions.

Note

The OrientableFlowLayout class is present only in Java 1.1 and later. It is currently not present in any vendor's Java implementation except Sun's. The most interesting thing about this is that it means someone at Sun is still working on the sun.awt package.

An OrientableFlowLayout is defined by seven integer parameters. Table 11-1 summarizes these parameters.

Table 11-1

OrientableFlowLayout parameters

Description	Abbreviation	Default	Meaning
orientation	orientation	horizontal	Components flow horizontally or vertically, that is, from left to right or from top to bottom—Orientable FlowLayout.HORIZONTAL and OrientableFlowLayout. VERTICAL— or set with the orientVertically() and orientHorizontally() methods
horizontal alignment	hAlign	centered	Left, right, or centered like FlowLayout.LEFT, FlowLayout.CENTER, and FlowLayout.RIGHT
vertical alignment	vAlign	centered	Top, bottom, or centered; given by the static variables OrientableFlowLayout.TOP, OrientableFlowLayout.BOTTOM, and OrientableFlowLayout.CENTER
horizontal gap between components when oriented horizontally	hHGap	5 pixels	An integral number of pixels
horizontal gap between components when oriented vertically	hVGap	5 pixels	An integral number of pixels
horizontal gap between components when oriented vertically	vHGap	5 pixels	An integral number of pixels
vertical gap between components when oriented vertically	vVGap	5 pixels	An integral number of pixels

The key difference between a regular java.awt.FlowLayout and a sun.awt. OrientableFlowLayout is the orientation of the OrientableFlowLayout. When oriented horizontally, an OrientableFlowLayout is very much like a java.awt. FlowLayout. Figure 11-10 shows three buttons laid out with an Orientable FlowLayout in horizontal orientation. Figure 11-11 shows the same three buttons laid out with an OrientableFlowLayout in vertical orientation.

Figure 11-10
Three buttons laid out with an OrientableFlowLayout in horizontal orientation.

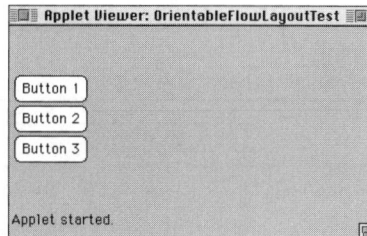

Figure 11-11
Three buttons laid out with an OrientableFlowLayout in vertical orientation.

In a FlowLayout, if there's not enough space to place all the components on one line, some will be shifted down to the next line. The same thing happens in an OrientableFlowLayout. However, if the layout is oriented vertically, then the excess components are shifted right to the next column instead. Figure 11-12 demonstrates.

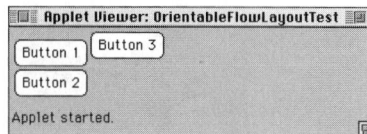

Figure 11-12
The right-shifting of an OrientableFlowLayout. Because there's not enough space for a third button in the first column, it's placed to the right.

If a FlowLayout has more space than the components need, then it can be left-aligned, right-aligned, or centered. The default is to center it. Orientable FlowLayouts also have alignments, but they have two: horizontal and vertical.

Possible horizontal alignments are FlowLayout.LEFT, FlowLayout.CENTER, and FlowLayout.RIGHT, just as for a FlowLayout. However, there are also three vertical alignments: OrientableFlowLayout.TOP, OrientableFlowLayout.CENTER, and OrientableFlowLayout.BOTTOM. Figures 11-13 through 11-15 show these three possibilities. Notice that alignment notwithstanding, the first component is always placed at the top, the second is placed one down from that, and so on. The alignment is with the bottom, but the flow is still top-to-bottom.

Note

The OrientableFlowLayout.CENTER field is inherited from FlowLayout.CENTER. It has the same value whether used for horizontal or vertical centering.

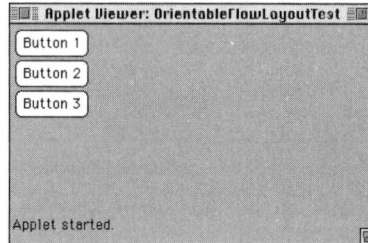

Figure 11-13
Three buttons arranged in a top-aligned OrientableFlowLayout.

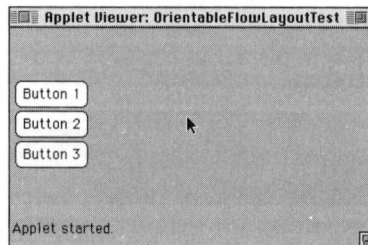

Figure 11-14
Three buttons arranged in a center-aligned OrientableFlowLayout.

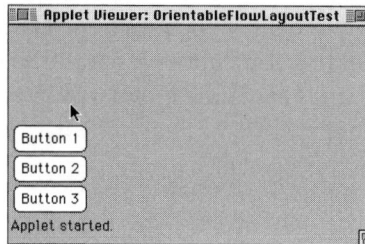

Figure 11-15
Three buttons arranged in a bottom-aligned OrientableFlowLayout.

You can set the vertical and horizontal alignments independently. The vertical alignment is used when the container is laid out vertically. The horizontal alignment is used when the container is laid out horizontally. You cannot, however, use two alignments at once. For example, there is no such thing as a vertically top aligned, horizontally right-aligned container in which the components group in the upper-right corner.

The final parameters to set are the amount of extra vertical space inserted between components and the amount of extra horizontal space inserted between components. These can have different values when the components are aligned vertically than they do when aligned horizontally. For example, you can specify that there are 15 pixels of vertical space between components when they're oriented vertically but only 5 pixels of vertical space when they're oriented horizontally.

The default is 5 pixels of vertical space in each direction, in each orientation. Figure 11-16 shows ten buttons with 15 pixels of vertical space between each row and 10 pixels of horizontal space between each column.

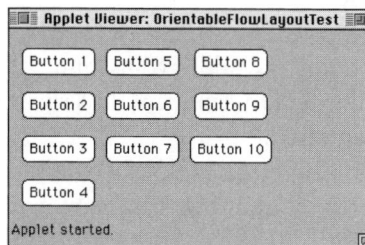

Figure 11-16
Ten buttons in a horizontal orientation with 15 pixels of vertical space and 10 pixels of horizontal space.

Most of the time, you set all these different parameters in the OrientableFlowLayout() constructors. There are four of them. This polymorphism lets you choose the number of parameters that you want to specify for a new OrientableFlowLayout. Any parameters not specified are set to the defaults.

```
public OrientableFlowLayout()
public OrientableFlowLayout(int orientation)
public OrientableFlowLayout(int orientation, int hAlign, int vAlign)
public OrientableFlowLayout(int orientation, int hAlign, int vAlign, int
hHGap, int hVGap, int vHGap, int vVGap)
```

Although most of the parameters that define an OrientableFlowLayout are immutable once the object is constructed, you can change the orientation of an OrientableFlowLayout object. This is done with the orientVertically() and orientHorizontally() methods:

```
public synchronized void orientHorizontally()
public synchronized void orientVertically()
```

Note

Changes made to a LayoutManager do not automatically change your program. You will not see the effect of a call to orientVertically() or orientHorizontally() until the container is invalidated and revalidated. To force the container to show your changes, you first call its invalidate() method and then its validate() method. An applet is its own container so invalidate(); validate(); is sufficient.

Containers are invalidated and revalidated automatically behind the scenes when you add or remove a component from a container. However, most containers have a fixed set of components, so you need to invalidate() them manually.

Finally, I'll note that OrientableFlowLayout has all the usual Layout Manager methods, like addLayoutComponent() and layoutContainer(), although it's unusual to call them directly. It also has a toString() method that prints the orientation.

Listing 11-4, OrientableFlowLayoutTest, is an applet that reads a series of parameters to set up an OrientableFlowLayout. This is used to position a number of buttons. The exact number of buttons is also read from a <PARAM> tag. Any parameters that are not found in the <PARAM> tag are set to reasonable defaults. The OrientableFlowLayout is constructed, and the buttons laid out. Most of the work in this applet involves reading parameters. Once you know the parameters that you want to use, constructing and setting the LayoutManager is almost trivial. This applet was used to produce all the pictures in this section.

Listing 11-4
The OrientableFlowLayoutTest

```
import sun.awt.OrientableFlowLayout;
import java.awt.*;
import java.applet.Applet;


public class OrientableFlowLayoutTest extends Applet {

  public void init() {

    String s;

    int hAlign = FlowLayout.CENTER;
    s = getParameter("hAlign");
    if (s != null && s.equalsIgnoreCase("Left")) {
      hAlign = FlowLayout.LEFT;
    }
    else if (s != null && s.equalsIgnoreCase("Right")) {
      hAlign = FlowLayout.RIGHT;
    }

    int vAlign = OrientableFlowLayout.CENTER;
    s = getParameter("vAlign");
    if (s != null && s.equalsIgnoreCase("Top")) {
      vAlign = OrientableFlowLayout.TOP;
    }
    else if (s != null && s.equalsIgnoreCase("Bottom")) {
      vAlign = OrientableFlowLayout.BOTTOM;
    }

    int orientation = OrientableFlowLayout.VERTICAL;
    s = getParameter("orientation");
    if (s != null && s.equalsIgnoreCase("horizontal")) {
      orientation = OrientableFlowLayout.HORIZONTAL;
    }

    int hHGap = readIntegerParameter("hHGAP", 5);
    int hVGap = readIntegerParameter("hVGAP", 5);
    int vHGap = readIntegerParameter("vHGAP", 5);
    int vVGap = readIntegerParameter("vVGAP", 5);
    int num_buttons = readIntegerParameter("num_buttons", 5);
```

(continued)

Listing 11-4
The OrientableFlowLayoutTest *(continued)*

```
OrientableFlowLayout theLayout = new OrientableFlowLayout
  (orientation, hAlign, vAlign, hHGap, hVGap, vHGap, vVGap);

setLayout(theLayout);

for (int i = 1; i <= num_buttons; i++) {
  add(new Button("Button " + i));
}

}


int readIntegerParameter(String name, int dflt) {

  try {
    String s = getParameter(name);
    int i = Integer.parseInt(s);
    return i;
  }
  catch (Exception e) {
    return dflt;
  }

}

}
```

FOCUSINGTEXTFIELD

Secret

The sun.awt. package contains one additional component: sun.awt.
FocusingTextField. This is a subclass of java.awt.TextField that moves the
focus from one TextField to the next when the user hits Return (or Enter).

For example, consider Figure 11-17. This is a standard form for data
entry. A user will type his or her name into this form, followed by an email
address, followed by a phone number. In traditional GUI environments,
when the user hits the Return key while the focus is on a TextField, the
focus jumps to the next field. This is normally more efficient than using the

mouse to click in each TextField. However, the java.awt.TextField class does not support this behavior. The sun.awt.FocusingTextField class does.

To create a FocusingTextField you use one of two constructors:

```
public FocusingTextField(int cols)
public FocusingTextField(int cols, boolean willSelect)
```

Figure 11-17
A data entry form.

The first is just like the standard java.awt.TextField constructor. The cols argument is roughly the size of the TextField in characters. The second constructor also requires a boolean that specifies the selection behavior of the TextField. If willSelect is true, then when the focus moves out of the field, its contents will be deselected. When the focus moves back into the TextField, the contents will be reselected if they were selected before. By default, willSelect is false. For example,

```
FocusingTextField name = new FocusingTextField(30, true);
FocusingTextField email = new FocusingTextField(30, true);
FocusingTextField phone = new FocusingTextField(30, true);
```

To make the focus jump from field to field when the user presses Return, you need two new methods: setNextField() and nextFocus(). Their signatures are

```
public void setNextField(TextField next)
public void nextFocus()
```

The setNextField() method lets you create an order for the fields to determine which TextField receives the focus after this one. Call it once for each FocusingTextFieldObject to set the field that will be jumped to when the field loses focus. For example,

```
name.setNextField(email);
email.setNextField(phone);
phone.setNextField(name);
```

The nextFocus() method actually moves the focus to the field. Call it in the action() method of the container that contains the FocusingTextField. In the action() method, you watch for FocusingTextField actions; and, when you spot one, you call the field's nextFocus() method. For example,

```
public boolean action(Event e, Object what) {

    if (e.target instanceof FocusingTextField) {
      FocusingTextField ftf = (FocusingTextField) e.target;
      ftf.nextFocus();
    }
    return false;

}
```

Of course, in a real-world action() method, you'll probably handle some additional components and do some more processing, too.

Finally, there are two more methods that let you get and set the boolean selection behavior of a FocusingTextField object. These are

```
public void setWillSelect(boolean willSelect)
public boolean getWillSelect()
```

Most of the time, however, you'll just set this in the constructor and not change it later.

Listing 11-5 puts this all together to draw the form shown in Figure 11-17. A VariableGridLayout is used to provide more accurate spacing.

Listing 11-5
FocusingTextFieldTest

```
import sun.awt.FocusingTextField;
import sun.awt.VariableGridLayout;
import java.awt.*;
import java.applet.Applet;

public class FocusingTextFieldTest extends Applet {

    FocusingTextField name = new FocusingTextField(30, true);
    FocusingTextField email = new FocusingTextField(30, true);
```

(continued)

FocusingTextFieldTest *(continued)*

```
FocusingTextField phone = new FocusingTextField(30, true);

public void init() {

  VariableGridLayout theLayout = new VariableGridLayout(3,2);
  theLayout.setColFraction(0, 0.25);
  setLayout(theLayout);

  name.setNextField(email);
  email.setNextField(phone);
  phone.setNextField(name);

  add(new Label("Name: "));
  add(name);
  add(new Label("Email: "));
  add(email);
  add(new Label("Phone: "));
  add(phone);

}

public boolean action(Event e, Object what) {

  if (e.target instanceof FocusingTextField) {
    FocusingTextField ftf = (FocusingTextField) e.target;
    ftf.nextFocus();
  }
  return false;

}

}
```

You're probably thinking that this is more work than it should be. The focus should track the chain of next fields automatically without any intervention from the programmer. Furthermore, as long as you know what the next field is, you might as well implement tabbing from field to field. And, as long as you're tabbing into the next field, why not have a previous field as well so you can shift-tab backwards? This component is in the sun classes rather than the java classes probably because it is half-baked. It adds a little to the standard TextField, but not enough to be significant. If you really need this functionality, then you probably need more than this component offers. Therefore, you're probably better off writing your own subclass of java.awt.TextField instead of using sun.awt.FocusingTextField.

CONTROLLING SCREEN UPDATING

Secret

The ScreenUpdater class is a subclass of Thread that runs at a low priority delivering messages to a list of objects. The objects to which the messages are delivered must implement the UpdateClient interface. The Screen UpdaterEntry class is used internally by the ScreenUpdate class to keep track of the objects that need to be updated.

The virtual machines run a ScreenUpdater thread to be sure that components and containers are repainted in a timely fashion. However, the timed callback mechanism that this class implements is quite general, and is by no means limited to updating the screen. You can use it to perform other actions that need to be taken after a certain amount of time has passed.

No more than one ScreenUpdater object exists in a virtual machine at a time. The constructor is declared private, so no class except the ScreenUpdater class itself can instantiate it:

```
private ScreenUpdater();
```

How, then, do you get an instance of the ScreenUpdater class? The answer is that there's a public static field in the ScreenUpdater class called updater that is initialized the first time the ClassLoader loads the class

```
public final static ScreenUpdater updater = new ScreenUpdater();
```

This is the only ScreenUpdater object that can exist in the virtual machine. The first time that the class is loaded, the constructor is invoked. All other times, you just get back the same object.

As soon as the updater object is constructed, it starts running itself. (Remember, it's a subclass of Thread.) It alternates between Thread. NORM_PRIORITY (5) and Thread.NORM_PRIORITY - 1 (4).

Now, the ScreenUpdater has a linked list of ScreenUpdaterEntry objects that need to be updated. (I'll explain how objects are placed in the list in a minute.) Each entry in this list has a time field that tells when the object next needs to be updated. This list is sorted according to when each object needs to be updated. Thus, objects in the list that should be updated at 5:00 P.M. are placed before objects in the list that need to be updated at 6:00 P.M.

As the ScreenUpdater thread runs, the ScreenUpdater retrieves the first entry in the list. Then it waits until it's time to update that entry. When the time comes, the entry is updated. Then the ScreenUpdater pulls the next entry from the list. It waits until the time when that object needs to be updated. Then it updates it.

To update objects in the list, the ScreenUpdater invokes their updateClient() method. This method is declared in the UpdateClient interface like this:

```
void updateClient(Object arg);
```

Only objects that implement the UpdateClient interface can be placed in the ScreenUpdater.

To add an object to the list, you call one of the three ScreenUpdater notify() methods:

```
public void notify(UpdateClient client)
public synchronized void notify(UpdateClient client, long delay)
public synchronized void notify(UpdateClient client, long delay, Object
arg)
```

The client argument is the object you want to update. The delay argument is how long you want to wait in milliseconds before the client is updated. If you don't specify this, 100 is used. The argument arg is optional and will be passed to the client's updateClient() method. If you don't specify this, null is used.

A lot of this, though interesting, consists of implementation details you don't need to know to use the class. To use the class, you just need to create objects that implement the UpdateClient interface and then call ScreenUpdater.updater.notify().

Listing 11-6 is a simple clock applet that uses the ScreenUpdater object to tell it when to redraw. It redraws once a second. The updateClient method updates the text in the TextField theTime. Then it tells the updater that it wants to be updated again in 1000 milliseconds (one second). Like all well-behaved applets, this one provides a simple and obvious mechanism for the user to stop it: in this case, a stop button.

Listing 11-6
The ScreenUpdaterTest applet

```java
import java.awt.*;
import sun.awt.*;
import java.applet.Applet;
import java.util.Date;


public class ScreenUpdaterTest extends Applet implements UpdateClient {

  TextField theTime = new TextField(30);
  boolean running = true;
  Button stopButton = new Button("Stop");
  Button startButton = new Button("Start");

  public void init() {
    theTime.setEditable(false);
    add(theTime);
    add(startButton);
    add(stopButton);
  }

  public void updateClient(Object arg) {
    Date d = new Date();
    theTime.setText(d.toString());
    if (running) ScreenUpdater.updater.notify(this, 1000);
  }

  public void start() {
    running = true;
    updateClient(null);
  }

  public void stop() {
    running = false;
  }

  public boolean action(Event e, Object what) {

    if (e.target == startButton) {
      start();
      return true;
    }
    else if (e.target == stopButton) {
      stop();
      return true;
    }
```

(continued)

The ScreenUpdaterTest applet *(continued)*

```
        return false;

    }

}
```

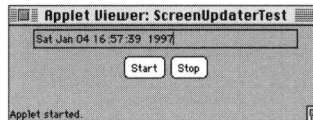

Figure 11-18
The ScreenUpdater clock.

SUMMARY

In this chapter, you learn the following:

- A HorizBagLayout object aligns components in a single row from left to right; this row runs off the right side of the panel when there's not enough space.

- A VerticalBagLayout object aligns components in a single column from top to bottom; this column runs off the bottom of the panel when there's not enough space.

- A VariableGridLayout is very much like a GridLayout, except that you can allot different percentages of the horizontal and vertical space to different rows and columns.

- An OrientableFlowLayout is exactly like a FlowLayout in horizontal orientation. In vertical orientation, components flow from top to bottom and then left to right when the first column runs out of space.

- A FocusingTextField is a subclass of TextField that shifts the focus to a different TextField when the user hits Return.

- The ScreenUpdater thread is a timed queue for events that will take place a specified number of milliseconds in the future.

Encoding and Decoding Data with the sun.misc Package

*T*he Seven-bit ASCII format is a convenient lowest common denominator format for computers. Even platforms for which ASCII is not the native tongue can generally speak it. However, not all files are ASCII. In fact, if the bits on a hard disk were randomly distributed, only about half the bytes on the disk would be valid ASCII characters.

Many gateways, especially e-mail gateways, understand only 7-bit ASCII and will set the high bit of all transmitted characters to zero. Naturally, this plays havoc with binary files, files made up of ISO Latin-1 or Unicode characters, and quite a lot more. For example, all your umlauts (¨) are turned into vertical bars (|), and your betas (β) become underscores (_). It's even worse for binary files, where changing a single bit can corrupt the entire file.

That's not all, either. The ASCII values from 0 to 30, as well as 127, are non-printing control characters. Some of these bytes have special meanings to particular hardware. For example, a terminal server may interpret ASCII 3 (end transmission) as the signal to break the connection. A dumb terminal may interpret ASCII 7 (bell) as the signal to ring a bell and then otherwise ignore the character.

Given these constraints, out of the 256 possible values for an 8-bit byte, the only ones that you can generally count on getting through all the different modems, terminal servers, terminals, gateways, and e-mail programs are the printable ASCII characters with values between 31 and 126. This may be enough for text messages, but it leaves something to be desired for file transfer.

There are a few other problems to watch out for, too. Some FTP programs will translate line endings present in a file, whether \n (ASCII 10), \r (ASCII 13), or \r\n (ASCII 10 followed by ASCII 13), into the preferred line ending format on the host system. Some other programs will insert extra line endings if a line grows to 72 characters or more without some sort of line break character. You can place a line break after each set of eight encoded characters to protect against programs that hard wrap your text, and ignore any \r or \n characters that occur when you're decoding or encoding. You might even add some unusual start of encoded data and finish of encoded data lines to guard against gateways that add headers or append signature files.

CODING BINARY DATA IN ASCII

What you need is a way to convert arbitrary, binary data into normal, printable, ASCII text in which each byte has a value between 31 and 126. It should be simple to do this. For example, you could encode each 8-bit byte as three ASCII digits between 000 and 255. In this scenario, zero would be 000; one would be 001; two would be 002; and so on. For example, the first four bytes of every Java class file are the magic number 0xCAFEBABE (in hex). This would be encoded as

```
202 254 186 190
```

Because the digits 0 through 9 are printable ASCII characters, this encoding should allow a binary file to get through any gateway that will pass ASCII text. This format is called *decimal dump*, because each byte of the file is presented as a decimal number.

Decimal dump is far from the most efficient encoding scheme that one could devise. Because each byte now takes up four bytes (three digits plus a space), the file size balloons to four times its original size. You can do a little better by leaving out the spaces and using two hexadecimal digits for each byte instead of three decimal digits. This shrinks the encoded file size down to only double the original size. Nonetheless, given random binary data, there is no way you can encode it into only the printable ASCII characters without making the file size grow somewhat. In the best case, you might make the file grow by no more than about 30 percent. If the binary data is not random, you might be able to do a little better yet.

There are a number of such codings in common use. These include, in rough order of commonness, uuencode, base-64, quoted-printable, and ucencode. Binhex is another popular binary-to-ASCII coding that has the added capability of combining the two forks of a Macintosh file into a single file.

Macintosh files each have two forks: a data fork and a resource fork. Most other operating systems consider each of these forks to be a separate file. For the most part, the MacOS hides the dichotomy from users, but it becomes visible when you transfer Macintosh files to other platforms. To programmers, the difference is more apparent. Java file I/O operates only on the data forks of Macintosh files. To get at the resource fork, you must use native methods.

The sun.misc package includes a number of classes that you can use to perform exactly this sort of encoding. The CharacterEncoder and CharacterDecoder classes are abstract superclasses for binary-to-ASCII conversions. Concrete subclasses are provided to handle Base64, uuencode, hexdump, and ucencode formats. Furthermore, you can write new subclasses that handle additional formats.

THE CHARACTERENCODER AND CHARACTERDECODER CLASSES

The sun.misc.CharacterEncoder class is an abstract superclass for classes that accept 8-bit binary data and encode it into ASCII. The sun.misc.Character Decoder class is an abstract superclass for classes that accept ASCII encoded data and decode it into 8-bit binary form. Concrete subclasses of these classes handle particular coding schemes like uunecode or Base-64.

These classes assume that the encoded data has roughly this form:

```
(Prefix)
(Line Prefix)(encoded data atoms)(Line Suffix)
(Buffer Suffix)
```

The prefix is a line that indicates the start of the encoded data. The suffix is a line that indicates the end of the encoded data. Everything before the prefix line and after the suffix line is ignored when decoding the file. Not all encoding schemes use prefixes and suffixes, but those that do can store multiple encoded files in a single file of text.

The line prefix is non-data that are placed at the beginning of each line of data. This often indicates the length of the line, and it may also contain checksums for the line, sequence numbers, or other housekeeping information. The line suffix is similar housekeeping information, but placed at the end of each line rather than at the beginning. Again, not all schemes use line prefixes or line suffixes.

The binary data itself is encoded in *data atoms*. In general, multiple data atoms are placed on each line of the file. A fixed number of data atoms always represents a fixed number of bytes. In the decimal dump format, 245 or 024 would be atoms. Each of these atoms represents exactly one byte of unencoded data.

The CharacterEncoder class has a single triply polymorphic, public method. This is encodeBuffer(). Its three polymorphic variants are

```
public void encodeBuffer(InputStream in, OutputStream out)
public void encodeBuffer(byte[] buf, OutputStream out) throws IOException
public String encodeBuffer(byte[] buf)
```

The first variant reads bytes from the InputStream in, encodes them, and sends the encoded data to the OutputStream out. This variant reads continuously until the InputStream is exhausted. The second variant reads the data from a byte array buf and sends the encoded data to the OutputStream out. The third variant also reads input from the byte array buf, but it stores the encoded data in a string of chars that it returns. As you might expect, the CharacterDecoder class has three complementary decodeBuffer() methods that convert encoded data into binary data. These are

```
public void decodeBuffer(InputStream in, OutputStream out) throws
IOException
public byte[] decodeBuffer(String inputString) throws IOException
public byte[] decodeBuffer(InputStream in) throws IOException
```

The first variant reads bytes from the InputStream in, decodes them, and sends the decoded data to the OutputStream out. It reads continuously until the InputStream is exhausted. The second variant reads the data from the string inputString and places the decoded data in a byte array that it returns. The third variant reads the encoded data from the InputStream argument in and returns the decoded data in a byte array.

There are four concrete subclasses of CharacterEncoder and three concrete subclasses of CharacterDecoder. These are

```
BASE64Decoder
BASE64Encoder
UUEncoder
UUDecoder
UCEncoder
UCDecoder
HexDumpEncoder
```

HexDump Encoding

The HexDumpEncoder is the simplest of the lot. It's also the only one that's not symmetrical; there's a HexDumpEncoder class but no corresponding HexDumpDecoder class (though one is provided in Listing 12-9 later in this chapter).

The HexDumpEncoder translates each byte in the input to a hexadecimal digit. For example, the byte value 255 becomes FF; 254 becomes FE; 253 becomes FD; and so on. An atom in this encoding is two hexadecimal digits. There is one encoded byte of data per atom.

Each line of output contains 16 two-digit bytes. Atoms are separated from each other by spaces. The line prefix is the offset into the file of the first byte in the line, given as a four-digit hex number. The line suffix is the ASCII representation of the data or '.' if a byte is not an ASCII printing character. For example,

```
0040: 28 4C 6A 61 76 61 2F 6C  61 6E 67 2F 53 74 72 69 (Ljava/lang/Stri
```

Listing 12-1 is a simple class that reads a set of filenames from the command line and dumps them to System.out in hex format.

Listing 12-1
The HexDumper class

```java
import java.io.*;
import sun.misc.*;


public class HexDumper {


  public static void main (String[] args) {

    for (int i=0; i <args.length; i++) {
      HexDumper hd = new HexDumper();
      hd.dumpFile(args[i]);
    }

  }


  public void dumpFile(String filename) {

    try {
      FileInputStream fin = new FileInputStream(filename);
      HexDumpEncoder hde = new HexDumpEncoder();
      hde.encodeBuffer(fin, System.out);
    }
    catch (Exception e) {
      System.err.println(e);
    }

  }

}
```

Here's the output you get when this program is used to dump HelloWorld.class:

```
0000:  CA FE BA BE 00 03 00 2D    00 1F 08 00 12 07 00 13    .......¯........
0010:  07 00 19 07 00 1A 07 00    1B 0A 00 04 00 09 09 00    ................
0020:  05 00 0A 0A 00 03 00 0B    0C 00 0E 00 0C 0C 00 1D    ................
0030:  00 16 0C 00 1E 00 0D 01    00 03 28 29 56 01 00 15    ..........()V...
0040:  28 4C 6A 61 76 61 2F 6C    61 6E 67 2F 53 74 72 69    (Ljava/lang/Stri
0050:  6E 67 3B 29 56 01 00 06    3C 69 6E 69 74 3E 01 00    ng;)V...<init>..
0060:  04 43 6F 64 65 01 00 0D    43 6F 6E 73 74 61 6E 74    .Code...Constant
0070:  56 61 6C 75 65 01 00 0A    45 78 63 65 70 74 69 6F    Value...Exceptio
0080:  6E 73 01 00 0B 48 65 6C    6C 6F 20 57 6F 72 6C 64    ns...Hello World
0090:  01 00 0A 48 65 6C 6C 6F    57 6F 72 6C 64 01 00 0F    ...HelloWorld...
00A0:  48 65 6C 6C 6F 57 6F 72    6C 64 2E 6A 61 76 61 01    HelloWorld.java.
00B0:  00 0F 4C 69 6E 65 4E 75    6D 62 65 72 54 61 62 6C    ..LineNumberTabl
00C0:  65 01 00 15 4C 6A 61 76    61 2F 69 6F 2F 50 72 69    e...Ljava/io/Pri
00D0:  6E 74 53 74 72 65 61 6D    3B 01 00 0E 4C 6F 63 61    ntStream;...Loca
00E0:  6C 56 61 72 69 61 62 6C    65 73 01 00 0A 53 6F 75    lVariables...Sou
00F0:  72 63 65 46 69 6C 65 01    00 13 6A 61 76 61 2F 69    rceFile...java/i
0100:  6F 2F 50 72 69 6E 74 53    74 72 65 61 6D 01 00 10    o/PrintStream...
0110:  6A 61 76 61 2F 6C 61 6E    67 2F 4F 62 6A 65 63 74    java/lang/Object
0120:  01 00 10 6A 61 76 61 2F    6C 61 6E 67 2F 53 79 73    ...java/lang/Sys
0130:  74 65 6D 01 00 04 6D 61    69 6E 01 00 03 6F 75 74    tem...main...out
0140:  01 00 05 70 72 69 6E 74    00 20 00 02 00 04 00 00    ...print. ......
0150:  00 00 00 02 00 09 00 1C    00 0C 00 01 00 0F 00 00    ................
0160:  00 25 00 02 00 00 00 00    00 09 B2 00 07 12 01 B6    .%.............
0170:  00 08 B1 00 00 00 01 00    15 00 00 00 0A 00 02 00    ................
0180:  00 00 07 00 08 00 04 00    00 00 0E 00 0C 00 01 00    ................
0190:  0F 00 00 00 1D 00 01 00    01 00 00 00 05 2A B7 00    .............*..
01A0:  06 B1 00 00 00 01 00 15    00 00 00 06 00 01 00 00    ................
01B0:  00 02 00 01 00 18 00 00    00 02 00 14              ............
```

There is no corresponding HexDump decoder class. Although it is not difficult to write one, there's little need for it in practice. The HexDump encoding is used primarily to inspect files, not to transmit them.

BASE64 ENCODING

Base64 encoding is defined in RFC2045 as part of the MIME (Multipurpose Internet Mail Extensions) specification. Like other encodings, Base64 represents arbitrary sequences of binary data in ASCII text. In fact, it uses only 65 ASCII characters, picked in such a fashion that the characters are the same in ASCII, EBCDIC, and all variants of ISO 646.

Table 12-1
The Base64 code

Bits	Value	Code	Bits	Value	Code	Bits	Value	Code	Bits	Value	Code
000000	0	A	010000	16	Q	100000	32	g	110000	48	w
000001	1	B	010001	17	R	100001	33	h	110001	49	x
000010	2	C	010010	18	S	100010	34	i	110010	50	y
000011	3	D	010011	19	T	100011	35	j	110011	51	z
000100	4	E	010100	20	U	100100	36	k	110100	52	0
000101	5	F	010101	21	V	100101	37	l	110101	53	1
000110	6	G	010110	22	W	100110	38	m	110110	54	2
000111	7	H	010111	23	X	100111	39	n	110111	55	3
001000	8	I	011000	24	Y	101000	40	o	111000	56	4
001001	9	J	011001	25	Z	101001	41	p	111001	57	5
001010	10	K	011010	26	a	101010	42	q	111010	58	6
001011	11	L	011011	27	b	101011	43	r	111011	59	7
001100	12	M	011100	28	c	101100	44	s	111100	60	8
001101	13	N	011101	29	d	101101	45	t	111101	61	9
001110	14	O	011110	30	e	101110	46	u	111110	62	+
001111	15	P	011111	31	f	101111	47	v	111111	63	/

You may have noted that 65 is one more than 64, which happens to be 2^6. This is not a coincidence. When encoding data into Base64, every 6-bit sequence maps onto exactly one character. Table 12-1 lists the encoding used. Thus, three 8-bit bytes are encoded as four ASCII characters where each character represents a run of six bits. An atom in Base64 is four ASCII characters, and there are three bytes per atom.

The values in Table 12-1 are formed by interpreting the bit patterns as 6-bit, unsigned integers.

Of course, two times out of three, the number of bits in a file will not be an even multiple of six. In these cases, either 8 or 16 extra zero bits (one or two null bytes) are added at the end of the input to round it up to an even multiple of 24 (the least common multiple of six and eight). If one null byte is added, the encoded data will end with one = character. If two null bytes are added, then two = characters are added. This equals sign is the 65th character allowed in Base64 encoding. It can occur only at the end of the encoded data and tells you how many extra bytes of padding were added to the input before it was encoded. One equals sign means one byte was added; two equals signs means two bytes were added; no equals signs means no padding was added.

To avoid problems with software that rewraps long lines, encoded data is presented in lines of no more than 76 characters. Lines are broken with carriage return-line feed pairs (\r\n). When decoding Base64 data, any character not represented as a value in Table 12-1 is ignored. Line breaks are the most common such characters, but theoretically any arbitrary characters that aren't included in Table 12-1 could be inserted in random locations in a Base64-encoded file without corrupting it.

Base64 does not specify any prefix or suffix for the encoded data. MIME handles that at a different level. Thus, when decoding Base64 data, you should assume that all the data you're handed is Base64 encoded.

Secret

The sun.misc.BASE64Encoder and sun.misc.BASE64Decoder classes do not have any public or protected members. You construct instances of these classes with the default noargs constructors, and you interact with them through the encodeBuffer() and decodeBuffer() methods of their respective superclasses.

Listing 12-2 is a program that converts the files specified on the command line into Base64 encoded files. There's no standard file name extension for Base64 files, so I chose .64.

Listing 12-2
The Base64Encoder class

```
import sun.misc.*;
import java.io.*;


public class Base64Encode {
  public static void main(String[] args) {

    if (args.length > 0) {
      for (int i = 0; i < args.length; i++) {
        try {
          InputStream is = new FileInputStream(args[i]);
          OutputStream os = new FileOutputStream(args[i] + ".64");
          BASE64Encoder b64ec = new BASE64Encoder();
          b64ec.encodeBuffer(is, os);
        }
        catch (IOException e) {
          System.err.println(e);
        }
      }  // end for
    } // end if

  }  // end main


}
```

It's not any harder to decode Base64 files. Listing 12-3 demonstrates this. The main difference is that Listing 12-3 only decodes one file at a time, because you also need to ask the user for the name of the file in which to place the decoded output.

Listing 12-3
The Base64Decoder class

```
import sun.misc.*;
import java.io.*;


public class Base64Decode {

  public static void main(String[] args) {

    if (args.length >= 2) {
      try {
        InputStream is = new FileInputStream(args[0]);
```

(continued)

The Base64Decoder class *(continued)*

```
        OutputStream os = new FileOutputStream(args[1]);
        BASE64Decoder b64dc = new BASE64Decoder();
        b64dc.decodeBuffer(is, os);
      }
    catch (IOException e) {
      System.err.println(e);
      }
    } // end if

  }  // end main


}
```

UUEncoding

Like Base64, uuencode converts 6-bit sextets of binary data to ASCII characters. Table 12-2 shows the encoding used. Unlike Base64, there's a simple algorithmic means of determining the ASCII value for a sextet in uuencoding. You treat the sextet as an unsigned 6-bit integer and add 32 (the value of the ASCII space character) to it.

Unlike Base64, uuencode depends on the ASCII English character set. Also unlike Base64, uuencode defines a line prefix and a line suffix to identify the start and the end of the uuencoded data. A uuencode line prefix looks like this:

```
begin [mode] [filename]
```

Here, [filename] is the name of the file and [mode] is a three-digit number like "644" corresponding to UNIX file permissions. If you're not on UNIX, you can pretty much ignore this number. This is followed by one or more lines of encoded data. Each line of encoded data has the format:

```
[length][data][data][data]...
```

Here, [length] is an unsigned byte that specifies the number of sextets encoded on this line. If the number of input bytes is not a multiple of three, then there may be padding at the end of the line to be ignored. When decoding, you should decode as many sextets as specified by the length byte and ignore any remaining characters on the line.

Table 12-2
UUCode

Bits	Value	Code	Bits	Value	Code	Bits	Value	Code	Bits	Value	Code
000000	0		010000	16	0	100000	32	@	110000	48	P
000001	1	!	010001	17	1	100001	33	A	110001	49	Q
000010	2	"	010010	18	2	100010	34	B	110010	50	R
000011	3	#	010011	19	3	100011	35	C	110011	51	S
000100	4	$	010100	20	4	100100	36	D	110100	52	T
000101	5	%	010101	21	5	100101	37	E	110101	53	U
000110	6	&	010110	22	6	100110	38	F	110110	54	V
000111	7	'	010111	23	7	100111	39	G	110111	55	W
001000	8	(	011000	24	8	101000	40	H	111000	56	X
001001	9	)	011001	25	9	101001	41	I	111001	57	Y
001010	10	*	011010	26	:	101010	42	J	111010	58	Z
001011	11	+	011011	27	;	101011	43	K	111011	59	[
001100	12	,	011100	28	<	101100	44	L	111100	60	\
001101	13	-	011101	29	=	101101	45	M	111101	61	]
001110	14	.	011110	30	>	101110	46	N	111110	62	^
001111	15	/	011111	31	?	101111	47	O	111111	63	_

There is no line suffix in uuencode. The end of the uuencoded data is signified by a line containing exactly one space character. This is followed by a line containing the word "end," just like this:

```
end
```

As long as you avoid any lines that look like the start of a uuencoded file, you can place any text you want before the start of the uuencoded data or after their end. This area is commonly used for human-readable ASCII that specifies the contents of the file.

Listing 12-4 is a typical, small, uuencoded file. The "cut here" line with many hyphens, although common (especially in the binary newsgroups of Usenet), is not part of the standard. It's not incompatible with the standard, however. As long as it's placed before the begin line, uudecode doesn't care.

Also, notice the *M* at the beginning of the first nine lines in the encoded data. The ASCII character M has the value 77. If you count the characters in those lines (including spaces but not including line breaks), you'll see that there are 61 characters in each of those lines. One of these is the length byte, M. The other sixty 8-bit characters encode 480 bits of data. Seventy-seven sextets is 462 bits of data. Therefore, the last two bytes of the line are padding, and the remainder should be decoded as data. There's nothing magical about 77. The tenth line of data begins with a G character, indicating that this line contains 71 sextets of data.

Listing 12-4
The HelloWorld.class file uuencoded

```
This file is the Java .class file for the HelloWorld program.
You can decode it with uuencode or any compatible decoder.
─────────────────────────────cut here─────────────────────────────
begin 644 HelloWorld.class
MROZZO@ # "T 'P@ $<@ $P< &0< &<@ &PH ! )"0 % H* , "PP #@ ,
M# = !8, !X #0$ R@5I5@@$ %%82B@S6!L6:.(3G1[;5J6! !!!b
M;FET/@$ !$-0984! U#;;Wm-gW3[5+[.QH!QYvjpW$a
M;&Q0(%=0<FQD 0 +K[i;&D7;W)L9 $ #[TAE;&Q05VJ]R;&0N:F%V80$ #TQI
M;F5.=6UB97)486J)L90$ %4QqJ879A+VE0+U!R:6YT4W1R96%M.P$ #nQ08V$L
M5F%R:6B:&5S 0 *V5]U<F-1FEL90$ $VqA=F$:6\ ')I;;G13b)&')
M !!J879A+VqA;F$<O3V)J96-T 0 0:F%V82]l86ONWLW$<W1E;0$ !&qA6X!
M -0=70! 5P<qFEN= @ ( ! @ ) !P # ! \ E (
M FR <2 ;8 "+$ ! !4 * ( ' @ ! X # ! \ =
G $ 0 4JMP &L0 $ %0 8 0 ( 08 @ 4

end
```

Secret

The sun.misc.UUEncoder class has the three polymorphic constructors. These allow you to set the filename and permissions that will be used in the begin line of the encoded data. These are

```
public UUEncoder()
public UUEncoder(String filename)
public UUEncoder(String filename, int mode)
```

Here, filename is the name of the file where the *decoded* data will be placed. Mode is the UNIX permissions that will be used for the file that holds the decoded data. The default filename is encoder.buf, and the default mode is 644.

After constructing a UUEncoder object, you interact with it through the encodeBuffer() methods of the superclass, sun.misc.CharacterEncoder. Listing 12-5 demonstrates by uuencoding files passed to it on the command line. The encoded files have the same name as the original file, plus the extension .uu on the end.

Listing 12-5
The UUEncoder program

```
import sun.misc.*;
import java.awt.*;
import java.io.*;

public class UUEncode {

  public static void main(String[] args) {

    if (args.length > 0) {
      for (int i = 0; i < args.length; i++) {
        try {
          InputStream is = new FileInputStream(args[i]);
          OutputStream os = new FileOutputStream(args[i] + ".uu");
          UUEncoder uuec = new UUEncoder(args[i]);
          uuec.encodeBuffer(is, os);
        }
        catch (IOException e) {
          System.err.println(e);
        }
      }  // end for
    } // end if

  }  // end main

}
```

The sun.misc.UUDecoder class is used to decode uuencoded files. It has no public methods (you can use the default noargs constructor), but it does have two public fields:

```
public String bufferName
public int mode
```

Here, bufferName is the name of the file into which the decoded data should be placed, and mode is the UNIX permissions that should be given to the file. These fields are set only after a file has been decoded. You interact with this class through the decodeBuffer methods of the superclass, sun.misc.CharacterDecoder. Listing 12-6 demonstrates by uudecoding files passed to it on the command line.

Listing 12-6
The UUDecoder program

```
import sun.misc.*;
import java.awt.*;
import java.io.*;


public class UUDecode {

  public static void main(String[] args) {

    if (args.length > 0) {
      for (int i = 0; i < args.length; i++) {
        try {
          UUDecoder uudc = new UUDecoder();
          InputStream is = new FileInputStream(args[i]);
          byte[] data = uudc.decodeBuffer(is);
          OutputStream os = new FileOutputStream(uudc.bufferName);
          os.write(data);
          os.close();
        }
        catch (IOException e) {
          System.err.println(e);
        }
      }  // end for
    } // end if

  }  // end main

}
```

UCENCODING

Secret

UCEncoding is unique to Java. It's designed to be similar to UUCode but to remove the dependency on ASCII. To the best of my knowledge, it is not yet actually used anywhere. The characters 0-9, A-Z, a-z,), and (are used to encode the sextets of data.

UCEncoding is algorithmic like uuencode, but the algorithm is more complex. Every two bytes are encoded into three ASCII characters. Thus, there are three characters in an atom and two bytes per atom. This expands the file size by almost exactly 50%.

Suppose you have two bytes, X and Y, with the bit patterns shown in Figure 12-1. X0 through X7 are the bits of byte X. Y0 through Y7 are the bits of byte Y.

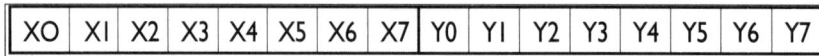

XO	XI	X2	X3	X4	X5	X6	X7	Y0	YI	Y2	Y3	Y4	Y5	Y6	Y7

Figure 12-1
Bits in two bytes.

These are encoded into three bytes as shown in Figure 12-2. Each of these bytes has the two high order bits equal to zero. Thus, each of the encoded bytes has a value between 0 and 63.

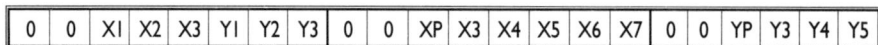

0	0	XI	X2	X3	YI	Y2	Y3	0	0	XP	X3	X4	X5	X6	X7	0	0	YP	Y3	Y4	Y5

Figure 12-2
The UCEncoded bits in two bytes.

XP is a parity bit for byte X, and YP is a parity bit for byte Y. XP is 1 if there is an odd number of one bits in byte X, and 0 if there is an even number of set bits in byte X. Similarly, YP is 1 if there is an odd number of one bits in byte Y, and 0 if there is an even number of 1 bits in byte Y. This provides rudimentary error detection in case the data is garbled in transmission.

These encoded bytes are now mapped into the 64 characters 0-9, A-Z, a-z, (, and) as shown in Table 12-3.

Next, 48 encoded bytes (72 characters) are placed on each line of the encoded file. Each line is formatted like this:

```
*[length][sequence][data][data][data]...[data][crc]\r\n
```

The line prefix has three parts. The first character in each line is the ASCII * character. This serves no purpose except to identify the line as a ucencode line. The second byte of each line is an unsigned length byte, much like the first byte of a uuencoded line. The next byte is an unsigned sequence number modulo 256. In other words, the first line of data has the sequence number 0; the second line of data has the sequence number 1; the third line has the sequence number 2; and so on. If there are more than 256 lines of data, then counting starts over at 0. The line prefix is followed by twenty-four 3-byte data atoms, each of which encodes two bytes of actual data as described above. If there are fewer than 24 atoms remaining, the remaining atoms are encoded, and then the line suffix is output.

Finally, the line suffix is a 2-byte CRC (Cyclic Redundancy Check) for the line. The CRG number itself is ucencoded in a 3-byte atom. The CRC includes the length byte, the sequence number, and all data bytes. It does not include any padding bytes that may be present. Finally, the line is terminated with a carriage return/linefeed pair.

UCEncoding is handled by the sun.misc.UCEncoder and sun.misc.UCDecoder classes. These classes do not have any public or protected members. You construct instances of these classes with the default noargs constructors, and you interact with them through the encodeBuffer() and decodeBuffer() methods of their respective superclasses.

Listing 12-6 is a simple command line program to ucencode files.

Decoding files is equally easy, as Listing 12-7 demonstrates. Both the file to decode and the file in which to place the decoded data are read from the command line.

Table 12-3
UCCode

Bits	Value	Code	Bits	Value	Code	Bits	Value	Code	Bits	Value	Code
000000	0	0	010000	16	G	100000	32	W	110000	48	m
000001	1	1	010001	17	H	100001	33	X	110001	49	n
000010	2	2	010010	18	I	100010	34	Y	110010	50	o
000011	3	3	010011	19	J	100011	35	Z	110011	51	p
000100	4	4	010100	20	K	100100	36	a	110100	52	q
000101	5	5	010101	21	L	100101	37	b	110101	53	r
000110	6	6	010110	22	M	100110	38	c	110110	54	s
000111	7	7	010111	23	N	100111	39	d	110111	55	t
001000	8	8	011000	24	O	101000	40	e	111000	56	u
001001	9	9	011001	25	P	101001	41	f	111001	57	v
001010	10	A	011010	26	Q	101010	42	g	111010	58	w
001011	11	B	011011	27	R	101011	43	h	111011	59	x
001100	12	C	011100	28	S	101100	44	i	111100	60	y
001101	13	D	011101	29	T	101101	45	j	111101	61	z
001110	14	E	011110	30	U	101110	46	k	111110	62	(
001111	15	F	011111	31	V	101111	47	l	111111	63	)

Listing 12-6
TheUCEncode class

```java
import sun.misc.*;
import java.awt.*;
import java.io.*;


public class UCEncode {

  public static void main(String[] args) {

    if (args.length > 0) {
      for (int i = 0; i < args.length; i++) {
        try {
          InputStream is = new FileInputStream(args[i]);
          OutputStream os = new FileOutputStream(args[i] + ".uc");
          UCEncoder ucec = new UCEncoder();
          ucec.encodeBuffer(is, os);
        }
        catch (IOException e) {
          System.err.println(e);
        }
      }  // end for
    } // end if

  }  // end main

}
```

Listing 12-7
TheUCDecode class

```java
import sun.misc.*;
import java.awt.*;
import java.io.*;


public class UCDecode {

  public static void main(String[] args) {

    if (args.length >= 2) {
      try {
        InputStream is = new FileInputStream(args[0]);
        OutputStream os = new FileOutputStream(args[1]);
        UCDecoder ucdc = new UCDecoder();
```

(continued)

Listing 12-7
TheUCDecode class *(continued)*

```
        ucdc.decodeBuffer(is, os);
      }
      catch (IOException e) {
        System.err.println(e);
      }
    } // end if

  }  // end main

  }
```

CREATING NEW ENCODINGS

Secret

In addition to using the four pre-supplied character encodings, you can create new ones by subclassing CharacterEncoder and CharacterDecoder. The first thing to note if you're trying to do this is that CharacterEncoder and CharacterDecoder have quite specific requirements for the codings they can handle. These codings

- Must have a fixed number of encoded characters per fixed number of encoded bytes. This rules out many formats such as Binhex that use run-length compression. It also rules out quoted-printable, which encodes many bytes as 1-byte atoms but encodes others as 3-byte atoms.

- Should not be state-dependent. In other words, how a particular sequence of bits is encoded should not depend on the bits that have come before it or that will come after it. You must be able to write a table that maps all valid bit sequences to characters.

If, indeed, you have a format for which this sort of encoding is true, you can write encoders and decoders for it relatively simply. Your encoder class must override three abstract methods in sun.misc.CharacterEncoder. These methods are

```
        protected abstract int bytesPerAtom()
        protected abstract int bytesPerLine()
        protected abstract void encodeAtom(OutputStream aStream, byte data[], int
offset, int length) throws IOException;
```

Your implementation of bytesPerAtom() should return the number of bytes encoded by each atom of encoded data. Your implementation of bytesPerLine() should return the maximum number of bytes which will be encoded on a single line. Finally, your encodeAtom() method should read as many bytes as it needs for an atom from the data[] array starting at offset, but should read no more than length bytes. If length is greater than the number of bytes you need, then ignore the extra bytes. If length is less than the number of bytes you need, you'll have to pad the data.

As an example, I'm going to implement the simple but inefficient decimal dump encoding described early in this chapter. In this, bytesPerAtom() returns 1; bytesPerLine() returns 16; and encodeAtom() converts a byte to a three-digit decimal number.

Listing 12-8
The DecimalDump program

```
import sun.misc.*;
import java.io.*;
import java.awt.*;

public class DecimalDump extends CharacterEncoder {

  int bytesPerAtom() {
    return 1;
  }
  int bytesPerLine()  {
    return 16;
  }

   void encodeAtom(OutputStream aStream, byte data[],
    int offset, int length) throws IOException {

    int c = data[offset];
    c = c < 0 ? -c + 127 : c;
    PrintStream p = new PrintStream(aStream);
    if (c < 100) p.print('0');
    if (c < 10) p.print('0');
    p.print(String.valueOf(c) + ' ');

  }

}
```

For more complicated encodings, you may also need to override some
non-abstract methods of the CharacterEncoder class. These are

```
protected PrintStream pStream;
protected void encodeBufferPrefix(OutputStream out) throws IOException
protected void encodeLinePrefix(OutputStream out, int length) throws
protected int readFully(InputStream in, byte[] buffer) throws
java.io.IOException
protected void encodeBufferSuffix(OutputStream out) throws IOException
protected void encodeLineSuffix(OutputStream out) throws IOException
```

The public encodeBuffer() methods from the superclass, sun.misc.
CharacterEncoder, drive the conversion. This method calls the above
methods in a certain order to process the input as shown in the flow chart in
Figure 12-3.

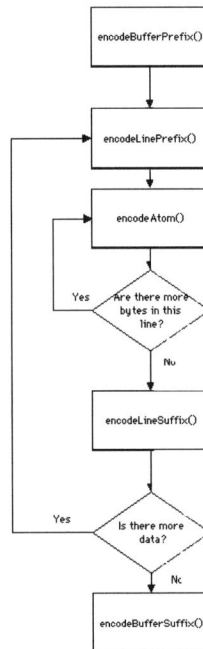

Figure 12-3
The encoding process.

The PrintStream pStream is the OutputStream used by and passed to all
the other methods in this class. It's opened by the encodeBufferPrefix()
method. By default, encodeBufferPrefix() just opens the PrintStream. If your

data format requires a buffer prefix, you'll want to write that on the PrintStream pStream (which is chained to the OutputStream out) in this method. Thus, your encodeBufferPrefix() method must do two things: one, chain out to pStream like this:

```
pStream = new PrintStream(out);
```

and two, write the buffer prefix on pStream.

Once you've written the buffer prefix, the encodeBuffer() method enters a loop that reads successive bytesPerLine() bytes at a time from the InputStream and stores them in a temporary array. These bytes are split into bytesPerAtom() chunks, and each chunk is encoded by calling encodeAtom().

When all the atoms on the line have been encoded, the encodeLineSuffix method is called to write the line suffix. The default encodeLineSuffix() just writes a \r\n to the OutputStream out. Override this if your encoding format has a more complicated line suffix than a bare \r\n.

Then encodeBuffer() reads the next bytesPerLine() bytes from the Input-Stream in and repeats the sequence. This continues until in is exhausted. At that point, encodeBufferSuffix() is called to write the buffer suffix, if any. The default version of this method does nothing. Override this if your encoding needs a buffer suffix.

How many and which of these methods you override is directly related to the complexity of the encoding format. The UCEncoder class overrides all of them. The DecimalDump class overrides none of them. Most cases fall somewhere between those two extremes.

The one method that you will probably not override is encodeBuffer(). The only case where you would override it would be if you were faced with a format like Binhex or quoted-printable, where there was not a fixed number of bytes per atom. However, in these cases you've moved so far away from the design of the superclass that there's really no reason to make your class a subclass of sun.misc.CharacterEncoder in the first place.

Writing your own decoders is quite similar. Your decoder class must override the three abstract methods in sun.misc.CharacterEncoder. These are

```
protected abstract int bytesPerAtom()
protected abstract int bytesPerLine()
protected abstract void decodeAtom(InputStream in, OutputStream out, int
length) throws IOException
```

Your implementation of bytesPerAtom() should return the number of bytes encoded by each atom of encoded data. Your implementation of bytesPerLine() should return the maximum number of bytes that will be encoded on a single line. These are each exactly the same as in the equivalent encoder class. Finally, your decodeAtom() method should read length bytes from the InputStream in, decode them, and write them on the OutputStream out.

As with the encoder class, you may also need to override some non-abstract methods, depending on the complexity of the format. These are:

```
    protected void decodeBufferPrefix(InputStream in, OutputStream out) throws
IOException
    protected int decodeLinePrefix(InputStream aStream, OutputStream out)
throws IOException
    protected void decodeLineSuffix(InputStream in, OutputStream out) throws
IOException
    protected void decodeBufferSuffix(InputStream in, OutputStream out) throws
IOException
```

One of the public decodeBuffer() methods in sun.misc.CharacterDecoder drives the conversion by calling these methods in a certain order. By default, these methods act as if there is no buffer prefix, line prefix, line suffix, or buffer suffix. This may be true for certain elementary formats like decimal dump and Base64. However, most of the time a format has at least some of these elements, and you need to override these methods to process them.

The decodeBufferSuffix() method is called first and should read the bufferSuffix, if any. When this method is finished, the InputStream in should be positioned at the start of the first line of encoded data.

Each line of encoded data is read by calling decodeLinePrefix() to decode the line prefix and then calling decodeAtom() as many times as necessary and then calling decodeLineSuffix(). Generally, the number of times to call decodeAtom() will be either fixed by the format or given as part of the line prefix. Each call to decodeAtom() results in some decoded data being written to the OutputStream out.

Finally, when all the lines of data have been processed, decodeBuffer-Suffix() is called to decode the buffer suffix, if any.

Listing 12-9 is a program that decodes the HexDump format produced by the HexDumpEncoder. It implements bytesPerAtom(), bytesPerLine(), and decodeAtom(), and overrides decodeLinePrefix and decodeLineSuffix(). The HexDump format does not have a buffer prefix or a buffer suffix, so the decodeBufferPrefix() and decodeBufferSuffix() methods do not need to be overridden.

Listing 12-9
The HexDumpDecoder class

```
import sun.misc.*;
import java.io.*;


public class HexDumpDecoder extends CharacterDecoder {

  int bytesPerAtom() {
    return 1;
  }

  int bytesPerLine()  {
    return 16;
  }

  void decodeAtom(InputStream in, OutputStream out, int l)
   throws IOException {
    int c = in.read();
    while (c == ' ') c = in.read();

    char c1 = (char) c;
    char c2 = (char) in.read();
    // read the space
    int i1 = Character.digit(c1, 16);
    int i2 = Character.digit(c2, 16);
    in.read();
    byte b = (byte) (i1*16 + i2);
    out.write(b);

  }

  int decodeLinePrefix(InputStream in, OutputStream out)
   throws IOException {
    //
    for (int i = 0; i < 6; i++) in.read();
   return (bytesPerLine());
  }

  void decodeLineSuffix(InputStream inStream, OutputStream outStream)
   throws java.io.IOException {

   int c;

   while (true) {
     c = inStream.read();
     if (c == -1) {
```

(continued)

Listing 12-9
The HexDumpDecoder class *(continued)*

```
            throw new CEStreamExhausted();
      }
      if ((c == '\n') || (c == '\r')) {
            break;
      }
    }

  }

 }
```

THE **CRC** CLASS

A Cyclic Redundancy Check, CRC for short, is the means by which a number can be assigned to a sequence of bits. Different bit sequences are likely to have different CRCs. The more bits in the CRC, the more unlikely it is that two random bit sequences will have the same CRC. There are 256 8-bit CRCs. Thus, using an 8-bit CRC, there's only a 1-in-256 chance that two random bit sequences will have the same CRC. Using a 16-bit CRC, that chance drops to 1 in 65,536. Using a 32-bit CRC, it drops down to less than one in four billion.

CRCs are commonly used to detect errors in streams of bits. The CRC is appended to the data before it's transmitted. If the data is corrupted in transit, then when it reaches its destination, the recalculated CRC is highly unlikely to match the corrupted data.

Note

The acronym CRC also stands for *class-responsibility-collaborator*, especially in object-oriented programming circles and especially when used in the phrase "CRC cards." CRC cards are a method of designing object-oriented applications. Although occasionally useful, CRC cards have nothing to do with cyclic redundancy checks.

Secret

The CRC used in the line suffix of the UCEncoding is produced by the sun.misc.CRC16 class. This class calculates a 16-bit CRC for a set of bytes.

This class has exactly one public constructor, one public field, and one public method. These are

```
public int value
public CRC16()
public void reset()
```

You create a new CRC object with the CRC16() noargs constructor like this:

```
CRC16 myCRC = new CRC16();
```

The CRC itself is stored in a public field called value, and this constructor sets it to zero. You can reset it to zero at any time with the reset() method. However to inspect it, you have to directly access the field. This is easy because value is public, but it's not very good object-oriented design. Would it have been that hard to add a getValue() method?

To calculate a CRC for a set of bytes, pass each byte in sequence to the update() method like this:

```
byte[] b;
// fill the byte array somehow
for (int i = 0; i < b.length; i++) {
  myCRC.update(b[i]);
}
System.out.println("CRC is " + myCRC.value);
```

Of course, how you fill the byte array is up to you. Listing 12-10 is a simple program that prints out a CRC number for each file entered on the command line.

Listing 12-10
The CRCCalculator class

```
import sun.misc.*;
import java.io.*;


public class CRCCalculator {

  public static void main(String[] args) {

    CRC16 myCRC = new CRC16();
    int b = 0;
```

(continued)

Listing 12-10

The CRCCalculator class *(continued)*

```
      for (int i=0; i < args.length; i++) {
//      int len = 0;
      try {
        FileInputStream fis = new FileInputStream(args[i]);
        while ((b = fis.read()) != -1) {
//      System.err.println(len++ + ":" + (char) b);
          myCRC.update((byte) b);
        }
        System.out.println(args[i] + " CRC: " + myCRC.value);
      }
      catch (IOException e) {
        System.err.println("Error reading file " + args[i] + "\n" + e);
      }

      myCRC.reset();
    }


    }


  }
```

SUMMARY

In this chapter, you learn the following:

- The sun.misc.CharacterEncoder class is an abstract superclass for classes that encode arbitrary binary data into an ASCII format that can survive mangling by most gateways and e-mail programs.

- The sun.misc.CharacterDecoder class is an abstract superclass for classes that decode the ASCII data back into its original binary format.

- Base64 is an encoding commonly used in MIME that works with both ASCII and EBCDIC. The sun.misc.BASE64Encoder and sun.misc.BASE64Decoder classes handle this format.

- UUEncode is an encoding format derived from UNIX that encodes not only the data in the file but also the filename and permissions. The sun.misc.UUEncoder and sun.misc.UUDecoder classes handle this format.

- UCEncode is an encoding format native to Java that is not dependent on ASCII. The sun.misc.UCEncoder and sun.misc.UCDecoder classes handle this format.

- You can create new encoders and decoders by subclassing sun.misc.CharacterEncoder and sun.misc.CharacterDecoder.

- The sun.misc.CRC class provides a mechanism for implementing cyclic redundancy checks for error detection.

NETWORK SERVERS AND CLIENTS IN THE SUN.NET PACKAGE

13

*T*he sun.net package includes two generic base classes for TCP-based network servers and clients: sun.net.Network-Server and sun.net.NetworkClient. As you might surmise, NetworkServer is a superclass for TCP/IP servers, and Network-Client is a superclass for TCP/IP clients.

TCP/IP stands for *Transmission Control Protocol/Internet Protocol*. It's the standard for data encoding and transmission on the Internet. The only alternative available to you as a Java programmer is UDP/IP or *User Datagram Protocol/Internet Protocol*. In Java, the java.net.Socket and java.net.ServerSocket classes handle TCP/IP, while the java.net.DatagramSocket and java.net.DatagramPacket classes handle UDP/IP.

Note

Most major Internet services, like the Web, news, and e-mail, use TCP/IP exclusively. However, a few of the simpler protocols, like echo, discard, and daytime, use both. All of this, and a lot more, is covered in great detail in my previous book, *Java Network Programming* (O'Reilly & Associates, 1997).

WRITING NETWORK SERVERS

TCP/IP servers can be implemented by subclassing the sun.net.Network-
Server class. This class provides a generic server that listens on a specified
port for connections.

The sun.net.NetworkServer Class

Secret

The sun.net.NetworkServer extends java.lang.Object and implements Runnable
and Cloneable. The NetworkServer class has one constructor, seven methods
(all public), and five fields (three of which are public). These are

```
public NetworkServer()
public Socket clientSocket
public PrintStream clientOutput
public InputStream clientInput
public static void main(String[] args)
final public void startServer(int port) throws IOException
public void close() throws IOException
public boolean clientIsOpen()
public void serviceRequest() throws IOException
final public void run() final public void startServer(int port) throws
IOException
public Object clone()
```

The NetworkServer() constructor is a default noargs constructor. It does
not initialize any of the fields.

The clientSocket field is a Socket object that represents the connection
with the client. The clientOutput field is a PrintStream object for sending
data to the client. The clientInput field is a buffered InputStream object for
reading input from the client.

Note

Because clientOutput is a PrintStream, it is limited to sending ASCII data.
If you want to send non-ASCII data, get a raw OutputStream from
clientSocket using clientSocket.getOutputStream() and chain it to the kind
of OutputStream you need.

Unlike most Sun classes, NetworkServer has a main() method. Thus, you
can start it from the command line and run it as an application. The main()
method constructs a new NetworkServer object and starts it listening on port
8888 by calling startServer(8888). Command line arguments are ignored.

The startServer() method constructs a new ServerSocket called serverSocket that listens on the specified port. serverSocket is a private field, and it will be null in many NetworkServer objects. The startServer() method also constructs a new Thread from this NetworkServer (which is runnable) and starts it running by calling the thread's start() method. This leads directly to the NetworkServer's run() method.

The run() method is the main loop of the NetworkServer class. In this loop, the first NetworkServer object that you create listens for incoming connections in an infinite while loop. Every time a new connection is detected, the NetworkServer clones itself with the clone() method and passes that connection off to its clone. Then it listens for the next connection. The clone handles the connection in the serviceRequest() method.

Note

It's important to clone the NetworkServer before handling the request in order to guarantee thread safety. Otherwise, input and output from different clients could easily be intermixed.

The default serviceRequest() method prints an identifier message, then waits for the user to input at least 300 bytes. It then echoes back these 300 bytes and waits for the user to input another 300 bytes. This continues until the client closes the connection. Listing 13-1 is the log of a connection with Telnet to a NetworkServer object.

Listing 13-1
A sample NetworkServer session. User input is in bold.

```
% java sun.net.NetworkServer &
[1] 2580
% telnet sunsite.unc.edu 8888
Trying 152.2.254.81...
Connected to sunsite.unc.edu.
Escape character is '^]'.
Echo server sun.net.NetworkServer
Hello there
Is anyone there?
Is anyone listening?
Why won't anyone listen to me?
Why won't you say anything?
Are you bored yet?
As you can see there is a bug in the NetworkServer class
in that it doesn't actually send any data until it's
filled its buffer which is 300 bytes long.
Of course this normally doesn't matter since the bug is
```

(continued)

Listing 13-1

A sample NetworkServer session. User input is in bold. *(continued)*

```
in the serviceRequest() method and you'll override that anyway.
Hello there
Let's see if I can force enough data through to force it to echo back
Let's see if I can force enough data through to force it to echo back
Hello there
Is anyone there?
Is anyone listening?
Why won't anyone listen to me?
Why won't you say anything?
Are you bored yet?
As you can see there is a bug in the NetworkServer class
in that it doesn't actually send any data until it's
filled its buffer which is 300 bytes long.
Of course this normally doesn't matter since the bug is
in the serviceRequest() method and you'll override that anyway.
Hello there
Let's see if I can force enough data through to force it to echo back
Let's see if I can force enough data through to force it to echo back
^]
telnet> close
Connection closed.
%
```

The close() method closes the clientSocket (that is, calls clientSocket.close()); then it sets all three public fields to null to allow them to be garbage collected. However, the underlying ServerSocket that listens for connections is not closed.

The clientIsOpen() method returns true if the clientSocket is non-null and false if the clientSocket is null. The clientSocket is always non-null as long as a client is connected to this NetworkServer object.

Subclassing NetworkServer

By itself, sun.net.NetworkServer isn't very interesting. It exists to be subclassed. As a general rule, your subclass should override serviceRequest(). Inside the serviceRequest() method; you interact with the client through the clientOutput and clientInput fields, and occasionally clientSocket, although you can use the other fields and methods if you need them.

Listing 13-2 is an echo server that adheres to RFC 862. RFC 862 defines both TCP and UDP echo services. Because NetworkServer is a TCP-based class, I will implement only that half of the protocol here. The echo server should listen for connections on port 7. Once a connection is established, any data received is echoed back until the client closes the connection.

Note

For more details about the echo protocol (and there really aren't many) see http://www.internic.net/rfc/rfc862.txt.

Listing 13-2
An EchoServer

```
import java.net.*;
import sun.net.NetworkServer;
import java.io.*;


public class EchoServer extends NetworkServer {

  public static void main(String[] args) {

    int port = 7;

    try {
      port = Integer.parseInt(args[0]);
    }
    catch (Exception e) {
      // no port specified on the command line so use the default
    }

    try {
      EchoServer es = new EchoServer ();
      es.startServer(port);
    }
    catch (IOException e) {
      System.err.println("Server failed to start: "+e);
    }

  }

  public void serviceRequest() throws IOException {

    while (true) {
      byte b = (byte) clientInput.read();
      clientOutput.write(b);
      clientOutput.flush();
    }

  }

}
```

The EchoServer class overrides two methods in NetworkServer: main() and serviceRequest(). The new main() method enables the user to enter a port number on the command line. This is useful when you want to run this program on a UNIX system but you don't have root access.

Note

On UNIX, you must be root to open a server socket on a port below 1024. Ports 1024 through 65,535 are available to any user on a first-come, first-served basis. On Windows and the Macintosh, all ports are accessible to all users.

Secret

However, the most often overridden method is serviceRequest(). This time, raw bytes are read in one at a time and echoed back as soon as they're read. The line-by-line output that you see as a result occurs because the telnet program doesn't send the data to the remote system until you hit Return. It's important to call clientOutput.flush() when you're ready to write data. Otherwise, the server may wait indefinitely for its output buffer to fill up before it actually sends anything.

Here's a sample session with this EchoServer. User input is bold.

```
% java EchoServer 1634 &
[1] 349
% telnet localhost 1634
Trying 127.0.0.1...
Connected to localhost.
Escape character is '^]'.
Hello
Hello
How are you?
How are you?
I'm fine, thank you.
I'm fine, thank you.
^]
telnet> close
Connection closed.
```

It's not hard to write servers for a lot of simple protocols using sun.net. NetworkServer. Listing 13-3 is a discard server that throws away all its input. The discard protocol is defined in RFC 21. By default, it listens on port 9.

Listing 13-3
The DiscardServer class

```
import java.net.*;
import sun.net.NetworkServer;
```

(continued)

The DiscardServer class *(continued)*

```
import java.io.*;


public class DiscardServer extends NetworkServer {

  public static void main(String[] args) {

    int port = 9;

    try {
      port = Integer.parseInt(args[0]);
    }
    catch (Exception e) {
      // no port specified on the command line so use the default
    }

    try {
      DiscardServer ds = new DiscardServer();
      ds.startServer(port);
    }
    catch (IOException e) {
      System.err.println("Server failed to start: "+e);
    }

  }

  public void serviceRequest() throws IOException {

    while (true) {
      int n = clientInput.read();
    }

  }

}
```

Here's a sample session interacting with this discard server. As usual, user input is in bold.

```
% java DiscardServer 2001 &
[2] 2522
% telnet localhost 2001
Trying 127.0.0.1...
Connected to localhost.
Escape character is '^]'.
Hello
Is anyone home?
```

```
I guess not.
Bye-bye now.
^]
telnet> close
Connection closed.
%
```

The daytime protocol, specified in RFC 867, requires a TCP server on port 13. When a client connects, the server sends the current date and time as ASCII text, and then closes the connection. Any data received is ignored. Listing 13-4 demonstrates.

Listing 13-4
The DaytimeServer class

```java
import java.net.*;
import sun.net.NetworkServer;
import java.io.*;
import java.util.Date;


public class DaytimeServer extends NetworkServer {

  public static void main(String[] args) {

    int port = 13;

    try {
      port = Integer.parseInt(args[0]);
    }
    catch (Exception e) {
      // no port specified on the command line so use the default
    }

    try {
      DaytimeServer ds = new DaytimeServer();
      ds.startServer(port);
    }
    catch (IOException e) {
      System.err.println("Server failed to start: "+e);
    }

  }

  public void serviceRequest() throws IOException {
```

(continued)

The DaytimeServer class *(continued)*

```
    clientOutput.println(new Date());
    clientOutput.flush();

  }

 }
```

To get the current time, Listing 13-4 creates a new java.util.Date object and sets it to the current time. When it is passed to println(), its toString() method is implicitly called.

Although the daytime service is supposed to close the connection, you'll notice that there's no explicit call to close(). When serviceRequest() returns, the run() method closes the connection. Listings 13-2 and 13-3 never closed because they had infinite loops in their serviceRequest() methods.

Here's a sample connection along with output from the UNIX date command for comparison. User input is shown in bold.

```
% java DaytimeServer 2034 &
[1] 6622
% telnet localhost 2034
Trying 127.0.0.1...
Connected to localhost.
Escape character is '^]'.
Wed Jan 08 15:51:53 EST 1997
Connection closed by foreign host.
% date
Wed Jan  8 15:51:57 EST 1997
%
```

WRITING NETWORK CLIENTS

The sun.net.NetworkClient class is a generic superclass for TCP Internet clients. It is slightly less capable than the NetworkServer class. It is not multi-threaded and cannot handle more than one connection at a time. It does not have a main() method, so it cannot run stand-alone. Like NetworkServer, it is useful primarily through the subclasses you can extend from it.

The sun.net.NetworkClient class

Secret

The A NetworkClient is an object that can connect to a remote server via TCP/IP and send exchange data with it.

The sun.net.NetworkClient class has two constructors, four methods (all public), and three fields (two public and one protected). These are

```
public NetworkClient()
public NetworkClient(String hostname, int port) throws IOException
public void openServer(String server, int port)
public void closeServer() throws IOException
public boolean serverIsOpen()
public NetworkClient(String host, int port) throws IOException
protected Socket        serverSocket
public PrintStream serverOutput
public InputStream serverInput
```

The NetworkClient() constructor is the default noargs constructor that does nothing. On the other hand, NetworkClient(String hostname, int port) not only constructs a NetworkClient object but also tries to connect it using openServer().

When openServer() is called, the Socket object serverSocket is connected to the specified host and port. If necessary, it is first disconnected from the host to which it's currently connected. Assuming that the connection attempt succeeds, serverInput and serverOutput are set to the serverSocket's input and output streams, respectively. While serverInput is a BufferedInputStream, serverOutput is a PrintStream.

Note

The identifier serverSocket is an unfortunate choice. It is *not* an instance of the ServerSocket class (java.net.ServerSocket), but rather of the Socket class (java.net.Socket). It is probably called serverSocket because it is the socket between the client and the server.

There are no built-in threading or serviceRequest() methods in the NetworkClient class as there are in the NetworkServer class. This remains to be implemented in the subclasses. There is a closeServer() method that terminates the connection to the server by calling serverSocket.close() and setting all the fields of the class to null. There is also a serverIsOpen() method which returns true if serverSocket is not null and false if it is null. In general, it should be true that serverSocket is non-null only when it is actually connected to the remote host.

Subclassing NetworkClient

You can use the NetworkClient class by constructing a NetworkClient object and using its serverOutput and serverInput fields to communicate with the remote host. However, this really doesn't gain you very much over using a raw Socket object. Most of the time, the NetworkClient class is used by subclassing it with classes that know how to handle specific protocols. In the next section, you'll learn about the TransferProtocolClient, which handles lockstep protocols. In the next three chapters, you'll see subclasses of NetworkClient that handle SMTP email, NNTP news servers, FTP file transfers, and HTTP Web servers. For now, I'd like to look at some simpler protocols.

There are several Internet protocols in which a client connects and then the server sends some ASCII text and closes the connection. From the client's standpoint, the only real difference between these protocols is the port on which the servers run. Table 13-1 lists these services, the ports on which they run, and what you can expect to see when you connect.

Table 13-1
Services that don't require any client input

Service	Port	Output
active users	11	A list of the users currently logged into the system
daytime	13	Date and time at the server
quote of the day	17	A quote
chargen	19	A continuous stream of data until the client closes the connection. The actual data sent is not specified, but it should contain a recognizable pattern.

Note

One common pattern of the chargen service is rotating 72-character lines of the ASCII printing characters. For example:

```
!"#$%&'()*+,-./0123456789:;<=>?<ABCDEFGHIJKLMNOPQRSTUVWXYZ[\]^_`abcdefgh
"#$%&'()*+,-./0123456789:;<=>?<ABCDEFGHIJKLMNOPQRSTUVWXYZ[\]^_`abcdefghi
#$%&'()*+,-./0123456789:;<=>?<ABCDEFGHIJKLMNOPQRSTUVWXYZ[\]^_`abcdefghij
```

and so on.

Note

Not all of these services are necessarily running on any particular host. In fact, unless the host is a UNIX workstation, it's unlikely that any of them are. In my testing, most UNIX hosts provided the daytime and chargen services, while relatively few provided active users or quote of the day services.

Listing 13-5 is a simple subclass of NetworkServer that connects to a user-specified host and port and presents the server's response to the user. In this example, the default port is set to 13, the daytime port. In subclasses, this can be overridden.

Listing 13-5
The ConnectClient

```
import sun.net.NetworkClient;
import java.net.*;
import java.io.*;


public class ConnectClient extends NetworkClient {

  static protected int defaultPort = 13;

  public static void main(String[] args) {

    int port = defaultPort;
    String hostname = "localhost";

    try {
      port = Integer.parseInt(args[1]);
    }
    catch (ArrayIndexOutOfBoundsException e) {
      // no problem, use the default port
    }
    catch (NumberFormatException e) {
      System.err.println("Usage: java ConnectClient host_name port_number");
    }

    try {
      hostname = args[0];
    }
    catch (ArrayIndexOutOfBoundsException e) {
     // no problem, use the local host
    }

    try {
      ConnectClient cc = new ConnectClient(hostname, port);
      String theLine;
```

(continued)

The ConnectClient *(continued)*

```
      BufferedReader br = new BufferedReader(new
       InputStreamReader(cc.serverInput));
      while ((theLine = br.readLine()) != null) {
        System.out.println(theLine);
      }
    }
    catch (IOException e) {
      System.err.println(e);
    }

  }

  public ConnectClient(String hostname, int port) throws IOException {
    super(hostname, port);
  }

}
```

The following shows the ConnectClient class being used to connect to the different services listed in Table 13-1.

```
% java ConnectClient localhost 13
Wed Jan  8 18:07:58 1997

% java ConnectClient localhost 19
 !"#$%&'()*+,-./0123456789:;<=>?<ABCDEFGHIJKLMNOPQRSTUVWXYZ[\]^_`abcdefg
!"#$%&'()*+,-./0123456789:;<=>?<ABCDEFGHIJKLMNOPQRSTUVWXYZ[\]^_`abcdefgh
"#$%&'()*+,-./0123456789:;<=>?<ABCDEFGHIJKLMNOPQRSTUVWXYZ[\]^_`abcdefghi
#$%&'()*+,-./0123456789:;<=>?<ABCDEFGHIJKLMNOPQRSTUVWXYZ[\]^_`abcdefghij
$%&'()*+,-./0123456789:;<=>?<ABCDEFGHIJKLMNOPQRSTUVWXYZ[\]^_`abcdefghijk
%&'()*+,-./0123456789:;<=>?<ABCDEFGHIJKLMNOPQRSTUVWXYZ[\]^_`abcdefghijkl
&'()*+,-./0123456789:;<=>?<ABCDEFGHIJKLMNOPQRSTUVWXYZ[\]^_`abcdefghijklm ^C
%
```

TRANSFERPROTOCOLCLIENT

The sun.net.TransferProtocolClient class is a generic superclass for TCP clients that speak *transfer protocols*. Transfer protocols are those in which the client sends a command in ASCII and the server issues a response as an ASCII-coded integer (for example, the 3-byte string "250" rather than a 4-byte, binary-coded integer).

Generally, a transfer protocol allows more than one request-response pair to be sent over a single connection. Common examples include SMTP, the Simple Mail Transfer Protocol; NNTP, the Net News Transfer Protocol; and FTP, the File Transfer Protocol. In the next three chapters, you'll encounter specific subclasses of TransferProtocolClient that handle these three protocols.

Note

HTTP 0.9 and 1.0 are relatively weak transfer protocols because the client sends exactly one request and gets exactly one response. HTTP 1.1, which allows multiple requests and responses on a single connection, is much more like a transfer protocol.

For example, here's a sample SMTP session. Client requests are in bold. The lines that begin with numbers are server responses.

```
220 elf.goodchildren.org Sendmail 4.1/SMI-4.1 ready at Fri, 9 Dec 97
13:13:01 MDT
HELO elf.goodchildren.org
250 elf.goodchildren.org Hello localhost [127.0.0.1], pleased to meet you
MAIL FROM: santa@northpole.org
250 santa@northpole.org... Sender ok
RCPT TO: john@goodchildren.org
250 john@goodchildren.org... Recipient ok
DATA
354 Enter mail, end with "." on a line by itself

Have you been a good child this year? Please let me know ASAP so I
know what to stock in my sleigh.

Sincerely,

Santa
.
250 Mail accepted
QUIT
221 elf.goodchildren.org delivering mail
```

Here, you see that as soon as the client connects, the server sends a brief identification message. This is quite common. Then the client sends the message

```
HELO elf.goodchildren.org
```

This identifies it to the server, which responds with the message

```
250 elf.goodchildren.org Hello localhost [127.0.0.1], pleased to meet you
```

This client message/server response duet continues until the client sends the QUIT message. The server responds with

```
221 elf.goodchildren.org delivering mail
```

and closes the connection.

The exact messages sent are completely dependent on the protocol. SMTP messages are not FTP messages, nor NNTP messages, and so on. However, all of these protocols and several more have this basic client message/server response format. The TransferProtocolClient class extends NetworkClient with special methods to make interacting with such a server easier.

The TransferProtocolClient class

The sun.net.TransferProtocolClient class is a subclass of sun.net. NetworkClient. It has two protected fields, two public constructors, and four public methods. These are

```
protected Vector serverResponse
protected int lastReplyCode
public TransferProtocolClient()
public TransferProtocolClient(String host, int port) throws IOException
public int readServerResponse() throws IOException
public void sendServer(String cmd)
public String getResponseString()
public Vector getResponseStrings()
```

This class is likely in the Sun classes because it's unfinished. It also contains one static class variable called debug which, when set to true, echo prints a lot of the actions taken by this class. It is set to false in the shipping versions of Java, but the field is still present in the source code and the .class files.

The noargs TransferProtocolClient constructor creates an uninitialized TransferProtocolClient. If you use this, you'll need to call openServer(String server, int port) later to make the connection. The openServer() method is inherited from the superclass, NetworkClient.

More often, you'll construct a TransferProtocolClient object with the second constructor, TransferProtocolClient(String host, int port). This actually attempts to open the connection to the server at the specified host and port. If this attempt fails, an IOException is thrown.

Once the connection is open, a transfer protocol consists of a series of client requests and server responses. To send a message, use the sendServer() method. To read the response code, an integer, first call the readServerResponse() method. This reads the integer code and stores any text that follows in the protected Vector serverResponse. Successive lines of text in the responses are stored as strings in the Vector.

If you're expecting no more than one line of text in response, you can get it with the getResponseString() method. If you think you might get more than one line of text, you should use getResponseStrings() instead and then enumerate the Vector that it returns. This Vector is just the protected field serverResponse. Before calling these methods, you must call readServerResponse(), which puts text into the Vector serverResponse. The getResponseString() and getResponseStrings() methods rely on the response already being in serverResponse. These methods do not read the response from the server themselves.

Finally, you can close the connection with the close() method inherited from the superclass.

Subclassing TransferProtocolClient

As with NetworkClient, it's quite rare to instantiate TransferProtocolClient directly. Instead, you normally subclass it with a class that understands the specifics of a protocol. The next three chapters present subclasses that handle SMTP, NNTP, and FTP.

What these protocols have in common is that their responses all begin with three digit, ASCII codes like this:

```
250 john@goodchildren.org... Recipient ok
```

These protocols learned from each other when they were being developed, so it's not surprising that they act alike. However, besides these three, there really aren't any other common protocols that look exactly like this. Thus, the TransferProtocolClient class isn't useful beyond acting as a generic superclass for sun.net.smtp.SmtpClient, sun.net.nntp.NntpClient, and sun.net.ftp.FtpClient. This may be one reason why this class is still in the sun packages instead of graduating to the java packages. Once you've written an SMTP client, an FTP client, and an NNTP client, there's not much else you can do with it.

SUMMARY

In this chapter, you learn the following:

- You create new network servers by inheriting from sun.net.NetworkServer and overriding serviceRequest().
- You create new NetworkClients by inheriting from sun.net.NetworkClient.
- The TransferProtocolClient class is a generic superclass for FTP, NNTP, and SMTP clients.

SENDING MAIL WITH THE SUN.NET.SMTP PACKAGE

14

*T*he sun.net.smtp package is a small, simple package with two classes (only one public) and one exception that's designed to facilitate the sending of e-mail. Its original purpose was probably to enable HotJava to handle mailto: URLs, but the Javasoft developers appear to have left it behind in the race to fix other, flashier parts of Java. Perhaps they will revive it and make it more robust in a future version of Java and extend it to handle both sending and receiving e-mail. For now, however, it supports only sending e-mail.

SMTPCLIENT

Secret

The sun.net.smtp.SmtpClient class lets you send e-mail. You are responsible for creating the message with proper headers, supplying the addresses to send to, supplying the address to send from, and specifying the name of the SMTP server to use.

sun.net.smtp.SmtpClient is a subclass of sun.net.Transfer-ProtocolClient, which is itself a subclass of sun.net.Network-Client. However, you will generally need only the methods of sun.net.smtp.SmtpClient itself and not any of the methods that it inherits from its superclasses.

SMTP stands for *Simple Mail Transfer Protocol*. SMTP is the protocol by which machines transfer messages on the Internet. SMTP is covered in more detail in my book *Java Network Programming* (O'Reilly & Associates, 1997). However, if you use the SmtpClient class, you really don't need to know much about the low-level details of the SMTP protocol.

Let me show you a simple example. Listing 14-1 is a command-line application that sends the e-mail message "Hello there!" with the subject "This is a test" from santa@northpole.org to elharo@sunsite.unc.edu. It demonstrates all the steps in sending e-mail with an SmtpClient object.

You first create a new SmtpClient object initialized with the name of the SMTP server using the SmtpClient() constructor. Then you set the e-mail address that the message is from with the from() method. Next, you set the email address to which the message is being sent with the to() method. Then you get a PrintStream object with the startMessage() method. Any additional headers, a blank line, and the body of the message are printed on this PrintStream. Finally, you finish the message and close the connection with the closeServer() method.

Listing 14-1
HelloMail

```
import java.io.*;
import sun.net.smtp.*;


public class HelloMail {

  public static void main(String[] args) {

    try {

      SmtpClient sc = new SmtpClient("sunsite.unc.edu");

      // from and to
      sc.from("santa@northpole.org");
      sc.to("elharo@sunsite.unc.edu");

      // additional headers, subject et al.
      PrintStream ps = sc.startMessage();
      ps.println("Subject: this is a test");

      // blank line separates the headers and message
      ps.println();
```

(continued)

HelloMail *(continued)*

```
    // message body
    ps.println("Hello there");
    sc.closeServer();

  }
  catch (IOException e) {
    System.err.println(e);
  }

  }

 }
```

The constructors

There are two polymorphic constructors in the SmtpClient class. They are as follows:

```
public SmtpClient(String server) throws IOException
public SmtpClient() throws IOException
```

The first constructor, which appears in Listing 15-1, requires you to specify the SMTP server that will send the e-mail. The second tries the host specified by the system property mailhost and the local host. The first constructor also tries to connect to mailhost and the local host if the attempt to connect to the SMTP server specified in the constructor fails.

In short, the SmtpClient attempts connections in the following order until one succeeds:

1. The host specified in the server argument to the constructor
2. The host specified in the mailhost system property
3. The localhost running the program
4. The machine named mailhost in the local domain of the machine running the program

Note: The fourth try needs a little more explanation. For example, if the program is running on www.idgbooks.com, Java will try to send the message by connecting to mailhost.idgbooks.com. This is not the most intelligent solution; mail would be a much better guess than mailhost at most sites.

If all four of these connections fail, then an IOException will be thrown the first time that you try to send data to the SMTP server. Ideally, you'd want the exception to be thrown immediately by the constructor, but that's not the case.

The methods

The SmtpClient class has four public methods:

```
public void to(String s) throws IOException
public void from(String s) throws IOException
public PrintStream startMessage() throws IOException
public void closeServer() throws IOException
```

The to() method sets the address to which the e-mail is sent. This should be a syntactically correct email address, like info@idgbooks.com or webmaster@macfaq.com. If you give it a malformed e-mail address, such as one that contains spaces, then an SmtpProtocolException (which is a subclass of IOException) will be thrown. Beyond formatting, no checks are done to make sure that the e-mail address is correct. E-mail that SmtpClient sends to an address that doesn't exist will be bounced back with an error message to the sender specified in the from() method.

The from() method sets the e-mail address from which the message will appear to have come. Like the String you pass to to(), the string you pass to from() must be a properly formatted e-mail address, or an IOException will be thrown. There's nothing to prevent you from forging e-mail. You can send from and to the e-mail address of your choice. Nothing prevents you from using fictitious addresses such as santa@northpole.org. Similarly, nothing prevents you from claiming to be someone who really does exist (such as president@whitehouse.gov). If nothing else, this should teach you not to trust suspicious e-mail that you receive without getting confirmation.

The startMessage() method returns a PrintStream object that you use to send the rest of the message. First, you send any other headers you want, most commonly Subject:, and then a blank line and then the body of your message. This is not well thought-out. You'd expect additional headers to be sent with some sort of sendHeader(String name, String value) method and the body to be sent with a sendBody(String body) method. Nonetheless, the current scheme is only slightly awkward. The main thing to remember is to send the blank line between the header and the body. Otherwise, the SMTP server will think the message is all header.

Note

More precisely, startMessage() returns a sun.net.smtp.SmtpPrintStream object. sun.net.smtp.SmtpPrintStream is a subclass of java.io.PrintStream. This is a package-protected class that is accessible only to other members of the sun.net.smtp package. It does some extra buffering necessary to handle connections over a network. The differences between PrintStream and SmtpPrintStream are completely internal and won't matter for the purposes of this chapter.

Finally, when the message is complete, you call the closeServer() method. This issues the QUIT command to the SMTP server and terminates the connection. Most fields of the SmtpClient object are set to null. There's another gotcha here: You cannot reuse an SmtpClient object once you've closed it, and you must close it to finish the transmission. Every message you send requires a new SmtpClient object.

Here are the eight steps for sending e-mail with the SmtpClient class:

1. Construct a new SmtpClient object with the SmtpClient() constructor. Pass the name of the SMTP server as an argument.
2. Set the To: field of the message header with the to() method.
3. Set the From: field with the from() method.
4. Get a PrintStream to send the rest of the message with the startMessage() method.
5. Print any additional headers you want in your message, like Subject:.
6. Print a blank line to separate the headers from the body.
7. Print the message body.
8. Close the connection with the closeServer() method.

Exceptions

The sun.net.smtp package defines one new exception: SmtpProtocol-Exception. This is a subclass of java.io.IOException. It's thrown when the SMTP server doesn't respond in the way that the SmtpClient object expects. All the methods of SmtpClient are declared to throw IOException, but you can use this class to handle protocol exceptions separately from other IOExceptions.

CHOOSING AN SMTP SERVER

The hosts to which an applet can connect for any purpose, including sending e-mail, are strictly limited. As a general rule, you can connect only to the system actually running the applet (the local host) and to the system from whence the applet came (the CODEBASE). Neither of these is always suitable.

Most hosts that run your applets will be personal computers that do not run an SMTP server. Therefore, often the best option is for clients to connect to the SMTP server on the host that served the applet. You can get the address of this host with the getCodeBase() method. This works as long as the Web server is also an SMTP server and no firewalls get in the way. If your Web server is not also an SMTP server, or if a firewall prevents external hosts from connecting, then you can set up a custom proxy server on your Web server and handle the protocol by hand. The applet will talk to the proxy, the proxy will talk to the SMTP server, and vice-versa.

If this fails, you're reduced to falling back on the defaults, the host specified in the system property mailhost (if any), the localhost (if it's running an SMTP server), and the machine in the local domain named mailhost (if such a machine exists). Because this is less than reliable, if even possible in some cases, you should try to run an SMTP server on the machine that serves your applets.

The issues involved are demonstrated with a simple applet that sends e-mail. Figure 14-1 shows a simple interface with a message area to type the message; with three TextFields to read the sender, the recipient, and the subject; and with a Send Message button to press when you're ready to send. The preferred SMTP is chosen to be the CODEBASE. In some cases, you may wish to set the recipient, and even the sender and subject, in a PARAM tag, but here the user is allowed to input it.

Creating the interface is straightforward so I won't say much more about it. However, you may wish to compare it to interfaces with similar functionality in programs such as Netscape Navigator.

Listing 14-2 is the source code for an applet that implements this interface. The init() method draws the interface. The action() method responds when the Send button is clicked. Specifically, it calls the void sendMail() method. sendMail() reads the contents of the different TextAreas and TextFields, constructs a message based on those contents, and sends it. Finally, it resets all the TextAreas and TextFields, except for sender, which is likely to be the same from message to message.

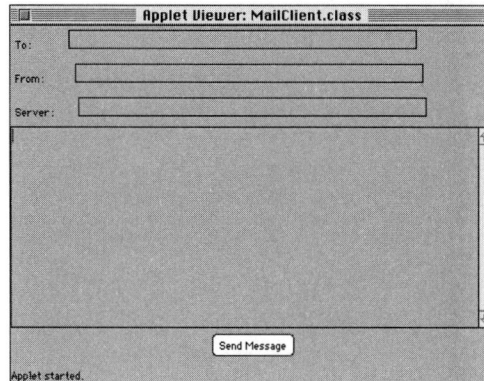

Figure 14-1
A user interface for a mail client.

Listing 14-2
The MailClient applet

```
import sun.net.smtp.*;
import java.applet.*;
import java.awt.*;
import java.io.*;


public class MailClient extends Applet {

  TextField sender;
  TextField addressee;
  TextField subject;
  TextArea message;
  Button send;

  public void init() {

    sender = new TextField(40);
    addressee = new TextField(40);
    subject = new TextField(40);
    message = new TextArea(70, 40);
    send = new Button("Send Message");
    setLayout(new BorderLayout());

    Panel n1 = new Panel();
```

(continued)

Listing 14-2
The MailClient applet *(continued)*

```
            n1.setLayout(new FlowLayout(FlowLayout.LEFT));
            n1.add(new Label("To:      "));
            n1.add(addressee);
            Panel n2 = new Panel();
            n2.setLayout(new FlowLayout(FlowLayout.LEFT));
            n2.add(new Label("From:    "));
            n2.add(sender);
            Panel n3 = new Panel();
            n3.setLayout(new FlowLayout(FlowLayout.LEFT));
            n3.add(new Label("Server: "));
            n3.add(subject);
            Panel headers = new Panel();
            headers.setLayout(new GridLayout(3, 1));
            headers.add(n1);
            headers.add(n2);
            headers.add(n3);
            add("North", headers);
            add("Center", message);
            Panel s1 = new Panel();
            s1.setLayout(new FlowLayout());
            s1.add(send);
            add("South", s1);

        }

    public boolean action(Event e, Object what) {

        if (e.target == send) {
          sendMail();
          return true;
        }
        return false;
    }

    protected void sendMail() {

        try {

          // from and to
          SmtpClient sc = new SmtpClient(getCodeBase().getHost());
          sc.from(sender.getText());
          sc.to(addressee.getText());
          PrintStream ps = sc.startMessage();

          // additional headers, subject et al.
          ps.println("Subject: " + subject.getText());
```

(continued)

The MailClient applet *(continued)*

```
        // blank line separates the headers and message
        ps.println();
        ps.println(message.getText());
        sc.closeServer();

        // clear the fields in preparation for the next message
        addressee.setText("");
        subject.setText("");
        message.setText("");
    }
    catch (IOException e) {
        // Should really put up a dialog box informing user of the error
        System.err.println(e);
    }


    }


}
```

SUMMARY

In this chapter, you learn how to send e-mail with the SmtpClient class:

- You construct a new SmtpClient object with the SmtpClient(String SmtpServerName) constructor. Pass the name of the SMTP server as an argument. For applets, this is likely to be the CODEBASE.

- You set the To: field of the message header with the to() method. You set the From: field with the from() method.

- The startMessage() method returns a PrintStream that you can use to print any other headers and the body of the message.

- The closeServer() method closes the connection to the server and sends the message on its way.

READING NEWS VIA NNTP WITH THE SUN.NET.NNTP PACKAGE

15

*N*NTP stands for *Net News Transfer Protocol*. It is the primary means by which Usenet news is transmitted between sites and from news servers to news clients like Newswatcher or Netscape.

The sun.net.nntp package includes three regular classes and two exception classes for communicating with NNTP servers. The sun.net.www.protocol.nntp package adds several more classes to implement a news protocol handler.

The main class in sun.net.nntp is NntpClient, a subclass of TransferProtocolClient, which represents an active connection to a news server. This class has methods for retrieving and posting articles, sending commands to the server, requesting headers, and setting the newsgroup to read.

The NewsgroupInfo class represents the state of a newsgroup on a server. This is represented by the name of the newsgroup, such as comp.lang.java.misc, and the article ID of the first and last articles in the group.

The NntpInputStream class is a subclass of FilterInputStream and is designed to handle the vagaries of data sent by NNTP servers. For the most part, you can treat it in your code as just another InputStream.

Finally, sun.net.nntp defines two new exception classes: NntpProtocolException and UnknownNewsgroupException. An NntpProtocolException is a subclass of java.io.IOexception that is thrown when the news server does something that the NntpClient doesn't expect. An UnknownNewsGroupException is a subclass of IOException that's thrown when the NntpClient asks the server to do something with an inactive newsgroup—that is, a newsgroup that's not available on the server. This may be because the newsgroup has been rmgrouped, because it is not received at that site or because its name was misspelled.

NEWSGROUPINFO

Secret

The NewsGroupInfo class contains three public fields and three public methods. These are

```
public String name;
public int firstArticle;
public int lastArticle;
public NewsgroupInfo(String name, int first, int last)
public void reload(NntpClient nntp) throws IOException
public String toString()
```

The name field is the name of the newsgroup, such as comp.lang.java. api. Each article in the newsgroup has an int ID. The ID for a given article can and generally will vary from server to server. As new articles enter the newspool, they're given successive IDs. The lowest article number in the group is stored in the firstArticle field. The highest article number is stored in the lastArticle field. Because of cancel messages and Expires: headers, not all numbers between the first ID and the last ID in the group may actually map to available articles, but most will.

Note

Each article also has a unique ID based on the server that originally posted the article and the time when it was posted. This looks something like 32243834.7B66@finjan.com. This is not what's discussed here.

Creating NewsGroupInfo objects

Theoretically, you can construct a new NewsgroupInfo object by passing the name of the group and the first and last article number to the NewsgroupInfo() constructor, like this:

```
NewsGroupInfo ni = new NewsGroupInfo("comp.lang.java.security", 63, 1098);
```

In practice, you don't know the numbers of the first and last article in the group. Therefore, you normally get NewsGroupInfo objects only with the getGroup() method of the NntpClient class, like this:

```
try {
  NntpClient nc = new NntpClient("news.myhost.com");
  NewsGroupInfo ni = nc.getGroup("comp.lang.java.security");
}
catch (IOException e) {
  System.err.println(e);
}
```

The NntpClient object knows how to ask the news server for the first and last article numbers.

Resetting article numbers

Once you have a NewsGroupInfo object, you can ask it to reset its first and last article numbers with the reload method. This might be important if you're reading news when the server suddenly expires a bunch of articles. For example,

```
try {
  ni.reload(new NntpClient("news.myhost.com"));
}
catch (IOException e) {
  System.err.println(e);
}
```

You must pass reload() an NntpClient object to make the connection to the news server.

NNTPCLIENT

The NntpClient class contains one public final static field, two public constructors, and ten public methods. These are

```
public static final int NNTP_PORT = 119;
public NntpClient ()
public NntpClient (String host) throws IOException
public void openServer(String name, int port) throws IOException
```

```
public int askServer(String cmd) throws IOException
public NewsgroupInfo getGroup(String name) throws IOException
public void setGroup(String name) throws IOException
public InputStream getArticle(int n) throws IOException
public InputStream getArticle(String id) throws IOException
public InputStream getHeader(int n) throws IOException
public InputStream getHeader(String id) throws IOException
public PrintStream startPost() throws IOException
public boolean finishPost() throws IOException
```

Opening a connection to the server

The NntpClient.NNTP_PORT field is always 119, the default port for news servers. News servers rarely run on any other port, but if they do, you can pick a different one by passing a port number to openServer().

Most of the time, you construct a new NntpClient object by using the NntpClient constructor with just a hostname like this:

```
try {
  NntpClient nc = new NntpClient("news.myhost.com");
}
catch (IOException e) {
  System.err.println(e);
}
```

This not only constructs the object but also attempts to connect to the requested news server by calling openServer("news.myhost.com", NNTP_PORT). If the connection fails, then an IOException is thrown. If you want to connect to a different port, you need to call NntpServer() with no arguments and then connect manually by calling openServer(), like this:

```
NntpClient nc = new NntpClient();
try {
  nc.openServer("news.myhost.com", 1119);
}
catch (IOException e) {
  System.err.println(e);
}
```

Reading articles

Now that you're connected to the server, you need to tell the server what group you want to read. You do this with the setGroup() method:

```
nc.setGroup("comp.lang.java.security");
```

To read the articles in the group, you ask for each one by number. The key is to know what's the first article and what's the last article. You get this information with a NewsgroupInfo object that you retrieve with getGroupInfo(), like this:

```
NewsgroupInfo ni = nc.getGroup("comp.lang.java.security");
int first = ni.firstArticle;
int last = ni.lastArticle;
for (int i = first; i <= last; i++) {
  // read the articles
}
```

To read an article, use the getArticle() method:

```
InputStream theArticle = nc.getArticle(i);
```

where *i* is the number of the article you want to read.

Listing 15-1 is a simple program that uses getArticle() and getGroup() to dump the entire contents of a newsgroup to System.out.

Listing 15-1
The DumpNews program

```
import sun.net.nntp.*;
import java.io.*;


public class DumpNews {

  public static void main(String[] args) {

    String server = "news";
    String newsgroup = "";

    try {
      newsgroup = args[0];
    }
    catch (ArrayIndexOutOfBoundsException e) {
      System.err.println("Usage: java DumpNews newsgroup server");
      System.exit(1);
    }

    try {
      server = args[1];
    }
    catch (ArrayIndexOutOfBoundsException e) {
```

(continued)

Listing 15-1
The DumpNews program *(continued)*

```
      }

      try {
        NntpClient nc = new NntpClient(server);
        nc.setGroup(newsgroup);
        NewsgroupInfo ni = nc.getGroup(newsgroup);
        int first = ni.firstArticle;
        int last = ni.lastArticle;
        for (int i = first; i <= last; i++) {
          try {
            InputStream theArticle = nc.getArticle(i);
            BufferedReader br = new BufferedReader(new
             InputStreamReader(theArticle));
            String theLine;
            System.out.println("---------\nArticle " + i);
            while ((theLine = br.readLine()) != null) {
              System.out.println(theLine);
            }
          }
          catch (NntpProtocolException ne) {
            // probably a canceled article, just skip it
          }
        }

      }
      catch (IOException e) {
        System.err.println(e);
      }

    }

  }
```

In some cases, you may want to present a list of the articles in a group to the user without downloading every message in that group. In a case like that, you can request just the headers of the articles with the getHeader() method, like this:

```
        InputStream theHeader = nc.getArticle(i);
```

You do not need to call getHeader() if you know that you want the entire article. The InputStream returned by getArticle() contains the headers of the article as well as its body.

Listing 15-2 is a simple variant of the DumpNews program that retrieves only the headers of the messages.

Listing 15-2
The DumpHeaders program

```
import sun.net.nntp.*;
import java.io.*;


public class DumpHeaders {

  public static void main(String[] args) {

    String server = "news";
    String newsgroup = "";

    try {
      newsgroup = args[0];
    }
    catch (ArrayIndexOutOfBoundsException e) {
      System.err.println("Usage: java DumpNews newsgroup server");
      System.exit(1);
    }

    try {
      server = args[1];
    }
    catch (ArrayIndexOutOfBoundsException e) {

    }

    try {
      NntpClient nc = new NntpClient(server);
      nc.setGroup(newsgroup);
      NewsgroupInfo ni = nc.getGroup(newsgroup);
      int first = ni.firstArticle;
      int last = ni.lastArticle;
      for (int i = first; i <= last; i++) {
        try {
          InputStream theHeader = nc.getHeader(i);
          BufferedReader br = new BufferedReader(new
           InputStreamReader(theHeader));
          String theLine;
          System.out.println("---------\nHeader " + i);
          while ((theLine = br.readLine()) != null) {
            System.out.println(theLine);
          }
        }
        catch (NntpProtocolException ne) {
          // probably a canceled article, just skip it
        }
```

(continued)

Listing 15-2
The DumpHeaders program *(continued)*

```
        }

    }
    catch (IOException e) {
      System.err.println(e);
    }

  }

}
```

Posting news

The remaining task for a news client is to post. The NewsClient class implements posting in the startPost() and finishPost() methods.

```
public PrintStream startPost() throws IOException
public boolean finishPost() throws IOException
```

The startPost() method returns a PrintStream to which you can send the new article. This article must be a fully formed news article according to RFC 1036. Lines must be terminated with a carriage return/linefeed pair (\r\n). The startPost() method returns null if posting is not allowed.

Modern news servers will fill in many of the news header fields if you don't. At a minimum, you should include a From: field, Subject: field, and Newsgroups: field. The minimum message you can post looks something like this:

```
From: elharo@sunsite.unc.edu (Elliotte Rusty Harold)
Newsgroups: inch.test
Subject: Example

The body of the message goes here after a blank line that
separates the header from the body.
```

When you're finished sending the article to the OutputStream, close it by calling finishPost(). If the news server accepts your article, then finishPost() returns true, and the server sends your article to the rest of the world. Otherwise, finishPost() returns false.

Listing 15-3 posts a simple article to the newsgroup inch.test. If you run it, change the newsgroup to your local test newsgroup. Please do not test by posting to a non-test newsgroup like comp.lang.java.misc.

Listing 15-3

The PostNews program

```
import sun.net.nntp.*;
import java.io.*;


public class PostNews {

  public static void main(String[] args) {

    String server = "news";
    String newsgroup = "inch.test";

    try {
      NntpClient nc = new NntpClient(server);
      nc.setGroup(newsgroup);
      OutputStream os = nc.startPost();
      if (os != null) {
        PrintStream p = new PrintStream(os);
        p.println("From: elharo@sunsite.unc.edu (Elliotte Harold)");
        p.println("Newsgroups: inch.test");
        p.println("Subject: Testing NntpClient");
        p.println("Followup-To: inch.test");
        p.println("Organization: Java Secrets");
        p.println("");
        p.println("The body of the message goes here after a blank line.");
        if (nc.finishPost()) {
          System.err.println("Success!");
        }
        else System.err.println("Failure");
      }
      else System.err.println("Posting not allowed");
    }
    catch (IOException e) {
      System.err.println(e);
    }

  }

}
```

Other commands

Posting articles and retrieving message headers and articles may be 90% of what a news program does, but the three commands used to do this are not 90% of the available commands that a client can send to a news server.

Commands consist of a command word, optionally followed by a parameter. Commands and parameters are separated from each other by spaces. Each command line should contain exactly one command with all necessary parameters and be terminated by a carriage return/linefeed pair. The command line should not be more than 512 characters long, including the terminating carriage-return/linefeed pair. Commands are not case-sensitive.

The NNTP commands and their meanings are defined in RFC 977. Most modern news servers should support all these commands. Many support additional commands as well. For those, you'll need to consult your news server's documentation or telnet to your news server and issue the HELP command like this:

```
% telnet news 119
Trying 204.178.32.254...
Connected to sleepy.inch.com.
Escape character is '^]'.
200 sleepy.inch.com InterNetNews NNRP server INN 1.4 22-Dec-93 ready
(posting ok
).
HELP
100 Legal commands
  authinfo user Name|pass Password
  article [MessageID|Number]
  body [MessageID|Number]
  date
  group newsgroup
  head [MessageID|Number]
  help
  ihave
  last
  list [active|newsgroups|distributions|schema]
  listgroup newsgroup
  mode reader
  newgroups yymmdd hhmmss ["GMT"] [<distributions>]
  newnews newsgroups yymmdd hhmmss ["GMT"] [<distributions>]
  next
  post
  slave
  stat [MessageID|Number]
  xgtitle [group_pattern]
  xhdr header [range|MessageID]
  xover [range]
  xpat header range|MessageID pat [morepat...]
  xpath xpath MessageID
Report problems to <usenet@inch.com>
```

```
     .
     QUIT
     205
     Connection closed by foreign host.
     %
```

For example, the LIST command returns a list of the active newsgroups on the server along with the article IDs of the first and last article in the group and a y or n indicating whether posting is or is not allowed. Parameters listed in brackets in the above list are optional parameters.

The askServer() method sends an arbitrary string to the news server. This string should be something that the news server can understand as a command. The startPost(), finishPost(), getGroup(), setGroup(), getArticle(), and getHeader() methods all indirectly call askServer(). However, those methods format the news command themselves. When you call askServer() directly, it is your responsibility to format the command properly.

Unfortunately, there's an annoying problem with askServer(). Although you can send a command to the server, the access protection on various methods and fields in the superclasses of NntpClient prevents you from reading the response. This makes askServer() essentially useless.

If you do want to send commands, you can send them manually with the public serverInput and serverOutput fields of the sun.net.NetworkClient class. For example, Listing 15-4 uses the HELP command to retrieve the list of supported commands from the server. In multiline responses like the one returned by the HELP command, a period (.) on a line by itself signifies the end of the response.

Listing 15-4
The GroupList class

```
import sun.net.nntp.*;
import sun.net.*;
import java.io.*;


public class ListGroups extends NntpClient {

  public static void main(String[] args) {

    String server = "news";

    try {
      NntpClient nc = new NntpClient(server);
      nc.serverOutput.println("HELP");
      String theLine = "";
```

(continued)

Listing 15-4

The GroupList class *(continued)*

```
        DataInputStream dis = new DataInputStream(nc.serverInput);
        while ((theLine = dis.readLine()) != null) {
          if (theLine.equals(".")) break;
          System.out.println(theLine);
        }
        nc.askServer("QUIT");
        nc.closeServer();
      }
      catch (IOException e) {
        System.err.println(e);
      }


    }


  }
```

SUMMARY

In this chapter, you learn the following:

- The sun.net.nntp.NntpClient class is a subclass of TransferProtocol Client, which is customized to communicate with an NNTP server.

- The sun.net.NewsgroupInfo class represents the state of a newsgroup on a server. Objects of this type are returned by the getGroup() method of NntpClient.

- Using the NntpClient class requires frequent use of methods inherited from its superclasses. If you can't find a method to do what you need in NntpClient, try looking in TransferProtocolClient or NetworkClient.

TRANSFERRING FILES WITH THE SUN.NET.FTP PACKAGE

16

*T*he file transfer protocol — FTP for short — is the predominant means of moving files from one host on the Internet to another. It is supported across a wide range of platforms including UNIX, VMS, Windows, DOS, MacOS, and, most importantly for this book, Java. Java supports FTP via the sun.net.ftp package.

OVERVIEW OF THE SUN.NET.FTP PACKAGE

Secret

The sun.net.ftp package contains three regular classes and two exception classes to handle FTP connections. The sun.net.ftp.FtpClient class is a subclass of sun.net.Transfer ProtocolClient that has the basic functionality needed in an FTP client. It can list files, put files, get files, and change directories. It cannot perform less common operations like creating directories, changing file permissions, or deleting files.

The FtpInputStream class is a subclass of sun.net. TelnetInputStream that behaves exactly like its superclass, but also holds a reference to the parent FtpClient. This prevents the

FtpClient object from being garbage-collected. This is quite a kludge. If anyone ever rewrites the sun.net.ftp package, he or she will probably revise the whole structure to avoid this problem with garbage collection by eliminating
this class.

There are two new exceptions in sun.net.ftp. FtpProtocolException is a subclass of java.io.IOException that indicates that the server has sent an error message in response to a client command. FtpLoginException is a subclass of FtpProtocolException that normally indicates a bad user name or password, or perhaps non-support of anonymous FTP. Both are checked exceptions that must be caught or declared in throws clauses. Most of the time, the more generic IOException is declared or caught instead.

The last class in the sun.net.ftp package is sun.net.ftp.IftpClient. This class is a subclass of FtpClient that passes its connections through a proxy server. In particular, it passes the connections through sun-barr.sun.com on port 4666. If this seems a little more specific than it should be to you, you're right. You can change the proxy server, but not the port. This was undoubtedly the proxy server that Jonathan Payne used when he developed this package. He probably meant to make it more general but never got around to it before he left Sun to join StarWave. In fact, this entire package has a very unfinished feel to it, even in 1.1. There are many debug lines commented out including comments like "This is bogus. It shouldn't send a password unless it needs to." It's likely that Payne meant to fix these classes, but didn't have time. They may be completed in the future, but it does not yet appear that anyone else on the Java team is working on this package.

THE FTP PROTOCOL

The FTP protocol is specified in RFC 959. FTP is a dual-channel protocol, wherein one socket called the *control connection* is opened for control messages like RETR and USER, and a separate socket called the *data connection* is used to actually transmit data. The client uses the control connection to tell the server which files to send or receive over the data connection. This contrasts with more common single-channel protocols like HTTP that use the same socket for both commands and data.

An FTP server listens for connections on the well-known port 21. When an FTP client wants to connect to this server, it opens a socket to port 21 on that host. This socket becomes the control connection. The client then sends a series of commands over the control connection. The server responds to each command with a reply code. Both common commands and common reply codes are included later in this chapter. The complete list of commands and replies is available in RFC 959.

Listing 16-1 shows a connection in which a client logs in to a server, changes directories, and tries to retrieve a file. Client requests are in bold. Text produced by the UNIX shell or the telnet program is italicized. Text returned by the FTP server is plain. Carriage-return/linefeed pairs (\r\n) terminate all lines.

Listing 16-1
A sample FTP session

```
% telnet ftp.javasoft.com 21
Trying 206.26.48.131...
Connected to ftp.javasoft.com.
Escape character is '^]'.
220 ftp2 FTP server (Version wu-2.4.2-academ[BETA-11](1) Fri Sep 20 13:46:36 PDT
1996) ready.
USER ftp
331 Guest login ok, send your complete e-mail address as password.
PASS elharo@sunsite.unc.edu
230-
230 Guest login ok, access restrictions apply.
CWD pub
250-
250-Please read the file README
250- it was last modified on Fri Nov 22 01:01:39 1996 - 57 days ago
250-Please read the file README.first
250- it was last modified on Fri Nov 22 01:05:50 1996 - 57 days ago
250 CWD command successful.
PORT 152,2,22,81,151,25
500 Illegal PORT Command
LIST
425 Can't build data connection: Connection refused.
RETR README
425 Can't build data connection: Connection refused.
QUIT
221 Goodbye.
Connection closed by foreign host.
%
```

Responses from the server are all three-digit ASCII numbers, like 250 or 331, followed by ASCII text. Immediately following the reply code is either a space or a hyphen. A hyphen means that the response is continued on the next line. A space means that this is the last line of this response. After the space or the hyphen is a line of text that the client program should display to the user.

As soon as the client connects, the server responds with a 220 code and a brief identification message. The client should then send the USER command followed by the username. This may be "anonymous" or "ftp" as in this example. If the username is valid on this system, the server responds with a 331 code. The client must now send the PASS command and the password. For anonymous login, this is the user's e-mail address. Assuming that the password is valid, the server sends another 230 response.

At this point, the client can navigate around the FTP file system. The CWD command changes the working directory. The TYPE I command switches the server into binary mode. The Type A command switches it into ASCII. However, before files or directory listings can be retrieved, the client must tell the server the address and port where it should send the data. This is done with the PORT command.

```
PORT 152,2,22,81,151,25
```

The first four numbers are the dotted decimal form of the client Internet address except that commas replace the dots. In other words, this command says that the data should be sent to the host at address 152.2.22.81. The last two numbers are the high and low order bytes, respectively, of the port number. Thus, the data should be sent to port $151*256 + 25$ — that is, port 38681.

Note

For reasons that I have not been able to determine, some FTP servers, notably ftp.javasoft.com, seem to have severe difficulties with this form of the PORT command.

The LIST command asks the server to open the data connection and send a list of the files in the current working directory over it. If successful, the server responds with the 125 or 150 code. The previous example was unsuccessful because no data channel was open to receive the listing. The RETR command asks the server to send the specified file over the data connection. If successful, the server responds with the 125 or 150 message. In the previous example, this command failed because no data connection was open.

Finally, when the client is finished, it sends the QUIT message, to which the server responds "221 Goodbye." Then the server closes the connection.

Notice that nowhere do you see the actual data of the file transferred or the list of files. That takes place over a separate connection from port 20 on the server to a random port on the client. The most common FTP commands appear in Table 16-1.

Table 16-1
Common FTP commands

Command	Parameter	Meaning
USER	username	Login name, such as "elharo" or "anonymous"
PASS	password	Password for the account specified by the USER command, such as "secret" or "elharo@sunsite.unc.edu"
PORT	h1,h2,h3,h4,p1,p2	The port and address to use for data transfer. The items h1 through h4 are the unsigned bytes of a dotted quad format Internet address, such as 199,1,32,67. The item p1 is the high order byte of the port number written as an ASCII string; p2 is the low order byte.
PWD		Print the name of the present working directory.
CWD	directory name	Change directory to the specified directory.
CDUP		Move up one directory. Same as "cd .." in UNIX or DOS or as Command-up arrow on the Mac.
MKD	dirname	Create the specified directory on the server.
RMD	dirname	Delete the named directory from the server.
LIST	dirname	List the files in the named directory or the current directory if no directory is named.
RETR	filename	Download the specified file from the current directory on the server to the client over the data connection.
STOR	filename	Copy the specified file from the client to the server.
DELE	filename	Delete the specified file in the current directory on the server.
QUIT		Wait for any ongoing file transfers to finish, then close the connection.

Each FTP reply code is a three-digit number. FTP reply codes are broken up into five centuries, much like HTTP reply codes. Reply codes with numeric values between 100 and 199 are "positive preliminary replies." The server has accepted the client's command and is processing it. The client should wait for another reply before sending any more commands. Reply codes between 200 and 299 are "positive completion replies." They indicate that the command has successfully finished. The client may issue a new command. Reply codes with numeric values between 300 and 399 are "positive intermediate replies." The server has accepted the command, but needs additional information from the client that the client should send in a

new command. For example, after a successful USER command, the server
sends a 331 reply to ask for a password.

Replies between 400 and 499 indicate "transient negative completion."
The command was rejected, but the client should try again. The command
may be accepted the next time. Finally reply codes between 500 and 599
indicate "permanent negative completion." The server rejected the command,
and the client should not try again. However, the user may wish to change
the command—for example, to correct a misspelled file name—and try the
corrected command. Table 16-2 lists the more common FTP replies.

Table 16-2
Common FTP replies adapted from Postel & Reynolds, RFC 959

Code	Meaning
125	The data connection is already open, and the transfer will begin.
150	The data connection will be opened, and the transfer begun.
200	Command Accepted, a generic response to commands that do not need answers that are more detailed
202	This command is not needed by this server. Continue.
220	Service ready
221	Closing control connection
225	Data connection open; no transfer in progress
226	File transfer completed successfully.
226	Closing data connection; the requested file action was successful.
230	Login successful
250	Requested file action okay, completed.
257	"PATHNAME" created, generally in response to a MKDIR command.
331	User name accepted; need password.
350	Requested file action pending further information.
425	Can't open data connection.
426	Connection closed; transfer aborted.
450	File was busy but may be available soon.
451	Local processing error
452	Disk full
500	Syntax error, command unrecognized
501	Syntax error in command arguments
502	Command not implemented
503	Bad sequence of commands, for example PASS before USER
504	Command not implemented for that parameter
530	Login unsuccessful
550	Access denied.
552	Disk quota exceeded.
553	Bad filename

THE FTPCLIENT CLASS

Secret

TheFtpClient class has four public static fields, one nonstatic public field, three public constructors, and ten public methods. These are

```
public static final int FTP_PORT = 21
public static boolean useFtpProxy
public static String ftpProxyHost
public static int ftpProxyPort
public String welcomeMsg
public FtpClient()
public FtpClient(String host) throws IOException
public FtpClient(String host, int port) throws IOException
public void openServer(String host) throws IOException
public void openServer(String host, int port) throws IOException
public void login(String user, String password) throws IOException
public TelnetInputStream list() throws IOException
public void cd(String remoteDirectory) throws IOException
public void binary() throws IOException
public void ascii() throws IOException
public sun.net.TelnetInputStream get(String filename)
public sun.net.TelnetOutputStream put(String filename) throws IOException
public void closeServer() throws IOException
```

The FtpClient class also has four protected methods. These are

```
protected int issueCommand(String cmd) throws IOException
protected void issueCommandCheck(String cmd) throws IOException
protected int readReply() throws IOException
protected Socket openDataConnection(String cmd) throws IOException
```

These methods are useful when you are subclassing this class, as you will see in the next section.

FtpClient has three constructors, all public. The first takes no arguments and creates an uninitialized FtpClient object that is not connected to anything. You can connect it by calling openServer(). The second variant of the constructor takes a string that is understood as a hostname. When this constructor is invoked, a connection is immediately opened to the requested host using openServer(host). The default FTP port, FtpClient.FTP_PORT or 21, is used. Finally, if you also pass an int to the constructor, then that int is used as the port number instead. This is rare because FTP servers running on non-standard ports are quite uncommon. If the connection fails, then an IOException is thrown. For example,

```
FtpClient fc = new FtpClient("ftp.javasoft.com");
```

Once the connection is established, you must send a username and password. This is done with the login() method like this:

```
fc.login("anonymous", "elharo@sunsite.unc.edu");
```

The first string is the username; the second is the password. If the connection fails, an FtpLoginException is thrown. This is a subclass of java.io.IOException.

Once you have logged into a server, you generally want to look around. The list() method is equivalent to the ls command of the standard UNIX FTP program or the LIST command to the FTP server. The list() method returns a sun.net.TelnetInputStream object. For now, just treat this as an InputStream containing lines of data to show to the user. For example,

```
try {
    BufferedReader theList = new BufferedReader(new
InputStreamReader(fc.list());
    String theLine;
    while ((theLine = theList.readLine()) != null)
System.out.println(theLine);
    }
    catch (IOException e) {
    }
```

To change directories, you invoke the cd() method, which is equivalent to using the cd command in the standard UNIX FTP program or sending a CWD command directly to the server. For example,

```
fc.cd("pub/java/1.1");
```

You can switch between ASCII and binary modes with the ascii() and binary() methods. ASCII mode FTP is used for text files, and it converts the line endings between platforms. Binary mode transfers a file as is, bit-per-bit. For example,

```
fc.ascii();
// get some text files
fc.binary();
// get some non-text files
```

The binary() method is the same as sending the "TYPE I" command and ascii() is the same as sending the "TYPE A" command.

One of the great hassles of cross-platform work is that even computers that agree on character sets do not agree on line endings. There are two ASCII characters commonly used to denote line endings: ASCII 10, carriage return, and ASCII 13, linefeed. Technically, a carriage return means move the platen to the leftmost position, whereas a linefeed means to scroll the paper up a line. Therefore, you need a combination of the two to move down one line and back to the left. This is what most PCs use. Every line is terminated by a carriage return/linefeed pair, "\r\n" in Java parlance.

However, because you almost never want to move to the left side of the page without also moving down a line, this wastes a byte on every line. Therefore, some systems use just a carriage return or a linefeed, but not both. Of course, no one can agree on which one should be used. UNIX uses a linefeed; the Mac uses a carriage return. This means that a lot of effort needs to be expended when text files are moved from one platform to another. In ASCII mode, the FTP programs will translate the line endings as necessary. In binary mode, they won't.

Of course, the whole point of the FTP protocol is file transfer. In Java, this is accomplished with the get() and put() commands. The get() method returns an InputStream you can use to read the contents of a file. Generally, you will copy what you read from the InputStream to a FileOutputStream to save the file. The put() method returns a TelnetOutputStream you use to send the contents of the file to the remote server. Generally, you'll copy data from a FileInputStream into the TelnetOutputStream. Of course, you don't have to get the data from a file or put it in a file. Streams can be redirected wherever it is convenient. For example,

```
try {
    String filename = "00Readme.txt"
    InputStream is = fc.get(filename);
    FileOutputStream fos = new FileOutputStream(filename);
    while (true) {
        int i = is.read();
        if (i == -1) break; // end of stream
        byte b = (byte) i;
        fos.write(b);
    }
    fos.close();
}
catch (IOException e) {
    System.err.println(e);
}
```

Unlike HTTP, FTP allows you to send multiple commands over a single connection. You can repeatedly call cd(), put(), get(), ascii(), binary(), and list() until you've got all the data you need. However, when you finish, you should call closeServer() to break the connection. Don't just leave an open connection laying around waiting for the server to kill it for inactivity. You can always make another connection with openServer() if you need to.

Listing 16-2 is a simple example that puts all this together to FTP a file. Both the file and the site from which to FTP it are specified on the command line. For example,

```
% java Download sunsite.unc.edu pub/languages/java/javafaq/test.txt
```

Listing 16-2
The Download class

```java
import java.io.*;
import sun.net.ftp.FtpClient;


public class Download {

  public static void main(String[] args) {

    FtpClient fc;
    String filename = "";
    String hostname = "";
    String username = "anonymous";
    String password = "";
    String directory = "";

    try {
      int lastSlash = args[1].lastIndexOf('/');
      filename = args[1].substring(lastSlash+1);
      directory = args[1].substring(0,lastSlash);
      hostname = args[0];
    }
    catch (ArrayIndexOutOfBoundsException e) {
      System.err.println("Usage: java Download host path/file username
password");
      System.exit(1);
    }
```

(continued)

The Download class *(continued)*

```
try {
  username = args[2];
}
catch (ArrayIndexOutOfBoundsException e) {
  username = "anonymous";
}

try {
  password = args[3];
}
catch (ArrayIndexOutOfBoundsException e) {
  password = username + "@";
}

try {
  fc = new FtpClient(hostname);
  fc.login(username, password);
  fc.binary();
  fc.cd(directory);
  InputStream theFile = fc.get(filename);
  int i = 0;
  FileOutputStream fos = new FileOutputStream(filename);
  while ((i = theFile.read()) != -1) {
    fos.write((byte) i);
  }
  fc.closeServer();
  fos.close();
}
catch (IOException e) {
  System.err.println(e);
}

}

}
```

This is hardly a perfect FTP client. The biggest problem is that the user needs to know both the name of the file and the directory where the file lives before downloading it. No provision is made for choosing a file from a list of files or for navigating a directory tree. In the next section, I'll show how to add methods for doing exactly that.

SUBCLASSING FTPCLIENT

The FtpClient class does not exercise the full power of the FTP protocol. For example you cannot make directories or delete files. The best way to add these features is by subclassing FtpClient with classes that understand a little more. You can also subclass FtpClient for other purposes. In this section you also see Sun's IftpClient class, which understands how to use a proxy server to connect to an FTP server, and a debugging client that lets you watch the interaction between the server and the client.

In addition to the public methods and fields you learned about in the last section, sun.net.FtpClient also has four protected methods you can call from inside your subclass. These are

```
protected int issueCommand(String cmd) throws IOException
protected void issueCommandCheck(String cmd) throws IOException
protected int readReply() throws IOException
protected Socket openDataConnection(String cmd) throws IOException
```

The issueCommand() method sends a raw FTP command like STOR or RETR to the server. It's used for commands wait for data to be sent over the data connection after they are issued. Commands that happen almost instantaneously and do not require data to be sent over the data connection, like CDUP and RMD, should use issueCommandCheck() instead. The issueCommand() method returns the reply code sent by the server. The issueCommandCheck() method does not, but you can get it by calling readReply() immediately after calling issueCommandCheck().

The openDataConnection() method opens a server socket on a random port. Then it issues a PORT command to tell the server on which host and port it's listening. The server will attempt to connect to this host and port.

IftpClient

The sun.net.IftpClient class is a subclass of FtpClient that uses a proxy server to connect to the remote server. It's a little limited in that it assumes the proxy server runs on port 4666, which, if I had to guess, I'd say was the port for the proxy server used by the person who wrote this class. If your proxy server uses a different port, this class won't be of much use to you.

Secret

The IftpClient class overrides the openServer(), checkExpectedReply(), and login() methods. You use these just as you use the equivalent methods in the superclass.

```
public void openServer(String host) throws IOException
boolean checkExpectedReply() throws IOException
public void login(String user, String password) throws IOException
```

There are two IftpClient() constructors. As with the superclass, the one that takes a hostname actually connects to the specified server, whereas the noargs constructor does not. If you use the noargs constructor, you must follow it with a call to openServer() when you're ready to connect.

```
public IftpClient(String hostname)
public IftpClient()
```

IftpClient also has one new method, setProxyServer(). This method lets you change the name of the proxy server that's used, though not the port. The default value of the proxyServer field is "sun-barr." Unless that also happens to be the name of your proxy server, call setProxyServer immediately after you construct a new IftpClient object.

```
public void setProxyServer(String proxy) throws IOException
```

DebugFtpClient

FTP is a relatively difficult protocol to explore with telnet because it uses two sockets at once, one for data and one for control messages. There are a couple of different ways that you can use Java to expose it, though. One would be to write subclasses of Socket and ServerSocket that logged all data transferred to a stream. The other, somewhat simpler way is to subclass FtpClient while overriding issueCommand() and TransferProtocol Client.readServerResponse(). All commands from the client to the server pass through issueCommand(), so by intercepting calls to issueCommand(), you can read the message from the client to the server and then pass it to super.issueCommand() to send the command. Similarly, all responses from the server to the client are passed through readServerResponse(). Therefore, by intercepting readServerResponse(), you can print out the server's message and then pass it to super.readServerResponse() for processing. Listing 16-5 demonstrates this.

Listing 16-5
The DebugFtpClient

```
import sun.net.ftp.FtpClient;
import java.io.IOException;
import java.util.Enumeration;


public class DebugFtpClient extends FtpClient {

  public DebugFtpClient(String s, int port) throws IOException {
    super(s, port);
  }

  public DebugFtpClient(String s) throws IOException {
    super(s);
  }

  public DebugFtpClient() throws IOException {
    super();
  }


  // all client commands are sent through here
  public int issueCommand(String cmd) throws IOException {
    System.err.println(cmd);
    return super.issueCommand(cmd);
  }

  public int readServerResponse() throws IOException {

    int result = super.readServerResponse();
    for (Enumeration e = serverResponse.elements(); e.hasMoreElements();) {
      System.out.println(e.nextElement());
    }
    return result;

  }

}
```

FullFtpClient

The FullFtpClient class adds a number of methods for common FTP commands that are not supported by sun.net.FtpClient. These include methods for deleting files, creating directories, removing directories,

changing file permissions, and a few more. All of these methods are
implemented relatively similarly, by passing the appropriate raw FTP
command from Table 16-1 to the protected issueCommandCheck() method
of the superclass. Nothing happens if the command is successful. However,
if the command fails, issueCommandCheck() throws an FtpProtocol
Exception containing the failed command. The FullFtpClient class passes
this on to whoever invoked it.

Listing 16-6
The FullFtpClient

```
/**
 * This class implements a more complete FTP client.
 *
 * @version 1.0, 01/19/97
 * @author  Elliotte Rusty Harold
 */

import java.io.IOException;
import sun.net.*;
import sun.net.ftp.*;
import java.util.Enumeration;
import java.util.Vector;


public class FullFtpClient extends FtpClient {

  /** New FullFtpClient connected to host <i>host</i>. */
  public FullFtpClient(String host) throws IOException {
    super(host);
  }

  /** New FullFtpClient connected to host <i>host</i>, port <i>port</i>. */
  public FullFtpClient(String host, int port) throws IOException {
    super(host, port);
  }

  /** Create an uninitialized FullFTP client. */
  public FullFtpClient() {}

  /** Move up one directory in the ftp file system */
  public void cdup() throws IOException {
    issueCommandCheck("CDUP");
  }

  /** Create a new directory named s in the ftp file system */
  public void mkdir(String s) throws IOException {
```

(continued)

The FullFtpClient *(continued)*

```
        issueCommandCheck("MKDIR " + s);
    }

    /** Delete the specified directory from the ftp file system */
    public void rmdir(String s) throws IOException {
      issueCommandCheck("RMD " + s);
    }

    /** Delete the file s from the ftp file system */
    public void delete(String s) throws IOException {
      issueCommandCheck("DELE " + s);
    }

    /** Get the name of the present working directory on the ftp file system */
    public String pwd() throws IOException {
      issueCommandCheck("PWD");
      StringBuffer result = new StringBuffer();
      for (Enumeration e = serverResponse.elements(); e.hasMoreElements();) {
        result.append((String) e.nextElement());
      }
      return result.toString();

    }

  }
```

SUMMARY

In this chapter, you learn the following:

- FTP stands for file transfer protocol. It's a platform-independent means of transferring both ASCII and binary files across the Internet.

- The sun.net.ftp.FtpClient class is a subclass of TransferProtocolClient that provides rudimentary support for FTP transfers.

- The sun.net.ftp.FtpInputStream, sun.net.FtpProtocolException, and sun.net.FtpLoginException classes support the FtpClient class. They do not normally need to be dealt with directly.

- The sun.net.IftpClient class is a subclass of FtpClient that uses a proxy server to connect to the remote server.

COMMUNICATING WITH WEB SERVERS

17

*T*he sun.net.www package contains several dozen poorly organized classes that allow Java applets to communicate with World Wide Web servers. The organizational problem with these classes is that the package tries to do too much. While the sun.net.smtp, sun.net.ftp, and sun.net.nntp packages covered in the last three chapters handle basic communication with SMTP, FTP, and NNTP servers, respectively, the sun.net. www package also includes the machinery for content and protocol handlers, HTTP servers, and a few other pieces besides. The real equivalent to the sun.net.smtp, sun.net.nntp, and sun.net.ftp packages is not sun.net.www, but rather sun. net.www.http.

MESSAGE FORMATS

The sun.net.www package includes several classes designed to handle various common Internet message formats used in e-mail, Usenet news, and HTTP. Historically, e-mail came first, and Usenet news headers were designed around the basic format provided by e-mail, with some additions. Later, the header format for both news and mail was used as the basis for the header format of MIME, the Multipurpose Internet Mail Extensions.

You might sometimes hear the acronym MIME expanded to "Multimedia Internet Mail Extensions" or "Multipart Internet Mail Extensions." However, "Multipurpose Internet Mail Extensions" is the official name.

MIME is a proposed Internet standard with many purposes, including the transmission of binary data through 7-bit channels and the inclusion of multiple parts in e-mail messages. It has been revised several times, most recently in Internet RFCs 2045 through 2049. What I discuss in this chapter is just one part of the broader standard, the message header format.

The basic message header format for MIME data is a key string that contains no white space, followed by a colon and a space, followed by a value string that may contain white space. The value string generally fits on a single line but it can be extended if a tab character precedes the following line. A blank line separates the header from the body of the message. For example, here is a simple MIME header from an e-mail message:

```
Date: Mon, 20 Jan 1997 09:23:36 -0500
From: Nancy Stevenson <7373.1147@compuserve.com>
Subject: Chapter 10
To: Elliotte Rusty Harold <elharo@sunsite.unc.edu>
```

This header has four fields. The first field has the key "Date" and the value "Mon, 20 Jan 1997 09:23:36 -0500." The second header has the key "From" and the value "Nancy Stevenson <7373.1147@compuserve.com>." The third field has the key "Subject" and the value "Chapter 10." Finally, the fourth field has the key "To" and the value "Elliotte Rusty Harold <elharo@sunsite.unc.edu>."

Of course, real message headers often have many more fields. However, each field has the same basic format of a string key followed immediately by a colon and a space, followed by a string value. Keys and values are always strings.

Different kinds of messages — that is, e-mail versus news versus MIME — are distinguished primarily by the different keys they contain. For example, email and news messages both contain Subject, Date, To, and From keys, but only an email message will contain a Message-ID field, and only a news message will contain an Article-ID field.

There is no standard that prohibits an e-mail message from containing an Article-ID field or a news header from containing a Message-ID field. It is just that they generally do not.

MessageHeader

The sun.net.www.MessageHeader class represents a message header that conforms to RFC 844. In the future, it will probably be extended to handle the more general format of RFC 2048, which allows message headers to include non-ASCII, international characters.

The MessageHeader class has two broad purposes: first, to allow easy creation of message headers and second, to allow easy parsing of message headers. Although both of these capabilities come in the same class, you use them almost completely separately. Let us first explore how to create a new message with a MessageHeader and then how to read one.

Writing message headers

To create a new MessageHeader for output, perhaps for sending to an SMTP or NNTP server, use the MessageHeader() constructor with no arguments:

```
public MessageHeader ()
```

You then add fields to the header with the add() and set() methods:

```
public void add(String key, String value)
public void set(String key, String value)
```

The add() method allows duplicate key values. However, the set() method replaces the first value with a given key if one already exists. Thus, you'd use set() for headers that shouldn't appear more than once in a message like "To" or "From" and add() for headers that may appear multiple times, such as "Received."

For example, to write a letter to the commander in chief you might do something like this:

```
MessageHeader mh = new MessageHeader();
mh.set("Date", (new Date()).toString());
mh.set("From", "elharo@sunsite.unc.edu");
mh.set("To", "president@whitehouse.gov");
mh.set("Subject", "Have you considered a spine transplant?");
```

Finally, once you have filled the header, there are two ways to print it. The simplest way is just to pass it to a print() or println() method and let its toString() method be called. Alternately, you can pass the PrintStream to the MessageHeader's print() method:

```
public void print(PrintStream p)
public String toString()
```

Passing toString() to a print method terminates lines with the host line-ending character, a linefeed on UNIX, a carriage return on the Mac, and a carriage return/linefeed pair on Windows. However, the print() method always ends lines with a carriage return/linefeed pair. This is required by some protocols, most notably HTTP, although servers are often forgiving of other line endings.

Reading message headers

The second purpose of the MessageHeader class is to parse headers that come from external sources like e-mail messages or Web server responses. For this purpose, you use a completely different set of methods. Generally, you construct a new MessageHeader object by passing an InputStream to the constructor:

```
public MessageHeader (InputStream is) throws java.io.IOException
```

This constructor reads the InputStream, parsing out the message header as it goes. Listing 17-1 is a simple program that enables you to select a file to read from the hard drive and print its MIME header:

Listing 17-1
The MessageHeaderTest class

```
import sun.net.www.*;
import java.io.*;
import java.awt.*;


public class MessageHeaderTest {

  public static void main(String[] args) {

    try {
      FileDialog fd = new FileDialog(new Frame(), "Choose the message");
      fd.show();
      FileInputStream fis = new FileInputStream(fd.getFile());
      MessageHeader mh = new MessageHeader(fis);
      System.out.println(mh);
    }
    catch (IOException e) {
      System.err.println(e);
    }


  }


  }
```

As an alternative, you can create a MessageHeader object with the noargs MessageHeader() constructor and then pass the InputStream to its parseHeader() method.

```
public void parseHeader(InputStream is) throws java.io.IOException
```

For example:

```
FileInputStream fis = new FileInputStream(fd.getFile());
MessageHeader mh = new MessageHeader();
mh.parseHeader(fis);
```

You can even pass multiple input streams to parseHeader(), thus accumulating several headers in one MessageHeader object. In this case, duplicate fields are added, not replaced. However, it is hard to imagine why you might want to do this.

Once the header has been parsed, several methods are available to help you retrieve information from it:

```
public String findValue(String k)
public String findNextValue(String k, String v)
public String getKey(int n)
public String getValue(int n)
public String canonicalID(String id)
```

The findValue() method returns the value of the first entry in the header whose key is k. If there are no entries in the header with the specified key, then null is returned.

Because there may be multiple entries in a header with the same key, the findNextValue() method returns the first entry in the header with the specified key after the entry whose value is v. For example, consider the following header:

```
X-Head: First header
X-Head: Second Header
X-Head: Third Header
```

To return the first value of "X-Head" after the one with the value of "Second Header," you would write

```
mh.findValue("X-Head", "Second Header");
```

If the specified key or value is not present, then null is returned. Thus, to loop through all the headers with the key k in MessageHeader mh, you might write

```
for(String v = mh.findValue(k); v != null; v = mh.findNextValue(k, v)) {
  System.out.println(k + ": " + v);
}
```

The getKey() and getValue() methods let you request field keys and values by number. The fields start counting at zero. Once you count past the last field, null is returned. Thus, to loop through all the fields in the MessageHeader mh, you might write

```
for(int i = 0 ; ; i++) {
  String key = mh.getKey(i);
  if (key == null) break;
  String value = mh.getValue(i);
  System.out.println(key + ": " + value);
}
```

In the special case that a line in the header has a value but no key (which isn't supposed to happen but often does), getKey() returns the string "NULLKEY".

Finally, the canonicalID() method is a very simple utility method. Given a string such as

```
<199701200924_MC1-F9F-6D2@compuserve.com>
```

canonicalID() returns the text between the angle brackets (<>). In this case, it would return

```
199701200924_MC1-F9F-6D2@compuserve.com
```

HeaderParser

The sun.net.www.HeaderParser class does almost exactly the same thing as the reading half of the MessageHeader class. It splits a string containing MIME-compliant headers into individual fields. I don't know why Java includes both the MessageHeader and the HeaderParser class:

```
public HeaderParser(String header)
public String findKey(int n)
public String findValue(int n)
public String findValue(String key)
public String findValue(String key, String default)
public int findInt(String key, int default)
```

The main difference is that a MessageHeader object is constructed from an InputStream while a HeaderParser is constructed from a string. Furthermore, HeaderParser only reads message headers; it does not write them. Finally, HeaderParser does not include any toString() or print() method. You must print its fields individually.

The findKey() method returns the nth key string in a header. The findValue() method is triply polymorphic, enabling you to find a value by position or by key. You can also specify a default value, in case the header is not found. If no default is specified and the value is not found, null is returned. Finally, findInt() will try to parse the value of the header with the specified key into an integer and return that.

Listing 17-2 is a simple program that reads a filename from the command line and parses it into individual headers.

Listing 17-2
The HeaderParserTest class

```
import sun.net.www.HeaderParser;
import java.io.*;


public class HeaderParserTest {

  public static void main(String[] args) {

    for (int i = 0; i < args.length; i++) {
      StringBuffer  buffer = new StringBuffer();
      try {
        FileInputStream fis = new FileInputStream(args[i]);
        DataInputStream dis = new DataInputStream(fis);
        String theLine;
        while ((theLine = dis.readLine()) != null) {
          buffer.append(theLine + "\r\n");
        }
        HeaderParser hp = new HeaderParser(buffer.toString());
        for (int j = 0; ; j++) {
          String key = hp.findKey(j);
          if (key == null) break;
          System.out.println(key + ": " + hp.findValue(j));
        }
      }
      catch (IOException e) {
        System.err.println(e);
      }

    }

  }

}
```

MIME types

One of the advantages of MIME is that it provides a platform-independent means of determining a file's type. However, not all protocols support MIME. Even among those that do, like HTTP, you will often find that servers are misconfigured and return incorrect MIME types. It is important for Java to be able to make reasonable guesses about the type of a file from the information it does have. This is provided primarily through the java.net.FileNameMap interface that is implemented by the sun.net.www.MimeTable class. This class contains a list of MimeEntry objects that associates MIME types with file extensions and the applications that understand that type of data.

The FileNameMap interface

The java.net.FileNameMap interface associates filenames like "sun.jpg" with MIME types like "image/jpeg." This interface declares a single method:

```
public abstract String getContentTypeFor(String fileName)
```

This interface is implemented by the sun.net.www.MimeTable class. Most of the time, you access it through the public static field URLConnection.fileNameMap. For example:

```
String mimetype =
URLConnection.fileNameMap.getContentTypeFor("sorlogo1.gif");
```

The MimeEntry class

A sun.net.www.MimeEntry object combines a string MIME type like "image/gif" with platform-specific information about how data with this MIME type is to be handled.

Secret

The state of a MimeEntry object is primarily determined by seven private fields:

```
private String typeName
private int action
private String command
private String description
private String imageFileName
private String fileExtensions[]
private String tempFileNameTemplate
```

The typeName specifies the MIME type, like "image/gif" or "text/html." The action is a numeric code that specifies how data of this MIME type should be handled. The string command is a platform-dependent command to be passed to System.exec() to launch a helper application to view the MIME type. The description string is a brief, human-readable description of the format. The imageFileName field is the name of an icon that can be used as a representation of the file type. The fileExtensions field is an array of the file extensions that map to this MIME type. For example, if typeName is "image/jpeg," then extensions are likely to be {".jpg", ".jpeg"}. Finally, tempNameTemplate is the name of a temporary file where data of this type can be saved to disk before it is loaded into an external helper application.

As a general rule, there are four ways that a Web browser can handle any particular MIME type.

- The browser itself can display it.
- The browser can save the data into a file.
- The browser can pass the data to a helper application to be displayed.
- The browser can do nothing.

The action field determines which of these options is taken for a MIME type. This field can have one of four values, each corresponding to one public final static int field in the MimeEntry class:

```
MimeEntry.LOAD_INTO_BROWSER
MimeEntry.SAVE_TO_FILE
MimeEntry.LAUNCH_APPLICATION
MimeEntry.UNKNOWN
```

If action is MimeEntry.LOAD_INTO_BROWSER, then the data is passed to the Web browser for handling. This would be routine for types that a browser can handle like text/html or image/gif. If action is MimeEntry. SAVE_TO_FILE, then the data is saved into a file. If action is MimeEntry. LAUNCH_APPLICATION, then a helper program is launched with System. exec() to view the data. Finally, if action is MimeEntry.UNKNOWN, then the data is generally ignored.

The constructors

There is only one public MimeEntry() constructor:

```
public MimeEntry(String mimetype)
```

For example:

```
MimeEntry me = new MimeEntry("application/octet-stream");
```

There are also three non-public constructors:

```
MimeEntry(String mimeType, String command, String tempFileNameTemplate)
MimeEntry(String mimeType, int action, String command, String
tempFileNameTemplate)
MimeEntry(String mimeType, int action, String command, String
tempFileNameTemplate, String[] extensions)
```

Each constructor simply passes its arguments to the last along with default values for the missing arguments. The action argument is, of course, a mnemonic constant specifying the action to be taken for this MIME type. The default value is MimeEntry.UNKNOWN. The command argument is the command to be used to launch an application to handle the data. The default is null. The tempFileNameTemplate argument is the name of a file into which the data can be saved for viewing with another program. This default is also null. Finally, extensions is an array of filename extensions that maps to the MIME type. For example, for "image/jpeg," extensions would be {".jpg", ".jpeg"}.

The mimeType and command arguments are used to set the typeName and command fields in the MimeEntry class.

Get and Set methods

Although the important fields of the MimeEntry class are private, most of them may be inspected or modified at any time with set and get methods:

```
public synchronized String getType()
public synchronized void setType(String mimeType)
public synchronized int getAction()
public synchronized void setAction(int action)
public synchronized void setAction(int action, String command)
public synchronized String getLaunchString()
public synchronized void setCommand(String command)
public synchronized String getDescription()
public synchronized void setDescription(String description)
public String getImageFileName()
public synchronized void setImageFileName(String filename)
public String getTempFileTemplate()
public synchronized String[] getExtensions()
public synchronized void setExtensions(String[] extensions_list)
```

The getLaunchString() method is really getCommand(); it's just named a little askew. The string returned by getLaunchString() is the same one set by setCommand() — that is, the command field. Other than that, these methods are completely predictable. For example:

```
MimeEntry director = new MimeEntry("application/x-director");
director.setExtensions({".dcr", ".dir", ".dxr"});
director.setAction(MimeEntry.LOAD_INTO_BROWSER);
```

In addition to the normal Set and Get methods that directly access and adjust the corresponding private fields, there's one slightly unusual get method. The method getExtensionsAsList() returns a single string containing the entire extensions list, separated by commas — for example, ".jpg, .jpeg".

```
public synchronized String getExtensionsAsList()
```

Utility methods

The toProperty() method returns a string representation of the MimeEntry object that is not intended for human eyes (as is the string representation returned by toString()), but rather for writing into a properties file like .hotjava/properties:

```
public synchronized String toProperty()
```

The string returned looks something like the ones shown in Listing 17-3.

Listing 17-3
MIME properties from Solaris 2.5

```
description=Unknown Data Type
action=browser; application=imagetool %s; icon=doc:/lib/images/ftp/jpeg.gif;
file_extensions=.jfif,.jfif-tbnl,.jpe,.jpg,.jpeg; description=JPEG Image
description=Unknown Content
action=save; icon=doc:/lib/images/ftp/tar.gif; file_extensions=.gtar
action=save; file_extensions=.ustar
file_extensions=.ief
action=save; icon=doc:/lib/images/ftp/zip.gif; file_extensions=.zip
action=application; application=xdvi %s; file_extensions=.dvi; description=TeX
DVI File
action=application; application=mpeg_play %s; icon=doc:/lib/images/ftp/mpeg.gif;
file_extensions=.mpg,.mpe,.mpeg; description=MPEG Video Clip
action=application; application=xterm -title troff -e sh -c "nroff %s | col |
more -w"; file_extensions=.t,.tr,.roff
file_extensions=.oda
file_extensions=.ras
file_extensions=.mime; description=Internet Email Message
action=browser; icon=doc:/lib/images/ftp/text.gif;
```

(continued)

Listing 17-3
MIME properties from Solaris 2.5 *(continued)*

```
file_extensions=.text,.c,.cc,.c++,.h,.pl,.txt,.java,.el; description=Plain Text
file_extensions=.movie,.mv
icon=doc:/lib/images/ftp/tiff.gif; file_extensions=.tif,.tiff; description=TIFF
Image
action=save; file_extensions=.sv4cpio
file_extensions=.src,.wsrc
icon=doc:/lib/images/ftp/avi.gif; file_extensions=.avi
file_extensions=.rgb
file_extensions=.saveme,.dump,.hqx,.arc,.o,.a,.bin,.exe,.z,.gz
action=save; file_extensions=.sh,.shar
action=application; application=xterm -title troff -e sh -c "nroff -ms %s | col
| more -w"; file_extensions=.ms
action=application; application=xterm -title troff -e sh -c "nroff -me %s | col
| more -w"; file_extensions=.me
action=application; application=audiotool %s;
icon=doc:/lib/images/ftp/audio.gif; file_extensions=.snd,.au
action=save; file_extensions=.cpio
file_extensions=.pgm
file_extensions=.pnm
file_extensions=.latex; description=LaTeX Source
file_extensions=.etx
icon=doc:/lib/images/ftp/html.gif; file_extensions=.htm,.html
file_extensions=.pdf; description=Adobe PDF Format
action=save; file_extensions=.hdf
file_extensions=.nc
action=application; application=imagetool %s; icon=doc:/lib/images/ftp/ps.gif;
file_extensions=.eps,.ai,.ps; description=Postscript File
file_extensions=.xbm,.xpm
file_extensions=.mov,.qt; description=QuickTime Video Clip
action=browser; icon=doc:/lib/images/ftp/gif.gif; file_extensions=.gif;
description=GIF Image
file_extensions=.xwd
action=save; file_extensions=.bcpio
file_extensions=.texinfo,.texi
icon=doc:/lib/images/ftp/aiff.gif; file_extensions=.aifc,.aif,.aiff
file_extensions=.tex; description=TeX Source
file_extensions=.ppm
file_extensions=.pbm
action=save; icon=doc:/lib/images/ftp/tar.gif; file_extensions=.tar
file_extensions=.tsv
action=save; file_extensions=.sv4crc
```

The toProperties() method is used primarily by the getAsProperties()
and saveAsProperties() methods in the MimeTable class:

```
public Object launch(URLConnection uc, InputStream is, MimeTable mt)
```

The launch() method tells the MimeEntry object to view some data. The uc argument is a URLConnection to the data; the is argument is normally the InputStream from the URL (that is uc.getInputStream()); and mt is the default MimeTable.

What the launch() method does for any given MIME type depends on the value of the action and command fields. If action is MimeEntry.SAVE_TO_FILE, then the method returns the is argument with no further ado. If action is MimeEntry.LOAD_INTO_BROWSER, then launch() returns uc.getContent(). If action is MimeEntry.LAUNCH_APPLICATION, then launch() returns the command String. For all other values of action, including MimeEntry.UNKNOWN, launch() returns null:

```
public boolean matches(String s)
```

The matches() method determines whether the String s is a MIME type that matches the typeName of this MimeEntry object. Strings match if they are the same as the typeName. However, they also match if the typeName is starred and the MIME type matches. For example, if typeName is "image/*" then "image/gif" and "image/jpeg" both match it.

Object methods

MimeEntry has the usual toString() method.

```
public String toString()
```

Listing 17-4 shows the format of the strings. These are taken from the same MimeEntry objects whose propertystrings you saw in Listing 17-3. The main difference between the strings produced by toString() and the ones produced by toProperty() is that toProperty() omits null fields and toString() includes the MIME type.

Listing 17-4
MimeEntry Strings

```
MimeEntry[contentType=unknown/unknown, image=null, action=0, command=null,
extensions=]
MimeEntry[contentType=image/jpeg, image=doc:/lib/images/ftp/jpeg.gif, action=1,
command=imagetool %s, extensions=.jfif,.jfif-tbnl,.jpe,.jpg,.jpeg]
MimeEntry[contentType=content/unknown, image=null, action=0, command=null,
extensions=]
MimeEntry[contentType=application/x-gtar, image=doc:/lib/images/ftp/tar.gif,
action=2, command=null, extensions=.gtar]
MimeEntry[contentType=application/x-ustar, image=null, action=2, command=null,
extensions=.ustar]
```

(continued)

Listing 17-4

MimeEntry Strings *(continued)*

```
MimeEntry[contentType=image/ief, image=null, action=0, command=null,
extensions=.ief]
MimeEntry[contentType=application/zip, image=doc:/lib/images/ftp/zip.gif,
action=2, command=null, extensions=.zip]
MimeEntry[contentType=application/x-dvi, image=null, action=3, command=xdvi %s,
extensions=.dvi]
MimeEntry[contentType=video/mpeg, image=doc:/lib/images/ftp/mpeg.gif, action=3,
command=mpeg_play %s, extensions=.mpg,.mpe,.mpeg]
MimeEntry[contentType=application/x-troff, image=null, action=3, command=xterm -
title troff -e sh -c "nroff %s | col | more -w", extensions=.t,.tr,.roff]
MimeEntry[contentType=application/oda, image=null, action=0, command=null,
extensions=.oda]
MimeEntry[contentType=image/x-cmu-rast, image=null, action=0, command=null,
extensions=.ras]
MimeEntry[contentType=message/rfc822, image=null, action=0, command=null,
extensions=.mime]
MimeEntry[contentType=text/plain, image=doc:/lib/images/ftp/text.gif, action=1,
command=null, extensions=.text,.c,.cc,.c++,.h,.pl,.txt,.java,.el]
MimeEntry[contentType=video/x-sgi-movie, image=null, action=0, command=null,
extensions=.movie,.mv]
MimeEntry[contentType=image/tiff, image=doc:/lib/images/ftp/tiff.gif, action=0,
command=null, extensions=.tif,.tiff]
MimeEntry[contentType=application/x-sv4cpio, image=null, action=2, command=null,
extensions=.sv4cpio]
MimeEntry[contentType=application/x-wais-source, image=null, action=0,
command=null, extensions=.src,.wsrc]
MimeEntry[contentType=application/x-troff-msvideo,
image=doc:/lib/images/ftp/avi.gif, action=0, command=null, extensions=.avi]
MimeEntry[contentType=image/x-rgb, image=null, action=0, command=null,
extensions=.rgb]
MimeEntry[contentType=application/octet-stream, image=null, action=0,
command=null, extensions=.saveme,.dump,.hqx,.arc,.o,.a,.bin,.exe,.z,.gz]
MimeEntry[contentType=application/x-shar, image=null, action=2, command=null,
extensions=.sh,.shar]
MimeEntry[contentType=application/x-troff-ms, image=null, action=3,
command=xterm -title troff -e sh -c "nroff -ms %s | col | more -w",
extensions=.ms]
MimeEntry[contentType=application/x-troff-me, image=null, action=3,
command=xterm -title troff -e sh -c "nroff -me %s | col | more -w",
extensions=.me]
MimeEntry[contentType=audio/basic, image=doc:/lib/images/ftp/audio.gif,
action=3, command=audiotool %s, extensions=.snd,.au]
MimeEntry[contentType=application/x-cpio, image=null, action=2, command=null,
extensions=.cpio]
MimeEntry[contentType=image/x-portable-graymap, image=null, action=0,
command=null, extensions=.pgm]
```

(continued)

MimeEntry Strings *(continued)*

```
MimeEntry[contentType=image/x-portable-anymap, image=null, action=0,
command=null, extensions=.pnm]
MimeEntry[contentType=application/x-latex, image=null, action=0, command=null,
extensions=.latex]
MimeEntry[contentType=text/x-setext, image=null, action=0, command=null,
extensions=.etx]
MimeEntry[contentType=text/html, image=doc:/lib/images/ftp/html.gif, action=0,
command=null, extensions=.htm,.html]
MimeEntry[contentType=application/pdf, image=null, action=0, command=null,
extensions=.pdf]
MimeEntry[contentType=application/x-hdf, image=null, action=2, command=null,
extensions=.hdf]
MimeEntry[contentType=application/x-netcdf, image=null, action=0, command=null,
extensions=.nc]
MimeEntry[contentType=audio/x-wav, image=doc:/lib/images/ftp/wav.gif, action=0,
command=null, extensions=.wav]
MimeEntry[contentType=application/x-troff-man, image=null, action=3,
command=xterm -title troff -e sh -c "nroff -man %s | col | more -w",
extensions=.man]
MimeEntry[contentType=application/postscript, image=doc:/lib/images/ftp/ps.gif,
action=3, command=imagetool %s, extensions=.eps,.ai,.ps]
MimeEntry[contentType=image/x-xbitmap, image=null, action=0, command=null,
extensions=.xbm,.xpm]
MimeEntry[contentType=video/quicktime, image=null, action=0, command=null,
extensions=.mov,.qt]
MimeEntry[contentType=image/gif, image=doc:/lib/images/ftp/gif.gif, action=1,
command=null, extensions=.gif]
MimeEntry[contentType=image/x-xwindowdump, image=null, action=0, command=null,
extensions=.xwd]
MimeEntry[contentType=application/x-bcpio, image=null, action=2, command=null,
extensions=.bcpio]
MimeEntry[contentType=application/x-texinfo, image=null, action=0, command=null,
extensions=.texinfo,.texi]
MimeEntry[contentType=audio/x-aiff, image=doc:/lib/images/ftp/aiff.gif,
action=0, command=null, extensions=.aifc,.aif,.aiff]
MimeEntry[contentType=application/x-tex, image=null, action=0, command=null,
extensions=.tex]
MimeEntry[contentType=image/x-portable-pixmap, image=null, action=0,
command=null, extensions=.ppm]
MimeEntry[contentType=image/x-portable-bitmap, image=null, action=0,
command=null, extensions=.pbm]
MimeEntry[contentType=application/x-tar, image=doc:/lib/images/ftp/tar.gif,
action=2, command=null, extensions=.tar]
MimeEntry[contentType=text/tab-separated-values, image=null, action=0,
command=null, extensions=.tsv]
MimeEntry[contentType=application/x-sv4crc, image=null, action=2, command=null,
extensions=.sv4crc]
```

Finally, MimeEntry implements Cloneable, and thus has a clone() method:

```
public Object clone()
```

MimeTable

Secret

The sun.net.www.MimeTable class associates lists of MimeEntry objects and filename extensions. That is, given a filename extension like .au, it finds the right MimeEntry object for that extension. It implements the java.net. FileNameMap interface.

Note

The difference between the extension list that a MimeTable handles and the extension list that a MimeEntry handles is that a MimeEntry's extension list has extensions for only one MIME type, whereas a MimeTable's extension list has extensions for all types. For example, a MimeEntry extension list might be {".jpg", ".jpeg"}, but would not be {".jpg", ".jpeg", ".gif", ".txt"} because that includes filename extensions for several different MIME types. However, a MimeTable's extension list might include ".jpg", ".jpeg", ".gif", ".txt", and several dozen more.

The key fields in a MimeTable object are two private Hashtables, entries and extensionMap:

```
private Hashtable entries;
private Hashtable extensionMap;
```

The extensionMap Hashtable holds a list of extensions like ".gif" and the associated MimeEntry objects. The extensions are the keys, and the MimeEntry objects are the values. The extensionMap Hashtable is used by the java.net.FileNameMap.getContentTypeFor() method as described above.

The entries Hashtable uses MIME type strings like "image/gif" as keys and MimeEntry objects as values. The MIME type strings are the keys and the MimeEntry objects are the values.

Thus, given either a filename extension like ".gif" or a MIME type like "image/gif," the MimeTable class can find the appropriate MimeEntry object.

Accessing the MimeTable

The MimeTable() constructor is declared private so you can't instantiate it yourself. Instead, a single instance is constructed and returned the first time you call the static getDefaultTable() method:

```
public static MimeTable getDefaultTable()
```

For example,

```
MimeTable mt = MimeTable.getDefaultTable();
```

Subsequent calls to MimeTable.getDefaultTable() return the same table. Therefore, there's only one MimeTable that exists in any virtual machine. Thus, in what follows, I'll refer to *the MimeTable* instead of *a MimeTable object*.

The MimeTable is preloaded with MimeEntry objects for many different MIME types. The exact set of MIME types and MimeEntry objects loaded into the table is platform- and host-dependent. On UNIX, Java creates the MimeEntry objects by reading and parsing the mailcap files. Java looks for mailcap files in these locations:

```
System.getProperty("user.mailcap")
~/.mailcap
/etc/mailcap
/usr/etc/mailcap
/usr/local/etc/mailcap",
System.getProperty("hotjava.home")/lib/mailcap
/usr/local/hotjava/lib/mailcap
```

The mailcap file contains a list of MIME types, filename extensions, descriptions of the types, filenames of icons for files of that type, and the preferred program to view that type — in other words, precisely the information needed to create a MimeEntry object. Listings 17-3 and 17-4 were created by printing all the MimeEntry objects in a MimeTable that had been filled by such a file. Listing 17-5 shows one relatively short mailcap file.

Listing 17-5
A sample mailcap file *(continued)*

```
# Copyright (c) 1991 Bell Communications Research, Inc. (Bellcore)
#
# Permission to use, copy, modify, and distribute this material
# for any purpose and without fee is hereby granted, provided
# that the above copyright notice and this permission notice
# appear in all copies, and that the name of Bellcore not be
# used in advertising or publicity pertaining to this
# material without the specific, prior written permission
# of an authorized representative of Bellcore. BELLCORE
# MAKES NO REPRESENTATIONS ABOUT THE ACCURACY OR SUITABILITY
# OF THIS MATERIAL FOR ANY PURPOSE. IT IS PROVIDED "AS IS",
# WITHOUT ANY EXPRESS OR IMPLIED WARRANTIES.
#
```

(continued)

Listing 17-5

A sample mailcap file *(continued)*

```
# Note that the effect of the following is to send ALL audio subtypes to the
# showaudio program, but to compose audio (e.g. in the mailto program)
# using "audio/basic" as the type.
audio/*; showaudio %s
audio/basic; showaudio %s; compose=audiocompose %s; edit=audiocompose %s;
description="An audio fragment"

# The following line is for sites where xv understands jpeg but xloadimage is
preferred.
image/jpeg; showpicture -viewer xv %s
# The following sends all other image subtypes to showpicture.
image/*; showpicture %s
# The following all appear AFTER the corresponding READING entries, and
# are for use in messages composition, e.g. in the "mailto" program
# In the following lines, the exit 0 junk is necessary because xwd
# doesn't always exit with a valid exit status!
# For sites with current (X11R5) pbm utilities
image/gif; showpicture %s; compose="xwd -frame | xwdtopnm | ppmtogif > %s\; exit
0"; description="An X11 window image dump in GIF format"
# For receiving X11 window image dumps from older versions of Andrew messages
image/x-xwd; showpicture %s; description="An X11 window image dump in X-XWD
format"

message/partial; showpartial %s %{id} %{number} %{total}
message/external-body; showexternal %s %{access-type} %{name} %{site}
%{directory} %{mode} %{server}; \
    needsterminal; composetyped = extcompose %s; \
    description="A reference to data stored in an external location"

# If you have an interactive Postscript interpreter, you should think carefully
# before replacing lpr with it in the following line, because PostScript
# can be an enormous security hole. It is RELATIVELY harmless
# when sent to the printer...
application/postscript ; lpr %s \; echo SENT FILE TO PRINTER ; description="A
Postscript File";\
    compose="getfilename Postscript %s"

# The following gives rudimentary capability for receiving
# text mail in the ISO-8859-1 character set, which covers many European
# languages, and the ISO-8859-8 character set, which includes Hebrew
# Note that the pipe to tr ensures that the "ISO" is case-insensitive.
text/richtext; shownonascii iso-8859-8 -e richtext -p %s; test=test "`echo
%{charset} | tr '[A-Z]' '[a-z]'`"  = iso-8859-8; copiousoutput
text/richtext; shownonascii iso-8859-1 -e richtext -p %s; test=test "`echo
%{charset} | tr '[A-Z]' '[a-z]'`"  = iso-8859-1; copiousoutput
text/plain; shownonascii iso-8859-8 %s; test=test "`echo %{charset} | tr '[A-Z]'
```

(continued)

A sample mailcap file *(continued)*

```
'[a-z]'`" = iso-8859-1; copiousoutput
text/enriched; shownonascii iso-8859-8 -e richtext -e -p %s; test=test "`echo
%{charset} | tr '[A-Z]' '[a-z]'`" = iso-8859-8; copiousoutput
text/enriched; shownonascii iso-8859-1 -e richtext -e -p %s; test=test "`echo
%{charset} | tr '[A-Z]' '[a-z]'`" = iso-8859-1; copiousoutput

# The following displays Japanese text at sites where the "kterm" program is
installed:
text/plain; kterm -geometry +0+0  -e more %s /dev/null; test=test "`echo
%{charset} | tr '[A-Z]' '[a-z]'`" = iso-2022-jp
```

Finding MIME data

The primary method of the MimeTable class is getContentTypeFor(). This
is a concrete implementation of the method of the same name in the java.net.
FileNameMap interface. This is used to guess a MIME type, given a filename.
For example,

```
String type = mt.getContentTypeFor("beefcake.jpg");
```

In addition to getContentTypeFor(), MimeTable has four find methods
that return MimeEntry objects. You can search by MIME type, file name,
file extension, or description:

```
public synchronized MimeEntry find(String type)
public MimeEntry findByFileName(String filename)
public synchronized MimeEntry findByExt(String extension)
public synchronized MimeEntry findByDescription(String description)
```

Modifying the table

There are three methods that add or remove entries from the MimeTable.
These are:

```
public synchronized void add(MimeEntry entry)
public synchronized MimeEntry remove(String name)
public synchronized MimeEntry remove(MimeEntry me)
```

Adding a new MIME type to the table is easy. Just create a MimeEntry
object for the type and pass it to the add() method:

```
MimeEntry zip = new MimeEntry("application/zip");
zip.setExtensions({".zip"});
```

```
zip.setAction(MimeEntry.LAUNCH_APPLICATION);
zip.setCommand("unzip %s");
MimeTable.getDefaultTable().add(me);
```

Removing entries from the table is even easier. You can either remove them by MimeType or remove them with a reference to a particular entry. For example,

```
MimeTable mt = MimeTable.getDefaultTable();
mt.remove("application/postscript");
MimeEntry me = mt.findByExt(".eps");
mt.remove(me);
me = mt.findByExt(".ai");
mt.remove(me);
me = mt.findByExt(".ps");
mt.remove(me);
```

Utility methods

The getSize() method simply tells you how many elements are in the MimeTable.

```
public synchronized int getSize()
```

The elements() method returns an Enumeration of all the MimeEntry objects in the MimeTable. It's useful, among other things, for exploring the MimeTable on different platforms.

```
public synchronized Enumeration elements()
```

Listing 17-6 is a simple program that prints each entry in the MimeTable so that you can see what MIME types are understood and what a browser is likely to do with them. Variants of this program produced Listings 17-3 and 17-4.

Listing 17-6
The MimeTypes class

```
import sun.net.www.*;
import java.util.*;

public class MimeTypes {

  public static void main(String[] args) {

    MimeTable mt = MimeTable.getDefaultTable();
```

(continued)

The MimeTypes class *(continued)*

```
    System.out.println("There are " + mt.getSize() + " entries in the
MimeTable.\n");
    for (Enumeration e = mt.elements(); e.hasMoreElements(); ) {
      MimeEntry me = (MimeEntry) e.nextElement();
      System.out.println(me);
    }

  }

}
```

Loading and saving the MimeTable

As vendors compete to produce the next Web standards for audio, video, artwork, and other formats, MIME types are proliferating at an unbelievable rate. Therefore, a Web browser should provide an interface to allow the user to add and change MIME type mappings. Figure 17-1 shows Netscape Navigator's MIME type preference dialog box (Macintosh version).

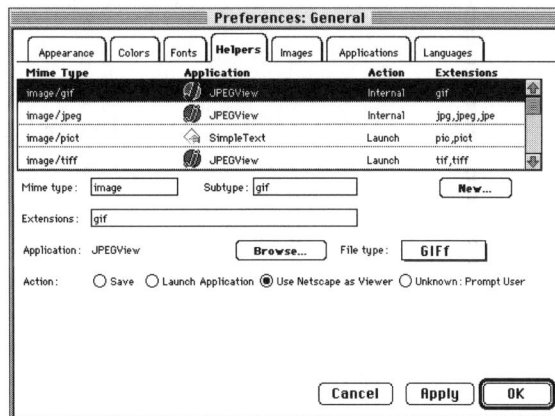

Figure 17-1
Netscape's dialog box for adjusting MIME preferences

Java does not provide such a convenient preference dialog box, but if you create your own, Java will let you save the preferences a user chooses for later runs. The save() and saveAsProperties() methods save the MimeTable into a file. The getAsProperties() and load() methods let you restore it.

```
    public synchronized void load()
    public synchronized boolean save(String filename)
```

```
public Properties getAsProperties()
protected boolean saveAsProperties(File f)
```

The save() method stores the MimeEntry properties in a named file. It also stores the name of the file in the System property content.types.user.table so that the file can be found later by the load() method. However, it's rare to call load() directly. Normally, this is invoked automatically the first time you call MimeTable.getDefaultTable(), and it does not need to be called again.

Similarly, you generally do not call getAsProperties() or saveAsProperties() directly. The saveAsProperties() method is called by save(), and getAsProperties() is called by load().

MimeLauncher

Secret

The sun.net.www.MimeLauncher class is a subclass of Thread that spawns external helper applications to view files with MIME types that Java itself can't deal with. This class has three methods, only one of which is public — run(). Even the constructor has only default access:

```
MimeLauncher (MimeEntry me, URLConnection uc, String gtt, String name)
    throws ApplicationLaunchException
```

Therefore you are extremely unlikely to instantiate this class or interact with it directly. Instead, it's called by the MimeEntry.launch() method when the MimeEntry's action field is set to MimeEntry.LAUNCH_APPLICATION.

When constructed, a MimeLauncher object checks to see if it can, in fact, find the command that must be executed to view the MimeEntry object me. If it can't find that command, then it throws an ApplicationLaunchException.

However, assuming the command is found, the caller then starts the thread, which results in its run() method being invoked.

```
public void run()
```

The run() method writes the data into the temporary file gtt, and tries to spawn a process to execute the command and view the file. Then it returns.

TRACKING DOWNLOADS: METERED STREAMS

Many Web servers are kind enough to tell clients how many bytes that they can expect to download. You can use this to provide feedback to users about how long they can expect to wait for an operation to complete, either with a progress bar or with a message like "47% of 108K" in the status bar of the browser. The MeteredStream class keeps track of how many bytes have been downloaded and how many it expects still to come.

Secret

The sun.net.www.MeteredStream class is a subclass of java.io. FilterInputStream, which keeps track of how many bytes have been received. It's useful for dealing with unreliable network connections that may unexpectedly stop delivering data. Most of the InputStreams returned by URL.getContent() or URL.openStream() are MeteredStreams.

Each MeteredStream has four protected instance fields:

```
protected boolean closed;
protected int expected;
protected int count;
protected ProgressEntry te;
```

The expected field is the number of bytes that this stream is supposed to read. The count field contains the number of bytes the stream has actually read. The closed field is a boolean variable that's false if the connection is open and true if it's not. Finally, te is a ProgressEntry object that's used to track the progress of all the instances of this class.

The constructors and the finalize() method adjust te to make sure it always represents the correct number of instances. Whenever a new instance is constructed, total_connections is incremented by one. When a MeteredStream is finalized, total_connections is decremented by one.

When you construct a MeteredStream object, you're expected to provide a ProgressEntry object that contains an estimate for the number of bytes that will be read from the stream. This number might come from a Content-length MIME header, for example.

```
public MeteredStream(InputStream is, ProgressEntry te)
protected void finalize()
```

The read(), close(), and skip() methods are overridden so that they track the number of bytes read and adjust expected, count, and te each time they're called. This happens privately, so you can use them exactly as you use the corresponding methods in the superclass.

```
public int read() throws IOException
public int read(byte b[], int off, int len) throws IOException
public void close() throws IOException
public long skip(long n) throws IOException
```

SUN.NET.WWW.URLCONNECTION

Secret

The sun.net.www.URLConnection class is an abstract subclass of java.net. URLConnection. Because it has the same name as java.net.URLConnection, it's fortunate that you rarely have cause to deal with it directly. You almost always work with either the superclass (java.net.URLConnection) or one of its subclasses (for example, sun.net.www.protocol.http.HttpURLConnection). If you do work directly with this class, you should use the fully qualified name — sun.net.www.URLConnection — instead of just URLConnection. The latter is too easy to confuse with java.net.URLConnection.

This class does not implement connect(), the only abstract method in java.net.URLConnection, but it overrides six methods:

```
public int getContentLength()
public String getContentType()
public void setRequestProperty(java.lang.String, java.lang.String)
public String getHeaderField(String name)
public String getHeaderFieldKey(int n)
public String getHeaderField(int n)
```

These methods have the same syntax as the corresponding methods in java.net.URLConnection. The difference is that they actually work. The equivalent methods in java.net.URLConnection all return null, except for getContentLength(), which returns -1.

This class also has three fields: two private (which should not need to, and indeed cannot, be accessed directly) and one protected field that is important to subclasses.

```
private String contentType
private int contentLength
protected MessageHeader properties
```

The contentType is the value of the Content-type header sent by the Web server, such as "text/html" or "application/octet-stream". If the Web server did not send a Content-type header, contentType is null. Similarly, contentLength is either the value of Content-length header sent by the Web server or -1 if no Content-length header was sent. Finally, the properties field is a MessageHeader object that contains a complete MIME header for a connection. These three fields are normally accessed through get and set methods:

```
public int getContentLength()
public String getContentType()
protected void setContentLength(int len)
```

```
public void setContentType(String mimetype)
public MessageHeader getProperties()
public void setProperties(MessageHeader properties)
```

Of course, this class also has a constructor:

```
public URLConnection(URL u)
```

Finally, this class has two unique methods of its own:

```
public boolean canCache()
public void close()
```

The close() method closes the connection and flushes any remaining data.

The canCache() method returns true if data from this URL may be cached and false if it should not be. Generally, CGI output is not cached, while most HTML and image files are cached.

SUN.NET.WWW.HTTP

The sun.net.www.http package contains several classes to communicate with HTTP servers. The primary class is HttpClient. The other classes, ClientVector, KeepAliveCache, KeepAliveKey, and KeepAliveStream, only support this class and are not normally used independently. Furthermore, HttpClient uses a number of classes in other packages extensively, particularly sun.net.www.MessageHeader. In many ways, this package is the counterpart of the sun.net.ftp, sun.net.nntp, and sun.net.smtp packages for their respective protocols.

HttpClient

The sun.net.www.HttpClient class is a subclass of sun.net.NetworkClient, which communicates with HTTP servers. The HTTP protocol handler uses it to download data from Web servers. You normally interact with this class indirectly through the URL, URLConnection, and HttpURLConnection classes. For now, let us look at how you can use it directly.

Creating HttpClient objects

The HttpClient class has four constructors, only one of which is public. These are

```
public HttpClient(URL u, String proxy, int proxy_port)
protected HttpClient(URL u, boolean)
private HttpClient(URL u, String proxy, int proxy_port, boolean useProxy)
private HttpClient(URL u)
```

The URL u is the URL to which this client connects. The string proxy argument is the hostname of the proxy server. Pass null if you aren't using a proxy server. The int argument proxy_port is the port on which the proxy server listens. Pass -1 if you aren't using a proxy server. Finally, the boolean argument useProxy is true if a proxy server will be used, false if it won't be. For example,

```
URL u = new URL("http://www.whitehouse.gov/");
HttpClient whitehouse = new HttpClient(u, null, -1);
```

In addition to the constructors, there's also an unusual public static method called New() that returns an HttpClient object for a particular URL. Its signature is

```
public static HttpClient New(URL u)
```

The difference between using a constructor and calling New() is that New() will reuse a connection to the server if one already exists and the server supports HTTP Keep-Alive. HTTP Keep-Alive is a new feature of HTTP 1.1 that lets clients send multiple requests over a single connection. It avoids much of the overhead of setting up and tearing down multiple TCP/IP connections. On fast connections, it can reduce the time that a Web page full of images takes to load by 50% or more.

The HttpClient class stores a list of active connections to HTTP servers in a sun.net.www.http.KeepAliveCache object. Rather than creating a completely new connection to the server, New() first checks the cache of currently open connections to see if there's a "kept alive" connection to the server. If there is, then New() returns the HttpClient object handling that connection. Otherwise, it constructs a new HttpClient object. Assuming you don't need to use a proxy, creating HttpClient objects with New() is more efficient than using the HttpClient() constructor when the server uses HTTP Keep-Alive. For example,

```
URL u = new URL("http://www.idgbooks.com/");
HttpClient IDG = HttpClient.New(u);
```

Communicating with the server

Leaving aside HTTP Keep-Alive for the moment, the interaction between an HTTP client and an HTTP server goes like this:

1. The client opens the connection to the server.
2. The client sends a request to the server.
3. The client receives a response from the server.
4. The client or the server, or both, closes the connection.

HTTP Keep-Alive lets the client repeat steps 2 and 3 multiple times before closing the connection.

The openServer() method is used to perform step 1—that is, to open the connection to the server.

```
public void openServer(String host, int port)
```

However, all of the constructors automatically call openServer() to open the connection to the server. The New() method also opens the connection if one isn't already open. Therefore, you generally do not need to call openServer() yourself. It will be called as soon as you construct an HttpClient object or call HttpClient.New().

Once the connection is open, the client sends a request that looks something like this:

```
GET /javafaq/index.html HTTP/1.0
Connection: Keep-Alive
User-Agent: Mozilla/3.01 (Macintosh; I; PPC)
Host: sunsite.unc.edu
Accept: image/gif, image/x-xbitmap, image/jpeg, image/pjpeg, */*
```

The first line tells the server to respond by sending the file /javafaq/index.html. It also says this client understands version 1.0 of the HTTP protocol. The remaining lines are a series of MIME headers that specify various information about the client. For example, this particular set of MIME headers says that this browser is the PowerMac version of Netscape 3.0.1, that the host part of the requested URL was sunsite.unc.edu, and that the browser can handle any MIME type (*/*). Finally, the request is terminated with a blank line.

Note

For a much more detailed look at the HTTP protocol, see my book *Java Network Programming* (O'Reilly & Associates, 1997).

An HttpClient object sends data to the server by writing it on its OutputStream, like this:

```
PrintStream ps = new PrintStream(IDG.getOutputStream());
ps.print("GET /javafaq/index.html HTTP/1.0\r\n");
ps.print("Connection: Keep-Alive\r\n");
ps.print("User-Agent: Mozilla/3.01 (Macintosh; I; PPC)\r\n");
ps.print("Host: sunsite.unc.edu\r\n")
ps.print(Accept: image/gif, image/x-xbitmap, image/jpeg, image/pjpeg,
*/*\r\n");
ps.print("\r\n"); // blank line to finish request
ps.flush();
```

Note that you need to terminate each line with a "\r\n." I do this manually with print() rather than using println() because println() generally sends only a linefeed, not a carriage return/linefeed pair.

Alternately, you can build a MessageHeader object and pass it to the writeRequests() method. Sending the first line is a little tricky because it's not really a MIME field. Use the prepend() method to add only the request as the name and pass null for the value.

```
public void writeRequests(MessageHeader request)
```

For example,

```
MessageHeader mh = new MessageHeader();
mh.add("Connection", "Keep-Alive");
mh.add("User-Agent", "Mozilla/3.01 (Macintosh; I; PPC)");
mh.add("Host", "sunsite.unc.edu");
mh.add("Accept", "image/gif, image/x-xbitmap, image/jpeg, image/pjpeg,
*/*");
mh.prepend("GET /javafaq/index.html HTTP/1.0", null);
IDG.writeRequests(mh);
```

Once the client has sent a request, the server sends a response. Most often, this will be an HTML file, but it may be binary image data or an error message. The server precedes the actual response data with a MIME header of its own, like this:

```
HTTP/1.1 200 OK
Date: Sun, 16 Feb 1997 17:19:15 GMT
Server: Apache/1.2b4
Connection: close
Content-Type: text/html
Last-Modified: Sat, 15 Feb 1997 15:28:54 GMT
ETag: "37aa03-24fb-3305d636"
```

```
Content-Length: 9467
Accept-Ranges: bytes
```

This is followed by the actual data of the requested file. To read this data, you first call parseHTTP():

```
public boolean parseHTTP(MessageHeader mh, ProgressEntry pe)
```

The MIME fields of the header are placed in the MessageHeader object mh. The ProgressEntry argument is an instance of the sun.net.ProgressEntry class. HotJava uses it to track downloads so that it can display messages like "37% of 95K loaded" in the status bar. All you really need to know about this class is the constructor:

```
public ProgressEntry(String filename, String MIMEType)
```

You can pass null for the second argument if you don't yet know the MIME type. For example,

```
IDG.parseHTTP(mh, new ProgressEntry(u.getFile(), null));
```

When parseHTTP() completes, the MIME header has been read and the InputStream is positioned at the first byte of the response data. You can get a reference to this InputStream with getInputStream():

```
public synchronized InputStream getInputStream()
```

The getInputStream() method can be called only after parseHttp() has been called. Otherwise, the fields in the HttpClient class won't be properly set up and a NullPointerException will be thrown. This means that you can't use this class to directly print out everything the server sends, including the MIME header. You can print the MIME header separately, but you can't simply read each line that the server sends and then print it.

If the server supports HTTP Keep-Alive, this request-response cycle may be repeated multiple times. However, when the client is through, it should close the connection by calling finished(). This adjusts the Keep-Alive count and then calls closeServer().

```
public static void finished(HttpClient hc)
public void closeServer()
```

Although closeServer() is public, you should not call it directly because it doesn't properly account for HTTP Keep-Alive. Call finished() instead, and let it call closeServer() for you.

Listing 17-7 puts this all together in an application that downloads a page from a Web site and prints it on System.out.

Listing 17-7
The PageGrabber class

```
import java.net.*;
import java.io.*;
import sun.net.www.*;
import sun.net.www.http.*;
import sun.net.*;


public class PageGrabber {

  MessageHeader request;
  MessageHeader response;


  public static void main(String[] args) {

    PageGrabber pg = new PageGrabber();

    for (int i = 0; i < args.length; i++) {
      try {
        URL u = new URL(args[i]);
        pg.getPage(u);
      }
      catch (MalformedURLException e) {
        System.err.println("Usage: java GrabPage URL1 URL2 ...");
      }
    }

  }


  public PageGrabber() {

    request = new MessageHeader();
    response = new MessageHeader();
    request.add("User-Agent", "PageGrabber 1.0");
    request.add("Accept", "text/html, text/plain, text/*");

  }


  public void getPage(URL u) {
```

(continued)

The PageGrabber class *(continued)*

```
    try {
      HttpClient hc = new HttpClient(u, null, -1);
      request.prepend("GET " + hc.getURLFile() + " " + "HTTP/1.0", null);
      hc.writeRequests(request);
      hc.parseHTTP(response, new ProgressEntry(u.getFile(), null));
      InputStreamReader isr = new InputStreamReader(hc.getInputStream());
      BufferedReader br = new BufferedReader(isr);
      while (true) {
        if (br.ready()) {
          String theLine = br.readLine();
          if (theLine == null) break;
          System.out.println(theLine);
        }
      }
      HttpClient.finished(hc);
    }
    catch (IOException e) {
      System.err.println(e);
    }

  }

}
```

This is very much a toy application. First of all, it's not thread safe. In addition, if you really needed something like this, you'd use the more portable URL classes instead. However, it does serve to demonstrate the use of the HttpClient class.

Clients can also post data to HTTP servers by retrieving an OutputStream object through getOutputStream().

```
public OutputStream getOutputStream()
```

This is used to handle POST and PUT requests.

```
public String getURLFile()
```

The getURLFile() method is very similar to URL.getFile(). In fact, if a proxy server isn't being used, getURLFile() just returns url.getFile() where url is the URL to which this client is connected. However, if a proxy server is being used, then getURLFile() prepends ://host:port to url.getFile(). In other words, it converts from the normal, unproxied URL to a URL the proxy server understands. This method is used elsewhere in the HttpClient class to convert unproxied URLs like http://sunsite.unc.edu:80/javafaq/books.html into proxied URL like http://proxy:8000/://sunsite.unc.edu:80/javafaq/books.html. The port number is omitted if it's not explicitly specified.

```
public final boolean isKeepingAlive()
```

The isKeepingAlive() method returns true if this client currently has an open connection to the Web server over which you can send additional requests. It returns false if a new connection needs to be opened.

```
public static synchronized void resetProperties()
```

The resetProperties() method restores a number of fields of the HttpClient to their default values as specified by various system properties. This method is also used to set the properties to their default values when an HttpClient object is created.

The proxyHost is set to the value of the system property http.proxyHost. If that's null, the system property proxyHost is used instead. If that's still null, proxyHost is set to null and no proxy is used. The proxyPort is set to the value of the system property http.proxyPort. If that fails, it's set to 80.

Next, the number of connections to store in the KeepAliveCache is set to the value of the system property http.maxConnections. If there's no such property, it's set to 2. Next, if the system property http.keepAlive exits and is "true," then HTTP Keep-Alive is turned on. Otherwise, it's turned off.

Finally, if proxyHost isn't null, then the system property http.nonProxyHosts is inspected for a list of hosts that should be connected to directly, rather than through the proxy. Generally, these are the hosts behind the firewall.

HttpClient also has the usual toString() method. This one returns the URL for this client in parentheses. For example,

```
(http://www.idgbooks.com/)
```

Finally, there are two protected methods, finalize() and getDefaultPort():

```
protected void finalize() throws Throwable
protected int getDefaultPort()
```

The finalize() method is empty. It exists only in case you want to override it in a subclass.

The getDefaultPort() method returns 80, the normal port for an HTTP server.

KeepAliveCache

Secret

The sun.net.www.http.KeepAliveCache class is a non-public subclass of Hashtable that the HttpClient class uses to keep a list of open connections. HttpClient has a static KeepAliveCache field called kac. When HttpClient. New() is called, Java checks the kac field to determine whether there's already an open connection to a particular server. If so, and if the server supports HTTP Keep-Alive, New() can reuse the object that's already in the cache rather than opening a new connection.

The KeepAliveCache class has three methods: put(), get(), and removeVector():

```
public synchronized void put(URL u, HttpClient hc)
public Object get(URL u)
synchronized void removeVector(KeepAliveKey key)
```

You might have guessed by these signatures that a KeepAliveCache Hashtable uses URL objects as keys and HttpClient objects as values. If you did, you were wrong. The KeepAliveCache class uses URLs and HttpClient objects to calculate the keys and the values, but they are not themselves the keys and the values. Before any elements are actually added to the Hashtable, the protocol, host, and port are stripped out of the URL and used to construct a new object of class KeepAliveKey. Similarly, the values in the Hashtable are ClientVector objects constructed with an HttpClient.

KeepAliveKey

Secret

The non-public sun.net.www.http.KeepAliveKey class has three private fields and three public methods:

```
private String protocol
private String host
private int port
public KeepAliveKey(URL u)
public boolean equals(Object object)
public int hashCode()
```

The constructor takes the protocol, host, and port from the URL u and stores them in the three private fields. However it ignores the file and ref of the URL. Thus, URLs that point to different files on the same server have the same KeepAliveKey. This allows Java to determine whether it already has an HttpClient object suitable for retrieving a particular URL.

ClientVector

Secret

ClientVector is a non-public class that extends java.util.Stack. It stores a list of requests made to a particular Web server, generally produced by the URL class. When objects are placed in the KeepAliveCache, the cache checks to see if there is already a Vector for that URL. If there is, it adds the new request to that Vector so it can be processed. If there isn't, it constructs a new ClientVector object. Subsequent requests for data from the same server are passed to the same ClientVector object.

```
ClientVector(KeepAliveCache kac, KeepAliveKey key, int nap)
synchronized HttpClient get()
synchronized void put(HttpClient httpClient)
public void run()
```

The ClientVector class implements Runnable. Every time the KeepAliveCache constructs a new ClientVector object, it also starts a relatively high priority thread using that object as the seed. This thread downloads data for each of the clients stored in the ClientVector in turn.

KeepAliveStream

Secret

The public class sun.net.www.http.KeepAliveStream is a subclass of sun.net.www.MeteredStream that the ClientVector class uses to download Web pages. The constructor takes an InputStream to chain to, a ProgressEntry object, and the HttpClient object that provides the data.

```
public KeepAliveStream(InputStream is, ProgressEntry pe, HttpClient hc)
```

The primary difference between the KeepAliveStream and the sun.net. www.MeteredStream is that KeepAliveStream does not support marking and resetting, whereas MeteredStream does. Thus, KeepAliveStream overrides the following methods from java.io.FilteredInputStream, sun.net.www.MeteredStream's superclass, to disallow marking:

```
public boolean markSupported()
public void mark(int i)
public void reset() throws IOException
```

The markSupported() method returns false; reset() immediately throws an IOException; and mark() does absolutely nothing.

The hurry() method is new in this class. Because KeepAliveStream is a subclass of MeteredStream, it knows how many more bytes it expects to read. The hurry() method tries to read these bytes all at once. This may not work over a network connection because some of the bytes may not yet have arrived. If so, hurry() returns false. If successful, hurry() returns true.

```
public synchronized boolean hurry()
```

Finally, there's a close() method. In addition to the usual stream closing operations, this method unregisters this stream from the ProgressData table.

```
public void close() throws IOException
```

SUN.NET.WWW.HTTPD AND THE BASICHTTPSERVER

The sun.net.www.httpd package contains a single class, BasicHttpServer, which extends sun.net.NetworkServer and provides a very rudimentary Web server. It has three public methods and five protected ones:

```
public static void main(String[] args)
public BasicHttpServer()
public final void serviceRequest()
protected void getRequest(URL u, String s)
protected void generateStatistics()
protected void startHtml(String s)
protected void generateProcessOutput(String s1, String s2)
protected void error(String s)
```

Because BasicHttpServer has a main() method, you can start it from the command line. By default, it listens on port 8888. For example,

```
% java sun.net.www.httpd.BasicHttpServer
```

There's no simple way to change the port from the command line. You would need to write a new class and instantiate a BasicHttpServer from your own code, like this:

```
BasicHttpServer myHttpServer = new BasicHttpServer();
myHttpServer.start(7000);
```

This class is hardly ready for prime time. In fact, I doubt that it's ready for the 1:00 A.M. to 5:00 A.M. insomniac bracket. For example, when the BasicHttpServer is sent this common request

```
GET / HTTP/1.0
```

it sends no data to the client, not even an error message, but produces this output on the server console:

```
Failed on /
java.io.FileNotFoundException:
/net/tachyon/export/disk1/Mosaic/docs//index.html
        at java.io.FileInputStream.<init>(FileInputStream.java)
        at
sun.net.www.httpd.BasicHttpServer.getRequest(BasicHttpServer.java:122)
        at
sun.net.www.httpd.BasicHttpServer.serviceRequest(BasicHttpServer.java:233)
        at sun.net.NetworkServer.run(NetworkServer.java:90)
        at java.lang.Thread.run(Thread.java)
```

This clues you in that the server is hard-coded with a document root of /net/tachyon/export/disk1/Mosaic/docs/. If you intend to use this class, you'll need to create your own directory with that path.

The server does understand a few requests that do not map to this hard-coded directory. These are

```
/statistics.html
/processes.html
/uptime.html
/echo.html
```

These correspond to different commands that one might run. The server runs them, much like a hard-wired CGI, and returns the result. For example, requesting /processes.html causes the BasicHttpServer to execute the UNIX command "/usr/ucb/ps -uaxwww" and return the result as a formatted Web page like this:

```
<html><head><title>Running processes</title></head>
<body><h1>Running processes</h1>
<pre>
USER        PID %CPU %MEM   SZ  RSS TT      S    START  TIME COMMAND
root       6521 3.6  1.0 2108 1948 pts/2   0 16:17:43  0:01 /usr/ucb/ps -
uaxwww
hiphop    13287 3.4  0.7 2012 1388 ?       S 01:00:16  3:41 eggdrop Saddam
root          3 0.8  0.0    0    0 ?       S    Feb 04 234:51 fsflush
prpatel    9968 0.6  5.01701210396 pts/6   S    Feb 14 37:31 netscape
elharo     6341 0.4  1.3 3996 2644 pts/2   S 15:58:59  0:02
/export/sunsite/users/elharo/java1.1b3/bin/../bin/sparc/green_threads/java sun.
```

I've truncated the output. BasicHttpServer leaves off the normal closing </body></html> tags, but frankly, this is the least of its problems.

Most of the other hard-wired paths are even more dysfunctional. The only one that's mildly useful is /echo.html. This echoes back the request the browser made. For example,

```
Echo reply

URL was http://president/echo.html

Socket was
Socket[addr=port122.dialup.inch.com/206.138.209.22,port=1334,localport=8888]

Connection: Keep-Alive
User-Agent: Mozilla/3.01 (Macintosh; I; PPC)
Host: president.oit.unc.edu:8888
Accept: image/gif, image/x-xbitmap, image/jpeg, image/pjpeg, */*
```

This is useful to CGI developers who want to see exactly what a particular Web browser is sending to the server.

There are also three "files" that generate a stack of binary data of the nonstandard MIME type application/chart. These are

```
/sin.dat
/stock.dat
/frac.dat
```

None of these appears to produce anything interesting, however.

In fact, this entire class seems to have little to no purpose whatsoever. Perhaps it was once used to test the NetworkServer class. This is the only subclass of NetworkServer in the JDK.

CONTENT HANDLERS

The sun.net.www.content package contains all of the JDK's content handlers. When a URL or URLConnection's getContent() method is invoked, the URLConnection object tries to find the right content handler for the URL. This depends not on the protocol, but on the MIME type, such as text/html. For protocols that don't support MIME, Java makes some reasonable guesses based on the file name.

If a ContentHandlerFactory is installed, it is asked for the right subclass of ContentHandler to handle the file. If the ContentHandlerFactory does not have the right handler for the MIME type, or if, as is often the case, no ContentHandlerFactory is installed, then Java looks for a class named

sun.net.www.content.*type.subtype* — for example, sun.net.www.content.
image.gif or sun.net.www.content.text.html.

The JDK does not include many content handlers. In fact, there are only
five: three image types and two text types. In each of the classes that follows,
the key method is getContent(). The getContent() method, which is declared
in the abstract class java.net.ContentHandler that these classes subclass,
reads from the URLConnection's InputStream (uc.getInputStream()) and
constructs and returns an object of an appropriate type.

```
public abstract Object getContent(URLConnection uc) throws IOException
```

Sun has never been very clear about what types of objects getContent()
is supposed to return, and some of the examples that they've published have
been positively misleading. In fact, the situation is so bad that many
programmers simply roll their own classes to handle content rather than
relying on the ContentHandler class.

However, inspecting the classes in this package makes the answer clear.
Content handlers for text types should return some form of InputStream.
Content handlers for image types should return an object that implements
the java.awt.image.ImageProducer interface.

Secret

The text content handlers

The sun.net.www.content.text package includes classes that handle content
types of text with various subtypes. Currently, the only subtypes supported
are plain and generic, which are essentially the same.

The text/plain content handler

The URL.getContent() method returns the sun.net.www.content.text.plain
class when the Web server indicates that the file that it is sending has type
text/plain. This is a very simple class with only a single method, getContent():

Secret

```
public Object getContent(URLConnection uc)
```

This method effectively returns uc.getInputStream(). However,
getContent() does not return uc.getInputStream() directly. Instead, it
chains uc.getInputStream() to a new PlainTextInputStream and returns

the PlainTextInputStream. If an IOException is thrown, it puts an error message in a StringBuffer and returns that instead.

The error handling here isn't very well thought out. Anyone who calls this method will be expecting an InputStream, not a StringBuffer. It would have been better to allow the exception to propagate by declaring that getContent() throws IOException. Alternately, the error message could have been returned in a StringBufferInputStream. This way the calling method would have been guaranteed to get an InputStream.

The PlainTextInputStream class

The sun.net.www.content.text.PlainTextInputStream class represents a stream of raw text. It has a single method, the default access constructor, PlainTextInputStream():

```
PlainTextInputStream(InputStream is)
```

PlainTextInputStream is a subclass of FilterInputStream that doesn't actually filter anything. Presumably, at some point in the future, they may rewrite the class to handle the conversion of raw ASCII bytes to the native character set, or some such function. However, right now this is just a do-nothing class.

The text/generic content handler

The URL.getContent() method returns the sun.net.www.content.text.generic class when the Web server indicates that the file it's sending has type text/generic. I've never actually seen a Web server use this MIME type, but apparently the programmer who wrote this class has.

The text/generic content handler is *exactly* the same as the text/plain content handler. It subclasses sun.net.www.content.text.plain but overrides no methods. Furthermore, the only new method in this class is the default noargs constructor:

```
public generic()
```

The only reason that this class exists is that Sun's scheme for locating content handlers requires it in order to handle the text/generic content type.

The image content handlers

Secret

The sun.net.www.content.image package includes content handlers for content type image. Three subtypes are supported: gif, jpeg, and x-xbitmap. These are supported by the sun.net.www.content.image.gif, sun.net.www. content.image.jpeg, and sun.net.www.content.image.x_xbitmap classes, respectively.

Note

There's also a sun.net.www.content.image.x_xpixmap class for handling X11 Pixmap images. However, this content handler always returns null. It didn't always, but the lines that would return something other than null have been commented out in the source code, apparently because the Pixmap image decoder was a little buggy.

Aside from their names, these classes are virtually identical. Each of them has exactly one real method, getContent(), plus the default noargs constructor.

```
public Object getContent(URLConnection uc) throws IOException
```

The getContent() method passes the URLConnection argument uc to the sun.awt.image.URLImageSource() constructor and returns the resulting URLImageSource object. The logic to recognize and handle each image type is contained in the URLImageSource class, *not* in the content handler itself.

The most important thing about the sun.awt.image.URLImageSource class is that it implements the java.awt.image.ImageProducer interface. An ImageProducer object provides bits for ImageConsumers that display the bits. ImageProducers need not produce all the bits at one time or even in order. ImageProducers and ImageConsumers work together to display as much of an image as can be shown at a given time. This is important when potentially large image files need to be loaded over slow network connections.

sun.awt.image.URLImageSource

Secret

The URLImageSource class is a subclass of sun.awt.image. InputStreamImageSource. Most of the logic for reading images from the network connection and feeding it to the registered ImageConsumer objects is in the InputStreamImageSource class. The URLImageSource class itself has four public constructors and one protected method — getDecoder():

```
public URLImageSource(URL u)
public URLImageSource(String href) throws MalformedURLException
public URLImageSource(URLConnection uc)
```

```
public URLImageSource(URL u, URLConnection uc)
protected ImageDecoder getDecoder()
```

The constructors perform some security checks on the host from which the image is being downloaded. (Remember, applets generally aren't allowed to connect to arbitrary hosts.)

The getDecoder() method reads the content type from the URLConnection and then tries to find and return the appropriate sun.awt.image.ImageDecoder object for that content type.

InputStreamImageSource

The InputStreamImageSource class extends java.lang.Object, but implements the java.awt.image.ImageProducer interface. Therefore, it has the following five methods:

```
public void addConsumer(ImageConsumer ic)
public synchronized boolean isConsumer(ImageConsumer ic)
public synchronized void removeConsumer(ImageConsumer ic)
public void startProduction(ImageConsumer ic)
public void requestTopDownLeftRightResend(ImageConsumer ic)
```

It also has several protected methods and one public method, doFetch():

```
protected abstract ImageDecoder getDecoder();
protected ImageDecoder decoderForType(InputStream is, String type)
protected ImageDecoder getDecoder(InputStream is)
public void doFetch()
```

The doFetch() method tells the InputStreamImageSource to begin loading data from its InputStream. However, the image data, which can be in any of several formats, must first be converted to Java's internal image format, essentially an uncompressed array of bytes with a 24-bit RGB color model. Therefore, the task of actually reading the bytes and translating them into Java's internal format is delegated to a decoder class. The doFetch() method invokes the protected getDecoder() method to choose the right decoder based on the MIME type of the image.

The ImageDecoder class

The getDecoder() method returns an instance of the abstract class sun.awt.image.ImageDecoder. The ImageDecoder class has four methods:

```
public ImageDecoder(InputStreamImageSource src, InputStream is)
```

```
    public abstract boolean catchupConsumer(InputStreamImageSource src,
ImageConsumer ic)
    public abstract void produceImage() throws IOException, ImageFormatException
    public synchronized void close()
```

The abstract methods catchupConsumer() and produceImage() are implemented in concrete subclasses for each specific image type. Currently, there are three concrete subclasses of ImageDecoder: GifImageDecoder, JPEGImageDecoder, and XbmImageDecoder. The URLImageSource calls the decoder object's produceImage() method to read the pixels and convert them into a Java format image.

To sum up, the main application constructs a URL object u, then calls u.getContent(). Next, u.getContent() calls u.openConnection() to get a URLConnection object uc. Then it calls uc.getContent(). The uc.getContent() method constructs a new URLImageSource object, uis, that reads from uc's InputStream. URLImageSource is a subclass of InputStreamImageSource. The object uis is passed back up the call chain to the original caller, which interprets it not as the class it is (URLImageSource) but rather as an instance of the ImageProducer interface.

The main application normally passes the ImageProducer — that is, the URLImageSource — to a createImage() method like the one in java.awt. Component. This method invokes the ImageProducer methods in URLImageSource to create a java.awt.Image object. The first time one of the ImageProducer methods is called, the URLImageSource creates an ImageDecoder for the MIME subtype. The ImageDecoder reads the raw bytes from the connection. As the data is read, the ImageDecoder translates it into the java.awt.Image format. This data is stored in the URLImageSource object, so it's available later without having to download it again.

PROTOCOL HANDLERS

Protocol handlers allow you to retrieve raw data from different URLs without concerning yourself excessively about the protocols used to retrieve the data. You just construct a conforming URL and then call openConnection(), openStream(), or getContent(); and the protocol handler provides you with the requested data. The protocol handler deals with any header that may be present — for example, the MIME header in an HTTP response — and only presents you with the actual data.

There is no java.net.ProtocolHandler class. Protocol handlers are normally divided into two main classes. A Handler class extends java.net. URL StreamHandler and parses the URL. Its openConnection() method is used to return the right subclass of java.net.URLConnection to handle the actual interaction with the server.

The sun.net.www.protocol package contains all of the JDK's protocol handlers. In the JDK, when you construct a new URL object like http://www. amazon.com/, the runtime looks for a URLStreamHandler object that can handle the protocol part of the URL, in this case HTTP. Other possible protocols include file, FTP, gopher, mailto, telnet, and news.

If a URLStreamHandlerFactory has been set, with the static URL. setURLStreamHandlerFactory() method, then the runtime first asks it to find an appropriate subclass of URLStreamHandler. By default, applets and applications tend not to have URLStreamHandlerFactories. If the URLStreamHandlerFactory does not exist or if Java is unable to find a URLStreamHandler for the requested protocol, then Java tries to instantiate a class named sun.net.www.protocol.http.Handler. The last sub-package name varies according to the protocol. For example, if you were instantiating a gopher URL, then Java would try to instantiate sun.net.www.protocol.gopher.Handler.

This is one of the very few instances in the JDK where classes in different packages share the same names. There are ten different classes named Handler in JDK 1.1, sun.net.www.protocol.appletresource.Handler, sun.net. www.protocol.doc.Handler, sun.net.www.protocol.file.Handler, sun.net.www. protocol.ftp.Handler, sun.net.www.protocol.gopher.Handler, sun.net.www. protocol.http.Handler, sun.net.www.protocol.mailto.Handler, sun.net.www. protocol.netdoc.Handler, sun.net.www.protocol.systemresource.Handler, and sun.net.www.protocol.verbatim.Handler. Using fully qualified names is highly recommended in these cases. However, in the interests of brevity, I'll often write just the subpackage before the class name in the following sections, for example mailto.Handler instead of sun.net.www.protocol. mailto.Handler.

The URLStreamHandler class's primary responsibility is to return the right kind of URLConnection object to handle the actual connection. The URLConnection object actually interacts with the remote server to provide data to the client. When you call a URL's openConnection(), openStream(), or getContent() method, the URLStreamHandler passes the request to the URLConnection.

Sun includes ten protocol handlers in the JDK 1.1. All major protocols except telnet are available, plus a few minor ones besides. This is a substantial improvement over the JDK 1.0 that supported only file and HTTP.

appletresource

Secret

Appletresource is a custom protocol used to load resource files into applets. Appletresource URLs have the following form:

```
appletresource:/base/+/member
```

Everything between the colon or the colon-slash and the /+/ is the *base*. Everything after /+/ is the *member*. The AppletResourceConnection() constructor splits these apart and stores them in private String fields called base and member, naturally enough. It also stores base+member in a new URL field called cachedURL.

Sun has warned that this representation may change between Java 1.1 and Java 1.1.1. They obviously have misgivings about this format. For now, you should not create appletresource URLs directly. Instead, you should retrieve resources by calling the getResource() method of java.lang.Class.

The appletresource.Handler class

The sun.net.www.protocol.appletresource.Handler class is a very simple subclass of URLStreamHandler with a single method, openConnection().

```
public URLConnection openConnection(URL u) throws IOException
```

This method simply passes the URL u to the AppletResourceConnection constructor and then returns the new AppletResourceConnection object. If the AppletResourceConnection() constructor throws any IOExceptions, this method passes them on. However, it does not create any new exceptions of its own.

The AppletResourceConnection class

The AppletResourceConnection class's state is defined primarily by four private fields:

```
private Object resource
private String base
```

```
private String member
private URL cachedURL
```

The constructor is protected. This isn't a big deal because you'd normally want to instantiate this class only through the appletresource.Handler class anyway.

```
protected AppletResourceConnection(URL u) throws MalformedURLException,
IOException
```

There are also three public methods:

```
public void connect() throws IOException
public Object getContent() throws IOException
public InputStream getInputStream() throws IOException
```

The connect() method sets the resource field to AppletResourceLoader. getLocalResource(cachedURL) (which may be null). This is a little different from most protocol handlers, where an InputStream field is is set to the InputStream from a file or network connection. The resource field will most likely be an AudioClip, an InputStream, or an ImageProducer.

The getContent() method calls connect() if you're not already connected. Then it returns the resource field.

The getInputStream() method, on the other hand, also calls connect if not already connected. However, it returns the resource field only if it's an instance of InputStream. Otherwise, it returns the resource at the cached URL as a stream.

> **Note**
> This class is still a little unfinished in Java 1.1. It includes some private debug methods and fields that probably should have been deleted before the final release version.

doc

> **Secret**
> Doc is a custom protocol used for HotJava's documentation. Doc URLs look like this:

```
doc:/lib/hotjava/whats-hot.html
```

When HotJava encounters a doc URL, it first tries to find the requested document on the local hard drive. If it can't find the file there, then it tries to find it in the equivalent location at http://java.sun.com/HotJava/ or at whatever URL the system property doc.url indicates. Thus, given the example above, it would try to load

```
http://java.sun.com/HotJava/lib/hotjava/whats-hot.html
```

The sun.net.www.protocol.doc package has just two classes, Handler and DocURLConnection. Between the two of them, they provide a convenient means to load help files and other documentation.

The doc.Handler class

The doc.Handler class has only one public method, openConnection():

```
public synchronized URLConnection openConnection(URL u) throws IOException
```

This method first tries to find the requested document in the install directory. The location of the install directory is normally given by the System property "hotjava.home." If that property is not set, then it makes a reasonable guess such as "/usr/local/hotjava" or "C:\hotjava." If the document is found in the install directory, then openConnection() returns a new DocURLConnection for the requested document, or throws an IOException if that fails.

If the necessary document cannot be located in the install directory, or perhaps if the install directory itself can't be located, then openConnection() next tries to find the document on the Internet. If the System property "doc.url" is set, then Java tries to find the document there. Otherwise, it looks at http://java.sun.com/HotJava/. If the document is found on the Web, then openConnection() returns a URLConnection, normally an HttpURL Connection, pointing to the requested document.

If none of this effort succeeds in finding the document, then an IOException is thrown.

The DocURLConnection class

Secret

The DocURLConnection class is used to read Java documentation. It has two public methods — connect() and getInputStream() — and two non-public fields:

```
InputStream is;
static String installDirectory;
```

The constructor is non-public, so you can't call it directly. It's invoked only by the doc.Handler class in the same package:

```
DocURLConnection(URL u)
```

The primary method in this class is connect(). Because documentation is expected to be present on the local hard drive, there's no actual connection to be made. Instead, this method looks for the file referenced by the file part of the URL u (that is, u.getFile) in the installation directory. It uses the MimeTable to determine the content-type of the file and the File.length() method to get the Content-length of the file. These are placed in a MessageHeader object for this connection.

```
public void connect() throws IOException
```

Next, the file is opened in a new FileInputStream. This is chained to a BufferedInputStream that is assigned to the InputStream field, is. If anything goes wrong, such as the file not being found, an IOException is thrown.

To actually read data from this connection, you normally use the getInputStream method. This merely calls connect() and then returns the is field. Because it calls connect(), this method can also throw an IOException.

```
public synchronized InputStream getInputStream()
```

file

The sun.net.www.protocol.file package contains a relatively simple protocol handler for file URLs — that is, URLs that point to a file on the local hard drive, such as:

```
file:///HD/Java/course/index.html
```

However, in the early days of the Web, file URLs were also used to refer to files on remote FTP sites like this:

```
file://sunsite.unc.edu/pub/languages/java/javafaq/examples.tar.gz
```

For the most part, this usage has died out and been replaced with FTP URLs. Nonetheless, the file protocol handler has to handle this case as well.

This protocol handler is made up of two classes: the expected sun.net. www.protocol.file.Handler and FileURLConnection classes, and a simple utility class, StringCompare.

The file.Handler class

As usual, the file.Handler class subclasses URLStreamHandler and has only a single method, an implementation of the abstract method openConnection() from the superclass:

```
public synchronized URLConnection openConnection(URL u) throws IOException
```

This method normally returns a sun.net.www.protocol. FileURLConnection object pointing to the file in question. However, because old file URLs may be FTP URLs in disguise, if openConnection() spots a file URL with a non-empty host part like sunsite.unc.edu, it rewrites the URL using the FTP protocol instead of the file protocol and passes the job to the FTP protocol handler by calling the openConnection() method of the new FTP URL. For example

```
URL ftpURL = new URL("ftp://" + fileURL.getHost() + fileURL.getFile());
return ftpURL.openConnection();
```

The actual code also handles ref parts of the URL, but you get the idea.

In the more normal case, where the file URL really does refer to a file on the local hard drive, then openConnection() returns a new FileURLConnection object. For example:

```
return new FileURLConnection(u);
```

The FileURLConnection class

The sun.net.www.protocol.FileURLConnection class has a single, non-public constructor, implements the abstract method connect(), and overrides getInputStream():

```
FileURLConnection(URL u)
public synchronized URLConnection connect(URL u)
public synchronized InputStream getInputStream()
```

Because the constructor has only package access, you can't instantiate this class directly. Instead, it's instantiated automatically the first time that you construct a URL with the file protocol.

The getInputStream() method calls connect() to open the connection and then returns an InputStream chained to the connection.

The primary method of this class, however, is connect(). This method must handle two distinct cases: one where the URL points to a file and one where it points to a directory. In the event that the file or directory doesn't exist, an IOException is thrown. It must fill the URLConnection's MessageHeader field

Because files don't normally have MIME headers, this method constructs a new one. It creates a new MessageHeader object. In that MessageHeader, it puts its best guess as to the file's MIME type, based on the filename. This comes from the MimeTable — for example

```
MessageHeader mh = new MessageHeader();
MimeEntry me = MimeTable.getDefaultTable().findByFileName(u.getFile());
if (me != null) mh.add("Content-type", me.getType());
```

If the URL points to a file and not a directory, the length of the file is placed in a Content-length header in the MIME header. Then a FileInputStream is opened from the file; a BufferedInputStream is chained to the FileInputStream; and the FileURLConnection's InputStream field is is set to this BufferedInputStream.

If the URL points to a directory, connect() sets the Content-type in the MessageHeader to "text/html." Then it creates a new StringBuffer filled with the alphabetically sorted contents of the directory and some HTML tags. Each filename is formatted as a clickable link. A StringBufferInputStream is constructed from this StringBuffer and the InputStream field, is, is set to that.

Note

In Java 1.0, this class looked for a file called index.html in the directory when faced with a directory URL and returned its contents. If no index file was found, an IOException was thrown.

Finally, the boolean field connected is set to true.

This class performs no security checks of its own. However, if you call it from an applet — that is, if you try to create a file URL from an applet — the IO classes will eventually complain, and you'll get a SecurityException.

The StringCompare class

Secret

The sun.net.www.protocol.File.StringCompare class is a short utility class that implements the sun.misc.Compare interface. Thus, it has the single method doCompare():

```
public int doCompare(Object o1, Object o2)
```

This method compares strings lexicographically with the String. compareTo() method, but is case-insensitive. It returns You pass it to the sun.misc.Sort class's quicksort() method to sort an array of strings. The file protocol handler uses it to sort directory listings.

FTP

The FTP protocol handler handles standard, ordinary, anonymous FTP URLs like

```
ftp://ftp.amug.org/
```

It cannot yet handle uploads or non-anonymous FTP URLs like

```
ftp://username:password@ftp.amug.org/
```

The FTP protocol handler is composed of the usual Handler and Ftp URLConnection classes plus one non-public helper class, FtpDirectoryThread, a subclass of java.lang.Thread used to read the contents of a directory. The sun.net.ftp.FtpClient class discussed in Chapter 15 handles the actual communication with the FTP server. Although you can consider it a part of the FTP protocol handler, it can also be used independently.

The ftp.Handler class

The sun.net.www.protocol.ftp.Handler class is the expected subclass of URLStreamHandler. It has the required openConnection() method and nothing more. A little unusually, this method is protected:

```
protected URLConnection openConnection(URL u)
```

This method normally returns a new FtpURLConnection object. However, if a proxy server is being used, then it returns an HttpURL Connection object instead. (Proxy servers are themselves HTTP servers.)

The FtpURLConnection class

An FtpURLConnection object is defined by two non-public fields, an InputStream is and an FtpClient object ftp:

```
InputStream is
FtpClient ftp
```

The constructor is trivial and doesn't really do much. It merely calls the matching superclass constructor.

```
public FtpURLConnection(URL uRL)
```

The real meat is in the connect() method:

```
public synchronized void connect() throws IOException
```

This method constructs a new FtpClient object for the FTP field and calls its login() method to connect. However, it does not actually retrieve the file.

The getInputStream() method connects, if not already connected, and retrieves the file from the FtpClient in binary mode. This method takes some reasonable guesses about the MIME type of the file and calculates its content length. These values are placed in the connections properties list. The InputStream that is returned contains the data in the file.

```
public InputStream getInputStream() throws IOException
```

The FtpDirectoryThread class

The sun.net.www.protocol.ftp.FtpDirectoryThread class is a subclass of java.lang.Thread. The FtpURLConnection spawns one of these threads when it needs to read the contents of an FTP directory. While running, this thread reads the directory and returns a stream of data containing an HTML-formatted version of the directory listing, not the raw ASCII list.

gopher

The gopher protocol handler is composed of the usual Handler and GopherURLConnection classes as well as the GopherClient and GopherInputStream classes. It handles standard gopher URLs like

```
gopher://spinaltap.micro.umn.edu:70/11/computer/prices/bookstore
```

The gopher.Handler class

The sun.net.www.protocol.gopher.Handler class is the expected subclass of URLStreamHandler. It has the required openConnection() method and nothing more.

```
public URLConnection openConnection(URL u)
```

This method normally returns a new GopherURLConnection object. However, if a proxy server is being used, then it returns an HttpURLConnection object instead. The proxy server makes the connection to the gopher server, and this class makes an HTTP connection to the proxy server.

The GopherURLConnection class

GopherURLConnection is a non-public subclass of sun.net.www. URLConnection. It doesn't do very much. Mostly it just passes requests to the GopherClient class.

GopherURLConnection has one constructor and two public methods:

```
GopherURLConnection(URL u)
public void connect()
public InputStream getInputStream()
```

The constructor is non-public, so this class is only instantiated from within its own package, generally by the gopher.Handler class. The constructor just passes the URL u to the superclass constructor.

The connect() method is a do-nothing method with an empty body — that is,

```
public void connect() {};
```

It does not actually connect to the server.

The getInputStream() method is the only one in this class that does much of anything. It creates a new GopherClient object gc connected to the URL u (from the constructor) and calls gc.openStream(). Then it returns that InputStream. All the work of actually interacting with the gopher server is delegated to the GopherClient class, so that's where I'll turn my attention next.

The GopherClient class

The GopherClient class is a subclass of sun.net.NetworkClient that implements java.lang.Runnable. It is to the gopher protocol as the FtpClient class is to the FTP protocol or as NntpClient is to the NNTP protocol. In other words, it's the standard means for interacting with a gopher server in Java.

However, unlike those clients, this class cannot stand on its own outside the gopher protocol handler, primarily because the constructor isn't public:

```
GopherClient(sun.net.www.URLConnection uc)
```

It's not clear why this class doesn't have a public constructor and isn't in its own separate sun.net.gopher package as FtpClient, NntpClient, HttpClient, and SmtpClient all are. Perhaps this just reflects the declining significance of the gopher protocol.

In addition to the fields it inherits from NetworkClient, GopherClient has three public static fields:

```
public static boolean useGopherProxy;
public static String gopherProxyHost;
public static int gopherProxyPort;
```

These obviously determine which proxy server is used and whether one is used at all. These are set when the class is loaded from the corresponding System properties gopherProxySet, gopherProxyHost, and gopherProxyPort.

There are two primary methods in this class. The first is the non-public method openStream():

```
InputStream openStream(URL u)
```

This actually returns a GopherInputStream. Furthermore, it constructs a MIME header for the gopher data. Finally, it starts a new thread using the GopherClient itself as the seed.

The second important method in this class is run(). The GopherClient class implements Runnable so it has to have a public run() method.

```
public void run()
```

The run() method makes the connection to the server and downloads the requested data. If the particular URL points to a directory listing or a search engine, run() reformats the data into HTML before returning.

The GopherInputStream class

GopherInputStream is a non-public subclass of java.io.FilterInputStream. It's returned by the openStream() method of the GopherClient class. The unique feature of this class is that it stores the NetworkClient object that created it in a field called parent — that is,

```
NetworkClient parent;
```

This field is set by the non-public GopherInputStream() constructor:

```
GopherInputStream(NetworkClient parent, InputStream is)
```

Because a GopherInputStream has a reference to the object that created it, it can call back to that object. In particular, the other method in this class, close(), uses the parent field to close the GopherClient object when the InputStream is closed.

```
public void close()
```

Of course, because GopherInputStream itself isn't public, you don't normally need to concern yourself with this. It takes place mostly behind the scenes.

HTTP

Secret

The HTTP protocol handler handles standard Web connections using the HttpClient class. It is by far the most commonly invoked protocol handler. It can handle a fairly broad spectrum of HTTP URLs. This protocol handler has the usual URLStreamHandler and URLConnection subclasses, as well as a couple of simple helper classes to handle authentication.

The http.Handler class

The sun.net.www.protocol.http.Handler class is a simple subclass of URLStreamHandler that understands proxy servers. It has two protected fields, proxy and proxyPort, which are set by the constructors:

```
protected String proxy;
protected int proxyPort;
public Handler()
public Handler(String proxy, int proxyPort)
```

The noargs constructor sets proxy to null and proxyPort to -1. The second constructor sets them to the specified values.

The remaining method is the required openConnection() method:

```
protected URLConnection openConnection(URL u) throws IOException
```

This method returns a new HttpURLConnection object pointing to the specified URL.

The HttpURLConnection class

The sun.net.www.protocol.http.HttpURLConnection is a subclass of java.net.HttpURLConnection. The java.net.HttpURLConnection is a subclass of java.net.URLConnection. This class handles the interaction with an HTTP server using an HttpClient object that is stored in a protected field called http. This class has two constructors — one public and one protected:

```
protected HttpURLConnection(URL u, Handler handler) throws IOException
public HttpURLConnection(URL u, String proxy, int proxyPort)
```

It also has two protected methods that return a new HttpClient object. Both just call the equivalent constructor.

```
protected HttpClient getNewClient(URL u) throws IOException
    protected HttpClient getProxiedClient(URL u, String proxy, int proxyPort)
throws IOException
```

Like all non-abstract URLConnection subclasses, this class must implement connect():

```
public void connect() throws IOException
```

If not already connected, this method creates a new HttpClient object for the use of this object. The boolean field connected is then set to true.

As usual, communication takes place through the getOutputStream() and getInputStream() methods:

```
public synchronized InputStream getInputStream() throws IOException
    public synchronized OutputStream getOutputStream() throws IOException
```

Assuming output to this URL is allowed, this method creates a new ByteArrayOutputStream stored in a field called poster. This stream is returned. If output is not allowed, an exception is thrown.

Assuming input from this URL is allowed, the first time that this method is called, it sends a MessageHeader request to the server. The server then responds with a MIME header and the response data. The server's MimeHeader response is read and parsed, and the actual response data is returned as an InputStream. Subsequent calls to getInputStream() return this same InputStream. If input is not allowed, an exception is thrown.

This method also handles a number of relatively common special cases.

If the server responds with a redirect message, this method transparently redirects the request to the new server. There is a maximum number of redirects allowed, five by default, but only one for applets controlled by the AppletSecurityManager.

If the server responds with a request for authentication, Java attempts to authenticate the user using the AuthenticationInfo class. It caches previous authentications, so you shouldn't need to reauthenticate every page of a password-protected site. The static setDefaultAuthenticator() method is used to determine the object that handles the authentication.

```
public static void setDefaultAuthenticator(HttpAuthenticator ha)
```

If the server responds with a HEAD or TRACE method, Java produces an EmptyInputStream, because there won't be any actual response data — only a header.

The disconnect() method closes the connection and performs some cleanup.

```
public synchronized void disconnect()
```

The usingProxy() method returns true if a proxy server is being used and false if it isn't:

```
public boolean usingProxy()
```

HttpURLConnection overrides the getHeaderField() and getHeaderFieldKey() methods from the superclass. Each of these methods calls getInputStream to make sure the MessageHeader is filled and then returns the requested item from the server's response MIME header.

```
public String getHeaderField(String name)
public String getHeaderField(int n)
public String getHeaderFieldKey(int n)
```

HttpURLConnection also overrides the setRequestProperty() and getRequestProperty() methods. These enable you to change or access the MIME fields in the MessageHeader that the client sends to the server as part of the request.

```
public void setRequestProperty(String string1, String string2)
public String getRequestProperty(String string)
```

Finally, there's a finalize method. It's not clear why, because it has a completely empty body:

```
public void finalize() {};
```

The EmptyInputStream class

The EmptyInputStream class is a subclass of InputStream that's used when a server responds to a TRACE or HEAD response that requires only a MIME header. It has only two very simple public methods:

```
public int available(){ return 0;}
public int read() { return -1;}
```

The available() method always returns 0 because there will never be any bytes available from an EmptyInputStream. The read() method returns -1, indicating the end of the data.

The AuthenticationInfo class

The AuthenticationInfo class is a wrapper for the data needed to authenticate a user to an HTTP server. This class holds two static Hashtables that store the data. Each AuthenticationInfo object has three strings and an int in non-public fields:

```
String host
int port
String realm
String auth
```

The host field holds the hostname of the server. The port field stores the port number. The realm field holds the name of the realm on the server for which this authentication info is valid. Finally, the auth String holds the username and password in the appropriate format for this host, port, and realm.

These fields are normally set via one of several constructors:

```
public AuthenticationInfo(URL u, String realm, String auth)
public AuthenticationInfo(URL u, String auth)
public AuthenticationInfo(String host, int port, String realm)
public AuthenticationInfo(String host, int port, String realm, String auth)
```

Several static methods store, retrieve, and remove particular AuthenticationInfo objects from the Hashtables:

```
public static void cacheInfo(AuthenticationInfo ai)
public static void cacheInfo(AuthenticationInfo ai, URL u)
public static void uncacheInfo(AuthenticationInfo ai)
public static void uncacheInfo(AuthenticationInfo ai, URL u)
public static AuthenticationInfo getAuth(URL u)
```

The only unique instance method in this class is getAuthString(). This returns the authentication string you might need to send to a Web server:

```
public String getAuthString()
```

Finally, Authentication overrides several methods from java.lang.Object. All three behave pretty much as you would expect:

```
public int hashCode()
public boolean equals(Object o)
public String toString()
```

The HttpAuthenticator interface

The HttpAuthenticator interface declares two methods:

```
public abstract boolean schemeSupported(String scheme);
public abstract String authString(URL u, String realm, String s);
```

The schemeSupported() method returns true if the specified scheme is supported and false if it isn't. Currently the only scheme Java supports is Basic authentication.

The authString() method returns the authentication string necessary for the given URL and realm.

mailto

Although mailto URLs are quite common, the mailto protocol handler is a little out of the ordinary. While most protocol handlers produce input streams, the mailto protocol handler must produce an output stream.

The mailto protocol handler (sun.net.www.protocol.mailto.Handler) handles classic mailto URLs like

```
mailto:elharo@sunsite.unc.edu
```

It cannot handle Netscape's extended mailto URL syntax that allows the specification of a subject line, like

```
action="mailto:santa@northpole.org?subject=Christmas list"
```

The mailto.Handler class

The public sun.net.www.protocol.mailto.Handler class has two methods:

```
public synchronized URLConnection openConnection(URL u)
public void parseURL(URL u, String spec, int start, int limit)
```

The openConnection() method returns a new MailToURLConnection to the URL u. It's so simple that it doesn't even throw any exceptions. However, the parseURL() method is a little more interesting.

Among other responsibilities, URLStreamHandlers need to parse URLs. The public sun.net.www.protocol.mailto.Handler class is the only protocol handler discussed here that can't just rely on the standard parsing routines that assume that everything looks like an HTTP URL. However, mailto URLs don't look like ordinary HTTP URLs, so this class has to override parseURL().

The parseURL() method converts the string spec into the URL object u by parsing its characters between start and limit. The protocol and port are copied from u, while the host is set to the empty string ("") and the file part of the URL is set to spec.substring(start, limit). In this case, the file part of the URL corresponds to the e-mail address.

The MailToURLConnection class

The MailToURLConnection class is a subclass of sun.net.www. URLConnection that provides input and output streams for sending e-mail. It has a non-public constructor, and is thus normally only instantiated by the mailto.Handler class.

```
MailToURLConnection(URL u)
```

The constructor calls the matching superclass constructor (super(u)) and creates a new MessageHeader for this object's properties with single entry, "Content-type: text/html."

Because MailToURLConnection subclasses URLConnection, it must implement connect, and it does. However, this connect method, like the GopherURLConnection connect() method, is completely empty — that is,

```
public void connect() throws IOException {};
```

Instead, this class relies on two non-public fields, the InputStream is and the OutputStream os, and two methods that initialize and return them, getOutputStream() and getInputStream().

```
InputStream is;
OutputStream os;
public synchronized OutputStream getOutputStream() throws IOException
public synchronized InputStream getInputStream() throws IOException
```

Both fields are initially null. You can call either getInputStream() or getOutputStream(), but you cannot call both on the same object. If you call getOutputStream(), calls to getInputStream() will return null. If you call getInputStream(), calls to getOutputStream() throw an IOException.

The getOutputStream() method constructs a new sun.net.SmtpClient object sc, sets its from and to fields, and sets os to sc.startMessage(). Finally, it returns os.

The to address is read from the URL. The from address is taken from the system property "user.fromaddr" or, if that fails, from the system property "user.name" at the system property "mail.host." If that fails, the from address is the system property "user.name" at InetAddress. getLocalHost().getHostName(), and if that fails the from address is simply the empty string "".

Subsequent calls to getOutputStream() simply return os.

The getInputStream() method returns an InputStream that contains a Web page. This Web page contains the sun.hotjava.applets. MailDocumentApplet. This package is not included in the JDK, but it is in HotJava. The fact that JDK method depends on something outside the JDK is a bit of an oversight on Sun's part.

Subsequent calls to getInputStream() return this same InputStream.

netdoc

Secret

The netdoc protocol handler is used by HotJava to show documentation files to the user. It doesn't really use any new network protocols. Rather, it just picks the most appropriate existing protocol. Therefore, this is the only protocol handler in the JDK that does not have its own subclass of URLConnection. It has only a Handler class, sun.net.www.protocol.netdoc. Handler.

In some sense, these are like relative URLs in <A HREF> tags. However, the base URL by which the final URL is calculated is read from the System property "doc.url."

The netdoc.Handler class

The netdoc.Handler class has a single method, openConnection():

```
public synchronized URLConnection openConnection(URL u) throws IOException
```

It also has one static non-public field, the URL object base:

```
static URL base;
```

The base is the location to which all other documentation URLs are relative. For example, a typical base URL might be http://www.javasoft. com/HotJava/. Then netdoc:/bookmarks/adding.html would really refer to the file at http://www.javasoft.com/HotJava/bookmarks/adding.html.

The first time that the openConnection() method is called, it checks the System property doc.url to find out what is the base location for the documentation. Then it forms a new URL object u2, pointing to the right file at the base. Next, it calls u2's openConnection method() and returns the resulting URLConnection object. The subclass of URLConnection returned is dependent upon the base. If the base URL is an HTTP URL, then the returned URLConnection will be an HttpURLConnection; if the base URL is an FTP URL, then the returned connection will be an FtpURLConnection, and so on.

The System property "newdoc.localonly" controls whether or not the browser is allowed to make a network connection to get the documentation. For example, if you're working off line, you may not want to dial out just to get a help file. Therefore, if "newdoc.localonly" is true, then openConnection() ignores the base field and instead tries to load the file from a platform-dependent location on the local disk via a file URL and the file protocol handler. On UNIX systems, it tries to load from the user's home directory (~).

If the connection to the documentation file can't be opened, then an IOException is thrown.

systemresource

Systemresource URLs are returned by the static ClassLoader. getSystemResource() method. They are similar to applet resources but refer to resources in the local CLASSPATH.

The systemresource.Handler class

The sun.net.www.protocol.systemresource.Handler class is a very simple subclass of URLStreamHandler with a single method, openConnection():

```
public URLConnection openConnection(URL u) throws IOException
```

This method simply passes the URL u to the SystemResourceConnection() constructor and then returns the new SystemResourceConnection object. If the SystemResourceConnection() constructor throws any IOExceptions, then this method passes them on. However, it does not create any new exceptions of its own.

The SystemResourceConnection class

A SystemResourceConnection object's state is defined by two private fields:

```
private Object resource;
private SystemResourceManager manager;
```

The Object field resource is the actual resource to which this URL Connection is connected. The manager field is an instance of the sun.net. www.protocol. systemresource.SystemResourceManager class. This class has a number of private and non-public methods the SystemResource Connection class calls on to find system resources. These include methods to read data from zip files. However, none of these methods is public.

The SystemResourceConnection() constructor is, as usual, non-public. It's normally called only by the systemresource.Handler class.

```
SystemResourceConnection(URL u) throws MalformedURLException, IOException
```

The connect() method calls the manager.getLocalResource() method and sets the resource field to the result (which may be null).

```
public void connect() throws IOException
```

The getContent() method calls connect() if not already connected and returns the resource field.

```
public Object getContent() throws IOException
```

The getInputStream() method calls connect() if not already connected. Then, if resource is some sort of InputStream, it returns that. Otherwise, it returns manager.getLocalResourceStream().

This class is still a little unfinished in Java 1.1. It includes some private debug methods and fields that probably should have been deleted before the final release version. Furthermore, it's unclear why SystemResourceManager was made a separate class, because its methods could easily have been rolled into the SystemResourceConnection class.

The ParseSystemURL class

The ParseSystemURL is a non-public class that breaks a systemresource URL into its constituent pieces. First, a ParseSystemURL object is constructed with this constructor:

```
public ParseSystemURL(URL u)
```

Then various methods are used to determine boolean information about the URL:

```
public boolean isValid()
public boolean isFile()
public boolean isZip()
public String getBase()
public String getMember()
```

Because the ParseSystemURL class itself is non-public, you're unlikely to use it directly. The SystemResourceManager class uses it internally.

verbatim

Verbatim is a non-standard protocol used when you want to retrieve some data but don't have a content handler for that MIME type. Verbatim URLs always return a MIME type of text/plain so the sun.net.www.content.text. plain content handler will handle them.

Verbatim URLs look like standard URLs to which the string "verbatim:" has been prepended. For example,

```
verbatim:http://altavista.digital.com/
verbatim:ftp://ftp.javasoft.com/
```

The URL that follows verbatim: is called the *sub URL*.

The verbatim.Handler class

As usual the sun.net.www.protocol.verbatim.Handler class subclasses URLStreamHandler and has only a single method, an implementation of the abstract method openConnection() from the superclass:

```
public URLConnection openConnection(URL u) throws IOException
```

This method constructs and returns a new sun.net.www.protocol. VerbatimConnection object. If there's a problem, it throws an IOException.

The VerbatimConnection class

The VerbatimConnection class is the usual subclass of URLConnection. However, instead of merely implementing connect(), it overrides almost every method in java.net.URLConnection. The only unique method is the constructor:

```
protected VerbatimConnection(URL u) throws MalformedURLException,
IOException
```

Because the constructor is protected, it can be instantiated only from subclasses. This class has a single non-public field called sub of type URLConnection. This holds the actual connection to the server. When a VerbatimConnection object is constructed, the "verbatim:" string is stripped off the front of the URL to get the sub-URL, and the sub-URL's openConnection() method is called to set the sub field. All but three of the overridden methods just call the corresponding methods of the sub field. These methods are as follows:

```
public void connect() throws IOException
public String getHeaderFieldKey(int i)
public Object getContent() throws IOException
public InputStream getInputStream() throws IOException
public OutputStream getOutputStream() throws IOException
public String toString()
public void setDoInput(boolean flag)
public boolean getDoInput()
public void setDoOutput(boolean flag)
public boolean getDoOutput()
public void setAllowUserInteraction(boolean flag)
public boolean getAllowUserInteraction()
public void setUseCaches(boolean flag)
```

```
public boolean getUseCaches()
public void setIfModifiedSince(long i)
public long getIfModifiedSince()
public void setRequestProperty(String string1, String string2)
public String getRequestProperty(String string)
```

Each of these methods merely calls the corresponding method of the sub field with the same arguments. For example, setIfModifiedSince(long i) just calls sub.setIfModifiedSince(i).

The only methods that behave differently in a VerbatimConnection than in the sub connection are the ones that can return the Content-type header. The obvious one is getContentType():

```
public String getContentType()
```

This always returns "text/plain" regardless of the MIME type returned by the server.

The polymorphic getHeaderField() method is also overridden to make sure that it returns "text/plain" for the content type. Before calling sub.getHeaderField(), each getHeaderField() method checks to see if it's being asked to get the "content-type" header field. (The check is case-insensitive.) If it is, it calls getContentType() so "text/plain" is returned. Otherwise, sub.getHeaderField() is returned.

```
public String getHeaderField(String name)
public String getHeaderField(int n)
```

SUMMARY

In this chapter you learn the following:

- MIME is an acronym for "Multipurpose Internet Mail Extensions." It's an Internet standard defined in RFCs 2045 through 2049. It has many purposes, including the encoding of binary data in ASCII text and attaching files to e-mail messages. However, this chapter is primarily concerned with the MIME header format. MIME headers are a series of lines of ASCII text. Each line has a keyword, followed by a colon and a space, followed by the value attached to the keyword. These headers are used in SMTP e-mail, Usenet news, and HTTP data transfer.

- The sun.net.www.MessageHeader class represents a MIME header.

- The sun.net.www.HeaderParser class splits a MIME header into its different fields by key and value.

- The MimeEntry class represents a MIME type and subtype like "text/plain" or "image/gif." A MimeEntry object encapsulates a MIME type and subtype, the file extensions mapped to that type and subtype, and the proper means of viewing data of that type.

- The sun.net.www.MimeTable class contains a list of all the different MIME types understood by the Java runtime. This class is the primary implementation of the java.net.FileNameMap interface that allows you to associate a filename extension like ".c" with a MIME type like "text/plain." No more than one of these objects exists in any given Java runtime, and this single instance of the class is retrieved with the MimeTable.getDefaultMimeTable() method.

- The sun.net.www.MeteredStream class is a subclass of java.io. FilterInputStream that tracks the amount of data expected to be read and the amount of data already read from the stream.

- The sun.net.www.URLConnection class is an abstract subclass of java. net.URLConnection that's specialized to handle connections with MIME headers.

- The sun.net.www.http package contains an HttpClient class and several support classes that handle basic HTTP operations, including advanced features like PUT and HTTP Keep-Alive.

- The sun.net.www.httpd package contains a single class, BasicHttpServer. This class is too dysfunctional for serious use.

- When no URLStreamHandlerFactory is installed, Java searches for URLStreamHandlers to handle specific protocols by trying to instantiate a class named Handler in the sun.net.www.protocol.*protocol_name* package. The JDK 1.1 includes protocol handlers for the appletresource, doc, file, FTP, gopher, HTTP, mailto, netdoc, systemresource, and verbatim protocols.

- When no ContentHandlerFactory is installed, Java searches for ContentHandlers to handle specific MIME types by trying to instantiate a class named sun.net.www.content.*type.subtype*. The JDK 1.1 includes content handlers for the text/generic, text/plain, image/gif, image/jpeg, and image/x-xbitmap content types.

III

PLATFORM-
DEPENDENT
JAVA

CHARACTER CONVERSION WITH SUN.IO

## 18

*A*lthough Java theoretically supports Unicode, in practice Unicode support is in its infancy, even in Java 1.1. (In Java 1.0 Unicode support was embryonic.) Using non-ISO Latin 1 characters in source code requires \u escapes, and many Java classes responsible for output, such as PrintStream, chop off the high-order bytes of all characters that they output. Even classes that do support Unicode are dependent on the fonts available on the host system. Few computers are prepared to display text written in English, Chinese, Hebrew, and Urdu.

Even those computers that can display text written in these languages often don't use Unicode to do it. Most commonly they use some 8-bit character set and change the font to present different glyphs.

Secret

The sun.io.ByteToCharConverter class is an abstract base class for subclasses that convert character data in an encoding used on the local system into Unicode characters. The sun.io. CharToByteConverter class is an abstract base class for subclasses that convert Unicode characters into the encoding used on the local system. The encoding used on the local system is sometimes referred to as *external encoding* (external to Java, that is).

This chapter is totally based on Java 1.1. There is nothing remotely like this available in Java 1.0. If you're still using Java 1.0, you should bypass this chapter until you upgrade.

Note

AVAILABLE CONVERSIONS

Secret

The sun.io package includes dozens of concrete subclasses of the abstract ByteToCharConverter and CharToByteConverter classes. Each subclass handles a specific conversion. For example, the ByteToCharMacIceland class converts from text written in the 1-byte Macintosh Icelandic character set to the 2-byte Unicode character set. The CharToByteMacIceland class converts from 2-byte Unicode to the 1-byte Macintosh Icelandic character set.

Table 18-1 lists all the conversions available in the sun.io package. The first column contains the name of the class that converts externally encoded bytes to Unicode chars. The second column contains the name of the class that converts Unicode chars to externally encoded bytes. The third column contains the name of the encoding. The fourth column lists the character sets that can be encoded with that external encoding.

Table 18-1

The classes in the sun.io package

ByteToChar classes	CharToByte classes	Name	Character Set
ByteToChar8859_1	CharToByte8859_1	8859_1	ISO 8859-1 (Latin-1) Danish, Dutch, English, Faroese, Finnish, Flemish, German, Hawaiian, Icelandic, Indonesian, Irish, Italian, Norwegian, Portuguese, Spanish, Swahili, Swedish
ByteToChar8859_2	CharToByte8859_2	8859_2	ISO 8859-2 (Latin Extended-A) When combined with Latin-1 this set will handle Afrikaans, Breton, Basque, Catalan, Croatian, Czech, Esperanto, Estonian, French, Frisian, Greenlandic, Hungarian, Latin, Latvian, Lithuanian, Maltese, Polish, Provençal, Rhaeto-Romanic, Romanian, Romany, Slavic, Slovenian, Sorbian, Turkish, Welsh, and many others.

(continued)

The classes in the sun.io package *(continued)*

ByteToChar classes	*CharToByte classes*	*Name*	*Character Set*
ByteToChar8859_3	CharToByte8859_3	8859_3	ISO 8859-3 (Latin Extended-B) Pinyin, Sami, Croatian, and a few others
ByteToChar8859_4	CharToByte8859_4	8859_4	ISO 8859-4 (Latin Extended-C)
ByteToChar8859_5	CharToByte8859_5	8859_5	ISO 8859-5 Latin/Cyrillic
ByteToChar8859_6	CharToByte8859_6	8859_6	ISO 8859-6 Latin/Arabic
ByteToChar8859_7	CharToByte8859_7	8859_7	ISO 8859-7 Latin/Greek
ByteToChar8859_8	CharToByte8859_8	8859_8	ISO 8859-8 Latin/Hebrew
ByteToChar8859_9	CharToByte8859_9	8859_9	ISO 8859-9 Latin/Turkish
ByteToCharBig5	CharToByteBig5	Big5	The Big 5 encoding for Chinese
ByteToChar CNS11643	CharToByte CNS11643	CNS11643	Chinese
ByteToCharCp037	CharToByteCp037	Cp037	EBCDIC American English
ByteToCharCp273	CharToByteCp273	Cp273	IBM273
ByteToCharCp277	CharToByteCp277	Cp277	EBCDIC Danish/Norwegian
ByteToCharCp278	CharToByteCp278	Cp278	EBCDIC Finnish/Swedish
ByteToCharCp280	CharToByteCp280	Cp280	EBCDIC Italian
ByteToCharCp284	CharToByteCp284	Cp284	EBCDIC Spanish
ByteToCharCp285	CharToByteCp285	Cp285	EBCDIC UK English
ByteToCharCp297	CharToByteCp297	Cp297	EBCDIC French
ByteToCharCp420	CharToByteCp420	Cp420	EBCDIC Arabic 1
ByteToCharCp424	CharToByteCp424	Cp424	EBCDIC Hebrew
ByteToCharCp437	CharToByteCp437	Cp437	The original DOS IBM PC character set, essentially ASCII with a few extra characters for drawing lines and boxes
ByteToCharCp500	CharToByteCp500	Cp500	EBCDIC Flemish/Romulsch
ByteToCharCp737	CharToByteCp737	Cp737	DOS Greek
ByteToCharCp775	CharToByteCp775	Cp775	DOS Baltic
ByteToCharCp850	CharToByteCp850	Cp850	DOS Latin-1
ByteToCharCp852	CharToByteCp852	Cp852	DOS Latin-2
ByteToCharCp855	CharToByteCp855	Cp855	DOS Cyrillic
ByteToCharCp856	CharToByteCp856	Cp856	IBM856
ByteToCharCp857	CharToByteCp857	Cp857	DOS Turkish
ByteToCharCp860	CharToByteCp860	Cp860	DOS Portuguese
ByteToCharCp861	CharToByteCp861	Cp861	DOS Icelandic
ByteToCharCp862	CharToByteCp862	Cp862	DOS Hebrew
ByteToCharCp863	CharToByteCp863	Cp863	DOS Canadian French
ByteToCharCp864	CharToByteCp864	Cp864	DOS Arabic
ByteToCharCp865	CharToByteCp865	Cp865	IBM865
ByteToCharCp866	CharToByteCp866	Cp866	IBM866
ByteToCharCp868	CharToByteCp868	Cp868	EBCDIC Arabic
ByteToCharCp869	CharToByteCp869	Cp869	DOS modern Greek

(continued)

Table 18-1

The classes in the sun.io package *(continued)*

ByteToChar classes	CharToByte classes	Name	Character Set
ByteToCharCp870	CharToByteCp870	Cp870	EBCDIC Serbian
ByteToCharCp871	CharToByteCp871	Cp871	EBCDIC Icelandic
ByteToCharCp874	CharToByteCp874	Cp874	Windows Thai
ByteToCharCp875	CharToByteCp875	Cp875	IBM875
ByteToCharCp918	CharToByteCp918	Cp918	EBCDIC Arabic 2
ByteToCharCp921	CharToByteCp921	Cp921	IBM921
ByteToCharCp922	CharToByteCp922	Cp922	IBM922
ByteToCharCp1006	CharToByteCp1006	Cp1006	IBM1006
ByteToCharCp1025	CharToByteCp1025	Cp1025	IBM1025
ByteToCharCp1026	CharToByteCp1026	Cp1026	IBM1026
ByteToCharCp1046	CharToByteCp1046	Cp1046	IBM1046
ByteToCharCp1097	CharToByteCp1097	Cp1097	IBM1097
ByteToCharCp1098	CharToByteCp1098	Cp1098	IBM1098
ByteToCharCp1112	CharToByteCp1112	Cp1112	IBM1112
ByteToCharCp1122	CharToByteCp1122	Cp1122	IBM1122
ByteToCharCp1123	CharToByteCp1123	Cp1123	IBM1123
ByteToCharCp1124	CharToByteCp1124	Cp1124	IBM1124
ByteToCharCp1250	CharToByteCp1250	Cp1250	Windows Eastern European (essentially ISO Latin-2)
ByteToCharCp1251	CharToByteCp1251	Cp1251	Windows Cyrillic
ByteToCharCp1252	CharToByteCp1252	Cp1252	Windows Western European (essentially ISO-Latin-1)
ByteToCharCp1253	CharToByteCp1253	Cp1253	Windows Greek
ByteToCharCp1254	CharToByteCp1254	Cp1254	Windows Turkish
ByteToCharCp1255	CharToByteCp1255	Cp1255	Windows Hebrew
ByteToCharCp1256	CharToByteCp1256	Cp1256	Windows Arabic
ByteToCharCp1257	CharToByteCp1257	Cp1257	Windows Baltic
ByteToCharCp1258	CharToByteCp1258	Cp1258	Windows Vietnamese
ByteToCharEUCJIS	CharToByteEUCJIS	EUCJIS	Japanese EUC
ByteToCharGB2312	CharToByteGB2312	GB2312	Chinese
ByteToCharJIS	CharToByteJIS	JIS	Japanese Hiragana
ByteToCharJIS0208	CharToByteJIS0208	JIS0208	Japanese
ByteToCharKSC5601	CharToByteKSC5601	KSC5601	Korean
ByteToCharMacArabic	CharToByteMacArabic	MacArabic	The Macintosh Arabic character set
ByteToChar MacCentralEurope	CharToByte MacCentralEurope	MacCentral Europe	The Macintosh Central European character set
ByteToCharMacCroatian	CharToByteMacCroatian	MacCroatian	The Macintosh Croatian character set
ByteToCharMacCyrillic	CharToByteMacCyrillic	MacCyrillic	The Macintosh Cyrillic character set
ByteToCharMacDingbat	CharToByteMacDingbat	MacDingbat	Zapf Dingbats

(continued)

The classes in the sun.io package *(continued)*

ByteToChar classes	*CharToByte classes*	*Name*	*Character Set*
ByteToCharMacGreek	CharToByteMacGreek	MacGreek	The Macintosh modern Greek character set
ByteToCharMacHebrew	CharToByteMacHebrew	MacHebrew	The Macintosh Hebrew character set
ByteToCharMacIceland	CharToByteMacIceland	MacIceland	The Macintosh Icelandic character set
ByteToCharMacRoman	CharToByteMacRoman	MacRoman	The Macintosh Roman character set
ByteToCharMacRomania	CharToByteMacRomania	MacRomania	The Macintosh Romanian character set
ByteToCharMacSymbol	CharToByteMacSymbol	MacSymbol	The Symbol font (includes a complete Greek alphabet is place of the usual roman letters)
ByteToCharMacThai	CharToByteMacThai	MacThai	The Macintosh Thai character set
ByteToChar MacTurkish	CharToByteMacTurkish	MacTurkish	The Macintosh Turkish character set
ByteToCharMacUkraine	CharToByteMacUkraine	MacUkraine	The Macintosh Ukrainian character set
ByteToCharSJIS	CharToByteSJIS	SJIS	Windows Japanese
ByteToCharUTF8	CharToByteUTF8	UTF8	UCS Transformation Format, 8-bit form as described in Chapter 3
ByteToCharUnicode	CharToByteUnicode	Unicode	Normal Unicode
ByteToCharUnicodeBig	CharToByteUnicodeBig	UnicodeBig	Unicode with big-endian byte order
ByteToCharUnicodeLittle	CharToByteUnicodeLittle	UnicodeLittle	Unicode with Little-Endian byte order
	CharToByte UnicodeBigUnmarked	Unicode BigUnmarked	Unicode with Big-Endian byte order without a FEFF marking the start of Unicode text
	CharToByte UnicodeLittleUnmarked	Unicode LittleUnmarked	Unicode with Little-Endian byte order without an FFFE marking the start of Unicode text

EBCDIC, used mainly by IBM mainframes, is an alternative to ASCII.

The Unicode standard explicitly does *not* specify the byte order used by Unicode characters. Big Endian and Little Endian encodings are both permitted. It is customary (though not required) to place the unsigned integer 65,279 at the start of a file of Unicode text. If the file is Big Endian, this will appear as FEFF. If the file is Little Endian this number will appear as FFFE.

The nine different ISO character sets all map to ASCII in the lower 128 characters. They differ in what characters are encoded in the upper 128 places. This helps ensure that at least ASCII data can be transmitted between computers using different character sets. Normally ASCII is enough to get your meaning across in English and most Latin script languages.

There are two more classes in the sun.io package not listed in Table 18-1. These are the abstract classes ByteToCharSingleByte and CharToByteSingle-Byte. These are subclasses of ByteToCharConverter and CharToByteConverter that handle conversions between Unicode and single byte character sets. They implement some (but not all) of the abstract methods of ByteToCharConverter and CharToByteConverter.

Depending on the platform, there may be a few more conversions available. The sun.awt.motif package, available only in the Solaris version of Java 1.1, contains eight more conversion classes to handle specific X-Windows fonts/character sets. Interestingly, this package contains only the CharToByte classes to convert from the X11 character sets to Unicode. The ByteToChar classes to convert in the other direction, from Unicode to these X11 character sets, are missing. Table 18-2 lists these additional conversions.

Table 18-2

X11 character set conversions available in sun.awt.motif

ByteToChar class	CharToByte class	Name	Description
CharToByte X11CNS11643P1	none	X11CNS11643P1	X Windows Chinese
CharToByte X11CNS11643P14	none	X11CNS11643P14	X Windows Chinese
CharToByte X11CNS11643P2	none	X11CNS11643P2	X Windows Chinese
CharToByteX11Dingbats	none	X11Dingbats	X Windows Dingbats
CharToByteX11GB2312	none	X11GB2312	X Windows Chinese
CharToByteX11JIS0201	none	X11JIS0201	X Windows Japanese
CharToByteX11JIS0208	none	X11JIS0208	X Windows Japanese
CharToByteX11KSC5601	none	X11KSC5601	X Windows Korean

USING THE CONVERTERS

Look at a simple example. Suppose you have the following string written in the Macintosh Symbol font:

```
This is a test
```

Now, suppose you want to convert that into the equivalent Unicode characters. Here's what you do:

```
// "This is a test";
int[] inSymbol = {84, 104, 105, 115, 32, 105, 115, 32, 97, 32, 116, 101,
115};
byte[] b = new byte[inSymbol.length];
for (int i = 0; i < inSymbol.length; i++) b[i] = (byte) inSymbol[i];
String inUnicode = new String(b, "MacSymbol");
```

Here, the first four lines are spent creating a byte array filled with the bytes for This is a test in the Symbol font. Normally, you'd probably read this out of a file.

Then you pass the byte array and the name of the encoding to the String() constructor. This builds a new string based on the MacSymbol converter.

Moving in the other direction is very similar. For example, assuming you've got the inUnicode string from the previous example,

```
byte[] temp = inUnicode.getBytes("MacSymbol");
String inSymbol = new String(temp);
```

If you print the string inSymbol, you will normally see something like this:

```
This is a test
```

You will see This is a test only if you're using the Mac Symbol font.

DIRECT CONVERSIONS

The previous section used the getBytes() method and String() constructor of java.lang.String to perform the conversions. However, strings are just arrays of chars (as you learned in Chapter 3), and sometimes it's easier or faster to work directly with arrays of chars rather than with strings. This also can give you more direct control over the conversion process. You can specify the sub-array to be converted, define what happens with unexpected input, and in general have more control over the conversion process.

You should be cautious about using the methods described in this section. Mark Reinhold of Javasoft has said, "An improved interface for access to low-level character conversion facilities is planned for a future release." (http://www.javasoft.com/products/jdk/1.1/docs/guide/io/b3-changes.html, February 4, 1997) It's not unlikely that some of the methods described here will be removed when that improved interface is in place.

The convertAll() method

To convert arrays of bytes to arrays of Unicode characters directly without intermediate Strings, use the convertAll() method of the ByteToCharConverter class.

```
public char[] convertAll(byte input[]) throws MalformedInputException
```

A sun.io.MalformedInputException is thrown if a byte or sequence of bytes in the input[] array is not, in fact, a valid character in the external encoding. For example, byte 135 is not defined in the MacSymbol character set. Therefore, if you were using a MacSymbol ByteToCharConverter and your input array contained the value 135, a MalformedInputException would be thrown. This can indicate either corrupt input data or that you've chosen the wrong conversion.

You can find out exactly where the malformed input occurred with the nextByteIndex() and getBadInputLength() methods. After a Malformed-InputException, nextByteIndex() will return the index of the first byte of the malformed input in the input[] array and getBadInputLength() will return the number of bytes of bad input, thus enabling you to fix the problem and move on.

```
public int nextByteIndex()
public int getBadInputLength()
```

All of this is mirrored in the CharToByteConverter class, which has a convertAll() method of its own that converts an array of Unicode characters to an array of bytes in an external encoding.

```
public byte[] convertAll(char input[]) throws MalformedInputException
```

Here, a MalformedInputException means that the input[] contained an invalid Unicode character. CharToByteConverter also has nextByteIndex() and getBadInputLength() methods so that you can fix the problem with the Unicode input and move on.

Note

In practice, problems with Unicode input are extremely rare. Even corrupted data streams are valid Unicode, if not exactly the Unicode that was originally planned.

The convert() method

Secret

The convert() method provides even more control over the conversion process. You can specify where in the input to read, in which array to put the output, and where in the array to put it. You can even split the input between calls to the convert() method, which may be useful when the data is coming off a slow network connection.

This is the signature of the convert() method in the ByteToChar Converter class:

```
public abstract int convert(byte input[], int inStart, int inEnd, char output[],
int outStart, int outEnd) throws MalformedInputException,
UnknownCharacterException, ConversionBufferFullException
```

Here, input[] is a byte array that contains the bytes to be converted to Unicode. Only the bytes between inStart and inEnd are converted. This allows you to select sub-arrays for conversion. To convert the entire input[] array, set inStart to 0 and inEnd to input.length - 1.

The converted Unicode, characters are placed in the char[] array output, specifically in the sub-array between outStart and outEnd. The maximum number of characters that will be placed in the output[] array is given by outEnd - outStart + 1. If fewer characters are present in the input, then the sub-array is not completely filled. The number of characters actually converted and placed in the output[] array is returned. If more characters are present in the input than the specified sub-array of output can hold, then as many characters as possible will be converted before a Conversion BufferFullException is thrown.

As with convertAll(), a MalformedInputException is thrown if a partial or invalid multibyte sequence is encountered. An UnknownCharacter-Exception is thrown if no Unicode character matches a particular byte or byte sequence in the input[] array.

The biggest difference between convert() and convertAll() is that convert() does not reset the converter object between calls. Thus, you can pass part of a stream in one call to convert and then pass the rest of the stream in a second call as more bytes are available. Even multibyte input sequences can be split between calls.

If a call to convert throws an exception, you can continue the conversion by fixing the arguments and calling convert() again. The nextByteIndex() method returns the index in the input[] array of the byte one past the last byte successfully converted by convert() — that is, the next byte to be converted. The nextCharIndex() method returns the index in the output[] array one past the last char sucessfully converted — that is, the position in the output[] array in which the next char to be converted will be placed. The getBadInputLength() method returns the length, in bytes, of the input that caused a MalformedInputException.

```
public int nextCharIndex()
public int nextByteIndex()
public int getBadInputLength()
```

When you are finished with a conversion performed with convert(), you should call flush(). Conversions performed with getBytes(), convertAll(), or other methods do not need to call flush() explicitly.

```
public abstract int flush(char output[], int outStart, int outEnd) throws
MalformedInputException, ConversionBufferFullException
```

The flush() method writes any remaining characters to the output[] array, beginning at outStart and ending at outEnd, and resets the converter so that it's ready to start a new conversion.

The flush() method throws a MalformedInputException if the output to be flushed contains a partial or invalid multibyte character sequence. Here, flush() writes as much as it can to the output buffer and resets the converter before throwing this exception.

The flush() method throws a ConversionBufferFullException if it fills the output array up to outEnd before it runs out of data to be flushed. In this case, the converter is not reset so you can call flush() again with a new output[] array to finish the job. No exception is thrown if flush() does not have enough data to fill the output array completely.

The CharToByteConverter class is, as you should expect, a reverse of the above. It has convert() and flush() methods just like the ByteToChar-Converter class. The only difference is that ByteToCharConverter converts an array of Unicode chars to an array of bytes in an external encoding rather than an array of bytes to an array of Unicode chars. The signatures of the ByteToCharConverter convert methods are

```
    public abstract int convert(char input[], int inStart, int inEnd, byte
output[], int outStart, int outEnd) throws MalformedInputException,
UnknownCharacterException, ConversionBufferFullException
    public abstract int flush(byte output[], int outStart, int outEnd) throws
MalformedInputException, ConversionBufferFullException
    public int nextCharIndex()
    public int nextByteIndex()
    public int getBadInputLength()
```

SUBSTITUTION MODE

A CharToByteConverter object contains a table (essentially a big array) of the characters it can handle. As it converts a string or array of chars to an array of bytes, it looks at each char in order, looks it up in the table to find out what the equivalent set of bytes is in the destination character set, and then places those bytes in the output array.

However, most character sets do not have equivalents for all Unicode characters. For example, Unicode contains thousands of Chinese pictographs. Most fonts and character sets contain exactly zero Chinese pictographs, so what is the converter to do if it needs to convert a Chinese pictograph into MacSymbol, for example?

There are three solutions to this problem. One is to throw a sun.io. UnknownCharacterException. This is a subclass of java.io.IOException. Because this is a checked exception, you must catch it or one of its superclasses when you call convert() or convertAll().

The second solution is to output a warning character indicating that the input Unicode character has no precise equivalent in the output character set. If you've ever used a Macintosh, I'm sure you've opened files to see occasional box characters like this: ❑. This is the Mac's way of letting you know that it can't represent that character in the present font. The box is a generic *substitution character* on the Mac.

In Java, you can, if you wish, pick a particular sequence of bytes that acts as a substitution character. That is, whenever a character that cannot be represented in the destination character set is encountered, these substitution bytes are written in the output instead. This avoids throwing

UnknownCharacterExceptions, although you still need to catch them because of the way the methods are declared.

By default, most converters use substitution mode. If you don't want substitution mode, but would rather have UnknownCharacterExceptions thrown, then you can turn it off with setSubstitutionMode(false):

```
public void setSubstitutionMode(boolean useSubstitution)
```

The default substitution character for most encodings is the ASCII English question mark ('?'). You can change this with the setSubstitution Bytes() method:

```
public void setSubstitutionBytes(byte subBytes[]) throws
IllegalArgumentException
```

The length of the subBytes[] array must be less than or equal to the maximum number of characters in the destination character set, most often one, sometimes two, and almost never more than four. Thus, you can't have a 2-byte substitution character in a 1-byte character set. If you try, an IllegalArgumentException will be thrown. You check the maximum number of bytes in a character in the destination character set with the getMaxBytes PerChar() method:

```
public abstract int getMaxBytesPerChar()
```

The third solution is to check each character before you attempt to convert it. Do this with the canConvert() method. This returns either true if the character can be converted with this CharToByteConverter, or false if it cannot:

```
public boolean canConvert(char c)
```

You can imagine other solutions such as outputting Unicode escapes like \u0763, but these are the ones that the CharToByteConverter class provides. The solutions are not orthogonal. In general, all possibilities are accessible at any time.

As you might guess, this tends to work in both directions. The ByteTo-CharConverter class also has setSubstitutionMode(), setSubstitutionChar(), and getMaxCharsPerByte() methods that are the mirror images of their CharToByteConverter counterparts. Unicode actually defines a specific character for the substitution character, number 65533. This is the default substitution character for substitution mode when converting from external encoding into Unicode. However, you can change it with setSubstitutionChar() if you prefer.

```
public int getMaxCharsPerByte()
public void setSubstitutionMode(boolean doSub)
public void setSubstitutionChars(char c[]) throws IllegalArgumentException
```

The one method that's missing from ByteToCharConverter that's present in CharToByteConverter, at least as of Java 1.1, is canConvert(). This makes the overly optimistic assumption that almost any character in an external character set has a Unicode equivalent. Perhaps this will be rectified in the future.

Listing 18-1 is a program that uses the ByteToCharConverter class to produce the Unicode equivalents to the Macintosh Symbol character set/font you see in Table 18-3.

Listing 18-1
The SymbolChart program

```
import java.io.*;
import sun.io.*;


public class SymbolChart {

  public static void main(String[] args) {

    try {
      FileOutputStream theChart = new FileOutputStream("chart.out");
      ByteToCharConverter SymbolToUnicode =
       ByteToCharConverter.getConverter("MacSymbol");
      byte[] symbol = new byte[256];
      for (int i = 0; i < 256; i++) symbol[i] = (byte) i;
      char[] unicode = SymbolToUnicode.convertAll(symbol);
      for (int i = 0; i < 256; i++) {
        theChart.write((byte) i);
        String s = "\t" + i + "\t" + ((int) unicode[i]) + "\n";
        theChart.write(s.getBytes());
      }
      theChart.close();
    }
    catch (Exception e) {
      System.err.println(e);
    }

  }

}
```

Characters 0 through 31 are non-printing control characters. Character 32 is the space character. Characters 128-160 are left undefined in the Mac Symbol font, although they are extra control codes in ISO Latin-1 and are defined in some other Macintosh fonts.

Table 18-3

Macintosh Symbol font values and Unicode equivalents.

Actual character	Numeric value in Mac Symbol font	Numeric value in unicode
_null	0	0
start of heading	1	1
_start of text	2	2
_end of text	3	3
_end of transmission	4	4
_enquiry	5	5
acknowledge	6	6
bell	7	7
backspace	8	8
tab (\t)	9	9
line feed (\n)	10	10
vertical tab	11	11
form feed	12	12
carriage return (\r)	13	13
shift out	14	14
shift in	15	15
datalink escape	16	16
device control 1	17	17
device control 2	18	18
device control 3	19	19
device control 4	20	20
negative acknowledge	21	21
synchronous idle	22	22
end of transmission block	23	23
cancel	24	24
end of medium	25	25
substitute	26	26
escape	27	27
file separator	28	28
group separator	29	29
record separator	30	30
unit separator	31	31
	32	32

(continued)

Macintosh Symbol font values and Unicode equivalents. *(continued)*

Actual character	Numeric value in Mac Symbol font	Numeric value in unicode
!	33	33
∀	34	8704
#	35	35
∃	36	8707
%	37	37
&	38	38
∍	39	8717
(	40	40
)	41	41
*	42	8727
+	43	43
,	44	44
−	45	8722
.	46	46
/	47	47
0	48	48
1	49	49
2	50	50
3	51	51
4	52	52
5	53	53
6	54	54
7	55	55
8	56	56
9	57	57
:	58	58
;	59	59
<	60	60
=	61	61
>	62	62
?	63	63
≅	64	8773
A	65	913
B	66	914
X	67	935
Δ	68	916
E	69	917
Φ	70	934
Γ	71	915

(continued)

Table 18-3

Macintosh Symbol font values and Unicode equivalents. *(continued)*

Actual character	Numeric value in Mac Symbol font	Numeric value in unicode
H	72	919
I	73	921
ϑ	74	977
K	75	922
Λ	76	923
M	77	924
N	78	925
O	79	927
Π	80	928
Θ	81	920
P	82	929
Σ	83	931
T	84	932
Y	85	933
ς	86	962
Ω	87	937
Ξ	88	926
Ψ	89	936
Z	90	918
[	91	91
∴	92	8756
]	93	93
⊥	94	8869
_	95	95
‾	96	65533
α	97	945
β	98	946
χ	99	967
δ	100	948
ε	101	949
φ	102	966
γ	103	947
η	104	951
ι	105	953
φ	106	981
κ	107	954
λ	108	955

(continued)

Macintosh Symbol font values and Unicode equivalents. *(continued)*

Actual character	Numeric value in Mac Symbol font	Numeric value in unicode
μ	109	956
ν	110	957
ο	111	959
π	112	960
θ	113	952
ρ	114	961
σ	115	963
τ	116	964
υ	117	965
ϖ	118	982
ω	119	969
ξ	120	958
ψ	121	968
ζ	122	950
{	123	123
		124	124
}	125	125
~	126	8764
delete	127	127
	128	65533
	129	65533
	130	65533
	131	65533
	132	65533
	133	65533
	134	65533
	135	65533
	136	65533
	137	65533
	138	65533
	139	65533
	140	65533
	141	65533
	142	65533
	143	65533
	144	65533
	145	65533

(continued)

Table 18-3

Macintosh Symbol font values and Unicode equivalents. *(continued)*

Actual character	Numeric value in Mac Symbol font	Numeric value in unicode
	146	65533
	147	65533
	148	65533
	149	65533
	150	65533
	151	65533
	152	65533
	153	65533
	154	65533
	155	65533
	156	65533
	157	65533
	158	65533
	159	65533
	160	65533
γ	161	978
′	162	8242
≤	163	8804
/	164	8260
∞	165	8734
ƒ	166	402
♣	167	9827
♦	168	9830
♥	169	9829
♠	170	9824
↔	171	8596
←	172	8592
↑	173	8593
→	174	8594
↓	175	8595
°	176	176
±	177	177
″	178	8243
≥	179	8805
×	180	215
∝	181	8733
∂	182	8706

(continued)

Macintosh Symbol font values and Unicode equivalents. *(continued)*

Actual character	Numeric value in Mac Symbol font	Numeric value in unicode
•	183	8226
÷	184	247
≠	185	8800
≡	186	8801
≈	187	8776
...	188	8230
|	189	65533
—	190	65533
⏎	191	8629
ℵ	192	8501
ℑ	193	8465
ℜ	194	8476
℘	195	8472
⊗	196	8855
⊕	197	8853
∅	198	8709
∩	199	8745
∪	200	8746
⊃	201	8835
⊇	202	8839
⊄	203	8836
⊂	204	8834
⊆	205	8838
∈	206	8712
∉	207	8713
∠	208	8736
∇	209	8711
®	210	174
©	211	169
™	212	8482
∏	213	8719
√	214	8730
⋅	215	8901
¬	216	172
∧	217	8743
∨	218	8744
⇔	219	8660
⇐	220	8656

(continued)

Table 18-3

Macintosh Symbol font values and Unicode equivalents. *(continued)*

Actual character	Numeric value in Mac Symbol font	Numeric value in unicode
⇑	221	8657
⇒	222	8658
⇓	223	8659
◊	224	8900
⟨	225	9001
®	226	65533
©	227	65533
™	228	65533
Σ	229	8721
⌠	230	65533
		231	65533
⌡	232	65533
	233	65533
		234	65533
⌊	235	65533
⌈	236	65533
	237	65533
⌊	238	65533
		239	65533
	240	65533
⟩	241	9002
∫	242	8747
⌠	243	8992
		244	65533
	245	8993
⌡	246	65533
		247	65533
⌡	248	65533
⌐	249	65533
		250	65533
	251	65533
⌐	252	65533
}	253	65533
⌡	254	65533
?	255	65533

Notice how many of the Unicode values are set to 65533 in Table 18-3. That's the substitution character defined for this conversion. These all represent either characters in the Mac Symbol font for which there is no precise Unicode equivalent or characters that are undefined in the Symbol font. Most fonts do not define glyphs or control codes for all 256 possible numeric values.

In a few cases, a value of 65533 indicates a deficiency in the ByteTo-CharConverter rather than in Unicode. For example Unicode does have ®, ©, and ™ symbols. They are Unicode values 174, 169, and 8482 respectively.

SUMMARY

In this chapter, you learn the following:

- The sun.io.ByteToCharConverter class is an abstract class for converting text written in external (non-Unicode) character sets into Unicode.

- The sun.io.CharToByteConverter class is an abstract class for converting text written in Unicode to external (non-Unicode) character sets.

- The sun.io package contains many concrete subclasses of these two classes. Each class handles a particular external character set. You do not instantiate these classes directly.

- Most of the time, you convert Unicode chars to externally encoded byte arrays with the java.lang.String.getBytes() method. However, the Char-ToByteConverter convert() and convertAll() methods can also be used.

- Most of the time, you convert byte arrays to Unicode chars with the java.lang.String.String() constructor. However, the ByteToChar-Converter convert() and convertAll() methods can also be used.

MIXED LANGUAGE PROGRAMMING WITH NATIVE METHODS

## 19

*D*espite all the hype surrounding Java, Java programs are severely handicapped compared to programs written in traditional languages like C or Fortran. Java's interpreted nature does exact a very real performance penalty relative to code written in a traditional language and compiled with a solid, optimizing compiler. In the best case, Java programs reach about 80 percent of the speed of compiled C++ code. In the worst case, they run intolerably slowly.

Raw speed is not always the problem. In many client-server and network programs, the speed of the network or the database is by far the tightest bottleneck on performance. However, in such programs, Java applications tend to look bad compared to the equivalent native program written in Visual Basic, an interpreted language whose speed Java can match, but which provides much stronger access to the native GUI.

Java's advantage relative to C, C++, Delphi, Visual Basic, and a host of other languages is that it's cross-platform. You can write Java code once and run it anywhere — at least, that's the theory. This is a huge boon to developers and largely explains why Java has become as popular as it has as quickly as it has.

However, as excited as developers get about true cross-platform code, end users who actually buy software don't care about this at all. End users buy the product that runs best on their hardware. On rare occasions, with truly groundbreaking products like Lotus 1-2-3 and Aldus Pagemaker, end users have bought the hardware that runs the software the best, but cross-platform applications are practically irrelevant to most of the people who actually purchase software.

Cross-platform development tools have been with us for over forty years, starting with Fortran. The problem with cross-platform development tools, however, is that they always make you give something up. They force you to write to the lowest common denominator of all the supported platforms. For example, Windows doesn't support hierarchical menus, so your Mac application can't have hierarchical menus either; the Mac doesn't have tabbed dialog boxes, so neither can your Windows application; and so on. In practice, this means that when you ship your carefully crafted cross-platform application, your competitors, who are shipping apps tied closely to the native GUI, will eat you for lunch.

Java's cross-platform nature is great for applets on Web pages. Java can handle applets on Web pages that C, C++, Delphi, Visual Basic, and dozens of other languages can't. Therefore, for applets on Web pages, you can afford the penalties imposed by cross-platform development. There really isn't any competition. However, if you want to sell genuine commercial software that is more than an applet on a Web page (for that matter even if you want to give it away), you need to be able to compete effectively with applications written in traditional languages like C and C++. Your application has to run as fast and look as good as every other application. In fact, if you're taking on a market leader, your application is generally going to need to be *better*, not just as good.

The solution to both problems, raw speed and native appearance, is native methods. Native methods let you write time- and appearance-critical portions of your program in a compiled language accessing the native GUI. Most of your program can still be written in Java, but those parts where speed or neatness counts can be provided in another language.

This chapter introduces the basics of using native code in Java through the Java Runtime Interface. You'll learn how to call C programs from Java and Java code from C. In the following chapter, I expand on the topics discussed here to show you how you can build fully executable, double-clickable applications that, to the casual user, are indistinguishable from programs written in traditional languages like C or Pascal. With these two chapters, you'll have the tools that you need to compete effectively with the hordes of C++ programmers currently coding the world.

DISADVANTAGES

Using native methods is not a decision to be taken lightly. Native methods have many disadvantages.

First and foremost, native methods increase your workload. Writing in Java is relatively simple. Writing in C or C++ is relatively hard. If you decide to use native methods, you immediately lose all the genuine benefits that Java's simplicity provides. Furthermore, you're placed in a position where you have to port code to dozens of platforms — exactly what Java is supposed to avoid.

You may decide to keep your workload manageable by providing your application only for Windows. Of course, this immediately cuts out about half of your potential market. Furthermore, you don't just lose all the potential buyers on the Mac, OS/2, UNIX, BeOS, network computers, and more. You actively alienate them. Advertising a "Java solution" that runs only on Windows is asking for flames. Excuses about "instability of VMs" or "insufficient resources" will not be accepted.

If you are not prepared to support over a dozen different platforms, you should be careful that your advertising and marketing does not even mention the words "Java" or "cross-platform." This shouldn't be too hard. Most software does not advertise the language in which it was written. If you do advertise Java software that does not run on all Java-capable platforms, many people will actively disparage your products, online and off, justly or unjustly. Macs, OS/2, UNIX, and many other platforms have many rabid fans whose day jobs may involve running networks of nothing but X86 Windows, but who will not even consider products from companies who have demonstrated insufficient obeisance to their platform god. You may argue in private about whether such religious fervor is truly helpful to business, but in public if you do not pay appropriate respect to the deity of choice, your product will not be bought.

Note: It may be helpful to remember that it was not the early Christians' belief in Christ that got them fed to the lions. It was their active disbelief in the Roman gods. Religious zealots can be surprisingly lenient about your worshipping at other temples as long as you tithe at their church, too, but you'd better have a mighty powerful deity on your side if you ignore *their* gods. Keep this in mind if you want to avoid becoming lion food.

The third disadvantage that you introduce by using native methods is the impossibility of running your program as an applet. You may claim that this is not significant, that your program is really a stand-alone application.

However, applets are the one area in which Java does have a real advantage to the end user as opposed to a program written in C or C++. It's not likely that your Java spreadsheet will outperform Microsoft Excel in speed, features, or ease of use. However, if it can be embedded in a Web page, then you've suddenly provided one killer feature that will convince users to use your product instead of Excel at least some of the time. The same is true of most other applications that you can imagine. There's a huge market for programs that repurpose old data into Web pages. Applets are often the best way to do that. You ignore this market only at significant cost to your bank account. You may not be able to provide full functionality in an applet, but the more you can provide, the more units you're likely to sell. This is a solid reason to try to keep native code to a minimum.

The fourth and perhaps most important disadvantage of native code is that it decreases security and introduces bugs. This isn't a problem just for applets, either. The biggest problem with software today isn't viruses; it isn't crackers or copy protection; it's bugs, plain and simple. Common, ordinary bugs are responsible for more lost productivity than all other software- and hardware-related failures combined. Java's designers went to substantial effort to eliminate common sources of bugs, such as memory leaks, pointer arithmetic, and obfuscated constructs like the C preprocessor. For the most part, they succeeded. However, as soon as you introduce native methods into your program, you're back to square one. You suddenly have memory leaks, dangling pointers, system crashes, and a whole lot more. Listing 19-1 shows the results of one of my early native methods. Fortunately, this was running on a relatively crash-proof UNIX system. On a Mac or Windows 95 system, I would have had a complete system failure and would have wasted several minutes while I rebooted.

Listing 19-1
The damage that native methods can do

```
% java NativeStaticTest
SIGSEGV   11* segmentation violation
    si_signo [11]: SIGSEGV   11* segmentation violation
    si_errno [0]: Error 0
    si_code [1]: SEGV_ACCERR [addr: 0x8692bbd4]

        stackbase=EFFFF93C, stackpointer=EFFFF538

Full thread dump:
    "Finalizer thread" (TID:0xee3002f8, sys_thread_t:0xef320de0, state:R) prio=1
```
(continued)

The damage that native methods can do (continued)

```
    "Async Garbage Collector" (TID:0xee3002b0, sys_thread_t:0xef350de0, state:R)
prio=1
    "Idle thread" (TID:0xee300268, sys_thread_t:0xef380de0, state:R) prio=0
    "Clock" (TID:0xee300180, sys_thread_t:0xef3b0de0, state:CW) prio=12
    "main" (TID:0xee300150, sys_thread_t:0x34050, state:R) prio=5: pending=java.
lang.NoSuchMethodError *current thread*
        NativeStaticTest.main(NativeStaticTest.java:7)
Monitor Cache Dump:
Registered Monitor Dump:
    Thread queue lock:      unowned
    Name and type hash table lock:      unowned
    String intern lock:     unowned
    JNI global reference lock:      unowned
    BinClass lock:      unowned
    Class loading lock:      unowned
    Java stack lock:     unowned
    Code rewrite lock:      unowned
    Heap lock:      unowned
    Has finalization queue lock:      unowned
    Finalize me queue lock:      unowned
    Monitor IO lock:      unowned
    Child death monitor:      unowned
    Event monitor:      unowned
    I/O monitor:      unowned
    Alarm monitor:      unowned
        Waiting to be notified:
            "Clock"
    Sbrk lock:      unowned
    Monitor cache expansion lock:      unowned
    Monitor registry:      monitor owner 34050: "main"
Thread Alarm Q:
Abort
%
```

Pure Java programs can't do this sort of damage, even when, as in this case, the programmer screws up. Later in this chapter, you'll see a corrected version of the C code that did this.

Don't think that you will be all right if you can just be careful; keep native code to a minimum, and test extensively. Programmers have thought this way for decades, and every year they produce code that is buggier and more crash-prone than the last.

CODE IN JAVA FIRST

Now that I've told you that you must write in native code to be competitive and that you must not write in native code or you'll be tarred, feathered, and run out of town on a rail, you may be feeling a little schizophrenic. Don't worry. There is a solution, and it's not a particularly difficult one. Here it is:

Write your application in Java first.

Before you even think about using native methods, you should produce a fairly complete prototype, written in 100% pure Java. This application should run on any platform with a Java VM. It may run slowly; it may not look beautiful; but it should run. This will be enough to keep yourself out of the line of fire of the religious zealots. Then optimize it as best you can for both performance and beauty. Finally, when you've gone as far as you can go in Java, provide native libraries as an optional enhancement on as many platforms as you can develop for.

Many experienced programmers are too quick to jump to the native code with they're familiar which when the limitations of Java become apparent. This is almost always a mistake. You shouldn't initially worry that a Gaussian blur is agonizingly slow in Java. Just write the algorithm and make sure it's debugged. You may wish to invest in an espresso machine so that you can go for good coffee while waiting for the program to run. That's okay. Just make sure the program runs.

The second step is to optimize the code as much as possible. The first step in optimization is quite easy: Compile with the -O option to turn on the built-in optimizer. This isn't as strong an optimizer as is present in some modern Fortran and C compilers, but it really is quite good, better in many cases than compilers that were in common use just a few years ago. A surprising number of Java programmers either don't know about or just don't use the built-in optimizer in javac. It's not hard to use. Just pass the -O flag on the command line, like this:

```
% javac -O FastFourier.java
```

At this point, it's probably best to use Sun's javac compiler. Most of the other companies publishing commercial Java compilers are concentrating on compilation speed, not execution speed. Furthermore, these compilers tend to have many bugs. Microsoft's Visual J++ is the worst offender in this respect. However, I do have high hopes for the GPL'd compiler, Guavac, which, although still a little buggy, does produce tighter code than javac in some cases. Guavac is available from `http://http.cs.berkeley.edu/~engberg/guavac/` and this is included on the CD.

Next, test your code with a JIT (just-in-time) compiler. JIT compilers have shown performance gains ranging from four times to over a hundred times faster. JIT compilers are available for most platforms, and more are coming soon.

Profiling

The next step is to hand-optimize your code. Rather than wasting time tweaking the last ounce of performance out of a method that is only rarely called, try using the -prof option to the Java interpreter to find out where your programs are spending most of their time. The profiler writes a sorted list of the most frequently called methods in the execution of a Java program to a file called java.prof in the current directory. Then optimize the heck out of those sections.

For example, let's consider the HexDumper program from Chapter 12. To profile it, just run it normally on a typical input file but use the -prof option, like this:

```
% java -prof HexDumper html/HelloWorldApplet.class
```

The HexDumper program still does exactly what it's supposed to do, but Java also writes a file full of useful information, as shown in Listing 19-2. The first number is the number of times that the method in question was called. For example, sun/io/CharToByte8859_1.flush([BII)I java/io/OutputStreamWriter.flushBuffer was called 4456 separate times.

The second column is the .class file style signature of the invoked method. This is decoded, as was discussed in Chapter 4. For example, the method in the first line is really sun.io.CharToByte8859_1.flush(byte[], int, int), which returns an int.

The third column is the method from which the method in the second column was invoked. Again, this is given in .class format rather than .java format. Thus, sun.io.CharToByte8859_1.flush(byte[], int, int) was called by the method java.io.OutputStreamWriter.flushBuffer(), which returned void.

The fourth column is the time in milliseconds that was actually spent in the method across all invocations. In this case, 58 milliseconds were spent in the flush() method invoked by the flushBuffer() method.

Listing 19-2

Profiling data for the HexDumper class

```
count callee caller time
4546 sun/io/CharToByte8859_1.flush([BII)I java/io/OutputStreamWriter.flushBuffer
()V 58
4044 sun/misc/HexDumpEncoder.bytesPerAtom()I
sun/misc/CharacterEncoder.encodeBuffer(Ljava/io/InputStream;Ljava/io/OutputStrea
m;)V 32
3811 java/io/PrintStream.write(I)V java/io/PrintStream.write(I)V 199
3811 java/io/BufferedOutputStream.write(I)V java/io/PrintStream.write(I)V 41
3036 java/io/PrintStream.write(I)V
sun/misc/HexDumpEncoder.hexDigit(Ljava/io/PrintStream;B)V 266
2295 java/lang/System.arraycopy(Ljava/lang/Object;ILjava/lang/Object;II)V
java/lang/String.getChars(II[CI)V 29
2273 java/io/PrintStream.write([BII)V java/io/PrintStream.write([BII)V 1891
2273 java/io/OutputStreamWriter.write([CII)V
java/io/BufferedWriter.flushBuffer()V 199
2273 java/io/PrintStream.write([BII)V java/io/OutputStreamWriter.flushBuffer()V
1972
2273 java/io/FileOutputStream.write([BII)V java/io/BufferedOutputStream.flush()V
 1495
2273 java/io/BufferedOutputStream.flush()V java/io/PrintStream.write([BII)V 1654
2273 java/io/BufferedWriter.write(Ljava/lang/String;II)V
java/io/Writer.write(Ljava/lang/String;)V 195
2273 java/io/OutputStream.flush()V java/io/BufferedOutputStream.flush()V 21
2273 java/lang/System.arraycopy(Ljava/lang/Object;ILjava/lang/Object;II)V
java/io/BufferedOutputStream.write([BII)V 20
2273 java/io/FileOutputStream.writeBytes([BII)V
java/io/FileOutputStream.write([BII)V 1395
2273 java/io/BufferedOutputStream.write([BII)V java/io/PrintStream.write([BII)V
101
2273 java/lang/String.getChars(II[CI)V
java/io/BufferedWriter.write(Ljava/lang/String;II)V 92
2273 sun/io/CharToByte8859_1.convert([CII[BII)I
java/io/OutputStreamWriter.write([CII)V 115
2188 java/io/Writer.write(Ljava/lang/String;)V
java/io/PrintStream.write(Ljava/lang/String;)V 250
2188 java/io/PrintStream.write(Ljava/lang/String;)V
java/io/PrintStream.print(Ljava/lang/String;)V 2747
2188 java/io/OutputStreamWriter.flushBuffer()V
java/io/PrintStream.write(Ljava/lang/String;)V 2123
2188 java/io/BufferedWriter.flushBuffer()V
java/io/PrintStream.write(Ljava/lang/String;)V 251
1432 java/io/PrintStream.print(Ljava/lang/String;)V
sun/misc/HexDumpEncoder.encodeAtom(Ljava/io/OutputStream;[BII)V 1763
```

(continued)

Profiling data for the HexDumper class *(continued)*

```
1349 java/io/FileInputStream.read()I
sun/misc/CharacterEncoder.readFully(Ljava/io/InputStream;[B)I 221
1348 sun/misc/HexDumpEncoder.encodeAtom(Ljava/io/OutputStream;[BII)V
sun/misc/CharacterEncoder.encodeBuffer(Ljava/io/InputStream;Ljava/io/OutputStrea
m;)V 2143
1348 sun/misc/HexDumpEncoder.hexDigit(Ljava/io/PrintStream;B)V
sun/misc/HexDumpEncoder.encodeAtom(Ljava/io/OutputStream;[BII)V 300
775 java/io/PrintStream.write(I)V
sun/misc/HexDumpEncoder.encodeLineSuffix(Ljava/io/OutputStream;)V 63
671 java/io/PrintStream.print(Ljava/lang/String;)V
sun/misc/HexDumpEncoder.encodeLineSuffix(Ljava/io/OutputStream;)V 920
441 java/lang/String.<init>(II[C)V <unknown caller> 4
383 java/lang/String.hashCode()I
java/util/Hashtable.put(Ljava/lang/Object;Ljava/lang/Object;)Ljava/lang/Object;
9
363 java/util/Hashtable.put(Ljava/lang/Object;Ljava/lang/Object;)Ljava/lang/Obje
ct; sun/io/CharacterEncoding.<clinit>()V 40
170 sun/misc/HexDumpEncoder.hexDigit(Ljava/io/PrintStream;B)V
sun/misc/HexDumpEncoder.encodeLinePrefix(Ljava/io/OutputStream;I)V 36
86 sun/misc/HexDumpEncoder.bytesPerLine()I
sun/misc/CharacterEncoder.encodeBuffer(Ljava/io/InputStream;Ljava/io/OutputStrea
m;)V 0
85 sun/misc/HexDumpEncoder.encodeLinePrefix(Ljava/io/OutputStream;I)V
sun/misc/CharacterEncoder.encodeBuffer(Ljava/io/InputStream;Ljava/io/OutputStrea
m;)V 166
85 sun/misc/CharacterEncoder.readFully(Ljava/io/InputStream;[B)I
sun/misc/CharacterEncoder.encodeBuffer(Ljava/io/InputStream;Ljava/io/OutputStrea
m;)V 271
85 java/io/PrintStream.print(Ljava/lang/String;)V sun/misc/HexDumpEncoder.encode
```

Listing 19-2 is only a part of the entire output of running the profiler. The actual output continues for several more pages, even on this relatively simple program. This shows why a profiler is so helpful. With even simple Java programs calling so many methods, it's generally impossible to hand-optimize them all. You have to allocate your resources to the most frequently invoked methods.

Looking at this output, it's clear that this program spends most of its time inside the sun.io and java.io packages. Programs like HexDumper are almost always I/O bound. Reading from and writing to disk, or worse yet the network, is almost always the most time-consuming operation in any program that does a lot of it. Thus, it's often a profitable target for hand-optimization.

You can't easily rewrite the sun or java classes, but you may be able to call them less often. In this case, the HexDumper class has only two methods that are easily accessible, main() and dumpFile(), and both are down in the noise region for this program.

```
   1 HexDumper.dumpFile(Ljava/lang/String;)V
HexDumper.main([Ljava/lang/String;)V 4017
   1 HexDumper.main([Ljava/lang/String;)V <unknown caller> 4017
```

Each of these methods takes about four seconds to execute. However, almost all of that time is spent in other methods. Neither method is called more than once. There's really not much room to optimize this program.

In some cases where your program spends most of its time executing in the API, you may be able to write a more efficient piece of code that does the same thing as the library class and call it instead.

Hand-Optimizing

Most of the optimization techniques with which you're familiar from other languages also apply to Java. This is not a book about optimization, but I will mention a few common techniques:

- Most importantly, make sure that you're using the best algorithm known to exist. Never use an $O(n)$ algorithm when an $O(\log n)$ algorithm is available.

- Avoid unnecessary calculations. Don't repeat the same unchanging calculation or part of a calculation with every pass through a loop.

- Not all calculations always need to be performed. If you know you're multiplying by zero or one, why bother with the multiplication at all?

- Buffer your reads and writes. Do not read or write to disk one byte or character at a time. Try reading at least 128 or 256 bytes at a shot. However, performance seems to degrade once you get past about 1024 bytes (less on a network connection), so keep your reads and writes between 128 and 1024.

- Recursive algorithms are often slower than their non-recursive equivalents.

- Declare any classes you don't subclass final. This allows javac to perform some additional optimizations.

- Clip your drawing. Never draw anything that hasn't changed or that the user can't see.

- Avoid method calls and instance variables, especially in tight loops. Replace them with local variables and manually inlined routines wherever possible.

- Use doubles and ints instead of floats, longs, shorts, or bytes.

- In switch statements and if-else blocks, test the most common cases first.

- Synchronization dramatically slows down execution. Avoid synchronization if at all possible. Use immutable objects and local variables instead to provide thread safety.

- Use a JAR archive to collect all your classes and media files.

Finally, once you've hand-optimized the sections of your code that take large fractions of execution time, if performance is still inadequate, consider recoding the most crucial methods in C.

THE JAVA NATIVE METHOD INTERFACE

The Java Native Method Interface is a platform-independent, virtual machine-independent description of how Java programs can call native methods written in C, C++, or assembler. Conversely, it is also a description of how these native methods can load Java classes, instantiate objects from those classes, invoke methods and get and set fields in those objects, handle Java exceptions, and perform runtime type checking.

Begin with a simple native method that takes no arguments, returns no values, and does not interact with Java in any way. This is not a common native method. Generally, if this is all you need, you can write the program in C and use Runtime.exec() to execute the program. This will get you started.

Listing 19-3 is a Java program that searches for and prints the first whole number (that is, the first integer greater than or equal to zero) that is not expressible as the sum of three perfect squares.

Listing 19-3
The firstNonSquareSum program

```
public class Sums {

  public static void main(String[] args) {

    Sums s = new Sums();
    s.firstNonSquareSum();

  }

  public void firstNonSquareSum() {

    int thisInt = 0;
    double max;
    int triple;
    boolean found = false;

    while (!found) {
      max = Math.sqrt(thisInt);
      iloop:
      for (int i = 0; i <= max; i++) {
        for (int j = 0; j <= i; j++) {
          for (int k = 0; k <= j; k++) {
            triple = i*i + j*j + k*k;
            if (triple == thisInt) {
              thisInt++;
              found = true;
              break iloop;
            }
          }
        }
      }
    }

    System.out.println(thisInt + " is not the sum of three cubes");

  }

}
```

Suppose that you need this program to run quite a bit faster. You can declare firstNonSquareSum() as native and recode it in C, and then recompile it into a shared library for each platform you support.

Note I admit that this is an artificial example. This method runs in essentially zero time, even on a slow machine. However, it's not uncommon for numerical algorithms to require rather large amounts of time. For such an example, add one extra for loop, and try to find what the first number is that's not the sum of four squares.

If you're curious why one might be interested in such a number, see *Shadows of the Mind* by Roger Penrose, page 68 (Oxford University Press, 1994).

Native methods are declared normally, except that they are prefixed with the keyword "native." They do not have method bodies. In this case, you have

```
public native void firstNonSquareSum();
```

Notice that there are no method body braces ({}), but there is a closing semicolon. Also note that the native keyword falls between the access specifier *public* and the return type *void*.

Of course, this method can't live on its own. It needs to be part of a class and may be part of a package as well. This class may have other methods and fields. In general, it's a full Java .class file, except that the method bodies of the native methods are missing. Listing 19-4 demonstrates.

Listing 19-4
The Sums class in the numbers package

```
package numbers;

public class Sums {

  static {
    System.loadLibrary("numbers");
  }

  public static void main(String[] args) {

    Sums s = new Sums();
    s.firstNonSquareSum();

  }

  public native void firstNonSquareSum();

}
```

In this class, I've added a static block that will be called the first time this class is loaded. The static block loads the native library named "numbers." This is where the native C code that actually implements the body of firstNonSquareSum() will be found.

The name of the native library is not important. It could just as easily have been "Fred" or "Jake," although, of course, the name should have something to do with the contents of the library. It will be translated into the format appropriate for native libraries on the host system — for example, libnumbers.so on UNIX and numbers.dll on Windows 95 and NT.

A single library can contain native code for native methods in many different classes and packages. In general, each class that relies on code in a particular native library should have a static block to load that library. Trying to load the same library more than once has no adverse effects.

Now that you've written the Java, you need to compile the Java program and use it to generate a C header file that will be used for the native program. This is done with the javah program using the -jni argument like this:

```
% javac -d . Sums.java
% javah -jni numbers.Sums
```

Getting the CLASSPATH correct is very important for native methods. That's why I used the -d flag to javac in the above. This puts the compiled .class files exactly where they need to go relative to the specified directory (in this case, the current working directory). Any necessary directories, such as numbers are created if they don't already exist.

Secret

You must compile the Java program that declares the native methods into a .class file *before* generating the header file with javah. Note that javah reads the compiled .class file, *not* the .java source code file.

jni stands for Java Native Interface. Without this argument, javah produces old-style stubs for Java 1.0.

Note

The javah program produces a header file to include in your C program. The file is named with the fully qualified class name with periods replaced by underscores, in this case, numbers_Sums.h. Listing 19-5 shows this header file.

Listing 19-5

numbers_Sums.h

```
/* DO NOT EDIT THIS FILE - it is machine generated */
#include <jni.h>
/* Header for class numbers_Sums */

#ifndef _Included_numbers_Sums
#define _Included_numbers_Sums
#ifdef __cplusplus
extern "C" {
#endif
/*
 * Class:     numbers_Sums
 * Method:    firstNonSquareSum
 * Signature: ()V
 */
JNIEXPORT void JNICALL Java_numbers_Sums_firstNonSquareSum
  (JNIEnv *, jobject);

#ifdef __cplusplus
}
#endif
#endif
```

The main thing to notice is these two lines:

```
JNIEXPORT void JNICALL Java_numbers_Sums_firstNonSquareSum
  (JNIEnv *, jobject);
```

Ignore JNIEXPORT and JNICALL for now. The rest of the lines tell you the signature that your C function has to have in order to match the Java method firstNonSquareSum(). That signature is

```
void JNICALL Java_numbers_Sums_firstNonSquareSum(JNIEnv *, jobject);
```

You need to add actual variables for the two arguments (the C headers just have types.) and include the numbers_Sums.h file at the top of your C program. Because this will be read from the same directory as your C code, instead of from your INCLUDE_PATH, use double quotes around numbers_Sums.h instead of angle brackets. Listing 19-6 is the completed numbers.c program that recodes the firstNonSquareSum() method in C.

Listing 19-6

The native C firstNonCubeSum() function

```c
#include <stdio.h>
#include <math.h>
#include "numbers_Sums.h"

void Java_numbers_Sums_firstNonSquareSum(JNIEnv * je, jobject jo) {

  int i, j, k;
  int thisInt = 0;
  double max;
  int triple;
  /* Wouldn't a Java boolean be much nicer? */
  int found = 0;

  while (!found) {
next:
    max = sqrt(thisInt);
    for (i = 0; i <= max; i++) {
      for (j = 0; j <= i; j++) {
        for (k = 0; k <= j; k++) {
          triple = i*i + j*j + k*k;
          if (triple == thisInt) {
            thisInt++;
            /* This is exactly what Java's labeled break lets you avoid */
            goto next;
          }
        }
      }
    }
    printf("%d is not the sum of three cubes\n", thisInt);
    found = 1;
  }

}
```

Now that the C program is written, you need to compile it into a shared library. This is a little different from compiling into a stand-alone application or linkable object file, but not that different. The exact details vary from platform to platform and compiler to compiler. The instructions here apply to gcc on most versions of UNIX and should work fairly well with other compilers also. For other platforms, you'll need to consult your compiler documentation.

With gcc on UNIX, you must first add the -shared command line flag. You also need to be sure that all the extra directories containing native method header files are in your INCLUDE_PATH. You can do this with the

-I option on the command line. Finally, you need to br sure that the compiled library has the proper name — for example, libnumbers.so or numbers.dll — and not a.out or some other improper name.

```
% gcc numbers.c -shared -lm -Ijava1.1b3/include -Ijava1.1b3/include/solaris
-o libnumbers.so
```

Once you've compiled the library, you have to put it where Java can find it. Again the exact details are platform-specific. On UNIX, the LD_LIBRARY_PATH environment variable determines where Java looks for files. For example,

```
% setenv LD_LIBRARY_PATH /usr/lib:/export/sunsite/users/elharo:/usr/
openwin/lib
```

Under Windows, you should be able to put the .dll file in one of the locations where Windows usually looks for libraries, such as the system directory.

If you're having trouble getting the library path properly configured, you can also load a library from an absolute path name using the System.load() method like this:

```
System.load("/export/sunsite/users/elharo/libnumbers.so");
```

This is good enough for debugging, but shipping applications shouldn't depend on absolute paths.

Now you're ready to run the program. Make a directory called numbers in one of the directories in your $CLASSPATH, and move the Sums class there. Then run the program in the usual way.

```
% mkdir numbers
% mv Sums.class numbers
% java numbers.Sums
7 is not the sum of three cubes
```

If the native library cannot be loaded, then an UnsatisfiedLinkError is thrown instead. This means that Java cannot find the native method that it needs. This may be because the library path is improperly set, because the C program was compiled into a regular object or executable file instead of a shared library, or because the Sums class is not in the right place in the CLASSPATH.

Returning primitive values from native methods

The biggest problem with native methods is that the data types, both reference and primitive, aren't guaranteed to match precisely the similarly named types on the host system. For example, a Java int is always a two's complement, 4-byte, signed integer. However, some C compilers use a two's complement, 2-byte, signed integer for the int and a 4-byte integer for the long.

The header files used by native methods typedef new types that are guaranteed to match the Java types. Each of these has the usual Java keyword prefixed with the letter j. For example, inside a C native metho; jboolean is a Java boolean; jint is a Java int; jshort is a Java short; jfloat is a Java float; and so on.

It's not particularly difficult to return a value of a primitive type — that is, long, int, char, short, byte, float, double, or boolean — from a native method. First, you declare the Java method to return the value of the appropriate type, as shown in Listing 19-7. Then firstNonSquareSum() returns an int, and the user interface is completely handled by Java. All that the native method does is calculate.

Listing 19-7
The Sums class in the numbers package

```
package numbers;

public class Sums {

  static {
   System.loadLibrary("numbers");
  }

  public static void main(String[] args) {

    Sums s = new Sums();
    int result = s.firstNonSquareSum();
    System.out.println(result + " is not the sum of three squares.");

  }

  public native int firstNonSquareSum();

}
```

Compile Listing 19-7 as usual; then run javah on it again. Anytime that you change the signature of a native method or add a new native method, you must rerun javah.

```
% javac -d . Sums.java
% javah -jni numbers.Sums
```

Inspecting the file numbers_Sums.h produced by javah, you see that the method signature for the C function has changed. It is now

```
jint Java_numbers_Sums_firstNonSquareSum(JNIEnv *, jobject);
```

You therefore know that your C function should return a jint. Because C is much looser about casting than Java, you can do most of your computations with the native C data types and then only cast to the Java type at the end. Listing 19-8 is the revised numbers.c program. Compile and load it exactly as before.

Listing 19-8
The native C firstNonCubeSum() function that returns a Java int

```c
#include <stdio.h>
#include <math.h>
#include "numbers_Sums.h"

jint Java_numbers_Sums_firstNonSquareSum(JNIEnv * je, jobject jo) {

  int i, j, k;
  int thisInt = 0;
  double max;
  int triple;
  /* Wouldn't a Java boolean be much nicer? */
  int found = 0;

  while (!found) {
next:
    max = sqrt(thisInt);
    for (i = 0; i <= max; i++) {
      for (j = 0; j <= i; j++) {
        for (k = 0; k <= j; k++) {
          triple = i*i + j*j + k*k;
          if (triple == thisInt) {
            thisInt++;
            /* This is exactly what Java's labeled break lets you avoid */
```

(continued)

Listing 19-8
The native C firstNonCubeSum() function that returns a Java int *(continued)*

```
              goto next;
          }
       }
     }
   }
   found = 1;
}

return (jint) thisInt;

}
```

Passing primitive data type arguments to native methods

Passing arguments of primitive data types to native methods is analogous to returning them. They're passed by value as the types jboolean, jbyte, jshort, jint, jlong, jfloat, jdouble, and jchar.

For example, suppose you want to use the following method:

```
public native int firstNonTripleSum(int power);
```

Here, rather than hard coding the power to which you raise each value, you pass it as an argument. If power is 0, you look for the first number that is not the sum of three numbers raised to the zeroth power. If power is 1, you look for the first number that is not the sum of three numbers raised to the first power. If power is 2, you look for the first number that is not the sum of three numbers raised to the second power, and so on. Listing 19-8 has the revised Java program.

Compile this program and run javah on the result as before. This time, when you look at the header file, you find this function signature:

```
jint Java_numbers_Sums_firstNonPowerSum (JNIEnv *, jobject, jint);
```

The difference is the third argument, a jint. This is the variable in which the first int argument to the Java method — power — is passed. The first two arguments are pointers to a Java environment structure and the actual object that called this native method. Just ignore them for now, but you'll need them in the next section.

Mathematically, this is a much trickier problem. Two and three are simple cases that stop almost immediately. However, one never stops. Any integer n equals $0^1 + 0^1 + n^1$. Listing 19-9 is the native method for this case. It has extra logic to check to see if an overflow condition has been encountered. If so, the method returns -1. Later you'll see how to throw an exception instead.

Listing 19-9
The native C firstNonPowerSum(int power) function

```
#include <stdio.h>
#include <math.h>
#include "numbers_Sums.h"

jint Java_numbers_Sums_firstNonPowerSum(JNIEnv * je, jobject jo, jint p) {

  int i, j, k;
  int thisInt = 0;
  double max;
  int triple;
  /* Wouldn't a Java boolean be much nicer? */
  int found = 0;
  int power = (int) p;

  while (!found) {
next:
    max = sqrt(thisInt);
    for (i = 0; i <= max; i++) {
      for (j = 0; j <= i; j++) {
        for (k = 0; k <= j; k++) {
          triple = pow(i, power) + pow(j, power) + pow(k, power);
          if (triple == thisInt) {
            thisInt++;
            /* This is exactly what Java's labeled break lets you avoid */
            goto next;
          }
          if (triple < 0) { // wrap around error
            thisInt = -1;
            goto end;
          }
        }
      }
    }
    found = 1;
  }
end:
  return (jint) thisInt;

}
```

USING OBJECTS IN NATIVE METHODS

Passing and returning primitive data types lets you perform most non-array numeric calculations that need the most speed possible. It also lets you call the native API to do things that Java doesn't allow you to do. However, you can go even further by allowing your native methods to interact with Java classes, objects, arrays, and exceptions.

Objects, unlike primitive data types, are passed and returned by reference. In other words, the native method gets a pointer to the object. Every native C function that implements a native Java method receives at least two arguments, even if the native method is void. The first argument is a pointer to a JNIEnv struct. This is used to call functions that access the fields and methods of Java objects. The second argument is a pointer to the object that called the native method. (In the case of a static method, the second argument is a pointer to the class that called the method.)

Note   Arguments are passed to and values are returned from native methods just as they are in pure Java. All primitive types are passed by value, and all object types are passed by reference.

I'm going to present a fairly artificial example here. Good, non-artificial examples are a little hard to come by for two reasons. First, the Java class library provides a very strong model for most of the things you might want to do. The only real holes tend to be extremely platform-specific (UNIX passwords, Apple Events, and the like), and I want to make this discussion intelligible to as wide an audience as possible. Second it's only rarely necessary for native methods to interact with Java objects directly. Ninety percent of the cases can be handled by passing primitive data types back and forth.

In this example, consider a java.util.Vector containing java.lang.Integer objects. The native method will calculate the factorial of each element in the Vector and return a Vector of java.lang.Long objects. Listing 19-10 is the Java program that drives the application.

In this example, the native method calculate() reads an object argument, uses the methods of that object to get at its data, and returns a new object made up of many other new objects. The only thing that this example does not demonstrate is field access.

After compiling Listing 19-10 and running javah on the .class file, you see that your native calculate() method needs this signature:

```
jobject Java_VectorFactorial_calculate(JNIEnv *, jobject, jobject);
```

Listing 19-10
The VectorFactorial class

```java
import java.util.*;


public class VectorFactorial {


  public static void main(String[] args) {

    int limit = 10;
    Vector intVector = new Vector(limit + 1);

    try {
      limit = Integer.parseInt(args[0]);
    }
    catch (NumberFormatException e) {

    }

    for (int i = 0; i <= limit; i++) {
      intVector.addElement(new Integer(i));
    }

    VectorFactorial vf = new VectorFactorial();
    Enumeration ef = (Enumeration) vf.calculate(intVector);

    while (ef.hasMoreElements()) {
      System.out.println((Long) ef.nextElement());
    }

  }

  public native Vector calculate(Vector input);

}
```

Notice that the native method does not retain the type of the object being passed to it or the object returned by it. All Java objects are treated the same. It's up to the programmer to remember to what class each object belongs. There is no compile-time type checking on object classes. Of course, this opens up many potentially lethal bugs. This is one more reason to try to keep as much of the method in Java as possible.

If this weren't a tutorial example designed to show you how to interface between your native methods and your Java objects, but rather a real program, I would have parsed the integers out in Java and passed one primitive int at a time to the native method and returned one long at a time.

It's convenient to split the native C program into two pieces: the calculation of the factorial and the parsing of the Vector. The factorial is quite simple and looks like this:

```
jlong jfactorial(jint n) {

  jlong result = 1;
  jint i;

  if (n < 0) return -1;
  for (i = n; i > 0; i--) result *= i;

  return result;

}
```

Notice that I've used jints and jlongs instead of ints and longs. On most architectures, a jint is an int and a jlong is a long, but this guarantees that the types match up, even on more obscure platforms. (Just because you're writing a native method in C doesn't mean you shouldn't try to make the method as portable as possible.)

The parsing of the Vector is much more complex. If I were to write it in Java, it would look like this:

```
Vector Java_VectorFactorial_calculate(Vector vec) {

  Vector result = new Vector(vec.size());
  for (int i = 0; i < vec.size(); i++) {
    Integer theInteger = (Integer) vec.elementAt(i);
    int j = theInteger.intValue();
    long l = factorial(j);
    Long L = new Long(l);
    result.addElement(L);
  }

  return result;

}
```

You can see that I'm going to need to call the size(), elementAt(), and Vector() methods of the Vector class; the Long() constructor, the intValue() method of the Integer class; and the factorial function in the native C code. There's also some type casting, but because of C's weaker types, this won't transfer over into the C program.

Invoking instance methods

Look at the first method you need to call: Vector.size(). Here, size() is an instance method in the java.util.Vector class that returns an int. The specific vector whose size you want is passed as the jobject argument vec to the Java_VectorFactorial_calculate() function.

You cannot call Java methods directly from C. Instead, you first need to get an ID for the class that contains the method and then an ID for the method itself. Finally, you use a C function to invoke the method through its class and method ID. Thus, there are three steps to calling an instance method from C:

1. Get the class ID using the FindClass() function.
2. Get the method ID using the GetMethodID() function.
3. Invoke the method with the appropriate CallTypeMethod function.

If you invoke a method more than once, only the third step needs to be repeated. You can save and reuse the results of the first two.

Loading Java classes from C

Assuming that your import statements are in order, a Java program can load a class as soon as you invoke it. C programs aren't as intelligent. You must explicitly load every class that you're going to use with the FindClass() function. This function searches the CLASSPATH to find the requested class. It does not look at the CODEBASE or anywhere other than the CLASSPATH. This is the signature for FindClass:

```
jclass FindClass(JNIEnv *jne, const char *name);
```

Recall that CLASSPATH is a system environment variable, not a property of the Java runtime. Therefore, it's one of the few Java-related items that are easy to get to from inside a native method.

The jne argument is just the Java environment pointer passed as the first argument to your native method. You can pass it along here. The jne argument is also a handle (that is, a pointer to a pointer) to a table of function pointers. Thus, to call one of the JNI functions from C, you prefix it with (*jne)->. For example, to call FindClass() you'd write

```
(*jne)->FindClass(jne, "java/util/Vector");
```

I use C in this chapter, but the JNI also works well with most C++ compilers. You do need to use "extern C" to declare that your native functions use C calling conventions. Assuming that you've done this, in C++ you can instead write

```
jne->FindClass("java/util/Vector");
```

C++ automatically passes a pointer to the object that invoked the method (the *this* pointer) as the first argument to each method. (At the level of the virtual machine, Java does this, too.)

The second argument, name, is a C string literal containing the name of the class. This function returns a jclass. Don't worry about what data type jclass is. You'll use it only by passing it to other JNI functions.

For example, to load the java.util.Vector class, as you'll do shortly, you would write

```
jclass VectorID;
VectorID = (*jne)->FindClass(jne, "java/util/Vector");
```

C programs don't understand imports, so you must use fully qualified class names, packages and all, with the periods replaced by forward slashes — for example, "java/util/Vector" instead of "java.util.Vector."

Finding method IDs

Once you know the ID for a class, you can request the IDs of the methods in the class with the GetMethodID() function. The GetMethodID() function has the following signature:

```
jmethodID GetMethodID(JNIEnv *jne, jclass clazz, const char *name, const char *sig);
```

The actual body of these methods is included from the VectorFactorial.h file, probably through several indirections, much as classes are imported into Java programs through the import statement.

The GetMethodID() function takes four arguments. The first argument, env, is the same java environment pointer as was passed to the native function. You can just pass it along. The second argument is a jclass item called clazz. (It's misspelled because class is a keyword in both Java and C++.) This is the value returned by the previous call to FindClass(). The third argument is a C string with the name of the class — for example, "Vector." The fourth argument is a C string with the signature of the Java method — for example, "()I" for a method like size that takes no arguments and returns an int. These signatures are the same ones that you encountered way back in Chapter 4 that are used in the .class files. For example, to get the Method ID for the size() method in the Vector class, you would write

```
jmethodID sizeID;
sizeID = (*jne)->GetMethodID(env, VectorID, "size", "()I");
```

I've adopted the convention of naming the different method and class IDs by the name of the class or method followed by ID. This works quite well, at least for non-polymorphic methods, and makes code much more legible. However, you are free to use whatever convention makes sense to you.

Calling Java methods from C

Once you have method and class IDs in place, you can invoke the method through one of the CallTypeMethod functions. There are ten, one for each of the primitive types that a Java method may return, plus one for void and one for all reference types (objects and arrays). For example, a method that returns an int like Vector.size() is invoked with the CallIntMethod() function.

The ten methods are:

```
void CallVoidMethod(JNIEnv *jne, jobject obj, jmethodID methodID, ...)
jobject CallObjectMethod(JNIEnv *jne, jobject obj, jmethodID methodID, ...)
jboolean CallBooleanMethod(JNIEnv *jne, jobject obj, jmethodID methodID,
...)
jbyte CallByteMethod(JNIEnv *jne, jobject obj, jmethodID methodID, ...)
```

```
jchar CallCharMethod(JNIEnv *jne, jobject obj, jmethodID methodID, ...)
jshort CallShortMethod(JNIEnv *jne, jobject obj, jmethodID methodID, ...)
jint CallIntMethod(JNIEnv *jne, jobject obj, jmethodID methodID, ...)
jlong CallLongMethod(JNIEnv *jne, jobject obj, jmethodID methodID, ...)
jfloat CallFloatMethod(JNIEnv *jne, jobject obj, jmethodID methodID, ...)
jdouble CallDoubleMethod(JNIEnv *jne, jobject obj, jmethodID methodID, ...)
```

For example, to invoke the size() method on the Vector vec, now that you know the Method ID, you would write

```
int size;
size = CallIntMethod(env, vec, sizeID);
```

The . . . in each method signature is where the arguments to the method can be passed. C, unlike Java, allows variable-length argument lists.

Passing arguments to Java methods

From the standpoint of a Java programmer, each of these methods has multiple signatures. The first three arguments are always the Java environment pointer, the object itself, and the Method ID for the method being invoked. For example,

```
int CallIntMethod(JNIEnv* jne, jobject obj, jmethodID methodID)
```

However, unlike Java, C allows variable-length argument lists. The same function may be called with varying numbers of arguments. (This is most common in the printf family of functions.) Thus, any additional arguments passed to one of the CallTypeMethod() functions are passed as arguments to the Java method. For example, the elementAt() method is invoked like this:

```
int elementAtID;
jobject thisInteger;
int i;
.
.
.
elementAtID = (*jne)->GetMethodID(jne, VectorID, "elementAt", "(I)I");
thisInteger = (*jne)->CallObjectMethod(jne, vec, elementAtID, i);
```

If a method takes more than one argument, just keep adding arguments to the end of your CallTypeMethod function.

> **Note**
>
> Despite this, the JNI cannot resolve polymorphic methods based on the signature of the CallTypeMethod function alone. You must pass different signatures as the third argument of GetMethodID() to choose between polymorphic methods.

Alternate method invocations

For reasons that aren't entirely clear, JNI defines two more separate but equivalent sets of functions for invoking Java methods. The three different sets differ only in how the arguments to the Java method are passed in the C function.

The CallTypeMethodA functions pass arguments to Java methods in an array of jvalues called args. The array is passed as the fourth argument to a CallTypeMethodA method. These functions are

```
    void CallVoidMethodA(JNIEnv *jne, jobject obj, jmethodID methodID, jvalue
*args)
    jobject CallObjectMethodA(JNIEnv *jne, jobject obj, jmethodID methodID,
jvalue *args)
    jboolean CallBooleanMethodA(JNIEnv *jne, jobject obj, jmethodID methodID,
jvalue *args)
    jbyte CallByteMethodA(JNIEnv *jne, jobject obj, jmethodID methodID, jvalue
*args)
    jchar CallCharMethodA(JNIEnv *jne, jobject obj, jmethodID methodID, jvalue
*args)
    jshort CallShortMethodA(JNIEnv *jne, jobject obj, jmethodID methodID,
jvalue *args)
    jint CallIntMethodA(JNIEnv *jne, jobject obj, jmethodID methodID, jvalue
*args)
    jlong CallLongMethodA(JNIEnv *jne, jobject obj, jmethodID methodID, jvalue
*args)
    jfloat CallFloatMethodA(JNIEnv *jne, jobject obj, jmethodID methodID,
jvalue *args)
    jdouble CallDoubleMethodA(JNIEnv *jne, jobject obj, jmethodID methodID,
jvalue *args)
```

> **Note**
>
> A va_list is a piece of C arcana that most C programmers never need to deal with. It's a C struct defined in <stdarg.h> precisely to handle variable-length argument lists. For more details, see *The C Programming Language*, Brian W. Kernighan and Dennis M. Ritchie, 2nd Edition (Prentice Hall, 1988).

The CallTypeMethodV functions pass arguments to Java methods in a va_list called args that is passed as the fourth argument to the CallTypeMethodV method. These functions are

```
    void CallVoidMethodV(JNIEnv *jne, jobject obj, jmethodID methodID, va_list
args)
    jobject CallObjectMethodV(JNIEnv *jne, jobject obj, jmethodID methodID,
va_list args)
    jboolean CallBooleanMethodV(JNIEnv *jne, jobject obj, jmethodID methodID,
va_list args)
    jbyte CallByteMethodV(JNIEnv *jne, jobject obj, jmethodID methodID, va_list
args)
    jchar CallCharMethodV(JNIEnv *jne, jobject obj, jmethodID methodID, va_list
args)
    jshort CallShortMethodV(JNIEnv *jne, jobject obj, jmethodID methodID,
va_list args)
    jint CallIntMethodV(JNIEnv *jne, jobject obj, jmethodID methodID, va_list
args)
    jlong CallLongMethodV(JNIEnv *jne, jobject obj, jmethodID methodID, va_list
args)
    jfloat CallFloatMethodV(JNIEnv *jne, jobject obj, jmethodID methodID,
va_list args)
    jdouble CallDoubleMethodV(JNIEnv *jne, jobject obj, jmethodID methodID,
va_list args)
```

Note

In essence, what you've got here is 30 different versions of the same method with 30 different argument lists. These three different sets of functions to call Java methods would be a perfect place for a little polymorphism, if only C supported it. Once again, I find myself wishing for the simplicity of Java.

Invoking constructors from C

Java has special syntax to invoke constructor methods. In C, Java constructors are invoked via the NewObject() function. However, the name used is the one in the .class file, <init>, and not the name of the class. For example, to create a new Vector object with the same size as the Vector object vec, you would write

```
    jmethodID VectorConstructorID;
    jobject LongVector;
    jclass VectorID;
    jint size;
```

```
        VectorID = (*jne)->FindClass(jne, "java/util/Vector");
        sizeID = (*jne)->GetMethodID(jne, VectorID, "size", "()V");
        VectorConstructorID = (*jne)->GetMethodID(jne, VectorID, "<init>",
"(I)V");

        size = (*jne)->CallIntMethod(jne, vec, sizeID);
        LongVector = (*jne)->NewObject(jne, LongID, "<init>", size);
```

In the signature part of the call, specify that the constructor returns void.

As with other methods, constructors can be called with variable length argument lists. The example passes one argument — size — to the Java Vector() constructor.

Access Protection in Native Methods

You may be wondering whether access protection — that is, private, protected, and public — extends to native methods. So far, I've shown you only public methods and classes.

Of course, once you're in C, you're no longer limited to playing by the rules. A C pointer can be the address of arbitrary points in memory, and with a lot of hacking, you could certainly use pointers to sneak around Java's access controls. The JNI only protects standard access to the Java environment. It does not and cannot protect against outright fraud. The Java byte code verifier can and does protect against fraud, but can protect only against fraudulent Java code, not fraudulent native code.

Listing 19-11 is the completed C code for the native method Java_VectorFactorial_calculate(). It uses constructors and method invocations extensively.

Listing 19-11
The calculate.c program

```
#include <stdio.h>
#include <stdlib.h>
#include <math.h>
#include "VectorFactorial.h"

jlong jfactorial(jint n) {

  jlong result = 1;
  jint i;
```

(continued)

Listing 19-11

The calculate.c program *(continued)*

```c
    if (n < 0) return -1;
    for (i = n; i > 0; i--) result *= i;

    return result;

}


jobject Java_VectorFactorial_calculate(JNIEnv* jne, jobject jo, jobject vec) {

    /* In Java this method would look like this */
    /*
    Vector result = new Vector(vec.size());
    for (int i = 0; i < vec.size(); i++) {
      Integer theInteger = vec.elementAt(i);
      int j = theInteger.intValue();
      long l = factorial(j);
      result.addElement(l);
    }

     return result;
     */

    jmethodID elementAtID, VectorConstructorID, sizeID, LongConstructorID,
intValueID, addElementID;
    jobject thisInteger, LongVector, thisLong;
    jclass VectorID, LongID, IntegerID;
    jint size, value;
    jlong fac;
    jint i;


    VectorID = (*jne)->FindClass(jne, "java/util/Vector");
    LongID = (*jne)->FindClass(jne, "java/lang/Long");
    IntegerID = (*jne)->FindClass(jne, "java/lang/Integer");
    intValueID = (*jne)->GetMethodID(jne, VectorID, "intValue", "()I");
    elementAtID = (*jne)->GetMethodID(jne, VectorID, "elementAt", "(I)I");
    addElementID = (*jne)->GetMethodID(jne, VectorID, "addElementID",
"(Ljava/lang/Object;)V");
    sizeID = (*jne)->GetMethodID(jne, VectorID, "size", "()V");
    VectorConstructorID = (*jne)->GetMethodID(jne, VectorID, "<init>", "(I)V");
    LongConstructorID = (*jne)->GetMethodID(jne, LongID, "<init>", "(I)V");

    size = (*jne)->CallIntMethod(jne, vec, sizeID);
    LongVector = (*jne)->NewObject(jne, LongID, LongConstructorID, size);
```

(continued)

The calculate.c program *(continued)*

```
    for (i = 0; i < size; i++) {
      thisInteger = (*jne)->CallObjectMethod(jne, vec, elementAtID, i);
      value = (*jne)->CallIntMethod(jne, thisInteger, intValueID);
      fac = jfactorial(value);
      thisLong = (*jne)->CallObjectMethod(jne, LongVector, LongConstructorID,
  fac);
      (*jne)->CallObjectMethod(jne, LongVector, addElementID, thisLong);
    }

    return LongVector;

  }
```

Using strings in native methods

As you learned in Chapter 3, Java implements strings as arrays of 2-byte, Unicode characters. C implements strings as pointers to null-terminated blocks of ASCII bytes. It isn't hard to convert from one to the other as long as the Unicode characters fit into the ASCII or ISO Latin-1 character sets, but because this is such a common operation, the JNI provides several methods to help you out.

The jstring type is used to represent Java strings within the C code.

The NewString() method constructs a new Java String object from an array of Unicode characters:

```
    jstring NewString(JNIEnv *jne, const jchar *unicodeChars, jsize len);
```

The GetStringLength() method returns the length of a jstring:

```
    jsize GetStringLength(JNIEnv *jne, jstring string);
```

The GetStringChars() function copies the characters from a jstring into an array of Unicode characters. It returns a pointer to that array:

```
    const jchar * GetStringChars(JNIEnv *jne, jstring string, jboolean
  *isCopy);
```

This pointer is valid until you call ReleaseStringChars(), which you should do when you're finished with the String to avoid memory leaks.

The isCopy argument is a pointer to a jboolean (that is, an unsigned char). Assuming that isCopy is not null, *isCopy is set to 1 (true) if the copy is successful and 0 (false) if the copy is unsuccessful.

The ReleaseStringChars() method frees the memory used by a particular jstring and its corresponding array of characters:

```
void ReleaseStringChars(JNIEnv *jne, jstring string,  const jchar *chars);
```

The chars argument should be NULL (the C equivalent of Java's null) or a pointer previously returned by invoking GetStringChars() on this string.

The NewStringUTF() function constructs a new Java string from an array of bytes encoding Unicode characters in UTF-8 format:

```
jstring NewStringUTF(JNIEnv *jne, const char *bytes, jsize length);
```

Because of the way that UTF-8 is defined, an ASCII C string (but not an ISO Latin-1 C string!) is a perfectly valid UTF-8 string. Therefore, if your C strings are pure ASCII, you can use them to produce Java strings very easily with this function. For example,

```
jstring jhello;
char* chello = "Hello";
hello = (*jne->) NewStringUTF(jne, chello, strlen(chello));
```

The GetStringUTFLength() function returns the number of bytes that a string would need to be encoded in UTF-8 format.

```
jsize GetStringUTFLength(JNIEnv *jne, jstring string);
```

The GetStringUTFChars() function returns a pointer to an array of UTF-8 characters.

```
jbyte* GetStringUTFChars(JNIEnv *jne, jstring string, jboolean *isCopy);
```

This pointer is valid until you call ReleaseStringUTFChars(), which you should do when you're finished with the string to avoid memory leaks.

These two functions are most commonly used to convert Java strings to C strings. For example

```
jstring s;
...
 const jbyte *str = (*jne)->GetStringUTFChars(jne, s, 0);
 /* work with the string
...
*/
(*jne)->ReleaseStringUTFChars(jne, s, str);
```

The isCopy argument is a pointer to a jboolean (that is, an unsigned char). Assuming isCopy is not null, then *isCopy is set to JNI_TRUE (1) if the copy is successful and JNI_FALSE (0) if the copy is unsuccessful.

The ReleaseStringUTFChars() function frees the memory used by a UTF-8 string:

```
void ReleaseStringUTFChars(JNIEnv *jne, jstring string, const jbyte *utf);
```

Using arrays in native methods

There are two fundamental kinds of array problems. The simplest is one in which the array is just a convenient data structure for a list of objects, but in which the components of the array don't have any particular relation to each other. Each component can be operated on individually. Most arrays of objects are of this type.

The more complicated problem is the one in which the components are more closely tied together and multiple array components must be used in each part of a calculation. Examples of the latter sort of problem include numeric integration, matrix multiplication, eigenvalue problems, Markov chains, coordinate transformation, Fourier transforms, and many other situations of scientific and engineering interest.

If the first case, simple lists of data, were all that native methods needed to deal with, then it would be sufficient to pass individual components of an array to native methods, one at a time. Indeed, the JNI provides functions to do exactly this, and this is the only way to access arrays of objects. However, it's the second case where raw performance truly becomes important, and one is far more likely to need to use native methods. For these cases, the overhead of making method calls or function invocations to access each and every array component would quickly overwhelm the speed benefits achieved by native methods. For example, passing a 100 by 100 component array would require 10,000 separate function calls. What's needed is a way to pass an entire array or sub-array to a native method with one function call.

In all languages and on all computer architectures, including the various Java virtual machines, an array is a contiguous block of memory. For example, an int array with four elements is 16 contiguous bytes of memory (four ints times four bytes per int). In Java, this memory is allocated in the heap.

In computer memory, multi-dimensional arrays are reduced to one-dimensional arrays, and the compiler generally handles the necessary overhead of converting between representations. A two-dimensional int array with 100 rows and 100 columns is 40,000 contiguous bytes of memory (100 times 100 ints times 4 bytes per int).

In C, an array is very close to a pointer to a block of memory. Array indexes and pointer arithmetic are different ways of accessing the same block of memory. Therefore, the obvious solution is to allow the runtime to pass a pointer to the memory used by the Java array. The C program can then just go ahead and use the array in its normal fashion.

> **Note** Contrary to popular belief, it's not quite true that arrays and pointers are the same thing in C, although it is close enough to the truth for my purposes in this chapter. For complete details about the relationship between arrays and pointers in C, see *Expert C Programming,* Peter van der Linden (Sunsoft Press/Prentice Hall, 1994).

The problem with this simple solution is that Java's garbage collector may move objects, including arrays, in the heap at unexpected times. Because Java is multithreaded, a native method may begin executing with a valid pointer to an array, but suddenly find that the array has moved out from where it was supposed to be. If the native function is reading from the array, it will get invalid data. If the native function is writing to the array, it may end up writing instead to empty space or inside the private data of another object in the heap. This sends the virtual machine crashing down in flames.

The solution is to provide native methods with a means of telling the virtual machine not to move a particular array in memory. This has the disadvantage of fragmenting Java's heap and possibly leading to OutOfMemoryErrors, especially with very large arrays. Therefore, these *pinning* functions may first copy a Java array or sub-array in a synchronized fashion to a block of memory outside the Java heap, and thus outside the control of the garbage collector, and then copy it back when the native function is through with it.

Accessing object components

The functions in this section return specific components in an array. These components are returned:

```
jobject GetObjectArrayElement(JNIEnv *jne, jarray a, jsize i);
```

This method returns a reference to the object at the *ith* position in the array a. As always, jne is the JNI interface pointer. This function will throw an ArrayIndexOutOfBoundsException if i is beyond the length of the array:

```
void SetObjectArrayElement(JNIEnv *jne, jarray a, jsize i, jobject o);
```

The SetObjectArrayElement() function stores the object o into the array a at the index i. This function throws an ArrayIndexOutOfBoundsException if i is beyond the bounds of the array, or an ArrayStoreException if the o's class is not a subclass of the component class of the array (for example, if you're trying to store an Integer object into an array of String objects).

Accessing scalar components

The GetScalarArrayElements() functions return a pointer to a block of memory that you can access as a native C array. This may or may not involve copying the array from the Java heap into the C heap. The ReleaseScalarArrayElements() functions copy the array back into the Java heap (if necessary) and invalidate the pointer. Different threads accessing the same array may or may not see the results of writes to the array before ReleaseScalarArrayElements() is called.

As usual, there are eight variations of GetScalarArrayElements, one for each primitive data type. These are

```
jboolean* GetBooleanArrayElements(JNIEnv *jne, jarray array, jboolean
*isCopy)
    jbyte* GetByteArrayElements(JNIEnv *jne, jarray array, jboolean *isCopy)
    jchar* GetCharArrayElements(JNIEnv *jne, jarray array, jboolean *isCopy)
    jshort* GetShortArrayElements(JNIEnv *jne, jarray array, jboolean *isCopy)
    jint* GetIntArrayElements(JNIEnv *jne, jarray array, jboolean *isCopy)
    jlong* GetLongArrayElements(JNIEnv *jne, jarray array, jboolean *isCopy)
    jfloat* GetFloatArrayElements(JNIEnv *jne, jarray array, jboolean *isCopy)
    jdouble* GetDoubleArrayElements(JNIEnv *jne, jarray array, jboolean
*isCopy)
```

As usual, jne is the Java Native Interface pointer. The array argument is, of course, the array from which the components will be copied. The isCopy argument is a pointer to a jboolean. The GetArrayElements() function sets isCopy to JNI_TRUE if the array elements were copied from the Java heap into a new block of memory and to JNI_FALSE if the components were not copied and the returned pointer points into the Java heap. You normally pass it using the C address-of operator &, like this:

```
jint* CData;
jboolean isCopy;
jarray javaData

...
CData = (*jne)->GetIntArrayElements(jne, javaData, &isCopy);
if (isCopy) {
...
```

There are also eight variations of ReleaseScalarArrayElements():

```
    void ReleaseBooleanArrayElements(JNIEnv *jne, jarray array, jboolean*
elems, jint mode)
    void ReleaseByteArrayElements(JNIEnv *jne, jarray array, jbyte* elems, jint
mode)
    void ReleaseCharArrayElements(JNIEnv *jne, jarray array, jchar* elems, jint
mode)
    void ReleaseShortArrayElements(JNIEnv *jne, jarray array, jshort* elems,
jint mode)
    void ReleaseIntArrayElements(JNIEnv *jne, jarray array, jint* elems, jint
mode)
    void ReleaseLongArrayElements(JNIEnv *jne, jarray array, jlong* elems, jint
mode)
    void ReleaseFloatArrayElements(JNIEnv *jne, jarray array, jfloat* elems,
jint mode)
    void ReleaseDoubleArrayElements(JNIEnv *jne, jarray jdata, jdouble* cdata,
jint mode)
```

As usual, jne is the Java Native Interface pointer. The jdata argument is the Java array from which the components were copied. The cdata argument is the pointer to the C array into which the elements were copied. These pointers may point to the same place, but you should not assume that.

Finally, mode should be zero or one of two defined constants, JNI_COMMIT and JNI_ABORT. This argument matters only if isCopy from GetScalarArrayElements is JNI_TRUE — that is, if a copy of the Java array was made for the C array. In this case, passing zero as the mode copies back the C array elements into the jdata array, and frees the C array cdata. However, if mode is set to JNI_COMMIT, then the C array elements are copied into the jdata array but the cdata array is not released. Another call to ReleaseArrayElements() is required to actually free the memory used by the C array.

On the other hand, if mode is set to JNI_ABORT, then the memory used by the C array is freed, but its elements are not copied into the jdata array. It's as if the original Java array was never changed.

Copying Sub-Arrays

The SetScalarArrayElements and ReleaseScalarArrayElements family of functions may or may not copy the data from the Java heap into the C heap, depending on the virtual machine. To guarantee that the data is copied, you should use the GetScalarArrayRegion and SetScalarArrayRegion functions. These methods ensure that your native C functions have exclusive access to their data while running. (Other threads may still change the Java arrays.)

The GetScalarArrayRegion functions copy data from a Java array into a C array. As usual, there is a version for each primitive Java data type:

```
void GetBooleanArrayRegion(JNIEnv *jne, jarray jdata, jsize start, jsize
len, jboolean *cdata)
void GetByteArrayRegion(JNIEnv *jne, jarray jdata, jsize start, jsize len,
jbyte *cdata)
void GetCharArrayRegion(JNIEnv *jne, jarray jdata, jsize start, jsize len,
jchar *cdata)
void GetShortArrayRegion(JNIEnv *jne, jarray jdata, jsize start, jsize len,
jshort *cdata)
void GetIntArrayRegion(JNIEnv *jne, jarray jdata, jsize start, jsize len,
jint *cdata)
void GetLongArrayRegion(JNIEnv *jne, jarray jdata, jsize start, jsize len,
jlong *cdata)
void GetFloatArrayRegion(JNIEnv *jne, jarray jdata, jsize start, jsize len,
jfloat *cdata)
void GetDoubleArrayRegion(JNIEnv *jne, jarray jdata, jsize start, jsize
len, jdouble* cdata)
```

The SetScalarArrayRegion functions copy data from a C array into a Java array:

```
void SetBooleanArrayRegion(JNIEnv *jne, jarray jdata, jsize start, jsize
len, jboolean *cdata)
void SetByteArrayRegion(JNIEnv *jne, jarray jdata, jsize start, jsize len,
jbyte *cdata)
void SetCharArrayRegion(JNIEnv *jne, jarray jdata, jsize start, jsize len,
jchar *cdata)
void SetShortArrayRegion(JNIEnv *jne, jarray jdata, jsize start, jsize len,
jshort *cdata)
```

```
    void SetIntArrayRegion(JNIEnv *jne, jarray jdata, jsize start, jsize len,
jint *cdata)
    void SetLongArrayRegion(JNIEnv *jne, jarray jdata, jsize start, jsize len,
jlong *cdata)
    void SetFloatArrayRegion(JNIEnv *jne, jarray jdata, jsize start, jsize len,
jfloat *cdata)
    void SetDoubleArrayRegion(JNIEnv *jne, jarray jdata, jsize start, jsize
len, jdouble* cdata)
```

As usual, jne is the Java Native Interface pointer; jdata is a reference to the java array; and cdata is a reference to the C array. The start argument is the index in the Java array where the copying from or to starts, and len is the number of elements to copy. (Data is always taken from or put into the cdata array starting at the beginning.) An ArrayIndexOutOfBoundsException will be thrown if (start + len - 1) is out of bounds for the Java array.

Other array operations

Java also provides methods to determine the length of the array and to create new arrays:

```
    jsize GetArrayLength(JNIEnv* jne, jarray array);
```

The GetArrayLength() function returns the number of components in the specified array. It is equivalent to returning array.length. This is often useful when you need to know how large a buffer to allocate for scalar data copied from a Java array.

```
    jarray NewObjectArray(JNIEnv* jne, jsize length, jclass componentClass,
jobject initialElement);
```

The NewObjectArray() function creates a new array of length objects, each of whose components is of the class componentClass. Each element of the array is set as a reference to the object initialElement (which may be null). If the array cannot be created, NULL is returned.

There are also eight functions to create scalar arrays, one for each primitive data type:

```
    jarray NewBooleanArray(JNIEnv* jne, jsize length)
    jarray NewByteArray(JNIEnv* jne, jsize length)
    jarray NewCharArray(JNIEnv* jne, jsize length)
    jarray NewShortArray(JNIEnv* jne, jsize length)
    jarray NewIntArray(JNIEnv* jne, jsize length)
    jarray NewLongArray(JNIEnv* jne, jsize length)
    jarray NewFloatArray(JNIEnv* jne, jsize length)
    jarray NewDoubleArray(JNIEnv* jne, jsize length)
```

As usual, *jne* is the Java Native Interface pointer, and *length* is the number of components in the array. Each of these methods returns a jarray, which will be NULL if the array cannot be created.

Accessing fields from native methods

Instance fields are accessed much as instance methods are. However, instead of jmethodID, there is a jfieldID; instead of calling the getMethodID() function, you call the getFieldID() function; and instead of CallIntMethod() and the like, there are GetIntField(), SetIntField() and the like.

The GetFieldID() takes a Java environment pointer, a jclass Class ID, a name of a field, and a signature of a field, and returns a jfieldID for that field. You then use this field ID in the various GetField and SetField functions.

```
jfieldID GetFieldID(JNIEnv *jne, jclass clazz, const char *name, const char *sig)
```

The only argument that really needs any explanation is the *sig*, or signature of the field. It is similar to method signatures, except not nearly as complex. Here, sig is a one-letter string that defines the type of the field, as shown in Table 19-1.

Table 19-1

The Field signature strings

Type	String
boolean	"Z"
byte	"B"
char	"C"
short	"S"
int	"I"
long	"J"
float	"F"
double	"D"
object	"Lpackage/subpackage/class;", e.g. "Ljava/lang/String;"

The GetTypeField() functions return the value of an instance field of an object. The field is specified by a field ID obtained from GetFieldID():

```
jobject GetObjectField(JNIEnv *jne, jobject obj, jfieldID fieldID)
jboolean GetBooleanField(JNIEnv *jne, jobject obj, jfieldID fieldID)
jbyte GetByteField(JNIEnv *jne, jobject obj, jfieldID fieldID)
jchar GetCharField(JNIEnv *jne, jobject obj, jfieldID fieldID)
jshort GetShortField(JNIEnv *jne, jobject obj, jfieldID fieldID)
jint GetIntField(JNIEnv *jne, jobject obj, jfieldID fieldID)
jlong GetLongField(JNIEnv *jne, jobject obj, jfieldID fieldID)
jfloat GetFloatField(JNIEnv *jne, jobject obj, jfieldID fieldID)
jdouble GetDoubleField(JNIEnv *jne, jobject obj, jfieldID fieldID)
```

There are nine corresponding SetField methods as well. Each returns void and takes one additional argument of the appropriate type:

```
void SetObjectField(JNIEnv *jne, jobject obj, jfieldID fieldID, jobject
value)
void SetBooleanField(JNIEnv *jne, jobject obj, jfieldID fieldID, jboolean
value)
void SetByteField(JNIEnv *jne, jobject obj, jfieldID fieldID, jbyte value)
void SetCharField(JNIEnv *jne, jobject obj, jfieldID fieldID, jchar value)
void SetShortField(JNIEnv *jne, jobject obj, jfieldID fieldID, jshort
value)
void SetIntField(JNIEnv *jne, jobject obj, jfieldID fieldID, jint value)
void SetLongField(JNIEnv *jne, jobject obj, jfieldID fieldID, jlong value)
void SetFloatField(JNIEnv *jne, jobject obj, jfieldID fieldID, jfloat
value)
void SetDoubleField(JNIEnv *jne, jobject obj, jfieldID fieldID, jdouble
value)
```

Static methods and fields in native methods

Static methods and fields are called from native methods, much as instance methods and fields are. However, wherever you'd pass a reference to an object (a jobject) to invoke an instance method or an instance field, you instead pass a reference to a class (a jclass). It would be nice if the C functions could be otherwise identical, but C is not polymorphic, so you must use slightly different method names instead. For methods, these are

```
jmethodID GetStaticMethodID(JNIEnv *jne, jclass clazz, const char *name,
const char *sig);
```

```
    void CallStaticVoidMethod(JNIEnv *jne, jclass clazz, jmethodID methodID,
...)
    jobject CallStaticObjectMethod(JNIEnv *jne, jclass clazz, jmethodID
methodID, ...)
    jboolean CallStaticBooleanMethod(JNIEnv *jne, jclass clazz, jmethodID
methodID, ...)
    jbyte CallStaticByteMethod(JNIEnv *jne, jclass clazz, jmethodID methodID,
...)
    jchar CallStaticCharMethod(JNIEnv *jne, jclass clazz, jmethodID methodID,
...)
    jshort CallStaticShortMethod(JNIEnv *jne, jclass clazz, jmethodID methodID,
...)
    jint CallStaticIntMethod(JNIEnv *jne, jclass clazz, jmethodID methodID,
...)
    jlong CallStaticLongMethod(JNIEnv *jne, jclass clazz, jmethodID methodID,
...)
    jfloat CallStaticFloatMethod(JNIEnv *jne, jclass clazz, jmethodID methodID,
...)
    jdouble CallStaticDoubleMethod(JNIEnv *jne, jclass clazz, jmethodID
methodID, ...)

    void CallStaticVoidMethodA(JNIEnv *jne, jclass clazz, jmethodID methodID,
jvalue *args)
    jobject CallStaticObjectMethodA(JNIEnv *jne, jclass clazz, jmethodID
methodID, jvalue *args)
    jboolean CallStaticBooleanMethodA(JNIEnv *jne, jclass clazz, jmethodID
methodID, jvalue *args)
    jbyte CallStaticByteMethodA(JNIEnv *jne, jclass clazz, jmethodID methodID,
jvalue *args)
    jchar CallStaticCharMethodA(JNIEnv *jne, jclass clazz, jmethodID methodID,
jvalue *args)
    jshort CallStaticShortMethodA(JNIEnv *jne, jclass clazz, jmethodID
methodID, jvalue *args)
    jint CallStaticIntMethodA(JNIEnv *jne, jclass clazz, jmethodID methodID,
jvalue *args)
    jlong CallStaticLongMethodA(JNIEnv *jne, jclass clazz, jmethodID methodID,
jvalue *args)
    jfloat CallStaticFloatMethodA(JNIEnv *jne, jclass clazz, jmethodID
methodID, jvalue *args)
    jdouble CallStaticDoubleMethodA(JNIEnv *jne, jclass clazz, jmethodID
methodID, ...)

    void CallStaticVoidMethodV(JNIEnv *jne, jclass clazz, jmethodID methodID,
va_list *args)
    jobject CallStaticObjectMethodV(JNIEnv *jne, jclass clazz, jmethodID
methodID, va_list *args)
    jboolean CallStaticBooleanMethodV(JNIEnv *jne, jclass clazz, jmethodID
methodID, va_list *args)
```

```
    jbyte CallStaticByteMethodV(JNIEnv *jne, jclass clazz, jmethodID methodID,
va_list *args)
    jchar CallStaticCharMethodV(JNIEnv *jne, jclass clazz, jmethodID methodID,
va_list *args)
    jshort CallStaticShortMethodV(JNIEnv *jne, jclass clazz, jmethodID
methodID, va_list *args)
    jint CallStaticIntMethodV(JNIEnv *jne, jclass clazz, jmethodID methodID,
va_list *args)
    jlong CallStaticLongMethodV(JNIEnv *jne, jclass clazz, jmethodID methodID,
va_list *args)
    jfloat CallStaticFloatMethodV(JNIEnv *jne, jclass clazz, jmethodID
methodID, va_list *args)
    jdouble CallStaticDoubleMethodV(JNIEnv *jne, jclass clazz, jmethodID
methodID, ...)
```

For fields, the relevant functions are

```
    jfieldID GetStaticFieldID(JNIEnv *jne, jclass clazz, const char *name,
const char *sig);

    jobject GetStaticObjectField(JNIEnv *jne, jclass clazz, jfieldID fieldID)
    jboolean GetStaticBooleanField(JNIEnv *jne, jclass clazz, jfieldID fieldID)
    jbyte GetStaticByteField(JNIEnv *jne, jclass clazz, jfieldID fieldID)
    jchar GetStaticCharField(JNIEnv *jne, jclass clazz, jfieldID fieldID)
    jshort GetStaticShortField(JNIEnv *jne, jclass clazz, jfieldID fieldID)
    jint GetStaticIntField(JNIEnv *jne, jclass clazz, jfieldID fieldID)
    jlong GetStaticLongField(JNIEnv *jne, jclass clazz, jfieldID fieldID)
    jfloat GetStaticFloatField(JNIEnv *jne, jclass clazz, jfieldID fieldID)
    jdouble GetStaticDoubleField(JNIEnv *jne, jclass clazz, jfieldID fieldID)

    jobject SetStaticObjectField(JNIEnv *jne, jclass clazz, jfieldID fieldID,
jobject value)
    jboolean SetStaticBooleanField(JNIEnv *jne, jclass clazz, jfieldID fieldID,
jboolean value)
    jbyte SetStaticByteField(JNIEnv *jne, jclass clazz, jfieldID fieldID, jbyte
value)
    jchar SetStaticCharField(JNIEnv *jne, jclass clazz, jfieldID fieldID, jchar
value)
    jshort SetStaticShortField(JNIEnv *jne, jclass clazz, jfieldID fieldID,
jshort value)
    jint SetStaticIntField(JNIEnv *jne, jclass clazz, jfieldID fieldID, jint
value)
    jlong SetStaticLongField(JNIEnv *jne, jclass clazz, jfieldID fieldID, jlong
value)
    jfloat SetStaticFloatField(JNIEnv *jne, jclass clazz, jfieldID fieldID,
jfloat value)
    jdouble SetStaticDoubleField(JNIEnv *jne, jclass clazz, jfieldID fieldID,
jdouble value)
```

Every one of these methods behaves exactly like the similarly named instance function, except for the single difference that you pass a Class ID instead of an object ID, so I won't bore you with the details. I'll just show a quick example of a C function that uses some of these functions to read several system properties through the static System.getProperty() method. Although I'm not going to do more than print them out here, in a real-world program, it would not be at all unusual to want to check the version and vendor of Java. Whereas most system properties are accessible through the standard C library getenv() function, the version and vendor of Java are not. You must use Java methods to get them.

Listing 19-11 is a very simple program that calls the native method printVersion() when launched from the command line.

Listing 19-11
The NativeStaticTest class

```
public class NativeStaticTest {

  public static void main(String[] args) {

    System.loadLibrary("print");
    printVersion();

  }

  public static native void printVersion();

}
```

The printVersion() method itself is declared static as well as native, so I also have an opportunity to show you how native static methods differ from native instance methods. The difference is exactly what you would guess. Instead of a jobject being passed as the second argument to the C function, a jclass is passed. After compiling NativeStaticTest.java with javac and running javah -jni on it, you see that your C function needs this signature:

```
void Java_NativeStaticTest_printVersion (JNIEnv *, jclass);
```

Listing 19-12 is the C function, printVersion. To call the System.getProperty() method, it first gets a class ID for the java.lang.System class using FindClass(), exactly as it would do if it were calling an instance

method. With this number, it can get a method ID for the getProperty()
method through the getStaticMethodID() function. With these two
numbers, it can invoke the System.getProperty method through
CallStaticVoidMethod().

Listing 19-12
printVersion.c

```c
#include <stdio.h>
#include <stdlib.h>
#include <string.h>
#include "NativeStaticTest.h"


void Java_NativeStaticTest_printVersion (JNIEnv *jne, jclass jc) {

  jmethodID getPropertyID, valueOfID, doubleValueID;
  jclass SystemID, DoubleID;
  jobject javaversion, tempdouble;
  jdouble version;

  SystemID = (*jne)->FindClass(jne, "java/lang/System");
  DoubleID = (*jne)->FindClass(jne, "java/lang/Double");
  getPropertyID = (*jne)->GetStaticMethodID(jne, SystemID, "getProperty",
   "(Ljava/lang/String;Ljava/lang/String;)Ljava/lang/String;");

  javaversion = (*jne)->CallStaticObjectMethod(jne, SystemID, getPropertyID,
"java.version", "unknown");

  /* Convert the returned String to a double and print it*/
  valueOfID = (*jne)->GetMethodID(jne, DoubleID, "valueOf",
   "(Ljava/lang/String;)Ljava/lang/Double;");
  tempdouble = (*jne)->CallStaticDoubleMethod(jne, DoubleID, valueOfID,
javaversion);
  doubleValueID = (*jne)->GetMethodID(jne, DoubleID, "doubleValue",
   "(Ljava/lang/String;)Ljava/lang/Double;");
  version = (*jne)->CallDoubleMethod(jne, tempdouble, doubleValueID);

  printf("This is version %f of Java", version);

}
```

Errors and exceptions in native methods

Native methods can throw exceptions. In fact, some of the functions that you've already seen occasionally throw exceptions and errors. For example, GetMethodID() throws a NoSuchMethodError if the requested method is not present in the class. Other methods such as FindClass() may return NULL if they fail to complete. So far, the examples in this chapter have ignored these problems, because unlike in Java, the C compiler does not force you to handle them. There are no checked exceptions in C. Still, it is the programmer's responsibility to check for and handle exceptional conditions appropriately.

The JNI provides several methods that you can use to throw new exceptions and handle ones thrown by the function library. Of course, you can also wrap your calls to the native method in the Java source code with try-catch blocks that handle the most common exceptions.

The basic Throw() function throws a previously created Throwable object:

```
jint Throw(JNIEnv *jne, jobject theThrowable)
```

It returns zero if the throw succeeded and a negative number if the throw failed.

On the other hand, to throw a new exception, pass the class of the Throwable and a string message to the ThrowNew() function:

```
jint ThrowNew(JNIEnv *jne, jclass clazz, const char *message);
```

This method also returns zero on success or a negative value on failure.

C does not have a try-catch mechanism, and the C++ mechanism does not merge well with Java's. However, you can use the ExceptionOccurred() function to determine whether an exception is currently being thrown:

```
jobject ExceptionOccurred(JNIEnv *jne);
```

The function returns the exception object that is currently being thrown or NULL if no exception is currently being thrown. If an exception is being thrown, you can use the ExceptionClear() function to clear it. If there's no such exception, ExceptionClear() does nothing:

```
void ExceptionClear(JNIEnv *jne)
```

The ExceptionDescribe() function is a useful debugging tool that prints a stack trace on stderr:

```
void ExceptionDescribe(JNIEnv *jne);
```

The FatalError() function essentially tells the VM to bail. There is little hope of recovery:

```
void FatalError(JNIEnv *jne, char* message);
```

Garbage collection and native methods

Passing objects to native methods presents a problem for the garbage collector because it has to know whether or not a native method is finished with an object. Thus, references used by native methods are divided into two groups: local and global references.

Local references are the most common. Objects passed to a native method are passed with a local reference, and the object can be garbage-collected as soon as the native method returns (assuming no other references to the object exist, of course). All of the references that you've seen so far in this chapter have been local references.

A global reference, on the other hand, is still valid after the native method returns. The garbage collector will not remove an object pointed to by a global reference until the reference is explicitly deleted. Local references may also be explicitly deleted when the native method is finished with them, but this isn't necessary.

```
jref NewGlobalRef(JNIEnv *jne, jref ref);
```

The NewGlobalRef() function creates a global reference to the object referred to by ref. The ref may itself be a global reference, but it is more commonly a local reference. Note that from C, there's no way to tell the difference between a local reference and a global reference. The distinction is relevant only to Java's garbage collector.

To allow an object referred to by a global reference to be eligible for garbage collection, you call DeleteGlobalRef().

```
void DeleteGlobalRef(JNIEnv *jne, jref *globalRef);
```

Of course, this does not guarantee that the object will be garbage collected, only that this global reference is no longer preventing it from being collected. There may be other references to the same object, either in Java or in native code.

If a native method is expected to execute for some time, you may not want to wait until the function returns before freeing all the memory that it has allocated for Java objects. If you're done with a local reference to an object, you can call DeleteLocalRef() to allow the referred object to be garbage collected. This is necessary only in very long-running native methods that use a lot of memory.

```
void DeleteLocalRef(JNIEnv *jne, jref *localRef);
```

Threading and native methods

Multithreading is a common source of bugs in Java code. Native methods are no different. In fact, the problems only get worse in native methods because of C's lack of inherent garbage collection and memory protection.

The best way to make your native methods thread safe is to avoid threads completely. Do not spawn threads in your native methods. Do not interface with threads other than the one that called the native method.

If this is not possible, if you absolutely must interact with multiple threads from within the same block of native code, then there are a few things about which you must be extremely careful. First, do not pass your JNIEnv pointer to different threads. Every thread has a separate Java environment and must use its own environment pointer.

If the same thread calls a native method repeatedly or calls multiple native methods, each of these will get a copy of the same JNIEnv pointer. However, different threads may call the same native method with different JNIEnv pointers.

The JNI does have two methods that enable you to perform basic synchronization on code, although, in general, I recommend synchronizing at the Java level instead. There are more than enough ways to cause problems in native methods without adding multithreading to the mix.

Recall that each Java object has a monitor or semaphore associated with it to let different threads lock an object for their exclusive use. In native code, you can request the monitor with the MonitorEnter() method:

```
jint MonitorEnter(JNIEnv *jne, jref ref)
```

Here, jref is a reference — that is, a jobject, jarray, or jstring that you're trying to lock. If the current thread already owns the monitor associated with this object, some housekeeping is performed, and execution continues. If no thread owns the object, then this thread gets a lock on the object, and execution continues. However, if some other thread has already locked the object, then this thread blocks until the lock is released and then tries again to assert ownership for itself. This method returns zero if it succeeds or a negative number if it fails.

When the native method is finished with an object that it locked, it should call MonitorExit() to release the lock so that other threads may use the object:

```
jint MonitorExit(JNIEnv *jne, jref ref)
```

This method returns zero if it succeeds or a negative number if it fails.

A thread may lock the same object multiple times. To release an object, it must call MonitorExit() once for each call it made to MonitorEnter().

DETERMINING AT RUNTIME WHETHER NATIVE CODE IS AVAILABLE

Using native code does not have to restrict your audience. You can provide native libraries on some platforms and provide pure Java on others. You can even use the same Java code on all platforms.

While you were testing the examples in this chapter, I suspect that you encountered more than a few UnsatisfiedLinkErrors or NoSuchMethod Errors. These are thrown when Java can't find a native library that it has been asked to load or a method in that library. So far, this has indicated only a problem in your environment that you need to fix. However, you can make these errors work *for* you by letting them alert you to the presence or absence of native code. If the native code is present, you can use it. If it's not, you can call alternative code written in Java instead.

As a general rule, the alternative Java code should provide as much functionality as possible. It may be slower; it may not look as pretty; but at least it will work. In some cases, you may want to completely hide native functionality that is not available in pure Java or on a particular platform. In a few cases, you may not be able to do more than put up an error message explaining the problem. However, under no circumstances should your program just quit and give up because a native library is not available!

Listing 19-13 revises the program from Listing 19-4. That program assumed that a native library was available. This uses one a native library if it's there, but falls back to Java if it's not.

Listing 19-13

The Sums class in the numbers package

```
package numbers;

public class Sums {

  static boolean useNative = true;

  static {
    try {
     System.loadLibrary("numbers");
     }
    catch(UnsatisfiedLinkError e) {
      useNative = false;
     }
  }

  public static void main(String[] args) {

    Sums s = new Sums();
    s.firstNonSquareSum();

  }

  public void firstNonSquareSum() {

    if (useNative) {
      nFirstNonSquareSum();
     }
    else jFirstNonSquareSum();

  }

  private native void nFirstNonSquareSum();

  private void jFirstNonSquareSum() {

    int thisInt = 0;
    double max;
    int triple;
    boolean found = false;

    while (!found) {
      max = Math.sqrt(thisInt);
      iloop:
      for (int i = 0; i <= max; i++) {
        for (int j = 0; j <= i; j++) {
          for (int k = 0; k <= j; k++) {
```

(continued)

Listing 19-13
The Sums class in the numbers package *(continued)*

```
            triple = i*i + j*j + k*k;
            if (triple == thisInt) {
              thisInt++;
              found = true;
              break iloop;
          }
        }
      }
    }

    System.out.println(thisInt + " is not the sum of three cubes");

  }

}
```

First, note the change in the static block. The program now tests to see if the loading of the library was successful. If it was, everything continues as before. However, if it wasn't, then the program sets a static boolean field called *useNative to false.*

Next, I change the firstNonSquareSum() method. It's no longer native. Instead, it's a wrapper method that checks the value of the useNative field. If useNative is true, it calls the native nFirstNonSquareSum() method. However, if useNative is false, it instead calls a new pure Java method jFirstNonSquareSum(), that does the same thing.

So far, I've tested only to see whether the numbers library exists. You can go even further to test whether specific methods inside the library exist. As with the library itself, there's no easy way to ask the question. You just have to call the method and be ready to catch yourself if it fails. For example,

```
    public void firstNonSquareSum() {

      if (useNative) {
        try {
          nFirstNonSquareSum();
        }
        catch(Throwable t) {
          jFirstNonSquareSum();
        }
      }
      else jFirstNonSquareSum();

    }
```

This handles any possible error that might be raised by the native method, including its very existence. If a problem does occur, it falls back to the more reliable Java method.

A Final Note

Writing this chapter has made me more grateful than ever for Java. When I started this chapter, it had been over a year since I'd done any serious work in C. Now I remember why. Although CLASSPATHs can be annoying in Java, they aren't nearly as big a bugbear as INCLUDE_PATHs and LD_LIBRARY_PATHs. Java has nothing as confusing as C's pointers to structs of function pointers and matching convoluted precedence ((jne)->). And the clarity of the best C code in this chapter alone doesn't come close to matching that of the worst Java in the entire book. The amount of time I spent on this chapter was completely disproportionate to its page count. Almost all of that time was spent debugging the C programs. In the entire rest of the book, only Chapter 7 on writing applet viewers came close to the difficulty level of the various simple C programs included here. After finishing this chapter, it is my fervent hope that I will never, ever have to write in C again.

SUMMARY

In this chapter, you learn the following:

- Native methods should be used only as a last resort. You should try to exhaust all avenues that use pure Java first. This is for both your own sake and your users.'

- The Java Native Method Interface is a collection of dozens of C functions that your native methods can call to interact with Java.

- Keep your native methods as simple as possible. Use primitive types in preference to object types. Try to avoid too much interaction with Java code to avoid problems with threading and garbage collection. Keep as much of the program logic in pure Java as possible.

- If possible, provide pure Java alternatives for all native methods. When calling native methods or loading native libraries, catch UnsatisfiedLink Errors and NoSuchMethodErrors and fall back to the pure Java version instead.

CREATING STAND-ALONE PROGRAMS

## 20

*U*ntil now, practical uses of Java have been limited to applets on Web pages. That's going to change soon. Java offers too many advantages as a language over C++, C, Basic, and other popular application development languages to restrict it only to Web pages. You should be able to write full stand-alone applications that can be run by double-clicking an icon or invoking them from the command line, just like applications written in C or other traditional languages.

In fact, you can write such applications, and you learn to do it in this chapter. There are two fundamental approaches. The first is to write a wrapper program that masquerades as the Java program, but is really just a shell script, batch file, or C program that invokes the Java interpreter. This is how HotJava and javac are written. The alternative is to embed a virtual machine inside the application itself. I explore both options in this chapter.

Like the native executable binary file format, the details are platform specific. By making an application of this type, you do restrict your program to one platform. Therefore, this chapter is broken up into sections about the three major platforms: UNIX, the Mac, and Windows32. The details can also vary from development environment to development environment. However, none of this is particularly hard if you have access to the platform on which you want to publish.

WRITING STAND-ALONE PROGRAMS FOR **UNIX**

The common means of creating a stand-alone Java program on UNIX platforms is to write a simple shell script that invokes the Java interpreter. This script needs to set a few environment variables and then pass the command-line arguments on to the Java program. This is how javacc, HotJava, and other pure Java applications are run.

Note

Sun uses the Korn shell (/bin/ksh) for many of their Solaris stand-alones. This is fine as long as you know that the Korn shell is installed. However, it's not installed on many non-Solaris systems, so I will use the more portable Bourne shell (sh) in what follows.

There are two fundamental steps that your shell script must perform:

1. Set the CLASSPATH environment variable to include your classes.
2. Pass the command line arguments to your program

I'll begin with a simple example. I will demonstrate how you might make the DecimalDump program of Listing 11-8 in Chapter 11 a stand-alone, character-mode application.

Listing 11-8 did not have a main() method or any real command line interface, so the first thing you must do is create one. Call this program ddencode, and model it after the elegantly simple uuencode program. This takes a single command line argument, the name of the file to be encoded. It encodes a single file at a time and displays a brief error message if the file is not specified. If you specify more than one file, it encodes only the last one. Like many UNIX programs, output goes to stdout by default but can be redirected to a file or pipe. For example:

```
% uuencode
Usage: uuencode [infile] remotefile
% uuencode Base64Decode.java      JackAndJill.java
begin 644 JackAndJill.java
M:6UP;W)T('-U;BYM:7-C+"!R96%D97(N"FEM<&]R="!J879A+F%W="XJ.R!0&
M:F%V82YI;RXJ.R!2XJ.PH*"G!U8FQI8R!C;&%S<R!"87-E-C1$96-O9&4@>PH*("!P
M=6)L:6,L<VAV<@<@0V%S92@'90:60;6%I;B3')I;F=;72!A<F=S*2!["@H@@
M:68@*&%R9W,N;&5N9W1H(#X](#$I('L*("!9(&QE*"(@0"(@=>")Y('L*("@Q*0@("!P"))
M;G!U=%-T<F5A;2(@(%R(]86YE26YP=71S=')E86T;(%)E86P=6=72!=;B'$L
M("!B(&]F("@@0@"@S<3>TW4(R'N'T5T4W1R96%M?'0N9V5T4W1R96%M?'0.()E
M86TE;G!U="!S='1S="@@"@"C1#3138T1T%5C;R!V,4E%0TQ"+4,Q1#A2(&%Y'R'$
M:&1F("@@0@"@`'@"!X96]D93$L%92@T83@5C)5-T5G%Y+5C(@$5$-C1$96-O9&4@
M:&%E<R"(]0\R1$""(!@0""@`'1F*"@@0@"@`'@8P5T4X5`00*B1%+S$W04,Y-R%4.C9=3B@F-$D
M("@G3"HH($""@`'@@E(S0^-RU4.38.5$Y.3<I4BLG(3H-C8'N;R9&0[(F%E<R"(]0(&'%N'4.)R@@@
```

```
B('T@+R\@96YD(&EF"@H@('T@("\0(&5N9"!M86EN"@I]"B @
```

```
end
%
```

Listing 20-1 is a class that provides a main method for the DecimalDump class of Listing 11-8. This main() method could have been provided inside the DecimalDump class itself. However, it's better to place platform-specific code into separate files.

Listing 20-1
The DDEncoder class

```java
import java.io.*;


public class DDEncoder {

    public static void main(String[] args) {

      try {
        File theFile = new File(args[args.length-1]);
        DecimalDump dd = new DecimalDump();
        FileInputStream fis = new FileInputStream(theFile);
        dd.encodeBuffer(fis, System.out);
      }
      catch (ArrayIndexOutOfBoundsException e) {
        System.err.println("Usage: ddencode infile");
      }
      catch (IOException e) {
        System.err.println("Usage: ddencode infile");
      }


    }


}
```

To prepare this file for distribution as a stand-alone application, you need to create a directory structure for it. This structure will eventually include all executable and .class files. For now, worry just about the .class files. This program requires three: DDEncoder.class, DecimalDump.class, and sun.misc.CharacterEncoder.class. Remember that although it's likely that the CharacterEncoder class will be installed on the host system, it is an undocumented Sun class, so you can't rely on it. Your classes directory should therefore look something like the one shown in Figure 20-1.

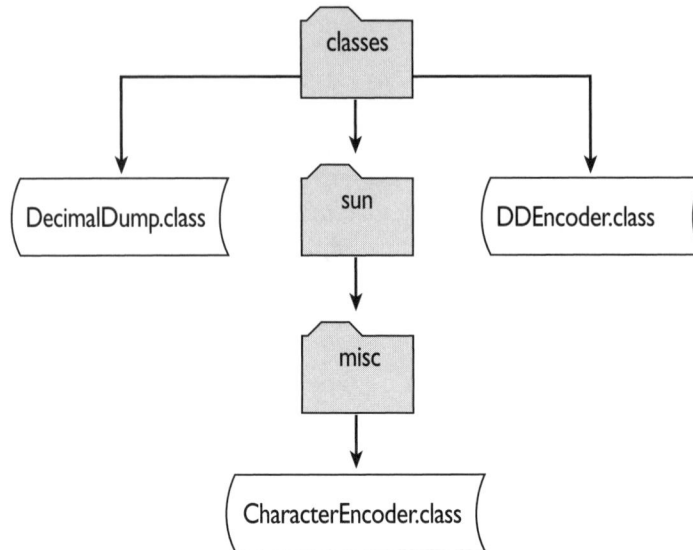

Figure 20-1
The classes directory for the ddencode program

Now you need to write a shell script that invokes this program. The simplest shell script that I can imagine is this:

```
#!/bin/sh

java DDEncoder /etc/passwd
```

Unlike Java programs, it doesn't matter what file you put this in, but for the sake of being definite, let's assume that it's in a file called *ddencode*.

The first line of this program tells UNIX to use /bin/sh to execute this file. The second line is blank. The third line is a simple command such as you might pass from the normal command prompt. Before you can execute this file, you'll need to set its executable bit (for example, chmod +x ddencode) and make sure the file is in your PATH.

Of course, you should generally pass any command-line arguments along to the Java program. Most of the time, the file you want to encode is not /etc/passwd. Command line arguments are passed to shell scripts in a series of variables called $1, $2, and so on. Just to pass along all the arguments, pass $* like this:

```
#!/bin/sh

java DDEncoder $*
```

In shell scripts, identifiers that begin with a dollar sign are variables. You can use these variables for a number of different purposes. The name of the file that contains the script is stored in the variable $0. This is not included in $*, however.

Next, you need to make sure that your classes are included in the user's CLASSPATH. Until now, I've assumed that they simply were. This is likely to be the case if . (*the current directory*) is in your CLASSPATH and you haven't moved too many files around. However, you should try to be a bit more definite than that.

The UNIX convention for software, including Java software, is that the executable files belong in a directory called bin, whereas support files belong in bin/../lib. Class files belong in either lib/classes or lib/classes.zip. This is shown in Figure 20-2. If you're familiar with UNIX, you should recognize that as shorthand for the lib directory in the parent directory of the bin directory. Software is normally distributed in a tar archive that retains the directory structure. All a user needs to do is add the bin directory to the PATH environment variable.

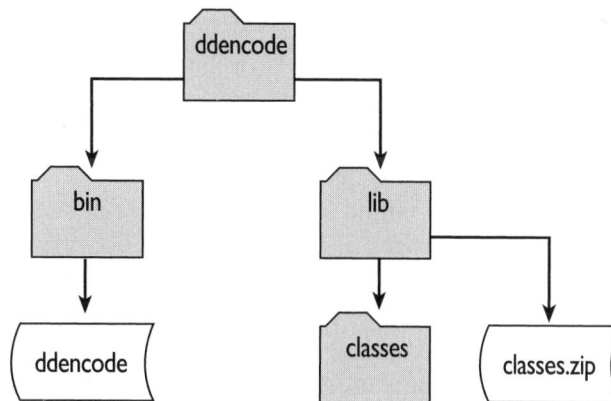

Figure 20-2
The ddencode hierarchy

Let's assume that the relevant directory structure is in place. You need to ensure that the CLASSPATH contains your lib directory. This takes a few more lines of code, primarily to find the bin directory where the executable file resides and to make sure that you only add to the existing CLASSPATH and that you don't nuke it entirely. The following script does that:

```sh
#!/bin/sh

# find out where this program is installed
EXE=`which $0`  >/dev/null 2>&1

# get the directory where this program is installed
EXEDIR=`dirname $EXE`

# get the directory where classes should be found
MYCLASSES="$EXEDIR/../lib/classes:$EXEDIR/../lib/classes.zip"

# add that directory to the CLASSPATH
if [ -z "$CLASSPATH" ]
then
  CLASSPATH="$MYCLASSES"
else
  CLASSPATH="$MYCLASSES:$CLASSPATH"
fi
export CLASSPATH
# echo $CLASSPATH

# execute the command
java -classpath $CLASSPATH DDEncoder $*
```

Most of this program just finds where the necessary classes are installed so they can be added to the CLASSPATH. The first line tells UNIX to use the program /bin/sh to execute this file. After that, you get straight to business of finding the classes.

The which command locates the executable with a given name. Here, the name of the program, which is the first command line argument, is stored in the variable $0. I could have written EXE="which ddencode" instead, but that would be a little less robust because the script would break if someone changed its filename. Stdout from the which command is piped to /dev/null because there's no reason to show it to the user. Similarly, stderr (output stream 2) is redirected to stdin and thus also ends up in /dev/null.

The which command produces a full path to the command like

```
/export/sunsite/users/elharo/ddencode/bin/ddencode
```

The dirname program is a convenience that strips off the filename leaving only the directory. For example:

```
/export/sunsite/users/elharo/ddencode/bin
```

This is stored in the variable EXEDIR.

Next the variable MYCLASSES is set to "$EXEDIR/../lib/classes:
$EXEDIR../lib/classes.zip". This evaluates to the actual location of the bin
directory. For example:

```
"/export/sunsite/users/elharo/ddencode/bin/../lib/classes:/export/sunsite/u
sers/elharo/ddencode/bin/../lib/classes.zip"
```

This finds both a classes directory in bin/../lib and a classes.zip file in
that directory. You normally don't need both of these, but it doesn't hurt.

Next, this path is prepended to any existing CLASSPATH. The -z
operator tests whether the environment variable CLASSPATH is null. If it is
null, CLASSPATH is set to MYCLASSES. If it isn't null — that is, if a
CLASSPATH variable has been set — then MYCLASSES is prepended to
the existing CLASSPATH. Then you export CLASSPATH so it will become
part of the environment.

You may want to echo the CLASSPATH — that is, print it on stdout —
for debugging purposes. If so, you can uncomment the next line by
removing the # sign.

Finally, the -classpath argument to the java program is used to set the
CLASSPATH for it. Otherwise, it would still miss the new classes.

Assuming the user has Java installed in his or her PATH somewhere,
this is all you need to do. If you want, you can check for that and add some
other likely locations to the PATH, such as /usr/local/java. However, this
still requires Java to be installed on the client system, so it doesn't add very
much. Here's the necessary code:

```
# make sure Java is installed
JAVAPROG=`which java`  >/dev/null 2>&1
if [ -x "$JAVAPROG" ]
then
# null command because sh requires something to be here
  :
else
  echo "$0 requires java"
  exit 1
fi
```

Again, the which command is used to get a full path for an executable
file. The -x command tests whether the file named by $JAVAPROG is
executable. Listing 20-2 contains the completed shell script:

Listing 20-2

The ddencode shell script

```
#!/bin/sh

    # make sure Java is installed
    JAVAPROG=`which java`  >/dev/null 2>&1

if [ -x "$JAVAPROG" ]
then
# null command because sh requires something to be here
  :
else
  echo "$0 requires java"
  exit 1
fi

# find out where this program is installed
EXE=`which $0`  >/dev/null 2>&1

# get the directory where this program is installed
EXEDIR=`dirname $EXE`

# get the directory where classes should be found
MYCLASSES="$EXEDIR/../lib/classes:$EXEDIR/../lib/classes.zip"

# add that directory to the CLASSPATH
if [ -z "$CLASSPATH" ]
then
  CLASSPATH="$MYCLASSES"
else
  CLASSPATH="$MYCLASSES:$CLASSPATH"
fi
export CLASSPATH
# echo $CLASSPATH

# execute the command
java -classpath $CLASSPATH DDEncoder $*
```

It's also possible to write essentially the same program in C and compile it into a fully executable file. This doesn't buy you a great deal under UNIX, where shell scripts are fairly portable, fast, and reliable. However, very similar C programs can be used on non-UNIX systems, like Windows and VMS, with only a few minor modifications. Listing 20-3 demonstrates:

Listing 20-3

A C wrapper for the ddencode program

```
#include <stdio.h>
#include <stdlib.h>
#include <string.h>

int main(int argc, char* argv[]) {

  /* Probably big enough to hold any string we'll need */
  char cmd[2048];
  char newclasspath[1024];
  char* oldclasspath;
  char which[256];
  char exe[256];
  char exedir[256];
  int i;
  FILE* temp;
  char* tempfile = NULL;

  tempfile = tmpnam(NULL);
  if (tempfile == NULL) {
    fprintf(stderr, "problem");
    exit(1);
  }
  sprintf(which, "which %s > %s", argv[0], tempfile);
  if (system(which) != 0) {
    fprintf(stderr, "Could not find encoder\n");
    exit(1);
  }
  printf("%s\n", tempfile);
  temp = fopen(tempfile, "r");
  fgets(exe, 256, temp);
  fclose(temp);

  strncpy(exedir, exe, strlen(exe)-(strlen(argv[0])+1));

  oldclasspath = getenv("CLASSPATH");
  if (oldclasspath != NULL) {
    sprintf(newclasspath, "%s../lib/classes:%s../lib/classes.zip:%s",
      exedir, exedir, oldclasspath);
  }
  else {
    sprintf(newclasspath, "%s../lib/classes:%s../lib/classes.zip", exedir,
exedir);
  }
```

(continued)

Listing 20-3

A C wrapper for the ddencode program *(continued)*

```
    sprintf(cmd, "java -classpath %s DDEncoder ", newclasspath);

    /* Remember that in C the first command line argument is argv[1],
    not argv[0] like in Java */
    for (i = 1; i < argc; i++) {

      strcat(cmd, " ");
      strcat(cmd, argv[i]);
    }

    return system(cmd);

  }
```

The trickiest and most platform-dependent part of this program is locating the executable file. The fundamental problem is that the standard C library has no real equivalent to the which program used in Listing 20-2 or the whence built-in of the Korn shell. There are a number of different ways to work around this omission. For example, you could write a function to search each directory in the PATH environment variable for an executable file named argv[0].

Because this is not a book about C, I've chosen the simplest and most obvious solution I could think of, although it's far from the most efficient. The system() function is used to execute the shell's which program. The result is stored in a temporary file and then read back in using standard C library functions.

> **Note**
> Interestingly enough, if this program were written in Java, you could have done this without a temporary file, because the System.exec() method returns a process object you can use to read the results from System.in. C, however, does not provide a simple means to read the output produced by a command executed through system().

CREATING STAND-ALONE PROGRAMS FOR THE MACOS

There are two ways to create what appears to be a double-clickable Macintosh application written in Java. The first is to use a .class file that launches the Java interpreter when double-clicked. The Java interpreter then executes the compiled .class file. This is relatively simple but does rely on the user, having the right Java interpreter installed. This is likely to become a feasible option in the Summer of 1997, assuming that Apple ships System 8 on time and includes the promised Java interpreter. The second option is to embed a Java runtime along with all necessary classes in the compiled, double-clickable file.

Exactly how you accomplish these options depends on your development environments. Here, I provide instructions using Apple's Macintosh Runtime for Java (MRJ) and Software Development Kit (SDK), which at the time of this writing provides the simplest environment for creating stand-alone applications for the Mac.

The Macintosh DDEncoder class

Listing 11-8 did not have a main() method or any real user interface, so the first thing you must do is create one. Call this program ddencode. When it starts up, it will bring up a standard file dialog box to ask the user to identify the file to encode. The result will be saved in a file of the same name with the additional suffix ".dd".

Listing 20-4 is a class that provides a main method for the DecimalDump class of Listing 11-8. This main() method could have been provided inside the DecimalDump class itself. However it's better to separate out platform-specific code into separate files.

Listing 20-4
The MacDDEncoder class

```
import java.io.*;


public class MacDDEncoder {

  public static void main(String[] args) {

    try {
      File theFile = new File(args[args.length-1]);
      DecimalDump dd = new DecimalDump();
      FileInputStream fis = new FileInputStream(theFile);
      dd.encodeBuffer(fis, System.out);
    }
    catch (ArrayIndexOutOfBoundsException e) {
      System.err.println("Usage: ddencode infile");
    }
    catch (IOException e) {
```

(continued)

Listing 20-4
The MacDDEncoder class *(continued)*

```
        System.err.println("Usage: ddencode infile");
    }

  }

}
```

Using type and creator codes

Every Macintosh file has a four-letter type code and a four-letter creator code. When you double-click a file, the Mac uses the four-letter code, together with information stored in the Desktop database, to determine what to do with it. If the file's type is APPL, then the file is presumed to be a double-clickable application and is launched. If the file type is anything else, the Mac looks at the creator code to see what application created the file. For example, SimpleText files have the type code "TEXT" and creator code "ttxt." Therefore, when the user double-clicks a file with type "TEXT" and creator code "ttxt," the Finder opens the file in SimpleText.

Note This is also how the Macintosh keeps track of which icons to display for which files in the Finder.

There are a number of freeware, shareware, and payware utilities that let you inspect, set, and modify type and creator codes. The most popular ones are Apple's free ResEdit, the shareware FileTyper, and the payware Disktop.

Sun's Java Development Kit for the Mac 1.0.2 includes the Java runner application for running stand-alone applications. This application uses the file type "COÂk" and the creator code "Javr" for Java .class files. If you set a .class file to have this type and creator code, then double-clicking the class file will open it in the Java Runner application. Compiling .java source code files with Sun's Java Compiler on the Macintosh automatically produces .class files with the right type and creator codes. However, files you download from the Internet or compile with a different compiler, such as Roaster, will need to be manually changed to these codes.

This technique doesn't produce a true stand-alone application by any means. You'll still have the Java Runner menu bars and icons in the application menu, but it does at least allow you to run an application by double-clicking it rather than by first opening a separate application and then opening the file you really want.

The Macintosh Runtime for Java

Apple's Macintosh Runtime for Java (MRJ) and the MRJ Software Development Kit (SDK) lets you build complete, stand-alone, double-clickable Macintosh applications. However, at the time of this writing, it does not allow you to bundle in the .class files. Those still need to be included separately. By the time you're reading this book, Apple should have released a tool called JBindery that lets you bundle in the .class files as well.

To build a stand-alone application with the MRJ SDK, you use Apple's JRunner tool. Using JRunner to build an application is easy and much simpler than using Sun's Java Runner. Mostly, using JRunner consists of filling in a few text fields in a GUI environment.

As usual, you'll first need to package your .class files into a zip file. In what follows, assume those classes are in a file called encoder.zip. Begin by launching the JRunner application. This brings up the dialog box shown in Figure 20-3.

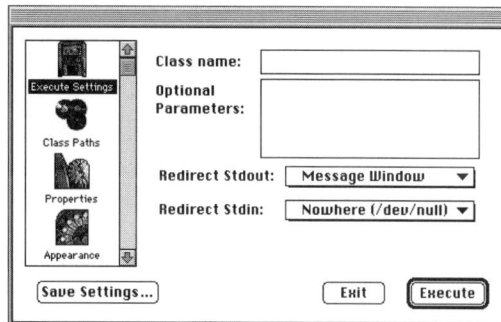

▌ Figure 20-3
The JRunner dialog.

The first thing you should do is to set the Class name to the class that contains the main() method, in this example MacDDEncoder Figure 20-4. The Optional Parameters field should contain anything you want to pass to your application from the command line. Then set both the Redirect Stdout: and Redirect Stdin: popup menus to "Nowhere (/dev/null)." Stdout and Stdin (System.out and System.in in Java parlance) are fine for debugging, but they don't belong in a real Macintosh application. If your program uses them, you'll need to rewrite it to use a GUI before porting it to the Mac.

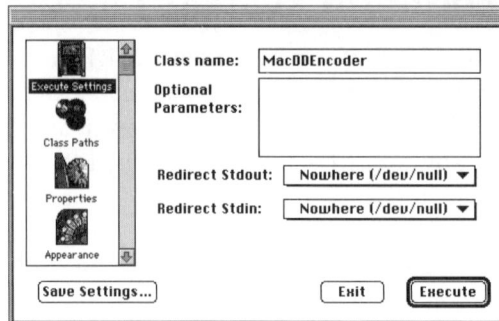

Figure 20-4
The JRunner dialog after setting the Execute settings.

Next you'll set the class paths, as shown in Figure 20-5. Here you should use a zip file. Other options are possible, but zip files are the simplest for the user. Click the "Add .zip file..." button and select the file that contains your classes. This zip file must be in the same folder as your finished application.

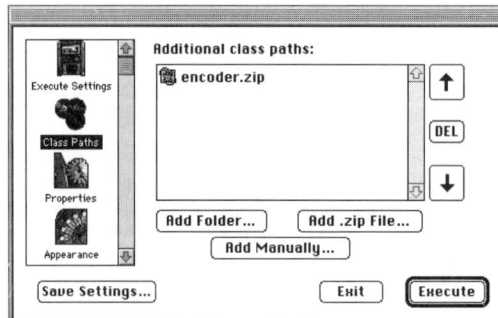

Figure 20-5
The JRunner dialog after setting the class paths.

Next, you have the option to add to Java's system properties list, as in Figure 20-6. You don't need to do that for this example, but if you want to, it's not hard to do. Just put the property name in the left TextField and the property value in the right TextField, and then click Add.

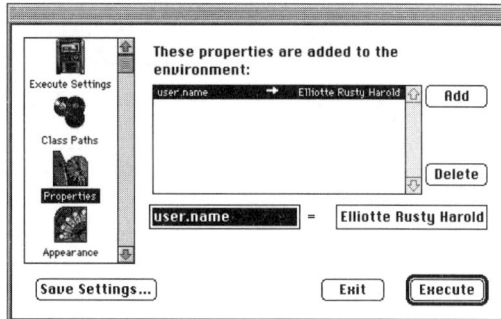

■ Figure 20-6
The JRunner dialog after setting the properties.

The Appearance settings shown in Figure 20-7 let you choose colors for Window, Title, and Frame backgrounds as well as whether or not grow boxes intrude into a window's visible area. Clicking any of the boxes to the right of Window Background:, Frame Background: or Title Background brings up a color picker dialog box you can use to select colors.

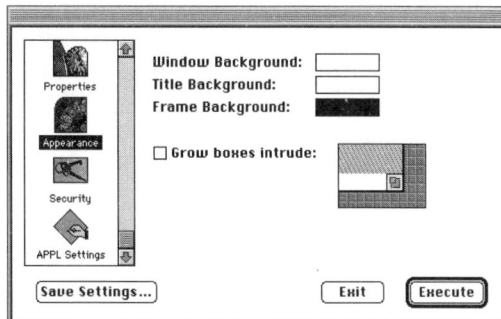

■ Figure 20-7
The JRunner dialog for adjusting the appearance of your application.

The security settings, shown in Figure 20-8, allow you to set whether or not Java verifies the byte codes before executing them. In general, you don't need to do this in an application, so it's customary to leave the box unchecked. You can also set various proxy servers. However, this generally needs to be left to the user to do, unless you're building an application that will only be distributed on a single intranet.

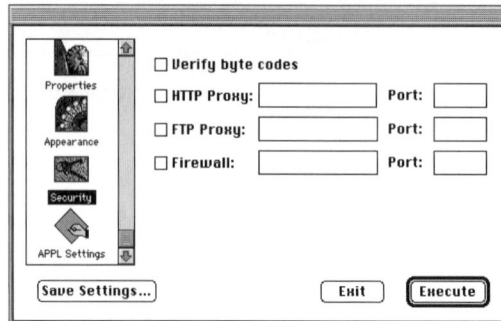

Figure 20-8
The JRunner dialog for adjusting security preferences.

Finally, the APPL settings panel shown in Figure 20-9 enables you to adjust some characteristics of the Macintosh Runtime. The signature is a four-letter Apple creator code. Before distributing an application, you need to register a signature with Apple to make sure yours doesn't conflict with any already in use. You can get more information and register your codes at `http://gemma.apple.com/dev/cftype`.

The minimum app heap is the minimum amount of RAM that will be used by the Java application heap. The maximum app heap is, of course, the maximum amount of RAM that will be used by the Java application heap.

Finally, you can add resources to the completed application. Most commonly, these would include icons for the Finder display. You can either drag and drop a resource file from the Finder into the indicated area or get a standard file dialog box to select a resource file by checking the Merge Resources From: checkbox.

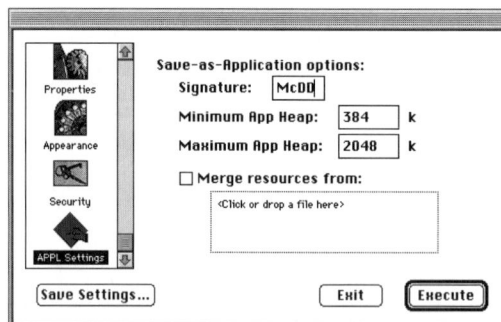

Figure 20-9
The APPL settings panel.

Finally, when all the preferences have been set, you're ready to create the stand-alone application. Click the Save Settings button (*not* the Execute button). In the standard file dialog box that appears, be sure to check the Save As Application checkbox.

That's all there is to it. You should now have a double-clickable, stand-alone Macintosh application.

CREATING STAND-ALONE WINDOWS PROGRAMS

Java programs can be made into stand-alone Windows programs in much the same way as they are made stand-alone on UNIX. However, instead of using a shell script, a batch file is written. The batch file needs to do pretty much the same thing the UNIX shell script does: set the CLASSPATH and call the java interpreter.

There are two fundamental steps that your shell script must perform:

1. Set the CLASSPATH environment variable to include your classes.
2. Pass the command-line arguments to your program.

As in the UNIX section, I demonstrate how you might make the DecimalDump program of Listing 11-8, a stand-alone, character-mode application. For this, I'll use Listing 20-1 given earlier in this chapter. However, I'll make one change to that interface. If more than one file is specified on the command line, the first one — not the last one — will be encoded. This makes wrapper a little easier to code within the limitations of .bat files.

Windows has even weaker support for locating files than UNIX does. As a general rule, most programs just define a directory in which they must be installed and provide an installer that places their files in the right place. If the user moves files from the expected location, or installs the program on a different drive, programs tend to break. The Windows 95 registry is a rough hack designed to partially alleviate the problem.

I do not want to discuss all the issues here. In fact, that could well be another book. For now, I'll assert that the program will be installed in the directory C:\ddencode. This directory will have the usual bin, lib, and bin\classes directories. You'll allow the user to adjust the location by setting an environment variable DDENCODE_HOME. Listing 20-5 accomplishes this task.

Listing 20-5

A DOS batch file wrapper for a Java program

```
@echo off

rem "Check to see if user is overriding the default location"
if "%DDENCODE_HOME%" == "" goto usedefault
   goto nodefault
:usedefault
   set DDENCODE_HOME=c:\ddencode
:nodefault

set CLASSPATH=%DDENCODE_HOME%\lib;%DDENCODE_HOME%\lib\classes.zip;%CLASSPATH%
set PATH=%DDENCODE_HOME%\bin;%PATH%
java DDEncoder %2
```

DOS batch files don't have a good equivalent for the UNIX sh $*
variable. %1 is the name of the program itself. %2 is the first command line
argument. %3 through %9 are the second through eighth command line
arguments. Therefore, you can pass up to eight command line arguments to
your main() methods like this:

```
java ClassName %2 %3 %4 %5 %6 %7 %8 %9
```

There's no problem if some of these arguments aren't present. In that
case, the later variables are just empty strings. It's not like Java or C where
you'll get an ArrayIndexOutOfBoundsException or a core dump if you try
to access more command line arguments than there really are.

DOS batch files are not as efficient or as well integrated into the
operating system as shell scripts are in UNIX. It's much more common to
see a wrapper for Windows written in C than a wrapper for UNIX. The
JDK 1.1 for Solaris uses Korn shell wrappers almost exclusively, whereas
the same distribution for Win32 only uses compiled .exe files.

SUMMARY

In this chapter, you learn the following:

- To make a Java program a stand-alone executable on UNIX, you
  normally write a shell script. C programs are also possible, though they
  must, of course, be recompiled for each platform.

- The easiest way to make a stand-alone, double-clickable application on the Macintosh is with Apple's JRunner utility, part of the Macintosh Runtime for Java SDK. You can also make a quick and dirty Mac stand-alone program by giving a custom icon to a JavaRunner document.

- Stand-alone Windows executables can be batch files or compiled programs written in a high-level language like C.

APPENDIXES

CLASS DEFINED IN INDEX

*T*his appendix lists all the classes defined in the sun and sunw packages alphabetically. This is useful when you encounter an unfamiliar class in source code or elsewhere, and want to know where it's defined.

AclEntryImpl: sun.security.acl

AclEnumerator: sun.security.acl

AclImpl: sun.security.acl

AddExpression: sun.tools.tree

Agent: sun.tools.debug

AgentConstants: sun.tools.debug

AgentIn: sun.tools.debug

AgentOutputStream: sun.tools.debug

AlgIdDSA: sun.security.x509

AlgorithmId: sun.security.x509

AllPermissionsImpl: sun.security.acl

AmbiguousClass: sun.tools.java

AmbiguousField: sun.tools.java

AndExpression: sun.tools.tree

AppletAudioClip: sun.applet

AppletClassEntry: sun.applet

AppletClassLoader: sun.applet

AppletCopyright: sun.applet

AppletIllegalArgumentException: sun.applet

AppletImageRef: sun.applet

AppletIOException: sun.applet

AppletMessageHandler: sun.applet

AppletObjectInputStream: sun.applet

AppletPanel: sun.applet

AppletProps: sun.applet

AppletResourceConnection: sun.net.www.protocol.appletresource

AppletResourceLoader: sun.applet

AppletSecurity: sun.applet

AppletSecurityException: sun.applet

AppletThreadGroup: sun.applet

AppletViewer: sun.applet

AppletViewerFactory: sun.applet

AppletViewerPanel: sun.applet

ApplicationLaunchException: sun.net.www

ArrayAccessExpression: sun.tools.tree

ArrayData: sun.tools.asm

ArrayExpression: sun.tools.tree

ArrayType: sun.tools.java

Assembler: sun.tools.asm

AssignAddExpression: sun.tools.tree

AssignBitAndExpression: sun.tools.tree

AssignBitOrExpression: sun.tools.tree

AssignBitXorExpression: sun.tools.tree

AssignDivideExpression: sun.tools.tree

AssignExpression: sun.tools.tree

AssignMultiplyExpression: sun.tools.tree

AssignRemainderExpression: sun.tools.tree

AssignShiftLeftExpression: sun.tools.tree

AssignShiftRightExpression: sun.tools.tree

AssignSubtractExpression: sun.tools.tree

AssignUnsignedShiftRightExpression: sun.tools.tree

AsyncConnector: sun.rmi.transport.proxy

AudioData: sun.audio

AudioDataStream: sun.audio

AudioDevice: sun.audio

AudioPlayer: sun.audio

AudioStream: sun.audio

AudioStreamSequence: sun.audio

AudioTranslatorStream: sun.audio

AuthenticationInfo: sun.net.www.protocol.http

AVA: sun.security.x509

AWTFinalizeable: sun.awt

AWTFinalizer: sun.awt

BASE64Decoder: sun.misc

BASE64Encoder: sun.misc

BasicHttpServer: sun.net.www.httpd

BatchEnvironment: sun.rmi.rmic, sun.tools.javac

BatchParser: sun.tools.javac

BigInt: sun.security.util

BinaryArithmeticExpression: sun.tools.tree

BinaryAssignExpression: sun.tools.tree

BinaryAttribute: sun.tools.java

BinaryBitExpression: sun.tools.tree

BinaryClass: sun.tools.java

BinaryCode: sun.tools.java

BinaryCompareExpression: sun.tools.tree

BinaryConstantPool: sun.tools.java

BinaryEqualityExpression: sun.tools.tree

BinaryExceptionHandler: sun.tools.java

BinaryExpression: sun.tools.tree

BinaryField: sun.tools.java

BinaryLogicalExpression: sun.tools.tree

BinaryShiftExpression: sun.tools.tree

BitAndExpression: sun.tools.tree

BitNotExpression: sun.tools.tree

BitOrExpression: sun.tools.tree

BitXorExpression: sun.tools.tree

BooleanExpression: sun.tools.tree

BoolEditor: sun.beans.editors

BreakpointHandler: sun.tools.debug

BreakpointQueue: sun.tools.debug

BreakpointSet: sun.tools.debug

BreakStatement: sun.tools.tree

ByteArrayImageSource: sun.awt.image

ByteEditor: sun.beans.editors

ByteExpression: sun.tools.tree

ByteToChar8859_1: sun.io

ByteToChar8859_2: sun.io

ByteToChar8859_3: sun.io

ByteToChar8859_4: sun.io

ByteToChar8859_5: sun.io

ByteToChar8859_6: sun.io

ByteToChar8859_7: sun.io

ByteToChar8859_8: sun.io

ByteToChar8859_9: sun.io

ByteToCharBig5: sun.io

ByteToCharCNS11643: sun.io

ByteToCharConverter: sun.io

ByteToCharCp037: sun.io

ByteToCharCp1006: sun.io

ByteToCharCp1025: sun.io

ByteToCharCp1026: sun.io

ByteToCharCp1046: sun.io

ByteToCharCp1097: sun.io

ByteToCharCp1098: sun.io

ByteToCharCp1112: sun.io

ByteToCharCp1122: sun.io

ByteToCharCp1123: sun.io

ByteToCharUnicode: sun.io
ByteToCharUnicodeBig: sun.io
ByteToCharUnicodeLittle: sun.io
ByteToCharUTF8: sun.io
Cache: sun.misc
CacheEntry: sun.misc
CacheEnumerator: sun.misc
CaseStatement: sun.tools.tree
CastExpression: sun.tools.tree
CatchData: sun.tools.asm
CatchStatement: sun.tools.tree
CEFormatException: sun.misc
CertAndKeyGen: sun.security.x509
CertException: sun.security.x509
CertParseError: sun.security.x509
CEStreamExhausted: sun.misc
CGIClientException: sun.rmi.transport.proxy
CGICommandHandler:
   sun.rmi.transport.proxy
CGIForwardCommand:
   sun.rmi.transport.proxy
CGIGethostnameCommand:
   sun.rmi.transport.proxy
CGIHandler: sun.rmi.transport.proxy
CGIPingCommand: sun.rmi.transport.proxy
CGIServerException: sun.rmi.transport.proxy
CGITryHostnameCommand:
   sun.rmi.transport.proxy
Channel: sun.rmi.transport
CharacterDecoder: sun.misc
CharacterEncoder: sun.misc
CharacterEncoding: sun.io
CharExpression: sun.tools.tree
CharsetString: sun.awt
CharToByte8859_1: sun.io
CharToByte8859_2: sun.io
CharToByte8859_3: sun.io
CharToByte8859_4: sun.io
CharToByte8859_5: sun.io
CharToByte8859_6: sun.io
CharToByte8859_7: sun.io
CharToByte8859_8: sun.io
CharToByte8859_9: sun.io

CharToByteBig5: sun.io
CharToByteCNS11643: sun.io
CharToByteConverter: sun.io
CharToByteCp037: sun.io
CharToByteCp1006: sun.io
CharToByteCp1025: sun.io
CharToByteCp1026: sun.io
CharToByteCp1046: sun.io
CharToByteCp1097: sun.io
CharToByteCp1098: sun.io
CharToByteCp1112: sun.io
CharToByteCp1122: sun.io
CharToByteCp1123: sun.io
CharToByteCp1124: sun.io
CharToByteCp1250: sun.io
CharToByteCp1251: sun.io
CharToByteCp1252: sun.io
CharToByteCp1253: sun.io
CharToByteCp1254: sun.io
CharToByteCp1255: sun.io
CharToByteCp1256: sun.io
CharToByteCp1257: sun.io
CharToByteCp1258: sun.io
CharToByteCp1381: sun.io
CharToByteCp1383: sun.io
CharToByteCp273: sun.io
CharToByteCp277: sun.io
CharToByteCp278: sun.io
CharToByteCp280: sun.io
CharToByteCp284: sun.io
CharToByteCp285: sun.io
CharToByteCp297: sun.io
CharToByteCp33722: sun.io
CharToByteCp420: sun.io
CharToByteCp424: sun.io
CharToByteCp437: sun.io
CharToByteCp500: sun.io
CharToByteCp737: sun.io
CharToByteCp775: sun.io
CharToByteCp838: sun.io
CharToByteCp850: sun.io
CharToByteCp852: sun.io

Compare: sun.misc
CompilerError: sun.tools.java
CompilerField: sun.tools.javac
ComponentBeanInfo: sun.beans.infos
CompoundStatement: sun.tools.tree
ConditionalExpression: sun.tools.tree
ConditionLock: sun.misc
ConditionVars: sun.tools.tree
Connection: sun.rmi.transport
ConnectionAcceptor: sun.rmi.transport.tcp
ConnectionInputStream: sun.rmi.transport
ConnectionMultiplexer: sun.rmi.transport.tcp
ConnectionOutputStream: sun.rmi.transport
ConstantExpression: sun.tools.tree
ConstantPool: sun.tools.asm
ConstantPoolData: sun.tools.asm
Constants: sun.tools.java
ConsumerQueue: sun.awt.image
ContentInfo: sun.security.pkcs
Context: sun.tools.tree
ContextEnvironment: sun.tools.tree
ContinueStatement: sun.tools.tree
ContinuousAudioDataStream: sun.audio
ConversionBufferFullException: sun.io
ConvertExpression: sun.tools.tree
Cover: sun.tools.asm
CRC16: sun.misc
CRC32OutputStream: sun.tools.jar
DebuggerCallback: sun.tools.debug
DeclarationStatement: sun.tools.tree
DerInputBuffer: sun.security.util
DerInputStream: sun.security.util
DerOutputStream: sun.security.util
DerValue: sun.security.util
DGCAckHandler: sun.rmi.transport
DGCClient: sun.rmi.transport
DGCImpl: sun.rmi.transport
DGCImpl_Skel: sun.rmi.transport
DGCImpl_Stub: sun.rmi.transport
Dispatcher: sun.rmi.server
DivideExpression: sun.tools.tree
DivRemExpression: sun.tools.tree

DocumentationGenerator: sun.tools.javadoc
DocURLConnection: sun.net.www.protocol.doc
DoStatement: sun.tools.tree
DoubleEditor: sun.beans.editors
DoubleExpression: sun.tools.tree
DrawingSurface: sun.awt
DrawingSurfaceInfo: sun.awt
DSA: sun.security.provider
DSAKeyPairGenerator: sun.security.provider
DSAPrivateKey: sun.security.provider
DSAPublicKey: sun.security.provider
EmbeddedFrame: sun.awt
EmptyApp: sun.tools.debug
EmptyInputStream: sun.net.www.protocol.http
EncodingException: sun.security.pkcs
Endpoint: sun.rmi.transport
Environment: sun.tools.java
EqualExpression: sun.tools.tree
ErrorConsumer: sun.tools.javac
ErrorMessage: sun.tools.javac
EventListener: sunw.util
EventObject: sunw.util
Expression: sun.tools.tree
ExpressionStatement: sun.tools.tree
ExprExpression: sun.tools.tree
Field: sun.tools.debug
FieldConstantData: sun.tools.asm
FieldDefinition: sun.tools.java
FieldExpression: sun.tools.tree
FIFOQueueEnumerator: sun.misc
FileDialogFilter: sun.awt.tiny
FileImageSource: sun.awt.image
FileURLConnection: sun.net.www.protocol.file
FinallyStatement: sun.tools.tree
FloatEditor: sun.beans.editors
FloatExpression: sun.tools.tree
FocusingTextField: sun.awt
FontDescriptor: sun.awt
FontEditor: sun.beans.editors
ForStatement: sun.tools.tree
FtpClient: sun.net.ftp

JdbcOdbc: sun.jdbc.odbc
JdbcOdbcBoundCol: sun.jdbc.odbc
JdbcOdbcBoundParam: sun.jdbc.odbc
JdbcOdbcCallableStatement: sun.jdbc.odbc
JdbcOdbcConnection: sun.jdbc.odbc
JdbcOdbcConnectionInterface: sun.jdbc.odbc
JdbcOdbcDatabaseMetaData: sun.jdbc.odbc
JdbcOdbcDriver: sun.jdbc.odbc
JdbcOdbcDriverAttribute: sun.jdbc.odbc
JdbcOdbcDriverInterface: sun.jdbc.odbc
JdbcOdbcInputStream: sun.jdbc.odbc
JdbcOdbcLimits: sun.jdbc.odbc
JdbcOdbcObject: sun.jdbc.odbc
JdbcOdbcPreparedStatement: sun.jdbc.odbc
JdbcOdbcPseudoCol: sun.jdbc.odbc
JdbcOdbcResultSet: sun.jdbc.odbc
JdbcOdbcResultSetInterface: sun.jdbc.odbc
JdbcOdbcResultSetMetaData: sun.jdbc.odbc
JdbcOdbcSQLWarning: sun.jdbc.odbc
JdbcOdbcStatement: sun.jdbc.odbc
JdbcOdbcTypeInfo: sun.jdbc.odbc
jpeg: sun.net.www.content.image
JPEGImageDecoder: sun.awt.image
KeepAlive: sun.rmi.transport
KeepAliveCache: sun.net.www.http
KeepAliveKey: sun.net.www.http
KeepAliveStream: sun.net.www.http
Label: sun.tools.asm
LeaseChecker: sun.rmi.transport
LeaseInfo: sun.rmi.transport
LeaseRenewer: sun.rmi.transport
LengthExpression: sun.tools.tree
LessExpression: sun.tools.tree
LessOrEqualExpression: sun.tools.tree
LIFOQueueEnumerator: sun.misc
LineNumber: sun.tools.debug
LiveRef: sun.rmi.transport
LoaderHandler: sun.rmi.server
LocalField: sun.tools.tree
LocalVariable: sun.tools.asm, sun.tools.debug
LocalVariableTable: sun.tools.asm
LocateDGC: sun.rmi.transport

Lock: sun.misc
LongEditor: sun.beans.editors
LongExpression: sun.tools.tree
MailToURLConnection: sun.net.www.protocol.mailto
Main: sun.rmi.rmic, sun.security.provider, sun.tools.jar, sun.tools.javac, sun.tools.javadoc, sun.tools.native2ascii
MainThread: sun.tools.debug
MalformedInputException: sun.io
Manifest: sun.tools.jar
MarshalInputStream: sun.rmi.server
MarshalOutputStream: sun.rmi.server
MButtonPeer: sun.awt.motif
MCanvasPeer: sun.awt.motif
MCheckboxMenuItemPeer: sun.awt.motif
MCheckboxPeer: sun.awt.motif
MChoiceMenu: sun.awt.motif
MChoicePeer: sun.awt.motif
MComponentPeer: sun.awt.motif
MD5: sun.security.provider
MDialogPeer: sun.awt.motif
MDrawingSurfaceInfo: sun.awt.motif
MEmbeddedFrame: sun.awt.motif
MEmbeddedFramePeer: sun.awt.motif
MessageHeader: sun.net.www
MessageUtils: sun.misc
MeteredStream: sun.net.www
MethodExpression: sun.tools.tree
MethodType: sun.tools.java
MFileDialogPeer: sun.awt.motif
MFontPeer: sun.awt.motif
MFramePeer: sun.awt.motif
MimeEntry: sun.net.www
MimeLauncher: sun.net.www
MimeTable: sun.net.www
MLabelPeer: sun.awt.motif
MListPeer: sun.awt.motif
MMenuBarPeer: sun.awt.motif
MMenuItemPeer: sun.awt.motif
MMenuPeer: sun.awt.motif
ModalThread: sun.awt.motif
MPanelPeer: sun.awt.motif

UPrintDialog: sun.awt.motif
URLCanonicalizer: sun.net
URLConnection: sun.net.www
URLImageSource: sun.awt.image
Utils: sun.rmi.transport
UUDecoder: sun.misc
UUEncoder: sun.misc
VarDeclarationStatement: sun.tools.tree
VariableGridLayout: sun.awt
VerbatimConnection:
  sun.net.www.protocol.verbatim
VerticalBagLayout: sun.awt
VM: sun.misc
VMNotification: sun.misc
VMNotifierThread: sun.misc
Vset: sun.tools.tree
WeakRef: sun.rmi.transport
WhileStatement: sun.tools.tree
WorldGroupImpl: sun.security.acl

WrappedSocket: sun.rmi.transport.proxy
X11Clipboard: sun.awt.motif
X11DrawingSurface: sun.awt
X11FontMetrics: sun.awt.motif
X11Graphics: sun.awt.motif
X11Image: sun.awt.motif
X11OffScreenImage: sun.awt.motif
X11Selection: sun.awt.motif
X11SelectionHolder: sun.awt.motif
X500Name: sun.security.x509
X500Signer: sun.security.x509
X509Cert: sun.security.x509
X509Key: sun.security.x509
XbmImageDecoder: sun.awt.image
x_xbitmap: sun.net.www.content.image
x_xbitmap: sun.net.www.content.image
x_xpixmap: sun.net.www.content.image
x_xpixmap: sun.net.www.content.image

METHOD DEFINED IN INDEX

*T*his appendix alphabetically lists all the methods that are defined in the sun and sunw packages. Each method is followed by an alphabetical list of the classes that define it.

accept(): sun.awt.tiny. FileDialogFilter, sun.rmi. transport.proxy. HttpAwareServerSocket, sun.rmi. transport.tcp.ConnectionAcceptor

acceptsURL(): sun.jdbc.odbc. JdbcOdbcDriver

action(): sun.applet.AppletCopyright, sun.applet.AppletProps, sun.awt. motif.MButtonPeer, sun.awt.motif. MCheckboxMenuItemPeer, sun.awt. motif.MListPeer, sun.awt.motif. MMenuItemPeer, sun.awt.motif. MTextFieldPeer, sun.awt.motif. UPrintDialog, sun.beans.editors. ColorEditor, sun.beans.editors. FontEditor, sun.rmi.rmic.UI, sun. tools.serialver.SerialVer, sun.tools. serialver.SerialVerFrame

add(): sun.awt.image.ImageFetcher, sun.awt.motif.MChoicePeer, sun. awt.motif.MListPeer, sun.awt.motif. MTinyChoicePeer, sun.awt.tiny. TinyChoicePeer, sun.awt.tiny. TinyListPeer, sun.misc.RegexpPool,

sun.net.www.MessageHeader, sun. net.www.MimeTable, sun.tools.asm. Assembler, sun.tools.asm.SwitchData, sun.tools.asm. TryData, sun.tools. jar.SignatureFile, sun.tools.tree.Vset

addArgument(): sun.tools.java.Parser

addAttribute(): sun.tools.java. BinaryField

addClass(): sun.tools.java.Imports

addConsumer(): sun.awt.image. InputStreamImageSource, sun.awt. image.OffScreenImageSource

addDependency(): sun.tools.java. BinaryClass, sun.tools.java. ClassDefinition, sun.tools.javac. SourceClass

addEntry(): sun.security.acl.AclImpl, sun.tools.jar.Manifest

addField(): sun.tools.java. ClassDefinition, sun.tools.javac. SourceClass

addFile(): sun.tools.jar.Manifest

addFiles(): sun.tools.jar.Manifest

addFinalizeable(): sun.awt.AWTFinalizer

addFlavorMap(): sun.awt.motif.Target

addHelpMenu(): sun.awt.motif.
MMenuBarPeer

addIdentity(): sun.security.provider.
IdentityDatabase

addItem(): sun.awt.motif.MChoicePeer, sun.
awt.motif.MListPeer, sun.awt.motif.
MMenuPeer, sun.awt.motif.
MTinyChoicePeer, sun.awt.tiny.
TinyChoicePeer, sun.awt.tiny. TinyListPeer,
sun.awt.tiny.TinyMenuPeer

addLayoutComponent(): sun.awt.
HorizBagLayout, sun.awt.
VerticalBagLayout

addMember(): sun.security.acl.GroupImpl

addMenu(): sun.awt.motif.MMenuBarPeer

addModifiers(): sun.tools.java.FieldDefinition

addNotifiable(): sun.rmi.transport.Notifier,
sun.rmi.transport.tcp.TCPChannel

addNotify(): sun.awt.EmbeddedFrame

addOwner(): sun.security.acl.OwnerImpl

addPackage(): sun.tools.java.Imports

addPermission(): sun.security.acl.AclEntryImpl

addPropertyChangeListener(): sun.beans.
editors.ColorEditor, sun.beans.editors.
FontEditor

addReference(): sun.tools.java.ClassDefinition

addScope(): sun.tools.jar.JarVerifierStream

addSeparator(): sun.awt.motif. MMenuPeer,
sun.awt.tiny.TinyMenuPeer

addSystemThread(): sun.tools.debug.Agent,
sun.tools.debug.RemoteDebugger

addTableCase(): sun.tools.asm.SwitchData

addVar(): sun.tools.tree.Vset

addVarUnassigned(): sun.tools.tree.Vset

addWatcher(): sun.awt.image.ImageWatched

allocBindBuf(): sun.jdbc.odbc.
JdbcOdbcPreparedStatement

allocBindDataBuffer(): sun.jdbc.odbc.
JdbcOdbcBoundParam

allocConnect(): sun.jdbc.odbc.JdbcOdbc

allocConnection(): sun.jdbc.odbc.
JdbcOdbcDriver, sun.jdbc.odbc.
JdbcOdbcDriverInterface

allocEnv(): sun.jdbc.odbc.JdbcOdbc

allocStmt(): sun.jdbc.odbc.JdbcOdbc

allowThreadSuspension(): sun.misc.VM

allProceduresAreCallable(): sun.jdbc.odbc.
JdbcOdbcDatabaseMetaData

allTablesAreSelectable(): sun.jdbc.odbc.
JdbcOdbcDatabaseMetaData

amFetcher(): sun.awt.image.ImageFetcher

annotateClass(): sun.rmi.server.
MarshalOutputStream

appletQuit(): sun.applet.AppletViewer

appletResize(): sun.applet.AppletPanel

arrayTypeName(): sun.tools.debug.
RemoteArray

asChange(): sun.misc.VM

asChange_otherthread(): sun.misc.VM

ascii(): sun.net.ftp.FtpClient

askServer(): sun.net.nntp.NntpClient

assessTrust(): sun.applet.AppletSecurity

authString(): sun.net.www.protocol.http.
HttpAuthenticator

available(): sun.jdbc.odbc.
JdbcOdbcInputStream, sun.net.www.
MeteredStream, sun.net.www.protocol.http.
EmptyInputStream, sun.rmi.transport.proxy.
HttpInputStream, sun.rmi.transport.proxy.
HttpSendInputStream, sun.rmi.transport.tcp.
MultiplexInputStream, sun.security.util.
DerInputStream

basicCheck(): sun.tools.java. ClassDefinition,
sun.tools.javac.SourceClass

beep(): sun.awt.motif.MToolkit, sun.awt.tiny.
TinyToolkit

beginClass(): sun.tools.java.Parser, sun.tools.
java.ParserActions, sun.tools. javac.
BatchParser

beginValidate(): sun.awt.motif.
MComponentPeer, sun.awt.tiny.
TinyComponentPeer, sun.awt.tiny.
TinyFileDialogPeer

binary(): sun.net.ftp.FtpClient

bind(): sun.rmi.registry.RegistryImpl, sun.rmi.
registry.RegistryImpl_Stub

bindColDefault(): sun.jdbc.odbc.JdbcOdbc

bindInParameterAtExec(): sun.jdbc.odbc.
JdbcOdbc

BinaryAssignExpression, sun.tools.tree.
CommaExpression, sun.tools.tree.
ConditionalExpression, sun.tools.tree.
Expression, sun.tools.tree.
IncDecExpression, sun.tools.tree.
MethodExpression, sun.tools.tree.
NewInstanceExpression

checkAccept(): sun.applet.AppletSecurity

checkAccess(): sun.applet.AppletSecurity

checkAmbigName(): sun.tools.tree.
ArrayAccessExpression, sun.tools.tree.
Expression, sun.tools.tree.FieldExpression,
sun.tools.tree.IdentifierExpression,
sun.tools.tree.TypeExpression

checkAssignOp(): sun.tools.tree.
ArrayAccessExpression, sun.tools.tree.
Expression, sun.tools.tree.FieldExpression,
sun.tools.tree.IdentifierExpression

checkAwtEventQueueAccess(): sun.applet.
AppletSecurity

checkBackBranch(): sun.tools.tree.Context

checkCondition(): sun.tools.tree.
AndExpression, sun.tools.tree.
BinaryLogicalExpression, sun.tools.tree.
BooleanExpression, sun.tools.tree.
ExprExpression, sun.tools.tree.Expression,
sun.tools.tree.NotExpression, sun.tools.tree.
OrExpression

checkConnect(): sun.applet.AppletSecurity

checkCreateClassLoader(): sun.applet.
AppletSecurity

checkExec(): sun.applet.AppletSecurity

checkExit(): sun.applet.AppletSecurity

checkFinalAssign(): sun.tools.tree.
FieldExpression

checkImage(): sun.awt.motif.MComponentPeer,
sun.awt.motif.MToolkit, sun.awt.tiny.
TinyComponentPeer, sun.awt.tiny.
TinyToolkit

checkInitializer(): sun.tools.tree.
ArrayExpression, sun.tools.tree.Expression

checkInsideClass(): sun.tools.javac.SourceClass

checkLHS(): sun.tools.tree.
ArrayAccessExpression, sun.tools.tree.
Expression, sun.tools.tree.FieldExpression,
sun.tools.tree.IdentifierExpression

checkLink(): sun.applet.AppletSecurity

checkListen(): sun.applet.AppletSecurity

checkLocalClass(): sun.tools.java.
ClassDefinition, sun.tools.javac.
SourceClass

checkMemberAccess(): sun.applet.
AppletSecurity

checkMethod(): sun.tools.tree.Statement

checkPackageAccess(): sun.applet.
AppletSecurity

checkPackageDefinition(): sun.applet.
AppletSecurity

checkPermission(): sun.security.acl.
AclEntryImpl, sun.security.acl.AclImpl

checkPrintJobAccess(): sun.applet.
AppletSecurity

checkPropertiesAccess(): sun.applet.
AppletSecurity

checkPropertyAccess(): sun.applet.
AppletSecurity

checkRead(): sun.applet.AppletSecurity

checkSecurityAccess(): sun.applet.
AppletSecurity

checkSetFactory(): sun.applet.AppletSecurity

checkSourceFile(): sun.tools.javac.SourceClass

checkSystemClipboardAccess(): sun.applet.
AppletSecurity

checkTopLevelWindow(): sun.applet.
AppletSecurity

checkValue(): sun.tools.tree.
ArrayAccessExpression, sun.tools.tree.
ArrayExpression, sun.tools.tree.
AssignExpression, sun.tools.tree.
AssignOpExpression, sun.tools.tree.
BinaryExpression, sun.tools.tree.
BinaryLogicalExpression, sun.tools.tree.
CastExpression, sun.tools.tree.
ConditionalExpression, sun.tools.tree.
ConvertExpression, sun.tools.tree.
Expression, sun.tools.tree.FieldExpression,
sun.tools.tree.IdentifierExpression,
sun.tools.tree.IncDecExpression,
sun.tools.tree.InstanceOfExpression,
sun.tools.tree. LengthExpression,
sun.tools.tree. MethodExpression,
sun.tools.tree. NewArrayExpression,
sun.tools.tree. NewInstanceExpression,
sun.tools.tree. SuperExpression,

sun.tools.tree.DeclarationStatement,
sun.tools.tree.DoStatement,
sun.tools.tree.Expression,
sun.tools.tree.ExpressionStatement,
sun.tools.tree.FinallyStatement,
sun.tools.tree.ForStatement,
sun.tools.tree.IfStatement,
sun.tools.tree.InlineMethodExpression,
sun.tools.tree.InlineNewInstanceExpression,
sun.tools.tree.InlineReturnStatement,
sun.tools.tree.InstanceOfExpression,
sun.tools.tree.NewInstanceExpression,
sun.tools.tree.PostDecExpression,
sun.tools.tree.PostIncExpression,
sun.tools.tree.PreDecExpression,
sun.tools.tree.PreIncExpression,
sun.tools.tree.ReturnStatement,
sun.tools.tree.Statement,
sun.tools.tree.SwitchStatement,
sun.tools.tree.SynchronizedStatement,
sun.tools.tree.ThrowStatement,
sun.tools.tree.TryStatement,
sun.tools.tree.VarDeclarationStatement,
sun.tools.tree.WhileStatement

codeArguments(): sun.tools.tree.
UplevelReference

codeInit(): sun.tools.java.FieldDefinition,
sun.tools.javac.SourceField

codeInitialization(): sun.tools.tree.
UplevelReference

codeValue(): sun.tools.tree.AddExpression,
sun.tools.tree.ArrayAccessExpression,
sun.tools.tree.ArrayExpression,
sun.tools.tree.AssignExpression,
sun.tools.tree.AssignOpExpression,
sun.tools.tree.BinaryBitExpression,
sun.tools.tree.BinaryExpression,
sun.tools.tree.BitNotExpression,
sun.tools.tree.BooleanExpression,
sun.tools.tree.CommaExpression,
sun.tools.tree.ConditionalExpression,
sun.tools.tree.ConvertExpression,
sun.tools.tree.DoubleExpression,
sun.tools.tree.Expression,
sun.tools.tree.FieldExpression,
sun.tools.tree.FloatExpression,
sun.tools.tree.IdentifierExpression,
sun.tools.tree.InlineMethodExpression,
sun.tools.tree.InlineNewInstanceExpression,

sun.tools.tree.InstanceOfExpression,
sun.tools.tree.IntegerExpression,
sun.tools.tree.LengthExpression,
sun.tools.tree.LongExpression,
sun.tools.tree.MethodExpression,
sun.tools.tree.NegativeExpression,
sun.tools.tree.NewArrayExpression,
sun.tools.tree.NewInstanceExpression,
sun.tools.tree.NullExpression,
sun.tools.tree.PostDecExpression,
sun.tools.tree.PostIncExpression,
sun.tools.tree.PreDecExpression,
sun.tools.tree.PreIncExpression,
sun.tools.tree.StringExpression,
sun.tools.tree.ThisExpression

colAttributes(): sun.jdbc.odbc.JdbcOdbc

colAttributesString(): sun.jdbc.odbc.JdbcOdbc

collect(): sun.tools.asm.Assembler

collectMethods(): sun.rmi.rmic.TopGRP

columnPrivileges(): sun.jdbc.odbc.JdbcOdbc

columns(): sun.jdbc.odbc.JdbcOdbc

commit(): sun.jdbc.odbc.
JdbcOdbcConnection

compile(): sun.rmi.rmic.Main, sun.tools.javac.
Main, sun.tools.javac.SourceClass

compileClass(): sun.tools.javac.SourceClass

computeStubHash(): sun.rmi.rmic.
GenerateRemoteProxy

connect(): sun.jdbc.odbc.JdbcOdbcDriver,
sun.net.www.protocol.appletresource.
AppletResourceConnection,
sun.net.www.protocol.doc.
DocURLConnection,
sun.net.www.protocol.file.
FileURLConnection,
sun.net.www.protocol.ftp.
FtpURLConnection,
sun.net.www.protocol.gopher.
GopherURLConnection,
sun.net.www.protocol.http.
HttpURLConnection,
sun.net.www.protocol.mailto.
MailToURLConnection,
sun.net.www.protocol.systemresource.
SystemResourceConnection,
sun.net.www.protocol.verbatim.
VerbatimConnection

connected(): sun.net.ProgressData, sun.net.
ProgressEntry

cont(): sun.misc.Timer, sun.tools.debug.
RemoteThread

containsDeprecated(): sun.tools.java.
ClassDefinition

convert(): sun.awt.CharToByteSymbol, sun.
awt.motif.CharToByteX11CNS11643P1,
sun.awt.motif.CharToByteX11CNS11643P2,
sun.awt.motif.CharToByteX11CNS11643P3,
sun.awt.motif.CharToByteX11Dingbats,
sun.awt.motif.CharToByteX11GB2312,
sun.awt.motif.CharToByteX11JIS0201,
sun.awt.motif.CharToByteX11JIS0208,
sun.awt.motif.CharToByteX11KSC5601,
sun.io.ByteToChar8859_1,
sun.io.ByteToCharBig5,
sun.io.ByteToCharCNS11643,
sun.io.ByteToCharConverter,
sun.io.ByteToCharCp33722,
sun.io.ByteToCharCp964,
sun.io.ByteToCharDBCS_ASCII,
sun.io.ByteToCharDBCS_EBCDIC,
sun.io.ByteToCharDefault,
sun.io.ByteToCharEUC,
sun.io.ByteToCharEUCJIS,
sun.io.ByteToCharGB2312,
sun.io.ByteToCharJIS,
sun.io.ByteToCharKSC5601,
sun.io.ByteToCharSJIS,
sun.io.ByteToCharSingleByte,
sun.io.ByteToCharUTF8,
sun.io.ByteToCharUnicode,
sun.io.CharToByte8859_1,
sun.io.CharToByteBig5,
sun.io.CharToByteCNS11643,
sun.io.CharToByteConverter,
sun.io.CharToByteCp933,
sun.io.CharToByteCp949,
sun.io.CharToByteCp970,
sun.io.CharToByteDBCS_ASCII,
sun.io.CharToByteDBCS_EBCDIC,
sun.io.CharToByteDefault,
sun.io.CharToByteEUC,
sun.io.CharToByteEUCJIS,
sun.io.CharToByteGB2312,
sun.io.CharToByteJIS,
sun.io.CharToByteKSC5601,
sun.io.CharToByteSJIS,
sun.io.CharToByteSingleByte,
sun.io.CharToByteUTF8,
sun.io.CharToByteUnicode,
sun.tools.native2ascii.Main,
sun.tools.tree.Node

convertAll(): sun.io.ByteToCharConverter,
sun.io.CharToByteConverter

convertData(): sun.jdbc.odbc.
JdbcOdbcInputStream

convertHangul(): sun.io.CharToByteKSC5601

convertWarning(): sun.jdbc.odbc.JdbcOdbc

copy(): sun.tools.tree.Vset

copyArea(): sun.awt.motif.PSGraphics,
sun.awt.motif.X11Graphics,
sun.awt.tiny.TinyGraphics

copyArguments(): sun.tools.tree.LocalField

copyInline(): sun.tools.tree.
ArrayAccessExpression, sun.tools.tree.
AssignOpExpression, sun.tools.tree.
BinaryAssignExpression, sun.tools.tree.
BinaryExpression, sun.tools.tree.
CatchStatement, sun.tools.tree.
CompoundStatement, sun.tools.tree.
ConditionalExpression, sun.tools.tree.
DoStatement, sun.tools.tree.Expression,
sun.tools.tree.ExpressionStatement, sun.
tools.tree.FieldExpression, sun.tools.tree.
FinallyStatement, sun.tools.tree.
ForStatement, sun.tools.tree.
IdentifierExpression, sun.tools.tree.
IfStatement, sun.tools.tree.
InlineMethodExpression, sun.tools.tree.
InlineNewInstanceExpression, sun.tools.
tree.InlineReturnStatement, sun.tools.tree.
LocalField, sun.tools.tree.MethodExpression,
sun.tools.tree.NaryExpression, sun.tools.
tree.NewArrayExpression, sun.tools.tree.
NewInstanceExpression, sun.tools.tree.
ReturnStatement, sun.tools.tree.Statement,
sun.tools.tree.SuperExpression, sun.tools.
tree.SwitchStatement, sun.tools.tree.
SynchronizedStatement, sun.tools.tree.
ThisExpression, sun.tools.tree.
ThrowStatement, sun.tools.tree.
TryStatement, sun.tools.tree.
UnaryExpression, sun.tools.tree.
VarDeclarationStatement, sun.tools.tree.
WhileStatement

costInline(): sun.tools.tree.AddExpression,
sun.tools.tree.ArrayAccessExpression,
sun.tools.tree.AssignAddExpression,
sun.tools.tree.AssignExpression,
sun.tools.tree.AssignOpExpression,
sun.tools.tree.BinaryAssignExpression,
sun.tools.tree.BinaryExpression,
sun.tools.tree.BreakStatement,
sun.tools.tree.CaseStatement,
sun.tools.tree.CastExpression,
sun.tools.tree.CompoundStatement,
sun.tools.tree.ConditionalExpression,
sun.tools.tree.ContinueStatement,
sun.tools.tree.DoStatement,
sun.tools.tree.Expression,
sun.tools.tree.ExpressionStatement,
sun.tools.tree.FieldExpression,
sun.tools.tree.ForStatement,
sun.tools.tree.IdentifierExpression,
sun.tools.tree.IfStatement,
sun.tools.tree.InlineReturnStatement,
sun.tools.tree.InstanceOfExpression,
sun.tools.tree.MethodExpression,
sun.tools.tree.NaryExpression,
sun.tools.tree.NewInstanceExpression,
sun.tools.tree.ReturnStatement,
sun.tools.tree.Statement,
sun.tools.tree.SwitchStatement,
sun.tools.tree.ThrowStatement,
sun.tools.tree.UnaryExpression,
sun.tools.tree.VarDeclarationStatement,
sun.tools.tree.WhileStatement

countApplets(): sun.applet.AppletViewer

covdata(): sun.tools.java.Environment

coverage(): sun.tools.java.Environment

create(): sun.awt.motif.PSGraphics,
sun.awt.motif.X11Graphics,
sun.awt.tiny.TinyGraphics

createAppletViewer(): sun.applet.
AppletViewerFactory, sun.applet.
StdAppletViewerFactory

createButton(): sun.awt.motif.MToolkit,
sun.awt.tiny.TinyToolkit

createCanvas(): sun.awt.motif.MToolkit,
sun.awt.tiny.TinyToolkit

createCheckbox(): sun.awt.motif.MToolkit,
sun.awt.tiny.TinyToolkit

createCheckboxMenuItem(): sun.awt.motif.
MToolkit, sun.awt.tiny.TinyToolkit

createChoice(): sun.awt.motif.MToolkit,
sun.awt.tiny.TinyToolkit

createDialog(): sun.awt.motif.MToolkit,
sun.awt.tiny.TinyToolkit

createFileDialog(): sun.awt.motif.MToolkit,
sun.awt.tiny.TinyToolkit

createFrame(): sun.awt.motif.MToolkit,
sun.awt.tiny.TinyToolkit

createIdentity(): sun.security.provider.Main

createImage(): sun.awt.motif.
MComponentPeer, sun.awt.motif.MToolkit,
sun.awt.tiny.TinyComponentPeer, sun.awt.
tiny.TinyToolkit

createIndexHash(): sun.tools.java.
BinaryConstantPool

createLabel(): sun.awt.motif.MToolkit,
sun.awt.tiny.TinyToolkit

createList(): sun.awt.motif.MToolkit,
sun.awt.tiny.TinyToolkit

createMenu(): sun.awt.motif.MToolkit,
sun.awt.tiny.TinyToolkit

createMenuBar(): sun.awt.motif.MToolkit,
sun.awt.tiny.TinyToolkit

createMenuItem(): sun.awt.motif.MToolkit,
sun.awt.tiny.TinyToolkit

createPanel(): sun.awt.motif.MToolkit,
sun.awt.tiny.TinyToolkit

createPopupMenu(): sun.awt.motif.MToolkit,
sun.awt.tiny.TinyToolkit

createScrollbar(): sun.awt.motif.MToolkit,
sun.awt.tiny.TinyToolkit

createScrollPane(): sun.awt.motif.MToolkit,
sun.awt.tiny.TinyToolkit

createServerSocket(): sun.rmi.transport.proxy.
RMIDirectSocketFactory, sun.rmi.transport.
proxy.RMIHttpToCGISocketFactory,
sun.rmi.transport.proxy.
RMIHttpToPortSocketFactory, sun.rmi.
transport.proxy.RMIMasterSocketFactory

createSigner(): sun.security.provider.Main

createSocket(): sun.rmi.transport.proxy.
RMIDirectSocketFactory, sun.rmi.transport.
proxy.RMIHttpToCGISocketFactory,
sun.rmi.transport.proxy.

dispose(): sun.awt.motif.MComponentPeer,
sun.awt.motif.MDialogPeer,
sun.awt.motif.MFramePeer,
sun.awt.motif.MMenuBarPeer,
sun.awt.motif.MMenuItemPeer,
sun.awt.motif.MMenuPeer,
sun.awt.motif.MPopupMenuPeer,
sun.awt.motif.MTextFieldPeer,
sun.awt.motif.MWindowPeer,
sun.awt.motif.PSGraphics,
sun.awt.motif.PageGraphics,
sun.awt.motif.X11Graphics,
sun.awt.tiny.TinyComponentPeer,
sun.awt.tiny.TinyDialogPeer,
sun.awt.tiny.TinyFramePeer,
sun.awt.tiny.TinyGraphics,
sun.awt.tiny.TinyMenuItemPeer,
sun.awt.tiny.TinyMenuPeer

doCompare(): sun.misc.Compare,
sun.net.www.protocol.file.StringCompare

doCompile(): sun.rmi.rmic.Main

doConnect(): sun.net.NetworkClient

doesMaxRowSizeIncludeBlobs(): sun.jdbc.
odbc.JdbcOdbcDatabaseMetaData

doFetch(): sun.awt.image.ImageFetchable,
sun.awt.image.InputStreamImageSource

doFinalization(): sun.awt.AWTFinalizeable,
sun.awt.image.ImageRepresentation,
sun.awt.motif.X11Graphics

doHashes(): sun.tools.jar.Manifest

done(): sun.rmi.server.UnicastRef,
sun.rmi.transport.StreamRemoteCall

doneWithArguments(): sun.tools.tree.
LocalField

DoubleByte(): sun.io.CharToByteJIS0208

down(): sun.tools.debug.RemoteThread

dragAbsolute(): sun.awt.motif.MScrollbarPeer

draw3DOval(): sun.awt.tiny.
TinyComponentPeer

draw3DRect(): sun.awt.tiny.
TinyComponentPeer

drawArc(): sun.awt.motif.PSGraphics,
sun.awt.motif.X11Graphics,
sun.awt.tiny.TinyGraphics

drawBytes(): sun.awt.motif.PSGraphics,
sun.awt.motif.X11Graphics,
sun.awt.tiny.TinyGraphics

drawBytesWidth(): sun.awt.motif.
X11Graphics

drawChars(): sun.awt.motif.PSGraphics,
sun.awt.motif.X11Graphics,
sun.awt.tiny.TinyGraphics

drawCharsWidth(): sun.awt.motif.
X11Graphics

drawImage(): sun.awt.image.
ImageRepresentation, sun.awt.motif.
PSGraphics, sun.awt.motif.X11Graphics,
sun.awt.tiny.TinyGraphics

drawLine(): sun.awt.motif.PSGraphics,
sun.awt.motif.X11Graphics,
sun.awt.tiny.TinyGraphics

drawOval(): sun.awt.motif.PSGraphics,
sun.awt.motif.X11Graphics,
sun.awt.tiny.TinyGraphics

drawPolygon(): sun.awt.motif.PSGraphics,
sun.awt.motif.X11Graphics,
sun.awt.tiny.TinyGraphics

drawPolyline(): sun.awt.motif.PSGraphics,
sun.awt.motif.X11Graphics,
sun.awt.tiny.TinyGraphics

drawRect(): sun.awt.motif.PSGraphics,
sun.awt.motif.X11Graphics

drawRoundRect(): sun.awt.motif.PSGraphics,
sun.awt.motif.X11Graphics,
sun.awt.tiny.TinyGraphics

drawScaledImage(): sun.awt.image.
ImageRepresentation

drawStretchImage(): sun.awt.image.
ImageRepresentation

drawString(): sun.awt.motif.PSGraphics,
sun.awt.motif.X11Graphics,
sun.awt.tiny.TinyGraphics

drawStringWidth(): sun.awt.motif.
X11Graphics

driverConnect(): sun.jdbc.odbc.JdbcOdbc

dump(): sun.misc.Queue,
sun.tools.java.Environment

dumpByte(): sun.jdbc.odbc.JdbcOdbcObject

dumpStack(): sun.tools.debug.RemoteThread

elements(): sun.misc.Cache, sun.misc.Queue,
sun.net.www.MimeTable

eliminate(): sun.tools.tree.Statement

sun.tools.asm.NameAndTypeData,
sun.tools.java.ClassDeclaration,
sun.tools.tree.BooleanExpression,
sun.tools.tree.ConvertExpression,
sun.tools.tree.DoubleExpression,
sun.tools.tree.Expression,
sun.tools.tree.FloatExpression,
sun.tools.tree.IdentifierExpression,
sun.tools.tree.IntExpression,
sun.tools.tree.IntegerExpression,
sun.tools.tree.LongExpression,
sun.tools.tree.NullExpression,
sun.tools.tree.StringExpression

equalsDefault(): sun.tools.tree.
BooleanExpression, sun.tools.tree.
DoubleExpression, sun.tools.tree.
Expression, sun.tools.tree.FloatExpression,
sun.tools.tree.IntegerExpression,
sun.tools.tree.LongExpression

error(): sun.jdbc.odbc.JdbcOdbc,
sun.net.www.httpd.BasicHttpServer,
sun.rmi.rmic.Main, sun.tools.jar.Main,
sun.tools.java.Environment,
sun.tools.javac.BatchEnvironment,
sun.tools.javac.Main

errorString(): sun.rmi.rmic.BatchEnvironment,
sun.tools.javac.BatchEnvironment

exceptionEvent(): sun.tools.debug.
DebuggerCallback, sun.tools.ttydebug.TTY

execDirect(): sun.jdbc.odbc.JdbcOdbc

execute(): sun.jdbc.odbc.JdbcOdbc, sun.jdbc.
odbc.JdbcOdbcPreparedStatement, sun.
jdbc.odbc.JdbcOdbcStatement, sun.misc.
Request, sun.rmi.transport.proxy.
CGICommandHandler, sun.rmi.transport.
proxy.CGIForwardCommand, sun.rmi.
transport.proxy.CGIGethostnameCommand,
sun.rmi.transport.proxy.CGIPingCommand,
sun.rmi.transport.proxy.CGITryHostname
Command

executeCall(): sun.rmi.transport.
StreamRemoteCall

executeQuery(): sun.jdbc.odbc.
JdbcOdbcPreparedStatement, sun.jdbc.
odbc.JdbcOdbcStatement

executeUpdate(): sun.jdbc.odbc.
JdbcOdbcPreparedStatement, sun.jdbc.
odbc.JdbcOdbcStatement

exists(): sun.tools.java.ClassFile,
sun.tools.java.Package

expect(): sun.tools.java.Parser

explicitCast(): sun.tools.java.Environment

exportCmd(): sun.security.provider.Main

exportObject(): sun.rmi.server.
UnicastServerRef, sun.rmi.transport.
Endpoint, sun.rmi.transport.LiveRef,
sun.rmi.transport.Transport,
sun.rmi.transport.tcp.TCPEndpoint,
sun.rmi.transport.tcp.TCPTransport

exprArgs(): sun.tools.java.Parser

fetch(): sun.jdbc.odbc.JdbcOdbc

fetchloop(): sun.awt.image.ImageFetcher

fillArc(): sun.awt.motif.PSGraphics,
sun.awt.motif.X11Graphics,
sun.awt.tiny.TinyGraphics

fillOval(): sun.awt.motif.PSGraphics,
sun.awt.motif.X11Graphics,
sun.awt.tiny.TinyGraphics

fillPolygon(): sun.awt.motif.PSGraphics,
sun.awt.motif.X11Graphics,
sun.awt.tiny.TinyGraphics

fillRect(): sun.awt.motif.PSGraphics,
sun.awt.motif.X11Graphics,
sun.awt.tiny.TinyGraphics

fillRoundRect(): sun.awt.motif.PSGraphics,
sun.awt.motif.X11Graphics,
sun.awt.tiny.TinyGraphics

finalize(): sun.awt.image.ImageRepresentation,
sun.awt.motif.X11Graphics,
sun.awt.tiny.TinyWindow,
sun.jdbc.odbc.JdbcOdbcConnection,
sun.jdbc.odbc.JdbcOdbcDriver,
sun.jdbc.odbc.JdbcOdbcResultSet,
sun.jdbc.odbc.JdbcOdbcStatement, sun.net.
www.MeteredStream, sun.net.www.http.
HttpClient, sun.net.www.protocol.http.
HttpURLConnection, sun.rmi.transport.
LiveRef, sun.rmi.transport.tcp.
ConnectionMultiplexer, sun.tools.debug.
RemoteObject

find(): sun.awt.motif.PSPaperSize,
sun.net.www.MimeTable

findAnyMethod(): sun.tools.java.
ClassDefinition

findByDescription(): sun.net.www.MimeTable

generateName(): sun.tools.javac.
BatchEnvironment

generateProcessOutput(): sun.net.www.httpd.
BasicHttpServer

generateStatistics(): sun.net.www.httpd.
BasicHttpServer

GenJCov(): sun.tools.asm.Assembler

GenVecJCov(): sun.tools.asm.Assembler

get(): sun.misc.Cache, sun.misc.Ref,
sun.net.ftp.FtpClient,
sun.net.www.http.KeepAliveCache,
sun.security.x509.AlgorithmId,
sun.tools.asm.SwitchData,
sun.tools.debug.RemoteBoolean,
sun.tools.debug.RemoteByte,
sun.tools.debug.RemoteChar,
sun.tools.debug.RemoteDebugger,
sun.tools.debug.RemoteDouble,
sun.tools.debug.RemoteFloat,
sun.tools.debug.RemoteInt,
sun.tools.debug.RemoteLong,
sun.tools.debug.RemoteShort

getAbsoluteName(): sun.tools.java.ClassFile,
sun.tools.javac.SourceClass

getAbstractFields(): sun.tools.java.
ClassDefinition

getAccessField(): sun.tools.java.
ClassDefinition

getAccessMethodTarget(): sun.tools.java.
FieldDefinition

getAccessUpdateField(): sun.tools.java.
FieldDefinition

getAction(): sun.net.www.MimeEntry

getAlgorithm(): sun.security.pkcs.PKCS8Key,
sun.security.x509.X509Key

getAlgorithmId(): sun.security.pkcs.PKCS8Key,
sun.security.x509.AlgorithmId,
sun.security.x509.X500Signer,
sun.security.x509.X509Key

getAllowUserInteraction(): sun.net.www.
protocol.verbatim.VerbatimConnection

getApparentClassName(): sun.tools.tree.
Context

getApparentField(): sun.tools.tree.Context

getApplet(): sun.applet.AppletPanel,
sun.applet.AppletViewer

getAppletContext(): sun.applet.AppletPanel,
sun.applet.AppletViewerPanel

getAppletHandlerThread(): sun.applet.
AppletPanel

getAppletHeight(): sun.applet.AppletPanel

getApplets(): sun.applet.AppletViewer

getAppletWidth(): sun.applet.AppletPanel

getArguments(): sun.tools.java.BinaryField,
sun.tools.java.FieldDefinition,
sun.tools.javac.SourceField

getArgumentTypes(): sun.tools.java.
MethodType, sun.tools.java.Type

getArrayDimension(): sun.tools.java.
ArrayType, sun.tools.java.Type

getArticle(): sun.net.nntp.NntpClient

getAscent(): sun.awt.motif.X11FontMetrics,
sun.awt.tiny.TinyFontMetrics

getAsciiStream(): sun.jdbc.odbc.
JdbcOdbcResultSet

getAsProperties(): sun.net.www.MimeTable

getAsText(): sun.beans.editors.BoolEditor,
sun.beans.editors.ColorEditor,
sun.beans.editors.FontEditor

getAttribute(): sun.tools.java.BinaryClass,
sun.tools.java.BinaryField

getAttributeProperties(): sun.jdbc.odbc.
JdbcOdbcDriver

getAudioClip(): sun.applet.AppletViewer

getAuth(): sun.net.www.protocol.http.
AuthenticationInfo

getAuthString(): sun.net.www.protocol.http.
AuthenticationInfo

getAutoCommit(): sun.jdbc.odbc.
JdbcOdbcConnection

getBackground(): sun.awt.image.Image

getBadInputLength(): sun.io.
ByteToCharConverter, sun.io.
CharToByteConverter

getBannerString(): sun.awt.motif.UPrintDialog

getBase(): sun.net.www.protocol.
systemresource.ParseSystemURL

getBaseMenuBar(): sun.applet.
AppletViewerFactory, sun.applet.
StdAppletViewerFactory

sun.io.ByteToCharCp1383,
sun.io.ByteToCharCp273,
sun.io.ByteToCharCp277,
sun.io.ByteToCharCp278,
sun.io.ByteToCharCp280,
sun.io.ByteToCharCp284,
sun.io.ByteToCharCp285,
sun.io.ByteToCharCp297,
sun.io.ByteToCharCp33722,
sun.io.ByteToCharCp420,
sun.io.ByteToCharCp424,
sun.io.ByteToCharCp437,
sun.io.ByteToCharCp500,
sun.io.ByteToCharCp737,
sun.io.ByteToCharCp775,
sun.io.ByteToCharCp838,
sun.io.ByteToCharCp850,
sun.io.ByteToCharCp852,
sun.io.ByteToCharCp855,
sun.io.ByteToCharCp856,
sun.io.ByteToCharCp857,
sun.io.ByteToCharCp860,
sun.io.ByteToCharCp861,
sun.io.ByteToCharCp862,
sun.io.ByteToCharCp863,
sun.io.ByteToCharCp864,
sun.io.ByteToCharCp865,
sun.io.ByteToCharCp866,
sun.io.ByteToCharCp868,
sun.io.ByteToCharCp869,
sun.io.ByteToCharCp870,
sun.io.ByteToCharCp871,
sun.io.ByteToCharCp874,
sun.io.ByteToCharCp875,
sun.io.ByteToCharCp918,
sun.io.ByteToCharCp921,
sun.io.ByteToCharCp922,
sun.io.ByteToCharCp930,
sun.io.ByteToCharCp933,
sun.io.ByteToCharCp935,
sun.io.ByteToCharCp937,
sun.io.ByteToCharCp939,
sun.io.ByteToCharCp942,
sun.io.ByteToCharCp948,
sun.io.ByteToCharCp949,
sun.io.ByteToCharCp950,
sun.io.ByteToCharCp964,
sun.io.ByteToCharCp970,
sun.io.ByteToCharDefault,
sun.io.ByteToCharEUCJIS,

sun.io.ByteToCharGB2312,
sun.io.ByteToCharJIS,
sun.io.ByteToCharKSC5601,
sun.io.ByteToCharMacArabic,
sun.io.ByteToCharMacCentralEurope,
sun.io.ByteToCharMacCroatian,
sun.io.ByteToCharMacCyrillic,
sun.io.ByteToCharMacDingbat,
sun.io.ByteToCharMacGreek,
sun.io.ByteToCharMacHebrew,
sun.io.ByteToCharMacIceland,
sun.io.ByteToCharMacRoman,
sun.io.ByteToCharMacRomania,
sun.io.ByteToCharMacSymbol,
sun.io.ByteToCharMacThai,
sun.io.ByteToCharMacTurkish,
sun.io.ByteToCharMacUkraine,
sun.io.ByteToCharSJIS,
sun.io.ByteToCharUTF8,
sun.io.ByteToCharUnicode,
sun.io.CharToByte8859_1,
sun.io.CharToByte8859_2,
sun.io.CharToByte8859_3,
sun.io.CharToByte8859_4,
sun.io.CharToByte8859_5,
sun.io.CharToByte8859_6,
sun.io.CharToByte8859_7,
sun.io.CharToByte8859_8,
sun.io.CharToByte8859_9,
sun.io.CharToByteBig5,
sun.io.CharToByteCNS11643,
sun.io.CharToByteConverter,
sun.io.CharToByteCp037,
sun.io.CharToByteCp1006,
sun.io.CharToByteCp1025,
sun.io.CharToByteCp1026,
sun.io.CharToByteCp1046,
sun.io.CharToByteCp1097,
sun.io.CharToByteCp1098,
sun.io.CharToByteCp1112,
sun.io.CharToByteCp1122,
sun.io.CharToByteCp1123,
sun.io.CharToByteCp1124,
sun.io.CharToByteCp1250,
sun.io.CharToByteCp1251,
sun.io.CharToByteCp1252,
sun.io.CharToByteCp1253,
sun.io.CharToByteCp1254,
sun.io.CharToByteCp1255,
sun.io.CharToByteCp1256,

getDigestAlgorithmIds(): sun.security.pkcs.
PKCS7

getDigestEncryptionAlgorithmId(): sun.
security.pkcs.SignerInfo

getDirectory(): sun.tools.java.ClassPath

getDisplay(): sun.awt.X11DrawingSurface,
sun.awt.motif.MDrawingSurfaceInfo

getDocumentation(): sun.tools.java.BinaryField,
sun.tools.java.ClassDefinition,
sun.tools.java.FieldDefinition

getDocumentBase(): sun.applet.AppletPanel,
sun.applet.AppletViewerPanel

getDoInput(): sun.net.www.protocol.
verbatim.VerbatimConnection

getDoOutput(): sun.net.www.protocol.
verbatim.VerbatimConnection

getDouble(): sun.jdbc.odbc.
JdbcOdbcCallableStatement, sun.jdbc.odbc.
JdbcOdbcResultSet

getDrawable(): sun.awt.X11DrawingSurface,
sun.awt.motif.MDrawingSurfaceInfo

getDrawingSurfaceInfo(): sun.awt.
DrawingSurface, sun.awt.motif.
MCanvasPeer, sun.awt.motif.
X11OffScreenImage

getDriverMajorVersion(): sun.jdbc.odbc.
JdbcOdbcDatabaseMetaData

getDriverMinorVersion(): sun.jdbc.odbc.
JdbcOdbcDatabaseMetaData

getDriverName(): sun.jdbc.odbc.
JdbcOdbcDatabaseMetaData

getDriverVersion(): sun.jdbc.odbc.
JdbcOdbcDatabaseMetaData

getElement(): sun.tools.debug.RemoteArray,
sun.tools.tree.Context

getElements(): sun.tools.debug.RemoteArray

getElementType(): sun.tools.debug.
RemoteArray, sun.tools.java.ArrayType,
sun.tools.java.Type

getEncoded(): sun.security.pkcs.PKCS8Key,
sun.security.x509.X509Key

getEncryptedDigest(): sun.security.pkcs.
SignerInfo

getEndLabel(): sun.tools.asm.TryData

getEndpoint(): sun.rmi.transport.Channel,
sun.rmi.transport.tcp.TCPChannel

getEndPos(): sun.tools.java.Scanner

getEntry(): sun.tools.jar.Manifest,
sun.tools.jar.SignatureFile

getError(): sun.tools.java.ClassDefinition

getEUC(): sun.io.CharToByteGB2312,
sun.io.CharToByteKSC5601

getExceptionCatchList(): sun.tools.debug.
RemoteDebugger

getExceptionHandlers(): sun.tools.java.
BinaryCode

getExceptionIds(): sun.tools.java.
FieldDefinition

getExceptions(): sun.tools.java.BinaryField,
sun.tools.java.FieldDefinition,
sun.tools.javac.SourceField

getExportedKeys(): sun.jdbc.odbc.
JdbcOdbcDatabaseMetaData

getExtensions(): sun.net.www.MimeEntry

getExtensionsAsList(): sun.net.www.
MimeEntry

getExtraNameCharacters(): sun.jdbc.odbc.
JdbcOdbcDatabaseMetaData

getField(): sun.tools.debug.RemoteClass,
sun.tools.debug.RemoteObject,
sun.tools.tree.Context

getFields(): sun.tools.debug.RemoteClass,
sun.tools.debug.RemoteObject

getFieldValue(): sun.tools.debug.RemoteClass,
sun.tools.debug.RemoteObject

getFile(): sun.tools.java.ClassPath

getFiles(): sun.tools.java.ClassPath

getFirstField(): sun.tools.java.ClassDefinition

getFirstMatch(): sun.tools.java.
ClassDefinition

getFlags(): sun.tools.java.Environment,
sun.tools.javac.BatchEnvironment

getFlatName(): sun.tools.java.Identifier

getFloat(): sun.jdbc.odbc.
JdbcOdbcCallableStatement,
sun.jdbc.odbc.JdbcOdbcResultSet

getFont(): sun.awt.motif.PSGraphics,
sun.awt.motif.X11Graphics,
sun.awt.tiny.TinyGraphics

getFontCharset(): sun.awt.PlatformFont,
sun.awt.motif.MFontPeer

getInfo(): sun.awt.image.ImageInfoGrabber, sun.jdbc.odbc.JdbcOdbc, sun.jdbc.odbc. JdbcOdbcDatabaseMetaData

getInfoBooleanString(): sun.jdbc.odbc. JdbcOdbcDatabaseMetaData

getInfoShort(): sun.jdbc.odbc.JdbcOdbc, sun.jdbc.odbc.JdbcOdbcDatabaseMetaData

getInfoString(): sun.jdbc.odbc.JdbcOdbc, sun.jdbc.odbc.JdbcOdbcDatabaseMetaData

getInitialValue(): sun.tools.java.FieldDefinition, sun.tools.javac.SourceField

getInnerClass(): sun.tools.java.ClassDefinition, sun.tools.java.FieldDefinition

getInnerClassField(): sun.tools.java. ClassDefinition

getInputStream(): sun.jdbc.odbc. JdbcOdbcBoundParam, sun.net.www.http. HttpClient, sun.net.www.protocol. appletresource.AppletResourceConnection, sun.net.www.protocol.doc. DocURLConnection, sun.net.www. protocol.file.FileURLConnection, sun.net. www.protocol.ftp.FtpURLConnection, sun.net.www.protocol.gopher. GopherURLConnection, sun.net.www. protocol.http.HttpURLConnection, sun.net. www.protocol.mailto. MailToURLConnection, sun.net.www.protocol.systemresource. SystemResourceConnection, sun.net.www.protocol.verbatim. VerbatimConnection, sun.rmi.transport. Connection, sun.rmi.transport. StreamRemoteCall, sun.rmi.transport. proxy.HttpSendSocket, sun.rmi.transport. proxy.WrappedSocket, sun.rmi.transport. tcp.TCPConnection, sun.tools.java.ClassFile

getInputStreamLen(): sun.jdbc.odbc. JdbcOdbcBoundParam

getInsets(): sun.awt.motif.MFramePeer, sun.awt.motif.MPanelPeer, sun.awt.motif.MWindowPeer, sun.awt.tiny.TinyPanelPeer, sun.awt.tiny.TinyScrollPanePeer, sun.awt.tiny.TinyWindowPeer

getInstanceField(): sun.tools.debug. RemoteClass

getInstanceFields(): sun.tools.debug. RemoteClass

getInt(): sun.jdbc.odbc. JdbcOdbcCallableStatement, sun.jdbc.odbc. JdbcOdbcResultSet

getInteger(): sun.security.util.DerInputStream, sun.security.util.DerValue, sun.tools.java.BinaryConstantPool

getInterfaces(): sun.tools.debug.RemoteClass, sun.tools.java.ClassDefinition

getInterval(): sun.misc.Timer

getIssuerAlgorithmId(): sun.security.x509. X509Cert

getIssuerName(): sun.security.pkcs.SignerInfo, sun.security.x509.X509Cert

getJarFiles(): sun.applet.AppletPanel, sun.applet.AppletViewerPanel

getJavaInitializationString(): sun.beans. editors.BoolEditor, sun.beans.editors. ByteEditor, sun.beans.editors.ColorEditor, sun.beans.editors.FloatEditor, sun.beans.editors.FontEditor, sun.beans.editors.LongEditor, sun.beans.editors.NumberEditor, sun.beans.editors.ShortEditor, sun.beans.editors.StringEditor

getKey(): sun.net.www.MessageHeader

getLabel(): sun.tools.asm.CatchData

getLabelContext(): sun.tools.tree.Context

getLaunchString(): sun.net.www.MimeEntry

getLeading(): sun.awt.motif.X11FontMetrics, sun.awt.tiny.TinyFontMetrics

getLength(): sun.audio.AudioStream, sun.audio.AudioTranslatorStream, sun.audio.NativeAudioStream, sun.jdbc.odbc.JdbcOdbcBoundCol

getLengthBuf(): sun.jdbc.odbc. JdbcOdbcPreparedStatement

getLineNumber(): sun.tools.debug. RemoteStackFrame

getLineNumbers(): sun.tools.debug. RemoteClass

getLocalAddress(): sun.rmi.transport.proxy. HttpSendSocket, sun.rmi.transport.proxy. WrappedSocket

getMaxDescent(): sun.awt.motif.
X11FontMetrics

getMaxFieldSize(): sun.jdbc.odbc.
JdbcOdbcStatement

getMaxIndexLength(): sun.jdbc.odbc.
JdbcOdbcDatabaseMetaData

getMaxLocals(): sun.tools.java.BinaryCode

getMaxProcedureNameLength(): sun.jdbc.
odbc.JdbcOdbcDatabaseMetaData

getMaxRows(): sun.jdbc.odbc.
JdbcOdbcStatement

getMaxRowSize(): sun.jdbc.odbc.
JdbcOdbcDatabaseMetaData

getMaxSchemaNameLength(): sun.jdbc.odbc.
JdbcOdbcDatabaseMetaData

getMaxStack(): sun.tools.java.BinaryCode

getMaxStatementLength(): sun.jdbc.odbc.
JdbcOdbcDatabaseMetaData

getMaxStatements(): sun.jdbc.odbc.
JdbcOdbcDatabaseMetaData

getMaxTableNameLength(): sun.jdbc.odbc.
JdbcOdbcDatabaseMetaData

getMaxTablesInSelect(): sun.jdbc.odbc.
JdbcOdbcDatabaseMetaData

getMaxUserNameLength(): sun.jdbc.odbc.
JdbcOdbcDatabaseMetaData

getMember(): sun.net.www.protocol.
systemresource.ParseSystemURL

getMemberNumber(): sun.tools.tree.Context

getMetaData(): sun.jdbc.odbc.
JdbcOdbcConnection, sun.jdbc.odbc.
JdbcOdbcResultSet

getMethod(): sun.tools.debug.RemoteClass

getMethodLineNumber(): sun.tools.debug.
RemoteClass

getMethodName(): sun.tools.debug.
RemoteStackFrame

getMethodNames(): sun.tools.debug.
RemoteClass

getMethods(): sun.tools.debug.RemoteClass

getMinimumSize(): sun.awt.motif.
MButtonPeer, sun.awt.motif.
MCheckboxPeer, sun.awt.motif.
MChoicePeer, sun.awt.motif.
MComponentPeer, sun.awt.motif.

MLabelPeer, sun.awt.motif.MListPeer,
sun.awt.motif.MScrollbarPeer,
sun.awt.motif.MTextAreaPeer,
sun.awt.motif.MTextFieldPeer,
sun.awt.motif.MTinyChoicePeer,
sun.awt.tiny.TinyButtonPeer,
sun.awt.tiny.TinyCheckboxPeer,
sun.awt.tiny.TinyChoicePeer,
sun.awt.tiny.TinyComponentPeer,
sun.awt.tiny.TinyLabelPeer,
sun.awt.tiny.TinyListPeer,
sun.awt.tiny.TinyScrollbarPeer,
sun.awt.tiny.TinyTextAreaPeer,
sun.awt.tiny.TinyTextFieldPeer

getMinorVersion(): sun.jdbc.odbc.
JdbcOdbcDriver

getModifiers(): sun.tools.debug.RemoteField,
sun.tools.java.ClassDefinition,
sun.tools.java.FieldDefinition,
sun.tools.java.IdentifierToken

getMoreData(): sun.security.x509.
CertException

getMoreResults(): sun.jdbc.odbc.
JdbcOdbcStatement

getName(): sun.jdbc.odbc.JdbcOdbcTypeInfo,
sun.rmi.transport.proxy.
CGICommandHandler, sun.rmi.transport.
proxy.CGIForwardCommand, sun.rmi.
transport.proxy.CGIGethostnameCommand,
sun.rmi.transport.proxy.CGIPingCommand,
sun.rmi.transport.proxy.
CGITryHostnameCommand, sun.security.
acl.AclImpl, sun.security.acl.GroupImpl,
sun.security.acl.PrincipalImpl, sun.security.
x509.AlgIdDSA, sun.security.x509.
AlgorithmId, sun.security.x509.X500Name,
sun.tools.debug.RemoteClass, sun.tools.
debug.RemoteField, sun.tools.debug.
RemoteStackVariable, sun.tools.debug.
RemoteThread, sun.tools.debug.
RemoteThreadGroup, sun.tools.jar.
SignatureFile, sun.tools.java.
ClassDeclaration, sun.tools.java
.ClassDefinition, sun.tools.java.ClassFile,
sun.tools.java.FieldDefinition, sun.tools.
java.Identifier, sun.tools.java.
IdentifierToken

getNameToHash(): sun.tools.jar. JarVerifierStream

getNative(): sun.io.CharToByteBig5, sun.io.CharToByteCNS11643

getNativeContainer(): sun.awt.motif.MToolkit

getNewClient(): sun.net.www.protocol.http. HttpURLConnection

getNext(): sun.tools.tree.UplevelReference

getNextEntry(): sun.tools.jar.JarVerifierStream

getNextField(): sun.tools.java.FieldDefinition

getNextFinalizeable(): sun.awt. AWTFinalizeable, sun.awt.image. ImageRepresentation, sun.awt.motif. X11Graphics

getNextMatch(): sun.tools.java. FieldDefinition

getNotAfter(): sun.security.x509.X509Cert

getNotBefore(): sun.security.x509.X509Cert

getNull(): sun.security.util.DerInputStream

getNumber(): sun.tools.tree.LocalField

getNumCopies(): sun.awt.motif.UPrintDialog

getNumericFunctions(): sun.jdbc.odbc. JdbcOdbcDatabaseMetaData

getObject(): sun.jdbc.odbc. JdbcOdbcCallableStatement, sun.jdbc.odbc.JdbcOdbcResultSet

getObjID(): sun.rmi.transport.LiveRef

getOctetString(): sun.security.util. DerInputStream, sun.security.util.DerValue

getODBCVer(): sun.jdbc.odbc. JdbcOdbcConnection, sun.jdbc.odbc. JdbcOdbcConnectionInterface

getOID(): sun.security.util.DerInputStream, sun.security.util.DerValue, sun.security.x509.AlgorithmId

getOp(): sun.tools.tree.Node

getOpcode(): sun.tools.asm.Instruction, sun.tools.debug.BreakpointHandler

getOperations(): sun.rmi.registry. RegistryImpl_Skel, sun.rmi.transport. DGCImpl_Skel

getOptionsString(): sun.awt.motif.UPrintDialog

getOrganization(): sun.security.x509. X500Name

getOrganizationalUnit(): sun.security.x509.

X500Name

getOrientation(): sun.awt.motif.UPrintDialog

getOuterArg(): sun.tools.tree. NewInstanceExpression, sun.tools.tree. SuperExpression

getOuterClass(): sun.tools.java.ClassDefinition

getOutputStream(): sun.net.www.http. HttpClient, sun.net.www.protocol.http. HttpURLConnection, sun.net.www. protocol.mailto.MailToURLConnection, sun.net.www.protocol.verbatim.VerbatimC onnection, sun.rmi.transport.Connection, sun.rmi.transport.StreamRemoteCall, sun.rmi.transport.proxy.HttpReceiveSocket, sun.rmi.transport.proxy.HttpSendSocket, sun.rmi.transport.proxy.WrappedSocket, sun.rmi.transport.tcp.TCPConnection

getP(): sun.security.x509.AlgIdDSA

getPackage(): sun.tools.java.Environment, sun.tools.javac.BatchEnvironment

getPageDimension(): sun.awt.motif.PSPrintJob

getPageResolution(): sun.awt.motif.PSPrintJob

getPaperSize(): sun.awt.motif.UPrintDialog

getParameter(): sun.applet.AppletPanel, sun.applet.AppletViewerPanel

getParamLength(): sun.jdbc.odbc. JdbcOdbcPreparedStatement

getParams(): sun.security.provider. DSAPrivateKey, sun.security.provider. DSAPublicKey

getParent(): sun.awt.EmbeddedFrame

getPath(): sun.tools.java.ClassFile

getPC(): sun.tools.debug.RemoteStackFrame

getPermissions(): sun.security.acl.AclImpl

getPort(): sun.rmi.transport.LiveRef, sun.rmi.transport.proxy.HttpReceiveSocket, sun.rmi.transport.proxy.HttpSendSocket, sun.rmi.transport.proxy.WrappedSocket, sun.rmi.transport.tcp.TCPEndpoint

getPrec(): sun.jdbc.odbc.JdbcOdbcTypeInfo

getPrecision(): sun.jdbc.odbc. JdbcOdbcResultSetMetaData, sun.jdbc. odbc.JdbcOdbcStatement

getPreferredSize(): sun.awt.motif. MComponentPeer, sun.awt.motif.

MListPeer, sun.awt.motif.MTextAreaPeer, sun.awt.motif.MTextFieldPeer, sun.awt. tiny.TinyComponentPeer, sun.awt.tiny. TinyListPeer, sun.awt.tiny. TinyTextAreaPeer, sun.awt.tiny. TinyTextFieldPeer

getPrimaryKeys(): sun.jdbc.odbc. JdbcOdbcDatabaseMetaData

getPrincipal(): sun.security.acl.AclEntryImpl, sun.security.x509.X509Cert

getPrintableString(): sun.security.util.DerValue

getPrintJob(): sun.awt.motif.MToolkit, sun.awt.motif.PSGraphics, sun.awt.tiny.TinyToolkit

getPrivateKey(): sun.security.x509. CertAndKeyGen

getProcedureColumns(): sun.jdbc.odbc. JdbcOdbcDatabaseMetaData

getProcedures(): sun.jdbc.odbc. JdbcOdbcDatabaseMetaData

getProcedureTerm(): sun.jdbc.odbc. JdbcOdbcDatabaseMetaData

getProperties(): sun.net.www.URLConnection

getProperty(): sun.awt.image.Image, sun.rmi.rmic.BatchEnvironment, sun.rmi.transport.Utils

getPropertyDescriptors(): sun.beans.infos. ComponentBeanInfo

getPropertyInfo(): sun.jdbc.odbc. JdbcOdbcDriver

getProtocol(): sun.jdbc.odbc.JdbcOdbcDriver

getProxiedClient(): sun.net.www.protocol. http.HttpURLConnection

getProxy(): sun.rmi.server.RemoteProxy

getPseudoCol(): sun.jdbc.odbc. JdbcOdbcResultSet, sun.jdbc.odbc. JdbcOdbcResultSetInterface

getPublicKey(): sun.security.x509. CertAndKeyGen, sun.security.x509. X509Cert

getQ(): sun.security.x509.AlgIdDSA

getQualifier(): sun.tools.java.Identifier

getQueryTimeout(): sun.jdbc.odbc. JdbcOdbcStatement

getRefClass(): sun.rmi.server.UnicastRef, sun.rmi.server.UnicastServerRef

getReference(): sun.tools.java.ClassDefinition

getReferenceName(): sun.tools.javadoc. DocumentationGenerator

getReferences(): sun.tools.java.ClassDefinition

getReferencesFrozen(): sun.tools.java. ClassDefinition

getRemainingTime(): sun.misc.Timer

getRemoteClass(): sun.tools.debug. RemoteStackFrame

getRequest(): sun.net.www.httpd. BasicHttpServer

getRequestProperty(): sun.net.www.protocol. http.HttpURLConnection, sun.net.www. protocol.verbatim.VerbatimConnection

getResource(): sun.applet.AppletClassLoader

getResourceAsName(): sun.applet. AppletResourceLoader

getResourceAsStream(): sun.applet. AppletClassLoader, sun.applet. AppletResourceLoader

getResourceLoader(): sun.applet. AppletClassLoader

getResponseString(): sun.net. TransferProtocolClient

getResponseStrings(): sun.net. TransferProtocolClient

getResultSet(): sun.jdbc.odbc. JdbcOdbcStatement

getResultStream(): sun.rmi.transport. StreamRemoteCall

getReturnContext(): sun.tools.tree.Context

getReturnType(): sun.tools.java.MethodType, sun.tools.java.Type

getRowCount(): sun.jdbc.odbc. JdbcOdbcResultSet, sun.jdbc.odbc. JdbcOdbcStatement

getRowFraction(): sun.awt.VariableGridLayout

getRowNumber(): sun.jdbc.odbc. JdbcOdbcResultSet

getScale(): sun.jdbc.odbc.JdbcOdbcResultSet, sun.jdbc.odbc.JdbcOdbcResultSetInterface, sun.jdbc.odbc.JdbcOdbcResultSetMetaData

getSchemaName(): sun.jdbc.odbc. JdbcOdbcResultSetMetaData

getSchemas(): sun.jdbc.odbc. JdbcOdbcDatabaseMetaData

getSubName(): sun.jdbc.odbc.JdbcOdbcDriver

getSubProtocol(): sun.jdbc.odbc. JdbcOdbcDriver

getSuperclass(): sun.tools.debug.RemoteClass

getSuperClass(): sun.tools.java.ClassDefinition

getSurface(): sun.awt.DrawingSurfaceInfo, sun.awt.motif.MDrawingSurfaceInfo

getSystemClipboard(): sun.awt.motif.MToolkit, sun.awt.tiny.TinyToolkit

getSystemEventQueueImpl(): sun.awt.motif. MToolkit, sun.awt.tiny.TinyToolkit

getSystemFunctions(): sun.jdbc.odbc. JdbcOdbcDatabaseMetaData

getTableName(): sun.jdbc.odbc. JdbcOdbcResultSetMetaData

getTablePrivileges(): sun.jdbc.odbc. JdbcOdbcDatabaseMetaData

getTables(): sun.jdbc.odbc. JdbcOdbcDatabaseMetaData

getTableTypes(): sun.jdbc.odbc. JdbcOdbcDatabaseMetaData

getTags(): sun.beans.editors.BoolEditor, sun.beans.editors.ColorEditor, sun.beans.editors.FontEditor

getTail(): sun.tools.java.Identifier

getTarget(): sun.rmi.transport.ObjectTable, sun.tools.tree.UplevelReference

getTcpNoDelay(): sun.rmi.transport.proxy. HttpSendSocket, sun.rmi.transport.proxy. WrappedSocket

getTempFileTemplate(): sun.net.www. MimeEntry

getText(): sun.awt.motif.MTextAreaPeer, sun.awt.motif.MTextFieldPeer, sun.awt.tiny.TinyTextAreaPeer, sun.awt.tiny.TinyTextFieldPeer, sun.tools. javac.Main, sun.tools.javadoc.Main

getThisArgument(): sun.tools.javac.SourceClass

getThisNumber(): sun.tools.tree.Context

getThreadGroup(): sun.applet. AppletClassLoader, sun.applet. AppletSecurity

getTime(): sun.jdbc.odbc. JdbcOdbcCallableStatement, sun.jdbc.odbc. JdbcOdbcResultSet

getTimeDateFunctions(): sun.jdbc.odbc. JdbcOdbcDatabaseMetaData

getTimerThread(): sun.misc.Timer

getTimestamp(): sun.jdbc.odbc. JdbcOdbcCallableStatement, sun.jdbc.odbc. JdbcOdbcResultSet

getToolkit(): sun.awt.motif.MComponentPeer, sun.awt.tiny.TinyComponentPeer

getTopClass(): sun.tools.java.ClassDefinition, sun.tools.java.FieldDefinition

getTopName(): sun.tools.java.Identifier

getTransactionIsolation(): sun.jdbc.odbc. JdbcOdbcConnection

getTransport(): sun.rmi.transport.Endpoint, sun.rmi.transport.tcp.TCPEndpoint

getType(): sun.jdbc.odbc.JdbcOdbcBoundCol, sun.net.www.MimeEntry, sun.tools.asm. CatchData, sun.tools.debug.RemoteField, sun.tools.debug.RemoteStackVariable, sun.tools.debug.RemoteValue, sun.tools. java.BinaryConstantPool, sun.tools.java. ClassDeclaration, sun.tools.java. ClassDefinition, sun.tools.java. FieldDefinition, sun.tools.tree.Expression

getTypeCode(): sun.tools.java.Type

getTypeCodeOffset(): sun.tools.java.Type

getTypedName(): sun.tools.debug.RemoteField

getTypeFromObject(): sun.jdbc.odbc. JdbcOdbcPreparedStatement

getTypeInfo(): sun.jdbc.odbc.JdbcOdbc, sun. jdbc.odbc.JdbcOdbcDatabaseMetaData

getTypeMask(): sun.tools.java.Type

getTypeSignature(): sun.tools.java.Type

getUnicodeStream(): sun.jdbc.odbc. JdbcOdbcResultSet

getUpdateCount(): sun.jdbc.odbc. JdbcOdbcStatement

getURL(): sun.jdbc.odbc.JdbcOdbcConnection, sun.jdbc.odbc.JdbcOdbcConnectionInterface, sun.jdbc.odbc.JdbcOdbcDatabaseMetaData

getURLFile(): sun.net.www.http.HttpClient

getUseCaches(): sun.net.www.protocol. verbatim.VerbatimConnection

getUserName(): sun.jdbc.odbc. JdbcOdbcDatabaseMetaData

handleKeyPress(): sun.awt.tiny.TinyWindow

handleKeyRelease(): sun.awt.tiny.TinyWindow

handleListChanged(): sun.awt.motif.MListPeer

handleMouseDown(): sun.awt.motif.
MTinyChoicePeer, sun.awt.tiny.TinyWindow

handleMouseDrag(): sun.awt.motif.
MTinyChoicePeer, sun.awt.tiny.TinyWindow

handleMouseEnter(): sun.awt.tiny.TinyWindow

handleMouseExit(): sun.awt.tiny.TinyWindow

handleMouseMove(): sun.awt.tiny.
TinyWindow

handleMouseUp(): sun.awt.motif.
MTinyChoicePeer, sun.awt.tiny.TinyWindow

handleMoved(): sun.awt.motif.MDialogPeer,
sun.awt.motif.MFramePeer

handleQuit(): sun.awt.motif.MDialogPeer,
sun.awt.motif.MFileDialogPeer,
sun.awt.motif.MFramePeer,
sun.awt.motif.MWindowPeer

handleResize(): sun.awt.motif.MDialogPeer,
sun.awt.motif.MFramePeer,
sun.awt.motif.MWindowPeer

handleSelected(): sun.awt.motif.
MFileDialogPeer

handleWindowEvent(): sun.awt.tiny.
TinyButtonPeer, sun.awt.tiny.
TinyCanvasPeer, sun.awt.tiny.
TinyCheckboxPeer, sun.awt.tiny.
TinyChoicePeer, sun.awt.tiny.TinyListPeer,
sun.awt.tiny.TinyPanelPeer,
sun.awt.tiny.TinyScrollPanePeer,
sun.awt.tiny.TinyScrollbarPeer,
sun.awt.tiny.TinyTextAreaPeer,
sun.awt.tiny.TinyTextFieldPeer

hasAbstractFields(): sun.tools.java.
ClassDefinition

hasBeenLoaded(): sun.tools.java.BinaryClass

hasConstructor(): sun.tools.java.
ClassDefinition

hasError(): sun.awt.image.Image

hashCode(): sun.applet.AppletClassEntry, sun.
net.www.http.KeepAliveKey, sun.net.www.
protocol.http.AuthenticationInfo, sun.rmi.
transport.LiveRef, sun.rmi.transport.
WeakRef, sun.rmi.transport.tcp.
TCPEndpoint, sun.security.acl.GroupImpl,
sun.security.acl.PrincipalImpl, sun.security.

util.ObjectIdentifier, sun.security.x509.
X509Cert, sun.tools.asm.
NameAndTypeData, sun.tools.tree.
IntExpression, sun.tools.tree.
StringExpression

hasLabel(): sun.tools.tree.Statement

hasMoreElements(): sun.misc.
CacheEnumerator, sun.misc.
FIFOQueueEnumerator, sun.misc.
LIFOQueueEnumerator, sun.security.acl.
AclEnumerator, sun.tools.asm.
SwitchDataEnumeration

hasProtocolName(): sun.net.
URLCanonicalizer

height(): sun.awt.motif.PSPaperSize

hexPad(): sun.jdbc.odbc.JdbcOdbcObject

hexPairToInt(): sun.jdbc.odbc.
JdbcOdbcObject

hexStringToByteArray(): sun.jdbc.odbc.
JdbcOdbcObject

hide(): sun.awt.motif.MComponentPeer,
sun.awt.tiny.TinyComponentPeer,
sun.awt.tiny.TinyWindowPeer

hurry(): sun.net.www.http.KeepAliveStream

I18N(): sun.rmi.rmic.UI,
sun.tools.serialver.SerialVer

identities(): sun.security.provider.
IdentityDatabase

ignoreExceptions(): sun.tools.debug.
RemoteClass

imageComplete(): sun.awt.image.
ImageInfoGrabber, sun.awt.image.
ImageRepresentation, sun.awt.image.
PixelStore

implementedBy(): sun.tools.java.
ClassDefinition

implicitCast(): sun.tools.java.Environment

importCertificate(): sun.security.provider.Main

importClass(): sun.tools.java.Parser,
sun.tools.java.ParserActions,
sun.tools.javac.BatchParser

importCmd(): sun.security.provider.Main

importPackage(): sun.tools.java.Parser,
sun.tools.java.ParserActions,
sun.tools.javac.BatchParser

index(): sun.tools.asm.ConstantPool

itrace(): sun.tools.debug.RemoteDebugger

jdbcCompliant(): sun.jdbc.odbc.
  JdbcOdbcDriver

jdbcTypeToOdbc(): sun.jdbc.odbc.OdbcDef

join(): sun.tools.tree.Vset

keyDown(): sun.awt.motif.NumericField

keys(): sun.misc.Cache

keyUp(): sun.beans.editors.ColorEditor

lastModified(): sun.tools.java.ClassFile

lastPageFirst(): sun.awt.motif.PSPrintJob

launch(): sun.net.www.MimeEntry

layoutContainer(): sun.awt.HorizBagLayout,
  sun.awt.OrientableFlowLayout,
  sun.awt.VariableGridLayout,
  sun.awt.VerticalBagLayout

length(): sun.tools.java.ClassFile

lineDown(): sun.awt.motif.MScrollbarPeer

lineUp(): sun.awt.motif.MScrollbarPeer

list(): sun.net.ftp.FtpClient,
  sun.rmi.registry.RegistryImpl,
  sun.rmi.registry.RegistryImpl_Stub,
  sun.security.provider.Main

listBreakpoints(): sun.tools.debug.
  RemoteDebugger

listClasses(): sun.tools.debug.
  RemoteDebugger

listing(): sun.tools.asm.Assembler

listThreadGroups(): sun.tools.debug.
  RemoteDebugger

listThreads(): sun.tools.debug.
  RemoteThreadGroup

listToArray(): sun.jdbc.odbc.JdbcOdbcDriver

load(): sun.net.www.MimeTable,
  sun.tools.java.BinaryClass,
  sun.tools.java.BinaryCode

loadClass(): sun.applet.AppletClassLoader,
  sun.rmi.server.LoaderHandler,
  sun.rmi.server.RMIClassLoader

loadDefinition(): sun.tools.java.Environment,
  sun.tools.javac.BatchEnvironment

loadSystemColors(): sun.awt.motif.MToolkit

localArgumentAvailable(): sun.tools.tree.
  UplevelReference

lock(): sun.awt.DrawingSurfaceInfo, sun.awt.
  motif.MDrawingSurfaceInfo, sun.misc.Lock

lockIfNecessary(): sun.jdbc.odbc.
  JdbcOdbcStatement

lockWhen(): sun.misc.ConditionLock

login(): sun.net.ftp.FtpClient, sun.net.ftp.
  IftpClient

lookup(): sun.rmi.registry.RegistryImpl,
  sun.rmi.registry.RegistryImpl_Stub,
  sun.tools.java.Identifier

lookupInner(): sun.tools.java.Identifier

loop(): sun.applet.AppletAudioClip

lostFocus(): sun.awt.FocusingTextField

lostSelectionOwnership(): sun.awt.motif.
  X11Clipboard, sun.awt.motif.
  X11SelectionHolder

main(): sun.applet.AppletViewer,
  sun.misc.MessageUtils, sun.misc.Regexp,
  sun.misc.RegexpPool,
  sun.net.NetworkServer,
  sun.net.www.httpd.BasicHttpServer,
  sun.rmi.registry.RegistryImpl,
  sun.rmi.rmic.Main,
  sun.rmi.transport.proxy.CGIHandler,
  sun.security.provider.Main,
  sun.tools.debug.EmptyApp,
  sun.tools.jar.Main, sun.tools.javac.Main,
  sun.tools.javadoc.Main,
  sun.tools.native2ascii.Main,
  sun.tools.serialver.SerialVer,
  sun.tools.ttydebug.TTY

mainInit(): sun.applet.AppletViewer

makeClassDefinition(): sun.tools.java.
  Environment, sun.tools.javac.
  BatchEnvironment

makeConnectionString(): sun.jdbc.odbc.
  JdbcOdbcDriver

makeFieldDefinition(): sun.tools.java.
  Environment, sun.tools.javac.
  BatchEnvironment

makeFieldReference(): sun.tools.tree.
  UplevelReference

makeLocalReference(): sun.tools.tree.
  UplevelReference

makeMultiCharsetString(): sun.awt.
  PlatformFont

makeReference(): sun.tools.tree.Context

makeStore(): sun.awt.image.GifImageDecoder,
  sun.awt.image.JPEGImageDecoder,

sun.tools.tree.ConditionalExpression,
sun.tools.tree.ContinueStatement,
sun.tools.tree.ConvertExpression,
sun.tools.tree.DeclarationStatement,
sun.tools.tree.DoStatement,
sun.tools.tree.DoubleExpression,
sun.tools.tree.Expression,
sun.tools.tree.ExpressionStatement,
sun.tools.tree.FieldExpression,
sun.tools.tree.FinallyStatement,
sun.tools.tree.FloatExpression,
sun.tools.tree.ForStatement,
sun.tools.tree.IdentifierExpression,
sun.tools.tree.IfStatement,
sun.tools.tree.InlineMethodExpression,
sun.tools.tree.InlineNewInstanceExpression,
sun.tools.tree.InlineReturnStatement,
sun.tools.tree.InstanceOfExpression,
sun.tools.tree.IntExpression,
sun.tools.tree.LongExpression,
sun.tools.tree.MethodExpression,
sun.tools.tree.NaryExpression,
sun.tools.tree.Node,
sun.tools.tree.NullExpression,
sun.tools.tree.ReturnStatement,
sun.tools.tree.ShortExpression,
sun.tools.tree.Statement,
sun.tools.tree.StringExpression,
sun.tools.tree.SuperExpression,
sun.tools.tree.SwitchStatement,
sun.tools.tree.SynchronizedStatement,
sun.tools.tree.ThisExpression,
sun.tools.tree.ThrowStatement,
sun.tools.tree.TryStatement,
sun.tools.tree.TypeExpression,
sun.tools.tree.UnaryExpression,
sun.tools.tree.VarDeclarationStatement,
sun.tools.tree.WhileStatement

printGetOperationsMethod(): sun.rmi.rmic.
GenerateRemoteProxy

printOperationDescriptor(): sun.rmi.rmic.
GenerateRemoteProxy

printSkeleton(): sun.rmi.rmic.
GenerateRemoteProxy

printStackTrace(): sun.tools.java.CompilerError

printStubHash(): sun.rmi.rmic.
GenerateRemoteProxy

printStubs(): sun.rmi.rmic.
GenerateRemoteProxy

printToConsole(): sun.tools.debug.
DebuggerCallback, sun.tools.ttydebug.TTY

procedureColumns(): sun.jdbc.odbc.JdbcOdbc

procedures(): sun.jdbc.odbc.JdbcOdbc

produceImage(): sun.awt.image.
GifImageDecoder, sun.awt.image.
ImageDecoder, sun.awt.image.
JPEGImageDecoder, sun.awt.image.
XbmImageDecoder

protectedAccess(): sun.tools.java.
ClassDefinition

proxyClassName(): sun.rmi.rmic.ProxyNames

pSetEditable(): sun.awt.motif.MTextAreaPeer,
sun.awt.motif.MTextFieldPeer

pushError(): sun.tools.javac.
BatchEnvironment, sun.tools.javac.
ErrorConsumer

put(): sun.misc.Cache, sun.net.ftp.FtpClient,
sun.net.www.http.KeepAliveCache,
sun.tools.asm.ConstantPool

putBitString(): sun.security.util.
DerOutputStream

putData(): sun.jdbc.odbc.JdbcOdbc

putDefault(): sun.tools.asm.SwitchData

putDerValue(): sun.security.util.
DerOutputStream

putIA5String(): sun.security.util.
DerOutputStream

putInteger(): sun.security.util.
DerOutputStream

putNull(): sun.security.util.DerOutputStream

putOctetString(): sun.security.util.
DerOutputStream

putOID(): sun.security.util.DerOutputStream

putParamData(): sun.jdbc.odbc.
JdbcOdbcPreparedStatement

putPrintableString(): sun.security.util.
DerOutputStream

putSequence(): sun.security.util.
DerOutputStream

putSet(): sun.security.util.DerOutputStream

putUTCTime(): sun.security.util.
DerOutputStream

quicksort(): sun.misc.Sort

resetCurrentFrameIndex(): sun.tools.debug.
RemoteThread

resetProperties(): sun.net.www.http.HttpClient

reshape(): sun.awt.motif.MComponentPeer,
sun.awt.tiny.TinyComponentPeer,
sun.awt.tiny.TinyScrollPanePeer,
sun.awt.tiny.TinyWindowPeer

resolve(): sun.tools.java.Environment,
sun.tools.java.ImportEnvironment,
sun.tools.java.Imports

resolveClass(): sun.applet.
AppletObjectInputStream, sun.rmi.server.
MarshalInputStream

resolveInnerClass(): sun.tools.java.
ClassDefinition

resolveName(): sun.tools.java.ClassDefinition,
sun.tools.java.Environment,
sun.tools.tree.ContextEnvironment

resolveNames(): sun.tools.java.Environment

resolvePackageQualifiedName(): sun.tools.
java.Environment

resolveSupers(): sun.tools.javac.SourceClass

resolveTypeStructure(): sun.tools.java.
ClassDefinition, sun.tools.java.
FieldDefinition, sun.tools.javac.
SourceClass, sun.tools.javac.SourceField

resume(): sun.tools.debug.RemoteThread

reverseElements(): sun.misc.Queue

rollback(): sun.jdbc.odbc.JdbcOdbcConnection

rowCount(): sun.jdbc.odbc.JdbcOdbc

run(): sun.applet.AppletPanel,
sun.audio.AudioPlayer,
sun.awt.AWTFinalizer,
sun.awt.ScreenUpdater,
sun.awt.image.ImageFetcher,
sun.awt.motif.InputThread,
sun.awt.motif.MToolkit,
sun.awt.motif.ModalThread,
sun.awt.motif.SelectionThread,
sun.awt.tiny.TinyEventThread,
sun.awt.tiny.TinyInputThread,
sun.awt.tiny.TinyScrollRepeater,
sun.misc.RequestProcessor,
sun.misc.TimerThread, sun.misc.
TimerTickThread, sun.misc.
VMNotifierThread, sun.net.NetworkServer,
sun.net.www.MimeLauncher, sun.net.

www.http.ClientVector, sun.net.www.
protocol.ftp.FtpDirectoryThread, sun.net.
www.protocol.gopher.GopherClient,
sun.rmi.rmic.Main, sun.rmi.rmic.UI,
sun.rmi.transport.DGCClient,
sun.rmi.transport.KeepAlive,
sun.rmi.transport.LeaseChecker,
sun.rmi.transport.LeaseRenewer,
sun.rmi.transport.Reaper, sun.rmi.
transport.UnreferencedObj, sun.rmi.
transport.proxy.AsyncConnector, sun.rmi.
transport.tcp.ConnectionAcceptor, sun.rmi.
transport.tcp.ConnectionMultiplexer,
sun.rmi.transport.tcp.Pinger,
sun.rmi.transport.tcp.TCPChannel,
sun.rmi.transport.tcp.TCPTransport,
sun.tools.debug.Agent,
sun.tools.debug.AgentIn,
sun.tools.debug.BreakpointHandler,
sun.tools.debug.MainThread,
sun.tools.debug.RemoteDebugger,
sun.tools.jar.Main

save(): sun.net.www.MimeTable,
sun.security.provider.IdentityDatabase

saveAsProperties(): sun.net.www.MimeTable

scan(): sun.tools.java.Parser,
sun.tools.java.Scanner

schemeSupported(): sun.net.www.protocol.
http.HttpAuthenticator

scroll(): sun.awt.tiny.TinyPanelPeer

scrolledHorizontal(): sun.awt.motif.
MScrollPanePeer

scrolledVertical(): sun.awt.motif.
MScrollPanePeer

searchTab(): sun.io.CharToByteBig5,
sun.io.CharToByteCNS11643

select(): sun.awt.motif.MChoicePeer,
sun.awt.motif.MListPeer,
sun.awt.motif.MTextAreaPeer,
sun.awt.motif.MTextFieldPeer,
sun.awt.motif.MTinyChoicePeer,
sun.awt.tiny.TinyChoicePeer,
sun.awt.tiny.TinyListPeer,
sun.awt.tiny.TinyTextAreaPeer,
sun.awt.tiny.TinyTextFieldPeer

sendEvent(): sun.applet.AppletPanel

sendHeaderInfo(): sun.awt.image.
JPEGImageDecoder

setVisible(): sun.awt.motif.MComponentPeer, sun.awt.tiny.TinyComponentPeer

setWarning(): sun.jdbc.odbc. JdbcOdbcResultSet, sun.jdbc.odbc. JdbcOdbcResultSetInterface, sun.jdbc.odbc. JdbcOdbcStatement

setWillSelect(): sun.awt.FocusingTextField

setXORMode(): sun.awt.motif.PSGraphics, sun.awt.motif.X11Graphics, sun.awt.tiny.TinyGraphics

show(): sun.awt.motif.MComponentPeer, sun.awt.motif.MDialogPeer, sun.awt.motif.MPopupMenuPeer, sun.awt.tiny.TinyComponentPeer, sun.awt.tiny.TinyWindowPeer

showAppletException(): sun.applet.AppletPanel

showAppletLog(): sun.applet.AppletPanel

showAppletStatus(): sun.applet.AppletPanel

showDocument(): sun.applet.AppletViewer

showStatus(): sun.applet.AppletViewer

shutDown(): sun.rmi.transport.tcp. ConnectionMultiplexer

shutdown(): sun.tools.java.Environment, sun.tools.javac.BatchEnvironment

sign(): sun.security.x509.X500Signer

SingleByte(): sun.io.CharToByteJIS0208

size(): sun.awt.motif.PSPaperSize, sun.misc. Cache, sun.security.provider.IdentityDatabase

skeleton(): sun.rmi.rmic.ProxyNames

skeletonClassName(): sun.rmi.rmic. ProxyNames

skeletonInterface(): sun.rmi.rmic.ProxyNames

skip(): sun.net.www.MeteredStream, sun.rmi. transport.proxy.HttpInputStream, sun.rmi. transport.proxy.HttpSendInputStream

sortClassDeclarations(): sun.rmi.rmic. GenerateRemoteProxy

sortedKeys(): sun.tools.asm.SwitchData

specialColumns(): sun.jdbc.odbc.JdbcOdbc**SQLAllocConnect()** : sun.jdbc.odbc.JdbcOdbc

SQLAllocEnv(): sun.jdbc.odbc.JdbcOdbc

SQLAllocStmt(): sun.jdbc.odbc.JdbcOdbc

SQLBindColDefault(): sun.jdbc.odbc. JdbcOdbc

SQLBindInParameterAtExec(): sun.jdbc.odbc. JdbcOdbc

SQLBindInParameterBinary(): sun.jdbc.odbc. JdbcOdbc

SQLBindInParameterDate(): sun.jdbc.odbc. JdbcOdbc

SQLBindInParameterDouble(): sun.jdbc.odbc. JdbcOdbc

SQLBindInParameterFloat(): sun.jdbc.odbc. JdbcOdbc

SQLBindInParameterInteger(): sun.jdbc.odbc. JdbcOdbc

SQLBindInParameterNull(): sun.jdbc.odbc. JdbcOdbc

SQLBindInParameterString(): sun.jdbc.odbc. JdbcOdbc

SQLBindInParameterTime(): sun.jdbc.odbc. JdbcOdbc

SQLBindInParameterTimestamp(): sun.jdbc. odbc.JdbcOdbc

SQLBindOutParameterString(): sun.jdbc. odbc.JdbcOdbc

SQLBrowseConnect(): sun.jdbc.odbc.JdbcOdbc

SQLCancel(): sun.jdbc.odbc.JdbcOdbc

SQLColAttributes(): sun.jdbc.odbc.JdbcOdbc

SQLColAttributesString(): sun.jdbc.odbc. JdbcOdbc

SQLColumnPrivileges(): sun.jdbc.odbc. JdbcOdbc

SQLColumns(): sun.jdbc.odbc.JdbcOdbc

SQLDescribeParamNullable(): sun.jdbc.odbc. JdbcOdbc

SQLDescribeParamPrecision(): sun.jdbc.odbc. JdbcOdbc

SQLDescribeParamScale(): sun.jdbc.odbc. JdbcOdbc

SQLDescribeParamType(): sun.jdbc.odbc. JdbcOdbc

SQLDisconnect(): sun.jdbc.odbc.JdbcOdbc

SQLDriverConnect(): sun.jdbc.odbc.JdbcOdbc

SQLExecDirect(): sun.jdbc.odbc.JdbcOdbc

SQLExecute(): sun.jdbc.odbc.JdbcOdbc

SQLFetch(): sun.jdbc.odbc.JdbcOdbc

SQLForeignKeys(): sun.jdbc.odbc.JdbcOdbc

SQLFreeConnect(): sun.jdbc.odbc.JdbcOdbc

sun.awt.motif.CharToByteX11KSC5601,
sun.awt.motif.MComponentPeer,
sun.awt.motif.PSGraphics,
sun.awt.motif.PSPaperSize,
sun.awt.motif.X11Graphics,
sun.awt.tiny.TinyComponentPeer,
sun.awt.tiny.TinyGraphics,
sun.io.ByteToCharConverter,
sun.io.CharToByteConverter, sun.misc.
QueueElement, sun.net.nntp.
NewsgroupInfo, sun.net.www.
MessageHeader, sun.net.www.MimeEntry,
sun.net.www. http.HttpClient,
sun.net.www.protocol.
http.AuthenticationInfo, sun.net.www.
protocol.verbatim.VerbatimConnection,
sun.rmi.transport.LiveRef, sun.rmi.
transport.proxy.HttpAwareServerSocket,
sun.rmi.transport.proxy.HttpReceiveSocket,
sun.rmi.transport.proxy.HttpSendSocket,
sun.rmi.transport.proxy.WrappedSocket,
sun.rmi.transport.tcp.TCPEndpoint,
sun.security.acl.AclEntryImpl, sun.security.
acl.AclImpl, sun.security.acl.GroupImpl,
sun.security.acl.PermissionImpl, sun.
security.acl.PrincipalImpl, sun.security.pkcs.
ContentInfo, sun.security.pkcs.PKCS10,
sun.security.pkcs.PKCS7, sun.security.
pkcs.PKCS8Key, sun.security.pkcs.
SignerInfo, sun.security.provider.DSA,
sun.security.provider.DSAPrivateKey,
sun.security.provider.DSAPublicKey,
sun.security.provider.IdentityDatabase,
sun.security.provider.SystemIdentity,
sun.security.provider.SystemSigner, sun.
security.util.BigInt, sun.security.util.
DerValue, sun.security.util.ObjectIdentifier,
sun.security.x509.AVA, sun.security.
x509.AlgIdDSA, sun.security.x509.
AlgorithmId, sun.security.x509.
CertException, sun.security.x509.RDN,
sun.security.x509.X500Name,
sun.security.x509.X509Cert, sun.security.
x509.X509Key, sun.tools.asm.
ClassConstantData, sun.tools.asm.
Instruction, sun.tools.asm. Label, sun.tools.
asm.LocalVariable, sun. tools.asm.
NameAndTypeData, sun.tools. asm.
StringConstantData, sun.tools.asm.
StringExpressionConstantData, sun.tools.

debug.BreakpointSet, sun.tools.debug.
RemoteArray, sun.tools.debug.
RemoteBoolean, sun.tools.debug.
RemoteByte, sun.tools.debug.RemoteChar,
sun.tools.debug.RemoteClass, sun.tools.
debug.RemoteDouble, sun.tools.debug.
RemoteField, sun.tools.debug.RemoteFloat,
sun.tools.debug.RemoteInt, sun.tools.
debug.RemoteLong, sun.tools.debug.
RemoteObject, sun.tools.debug.
RemoteShort, sun.tools.debug.
RemoteString, sun.tools.debug.StackFrame,
sun.tools.java.ClassDeclaration, sun.tools.
java.ClassDefinition, sun.tools.java.
ClassFile, sun.tools.java.ClassPath, sun.
tools.java.FieldDefinition, sun.tools.java.
Identifier, sun.tools.java.IdentifierToken,
sun.tools.java.Type, sun.tools.tree.Node,
sun.tools.tree.UplevelReference,
sun.tools.tree.Vset

totalMemory(): sun.tools.debug.
RemoteDebugger

trace(): sun.jdbc.odbc.JdbcOdbcObject,
sun.tools.debug.RemoteDebugger

transact(): sun.jdbc.odbc.JdbcOdbc

translate(): sun.awt.motif.PSGraphics,
sun.awt.motif.X11Graphics,
sun.awt.tiny.TinyGraphics

tType(): sun.tools.java.Type

typeName(): sun.tools.debug.RemoteArray,
sun.tools.debug.RemoteBoolean,
sun.tools.debug.RemoteByte,
sun.tools.debug.RemoteChar,
sun.tools.debug.RemoteClass,
sun.tools.debug.RemoteDouble,
sun.tools.debug.RemoteFloat,
sun.tools.debug.RemoteInt,
sun.tools.debug.RemoteLong,
sun.tools.debug.RemoteObject,
sun.tools.debug.RemoteShort,
sun.tools.debug.RemoteString,
sun.tools.debug.RemoteValue

typeString(): sun.tools.java.ArrayType, sun.
tools.java.ClassType, sun.tools.java.
MethodType, sun.tools.java.Type

unbind(): sun.rmi.registry.RegistryImpl,
sun.rmi.registry.RegistryImpl_Stub

SUB-CLASS INDEX

C

*T*his appendix alphabetically lists all the classes that are extended by classes defined in the sun and sunw packages. This is especially useful for abstract classes that are always subclassed.

java.applet.Applet:
sun.tools.serialver.SerialVer

java.awt.Canvas:
sun.awt.motif.Separator,
sun.awt.tiny.Separator

java.awt.Dialog:
sun.awt.motif.UPrintDialog,
sun.awt.tiny.TinyFileDialogPeer

java.awt.FlowLayout:
sun.awt.OrientableFlowLayout

java.awt.FontMetrics:
sun.awt.motif.X11FontMetrics,
sun.awt.tiny.TinyFontMetrics

java.awt.Frame:
sun.applet.AppletCopyright,
sun.applet.AppletProps,
sun.applet.AppletViewer,
sun.applet.TextFrame,
sun.awt.EmbeddedFrame,
sun.rmi.rmic.UI,
sun.tools.serialver.SerialVerFrame

java.awt.Graphics:
sun.awt.motif.PSGraphics,
sun.awt.motif.X11Graphics,
sun.awt.tiny.TinyGraphics

java.awt.GridLayout:
sun.awt.VariableGridLayout

java.awt.Image: sun.awt.image.Image

java.awt.Panel: sun.applet.AppletPanel,
sun.beans.editors.ColorEditor,
sun.beans.editors.FontEditor

java.awt.PrintJob:
sun.awt.motif.PSPrintJob

java.awt.TextField:
sun.awt.FocusingTextField,
sun.awt.motif.NumericField

java.awt.Toolkit:
sun.awt.motif.MToolkit,
sun.awt.tiny.TinyToolkit

java.awt.Window:
sun.awt.motif.MChoiceMenu

java.awt.datatransfer.Clipboard:
sun.awt.motif.X11Clipboard

java.beans.PropertyEditorSupport:
sun.beans.editors.BoolEditor,
sun.beans.editors.NumberEditor,
sun.beans.editors.StringEditor

java.beans.SimpleBeanInfo:
sun.beans.infos.ComponentBeanInfo

java.io.BufferedOutputStream:
sun.net.TelnetOutputStream,
sun.tools.debug.ResponseStream

java.io.ByteArrayInputStream:
sun.audio.AudioDataStream,
sun.security.util.DerInputBuffer

java.io.ByteArrayOutputStream:
sun.rmi.transport.proxy.HttpOutputStream,
sun.security.util.DerOutputStream

java.io.CharConversionException:
sun.io.ConversionBufferFullException,
sun.io.MalformedInputException,
sun.io.UnknownCharacterException

java.io.FilterInputStream:
sun.audio.AudioStream,
sun.audio.NativeAudioStream,
sun.net.TelnetInputStream,
sun.net.nntp.NntpInputStream,
sun.net.www.MeteredStream,
sun.net.www.content.text.
PlainTextInputStream,
sun.net.www.protocol.gopher.
GopherInputStream,
sun.rmi.transport.proxy.HttpInputStream,
sun.rmi.transport.proxy.
HttpSendInputStream

java.io.FilterOutputStream:
sun.rmi.transport.proxy.
HttpSendOutputStream, sun.tools.debug.
AgentOutputStream

java.io.FilterReader:
sun.tools.java.ScannerInputStream

java.io.IOException:
sun.applet.AppletIOException,
sun.audio.InvalidAudioFormatException,
sun.misc.CEFormatException,
sun.misc.CEStreamExhausted,
sun.net.TelnetProtocolException,
sun.net.ftp.FtpProtocolException,
sun.net.nntp.NntpProtocolException,
sun.net.nntp.UnknownNewsgroupException,

sun.net.smtp.SmtpProtocolException,
sun.security.pkcs.ParsingException,
sun.tools.jar.JarException

java.io.InputStream:
sun.jdbc.odbc.JdbcOdbcInputStream,
sun.net.www.protocol.http.
EmptyInputStream,
sun.rmi.transport.tcp.MultiplexInputStream

java.io.ObjectInputStream:
sun.applet.AppletObjectInputStream,
sun.rmi.server.MarshalInputStream

java.io.ObjectOutputStream:
sun.rmi.server.MarshalOutputStream

java.io.OutputStream:
sun.rmi.rmic.TextAreaOutput,
sun.rmi.transport.tcp.
MultiplexOutputStream,
sun.tools.jar.CRC32OutputStream

java.io.PrintStream:
sun.net.smtp.SmtpPrintStream,
sun.rmi.rmic.ProxyStream

java.io.SequenceInputStream:
sun.audio.AudioStreamSequence

java.lang.ClassLoader:
sun.applet.AppletClassLoader

java.lang.Error: sun.tools.java.CompilerError

java.lang.Exception:
sun.awt.image.ImageFormatException,
sun.misc.REException,
sun.net.www.ApplicationLaunchException,
sun.rmi.transport.proxy.CGIClientException,
sun.rmi.transport.proxy.CGIServerException,
sun.security.pkcs.EncodingException,
sun.tools.debug.InvalidPCException,
sun.tools.debug.NoSessionException,
sun.tools.debug.
NoSuchLineNumberException,
sun.tools.java.AmbiguousField,
sun.tools.java.ClassNotFound,
sun.tools.java.SyntaxError

java.lang.IllegalArgumentException:
sun.applet.AppletIllegalArgumentException

java.lang.Object: sun.applet.AppletAudioClip,
sun.applet.AppletClassEntry,
sun.applet.AppletMessageHandler,
sun.applet.AppletResourceLoader,
sun.applet.HashValues,
sun.applet.StdAppletViewerFactory,
sun.audio.AudioData,

sun.rmi.transport.tcp.ConnectionMultiplexer,
sun.rmi.transport.tcp.InEntry,
sun.rmi.transport.tcp.
MultiplexConnectionInfo,
sun.rmi.transport.tcp.Pinger,
sun.rmi.transport.tcp.TCPChannel,
sun.rmi.transport.tcp.TCPConnection,
sun.rmi.transport.tcp.TCPEndpoint,
sun.security.acl.AclEntryImpl,
sun.security.acl.AclEnumerator,
sun.security.acl.GroupImpl,
sun.security.acl.OwnerImpl,
sun.security.acl.PermissionImpl,
sun.security.acl.PrincipalImpl,
sun.security.pkcs.ContentInfo,
sun.security.pkcs.PKCS10,
sun.security.pkcs.PKCS7,
sun.security.pkcs.PKCS8Key,
sun.security.pkcs.SignerInfo,
sun.security.provider.Main,
sun.security.util.BigInt,
sun.security.util.DerInputStream,
sun.security.util.DerValue,
sun.security.util.ObjectIdentifier,
sun.security.x509.AVA,
sun.security.x509.AlgorithmId,
sun.security.x509.CertAndKeyGen,
sun.security.x509.RDN,
sun.security.x509.X500Name,
sun.security.x509.X500Signer,
sun.security.x509.X509Cert,
sun.security.x509.X509Key,
sun.tools.asm.ArrayData,
sun.tools.asm.Assembler,
sun.tools.asm.CatchData,
sun.tools.asm.ConstantPool,
sun.tools.asm.ConstantPoolData,
sun.tools.asm.Cover,
sun.tools.asm.Instruction,
sun.tools.asm.LocalVariable,
sun.tools.asm.LocalVariableTable,
sun.tools.asm.NameAndTypeData,
sun.tools.asm.SwitchData,
sun.tools.asm.SwitchDataEnumeration,
sun.tools.asm.TryData,
sun.tools.debug.Agent,
sun.tools.debug.AgentIn,
sun.tools.debug.BreakpointQueue,
sun.tools.debug.BreakpointSet,
sun.tools.debug.EmptyApp,

sun.tools.debug.Field,
sun.tools.debug.LineNumber,
sun.tools.debug.LocalVariable,
sun.tools.debug.RemoteAgent,
sun.tools.debug.RemoteDebugger,
sun.tools.debug.RemoteValue,
sun.tools.debug.StackFrame,
sun.tools.jar.Main, sun.tools.jar.Manifest,
sun.tools.jar.SignatureFile,
sun.tools.java.BinaryAttribute,
sun.tools.java.BinaryCode,
sun.tools.java.BinaryConstantPool,
sun.tools.java.BinaryExceptionHandler,
sun.tools.java.ClassDeclaration,
sun.tools.java.ClassDefinition,
sun.tools.java.ClassFile,
sun.tools.java.ClassPath,
sun.tools.java.ClassPathEntry,
sun.tools.java.Environment,
sun.tools.java.FieldDefinition,
sun.tools.java.Identifier,
sun.tools.java.IdentifierToken,
sun.tools.java.Imports,
sun.tools.java.Package,
sun.tools.java.Scanner,
sun.tools.java.Type,
sun.tools.javac.CompilerField,
sun.tools.javac.ErrorMessage,
sun.tools.javac.Main,
sun.tools.javadoc.DocumentationGenerator,
sun.tools.javadoc.Main,
sun.tools.native2ascii.Main,
sun.tools.tree.ConditionVars,
sun.tools.tree.Context, sun.tools.tree.Node,
sun.tools.tree.UplevelReference,
sun.tools.tree.Vset, sun.tools.ttydebug.TTY

java.lang.SecurityException:
sun.applet.AppletSecurityException,
sun.security.x509.CertException

java.lang.SecurityManager:
sun.applet.AppletSecurity

java.lang.Thread: sun.audio.AudioPlayer,
sun.awt.AWTFinalizer,
sun.awt.ScreenUpdater,
sun.awt.image.ImageFetcher,
sun.awt.motif.InputThread,
sun.awt.motif.ModalThread,
sun.awt.motif.SelectionThread,
sun.awt.tiny.TinyEventThread,

sun.awt.EmbeddedFrame:
sun.awt.motif.MEmbeddedFrame

sun.awt.PlatformFont:
sun.awt.motif.MFontPeer

sun.awt.image.Image:
sun.awt.motif.X11Image,
sun.awt.tiny.TinyImage

sun.awt.image.ImageDecoder:
sun.awt.image.GifImageDecoder,
sun.awt.image.JPEGImageDecoder,
sun.awt.image.XbmImageDecoder

sun.awt.image.ImageWatched:
sun.awt.image.ImageInfoGrabber,
sun.awt.image.ImageRepresentation

sun.awt.image.InputStreamImageSource:
sun.awt.image.ByteArrayImageSource,
sun.awt.image.FileImageSource,
sun.awt.image.URLImageSource

sun.awt.image.PixelStore:
sun.awt.image.PixelStore32,
sun.awt.image.PixelStore8

sun.awt.image.URLImageSource:
sun.tools.jar.JarImageSource

sun.awt.motif.MCanvasPeer:
sun.awt.motif.MPanelPeer,
sun.awt.motif.MTinyChoicePeer

sun.awt.motif.MComponentPeer:
sun.awt.motif.MButtonPeer,
sun.awt.motif.MCanvasPeer,
sun.awt.motif.MCheckboxPeer,
sun.awt.motif.MChoicePeer,
sun.awt.motif.MLabelPeer,
sun.awt.motif.MListPeer,
sun.awt.motif.MScrollbarPeer,
sun.awt.motif.MTextAreaPeer,
sun.awt.motif.MTextFieldPeer

sun.awt.motif.MDialogPeer:
sun.awt.motif.MFileDialogPeer

sun.awt.motif.MFramePeer:
sun.awt.motif.MEmbeddedFramePeer

sun.awt.motif.MMenuItemPeer:
sun.awt.motif.MCheckboxMenuItemPeer,
sun.awt.motif.MMenuPeer

sun.awt.motif.MMenuPeer:
sun.awt.motif.MPopupMenuPeer

sun.awt.motif.MPanelPeer:
sun.awt.motif.MDialogPeer,

sun.awt.motif.MFramePeer,
sun.awt.motif.MScrollPanePeer,
sun.awt.motif.MWindowPeer

sun.awt.motif.PSGraphics:
sun.awt.motif.PageGraphics

sun.awt.motif.X11Image:
sun.awt.motif.X11OffScreenImage

sun.awt.tiny.TinyCanvasPeer:
sun.awt.tiny.TinyPanelPeer

sun.awt.tiny.TinyComponentPeer:
sun.awt.tiny.TinyButtonPeer,
sun.awt.tiny.TinyCanvasPeer,
sun.awt.tiny.TinyCheckboxPeer,
sun.awt.tiny.TinyChoicePeer,
sun.awt.tiny.TinyLabelPeer,
sun.awt.tiny.TinyListPeer,
sun.awt.tiny.TinyScrollPanePeer,
sun.awt.tiny.TinyScrollbarPeer,
sun.awt.tiny.TinyTextAreaPeer,
sun.awt.tiny.TinyTextFieldPeer

sun.awt.tiny.TinyFrame:
sun.awt.tiny.TinyWinManagerFrame

sun.awt.tiny.TinyMenuItemPeer:
sun.awt.tiny.TinyCheckboxMenuItemPeer

sun.awt.tiny.TinyPanelPeer:
sun.awt.tiny.TinyWindowPeer

sun.awt.tiny.TinyVerticalScrollbar:
sun.awt.tiny.TinyHorizontalScrollbar

sun.awt.tiny.TinyWindow:
sun.awt.tiny.TinyChoiceMenu,
sun.awt.tiny.TinyComponentPeer,
sun.awt.tiny.TinyFrame,
sun.awt.tiny.TinyMenuPeer,
sun.awt.tiny.TinyMenuWindow

sun.awt.tiny.TinyWindowPeer:
sun.awt.tiny.TinyDialogPeer,
sun.awt.tiny.TinyFramePeer

sun.beans.editors.NumberEditor:
sun.beans.editors.ByteEditor,
sun.beans.editors.DoubleEditor,
sun.beans.editors.FloatEditor,
sun.beans.editors.IntEditor,
sun.beans.editors.LongEditor,
sun.beans.editors.ShortEditor

sun.io.ByteToCharConverter:
sun.io.ByteToChar8859_1,
sun.io.ByteToCharBig5,
sun.io.ByteToCharCNS11643,

sun.io.ByteToCharMacDingbat,
sun.io.ByteToCharMacGreek,
sun.io.ByteToCharMacHebrew,
sun.io.ByteToCharMacIceland,
sun.io.ByteToCharMacRoman,
sun.io.ByteToCharMacRomania,
sun.io.ByteToCharMacSymbol,
sun.io.ByteToCharMacThai,
sun.io.ByteToCharMacTurkish,
sun.io.ByteToCharMacUkraine

sun.io.ByteToCharUnicode:
sun.io.ByteToCharUnicodeBig,
sun.io.ByteToCharUnicodeLittle

sun.io.CharToByte8859_1:
sun.awt.CharToByteSymbol,
sun.awt.motif.CharToByteX11Dingbats,
sun.awt.motif.CharToByteX11JIS0201

sun.io.CharToByteCNS11643:
sun.awt.motif.CharToByteX11CNS11643P1,
sun.awt.motif.CharToByteX11CNS11643P2,
sun.awt.motif.CharToByteX11CNS11643P3

sun.io.CharToByteConverter:
sun.io.CharToByte8859_1,
sun.io.CharToByteBig5,
sun.io.CharToByteCNS11643,
sun.io.CharToByteCp933,
sun.io.CharToByteCp949,
sun.io.CharToByteCp970,
sun.io.CharToByteDBCS_ASCII,
sun.io.CharToByteDBCS_EBCDIC,
sun.io.CharToByteDefault,
sun.io.CharToByteEUC,
sun.io.CharToByteGB2312,
sun.io.CharToByteJIS0208,
sun.io.CharToByteKSC5601,
sun.io.CharToByteSingleByte,
sun.io.CharToByteUTF8,
sun.io.CharToByteUnicode

sun.io.CharToByteDBCS_ASCII:
sun.io.CharToByteCp1381,
sun.io.CharToByteCp1383,
sun.io.CharToByteCp942,
sun.io.CharToByteCp948,
sun.io.CharToByteCp950

sun.io.CharToByteDBCS_EBCDIC:
sun.io.CharToByteCp930,
sun.io.CharToByteCp935,
sun.io.CharToByteCp937,
sun.io.CharToByteCp939

sun.io.CharToByteEUC:
sun.io.CharToByteCp33722,
sun.io.CharToByteCp964

sun.io.CharToByteEUCJIS:
sun.awt.motif.CharToByteX11JIS0208

sun.io.CharToByteGB2312:
sun.awt.motif.CharToByteX11GB2312

sun.io.CharToByteJIS0208:
sun.io.CharToByteEUCJIS,
sun.io.CharToByteJIS,
sun.io.CharToByteSJIS

sun.io.CharToByteKSC5601:
sun.awt.motif.CharToByteX11KSC5601

sun.io.CharToByteSingleByte:
sun.io.CharToByte8859_2,
sun.io.CharToByte8859_3,
sun.io.CharToByte8859_4,
sun.io.CharToByte8859_5,
sun.io.CharToByte8859_6,
sun.io.CharToByte8859_7,
sun.io.CharToByte8859_8,
sun.io.CharToByte8859_9,
sun.io.CharToByteCp037,
sun.io.CharToByteCp1006,
sun.io.CharToByteCp1025,
sun.io.CharToByteCp1026,
sun.io.CharToByteCp1046,
sun.io.CharToByteCp1097,
sun.io.CharToByteCp1098,
sun.io.CharToByteCp1112,
sun.io.CharToByteCp1122,
sun.io.CharToByteCp1123,
sun.io.CharToByteCp1124,
sun.io.CharToByteCp1250,
sun.io.CharToByteCp1251,
sun.io.CharToByteCp1252,
sun.io.CharToByteCp1253,
sun.io.CharToByteCp1254,
sun.io.CharToByteCp1255,
sun.io.CharToByteCp1256,
sun.io.CharToByteCp1257,
sun.io.CharToByteCp1258,
sun.io.CharToByteCp273,
sun.io.CharToByteCp277,
sun.io.CharToByteCp278,
sun.io.CharToByteCp280,
sun.io.CharToByteCp284,
sun.io.CharToByteCp285,
sun.io.CharToByteCp297,
sun.io.CharToByteCp420,

sun.net.www.protocol.ftp.
FtpURLConnection,
sun.net.www.protocol.gopher.
GopherURLConnection,
sun.net.www.protocol.mailto.
MailToURLConnection,
sun.net.www.protocol.systemresource.
SystemResourceConnection

sun.net.www.content.text.plain:
sun.net.www.content.text.Generic

sun.rmi.rmic.ProxyNames:
sun.rmi.rmic.GenerateMarshaling,
sun.rmi.rmic.GenerateRemoteProxy,
sun.rmi.rmic.TopGRP

sun.rmi.server.MarshalInputStream:
sun.rmi.transport.ConnectionInputStream

sun.rmi.server.MarshalOutputStream:
sun.rmi.transport.ConnectionOutputStream

sun.rmi.server.UnicastRef:
sun.rmi.server.UnicastServerRef

sun.rmi.transport.Transport:
sun.rmi.transport.tcp.TCPTransport

sun.rmi.transport.proxy.WrappedSocket:
sun.rmi.transport.proxy.HttpReceiveSocket

sun.security.acl.GroupImpl:
sun.security.acl.WorldGroupImpl

sun.security.acl.OwnerImpl:
sun.security.acl.AclImpl

sun.security.acl.PermissionImpl:
sun.security.acl.AllPermissionsImpl

sun.security.pkcs.PKCS8Key:
sun.security.provider.DSAPrivateKey

sun.security.x509.AlgorithmId:
sun.security.x509.AlgIdDSA

sun.security.x509.CertException:
sun.security.x509.CertParseError

sun.security.x509.X509Key:
sun.security.provider.DSAPublicKey

sun.tools.asm.ConstantPoolData:
sun.tools.asm.ClassConstantData,
sun.tools.asm.FieldConstantData,
sun.tools.asm.NameAndTypeConstantData,
sun.tools.asm.NumberConstantData,
sun.tools.asm.StringConstantData,
sun.tools.asm.StringExpressionConstantData

sun.tools.asm.Instruction: sun.tools.asm.Label

sun.tools.debug.Field:
sun.tools.debug.RemoteField

sun.tools.debug.LocalVariable:
sun.tools.debug.RemoteStackVariable

sun.tools.debug.RemoteObject:
sun.tools.debug.RemoteArray,
sun.tools.debug.RemoteClass,
sun.tools.debug.RemoteString,
sun.tools.debug.RemoteThread,
sun.tools.debug.RemoteThreadGroup

sun.tools.debug.RemoteValue:
sun.tools.debug.RemoteBoolean,
sun.tools.debug.RemoteByte,
sun.tools.debug.RemoteChar,
sun.tools.debug.RemoteDouble,
sun.tools.debug.RemoteFloat,
sun.tools.debug.RemoteInt,
sun.tools.debug.RemoteLong,
sun.tools.debug.RemoteObject,
sun.tools.debug.RemoteShort

sun.tools.debug.StackFrame:
sun.tools.debug.RemoteStackFrame

sun.tools.java.ClassDefinition:
sun.tools.java.BinaryClass,
sun.tools.javac.SourceClass

sun.tools.java.ClassNotFound:
sun.tools.java.AmbiguousClass

sun.tools.java.Environment:
sun.tools.java.ImportEnvironment,
sun.tools.javac.BatchEnvironment,
sun.tools.tree.ContextEnvironment

sun.tools.java.FieldDefinition:
sun.tools.java.BinaryField,
sun.tools.javac.SourceField,
sun.tools.tree.LocalField

sun.tools.java.Parser:
sun.tools.javac.BatchParser

sun.tools.java.Scanner: sun.tools.java.Parser

sun.tools.java.Type:
sun.tools.java.ArrayType,
sun.tools.java.ClassType,
sun.tools.java.MethodType

sun.tools.javac.BatchEnvironment:
sun.rmi.rmic.BatchEnvironment

sun.tools.javadoc.DocumentationGenerator:
sun.tools.javadoc.
HTMLDocumentationGenerator

sun.tools.tree.ContinueStatement,
sun.tools.tree.DeclarationStatement,
sun.tools.tree.DoStatement,
sun.tools.tree.ExpressionStatement,
sun.tools.tree.FinallyStatement,
sun.tools.tree.ForStatement,
sun.tools.tree.IfStatement,
sun.tools.tree.InlineReturnStatement,
sun.tools.tree.ReturnStatement,
sun.tools.tree.SwitchStatement,
sun.tools.tree.SynchronizedStatement,
sun.tools.tree.ThrowStatement,
sun.tools.tree.TryStatement,
sun.tools.tree.VarDeclarationStatement,
sun.tools.tree.WhileStatement

sun.tools.tree.ThisExpression:
sun.tools.tree.SuperExpression

sun.tools.tree.UnaryExpression:
sun.tools.tree.ArrayAccessExpression,
sun.tools.tree.BinaryExpression,
sun.tools.tree.BitNotExpression,
sun.tools.tree.ConvertExpression,
sun.tools.tree.ExprExpression,
sun.tools.tree.FieldExpression,
sun.tools.tree.IncDecExpression,
sun.tools.tree.LengthExpression,
sun.tools.tree.NaryExpression,
sun.tools.tree.NegativeExpression,
sun.tools.tree.NotExpression,
sun.tools.tree.PositiveExpression

Interface Implemented by Index

*T*his appendix alphabetically lists all the interfaces that are implemented by classes defined in the sun and sunw packages. Many methods in the java packages return objects that are merely defined as implementing a particular interface. This list gives you the possible classes that can be returned by such a method.

java.applet.AppletContext:
sun.applet.AppletViewer

java.applet.AppletStub:
sun.applet.AppletPanel

java.applet.AudioClip:
sun.applet.AppletAudioClip

java.awt.LayoutManager:
sun.awt.HorizBagLayout,
sun.awt.VerticalBagLayout

java.awt.PrintGraphics:
sun.awt.motif.PSGraphics

java.awt.image.ImageConsumer:
sun.awt.image.ImageInfoGrabber,
sun.awt.image.ImageRepresentation

java.awt.image.ImageProducer:
sun.awt.image.
InputStreamImageSource,
sun.awt.image.OffScreenImageSource

java.awt.peer.ButtonPeer:
sun.awt.motif.MButtonPeer,

sun.awt.tiny.TinyButtonPeer

java.awt.peer.CanvasPeer:
sun.awt.motif.MCanvasPeer,
sun.awt.tiny.TinyCanvasPeer

java.awt.peer.CheckboxMenuItemPeer:
sun.awt.motif.
MCheckboxMenuItemPeer,
sun.awt.tiny.
TinyCheckboxMenuItemPeer

java.awt.peer.CheckboxPeer:
sun.awt.motif.MCheckboxPeer,
sun.awt.tiny.TinyCheckboxPeer

java.awt.peer.ChoicePeer:
sun.awt.motif.MChoicePeer,
sun.awt.motif.MTinyChoicePeer,
sun.awt.tiny.TinyChoicePeer

java.awt.peer.ComponentPeer:
sun.awt.motif.MComponentPeer,
sun.awt.tiny.TinyComponentPeer

java.awt.peer.DialogPeer:
 sun.awt.motif.MDialogPeer,
 sun.awt.tiny.TinyDialogPeer

java.awt.peer.FileDialogPeer:
 sun.awt.motif.MFileDialogPeer,
 sun.awt.tiny.TinyFileDialogPeer

java.awt.peer.FontPeer: sun.awt.PlatformFont

java.awt.peer.FramePeer:
 sun.awt.motif.MFramePeer,
 sun.awt.tiny.TinyFramePeer

java.awt.peer.LabelPeer:
 sun.awt.motif.MLabelPeer,
 sun.awt.tiny.TinyLabelPeer

java.awt.peer.ListPeer:
 sun.awt.motif.MListPeer,
 sun.awt.tiny.TinyListPeer

java.awt.peer.MenuBarPeer:
 sun.awt.motif.MMenuBarPeer

java.awt.peer.MenuItemPeer:
 sun.awt.motif.MMenuItemPeer,
 sun.awt.tiny.TinyMenuItemPeer

java.awt.peer.MenuPeer:
 sun.awt.motif.MMenuPeer,
 sun.awt.tiny.TinyMenuPeer

java.awt.peer.PanelPeer:
 sun.awt.motif.MPanelPeer,
 sun.awt.tiny.TinyPanelPeer

java.awt.peer.PopupMenuPeer:
 sun.awt.motif.MPopupMenuPeer

java.awt.peer.ScrollPanePeer:
 sun.awt.motif.MScrollPanePeer,
 sun.awt.tiny.TinyScrollPanePeer

java.awt.peer.ScrollbarPeer:
 sun.awt.motif.MScrollbarPeer,
 sun.awt.tiny.TinyScrollbarPeer

java.awt.peer.TextAreaPeer:
 sun.awt.motif.MTextAreaPeer,
 sun.awt.tiny.TinyTextAreaPeer

java.awt.peer.TextFieldPeer:
 sun.awt.motif.MTextFieldPeer,
 sun.awt.tiny.TinyTextFieldPeer

java.awt.peer.WindowPeer:
 sun.awt.motif.MWindowPeer,
 sun.awt.tiny.TinyWindowPeer

java.beans.PropertyEditor:
 sun.beans.editors.ColorEditor,
 sun.beans.editors.FontEditor

java.io.Externalizable:
 sun.rmi.transport.LiveRef

java.io.FilenameFilter:
 sun.awt.tiny.FileDialogFilter

java.io.Serializable: sun.rmi.server.UnicastRef,
 sun.rmi.transport.tcp.TCPEndpoint,
 sun.security.provider.DSAPrivateKey,
 sun.security.provider.DSAPublicKey,
 sun.security.provider.IdentityDatabase,
 sun.security.provider.SystemIdentity,
 sun.security.util.ObjectIdentifier,
 sun.security.x509.AlgorithmId,
 sun.security.x509.X509Cert

java.lang.Cloneable: sun.net.NetworkServer,
 sun.net.www.MimeEntry,
 sun.security.provider.MD5,
 sun.security.provider.SHA,
 sun.security.util.DerInputBuffer,
 sun.tools.tree.Node

java.lang.Runnable: sun.applet.AppletPanel,
 sun.awt.motif.MToolkit,
 sun.misc.RequestProcessor,
 sun.net.NetworkServer,
 sun.net.www.http.ClientVector,
 sun.net.www.protocol.gopher.GopherClient,
 sun.rmi.rmic.Main, sun.rmi.rmic.UI,
 sun.rmi.transport.DGCClient,
 sun.rmi.transport.KeepAlive,
 sun.rmi.transport.LeaseChecker,
 sun.rmi.transport.LeaseRenewer,
 sun.rmi.transport.Reaper,
 sun.rmi.transport.UnreferencedObj,
 sun.rmi.transport.proxy.AsyncConnector,
 sun.rmi.transport.tcp.ConnectionAcceptor,
 sun.rmi.transport.tcp.Pinger,
 sun.rmi.transport.tcp.TCPChannel,
 sun.rmi.transport.tcp.TCPTransport,
 sun.tools.debug.Agent,
 sun.tools.debug.AgentIn

java.net.FileNameMap:
 sun.net.www.MimeTable

java.rmi.Remote:
 sun.rmi.registry.RegistryImpl_Stub

java.rmi.dgc.DGC:
 sun.rmi.transport.DGCImpl,
 sun.rmi.transport.DGCImpl_Stub

java.rmi.registry.Registry:
 sun.rmi.registry.RegistryImpl,
 sun.rmi.registry.RegistryImpl_Stub

java.rmi.registry.RegistryHandler:
sun.rmi.registry.RegistryHandler

java.rmi.server.LoaderHandler:
sun.rmi.server.LoaderHandler

java.rmi.server.RemoteCall:
sun.rmi.transport.StreamRemoteCall

java.rmi.server.RemoteRef:
sun.rmi.server.UnicastRef

java.rmi.server.ServerRef:
sun.rmi.server.UnicastServerRef

java.rmi.server.Skeleton:
sun.rmi.registry.RegistryImpl_Skel,
sun.rmi.transport.DGCImpl_Skel

java.security.Certificate:
sun.security.x509.X509Cert

java.security.Principal:
sun.security.acl.PrincipalImpl,
sun.security.x509.X500Name

java.security.PrivateKey:
sun.security.pkcs.PKCS8Key

java.security.PublicKey:
sun.security.x509.X509Key

java.security.acl.Acl: sun.security.acl.AclImpl

java.security.acl.AclEntry:
sun.security.acl.AclEntryImpl

java.security.acl.Group:
sun.security.acl.GroupImpl

java.security.acl.Owner:
sun.security.acl.OwnerImpl

java.security.acl.Permission:
sun.security.acl.PermissionImpl

java.security.interfaces.DSAKeyPairGenerator:
sun.security.provider.DSAKeyPairGenerator

java.security.interfaces.DSAParams:
sun.security.x509.AlgIdDSA

java.security.interfaces.DSAPrivateKey:
sun.security.provider.DSAPrivateKey

java.security.interfaces.DSAPublicKey:
sun.security.provider.DSAPublicKey

java.sql.CallableStatement:
sun.jdbc.odbc.JdbcOdbcCallableStatement

java.sql.Connection:
sun.jdbc.odbc.JdbcOdbcConnectionInterface

java.sql.DatabaseMetaData:
sun.jdbc.odbc.JdbcOdbcDatabaseMetaData

java.sql.Driver:
sun.jdbc.odbc.JdbcOdbcDriverInterface

java.sql.PreparedStatement:
sun.jdbc.odbc.JdbcOdbcPreparedStatement

java.sql.ResultSet:
sun.jdbc.odbc.JdbcOdbcResultSetInterface

java.sql.ResultSetMetaData:
sun.jdbc.odbc.JdbcOdbcResultSetMetaData

java.sql.Statement:
sun.jdbc.odbc.JdbcOdbcStatement

java.util.Enumeration:
sun.misc.CacheEnumerator,
sun.misc.FIFOQueueEnumerator,
sun.misc.LIFOQueueEnumerator,
sun.security.acl.AclEnumerator,
sun.tools.asm.SwitchDataEnumeration

sun.applet.AppletViewerFactory:
sun.applet.StdAppletViewerFactory

sun.awt.AWTFinalizeable:
sun.awt.image.ImageRepresentation,
sun.awt.motif.X11Graphics

sun.awt.DrawingSurface:
sun.awt.motif.MCanvasPeer,
sun.awt.motif.X11OffScreenImage

sun.awt.DrawingSurfaceInfo:
sun.awt.motif.MDrawingSurfaceInfo

sun.awt.PhysicalDrawingSurface:
sun.awt.X11DrawingSurface

sun.awt.UpdateClient:
sun.awt.motif.MComponentPeer,
sun.awt.tiny.TinyComponentPeer

sun.awt.X11DrawingSurface:
sun.awt.motif.MDrawingSurfaceInfo

sun.awt.image.ImageFetchable:
sun.awt.image.InputStreamImageSource

sun.awt.motif.X11SelectionHolder:
sun.awt.motif.X11Clipboard

sun.awt.tiny.TinyScrollbarClient:
sun.awt.tiny.TinyListPeer,
sun.awt.tiny.TinyScrollPanePeer,
sun.awt.tiny.TinyScrollbarPeer,
sun.awt.tiny.TinyTextAreaPeer

sun.jdbc.odbc.JdbcOdbcConnectionInterface:
sun.jdbc.odbc.JdbcOdbcConnection

sun.jdbc.odbc.JdbcOdbcDriverInterface:
sun.jdbc.odbc.JdbcOdbcDriver

sun.jdbc.odbc.JdbcOdbcResultSetInterface:
sun.jdbc.odbc.JdbcOdbcResultSet

sun.misc.Compare:
sun.net.www.protocol.file.StringCompare

sun.rmi.server.Dispatcher:
sun.rmi.server.UnicastServerRef

sun.rmi.transport.Channel:
sun.rmi.transport.tcp.TCPChannel

sun.rmi.transport.Connection:
sun.rmi.transport.tcp.TCPConnection

sun.rmi.transport.Endpoint:
sun.rmi.transport.tcp.TCPEndpoint

sun.rmi.transport.Notifiable:
sun.rmi.transport.DGCAckHandler

sun.rmi.transport.Notifier:
sun.rmi.transport.Channel

sun.rmi.transport.proxy.CGICommandHandler:
sun.rmi.transport.proxy.
CGIForwardCommand,
sun.rmi.transport.proxy.
CGIGethostnameCommand,
sun.rmi.transport.proxy.CGIPingCommand,
sun.rmi.transport.proxy.
CGITryHostnameCommand

sun.rmi.transport.proxy.RMISocketInfo:
sun.rmi.transport.proxy.HttpReceiveSocket,
sun.rmi.transport.proxy.HttpSendSocket

sun.tools.debug.AgentConstants:
sun.tools.debug.Agent,
sun.tools.debug.AgentIn,
sun.tools.debug.AgentOutputStream,
sun.tools.debug.BreakpointHandler,
sun.tools.debug.BreakpointSet,
sun.tools.debug.RemoteAgent,
sun.tools.debug.RemoteField,
sun.tools.debug.RemoteStackVariable,
sun.tools.debug.RemoteValue

sun.tools.debug.DebuggerCallback:
sun.tools.ttydebug.TTY

sun.tools.java.Constants:
sun.rmi.rmic.GenerateMarshaling,
sun.rmi.rmic.GenerateRemoteProxy,
sun.rmi.rmic.Main, sun.rmi.rmic.TopGRP,
sun.tools.asm.Assembler,
sun.tools.asm.Instruction,
sun.tools.debug.AgentConstants,
sun.tools.java.BinaryAttribute,
sun.tools.java.BinaryClass,
sun.tools.java.BinaryCode,
sun.tools.java.BinaryConstantPool,
sun.tools.java.ClassDeclaration,
sun.tools.java.ClassDefinition,
sun.tools.java.Environment,
sun.tools.java.FieldDefinition,
sun.tools.java.Identifier,
sun.tools.java.Imports,
sun.tools.java.Parser,
sun.tools.java.Scanner,
sun.tools.java.ScannerInputStream,
sun.tools.java.Type, sun.tools.javac.Main,
sun.tools.javac.SourceField,
sun.tools.javadoc.DocumentationGenerator,
sun.tools.javadoc.HTMLDocumentationGe
nerator, sun.tools.javadoc.Main,
sun.tools.tree.Context, sun.tools.tree.Node,
sun.tools.tree.UplevelReference,
sun.tools.tree.Vset

sun.tools.java.ParserActions:
sun.tools.java.Parser

sun.tools.java.RuntimeConstants:
sun.tools.asm.ConstantPool,
sun.tools.asm.ConstantPoolData,
sun.tools.java.Constants

sun.tools.javac.ErrorConsumer:
sun.tools.javac.BatchEnvironment

CLASS RETURNED BY INDEX

*T*his appendix lists all the public and protected methods in the sun and sunw packages that return objects of the given class. The classes are ordered alphabetically.

java.applet.Applet:
sun.applet.AppletPanel.getApplet(),
sun.applet.AppletViewer.getApplet()

java.applet.AppletContext:
sun.applet.AppletPanel.
getAppletContext(),
sun.applet.AppletViewerPanel.
getAppletContext()

java.applet.AudioClip:
sun.applet.AppletViewer.
getAudioClip()

java.awt.Color:
sun.awt.image.Image.getBackground(),
sun.awt.motif.PSGraphics.getColor(),
sun.awt.motif.X11Graphics.
getColor(),
sun.awt.tiny.TinyComponentPeer.get
WinBackground(),
sun.awt.tiny.TinyGraphics.getColor()

java.awt.Dimension:
sun.applet.AppletPanel.
minimumSize(),
sun.applet.AppletPanel.
preferredSize(),

sun.awt.HorizBagLayout.
minimumLayoutSize(),
sun.awt.HorizBagLayout.
preferredLayoutSize(),
sun.awt.OrientableFlowLayout.
minimumLayoutSize(),
sun.awt.OrientableFlowLayout.
preferredLayoutSize(),
sun.awt.VerticalBagLayout.
minimumLayoutSize(),
sun.awt.VerticalBagLayout.
preferredLayoutSize(),
sun.awt.motif.MButtonPeer.
getMinimumSize(),
sun.awt.motif.MButtonPeer.
minimumSize(),
sun.awt.motif.MCheckboxPeer.
getMinimumSize(),
sun.awt.motif.MCheckboxPeer.
minimumSize(),
sun.awt.motif.MChoicePeer.
getMinimumSize(),
sun.awt.motif.MChoicePeer.
minimumSize(),

sun.awt.motif.MComponentPeer.
getMinimumSize(), sun.awt.motif.
MComponentPeer.
getPreferredSize(), sun.awt.motif.
MComponentPeer.minimumSize(),
sun.awt.motif.MComponentPeer.
preferredSize(), sun.awt.motif.MLabelPeer.
getMinimumSize(),
sun.awt.motif.MLabelPeer.minimumSize(),
sun.awt.motif.MListPeer.getMinimumSize(),
sun.awt.motif.MListPeer.getPreferredSize(),
sun.awt.motif.MListPeer.minimumSize(),
sun.awt.motif.MListPeer.minimumSize(),
sun.awt.motif.MListPeer.preferredSize(),
sun.awt.motif.MScrollbarPeer.
getMinimumSize(),
sun.awt.motif.MScrollbarPeer.
minimumSize(),
sun.awt.motif.MTextAreaPeer.
getMinimumSize(),
sun.awt.motif.MTextAreaPeer.g
etMinimumSize(),
sun.awt.motif.MTextAreaPeer.
getPreferredSize(),
sun.awt.motif.MTextAreaPeer.
minimumSize(),
sun.awt.motif.MTextAreaPeer.
minimumSize(),
sun.awt.motif.MTextAreaPeer.
preferredSize(),
sun.awt.motif.MTextFieldPeer.
getMinimumSize(),
sun.awt.motif.MTextFieldPeer.
getMinimumSize(),
sun.awt.motif.MTextFieldPeer.
getPreferredSize(),
sun.awt.motif.MTextFieldPeer.
minimumSize(),
sun.awt.motif.MTextFieldPeer.
minimumSize(),
sun.awt.motif.MTextFieldPeer.
preferredSize(),
sun.awt.motif.MTinyChoicePeer.
getMinimumSize(),
sun.awt.motif.MTinyChoicePeer.
minimumSize(),
sun.awt.motif.MToolkit.getScreenSize(),
sun.awt.motif.PSPaperSize.size(),
sun.awt.motif.PSPrintJob.
getPageDimension(),

sun.awt.tiny.TinyButtonPeer.
getMinimumSize(),
sun.awt.tiny.TinyButtonPeer.minimumSize(),
sun.awt.tiny.TinyCheckboxPeer.
getMinimumSize(),
sun.awt.tiny.TinyCheckboxPeer.
minimumSize(),
sun.awt.tiny.TinyChoicePeer.
getMinimumSize(),
sun.awt.tiny.TinyChoicePeer.minimumSize(),
sun.awt.tiny.TinyComponentPeer.
getMinimumSize(),
sun.awt.tiny.TinyComponentPeer.
getPreferredSize(),
sun.awt.tiny.TinyComponentPeer.
minimumSize(),
sun.awt.tiny.TinyComponentPeer.
preferredSize(), sun.awt.tiny.TinyLabelPeer.
getMinimumSize(),
sun.awt.tiny.TinyLabelPeer.minimumSize(),
sun.awt.tiny.TinyListPeer.
getMinimumSize(),
sun.awt.tiny.TinyListPeer.getPreferredSize(),
sun.awt.tiny.TinyListPeer.minimumSize(),
sun.awt.tiny.TinyListPeer.minimumSize(),
sun.awt.tiny.TinyListPeer.preferredSize(),
sun.awt.tiny.TinyScrollbarPeer.
getMinimumSize(),
sun.awt.tiny.TinyScrollbarPeer.
minimumSize(),
sun.awt.tiny.TinyTextAreaPeer.
getMinimumSize(),
sun.awt.tiny.TinyTextAreaPeer.
getMinimumSize(),
sun.awt.tiny.TinyTextAreaPeer.
getPreferredSize(),
sun.awt.tiny.TinyTextAreaPeer.
minimumSize(),
sun.awt.tiny.TinyTextAreaPeer.
minimumSize(),
sun.awt.tiny.TinyTextAreaPeer.
preferredSize(),
sun.awt.tiny.TinyTextFieldPeer.
getMinimumSize(),
sun.awt.tiny.TinyTextFieldPeer.
getMinimumSize(),
sun.awt.tiny.TinyTextFieldPeer.
getPreferredSize(),
sun.awt.tiny.TinyTextFieldPeer.
minimumSize(),

sun.awt.motif.ImageGrabber.
getColorModel(),
sun.awt.motif.MComponentPeer.
getColorModel(),
sun.awt.motif.MToolkit.getColorModel(),
sun.awt.tiny.TinyComponentPeer.
getColorModel(),
sun.awt.tiny.TinyToolkit.getColorModel()

java.awt.image.ImageProducer:
sun.awt.image.Image.getSource()

java.awt.peer.ButtonPeer:
sun.awt.motif.MToolkit.createButton(),
sun.awt.tiny.TinyToolkit.createButton()

java.awt.peer.CanvasPeer:
sun.awt.motif.MToolkit.createCanvas(),
sun.awt.tiny.TinyToolkit.createCanvas()

java.awt.peer.CheckboxMenuItemPeer:
sun.awt.motif.MToolkit.
createCheckboxMenuItem(),
sun.awt.tiny.TinyToolkit.
createCheckboxMenuItem()

java.awt.peer.CheckboxPeer:
sun.awt.motif.MToolkit.createCheckbox(),
sun.awt.tiny.TinyToolkit.createCheckbox()

java.awt.peer.ChoicePeer:
sun.awt.motif.MToolkit.createChoice(),
sun.awt.tiny.TinyToolkit.createChoice()

java.awt.peer.DialogPeer:
sun.awt.motif.MToolkit.createDialog(),
sun.awt.tiny.TinyToolkit.createDialog()

java.awt.peer.FileDialogPeer:
sun.awt.motif.MToolkit.createFileDialog(),
sun.awt.tiny.TinyToolkit.createFileDialog()

java.awt.peer.FontPeer:
sun.awt.motif.MToolkit.getFontPeer(),
sun.awt.tiny.TinyToolkit.getFontPeer()

java.awt.peer.FramePeer:
sun.awt.motif.MToolkit.createFrame(),
sun.awt.tiny.TinyToolkit.createFrame()

java.awt.peer.LabelPeer:
sun.awt.motif.MToolkit.createLabel(),
sun.awt.tiny.TinyToolkit.createLabel()

java.awt.peer.ListPeer:
sun.awt.motif.MToolkit.createList(),
sun.awt.tiny.TinyToolkit.createList()

java.awt.peer.MenuBarPeer:
sun.awt.motif.MToolkit.createMenuBar(),
sun.awt.tiny.TinyToolkit.createMenuBar()

java.awt.peer.MenuItemPeer:
sun.awt.motif.MToolkit.createMenuItem(),
sun.awt.tiny.TinyToolkit.createMenuItem()

java.awt.peer.MenuPeer:
sun.awt.motif.MToolkit.createMenu(),
sun.awt.tiny.TinyToolkit.createMenu()

java.awt.peer.PanelPeer:
sun.awt.motif.MToolkit.createPanel(),
sun.awt.tiny.TinyToolkit.createPanel()

java.awt.peer.PopupMenuPeer:
sun.awt.motif.MToolkit.createPopupMenu(),
sun.awt.tiny.TinyToolkit.createPopupMenu()

java.awt.peer.ScrollPanePeer:
sun.awt.motif.MToolkit.createScrollPane(),
sun.awt.tiny.TinyToolkit.createScrollPane()

java.awt.peer.ScrollbarPeer:
sun.awt.motif.MToolkit.createScrollbar(),
sun.awt.tiny.TinyToolkit.createScrollbar()

java.awt.peer.TextAreaPeer:
sun.awt.motif.MToolkit.createTextArea(),
sun.awt.tiny.TinyToolkit.createTextArea()

java.awt.peer.TextFieldPeer:
sun.awt.motif.MToolkit.createTextField(),
sun.awt.tiny.TinyToolkit.createTextField()

java.awt.peer.WindowPeer:
sun.awt.motif.MToolkit.createWindow(),
sun.awt.tiny.TinyToolkit.createWindow()

java.io.ByteToCharConverter:
sun.html.Parser.getCharConverter()

java.io.CharToByteConverter:
sun.awt.PlatformFont.getFontCharset(),
sun.awt.motif.MFontPeer.getFontCharset()

java.io.File:
sun.tools.java.Environment.getcovFile(),
sun.tools.javac.BatchEnvironment.
getcovFile()

java.io.InputStream:
sun.applet.AppletClassLoader.
getResourceAsStream(),
sun.applet.AppletResourceLoader.
getLocalResourceStream(),
sun.applet.AppletResourceLoader.
getResourceAsStream(),
sun.html.Entity.getInputStream(),
sun.net.nntp.NntpClient.getArticle(),
sun.net.nntp.NntpClient.getArticle(),
sun.net.nntp.NntpClient.getHeader(),
sun.net.nntp.NntpClient.getHeader(),

sun.net.www.http.HttpClient.
getInputStream(),
sun.net.www.protocol.appletresource.
AppletResourceConnection.getInputStream(),
sun.net.www.protocol.file.
FileURLConnection.getInputStream(),
sun.net.www.protocol.ftp.
FtpURLConnection.getInputStream(),
sun.net.www.protocol.gopher.
GopherURLConnection.getInputStream(),
sun.net.www.protocol.http.
HttpURLConnection.getInputStream(),
sun.net.www.protocol.mailto.
MailToURLConnection.getInputStream(),
sun.net.www.protocol.systemresource.
SystemResourceConnection.getInputStream(),
sun.net.www.protocol.verbatim.
VerbatimConnection.getInputStream(),
sun.rmi.transport.Connection.
getInputStream(),
sun.rmi.transport.proxy.HttpSendSocket.
getInputStream(),
sun.rmi.transport.proxy.HttpSendSocket.
readNotify(),
sun.rmi.transport.proxy.WrappedSocket.
getInputStream(),
sun.rmi.transport.tcp.TCPConnection.
getInputStream(),
sun.tools.debug.RemoteClass.getSourceFile(),
sun.tools.java.ClassFile.getInputStream()

java.io.ObjectInput:
sun.rmi.transport.StreamRemoteCall.
getInputStream()

java.io.ObjectOutput:
sun.rmi.transport.StreamRemoteCall.
getOutputStream(),
sun.rmi.transport.StreamRemoteCall.
getResultStream()

java.io.OutputStream:
sun.net.www.http.HttpClient.
getOutputStream(),
sun.net.www.protocol.http.
HttpURLConnection.getOutputStream(),
sun.net.www.protocol.mailto.
MailToURLConnection.getOutputStream(),
sun.net.www.protocol.verbatim.
VerbatimConnection.getOutputStream(),
sun.rmi.transport.Connection.
getOutputStream(),

sun.rmi.transport.proxy.HttpReceiveSocket.
getOutputStream(),
sun.rmi.transport.proxy.HttpSendSocket.
getOutputStream(),
sun.rmi.transport.proxy.HttpSendSocket.
writeNotify(),
sun.rmi.transport.proxy.WrappedSocket.
getOutputStream(),
sun.rmi.transport.tcp.TCPConnection.
getOutputStream()

java.io.PrintStream:
sun.net.nntp.NntpClient.startPost(),
sun.net.smtp.SmtpClient.startMessage()

java.lang.Bignum:
sun.security.provider.AlgIdDSA.getG(),
sun.security.provider.AlgIdDSA.getP(),
sun.security.provider.AlgIdDSA.getQ(),
sun.security.provider.DSAPublicKey.getY(),
sun.security.util.BigInt.toBignum()

java.lang.Class:
sun.applet.AppletClassLoader.loadClass(),
sun.applet.AppletClassLoader.loadClass(),
sun.applet.
AppletObjectInputStream.resolveClass(),
sun.rmi.server.LoaderHandler.loadClass(),
sun.rmi.server.LoaderHandler.loadClass(),
sun.rmi.server.MarshalInputStream.
resolveClass(),
sun.rmi.server.RMIClassLoader.loadClass()

java.lang.Object:
sun.applet.AppletImageRef.reconstitute(),
sun.applet.AppletResourceLoader.getLocal
Resource(), sun.applet.AppletSecurity.
getSecurityContext(),
sun.awt.image.Image.getProperty(),
sun.awt.image.PixelStore.reconstitute(),
sun.awt.motif.ImageGrabber.getPixels(),
sun.awt.motif.MToolkit.targetToPeer(),
sun.html.Attributes.clone(),
sun.misc.Cache.get(), sun.misc.Cache.put(),
sun.misc.Cache.remove(),
sun.misc.CacheEntry.reconstitute(),
sun.misc.CacheEnumerator.nextElement(),
sun.misc.FIFOQueueEnumerator.
nextElement(),
sun.misc.LIFOQueueEnumerator.
nextElement(), sun.misc.Queue.dequeue(),
sun.misc.Queue.dequeue(),
sun.misc.Ref.check(), sun.misc.Ref.get(),

sun.misc.Ref.reconstitute(),
sun.misc.RegexpPool.delete(),
sun.misc.RegexpPool.match(),
sun.misc.RegexpPool.matchNext(),
sun.misc.RegexpTarget.found(),
sun.net.NetworkServer.clone(),
sun.net.www.MimeEntry.launch(),
sun.net.www.content.image.gif.getContent(),
sun.net.www.content.image.jpeg.
getContent(),
sun.net.www.content.image.x_xbitmap.
getContent(),
sun.net.www.content.image.x_xpixmap.
getContent(),
sun.net.www.content.text.plain.
getContent(),
sun.net.www.http.KeepAliveCache.get(),
sun.net.www.protocol.appletresource.
AppletResourceConnection.getContent(),
sun.net.www.protocol.systemresource.
SystemResourceConnection.getContent(),
sun.net.www.protocol.verbatim.
VerbatimConnection.getContent(),
sun.rmi.server.MarshalOutputStream.
replaceObject(),
sun.rmi.transport.WeakRef.reconstitute(),
sun.rmi.transport.proxy.HttpSendSocket.
getOption(),
sun.security.acl.AclEntryImpl.clone(),
sun.security.acl.AclEnumerator.
nextElement(), sun.security.provider.DSA.
engineGetParameter(),
sun.tools.asm.CatchData.getType(),
sun.tools.asm.Instruction.getValue(),
sun.tools.asm.SwitchDataEnumeration.
nextElement(),
sun.tools.java.BinaryConstantPool.
getConstant(),
sun.tools.java.BinaryConstantPool.
getValue(),
sun.tools.java.ClassDefinition.getSource(),
sun.tools.java.Environment.getSource(),
sun.tools.java.FieldDefinition.
getInitialValue(),
sun.tools.javac.SourceField.getInitialValue(),
sun.tools.tree.BooleanExpression.getValue(),
sun.tools.tree.DoubleExpression.getValue(),
sun.tools.tree.Expression.getValue(),
sun.tools.tree.FloatExpression.getValue(),
sun.tools.tree.IntegerExpression.getValue(),

sun.tools.tree.LongExpression.getValue(),
sun.tools.tree.Node.clone(),
sun.tools.tree.StringExpression.getValue()

java.lang.String:
sun.applet.AppletAudioClip.toString(),
sun.applet.AppletClassLoader.
getResourceAsName(),
sun.applet.AppletIOException.
getLocalizedMessage(), sun.applet.
AppletIllegalArgumentException.getLoca-
lizedMessage(),
sun.applet.AppletPanel.getParameter(),
sun.applet.AppletResourceLoader.
getResourceAsName(),
sun.applet.AppletSecurityException.
getLocalizedMessage(),
sun.applet.AppletViewerPanel.
getParameter(),
sun.awt.HorizBagLayout.toString(),
sun.awt.OrientableFlowLayout.toString(),
sun.awt.PlatformFont.styleStr(),
sun.awt.VariableGridLayout.toString(),
sun.awt.VerticalBagLayout.toString(),
sun.awt.image.ConsumerQueue.toString(),
sun.awt.motif.
CharToByteX11CNS11643P1.toString(),
sun.awt.motif.
CharToByteX11CNS11643P14.toString(),
sun.awt.motif.
CharToByteX11CNS11643P2.toString(),
sun.awt.motif.CharToByteX11Dingbats.
toString(),
sun.awt.motif.CharToByteX11GB2312.
toString(),
sun.awt.motif.CharToByteX11JIS0201.
toString(),
sun.awt.motif.CharToByteX11JIS0208.
toString(),
sun.awt.motif.CharToByteX11KSC5601.
toString(),
sun.awt.motif.MComponentPeer.toString(),
sun.awt.motif.MTextAreaPeer.getText(),
sun.awt.motif.MTextFieldPeer.getText(),
sun.awt.motif.PSPaperSize.name(),
sun.awt.motif.PSPaperSize.
toPostScriptCode(),
sun.awt.motif.PSPaperSize.
toPostScriptCode(),
sun.awt.motif.PSPaperSize.toString(),

sun.io.ByteToCharCp284.
getCharacterEncoding(),
sun.io.ByteToCharCp285.
getCharacterEncoding(),
sun.io.ByteToCharCp297.
getCharacterEncoding(),
sun.io.ByteToCharCp420.
getCharacterEncoding(),
sun.io.ByteToCharCp424.
getCharacterEncoding(),
sun.io.ByteToCharCp437.
getCharacterEncoding(),
sun.io.ByteToCharCp500.
getCharacterEncoding(),
sun.io.ByteToCharCp737.
getCharacterEncoding(),
sun.io.ByteToCharCp775.
getCharacterEncoding(),
sun.io.ByteToCharCp850.
getCharacterEncoding(),
sun.io.ByteToCharCp852.
getCharacterEncoding(),
sun.io.ByteToCharCp855.
getCharacterEncoding(),
sun.io.ByteToCharCp856.
getCharacterEncoding(),
sun.io.ByteToCharCp857.
getCharacterEncoding(),
sun.io.ByteToCharCp860.
getCharacterEncoding(),
sun.io.ByteToCharCp861.
getCharacterEncoding(),
sun.io.ByteToCharCp862.
getCharacterEncoding(),
sun.io.ByteToCharCp863.
getCharacterEncoding(),
sun.io.ByteToCharCp864.
getCharacterEncoding(),
sun.io.ByteToCharCp865.
getCharacterEncoding(),
sun.io.ByteToCharCp866.
getCharacterEncoding(),
sun.io.ByteToCharCp868.
getCharacterEncoding(),
sun.io.ByteToCharCp869.
getCharacterEncoding(),
sun.io.ByteToCharCp870.
getCharacterEncoding(),
sun.io.ByteToCharCp871.
getCharacterEncoding(),

sun.io.ByteToCharCp874.
getCharacterEncoding(),
sun.io.ByteToCharCp875.
getCharacterEncoding(),
sun.io.ByteToCharCp918.
getCharacterEncoding(),
sun.io.ByteToCharCp921.
getCharacterEncoding(),
sun.io.ByteToCharCp922.
getCharacterEncoding(),
sun.io.ByteToCharEUCJIS.
getCharacterEncoding(),
sun.io.ByteToCharGB2312.
getCharacterEncoding(),
sun.io.ByteToCharJIS.
getCharacterEncoding(),
sun.io.ByteToCharKSC5601.
getCharacterEncoding(),
sun.io.ByteToCharMacArabic.
getCharacterEncoding(),
sun.io.ByteToCharMacCentralEurope.
getCharacterEncoding(),
sun.io.ByteToCharMacCroatian.
getCharacterEncoding(),
sun.io.ByteToCharMacCyrillic.
getCharacterEncoding(),
sun.io.ByteToCharMacDingbat.
getCharacterEncoding(),
sun.io.ByteToCharMacGreek.
getCharacterEncoding(),
sun.io.ByteToCharMacHebrew.
getCharacterEncoding(),
sun.io.ByteToCharMacIceland.
getCharacterEncoding(),
sun.io.ByteToCharMacRoman.
getCharacterEncoding(),
sun.io.ByteToCharMacRomania.
getCharacterEncoding(),
sun.io.ByteToCharMacSymbol.
getCharacterEncoding(),
sun.io.ByteToCharMacThai.
getCharacterEncoding(),
sun.io.ByteToCharMacTurkish.
getCharacterEncoding(),
sun.io.ByteToCharMacUkraine.
getCharacterEncoding(),
sun.io.ByteToCharSJIS.
getCharacterEncoding(),
sun.io.ByteToCharUTF8.
getCharacterEncoding(),

sun.io.CharToByteCp860.
getCharacterEncoding(),
sun.io.CharToByteCp861.
getCharacterEncoding(),
sun.io.CharToByteCp862.
getCharacterEncoding(),
sun.io.CharToByteCp863.
getCharacterEncoding(),
sun.io.CharToByteCp864.
getCharacterEncoding(),
sun.io.CharToByteCp865.
getCharacterEncoding(),
sun.io.CharToByteCp866.
getCharacterEncoding(),
sun.io.CharToByteCp868.
getCharacterEncoding(),
sun.io.CharToByteCp869.
getCharacterEncoding(),
sun.io.CharToByteCp870.
getCharacterEncoding(),
sun.io.CharToByteCp871.
getCharacterEncoding(),
sun.io.CharToByteCp874.
getCharacterEncoding(),
sun.io.CharToByteCp875.
getCharacterEncoding(),
sun.io.CharToByteCp918.
getCharacterEncoding(),
sun.io.CharToByteCp921.
getCharacterEncoding(),
sun.io.CharToByteCp922.
getCharacterEncoding(),
sun.io.CharToByteEUCJIS.
getCharacterEncoding(),
sun.io.CharToByteGB2312.
getCharacterEncoding(),
sun.io.CharToByteJIS.
getCharacterEncoding(),
sun.io.CharToByteKSC5601.
getCharacterEncoding(),
sun.io.CharToByteMacArabic.
getCharacterEncoding(),
sun.io.CharToByteMacCentralEurope.
getCharacterEncoding(),
sun.io.CharToByteMacCroatian.
getCharacterEncoding(),
sun.io.CharToByteMacCyrillic.
getCharacterEncoding(),
sun.io.CharToByteMacDingbat.
getCharacterEncoding(),

sun.io.CharToByteMacGreek.
getCharacterEncoding(),
sun.io.CharToByteMacHebrew.
getCharacterEncoding(),
sun.io.CharToByteMacIceland.
getCharacterEncoding(),
sun.io.CharToByteMacRoman.
getCharacterEncoding(),
sun.io.CharToByteMacRomania.
getCharacterEncoding(),
sun.io.CharToByteMacSymbol.
getCharacterEncoding(),
sun.io.CharToByteMacThai.
getCharacterEncoding(),
sun.io.CharToByteMacTurkish.
getCharacterEncoding(),
sun.io.CharToByteMacUkraine.
getCharacterEncoding(),
sun.io.CharToByteSJIS.
getCharacterEncoding(),
sun.io.CharToByteUTF8.
getCharacterEncoding(),
sun.io.CharToByteUnicode.
getCharacterEncoding(),
sun.misc.CharacterEncoder.encode(),
sun.misc.CharacterEncoder.encodeBuffer(),
sun.misc.MessageUtils.subst(),
sun.misc.MessageUtils.subst(),
sun.misc.MessageUtils.subst(),
sun.misc.MessageUtils.subst(),
sun.misc.MessageUtils.substProp(),
sun.misc.MessageUtils.substProp(),
sun.misc.MessageUtils.substProp(),
sun.misc.QueueElement.toString(),
sun.net.TransferProtocolClient.
getResponseString(),
sun.net.URLCanonicalizer.canonicalize(),
sun.net.nntp.NewsgroupInfo.toString(),
sun.net.www.HeaderParser.findKey(),
sun.net.www.HeaderParser.findValue(),
sun.net.www.HeaderParser.findValue(),
sun.net.www.HeaderParser.findValue(),
sun.net.www.MessageHeader.canonicalID(),
sun.net.www.MessageHeader.
findNextValue(),
sun.net.www.MessageHeader.findValue(),
sun.net.www.MessageHeader.getKey(),
sun.net.www.MessageHeader.getValue(),
sun.net.www.MessageHeader.toString(),

sun.security.provider.AlgIdDSA.getName(),
sun.security.provider.AlgIdDSA.
paramsToString(),
sun.security.provider.AlgIdDSA.toString(),
sun.security.provider.DSA.
engineGetAlgorithm(),
sun.security.provider.DSA.engineToString(),
sun.security.provider.DSAPublicKey.
toString(),
sun.security.provider.IdentityDatabase.
toString(),
sun.security.provider.SystemIdentity.
toString(),
sun.security.provider.SystemSigner.
toString(), sun.security.util.BigInt.toString(),
sun.security.util.DerValue.
getPrintableString(),
sun.security.util.DerValue.toString(),
sun.security.util.ObjectIdentifier.toString(),
sun.security.x509.AVA.toString(),
sun.security.x509.AlgorithmId.getFormat(),
sun.security.x509.AlgorithmId.getName(),
sun.security.x509.AlgorithmId.
paramsToString(),
sun.security.x509.AlgorithmId.toString(),
sun.security.x509.CertException.
getMoreData(),
sun.security.x509.CertException.
getVerfDescription(),
sun.security.x509.CertException.toString(),
sun.security.x509.RDN.toString(),
sun.security.x509.X500Name.
getCommonName(),
sun.security.x509.X500Name.getCountry(),
sun.security.x509.X500Name.getLocality(),
sun.security.x509.X500Name.getName(),
sun.security.x509.X500Name.
getOrganization(),
sun.security.x509.X500Name.
getOrganizationalUnit(),
sun.security.x509.X500Name.getState(),
sun.security.x509.X500Name.toString(),
sun.security.x509.X509Cert.getFormat(),
sun.security.x509.X509Cert.toString(),
sun.security.x509.X509Cert.toString(),
sun.security.x509.X509Key.toString(),
sun.tools.asm.ClassConstantData.toString(),
sun.tools.asm.Instruction.toString(),
sun.tools.asm.Label.toString(),
sun.tools.asm.LocalVariable.toString(),

sun.tools.asm.NameAndTypeData.toString(),
sun.tools.asm.StringConstantData.toString(),
sun.tools.asm.
StringExpressionConstantData.toString(),
sun.tools.debug.BreakpointSet.toString(),
sun.tools.debug.RemoteArray.
arrayTypeName(),
sun.tools.debug.RemoteArray.description(),
sun.tools.debug.RemoteArray.toString(),
sun.tools.debug.RemoteArray.typeName(),
sun.tools.debug.RemoteBoolean.toString(),
sun.tools.debug.RemoteBoolean.typeName(),
sun.tools.debug.RemoteByte.toString(),
sun.tools.debug.RemoteByte.typeName(),
sun.tools.debug.RemoteChar.toString(),
sun.tools.debug.RemoteChar.typeName(),
sun.tools.debug.RemoteClass.
clearBreakpoint(),
sun.tools.debug.RemoteClass.
clearBreakpointLine(),
sun.tools.debug.RemoteClass.
clearBreakpointMethod(),
sun.tools.debug.RemoteClass.description(),
sun.tools.debug.RemoteClass.getName(),
sun.tools.debug.RemoteClass.
getSourceFileName(),
sun.tools.debug.RemoteClass.
setBreakpointLine(),
sun.tools.debug.RemoteClass.
setBreakpointMethod(),
sun.tools.debug.RemoteClass.toString(),
sun.tools.debug.RemoteClass.typeName(),
sun.tools.debug.RemoteDebugger.
getSourcePath(),
sun.tools.debug.RemoteDouble.toString(),
sun.tools.debug.RemoteDouble.typeName(),
sun.tools.debug.RemoteField.getModifiers(),
sun.tools.debug.RemoteField.getName(),
sun.tools.debug.RemoteField.getTypedName(),
sun.tools.debug.RemoteField.toString(),
sun.tools.debug.RemoteFloat.toString(),
sun.tools.debug.RemoteFloat.typeName(),
sun.tools.debug.RemoteInt.toString(),
sun.tools.debug.RemoteInt.typeName(),
sun.tools.debug.RemoteLong.toString(),
sun.tools.debug.RemoteLong.typeName(),
sun.tools.debug.RemoteObject.description(),
sun.tools.debug.RemoteObject.toString(),
sun.tools.debug.RemoteObject.typeName(),
sun.tools.debug.RemoteShort.toString(),

sun.tools.debug.RemoteShort.typeName(),
sun.tools.debug.RemoteStackFrame.
getMethodName(),
sun.tools.debug.RemoteStackVariable.
getName(),
sun.tools.debug.RemoteString.description(),
sun.tools.debug.RemoteString.toString(),
sun.tools.debug.RemoteString.typeName(),
sun.tools.debug.RemoteThread.getName(),
sun.tools.debug.RemoteThread.getStatus(),
sun.tools.debug.RemoteThreadGroup.
getName(),
sun.tools.debug.RemoteValue.description(),
sun.tools.debug.RemoteValue.toHex(),
sun.tools.debug.RemoteValue.typeName(),
sun.tools.debug.StackFrame.toString(),
sun.tools.jar.SignatureFile.getBlockName(),
sun.tools.jar.SignatureFile.getName(),
sun.tools.java.ArrayType.typeString(),
sun.tools.java.BinaryConstantPool.
getString(), sun.tools.java.BinaryField.
getDocumentation(),
sun.tools.java.ClassDeclaration.toString(),
sun.tools.java.ClassDefinition.
getDocumentation(),
sun.tools.java.ClassDefinition.toString(),
sun.tools.java.ClassFile.getAbsoluteName(),
sun.tools.java.ClassFile.getName(),
sun.tools.java.ClassFile.getPath(),
sun.tools.java.ClassFile.toString(),
sun.tools.java.ClassPath.toString(),
sun.tools.java.ClassType.typeString(),
sun.tools.java.FieldDefinition.
getDocumentation(),
sun.tools.java.FieldDefinition.toString(),
sun.tools.java.Identifier.toString(),
sun.tools.java.IdentifierToken.toString(),
sun.tools.java.MethodType.typeString(),
sun.tools.java.Type.getTypeSignature(),
sun.tools.java.Type.toString(),
sun.tools.java.Type.typeString(),
sun.tools.java.Type.typeString(),
sun.tools.javac.BatchEnvironment.
errorString(),
sun.tools.javac.BatchEnvironment.
getProperty(), sun.tools.javac.SourceClass.
getAbsoluteName(),
sun.tools.javadoc.DocumentationGenerator.
getReferenceName(),

sun.tools.javadoc.DocumentationGenerator.
getReferenceName(),
sun.tools.serialver.SerialVer.I18N(),
sun.tools.serialver.SerialVer.I18N(),
sun.tools.serialver.SerialVer.I18N(),
sun.tools.tree.Node.toString(),
sun.tools.tree.Vset.toString()

java.lang.Thread: sun.applet.AppletPanel.
getAppletHandlerThread(),
sun.misc.Timer.getTimerThread()

java.lang.ThreadGroup:
sun.applet.AppletClassLoader.
getThreadGroup(),
sun.applet.AppletSecurity.
getThreadGroup()

java.net.InetAddress:
sun.rmi.transport.proxy.HttpReceiveSocket.
getInetAddress(),
sun.rmi.transport.proxy.HttpSendSocket.
getInetAddress(),
sun.rmi.transport.proxy.WrappedSocket.
getInetAddress()

java.net.ServerSocket:
sun.rmi.transport.proxy.
RMIDirectSocketFactory.
createServerSocket(),
sun.rmi.transport.proxy.
RMIHttpToCGISocketFactory.
createServerSocket(),
sun.rmi.transport.proxy.
RMIHttpToPortSocketFactory.
createServerSocket(),
sun.rmi.transport.proxy.
RMIMasterSocketFactory.
createServerSocket()

java.net.Socket:
sun.net.ftp.FtpClient.openDataConnection(),
sun.rmi.transport.proxy.
HttpAwareServerSocket.accept(),
sun.rmi.transport.proxy.
RMIDirectSocketFactory.createSocket(),
sun.rmi.transport.proxy.
RMIHttpToCGISocketFactory.
createSocket(), sun.rmi.transport.proxy.
RMIHttpToPortSocketFactory.
createSocket(),
sun.rmi.transport.proxy.RMIMasterSocket
Factory.createSocket()

java.net.URL: sun.applet.AppletClassLoader.
getCodeBase(),
sun.applet.AppletPanel.getCodeBase(),
sun.applet.AppletPanel.getDocumentBase(),
sun.applet.AppletViewerPanel.
getCodeBase(),
sun.applet.AppletViewerPanel.
getDocumentBase(),
sun.html.PublicMapping.get(),
sun.rmi.server.RMIClassLoader.
getCodeBase()

java.net.URLConnection:
sun.net.www.protocol.appletresource.
Handler.openConnection(),
sun.net.www.protocol.doc.Handler.
openConnection(),
sun.net.www.protocol.file.Handler.
openConnection(),
sun.net.www.protocol.ftp.Handler.
openConnection(),
sun.net.www.protocol.gopher.Handler.
openConnection(),
sun.net.www.protocol.http.Handler.
openConnection(),
sun.net.www.protocol.mailto.Handler.
openConnection(),
sun.net.www.protocol.netdoc.Handler.
openConnection(),
sun.net.www.protocol.systemresource.
Handler.openConnection(),
sun.net.www.protocol.verbatim.Handler.
openConnection()

java.rmi.Remote:
sun.rmi.registry.RegistryImpl.lookup(),
sun.rmi.registry.RegistryImpl_Stub.lookup()

java.rmi.dgc.Lease:
sun.rmi.transport.DGCImpl.dirty(),
sun.rmi.transport.DGCImpl_Stub.dirty()

java.rmi.registry.Registry:
sun.rmi.registry.RegistryHandler.
registryImpl(),
sun.rmi.registry.RegistryHandler.
registryStub()

java.rmi.server.ObjID:
sun.rmi.registry.RegistryImpl.getID(),
sun.rmi.transport.LiveRef.getObjID()

java.rmi.server.RemoteCall:
sun.rmi.server.UnicastRef.newCall()

java.rmi.server.RemoteStub:
sun.rmi.server.RemoteProxy.getProxy(),
sun.rmi.server.RemoteProxy.getStub(),
sun.rmi.server.RemoteProxy.getStub(),
sun.rmi.server.RemoteProxy.getStub(),
sun.rmi.server.UnicastServerRef.
exportObject(),
sun.rmi.server.UnicastServerRef.
setSkeleton(),
sun.rmi.transport.Target.getStub()

java.rmi.server.Skeleton:
sun.rmi.server.RemoteProxy.getSkeleton()

java.security.Identity:
sun.security.provider.IdentityDatabase.
getIdentity(),
sun.security.provider.IdentityDatabase.
getIdentity()

java.security.KeyPair:
sun.security.provider.DSA.
engineGenerateKeyPair()

java.security.Principal:
sun.security.acl.AclEntryImpl.getPrincipal(),
sun.security.x509.X509Cert.
getGuarantor(),
sun.security.x509.X509Cert.getPrincipal()

java.security.PrivateKey:
sun.security.x509.CertAndKeyGen.
getPrivateKey()

java.security.PublicKey:
sun.security.x509.X509Cert.getPublicKey()

java.security.Signature:
sun.security.x509.X509Cert.getVerifier()

java.security.interfaces.DSAParams:
sun.security.provider.DSAPrivateKey.
getParams(),
sun.security.provider.DSAPublicKey.
getParams()

java.util.Date:
sun.security.util.DerInputStream.
getUTCTime(),
sun.security.x509.X509Cert.getNotAfter(),
sun.security.x509.X509Cert.getNotBefore()

java.util.Enumeration:
sun.applet.AppletViewer.getApplets(),
sun.html.AttributeList.getValues(),
sun.misc.Cache.elements(),
sun.misc.Cache.keys(),
sun.misc.Queue.elements(),

sun.html.Tag.getElement(),
sun.html.TagStack.first(),
sun.html.UnknownTag.getElement()

sun.html.Entity: sun.html.DTD.defEntity(),
sun.html.DTD.defEntity(),
sun.html.DTD.defineEntity(),
sun.html.DTD.getEntity(),
sun.html.DTD.getEntity()

sun.html.Tag: sun.html.Parser.makeTag()

sun.misc.Ref:
sun.applet.AppletResourceLoader.
getImageRef()

sun.misc.TimerTickThread:
sun.misc.TimerTickThread.call()

sun.net.TelnetInputStream:
sun.net.ftp.FtpClient.get(),
sun.net.ftp.FtpClient.list()

sun.net.TelnetOutputStream:
sun.net.ftp.FtpClient.put()

sun.net.nntp.NewsgroupInfo:
sun.net.nntp.NntpClient.getGroup()

sun.net.www.MessageHeader:
sun.net.www.URLConnection.
getProperties(),
sun.tools.jar.Manifest.entryAt(),
sun.tools.jar.Manifest.getEntry(),
sun.tools.jar.SignatureFile.entryAt(),
sun.tools.jar.SignatureFile.getEntry()

sun.net.www.MimeEntry:
sun.net.www.MimeTable.find(),
sun.net.www.MimeTable.findByExt(),
sun.net.www.MimeTable.findByFileName()

sun.net.www.MimeTable:
sun.net.www.MimeTable.getDefaultTable()

sun.net.www.http.HttpClient:
sun.net.www.http.HttpClient.New()

sun.net.www.protocol.http.AuthenticationInfo:
sun.net.www.protocol.http.
AuthenticationInfo.getAuth(),
sun.net.www.protocol.http.
AuthenticationInfo.getAuth()

sun.rmi.server.RMIClassLoader:
sun.rmi.server.RMIClassLoader.
getClassLoader(),
sun.rmi.server.RMIClassLoader.
getLocalLoader()

sun.rmi.transport.Channel:
sun.rmi.transport.Connection.getChannel(),

sun.rmi.transport.Endpoint.getChannel(),
sun.rmi.transport.LiveRef.getChannel(),
sun.rmi.transport.Transport.getChannel(),
sun.rmi.transport.tcp.TCPConnection.
getChannel(),
sun.rmi.transport.tcp.TCPEndpoint.
getChannel(),
sun.rmi.transport.tcp.TCPTransport.
getChannel(),
sun.rmi.transport.tcp.TCPTransport.
getCurrentChannel()

sun.rmi.transport.Connection:
sun.rmi.transport.Channel.newConnection(),
sun.rmi.transport.StreamRemoteCall.
getConnection(),
sun.rmi.transport.tcp.TCPChannel.
newConnection()

sun.rmi.transport.Endpoint:
sun.rmi.transport.Channel.getEndpoint(),
sun.rmi.transport.Transport.thisEndpoint(),
sun.rmi.transport.tcp.TCPChannel.
getEndpoint(),
sun.rmi.transport.tcp.TCPTransport.
thisEndpoint()

sun.rmi.transport.Target:
sun.rmi.transport.ObjectTable.getTarget()

sun.rmi.transport.Transport:
sun.rmi.transport.Endpoint.getTransport(),
sun.rmi.transport.tcp.TCPEndpoint.
getTransport()

sun.rmi.transport.tcp.TCPConnection:
sun.rmi.transport.tcp.
ConnectionMultiplexer.openConnection()

sun.rmi.transport.tcp.TCPEndpoint:
sun.rmi.transport.tcp.TCPEndpoint.
getLocalEndpoint(),
sun.rmi.transport.tcp.TCPEndpoint.
read()

sun.security.pkcs.ContentInfo:
sun.security.pkcs.PKCS7.getContentInfo()

sun.security.pkcs.PKCS10:
sun.security.x509.CertAndKeyGen.
getCertRequest()

sun.security.pkcs.PKCS7:
sun.tools.jar.SignatureFile.getBlock()

sun.security.pkcs.PKCS8Key:
sun.security.pkcs.PKCS8Key.parse()

sun.security.pkcs.SignerInfo:
sun.security.pkcs.PKCS7.verify()

sun.tools.java.Type:
sun.tools.debug.RemoteField.getType(),
sun.tools.debug.RemoteStackVariable.
getType(),
sun.tools.java.ArrayType.getElementType(),
sun.tools.java.BinaryConstantPool.getType(),
sun.tools.java.ClassDeclaration.getType(),
sun.tools.java.ClassDefinition.getType(),
sun.tools.java.Environment.resolveNames(),
sun.tools.java.FieldDefinition.getType(),
sun.tools.java.MethodType.getReturnType(),
sun.tools.java.Parser.parseArrayBrackets(),
sun.tools.java.Parser.parseType(),
sun.tools.java.Type.getElementType(),
sun.tools.java.Type.getReturnType(),
sun.tools.java.Type.tArray(),
sun.tools.java.Type.tClass(),
sun.tools.java.Type.tMethod(),
sun.tools.java.Type.tMethod(),
sun.tools.java.Type.tType(),
sun.tools.tree.Expression.getType()

sun.tools.tree.CheckContext:
sun.tools.tree.Context.getReturnContext()

sun.tools.tree.ConditionVars:
sun.tools.tree.Expression.checkCondition()

sun.tools.tree.Context:
sun.tools.tree.Context.getBreakContext(),
sun.tools.tree.Context.getContinueContext(),
sun.tools.tree.Context.getLabelContext()

sun.tools.tree.Expression:
sun.tools.java.Parser.parseBinaryExpression(),
sun.tools.java.Parser.parseExpression(),
sun.tools.java.Parser.
parseMethodExpression(),
sun.tools.java.Parser.
parseNewInstanceExpression(),
sun.tools.java.Parser.parseTerm(),
sun.tools.java.Parser.parseTypeExpression(),
sun.tools.tree.ArrayAccessExpression.
copyInline(),
sun.tools.tree.ArrayAccessExpression.
inline(),
sun.tools.tree.ArrayAccessExpression.
inlineLHS(),
sun.tools.tree.ArrayAccessExpression.
inlineValue(),
sun.tools.tree.ArrayExpression.inline(),
sun.tools.tree.ArrayExpression.inlineValue(),
sun.tools.tree.AssignOpExpression.
copyInline(),

sun.tools.tree.AssignOpExpression.
inlineValue(),
sun.tools.tree.BinaryAssignExpression.
copyInline(),
sun.tools.tree.BinaryAssignExpression.
getImplementation(),
sun.tools.tree.BinaryAssignExpression.
inline(),
sun.tools.tree.BinaryAssignExpression.
inlineValue(),
sun.tools.tree.BinaryAssignExpression.
order(),
sun.tools.tree.BinaryExpression.copyInline(),
sun.tools.tree.BinaryExpression.inline(),
sun.tools.tree.BinaryExpression.inlineValue(),
sun.tools.tree.BinaryExpression.order(),
sun.tools.tree.BinaryLogicalExpression.
inline(),
sun.tools.tree.CastExpression.inline(),
sun.tools.tree.CastExpression.inlineValue(),
sun.tools.tree.CommaExpression.inline(),
sun.tools.tree.CommaExpression.
inlineValue(),
sun.tools.tree.CompoundStatement.
firstConstructor(),
sun.tools.tree.ConditionalExpression.
copyInline(),
sun.tools.tree.ConditionalExpression.inline(),
sun.tools.tree.ConditionalExpression.
inlineValue(),
sun.tools.tree.ConditionalExpression.
order(),
sun.tools.tree.Context.findOuterLink(),
sun.tools.tree.Context.findOuterLink(),
sun.tools.tree.Context.getAvailableValue(),
sun.tools.tree.ConvertExpression.inline(),
sun.tools.tree.DivRemExpression.inline(),
sun.tools.tree.Expression.copyInline(),
sun.tools.tree.Expression.firstConstructor(),
sun.tools.tree.Expression.
getImplementation(),
sun.tools.tree.Expression.inline(),
sun.tools.tree.Expression.inlineLHS(),
sun.tools.tree.Expression.inlineValue(),
sun.tools.tree.Expression.order(),
sun.tools.tree.ExpressionStatement.
firstConstructor(),
sun.tools.tree.FieldExpression.copyInline(),
sun.tools.tree.FieldExpression.
getImplementation(),
sun.tools.tree.FieldExpression.inline(),

sun.tools.tree.ForStatement.inline(),
sun.tools.tree.IfStatement.copyInline(),
sun.tools.tree.IfStatement.inline(),
sun.tools.tree.InlineReturnStatement.
copyInline(),
sun.tools.tree.InlineReturnStatement.
inline(),
sun.tools.tree.ReturnStatement.copyInline(),
sun.tools.tree.ReturnStatement.inline(),
sun.tools.tree.Statement.copyInline(),
sun.tools.tree.Statement.eliminate(),
sun.tools.tree.Statement.inline(),
sun.tools.tree.Statement.insertStatement(),
sun.tools.tree.SwitchStatement.copyInline(),
sun.tools.tree.SwitchStatement.inline(),
sun.tools.tree.SynchronizedStatement.
copyInline(),
sun.tools.tree.SynchronizedStatement.
inline(),
sun.tools.tree.ThrowStatement.copyInline(),
sun.tools.tree.ThrowStatement.inline(),
sun.tools.tree.TryStatement.copyInline(),
sun.tools.tree.TryStatement.inline(),
sun.tools.tree.VarDeclarationStatement.
copyInline(),
sun.tools.tree.VarDeclarationStatement.
inline(),
sun.tools.tree.WhileStatement.copyInline(),
sun.tools.tree.WhileStatement.inline()

sun.tools.tree.Vset:
sun.tools.java.ClassDefinition.
checkLocalClass(),
sun.tools.java.FieldDefinition.check(),
sun.tools.javac.SourceClass.
checkInsideClass(),
sun.tools.javac.SourceClass.
checkLocalClass(),
sun.tools.javac.SourceField.check(),
sun.tools.tree.ArrayAccessExpression.
checkAmbigName(),
sun.tools.tree.ArrayAccessExpression.
checkAssignOp(),
sun.tools.tree.ArrayAccessExpression.
checkLHS(),
sun.tools.tree.ArrayAccessExpression.
checkValue(),
sun.tools.tree.ArrayExpression.
checkInitializer(),
sun.tools.tree.ArrayExpression.checkValue(),
sun.tools.tree.AssignExpression.

checkValue(),
sun.tools.tree.AssignOpExpression.
checkValue(),
sun.tools.tree.BinaryAssignExpression.
check(),
sun.tools.tree.BinaryExpression.checkValue(),
sun.tools.tree.BinaryLogicalExpression.
checkValue(),
sun.tools.tree.CastExpression.checkValue(),
sun.tools.tree.CommaExpression.check(),
sun.tools.tree.ConditionalExpression.
check(),
sun.tools.tree.ConditionalExpression.
checkValue(), sun.tools.tree.Context.
removeAdditionalVars(),
sun.tools.tree.ConvertExpression.
checkValue(),
sun.tools.tree.Expression.check(),
sun.tools.tree.Expression.checkAmbigName(),
sun.tools.tree.Expression.checkAssignOp(),
sun.tools.tree.Expression.checkInitializer(),
sun.tools.tree.Expression.checkLHS(),
sun.tools.tree.Expression.checkValue(),
sun.tools.tree.FieldExpression.
checkAmbigName(),
sun.tools.tree.FieldExpression.
checkAssignOp(),
sun.tools.tree.FieldExpression.
checkFinalAssign(),
sun.tools.tree.FieldExpression.
checkLHS(),
sun.tools.tree.FieldExpression.checkValue(),
sun.tools.tree.IdentifierExpression.
checkAmbigName(),
sun.tools.tree.IdentifierExpression.
checkAssignOp(),
sun.tools.tree.IdentifierExpression.
checkLHS(),
sun.tools.tree.IdentifierExpression.
checkValue(),
sun.tools.tree.IncDecExpression.check(),
sun.tools.tree.IncDecExpression.
checkValue(),
sun.tools.tree.InstanceOfExpression.
checkValue(),
sun.tools.tree.LengthExpression.
checkValue(),
sun.tools.tree.MethodExpression.check(),
sun.tools.tree.MethodExpression.
checkValue(),

sun.tools.tree.NewArrayExpression.
checkValue(),
sun.tools.tree.NewInstanceExpression.
check(),
sun.tools.tree.NewInstanceExpression.
checkValue(),
sun.tools.tree.Statement.checkMethod(),
sun.tools.tree.SuperExpression.checkValue(),
sun.tools.tree.ThisExpression.checkValue(),
sun.tools.tree.TypeExpression.
checkAmbigName(),

sun.tools.tree.TypeExpression.checkValue(),
sun.tools.tree.UnaryExpression.checkValue(),
sun.tools.tree.Vset.add(),
sun.tools.tree.Vset.addVar(),
sun.tools.tree.Vset.addVarUnassigned(),
sun.tools.tree.Vset.clearDeadEnd(),
sun.tools.tree.Vset.clearVar(),
sun.tools.tree.Vset.copy(),
sun.tools.tree.Vset.join(),
sun.tools.tree.Vset.removeAdditionalVars()

CLASS PASSED TO INDEX

F

*T*his appendix lists all the classes that are passed to public and protected methods in the sun and sunw packages. The classes are ordered alphabetically.

java.awt.AWTEvent: sun.awt.motif. MComponentPeer.handleEvent(), sun.awt.tiny.TinyComponentPeer. handleEvent(), sun.awt.tiny. TinyFileDialogPeer.handleEvent()

java.awt.Adjustable: sun.awt.motif. MScrollPanePeer.setUnitIncrement(), sun.awt.motif.MScrollPanePeer. setValue(), sun.awt.tiny. TinyScrollPanePeer.setUnitIncrement(), sun.awt.tiny.TinyScrollPanePeer. setValue()

java.awt.Button: sun.awt.motif. MToolkit.createButton(), sun.awt. tiny.TinyToolkit.createButton()

java.awt.Canvas: sun.awt.motif. MToolkit.createCanvas(), sun.awt. tiny.TinyToolkit.createCanvas()

java.awt.Checkbox: sun.awt.motif. MToolkit.createCheckbox(), sun.awt. tiny.TinyToolkit.createCheckbox()

java.awt.CheckboxGroup: sun.awt. motif.MCheckboxPeer. setCheckboxGroup(),

sun.awt.tiny.TinyCheckboxPeer. setCheckboxGroup()

java.awt.CheckboxMenuItem: sun.awt. motif.MToolkit.createCheckbox MenuItem(), sun.awt.tiny. TinyToolkit.createCheckboxMenu Item()

java.awt.Choice: sun.awt.motif. MToolkit.createChoice(), sun.awt. tiny.TinyToolkit.createChoice()

java.awt.Color: sun.awt.image. ImageRepresentation.drawImage(), sun.awt.image.ImageRepresentation. drawScaledImage(), sun.awt.image.ImageRepresentation. drawStretchImage(), sun.awt.motif. MChoicePeer. setBackground(), sun.awt.motif.MChoicePeer. setForeground(), sun.awt.motif. MComponentPeer.setBackground(), sun.awt.motif.MComponentPeer. setForeground(), sun.awt.motif. MTextAreaPeer.setBackground(), sun.awt.motif.MTextAreaPeer.

setTextBackground(), sun.awt.motif.
MTextFieldPeer.setBackground(), sun.awt.
motif.PSGraphics.drawImage(),
sun.awt.motif.PSGraphics.setColor(),
sun.awt.motif.PSGraphics.setXORMode(),
sun.awt.motif.X11Graphics.drawImage(),
sun.awt.motif.X11Graphics.setColor(),
sun.awt.motif.X11Graphics.setXORMode(),
sun.awt.tiny.TinyComponentPeer.
setBackground(), sun.awt.tiny.
TinyComponentPeer.setForeground(),
sun.awt.tiny.TinyGraphics.drawImage(),
sun.awt.tiny.TinyGraphics.setColor(),
sun.awt.tiny.TinyGraphics.setXORMode()

java.awt.Component: sun.awt.
HorizBagLayout.addLayoutComponent(),
sun.awt.HorizBagLayout.
removeLayoutComponent(), sun.awt.
VerticalBagLayout.addLayoutComponent(),
sun.awt.VerticalBagLayout.
removeLayoutComponent(), sun.awt.motif.
MToolkit.getNativeContainer()

java.awt.Container: sun.awt.
HorizBagLayout.layoutContainer(), sun.awt.
HorizBagLayout.minimumLayoutSize(), sun.
awt.HorizBagLayout.preferredLayoutSize(),
sun.awt.OrientableFlowLayout.
layoutContainer(), sun.awt. OrientableFlow
Layout.minimumLayoutSize(), sun.awt.
OrientableFlowLayout.preferredLayoutSize(),
sun.awt.VariableGridLayout.
layoutContainer(), sun.awt.
VerticalBagLayout.layoutContainer(),
sun.awt.VerticalBagLayout.
minimumLayoutSize(), sun.awt.
VerticalBagLayout.preferredLayoutSize()

java.awt.Cursor: sun.awt.motif.
MComponentPeer.setCursor(), sun.awt.
tiny.TinyComponentPeer.setCursor()

java.awt.Dialog: sun.awt.motif.MToolkit.
createDialog(), sun.awt.tiny.TinyToolkit.
createDialog()

java.awt.Event: sun.applet.AppletCopyright.
action(), sun.applet.AppletPanel.sendEvent(),
sun.applet.AppletProps.action(),
sun.applet.AppletViewer.handleEvent(),
sun.applet.TextFrame.handleEvent(),
sun.awt.FocusingTextField.gotFocus(),
sun.awt.FocusingTextField.lostFocus(),
sun.awt.motif.MPopupMenuPeer.show(),
sun.awt.motif.NumericField.keyDown(),
sun.awt.motif.UPrintDialog.action(), sun.
awt.motif.UPrintDialog.handleEvent(), sun.
awt.tiny.TinyButtonPeer.
handleWindowEvent(), sun.awt.tiny.
TinyCanvasPeer.handleWindowEvent(),
sun.awt.tiny.TinyCheckboxPeer.
handleWindowEvent(), sun.awt.tiny.
TinyChoicePeer.handleWindowEvent(),
sun.awt.tiny.TinyComponentPeer.
handleEvent(), sun.awt.tiny.
TinyComponentPeer.targetEvent(), sun.awt.
tiny.TinyFileDialogPeer.handleEvent(), sun.
awt.tiny.TinyListPeer.handleWindowEvent(),
sun.awt.tiny.TinyPanelPeer.handleWindow
Event(), sun.awt.tiny.TinyScrollPanePeer.
handleWindowEvent(), sun.awt.tiny.
TinyScrollbarPeer.handleWindowEvent(),
sun.awt.tiny.TinyTextAreaPeer.handle
WindowEvent(), sun.awt.tiny.
TinyTextFieldPeer.handleWindowEvent(),
sun.beans.editors.ColorEditor.action(),
sun.beans.editors.ColorEditor.keyUp(),
sun.beans.editors.FontEditor.action(),
sun.rmi.rmic.UI.action(),
sun.rmi.rmic.UI.handleEvent(), sun.tools.
serialver.SerialVer.action(), sun.tools.
serialver.SerialVer.handleEvent(), sun.tools.
serialver.SerialVerFrame.action(), sun.tools.
serialver.SerialVerFrame.handleEvent()

java.awt.FileDialog: sun.awt.motif.MToolkit.
createFileDialog(), sun.awt.tiny.
TinyToolkit.createFileDialog()

java.awt.Font: sun.awt.motif.MChoicePeer.
setFont(), sun.awt.motif.MComponentPeer.
getFontMetrics(), sun.awt.motif.
MComponentPeer.setFont(),
sun.awt.motif.MFileDialogPeer.setFont(),
sun.awt.motif.MTextAreaPeer.setFont(),
sun.awt.motif.MTextFieldPeer.setFont(),
sun.awt.motif.MToolkit.getFontMetrics(),
sun.awt.motif.PSGraphics.getFontMetrics(),
sun.awt.motif.PSGraphics.setFont(), sun.
awt.motif.X11Graphics.getFontMetrics(),
sun.awt.motif.X11Graphics.setFont(), sun.
awt.tiny.TinyComponentPeer.
getFontMetrics(), sun.awt.tiny.
TinyComponentPeer.setFont(), sun.awt.

java.awt.Panel: sun.awt.motif.MToolkit. createPanel(), sun.awt.tiny.TinyToolkit. createPanel()

java.awt.PopupMenu: sun.awt.motif. MToolkit.createPopupMenu(), sun.awt. tiny.TinyToolkit.createPopupMenu()

java.awt.Rectangle: sun.beans.editors ColorEditor.paintValue(), sun.beans. editors.FontEditor.paintValue()

java.awt.ScrollPane: sun.awt.motif.MToolkit. createScrollPane(), sun.awt.tiny. TinyToolkit.createScrollPane()

java.awt.Scrollbar: sun.awt.motif.MToolkit. createScrollbar(), sun.awt.tiny.TinyToolkit. createScrollbar()

java.awt.Shape: sun.awt.motif.PSGraphics. setClip(), sun.awt.motif.X11Graphics. setClip(), sun.awt.tiny.TinyGraphics.setClip()

java.awt.TextArea: sun.awt.motif.MToolkit. createTextArea(), sun.awt.tiny.TinyToolkit. createTextArea()

java.awt.TextField: sun.awt.FocusingTextField. setNextField(), sun.awt.motif.MToolkit. createTextField(), sun.awt.tiny.TinyToolkit. createTextField()

java.awt.Window: sun.awt.motif.MToolkit. createWindow(), sun.awt.tiny.TinyToolkit. createWindow()

java.awt.datatransfer.ClipboardOwner: sun. awt.motif.X11Clipboard.setContents()

java.awt.datatransfer.DataFlavor: sun. awt.motif.Target.addFlavorMap()

java.awt.datatransfer.Transferable: sun. awt.motif.X11Clipboard.setContents()

java.awt.image.ColorModel: sun.awt.image. ImageInfoGrabber.setColorModel(), sun. awt.image.ImageInfoGrabber.setPixels(), sun.awt.image.ImageRepresentation. setColorModel(), sun.awt.image. ImageRepresentation.setPixels(), sun.awt.image.PixelStore.setColorModel()

java.awt.image.ImageConsumer: sun.awt. image.GifImageDecoder.catchupConsumer(), sun.awt.image.ImageDecoder. catchupConsumer(), sun.awt.image. InputStreamImageSource.addConsumer(), sun.awt.image.InputStreamImageSource.

isConsumer(), sun.awt.image. InputStreamImageSource.removeConsumer(), sun.awt.image.InputStreamImageSource. requestTopDownLeftRightResend(), sun. awt.image.InputStreamImageSource. startProduction(), sun.awt.image. JPEGImageDecoder.catchupConsumer(), sun.awt.image.OffScreenImageSource. addConsumer(), sun.awt.image. OffScreenImageSource.isConsumer(), sun.awt.image.OffScreenImageSource. removeConsumer(), sun.awt.image. OffScreenImageSource. requestTopDownLeftRightResend(), sun.awt.image.OffScreenImageSource. startProduction(), sun.awt.image.PixelStore. replay(), sun.awt.image.XbmImageDecoder. catchupConsumer()

java.awt.image.ImageObserver: sun.awt. image.Image.check(), sun.awt.image.Image. getHeight(), sun.awt.image.Image. getProperty(), sun.awt.image.Image. getWidth(), sun.awt.image.Image.preload(), sun.awt.image.ImageRepresentation.check(), sun.awt.image.ImageRepresentation. drawImage(), sun.awt.image. ImageRepresentation.drawScaledImage(), sun.awt.image.ImageRepresentation. drawStretchImage(), sun.awt.image. ImageRepresentation.prepare(), sun.awt. image.ImageRepresentation. removeWatcher(), sun.awt.image. ImageWatched.addWatcher(), sun.awt. image.ImageWatched.isWatcher(), sun.awt. image.ImageWatched.removeWatcher(), sun. awt.motif.MComponentPeer.checkImage(), sun.awt.motif.MComponentPeer. prepareImage(), sun.awt.motif.MToolkit. checkImage(), sun.awt.motif.MToolkit. prepareImage(), sun.awt.motif.PSGraphics. drawImage(), sun.awt.motif.X11Graphics. drawImage(), sun.awt.tiny. TinyComponentPeer.checkImage(), sun.awt. tiny.TinyComponentPeer.prepareImage(), sun.awt.tiny.TinyGraphics.drawImage(), sun.awt.tiny.TinyToolkit.checkImage(), sun.awt.tiny.TinyToolkit.prepareImage()

java.awt.image.ImageProducer: sun.awt. image.PixelStore.replay(), sun.awt.motif.

MComponentPeer.createImage(), sun.awt.
motif.MToolkit.createImage(), sun.awt.
tiny.TinyComponentPeer.createImage(),
sun.awt.tiny.TinyToolkit.createImage()

java.awt.peer.ComponentPeer: sun.awt.
EmbeddedFrame.setPeer()

java.beans.PropertyChangeListener: sun.beans.
editors.ColorEditor.addPropertyChange
Listener(), sun.beans.editors.ColorEditor.
removePropertyChangeListener(), sun.beans.
editors.FontEditor.addPropertyChange
Listener(), sun.beans.editors.FontEditor.
removePropertyChangeListener()

java.io.DataInput: sun.rmi.transport.tcp.
TCPEndpoint.read()

java.io.DataInputStream: sun.tools.java.
BinaryClass.load()

java.io.DataOutput: sun.rmi.transport.tcp.
TCPEndpoint.write()

java.io.DataOutputStream: sun.tools.asm.
Assembler.write(), sun.tools.asm.Assembler.
writeCoverageTable(), sun.tools.asm.
Assembler.writeLineNumberTable(), sun.
tools.asm.Assembler.writeLocalVariable
Table(), sun.tools.asm.ConstantPool.write(),
sun.tools.java.BinaryConstantPool.write()

java.io.File: sun.awt.tiny.FileDialogFilter.
accept(), sun.net.www.MimeTable.
saveAsProperties(), sun.rmi.rmic.TopGRP.
generate(), sun.rmi.rmic.TopGRP.
streamName(), sun.security.provider.
IdentityDatabase.fromFile(), sun.tools.jar.
Manifest.addFile(), sun.tools.jar.Manifest.
addFiles()

java.io.FileDescriptor: sun.applet.
AppletSecurity.checkRead(), sun.applet.
AppletSecurity.checkWrite()

java.io.FilenameFilter: sun.awt.motif.
MFileDialogPeer.setFilenameFilter(), sun.awt.
tiny.TinyFileDialogPeer.setFilenameFilter()

java.io.InputStream: sun.audio.AudioDevice.
closeChannel(), sun.audio.AudioDevice.
openChannel(), sun.audio.AudioPlayer.
start(), sun.audio.AudioPlayer.stop(),
sun.awt.image.InputStreamImageSource.
decoderForType(), sun.awt.image.
InputStreamImageSource.getDecoder(), sun.
jdbc.odbc.JdbcOdbcBoundParam.

setInputStream(), sun.jdbc.odbc.
JdbcOdbcPreparedStatement.setAsciiStream(),
sun.jdbc.odbc.JdbcOdbcPreparedStatement.
setBinaryStream(), sun.jdbc.odbc.
JdbcOdbcPreparedStatement.setStream(),
sun.jdbc.odbc.JdbcOdbcPreparedStatement.
setUnicodeStream(), sun.misc.
BASE64Decoder.decodeAtom(), sun.misc.
CharacterDecoder.decodeAtom(), sun.misc.
CharacterDecoder.decodeBuffer(), sun.misc.
CharacterDecoder.decodeBufferPrefix(), sun.
misc.CharacterDecoder.decodeBufferSuffix(),
sun.misc.CharacterDecoder.
decodeLinePrefix(), sun.misc.
CharacterDecoder.decodeLineSuffix(),
sun.misc.CharacterDecoder.readFully(),
sun.misc.CharacterEncoder.encode(),
sun.misc.CharacterEncoder.encodeBuffer(),
sun.misc.CharacterEncoder.readFully(),
sun.misc.UCDecoder.decodeAtom(),
sun.misc.UCDecoder.decodeBufferPrefix(),
sun.misc.UCDecoder.decodeLinePrefix(),
sun.misc.UCDecoder.decodeLineSuffix(),
sun.misc.UUDecoder.decodeAtom(),
sun.misc.UUDecoder.decodeBufferPrefix(),
sun.misc.UUDecoder.decodeBufferSuffix(),
sun.misc.UUDecoder.decodeLinePrefix(),
sun.misc.UUDecoder.decodeLineSuffix(),
sun.net.www.MessageHeader.parseHeader(),
sun.net.www.MimeEntry.launch(), sun.
security.pkcs.PKCS8Key.decode(), sun.
security.provider.IdentityDatabase.
fromStream(), sun.security.x509.X509Cert.
decode(), sun.security.x509.X509Key.
decode(), sun.tools.java.Scanner.
useInputStream()

java.io.ObjectInput: sun.rmi.server.UnicastRef.
readExternal(), sun.rmi.server.
UnicastServerRef.readExternal(),
sun.rmi.transport.LiveRef.readExternal()

java.io.ObjectOutput: sun.rmi.server.
UnicastRef.getRefClass(), sun.rmi.server.
UnicastRef.writeExternal(), sun.rmi.server.
UnicastServerRef.getRefClass(),
sun.rmi.server.UnicastServerRef.
writeExternal(), sun.rmi.transport.LiveRef.
writeExternal()

java.io.ObjectStreamClass: sun.applet.
AppletObjectInputStream.resolveClass(),

sun.rmi.server.MarshalInputStream.
resolveClass()

java.io.OutputStream: sun.misc.
BASE64Decoder.decodeAtom(),
sun.misc.BASE64Encoder.encodeAtom(),
sun.misc.CharacterDecoder.decodeAtom(),
sun.misc.CharacterDecoder.decodeBuffer(),
sun.misc.CharacterDecoder.
decodeBufferPrefix(), sun.misc.
CharacterDecoder.decodeBufferSuffix(),
sun.misc.CharacterDecoder.
decodeLinePrefix(), sun.misc.
CharacterDecoder.decodeLineSuffix(),
sun.misc.CharacterEncoder.encode(),
sun.misc.CharacterEncoder.encodeAtom(),
sun.misc.CharacterEncoder.encodeBuffer(),
sun.misc.CharacterEncoder.
encodeBufferPrefix(), sun.misc.
CharacterEncoder.encodeBufferSuffix(),
sun.misc.CharacterEncoder.
encodeLinePrefix(), sun.misc.
CharacterEncoder.encodeLineSuffix(),
sun.misc.HexDumpEncoder.encodeAtom(),
sun.misc.HexDumpEncoder.
encodeBufferPrefix(), sun.misc.
HexDumpEncoder.encodeLinePrefix(),
sun.misc.HexDumpEncoder.
encodeLineSuffix(), sun.misc.UCDecoder.
decodeAtom(), sun.misc.UCDecoder.
decodeBufferPrefix(),
sun.misc.UCDecoder.decodeLinePrefix(),
sun.misc.UCDecoder.decodeLineSuffix(),
sun.misc.UCEncoder.encodeAtom(),
sun.misc.UCEncoder.encodeBufferPrefix(),
sun.misc.UCEncoder.encodeLinePrefix(),
sun.misc.UCEncoder.encodeLineSuffix(),
sun.misc.UUDecoder.decodeAtom(),
sun.misc.UUDecoder.decodeBufferPrefix(),
sun.misc.UUDecoder.decodeBufferSuffix(),
sun.misc.UUDecoder.decodeLinePrefix(),
sun.misc.UUDecoder.decodeLineSuffix(),
sun.misc.UUEncoder.encodeAtom(), sun.
misc.UUEncoder.encodeBufferPrefix(), sun.
misc.UUEncoder.encodeBufferSuffix(), sun.
misc.UUEncoder.encodeLinePrefix(), sun.
misc.UUEncoder.encodeLineSuffix(), sun.
security.pkcs.PKCS7.encodeSignedData(),
sun.security.provider.IdentityDatabase.
save(), sun.security.x509.AlgorithmId.

encode(), sun.security.x509.X509Cert.
encode(), sun.tools.jar.Manifest.stream(),
sun.tools.jar.SignatureFile.stream(),
sun.tools.java.BinaryClass.write(),
sun.tools.javac.SourceClass.compile(),
sun.tools.javac.SourceClass.compileClass()

java.io.PrintStream: sun.applet.AppletViewer.
parse(), sun.misc.RegexpPool.print(),
sun.net.www.MessageHeader.print(),
sun.security.pkcs.PKCS10.print(),
sun.tools.asm.Assembler.listing(),
sun.tools.java.ClassDefinition.print(),
sun.tools.java.FieldDefinition.print(),
sun.tools.javac.SourceField.print(), sun.
tools.tree.ArrayAccessExpression.print(),
sun.tools.tree.AssignOpExpression.print(),
sun.tools.tree.BinaryExpression.print(),
sun.tools.tree.BooleanExpression.print(),
sun.tools.tree.BreakStatement.print(),
sun.tools.tree.ByteExpression.print(),
sun.tools.tree.CaseStatement.print(),
sun.tools.tree.CastExpression.print(),
sun.tools.tree.CatchStatement.print(),
sun.tools.tree.CharExpression.print(),
sun.tools.tree.CompoundStatement.print(),
sun.tools.tree.ConditionalExpression.print(),
sun.tools.tree.ContinueStatement.print(),
sun.tools.tree.ConvertExpression.print(),
sun.tools.tree.DeclarationStatement.print(),
sun.tools.tree.DoStatement.print(),
sun.tools.tree.DoubleExpression.print(),
sun.tools.tree.Expression.print(),
sun.tools.tree.ExpressionStatement.print(),
sun.tools.tree.FieldExpression.print(),
sun.tools.tree.FinallyStatement.print(),
sun.tools.tree.FloatExpression.print(),
sun.tools.tree.ForStatement.print(),
sun.tools.tree.IdentifierExpression.print(),
sun.tools.tree.IfStatement.print(), sun.
tools.tree.InlineMethodExpression.print(),
sun.tools.tree.InlineNewInstanceExpression.
print(), sun.tools.tree.InlineReturnStatement.
print(), sun.tools.tree.InstanceOfExpression.
print(), sun.tools.tree.IntExpression.print(),
sun.tools.tree.LongExpression.print(),
sun.tools.tree.MethodExpression.print(),
sun.tools.tree.NaryExpression.print(),
sun.tools.tree.Node.print(),
sun.tools.tree.NullExpression.print(),

sun.tools.java.Environment.
makeFieldDefinition(), sun.tools.javac.
BatchEnvironment.error(), sun.tools.javac.
BatchEnvironment.errorString(),
sun.tools.javac.BatchEnvironment.
makeFieldDefinition(), sun.tools.javac.
BatchEnvironment.reportError(),
sun.tools.serialver.SerialVer.action(),
sun.tools.serialver.SerialVerFrame.action(),
sun.tools.tree.IntExpression.equals(),
sun.tools.tree.StringExpression.equals()

java.lang.Runnable: sun.rmi.transport.
RMIThread.newThread()

java.lang.String: sun.applet.
AppletClassLoader.getResource(),
sun.applet.AppletClassLoader.
getResourceAsStream(), sun.applet.
AppletClassLoader.loadClass(),
sun.applet.AppletPanel.getParameter(), sun.
applet.AppletPanel.showAppletLog(), sun.
applet.AppletPanel.showAppletStatus(), sun.
applet.AppletResourceLoader.
getResourceAsName(),
sun.applet.AppletResourceLoader.
getResourceAsStream(),
sun.applet.AppletSecurity.checkAccept(),
sun.applet.AppletSecurity.checkConnect(),
sun.applet.AppletSecurity.checkExec(),
sun.applet.AppletSecurity.checkLink(), sun.
applet.AppletSecurity.checkPackageAccess(),
sun.applet.AppletSecurity.checkPackage
Definition(), sun.applet.AppletSecurity.
checkPropertyAccess(),
sun.applet.AppletSecurity.checkRead(), sun.
applet.AppletSecurity.checkSecurityAccess(),
sun.applet.AppletSecurity.checkWrite(),
sun.applet.AppletSecurity.debug(),
sun.applet.AppletViewer.getApplet(),
sun.applet.AppletViewer.showDocument(),
sun.applet.AppletViewer.showStatus(), sun.
applet.AppletViewerPanel.getParameter(),
sun.awt.EmbeddedFrame.setTitle(), sun.awt.
HorizBagLayout.addLayoutComponent(),
sun.awt.PlatformFont.getFontCharset(), sun.
awt.PlatformFont.makeMultiCharsetString(),
sun.awt.VerticalBagLayout.addLayout
Component(), sun.awt.image.Image.
getProperty(), sun.awt.image.
InputStreamImageSource.decoderForType(),

sun.awt.motif.MButtonPeer.setLabel(),
sun.awt.motif.MCheckboxPeer.setLabel(),
sun.awt.motif.MChoicePeer.add(),
sun.awt.motif.MChoicePeer.addItem(),
sun.awt.motif.MDialogPeer.setTitle(), sun.
awt.motif.MFileDialogPeer.handleSelected(),
sun.awt.motif.MFileDialogPeer.setDirectory(),
sun.awt.motif.MFileDialogPeer.setFile(),
sun.awt.motif.MFontPeer.getFontCharset(),
sun.awt.motif.MFramePeer.setTitle(),
sun.awt.motif.MLabelPeer.setText(),
sun.awt.motif.MListPeer.add(),
sun.awt.motif.MListPeer.addItem(),
sun.awt.motif.MMenuItemPeer.setLabel(),
sun.awt.motif.MTextAreaPeer.insert(), sun.
awt.motif.MTextAreaPeer.insertText(), sun.
awt.motif.MTextAreaPeer.replaceRange(),
sun.awt.motif.MTextAreaPeer.replaceText(),
sun.awt.motif.MTextAreaPeer.setText(),
sun.awt.motif.MTextFieldPeer.setText(),
sun.awt.motif.MTinyChoicePeer.add(),
sun.awt.motif.MTinyChoicePeer.addItem(),
sun.awt.motif.MToolkit.getFontPeer(),
sun.awt.motif.MToolkit.getImage(), sun.awt.
motif.MToolkit.getPrintJob(), sun.awt.
motif.PSGraphics.drawString(), sun.awt.
motif.PSPaperSize.find(), sun.awt.motif.
PSPrintControl.initJob(), sun.awt.motif.
UPrintDialog.setBannerString(), sun.awt.
motif.UPrintDialog.setDestString(), sun.awt.
motif.UPrintDialog.setDocumentTitle(), sun.
awt.motif.UPrintDialog.setOptionsString(),
sun.awt.motif.X11FontMetrics.stringWidth(),
sun.awt.motif.X11Graphics.drawString(),
sun.awt.motif.X11Graphics.
drawStringWidth(), sun.awt.tiny.
FileDialogFilter.accept(), sun.awt.tiny.
TinyButtonPeer.setLabel(), sun.awt.tiny.
TinyCheckboxPeer.setLabel(),
sun.awt.tiny.TinyChoicePeer.add(),
sun.awt.tiny.TinyChoicePeer.addItem(),
sun.awt.tiny.TinyDialogPeer.setTitle(), sun.
awt.tiny.TinyFileDialogPeer.setDirectory(),
sun.awt.tiny.TinyFileDialogPeer.setFile(),
sun.awt.tiny.TinyFramePeer.setTitle(),
sun.awt.tiny.TinyGraphics.drawString(),
sun.awt.tiny.TinyLabelPeer.setText(),
sun.awt.tiny.TinyListPeer.add(),
sun.awt.tiny.TinyListPeer.addItem(),

getPropertyInfo(), sun.jdbc.odbc.
JdbcOdbcDriver.getProtocol(), sun.jdbc.
odbc.JdbcOdbcDriver.getSubName(), sun.
jdbc.odbc.JdbcOdbcDriver.getSubProtocol(),
sun.jdbc.odbc.JdbcOdbcDriver.listToArray(),
sun.jdbc.odbc.JdbcOdbcObject.hexPad(),
sun.jdbc.odbc.JdbcOdbcObject.
hexPairToInt(), sun.jdbc.odbc.
JdbcOdbcObject.hexStringToByteArray(),
sun.jdbc.odbc.JdbcOdbcObject.trace(),
sun.jdbc.odbc.JdbcOdbcPreparedStatement.
executeQuery(),
sun.jdbc.odbc.JdbcOdbcPreparedStatement.
executeUpdate(),
sun.jdbc.odbc.JdbcOdbcPreparedStatement.
setChar(),
sun.jdbc.odbc.JdbcOdbcPreparedStatement.
setString(), sun.jdbc.odbc.
JdbcOdbcResultSet.findColumn(), sun.jdbc.
odbc.JdbcOdbcResultSet.getAsciiStream(),
sun.jdbc.odbc.JdbcOdbcResultSet.
getBigDecimal(), sun.jdbc.odbc.
JdbcOdbcResultSet.getBinaryStream(),
sun.jdbc.odbc.JdbcOdbcResultSet.
getBoolean(), sun.jdbc.odbc.
JdbcOdbcResultSet.getByte(), sun.jdbc.
odbc.JdbcOdbcResultSet.getBytes(),
sun.jdbc.odbc.JdbcOdbcResultSet.getDate(),
sun.jdbc.odbc.JdbcOdbcResultSet.
getDouble(), sun.jdbc.odbc.
JdbcOdbcResultSet.getFloat(), sun.jdbc.
odbc.JdbcOdbcResultSet.getInt(), sun.jdbc.
odbc.JdbcOdbcResultSet.getLong(), sun.
jdbc.odbc.JdbcOdbcResultSet.getObject(),
sun.jdbc.odbc.JdbcOdbcResultSet.getShort(),
sun.jdbc.odbc.JdbcOdbcResultSet.getString(),
sun.jdbc.odbc.JdbcOdbcResultSet.getTime(),
sun.jdbc.odbc.JdbcOdbcResultSet.
getTimestamp(), sun.jdbc.odbc.
JdbcOdbcResultSet.getUnicodeStream(), sun.
jdbc.odbc.JdbcOdbcStatement.execute(),
sun.jdbc.odbc.JdbcOdbcStatement.
executeQuery(), sun.jdbc.odbc.
JdbcOdbcStatement.executeUpdate(), sun.
jdbc.odbc.JdbcOdbcStatement.
lockIfNecessary(), sun.jdbc.odbc.
JdbcOdbcStatement.setCursorName(),
sun.jdbc.odbc.JdbcOdbcTypeInfo.
setName(), sun.misc.CharacterDecoder.
decodeBuffer(), sun.misc.MessageUtils.

subst(), sun.misc.MessageUtils.substProp(),
sun.misc.Queue.dump(),
sun.misc.RegexpPool.add(),
sun.misc.RegexpPool.delete(),
sun.misc.RegexpPool.match(),
sun.misc.RegexpPool.matchNext(),
sun.misc.RegexpPool.replace(),
sun.misc.RegexpTarget.found(),
sun.net.NetworkClient.doConnect(),
sun.net.NetworkClient.openServer(),
sun.net.ProgressEntry.setType(), sun.net.
TransferProtocolClient.sendServer(), sun.
net.URLCanonicalizer.canonicalize(), sun.
net.URLCanonicalizer.hasProtocolName(),
sun.net.URLCanonicalizer.
isSimpleHostName(), sun.net.ftp.FtpClient.
cd(), sun.net.ftp.FtpClient.get(), sun.net.ftp.
FtpClient.issueCommand(), sun.net.ftp.
FtpClient.issueCommandCheck(), sun.net.
ftp.FtpClient.login(), sun.net.ftp.FtpClient.
openDataConnection(),
sun.net.ftp.FtpClient.openServer(),
sun.net.ftp.FtpClient.put(),
sun.net.ftp.IftpClient.login(),
sun.net.ftp.IftpClient.openServer(),
sun.net.ftp.IftpClient.setProxyServer(),
sun.net.nntp.NntpClient.askServer(),
sun.net.nntp.NntpClient.getArticle(),
sun.net.nntp.NntpClient.getGroup(),
sun.net.nntp.NntpClient.getHeader(),
sun.net.nntp.NntpClient.openServer(),
sun.net.nntp.NntpClient.setGroup(),
sun.net.smtp.SmtpClient.from(),
sun.net.smtp.SmtpClient.to(),
sun.net.smtp.SmtpPrintStream.print(),
sun.net.www.HeaderParser.findInt(),
sun.net.www.HeaderParser.findValue(),
sun.net.www.MessageHeader.add(), sun.
net.www.MessageHeader.canonicalID(), sun.
net.www.MessageHeader.findNextValue(),
sun.net.www.MessageHeader.findValue(),
sun.net.www.MessageHeader.prepend(),
sun.net.www.MessageHeader.set(),
sun.net.www.MimeEntry.matches(),
sun.net.www.MimeEntry.setAction(), sun.
net.www.MimeEntry.setCommand(), sun.
net.www.MimeEntry.setDescription(), sun.
net.www.MimeEntry.setExtensions(), sun.
net.www.MimeEntry.setImageFileName(),
sun.net.www.MimeEntry.setType(),

AlgorithmId.getAlgorithmId(),
sun.security.x509.X509Cert.getVerifier(),
sun.tools.debug.DebuggerCallback.
exceptionEvent(), sun.tools.debug.
DebuggerCallback.printToConsole(), sun.
tools.debug.RemoteClass.getField(), sun.
tools.debug.RemoteClass.getFieldValue(),
sun.tools.debug.RemoteClass.getMethod(),
sun.tools.debug.RemoteClass.
getMethodLineNumber(), sun.tools.debug.
RemoteDebugger.findClass(), sun.tools.
debug.RemoteDebugger.setSourcePath(),
sun.tools.debug.RemoteObject.getField(),
sun.tools.debug.RemoteObject.
getFieldValue(), sun.tools.debug.
RemoteObject.setField(), sun.tools.debug.
RemoteStackFrame.getLocalVariable(),
sun.tools.debug.RemoteThread.
getStackVariable(),
sun.tools.debug.RemoteValue.fromHex(),
sun.tools.jar.Main.error(),
sun.tools.jar.Main.output(),
sun.tools.jar.Manifest.getEntry(),
sun.tools.jar.Manifest.isManifestName(),
sun.tools.jar.SignatureFile.add(),
sun.tools.jar.SignatureFile.getEntry(), sun.
tools.java.ArrayType.typeString(), sun.tools.
java.BinaryConstantPool.indexString(),
sun.tools.java.ClassDefinition.
containsDeprecated(),
sun.tools.java.ClassPath.getDirectory(),
sun.tools.java.ClassPath.getFile(),
sun.tools.java.ClassPath.getFiles(),
sun.tools.java.ClassType.typeString(),
sun.tools.java.Environment.error(),
sun.tools.java.Environment.
makeClassDefinition(), sun.tools.java.
Environment.makeFieldDefinition(),
sun.tools.java.Environment.output(),
sun.tools.java.Environment.
setCharacterEncoding(),
sun.tools.java.Identifier.lookup(),
sun.tools.java.MethodType.typeString(),
sun.tools.java.Package.getSourceFile(),
sun.tools.java.Parser.beginClass(),
sun.tools.java.Parser.defineField(),
sun.tools.java.Parser.parseClassBody(),
sun.tools.java.Parser.parseNamedClass(),
sun.tools.java.ParserActions.beginClass(),
sun.tools.java.ParserActions.defineField(),

sun.tools.java.Type.tType(),
sun.tools.java.Type.typeString(),
sun.tools.javac.BatchEnvironment.error(),
sun.tools.javac.BatchEnvironment.
errorString(), sun.tools.javac.
BatchEnvironment.insertError(),
sun.tools.javac.BatchEnvironment.
makeClassDefinition(), sun.tools.javac.B
atchEnvironment.makeFieldDefinition(),
sun.tools.javac.BatchEnvironment.output(),
sun.tools.javac.BatchEnvironment.
pushError(), sun.tools.javac.
BatchEnvironment.reportError(),
sun.tools.javac.BatchParser.beginClass(),
sun.tools.javac.BatchParser.defineField(),
sun.tools.javac.ErrorConsumer.pushError(),
sun.tools.javac.Main.error(),
sun.tools.javac.Main.getText(),
sun.tools.javac.Main.output(),
sun.tools.javac.Main.warning(), sun.tools.
javadoc.DocumentationGenerator.init(),
sun.tools.javadoc.Main.getText(),
sun.tools.serialver.SerialVer.I18N(),
sun.tools.tree.Expression.equals(),
sun.tools.tree.StringExpression.equals(),
sun.tools.ttydebug.TTY.exceptionEvent(),
sun.tools.ttydebug.TTY.printToConsole()

java.lang.Thread: sun.applet.
AppletSecurity.checkAccess(), sun.applet.
AppletSecurity.inThreadGroup(), sun.awt.
image.ImageFetcher.fetchloop(), sun.awt.
image.ImageFetcher.isFetcher(), sun.tools.
debug.Agent.addSystemThread(), sun.tools.
debug.Agent.removeSystemThread(),
sun.tools.debug.Agent.systemThread(),
sun.tools.debug.RemoteDebugger.
addSystemThread()

java.lang.ThreadGroup: sun.applet.
AppletSecurity.checkAccess(),
sun.applet.AppletSecurity.inThreadGroup(),
sun.misc.VM.allowThreadSuspension()

java.lang.Throwable: sun.applet.AppletPanel.
showAppletException()

java.math.BigDecimal: sun.jdbc.odbc.
JdbcOdbcPreparedStatement.
setBigDecimal(), sun.jdbc.odbc.
JdbcOdbcPreparedStatement.setDecimal()

java.math.BigInteger: sun.security.provider.
DSAKeyPairGenerator.generateKeyPair()

java.rmi.server.RemoteObject: sun.rmi.server. UnicastRef.newCall()

java.rmi.server.RemoteRef: sun.rmi.server. RemoteProxy.getStub(), sun.rmi.server. UnicastRef.remoteEquals()

java.rmi.server.UID: sun.rmi.transport. DGCAckHandler.received()

java.security.Identity: sun.security.provider. IdentityDatabase.addIdentity(), sun.security.provider.IdentityDatabase. removeIdentity(), sun.security.provider. Main.list()

java.security.IdentityScope: sun.security. provider.Main.setScope(), sun.tools.jar. JarVerifierStream.addScope(), sun.tools.jar. JarVerifierStream.removeScope()

java.security.Principal: sun.security.acl. AclEntryImpl.setPrincipal(), sun.security.acl.AclImpl.addEntry(), sun.security.acl.AclImpl.checkPermission(), sun.security.acl.AclImpl.getPermissions(), sun.security.acl.AclImpl.removeEntry(), sun.security.acl.AclImpl.setName(), sun.security.acl.GroupImpl.addMember(), sun.security.acl.GroupImpl.isMember(), sun. security.acl.GroupImpl.removeMember(), sun.security.acl.OwnerImpl.addOwner(), sun.security.acl.OwnerImpl.deleteOwner(), sun.security.acl.OwnerImpl.isOwner(), sun. security.acl.WorldGroupImpl.isMember()

java.security.PrivateKey: sun.security. provider.DSA.engineInitSign(), sun.security.x509.X509Cert.getSigner()

java.security.PublicKey: sun.security. provider.DSA.engineInitVerify(), sun.security.provider.IdentityDatabase. getIdentity(), sun.security.x509.X509Cert. verify()

java.security.SecureRandom: sun.security. provider.DSAKeyPairGenerator. generateKeyPair(), sun.security.provider. DSAKeyPairGenerator.initialize(), sun.security.x509.CertAndKeyGen. setRandom()

java.security.acl.AclEntry: sun.security.acl. AclImpl.addEntry(), sun.security.acl. AclImpl.removeEntry()

java.security.acl.Group: sun.security.acl. GroupImpl.equals()

java.security.acl.Permission: sun.security.acl. AclEntryImpl.addPermission(), sun.security. acl.AclEntryImpl.checkPermission(), sun.security.acl.AclEntryImpl. removePermission(), sun.security.acl. AclImpl.checkPermission(), sun.security.acl. AllPermissionsImpl.equals()

java.security.interfaces.DSAParams: sun. security.provider.DSAKeyPairGenerator. initialize()

java.sql.Date: sun.jdbc.odbc.JdbcOdbc. SQLBindInParameterDate(), sun.jdbc.odbc. JdbcOdbcPreparedStatement.setDate()

java.sql.SQLWarning: sun.jdbc.odbc. JdbcOdbcResultSet.setWarning(), sun.jdbc. odbc.JdbcOdbcResultSetInterface. setWarning(), sun.jdbc.odbc. JdbcOdbcStatement.setWarning()

java.sql.Statement: sun.jdbc.odbc. JdbcOdbcConnection.deregisterStatement(), sun.jdbc.odbc.JdbcOdbcConnection. registerStatement(), sun.jdbc.odbc. JdbcOdbcConnectionInterface. deregisterStatement(), sun.jdbc.odbc. JdbcOdbcResultSet.initialize()

java.sql.Time: sun.jdbc.odbc.JdbcOdbc. SQLBindInParameterTime(), sun.jdbc.odbc.JdbcOdbcPreparedStatement. setTime()

java.sql.Timestamp: sun.jdbc.odbc.JdbcOdbc. SQLBindInParameterTimestamp(), sun.jdbc. odbc.JdbcOdbcPreparedStatement.setTimes tamp()

java.util.Date: sun.security.util. DerOutputStream.putUTCTime()

java.util.Hashtable: sun.applet. AppletViewerFactory.createAppletViewer(), sun.applet.StdAppletViewerFactory. createAppletViewer(), sun.awt.image. ImageInfoGrabber.setProperties(), sun.awt. image.ImageRepresentation.setProperties(), sun.awt.image.PixelStore.setProperties(), sun.jdbc.odbc.JdbcOdbcPreparedStatement. initialize(), sun.jdbc.odbc. JdbcOdbcStatement.initialize(), sun.rmi.rmic.TopGRP.collectMethods(), sun.tools.tree.AndExpression. checkCondition(), sun.tools.tree. ArrayAccessExpression.checkAmbigName(), sun.tools.tree.ArrayAccessExpression. checkAssignOp(), sun.tools.tree. ArrayAccessExpression.checkLHS(), sun.tools.tree.ArrayAccessExpression. checkValue(), sun.tools.tree. ArrayExpression.checkInitializer(), sun. tools.tree.ArrayExpression.checkValue(), sun.tools.tree.AssignExpression. checkValue(), sun.tools.tree. AssignOpExpression.checkValue(), sun. tools.tree.BinaryAssignExpression.check(), sun.tools.tree.BinaryExpression. checkValue(), sun.tools.tree. BinaryLogicalExpression.checkCondition(), sun.tools.tree.BinaryLogicalExpression. checkValue(), sun.tools.tree. BooleanExpression.checkCondition(), sun.tools.tree.CastExpression.checkValue(), sun.tools.tree.CommaExpression.check(), sun.tools.tree.ConditionalExpression.check(), sun.tools.tree.ConditionalExpression.check Value(), sun.tools.tree.ConvertExpression. checkValue(), sun.tools.tree. ExprExpression.checkCondition(), sun.tools.tree.Expression.check(), sun.tools. tree.Expression.checkAmbigName(), sun.tools.tree.Expression.checkAssignOp(), sun.tools.tree.Expression.checkCondition(), sun.tools.tree.Expression.checkInitializer(), sun.tools.tree.Expression.checkLHS(), sun.tools.tree.Expression.checkValue(), sun.tools.tree.FieldExpression. checkAmbigName(), sun.tools.tree. FieldExpression.checkAssignOp(), sun.tools.tree.FieldExpression.checkLHS(), sun.tools.tree.FieldExpression.checkValue(), sun.tools.tree.IdentifierExpression. checkAmbigName(), sun.tools.tree. IdentifierExpression.checkAssignOp(), sun.tools.tree.IdentifierExpression. checkLHS(), sun.tools.tree. IdentifierExpression.checkValue(), sun.tools.tree.IncDecExpression.check(), sun. tools.tree.IncDecExpression.checkValue(), sun.tools.tree.InstanceOfExpression. checkValue(), sun.tools.tree. LengthExpression.checkValue(),

sun.tools.tree.MethodExpression.check(), sun.tools.tree.MethodExpression. checkValue(), sun.tools.tree. NewArrayExpression.checkValue(), sun.tools.tree.NewInstanceExpression. check(), sun.tools.tree. NewInstanceExpression.checkValue(), sun. tools.tree.NotExpression.checkCondition(), sun.tools.tree.OrExpression. checkCondition(), sun.tools.tree.Statement. checkMethod(), sun.tools.tree. SuperExpression.checkValue(), sun.tools. tree.ThisExpression.checkValue(), sun.tools. tree.TypeExpression.checkAmbigName(), sun.tools.tree.TypeExpression.checkValue(), sun.tools.tree.UnaryExpression. checkValue()

java.util.Properties: sun.awt.motif.MToolkit. getPrintJob(), sun.awt.motif.PSPrintControl. initJob(), sun.awt.tiny.TinyToolkit. getPrintJob(), sun.jdbc.odbc. JdbcOdbcConnection.initialize(), sun.jdbc. odbc.JdbcOdbcDriver.connect(), sun.jdbc. odbc.JdbcOdbcDriver.getPropertyInfo(), sun.jdbc.odbc.JdbcOdbcDriver. makeConnectionString()

java.util.Vector: sun.tools.java.Parser. parseClassBody(), sun.tools.java.Parser. parseInheritance(), sun.tools.javadoc. DocumentationGenerator.init()

sun.applet.AppletViewerFactory: sun.applet. AppletViewer.parse()

sun.awt.AWTFinalizeable: sun.awt. AWTFinalizeable.setNextFinalizeable(), sun.awt.AWTFinalizer.addFinalizeable(), sun.awt.image.ImageRepresentation. setNextFinalizeable(), sun.awt.motif. X11Graphics.setNextFinalizeable()

sun.awt.UpdateClient: sun.awt. ScreenUpdater.notify(), sun.awt. ScreenUpdater.removeClient()

sun.awt.image.ImageFetchable: sun.awt. image.ImageFetcher.add()

sun.awt.image.InputStreamImageSource: sun. awt.image.GifImageDecoder. catchupConsumer(), sun.awt.image. ImageDecoder.catchupConsumer(), sun.awt. image.JPEGImageDecoder.catchup

Consumer(), sun.awt.image.
XbmImageDecoder.catchupConsumer()

sun.awt.motif.MComponentPeer: sun.awt.
motif.MScrollPanePeer.setScrollChild()

sun.awt.tiny.TinyVerticalScrollbar: sun.awt.
tiny.TinyScrollRepeater.setScrollbar()

sun.jdbc.odbc.JdbcOdbc: sun.jdbc.odbc.
JdbcOdbcPreparedStatement.initialize(), sun.
jdbc.odbc.JdbcOdbcResultSet.initialize(),
sun.jdbc.odbc.JdbcOdbcStatement.initialize()

sun.jdbc.odbc.JdbcOdbcInputStream: sun.
jdbc.odbc.JdbcOdbcBoundCol.
setInputStream(), sun.jdbc.odbc.
JdbcOdbcResultSet.setInputStream()

sun.jdbc.odbc.JdbcOdbcSQLWarning: sun.
jdbc.odbc.JdbcOdbc.convertWarning()

sun.misc.Compare: sun.misc.Sort.quicksort()

sun.misc.Request: sun.misc.RequestProcessor.
postRequest()

sun.misc.Timer: sun.misc.Timeable.tick(),
sun.misc.TimerThread.dequeue(),
sun.misc.TimerThread.enqueue(),
sun.misc.TimerThread.requeue(),
sun.misc.TimerTickThread.call()

sun.misc.VMNotification: sun.misc.VM.
registerVMNotification()

sun.net.ProgressEntry: sun.net.ProgressData.
register(), sun.net.ProgressData.unregister(),
sun.net.ProgressData.update(),
sun.net.www.http.HttpClient.parseHTTP()

sun.net.nntp.NntpClient: sun.net.nntp.
NewsgroupInfo.reload()

sun.net.www.MessageHeader: sun.net.www.
URLConnection.setProperties(), sun.net.
www.http.HttpClient.parseHTTP(), sun.
net.www.http.HttpClient.writeRequests(),
sun.tools.jar.Manifest.addEntry(),
sun.tools.jar.Manifest.doHashes()

sun.net.www.MimeEntry: sun.net.www.
MimeTable.add(), sun.net.www.
MimeTable.remove()

sun.net.www.MimeTable: sun.net.www.
MimeEntry.launch()

sun.net.www.http.HttpClient: sun.net.www.
http.HttpClient.finished(), sun.net.www.
http.KeepAliveCache.put()

sun.net.www.protocol.http.AuthenticationInfo:
sun.net.www.protocol.http.
AuthenticationInfo.cacheInfo(), sun.net.
www.protocol.http.AuthenticationInfo.
uncacheInfo()

sun.net.www.protocol.http.HttpAuthenticator:
sun.net.www.protocol.http.
HttpURLConnection.
setDefaultAuthenticator()

sun.rmi.rmic.BatchEnvironment: sun.rmi.
rmic.TopGRP.generate()

sun.rmi.rmic.ProxyStream: sun.rmi.rmic.
GenerateMarshaling.marshalArgument(),
sun.rmi.rmic.GenerateMarshaling.
marshalArguments(), sun.rmi.rmic.
GenerateMarshaling.unmarshalArgument(),
sun.rmi.rmic.GenerateMarshaling.
unmarshalArguments()

sun.rmi.transport.Connection: sun.rmi.
transport.Channel.free(), sun.rmi.transport.
tcp.ConnectionAcceptor.accept(),
sun.rmi.transport.tcp.TCPChannel.free()

sun.rmi.transport.Endpoint: sun.rmi.
transport.DGCAckHandler.notify(), sun.
rmi.transport.Notifiable.notify(), sun.
rmi.transport.Notifier.addNotifiable(), sun.
rmi.transport.Notifier.removeNotifiable(),
sun.rmi.transport.Transport.getChannel(),
sun.rmi.transport.tcp.TCPChannel.
addNotifiable(), sun.rmi.transport.tcp.
TCPChannel.removeNotifiable(),
sun.rmi.transport.tcp.TCPTransport.
getChannel()

sun.rmi.transport.Notifiable: sun.rmi.
transport.Notifier.addNotifiable(), sun.rmi.
transport.Notifier.removeNotifiable(),
sun.rmi.transport.tcp.TCPChannel.
addNotifiable(), sun.rmi.transport.tcp.
TCPChannel.removeNotifiable()

sun.rmi.transport.Target: sun.rmi.transport.
Endpoint.exportObject(),
sun.rmi.transport.LiveRef.exportObject(),
sun.rmi.transport.Transport.exportObject(),
sun.rmi.transport.tcp.TCPEndpoint.
exportObject(), sun.rmi.transport.tcp.
TCPTransport.exportObject()

sun.tools.tree.NegativeExpression.
codeValue(), sun.tools.tree.
NewArrayExpression.codeValue(), sun.
tools.tree.NewInstanceExpression.code(),
sun.tools.tree.NewInstanceExpression.
codeValue(), sun.tools.tree.NullExpression.
codeValue(), sun.tools.tree.
PostDecExpression.code(), sun.tools.tree.
PostDecExpression.codeValue(), sun.tools.
tree.PostIncExpression.code(), sun.tools.
tree.PostIncExpression.codeValue(),
sun.tools.tree.PreDecExpression.code(), sun.
tools.tree.PreDecExpression.codeValue(),
sun.tools.tree.PreIncExpression.code(),
sun.tools.tree.PreIncExpression.codeValue(),
sun.tools.tree.ReturnStatement.code(),
sun.tools.tree.Statement.code(),
sun.tools.tree.StringExpression.codeValue(),
sun.tools.tree.SwitchStatement.code(),
sun.tools.tree.SynchronizedStatement.code(),
sun.tools.tree.ThisExpression.codeValue(),
sun.tools.tree.ThrowStatement.code(), sun.
tools.tree.TryStatement.code(), sun.tools.
tree.UplevelReference.codeArguments(),
sun.tools.tree.UplevelReference.
codeInitialization(), sun.tools.tree.
VarDeclarationStatement.code(),
sun.tools.tree.WhileStatement.code()

sun.tools.asm.ConstantPool: sun.tools.asm.
Assembler.collect(), sun.tools.asm.
Assembler.write(), sun.tools.asm.Assembler.
writeCoverageTable(), sun.tools.asm.
Assembler.writeLineNumberTable(),
sun.tools. asm.Assembler.
writeLocalVariableTable()

sun.tools.asm.Instruction: sun.tools.asm.
Assembler.add()

sun.tools.asm.Label: sun.tools.asm.
SwitchData.add()

sun.tools.debug.RemoteField: sun.tools.debug.
RemoteClass.clearBreakpointMethod(),
sun.tools.debug.RemoteClass.
setBreakpointMethod()

sun.tools.debug.RemoteObject: sun.tools.
debug.RemoteObject.setField()

sun.tools.debug.RemoteThread: sun.tools.
debug.DebuggerCallback.breakpointEvent(),
sun.tools.debug.DebuggerCallback.

exceptionEvent(), sun.tools.debug.
DebuggerCallback.threadDeathEvent(),
sun.tools.ttydebug.TTY.breakpointEvent(),
sun.tools.ttydebug.TTY.exceptionEvent(),
sun.tools.ttydebug.TTY.threadDeathEvent()

sun.tools.debug.RemoteThreadGroup: sun.
tools.debug.RemoteDebugger.
listThreadGroups()

sun.tools.java.BinaryConstantPool: sun.tools.
java.BinaryCode.load()

sun.tools.java.BinaryField: sun.tools.java.
BinaryCode.load()

sun.tools.java.ClassDeclaration: sun.tools.
java.BinaryClass.addDependency(),
sun.tools.java.ClassDefinition.
addDependency(), sun.tools.java.
ClassDefinition.canAccess(), sun.tools.java.
ClassDefinition.implementedBy(), sun.tools.
java.ClassDefinition.subClassOf(), sun.
tools.java.ClassDefinition.superClassOf(),
sun.tools.java.Environment.loadDefinition(),
sun.tools.javac.BatchEnvironment.
loadDefinition(), sun.tools.javac.
SourceClass.addDependency(), sun.tools.
javadoc.DocumentationGenerator.
getClassDefinition()

sun.tools.java.ClassDefinition: sun.rmi.rmic.
TopGRP.collectMethods(), sun.rmi.rmic.
TopGRP.generate(), sun.rmi.rmic.TopGRP.
remotable(), sun.rmi.rmic.TopGRP.
streamName(), sun.tools.asm.Assembler.
GenVecJCov(), sun.tools.asm.Assembler.
writeCoverageTable(), sun.tools.java.
ClassDeclaration.setDefinition(), sun.tools.
java.ClassDefinition.checkLocalClass(), sun.
tools.java.ClassDefinition.enclosingClassOf(),
sun.tools.java.ClassDefinition.
matchMethod(), sun.tools.java.
ClassDefinition.noteUsedBy(), sun.tools.
java.ClassDefinition.setOuterClass(),
sun.tools.java.Environment.
makeClassDefinition(), sun.tools.java.
Environment.makeFieldDefinition(),
sun.tools.java.Environment.resolve(),
sun.tools.java.Environment.resolveNames(),
sun.tools.java.Parser.defineField(),
sun.tools.java.Parser.endClass(),
sun.tools.java.Parser.recoverField(),

sun.tools.java.FieldDefinition.isInlineable(),
sun.tools.java.FieldDefinition.
reportDeprecated(), sun.tools.java.
FieldDefinition.resolveTypeStructure(),
sun.tools.java.Imports.forceResolve(),
sun.tools.java.Imports.newEnvironment(),
sun.tools.java.Imports.resolve(),
sun.tools.javac.BatchEnvironment.
makeClassDefinition(), sun.tools.javac.
BatchEnvironment.makeFieldDefinition(),
sun.tools.javac.SourceClass.addField(),
sun.tools.javac.SourceClass.basicCheck(),
sun.tools.javac.SourceClass.check(), sun.
tools.javac.SourceClass.checkInsideClass(),
sun.tools.javac.SourceClass.
checkLocalClass(), sun.tools.javac.
SourceClass.checkSourceFile(), sun.tools.
javac.SourceClass.compileClass(), sun.tools.
javac.SourceClass.inlineLocalClass(),
sun.tools.javac.SourceClass.noteUsedBy(),
sun.tools.javac.SourceClass.
reportDeprecated(), sun.tools.javac.
SourceClass.resolveSupers(), sun.tools.
javac.SourceClass.resolveTypeStructure(),
sun.tools.javac.SourceClass.setupEnv(),
sun.tools.javac.SourceField.check(),
sun.tools.javac.SourceField.code(),
sun.tools.javac.SourceField.codeInit(),
sun.tools.javac.SourceField.getExceptions(),
sun.tools.javac.SourceField.getValue(), sun.
tools.javac.SourceField.isInlineable(), sun.
tools.javac.SourceField.reportDeprecated(),
sun.tools.javac.SourceField.
resolveTypeStructure(), sun.tools.tree.
AddExpression.codeValue(), sun.tools.tree.
AddExpression.costInline(), sun.tools.tree.
AndExpression.checkCondition(),
sun.tools.tree.ArrayAccessExpression.
checkAmbigName(), sun.tools.tree.
ArrayAccessExpression.checkAssignOp(),
sun.tools.tree.ArrayAccessExpression.
checkLHS(), sun.tools.tree.
ArrayAccessExpression.checkValue(),
sun.tools.tree.ArrayAccessExpression.
codeValue(), sun.tools.tree.
ArrayAccessExpression.costInline(), sun.
tools.tree.ArrayAccessExpression.inline(),
sun.tools.tree.ArrayAccessExpression.
inlineLHS(), sun.tools.tree.
ArrayAccessExpression.inlineValue(),

sun.tools.tree.ArrayExpression.
checkInitializer(), sun.tools.tree.
ArrayExpression.checkValue(),
sun.tools.tree.ArrayExpression.codeValue(),
sun.tools.tree.ArrayExpression.inline(), sun.
tools.tree.ArrayExpression.inlineValue(), sun.
tools.tree.AssignAddExpression.costInline(),
sun.tools.tree.AssignExpression.
checkValue(), sun.tools.tree.
AssignExpression.code(), sun.tools.tree.
AssignExpression.codeValue(),
sun.tools.tree.AssignExpression.costInline(),
sun.tools.tree.AssignOpExpression.
checkValue(), sun.tools.tree.
AssignOpExpression.code(), sun.tools.tree.
AssignOpExpression.codeValue(), sun.tools.
tree.AssignOpExpression.costInline(), sun.
tools.tree.AssignOpExpression.inlineValue(),
sun.tools.tree.BinaryAssignExpression.
check(), sun.tools.tree.
BinaryAssignExpression.costInline(), sun.
tools.tree.BinaryAssignExpression.inline(),
sun.tools.tree.BinaryAssignExpression.
inlineValue(), sun.tools.tree.
BinaryBitExpression.codeValue(), sun.tools.
tree.BinaryExpression.checkValue(), sun.
tools.tree.BinaryExpression.codeValue(),
sun.tools.tree.BinaryExpression.costInline(),
sun.tools.tree.BinaryExpression.inline(), sun.
tools.tree.BinaryExpression.inlineValue(),
sun.tools.tree.BinaryLogicalExpression.
checkCondition(), sun.tools.tree.
BinaryLogicalExpression.checkValue(), sun.
tools.tree.BinaryLogicalExpression.inline(),
sun.tools.tree.BitNotExpression.
codeValue(), sun.tools.tree.
BooleanExpression.checkCondition(), sun.
tools.tree.BooleanExpression.codeValue(),
sun.tools.tree.BreakStatement.code(),
sun.tools.tree.BreakStatement.costInline(),
sun.tools.tree.CaseStatement.costInline(),
sun.tools.tree.CastExpression.checkValue(),
sun.tools.tree.CastExpression.costInline(),
sun.tools.tree.CastExpression.inline(),
sun.tools.tree.CastExpression.inlineValue(),
sun.tools.tree.CatchStatement.code(),
sun.tools.tree.CatchStatement.inline(),
sun.tools.tree.CommaExpression.check(),
sun.tools.tree.CommaExpression.code(),
sun.tools.tree.CommaExpression.

DocumentationGenerator.
getReferenceName(), sun.tools.tree.Context.
getApparentClassName(), sun.tools.tree.
Context.getApparentField(), sun.tools.tree.
Context.getBreakContext(), sun.tools.tree.
Context.getContinueContext(), sun.tools.
tree.Context.getField(), sun.tools.tree.
Context.getLabelContext(), sun.tools.tree.
Context.getLocalClass(), sun.tools.tree.
Context.getLocalField(), sun.tools.tree.
ContextEnvironment.resolveName(),
sun.tools.tree.Expression.equals(),
sun.tools.tree.IdentifierExpression.equals(),
sun.tools.tree.Statement.hasLabel()

sun.tools.java.IdentifierToken: sun.tools.java.
Environment.makeClassDefinition(), sun.
tools.java.IdentifierToken.getWhere(),
sun.tools.java.Imports.addClass(),
sun.tools.java.Imports.addPackage(),
sun.tools.java.Parser.beginClass(),
sun.tools.java.Parser.defineField(),
sun.tools.java.Parser.importClass(),
sun.tools.java.Parser.importPackage(),
sun.tools.java.Parser.packageDeclaration(),
sun.tools.java.Parser.parseClassBody(),
sun.tools.java.ParserActions.beginClass(),
sun.tools.java.ParserActions.defineField(),
sun.tools.java.ParserActions.importClass(),
sun.tools.java.ParserActions.importPackage(),
sun.tools.java.ParserActions.
packageDeclaration(), sun.tools.javac.
BatchEnvironment.makeClassDefinition(),
sun.tools.javac.BatchParser.beginClass(),
sun.tools.javac.BatchParser.defineField(),
sun.tools.javac.BatchParser.importClass(),
sun.tools.javac.BatchParser.importPackage(),
sun.tools.javac.BatchParser.
packageDeclaration()

sun.tools.java.Type: sun.rmi.rmic.
GenerateMarshaling.marshalArgument(),
sun.rmi.rmic.GenerateMarshaling.
unmarshalArgument(), sun.tools.java.
ClassDefinition.findMethod(), sun.tools.
java.ClassDefinition.protectedAccess(), sun.
tools.java.Environment.classExists(), sun.
tools.java.Environment.explicitCast(),
sun.tools.java.Environment.
getClassDeclaration(), sun.tools.java.
Environment.getClassDefinition(),

sun.tools.java.Environment.implicitCast(),
sun.tools.java.Environment.isMoreSpecific(),
sun.tools.java.Environment.
makeFieldDefinition(), sun.tools.java.
Environment.resolve(), sun.tools.java.
Environment.resolveNames(), sun.tools.
java.MethodType.equalArguments(),
sun.tools.java.Parser.defineField(),
sun.tools.java.Parser.parseArrayBrackets(),
sun.tools.java.ParserActions.defineField(),
sun.tools.java.Type.equalArguments(),
sun.tools.java.Type.tArray(), sun.tools.java.
Type.tMethod(), sun.tools.javac.
BatchEnvironment.getClassDeclaration(),
sun.tools.javac.BatchEnvironment.
makeFieldDefinition(), sun.tools.javac.
BatchParser.defineField(), sun.tools.tree.
ArrayExpression.checkInitializer(),
sun.tools.tree.Expression.checkInitializer(),
sun.tools.tree.Expression.fitsType(),
sun.tools.tree.IntegerExpression.fitsType(),
sun.tools.tree.Node.convert()

sun.tools.tree.ConditionVars: sun.tools.tree.
AndExpression.checkCondition(),
sun.tools.tree.BinaryLogicalExpression.
checkCondition(), sun.tools.tree.
BooleanExpression.checkCondition(), sun.
tools.tree.ExprExpression.checkCondition(),
sun.tools.tree.Expression.checkCondition(),
sun.tools.tree.NotExpression.
checkCondition(), sun.tools.tree.
OrExpression.checkCondition()

sun.tools.tree.Context: sun.tools.java.
ClassDefinition.checkLocalClass(), sun.
tools.java.ClassDefinition.getAccessField(),
sun.tools.java.FieldDefinition.check(),
sun.tools.java.FieldDefinition.codeInit(),
sun.tools.java.FieldDefinition.
getAccessUpdateField(), sun.tools.javac.
SourceClass.checkInsideClass(), sun.tools.
javac.SourceClass.checkLocalClass(),
sun.tools.javac.SourceField.check(),
sun.tools.javac.SourceField.codeInit(), sun.
tools.tree.AddExpression.codeValue(), sun.
tools.tree.AddExpression.costInline(), sun.
tools.tree.AndExpression.checkCondition(),
sun.tools.tree.ArrayAccessExpression.
checkAmbigName(), sun.tools.tree.
ArrayAccessExpression.checkAssignOp(),

sun.tools.tree.ArrayAccessExpression.
checkLHS(), sun.tools.tree.
ArrayAccessExpression.checkValue(),
sun.tools.tree.ArrayAccessExpression.
codeValue(), sun.tools.tree.
ArrayAccessExpression.copyInline(), sun.
tools.tree.ArrayAccessExpression.costInline(),
sun.tools.tree.ArrayAccessExpression.inline(),
sun.tools.tree.ArrayAccessExpression.
inlineLHS(), sun.tools.tree.
ArrayAccessExpression.inlineValue(), sun.
tools.tree.ArrayExpression.checkInitializer(),
sun.tools.tree.ArrayExpression.checkValue(),
sun.tools.tree.ArrayExpression.codeValue(),
sun.tools.tree.ArrayExpression.inline(),
sun.tools.tree.ArrayExpression.inlineValue(),
sun.tools.tree.AssignAddExpression.
costInline(), sun.tools.tree.
AssignExpression.checkValue(), sun.tools.
tree.AssignExpression.code(), sun.tools.tree.
AssignExpression.codeValue(), sun.tools.
tree.AssignExpression.costInline(), sun.
tools.tree.AssignOpExpression.checkValue(),
sun.tools.tree.AssignOpExpression.code(),
sun.tools.tree.AssignOpExpression.
codeValue(), sun.tools.tree.
AssignOpExpression.copyInline(), sun.tools.
tree.AssignOpExpression.costInline(), sun.
tools.tree.AssignOpExpression.inlineValue(),
sun.tools.tree.BinaryAssignExpression.
check(), sun.tools.tree.
BinaryAssignExpression.copyInline(),
sun.tools.tree.BinaryAssignExpression.
costInline(), sun.tools.tree.
BinaryAssignExpression.inline(), sun.tools.
tree.BinaryAssignExpression.inlineValue(),
sun.tools.tree.BinaryBitExpression.
codeValue(), sun.tools.tree.
BinaryExpression.checkValue(), sun.tools.
tree.BinaryExpression.codeValue(), sun.
tools.tree.BinaryExpression.copyInline(),
sun.tools.tree.BinaryExpression.costInline(),
sun.tools.tree.BinaryExpression.inline(),
sun.tools.tree.BinaryExpression.inlineValue(),
sun.tools.tree.BinaryLogicalExpression.
checkCondition(), sun.tools.tree.
BinaryLogicalExpression.checkValue(),
sun.tools.tree.BinaryLogicalExpression.
inline(), sun.tools.tree.BitNotExpression.
codeValue(), sun.tools.tree.

BooleanExpression.checkCondition(), sun.
tools.tree.BooleanExpression.codeValue(),
sun.tools.tree.BreakStatement.code(),
sun.tools.tree.BreakStatement.costInline(),
sun.tools.tree.CaseStatement.costInline(),
sun.tools.tree.CastExpression.checkValue(),
sun.tools.tree.CastExpression.costInline(),
sun.tools.tree.CastExpression.inline(),
sun.tools.tree.CastExpression.inlineValue(),
sun.tools.tree.CatchStatement.code(),
sun.tools.tree.CatchStatement.copyInline(),
sun.tools.tree.CatchStatement.inline(),
sun.tools.tree.CommaExpression.check(),
sun.tools.tree.CommaExpression.code(),
sun.tools.tree.CommaExpression.
codeValue(), sun.tools.tree.
CommaExpression.inline(), sun.tools.tree.
CommaExpression.inlineValue(), sun.tools.
tree.CompoundStatement.code(), sun.tools.
tree.CompoundStatement.copyInline(), sun.
tools.tree.CompoundStatement.costInline(),
sun.tools.tree.CompoundStatement.inline(),
sun.tools.tree.ConditionalExpression.
check(), sun.tools.tree.
ConditionalExpression.checkValue(), sun.
tools.tree.ConditionalExpression.code(),
sun.tools.tree.ConditionalExpression.
codeValue(), sun.tools.tree.
ConditionalExpression.copyInline(), sun.
tools.tree.ConditionalExpression.costInline(),
sun.tools.tree.ConditionalExpression.
inline(), sun.tools.tree.ConditionalExpression.
inlineValue(), sun.tools.tree.Context.
newEnvironment(), sun.tools.tree.
ContinueStatement.code(), sun.tools.tree.
ContinueStatement.costInline(), sun.tools.
tree.ConvertExpression.checkValue(), sun.
tools.tree.ConvertExpression.codeValue(),
sun.tools.tree.ConvertExpression.inline(),
sun.tools.tree.DeclarationStatement.code(),
sun.tools.tree.DeclarationStatement.inline(),
sun.tools.tree.DivRemExpression.inline(),
sun.tools.tree.DoStatement.code(),
sun.tools.tree.DoStatement.copyInline(),
sun.tools.tree.DoStatement.costInline(),
sun.tools.tree.DoStatement.inline(), sun.
tools.tree.DoubleExpression.codeValue(),
sun.tools.tree.ExprExpression.
checkCondition(), sun.tools.tree.Expression.
check(), sun.tools.tree.Expression.

checkAmbigName(), sun.tools.tree.
Expression.checkAssignOp(), sun.tools.tree.
Expression.checkCondition(), sun.tools.
tree.Expression.checkInitializer(),
sun.tools.tree.Expression.checkLHS(),
sun.tools.tree.Expression.checkValue(),
sun.tools.tree.Expression.code(),
sun.tools.tree.Expression.codeValue(),
sun.tools.tree.Expression.copyInline(),
sun.tools.tree.Expression.costInline(),
sun.tools.tree.Expression.inline(),
sun.tools.tree.Expression.inlineLHS(),
sun.tools.tree.Expression.inlineValue(),
sun.tools.tree.ExpressionStatement.code(),
sun.tools.tree.ExpressionStatement.
copyInline(), sun.tools.tree.
ExpressionStatement.costInline(), sun.tools.
tree.ExpressionStatement.inline(), sun.tools.
tree.FieldExpression.checkAmbigName(),
sun.tools.tree.FieldExpression.
checkAssignOp(), sun.tools.tree.
FieldExpression.checkFinalAssign(),
sun.tools.tree.FieldExpression.checkLHS(),
sun.tools.tree.FieldExpression.checkValue(),
sun.tools.tree.FieldExpression.codeValue(),
sun.tools.tree.FieldExpression.copyInline(),
sun.tools.tree.FieldExpression.costInline(),
sun.tools.tree.FieldExpression.inline(),
sun.tools.tree.FieldExpression.inlineLHS(),
sun.tools.tree.FieldExpression.inlineValue(),
sun.tools.tree.FinallyStatement.code(),
sun.tools.tree.FinallyStatement.copyInline(),
sun.tools.tree.FinallyStatement.inline(),
sun.tools.tree.FloatExpression.codeValue(),
sun.tools.tree.ForStatement.code(),
sun.tools.tree.ForStatement.copyInline(),
sun.tools.tree.ForStatement.costInline(),
sun.tools.tree.ForStatement.inline(),
sun.tools.tree.IdentifierExpression.
checkAmbigName(), sun.tools.tree.
IdentifierExpression.checkAssignOp(), sun.
tools.tree.IdentifierExpression.checkLHS(),
sun.tools.tree.IdentifierExpression.
checkValue(), sun.tools.tree.
IdentifierExpression.codeValue(), sun.tools.
tree.IdentifierExpression.copyInline(), sun.
tools.tree.IdentifierExpression.costInline(),
sun.tools.tree.IdentifierExpression.inline(),
sun.tools.tree.IdentifierExpression.
inlineLHS(), sun.tools.tree.

IdentifierExpression.inlineValue(),
sun.tools.tree.IfStatement.code(),
sun.tools.tree.IfStatement.copyInline(),
sun.tools.tree.IfStatement.costInline(),
sun.tools.tree.IfStatement.inline(), sun.tools.
tree.IncDecExpression.check(), sun.tools.
tree.IncDecExpression.checkValue(), sun.
tools.tree.IncDecExpression.inline(), sun.
tools.tree.IncDecExpression.inlineValue(),
sun.tools.tree.InlineMethodExpression.
code(), sun.tools.tree.
InlineMethodExpression.codeValue(),
sun.tools.tree.InlineMethodExpression.
copyInline(), sun.tools.tree.
InlineMethodExpression.inline(), sun.tools.
tree.InlineMethodExpression.inlineValue(),
sun.tools.tree.InlineNewInstanceExpression.
code(), sun.tools.tree.
InlineNewInstanceExpression.codeValue(),
sun.tools.tree.InlineNewInstanceExpression.
copyInline(), sun.tools.tree.
InlineNewInstanceExpression.inline(),
sun.tools.tree.InlineNewInstanceExpression.
inlineValue(), sun.tools.tree.
InlineReturnStatement.code(), sun.tools.
tree.InlineReturnStatement.copyInline(),
sun.tools.tree.InlineReturnStatement.
costInline(), sun.tools.tree.
InlineReturnStatement.inline(), sun.tools.
tree.InstanceOfExpression.checkValue(),
sun.tools.tree.InstanceOfExpression.code(),
sun.tools.tree.InstanceOfExpression.
codeValue(), sun.tools.tree.
InstanceOfExpression.costInline(), sun.tools.
tree.InstanceOfExpression.inline(), sun.
tools.tree.InstanceOfExpression.inlineValue(),
sun.tools.tree.IntegerExpression.codeValue(),
sun.tools.tree.LengthExpression.checkValue(),
sun.tools.tree.LengthExpression.codeValue(),
sun.tools.tree.LocalField.copyArguments(),
sun.tools.tree.LocalField.copyInline(), sun.
tools.tree.LocalField.doneWithArguments(),
sun.tools.tree.LocalField.
getCurrentInlineCopy(), sun.tools.tree.
LocalField.getNumber(), sun.tools.tree.
LongExpression.codeValue(), sun.tools.tree.
MethodExpression.check(), sun.tools.tree.
MethodExpression.checkValue(), sun.tools.
tree.MethodExpression.codeValue(), sun.
tools.tree.MethodExpression.copyInline(),

sun.tools.tree.MethodExpression.costInline(),
sun.tools.tree.MethodExpression.inline(), sun.
tools.tree.MethodExpression.inlineValue(),
sun.tools.tree.NaryExpression.copyInline(),
sun.tools.tree.NaryExpression.costInline(),
sun.tools.tree.NegativeExpression.
codeValue(), sun.tools.tree.
NewArrayExpression.checkValue(), sun.
tools.tree.NewArrayExpression.codeValue(),
sun.tools.tree.NewArrayExpression.
copyInline(), sun.tools.tree.
NewArrayExpression.inline(), sun.tools.
tree.NewArrayExpression.inlineValue(), sun.
tools.tree.NewInstanceExpression.check(),
sun.tools.tree.NewInstanceExpression.
checkValue(), sun.tools.tree.
NewInstanceExpression.code(), sun.tools.
tree.NewInstanceExpression.codeValue(),
sun.tools.tree.NewInstanceExpression.
copyInline(), sun.tools.tree.
NewInstanceExpression.costInline(), sun.
tools.tree.NewInstanceExpression.inline(),
sun.tools.tree.NewInstanceExpression.
inlineValue(), sun.tools.tree.
NewInstanceExpression.insertOuterLink(),
sun.tools.tree.Node.convert(), sun.tools.
tree.NotExpression.checkCondition(), sun.
tools.tree.NullExpression.codeValue(), sun.
tools.tree.OrExpression.checkCondition(),
sun.tools.tree.PostDecExpression.code(), sun.
tools.tree.PostDecExpression.codeValue(),
sun.tools.tree.PostIncExpression.code(), sun.
tools.tree.PostIncExpression.codeValue(),
sun.tools.tree.PreDecExpression.code(), sun.
tools.tree.PreDecExpression.codeValue(),
sun.tools.tree.PreIncExpression.code(),
sun.tools.tree.PreIncExpression.codeValue(),
sun.tools.tree.ReturnStatement.code(),
sun.tools.tree.ReturnStatement.copyInline(),
sun.tools.tree.ReturnStatement.costInline(),
sun.tools.tree.ReturnStatement.inline(),
sun.tools.tree.Statement.checkMethod(),
sun.tools.tree.Statement.code(),
sun.tools.tree.Statement.copyInline(),
sun.tools.tree.Statement.costInline(),
sun.tools.tree.Statement.inline(),
sun.tools.tree.StringExpression.codeValue(),
sun.tools.tree.SuperExpression.checkValue(),
sun.tools.tree.SuperExpression.copyInline(),
sun.tools.tree.SwitchStatement.code(),

sun.tools.tree.SwitchStatement.copyInline(),
sun.tools.tree.SwitchStatement.costInline(),
sun.tools.tree.SwitchStatement.inline(), sun.
tools.tree.SynchronizedStatement.code(),
sun.tools.tree.SynchronizedStatement.
copyInline(), sun.tools.tree.
SynchronizedStatement.inline(),
sun.tools.tree.ThisExpression.checkValue(),
sun.tools.tree.ThisExpression.codeValue(),
sun.tools.tree.ThisExpression.copyInline(),
sun.tools.tree.ThisExpression.inlineValue(),
sun.tools.tree.ThrowStatement.code(),
sun.tools.tree.ThrowStatement.copyInline(),
sun.tools.tree.ThrowStatement.costInline(),
sun.tools.tree.ThrowStatement.inline(),
sun.tools.tree.TryStatement.code(), sun.
tools.tree.TryStatement.copyInline(), sun.
tools.tree.TryStatement.inline(), sun.tools.
tree.TypeExpression.checkAmbigName(),
sun.tools.tree.TypeExpression.checkValue(),
sun.tools.tree.TypeExpression.inline(), sun.
tools.tree.UnaryExpression.checkValue(),
sun.tools.tree.UnaryExpression.copyInline(),
sun.tools.tree.UnaryExpression.costInline(),
sun.tools.tree.UnaryExpression.inline(), sun.
tools.tree.UnaryExpression.inlineValue(),
sun.tools.tree.UplevelReference.
codeArguments(), sun.tools.tree.
UplevelReference.codeInitialization(),
sun.tools.tree.UplevelReference.
localArgumentAvailable(), sun.tools.tree.
UplevelReference.makeFieldReference(),
sun.tools.tree.UplevelReference.
makeLocalReference(), sun.tools.tree.
UplevelReference.noteReference(), sun.tools.
tree.UplevelReference.willCodeArguments(),
sun.tools.tree.VarDeclarationStatement.
code(), sun.tools.tree.
VarDeclarationStatement.copyInline(),
sun.tools.tree.VarDeclarationStatement.
costInline(), sun.tools.tree.
VarDeclarationStatement.inline(),
sun.tools.tree.WhileStatement.code(),
sun.tools.tree.WhileStatement.copyInline(),
sun.tools.tree.WhileStatement.costInline(),
sun.tools.tree.WhileStatement.inline()

sun.tools.tree.Expression: sun.tools.java.Parser.
parseBinaryExpression(), sun.tools.java.
Parser.parseDeclaration(), sun.tools.java.
Parser.parseMethodExpression(), sun.tools.

java.Parser.parseNewInstanceExpression(),
sun.tools.java.Parser.topLevelExpression(),
sun.tools.tree.ArrayAccessExpression.
checkAssignOp(), sun.tools.tree.Expression.
checkAssignOp(), sun.tools.tree.
FieldExpression.checkAssignOp(),
sun.tools.tree.FieldExpression.toIdentifier(),
sun.tools.tree.IdentifierExpression.
checkAssignOp(), sun.tools.tree.
NewInstanceExpression.insertOuterLink(),
sun.tools.tree.Node.convert(),
sun.tools.tree.Statement.setLabel()

sun.tools.tree.LocalField: sun.tools.java.
ClassDefinition.addReference(), sun.tools.
java.ClassDefinition.getReference(),
sun.tools.tree.Context.declare(),
sun.tools.tree.Context.isInScope(),
sun.tools.tree.Context.makeReference(),
sun.tools.tree.Context.noteReference()

sun.tools.tree.Node: sun.tools.java.
FieldDefinition.setValue(),
sun.tools.java.Parser.addArgument(),
sun.tools.java.Parser.defineField(),
sun.tools.java.ParserActions.defineField(),
sun.tools.javac.BatchParser.defineField()

sun.tools.tree.Statement: sun.tools.tree.
CompoundStatement.insertStatement(),
sun.tools.tree.Context.checkBackBranch(),
sun.tools.tree.Statement.eliminate(),
sun.tools.tree.Statement.insertStatement()

sun.tools.tree.UnaryExpression: sun.tools.tree.
ArrayAccessExpression.checkAmbigName(),
sun.tools.tree.Expression.checkAmbigName(),
sun.tools.tree.FieldExpression.
checkAmbigName(), sun.tools.tree.
IdentifierExpression.checkAmbigName(),
sun.tools.tree.TypeExpression.
checkAmbigName()

sun.tools.tree.UplevelReference: sun.tools.
tree.UplevelReference.insertInto(), sun.
tools.tree.UplevelReference.isEarlierThan()

sun.tools.tree.Vset: sun.tools.java.
ClassDefinition.checkLocalClass(), sun.
tools.java.FieldDefinition.check(), sun.tools.
javac.SourceClass.checkInsideClass(), sun.
tools.javac.SourceClass.checkLocalClass(),
sun.tools.javac.SourceField.check(), sun.
tools.tree.AndExpression.checkCondition(),
sun.tools.tree.ArrayAccessExpression.

checkAmbigName(), sun.tools.tree.
ArrayAccessExpression.checkAssignOp(),
sun.tools.tree.ArrayAccessExpression.
checkLHS(), sun.tools.tree.
ArrayAccessExpression.checkValue(), sun.
tools.tree.ArrayExpression.checkInitializer(),
sun.tools.tree.ArrayExpression.checkValue(),
sun.tools.tree.AssignExpression.checkValue(),
sun.tools.tree.AssignOpExpression.
checkValue(), sun.tools.tree.
BinaryAssignExpression.check(), sun.tools.
tree.BinaryExpression.checkValue(),
sun.tools.tree.BinaryLogicalExpression.
checkCondition(), sun.tools.tree.
BinaryLogicalExpression.checkValue(),
sun.tools.tree.BooleanExpression.
checkCondition(), sun.tools.tree.
CastExpression.checkValue(), sun.tools.
tree.CommaExpression.check(), sun.tools.
tree.ConditionalExpression.check(), sun.tools.
tree.ConditionalExpression.checkValue(),
sun.tools.tree.Context.checkBackBranch(),
sun.tools.tree.Context.removeAdditional
Vars(), sun.tools.tree.ConvertExpression.
checkValue(), sun.tools.tree.ExprExpression.
checkCondition(), sun.tools.tree.Expression.
check(), sun.tools.tree.Expression.
checkAmbigName(), sun.tools.tree.
Expression.checkAssignOp(), sun.tools.tree.
Expression.checkCondition(), sun.tools.tree.
Expression.checkInitializer(), sun.tools.tree.
Expression.checkLHS(), sun.tools.tree.
Expression.checkValue(), sun.tools.tree.
FieldExpression.checkAmbigName(), sun.
tools.tree.FieldExpression.checkAssignOp(),
sun.tools.tree.FieldExpression.
checkFinalAssign(), sun.tools.tree.
FieldExpression.checkLHS(), sun.tools.tree.
FieldExpression.checkValue(), sun.tools.tree.
IdentifierExpression.checkAmbigName(),
sun.tools.tree.IdentifierExpression.
checkAssignOp(), sun.tools.tree.
IdentifierExpression.checkLHS(), sun.tools.
tree.IdentifierExpression.checkValue(), sun.
tools.tree.IncDecExpression.check(), sun.
tools.tree.IncDecExpression.checkValue(),
sun.tools.tree.InstanceOfExpression.
checkValue(), sun.tools.tree.
LengthExpression.checkValue(), sun.tools.
tree.MethodExpression.check(), sun.tools.

SUN CLASS HIERARCHY DIAGRAMS

G

*T*his appendix contains class hierarchy diagrams for the sun packages discussed in this book and a few more besides. In these diagrams, classes appear as rectangles containing the class names. Concrete classes are white; abstract classes are gray. Interfaces appear as rounded rectangles. A solid arrow connects the superclass to the subclass. A dashed arrow connects an interface to the class or classes that implement it. Each shape includes the name of the class or interface it represents. If a class is not a member of the package being diagrammed, then the package name also appears.

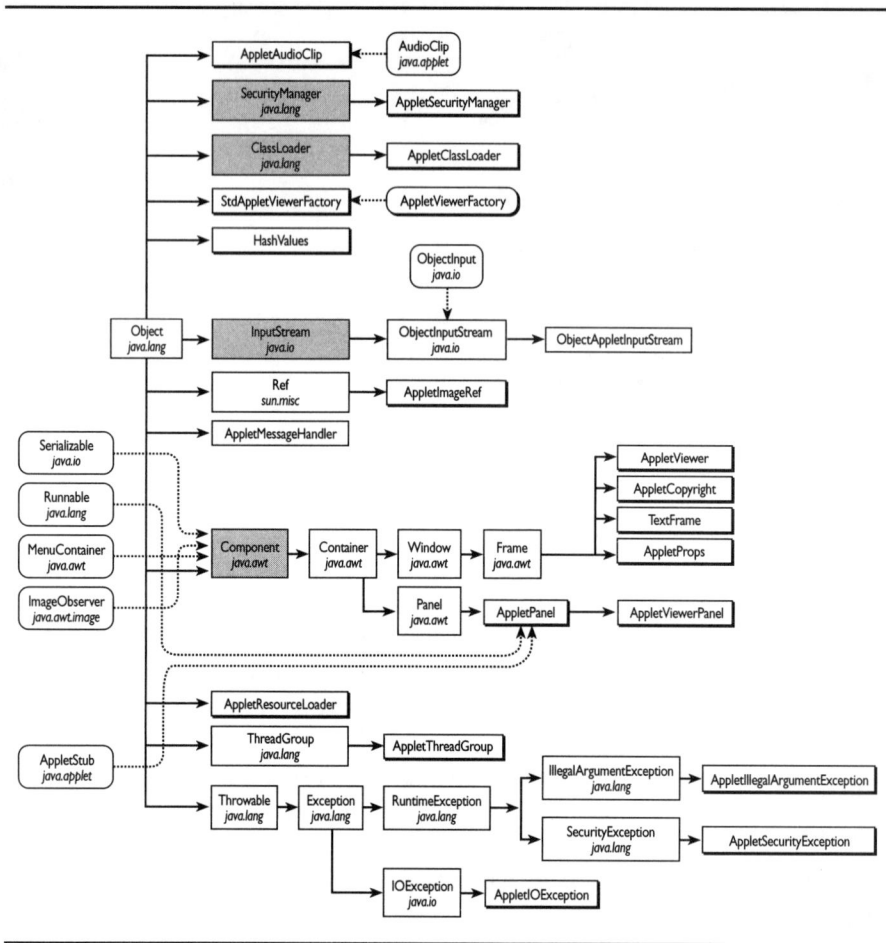

Figure G-1
The sun.applet package.

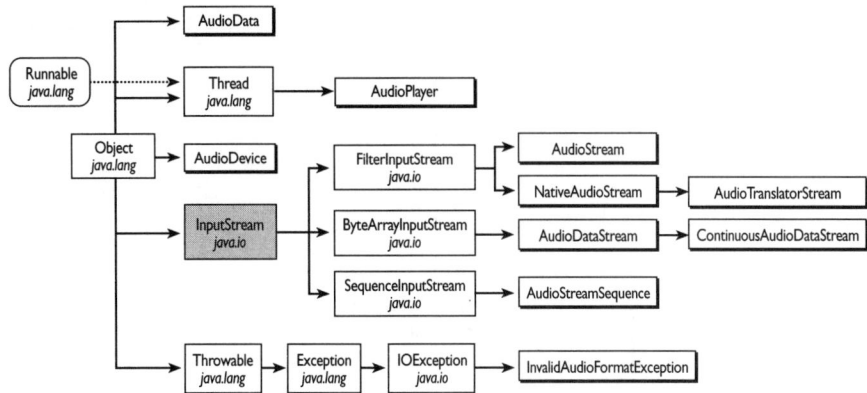

Figure G-2
The sun.audio package.

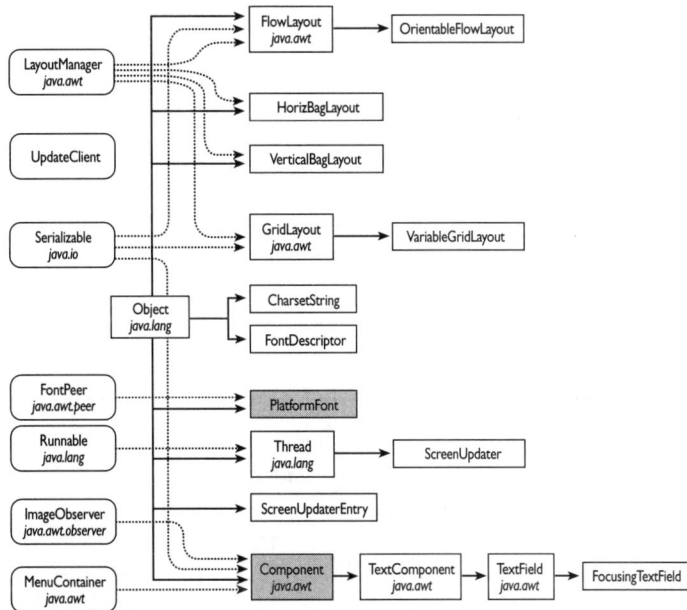

Figure G-3
The sun.beans.editors package.

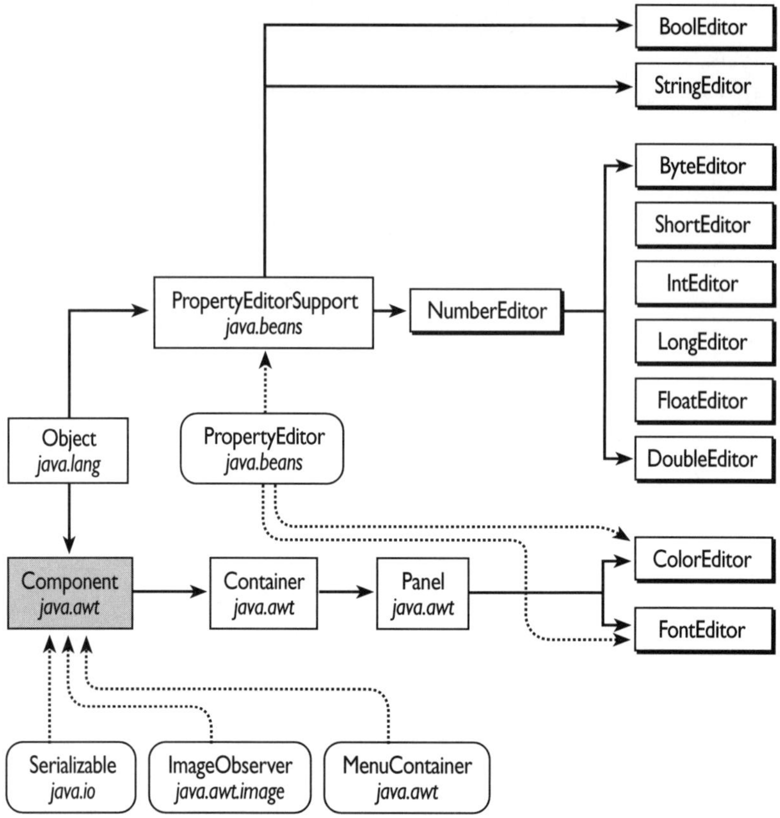

Figure G-4
The sun.beans.info package.

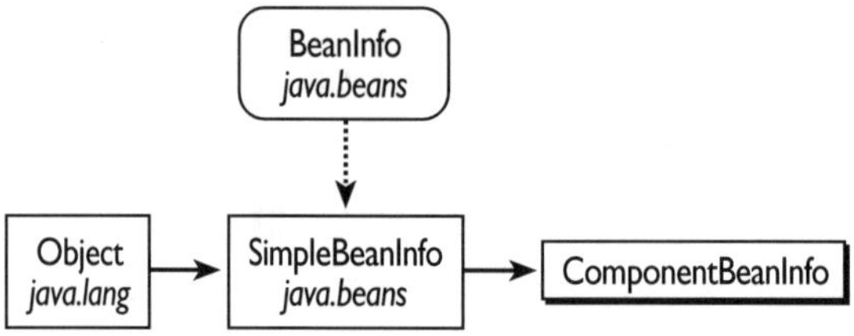

Figure G-5
The sun.html package was included in some early betas of Java 1.1. It was removed from the release version. It may reappear in the future or as part of HotJava.

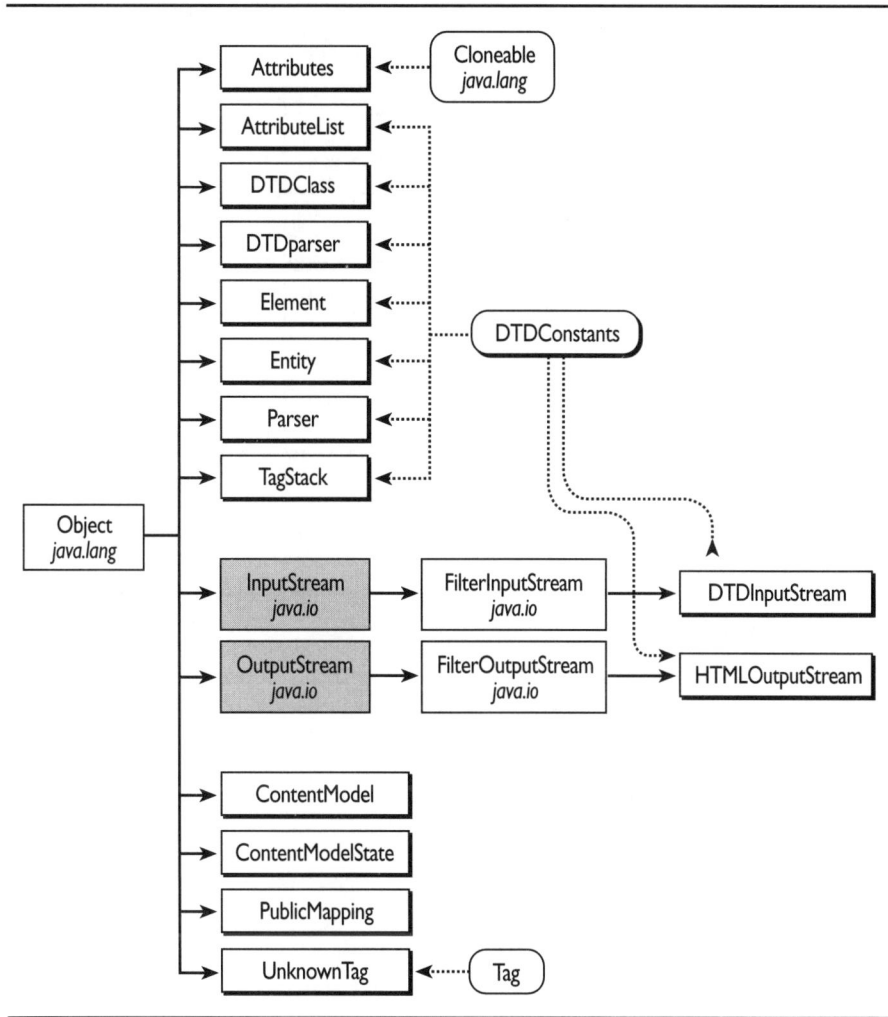

Figure G-6
The sun.jdbc.odbc package.

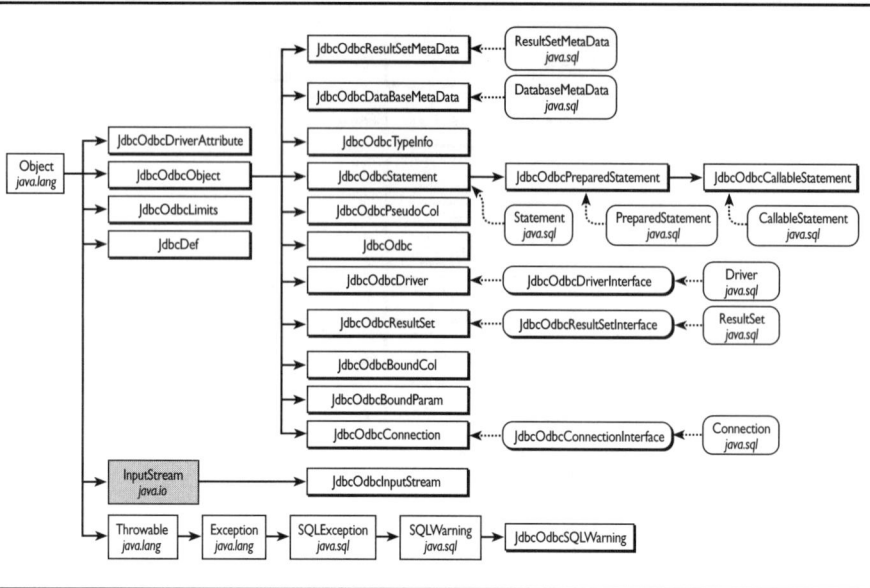

Figure G-7
The sun.misc package.

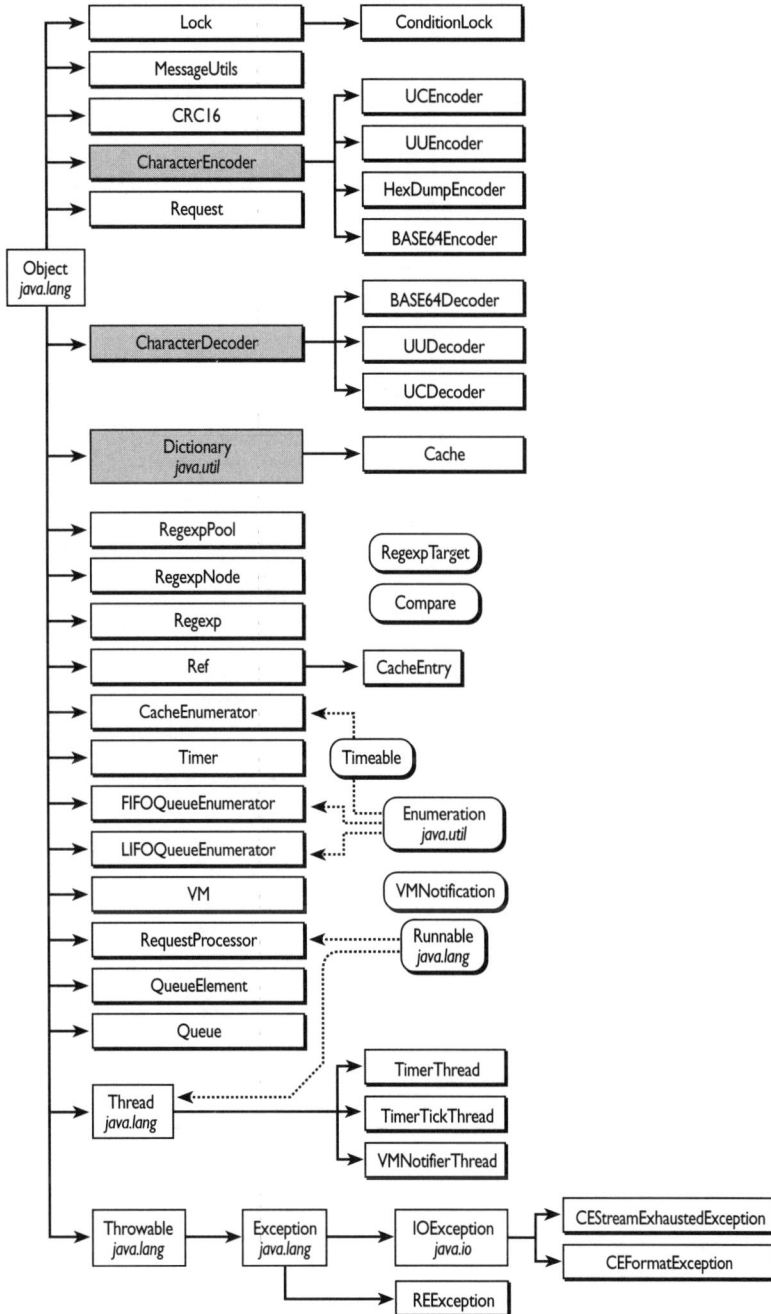

Figure G-8

The sun.net package.

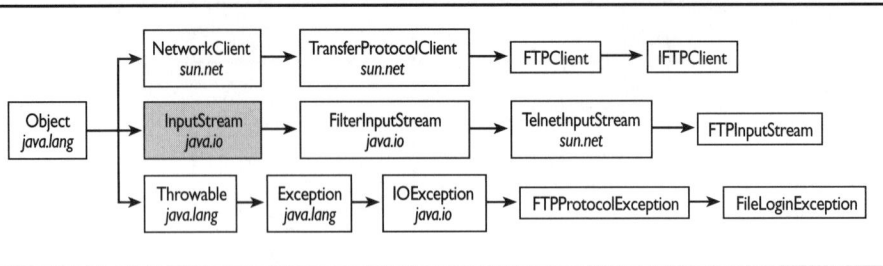

Figure G-9
The sun.net.ftp package.

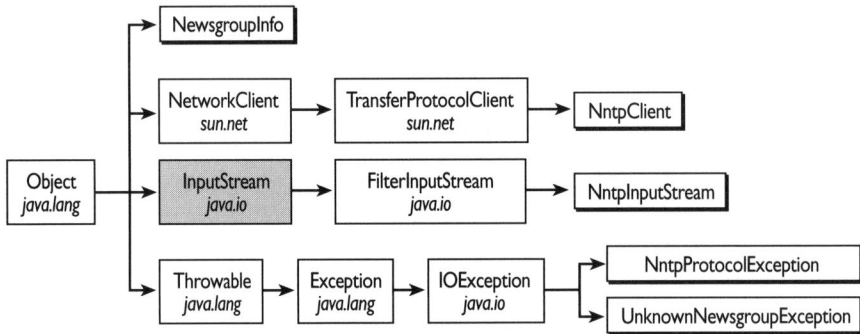

Figure G-10
The sun.net.nntp package.

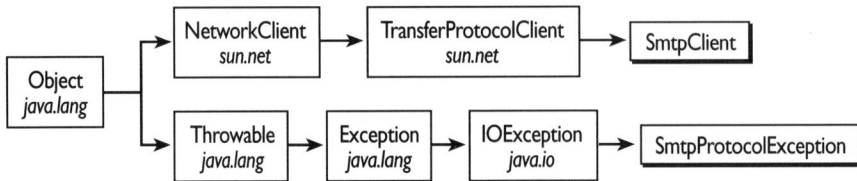

Figure G-11
The sun.net.smtp package.

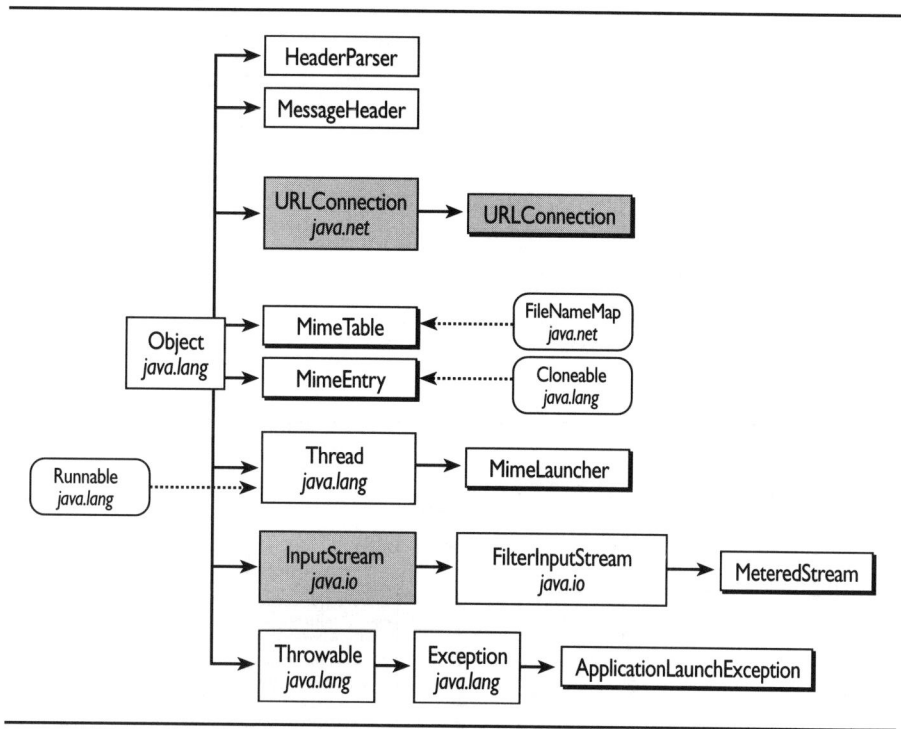

Figure G-12
The sun.net.www package.

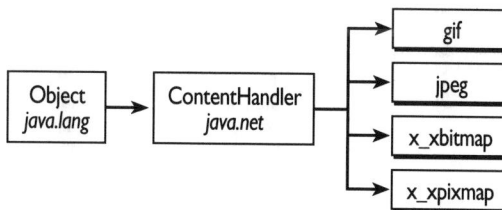

Figure G-13
The sun.net.www.content.image package.

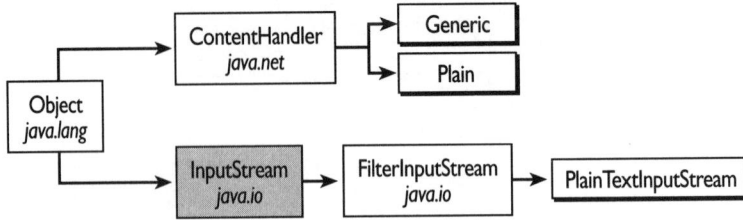

Figure G-14
The sun.net.www.content.text package.

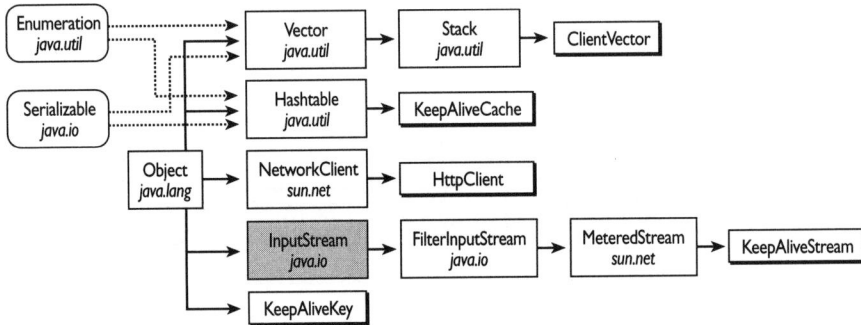

Figure G-15
The sun.net.www.http package.

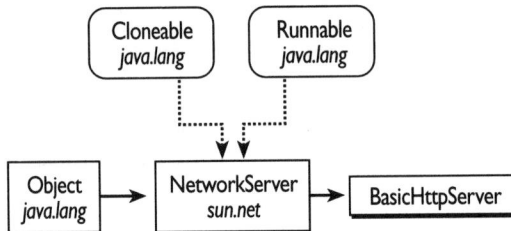

Figure G-16
The sun.net.www.httpd package.

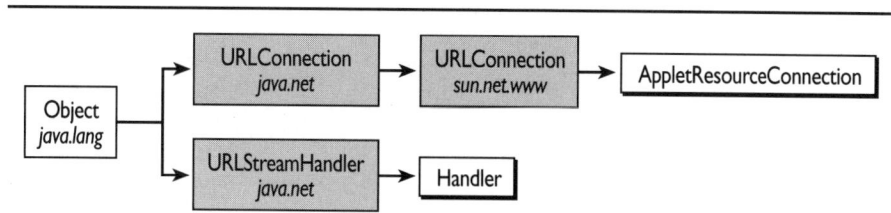

Figure G-17
The sun.net.www.protocol.appletresource package.

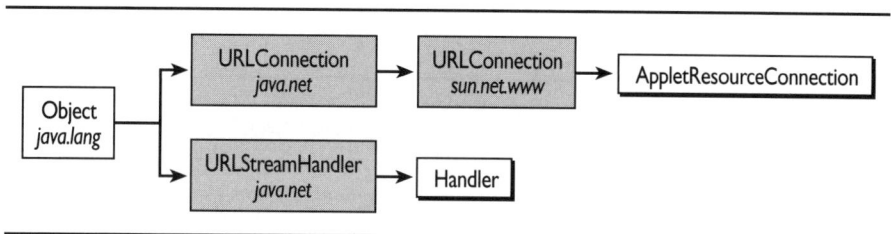

Figure G-18
The sun.net.www.protocol.PCT package.

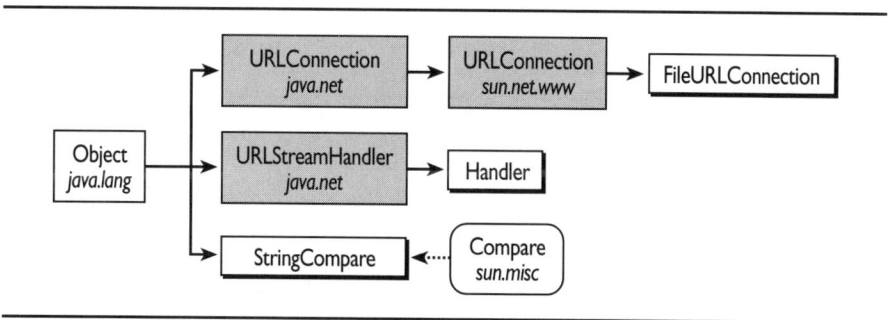

Figure G-19
The sun.net.www.protocol.file package.

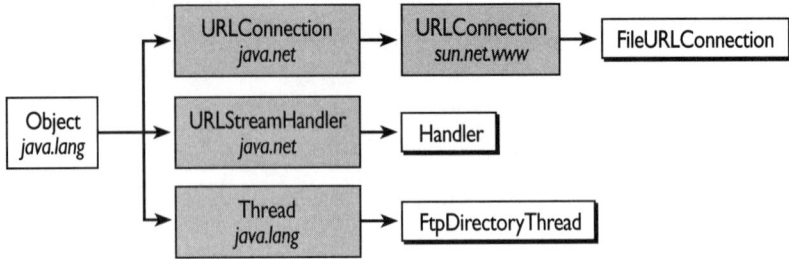

Figure G-20
The sun.net.www.protocol.ftp package.

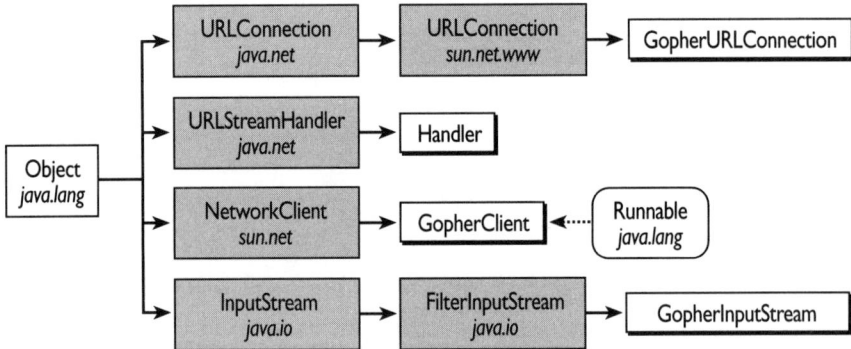

Figure G-21
The sun.net.www.protocol.gopher package.

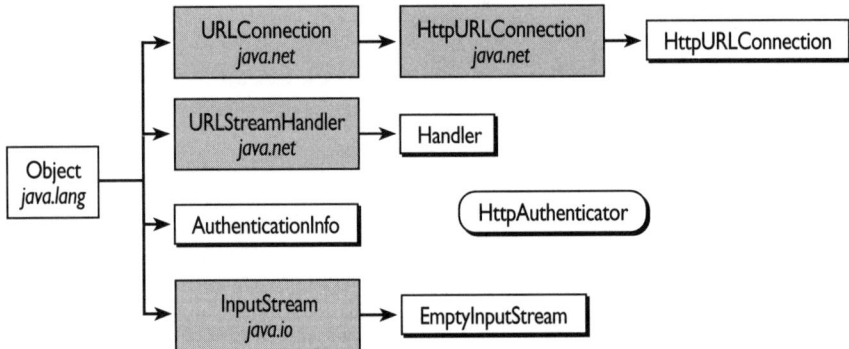

Figure G-22
The sun.net.www.protocol.http package.

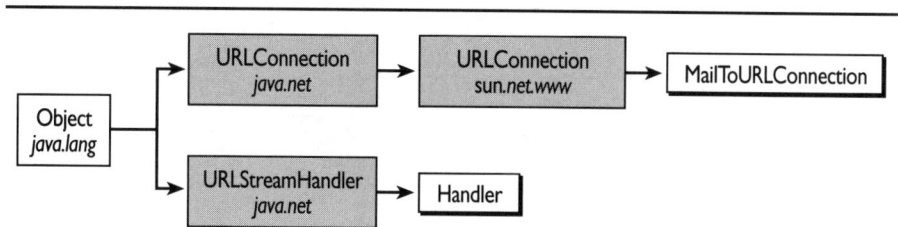

Figure G-23
The sun.net.www.protocol.mailto package.

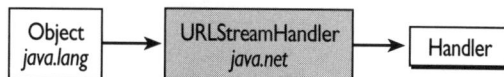

Figure G-24
The sun.net.www.protocol.netdoc package.

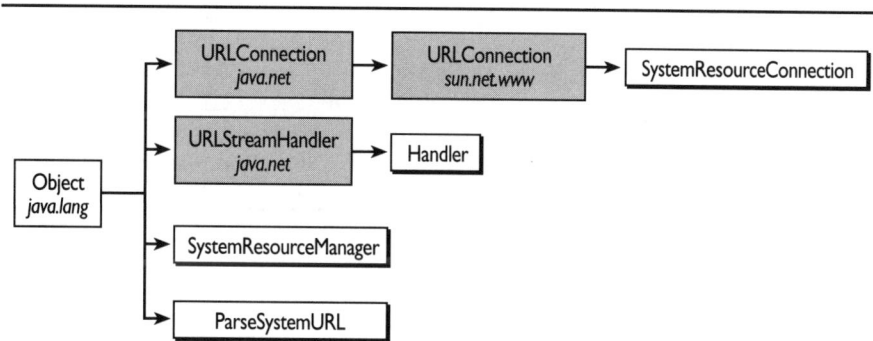

Figure G-25
The sun.net.www.protocol.systemresource package.

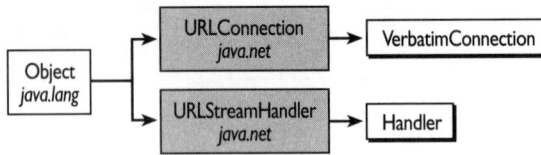

Figure G-26
The sun.net.www.protocol.verbatim package.

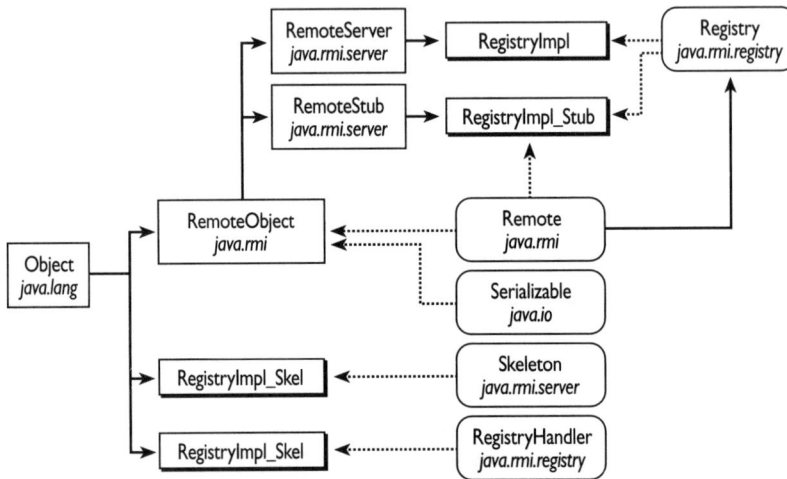

Figure G-27
The sun.rmi.registry package.

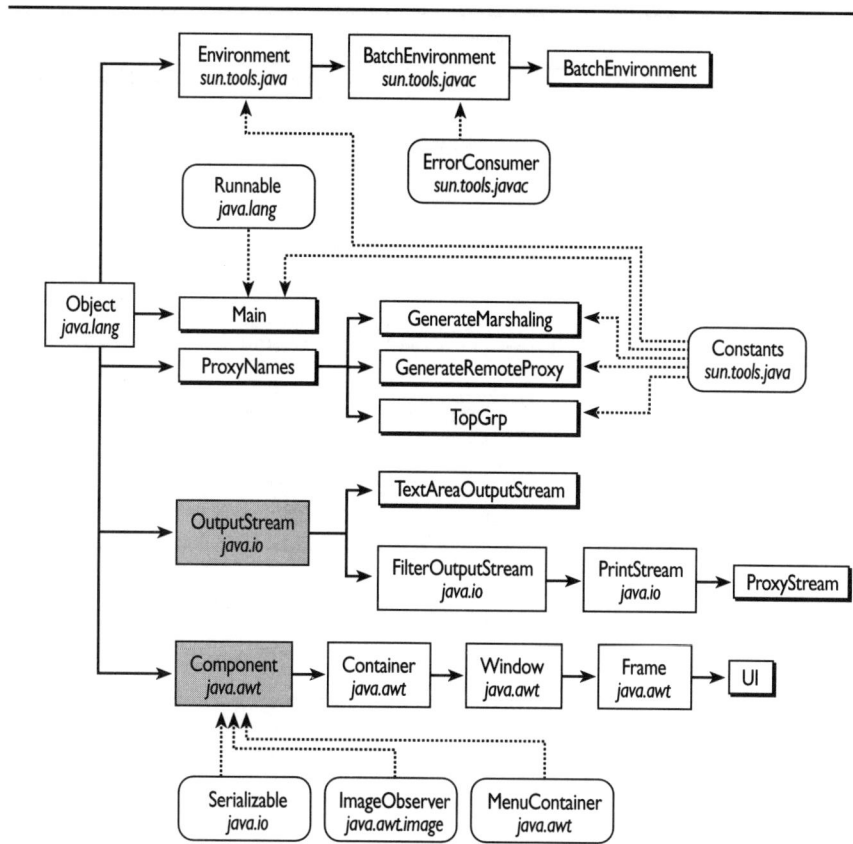

Figure G-28
The sun.rmi.rmic package.

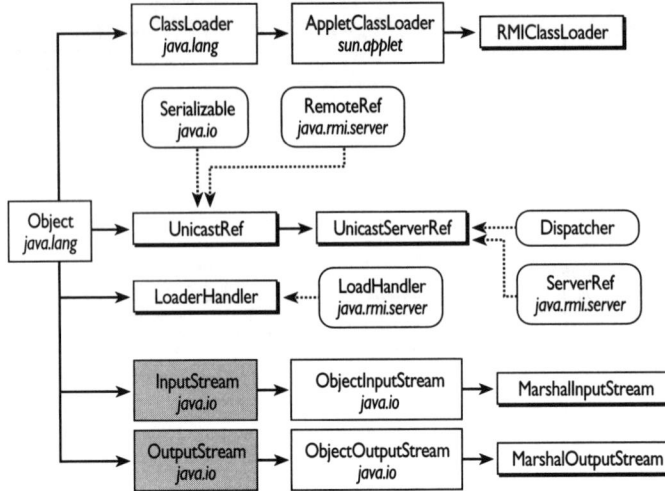

Figure G-29
The sun.rmi.server package.

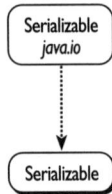

Figure G-30
The sunw.io package.

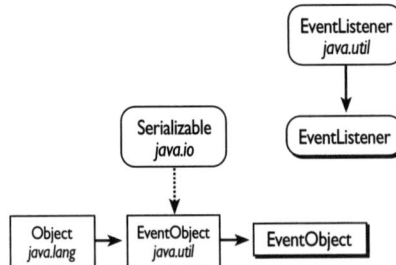

Figure G-31
The sunw.util package.

ABOUT THE CD-ROM

*T*his CD-ROM contains Java development tools I find intriguing. What drives my choices is that they all work at a very low level. This isn't just another collection of applets and publisher's editions. Instead, the CD-ROM is full of hardcore hacking tools for Java. As such, some of these tools are a little rough-edged, so exercise a bit of caution when using them.

Nonetheless, I've found these tools to be useful and thought-provoking. When you put them all together, you've got both the foundation of an almost complete Java environment (runtime, compilers, and so on) and a complete package for reverse engineering Java files (decompiler, disassembler, class browser, and so on). Many of these tools are GPL'd (published under the Free Software Foundation's General Public License) and thus, in many cases, source code is included. Even if you don't replace your Sun-supplied compilers and runtimes with these versions, you can still learn a lot about Java by studying the source code for these programs.

The one piece I was not able to include on the CD-ROM that I really, really wanted was an independent implementation of the AWT with source code. However, I do suggest that you check out `http://www.biss-net/bis-awt.html` to learn about the BISS AWT package. While you're at it, you should also learn about the Jolt project (`http://www.redhat.com/linux-info/jolt/`) that's attempting to produce a freely redistributable, clean-room clone of Java using many of the pieces on this very CD-ROM.

I also hoped to include the complete source code for Sun's Java here, as well. However, the standard JDK does include the source code for at least the java packages. Unzip the src.zip file in the main JDK directory.

WHAT IS INCLUDED ON THE CD-ROM

The tools you will find on this disc include the following:

- David Engberg's guavac compiler
- Tim Wilkinson's Kaffe virtual machine and JIT
- Robert Raud's ClassViewer class browser
- Aart Bik's JAVAR thread optimizer
- Wingsoft's Wingdis decompiler
- PFP Software GmbH's DeJAVA disassembler
- KB Sriram's Hashjava obfuscator, Jas byte code assembler, and Jinstall installer maker

I've also included Per Bothner's Kawa Scheme compiler that outputs Java byte code and Colin J. Taylor's Java Lambda Calculus Interpreter, which is written entirely in Java.

These tools are included on the disk uncompressed, unarchived form. Where you find a zip file, it is an uncompressed zip file that stores a Java package or packages that you should place in your class path. In all cases you should mount the CD in the usual fashion for you operating system, and then copy the directories you're interested in onto your hard drive. These directories are:

CLASSVIEWER

DEJAVA

GUAVAC

JAS

JAVAR

JINSTAFF

KAFFE

KAWA

LAMBDA

There are also a SOURCE directory which contains source code from this book and a README file which is essentially this appendix. Information about the specific packages follows.

A Word About the Programs

Guavac is a Java compiler written in C++ by Effective Edge Technologies and distributed under the Gnu General Public License. You should feel free to use, copy, and modify it, based on the terms in the COPYING file included in this distribution. Guavac is distributed free of charge in the hopes that other people will find it useful and possibly enhance its utility in turn.

Guavac should produce correct byte code for valid Java input, but you may encounter some difficulties in compiling Guavac itself, which may make Guavac impractical for inexperienced programmers. Guavac is written in C++, so it requires a decent C++ compiler and a class library that implements the standard C++ libraries defined in the current C++ standard. To be more specific, Guavac uses a few STL collection classes (like map and deque) as well as the standard string class, which is used for Java's 16-bit (Unicode) strings. This has only been tested using gcc (Version 2.7.2) and libg++ (Version 2.7.1), which seem to work out of the box on Linux, OSF, Irix, and Solaris. Older versions of gcc will *not* work. The C++ code you use should be reasonably portable to an alternate C++ compiler that also supports the standard templates. The only blatantly non-portable code that may require changing is in dynamic_cast.h. Read the comments there for more information.

Tim Wilkinson's Kaffe 0.83 is a virtual machine design for most Unix-like systems. Kaffe performs *just-in-time* compilation. If full JIT support isn't possible, the system defaults to an interpreter. The Kaffe home page is at http://www.kaffe.org.

Robert Raud's ClassViewer displays the methods and fields defined in a Java .class file. You can browse into other classes referred to in the .class file and decompile the class file if you also have Mocha installed. This is useful when source code is not available and as a verification and troubleshooting tool. Files can be locally stored or downloaded from a Web site. The Java

ClassViewer is written in Java and works on any platform where Java is supported. The ClassViewer home page is at `http://www.intac.com/~robraud/classinfo.html`.

Aart Bik's JAVAR, Version 1.2 beta, is a prototype restructuring compiler that can be used to make implicit parallelism in Java programs explicit by means of multi-threading. This prototype tool does not provide a complete Java front-end (for instance, unicode escapes are not supported and only limited semantic analysis has been implemented). Therefore, applying JAVAR to a program should be postponed until after a program has been thoroughly tested using a full Java compiler. Moreover, JAVAR relies completely on the identification of implicit parallelism by means of annotations. However, the tool provides sufficient functionality to make the parallelization less complex and less error-prone. The JAVAR Web page can be found at `http://www.extreme.indiana.edu/hpjava/`.

WingDis 2.0.3 is a command-line decompiler that allows users to convert a Java class or Java byte code file to a Java-like program. The eventual goal of WingDis is to generate an equivalent and compilable Java source code (text) from a Java class file (binary). The Wingsoft home page is at `http://www.wingsoft.com/`.

PFP Software GmbH's DeJAVA, Version 1.13, is a Windows 95/NT console mode application that disassembles .class byte code files, much like the javap utility that ships with Sun's JDK.

Colin J. Taylor's Java Lambda Calculus Interpreter 1.00 is a GPL'd lambda calculus interpreter that uses call-by-name semantics written in Java. The language is mostly Church's simple untyped lambda calculus; the only concession for usefulness is the addition of numbers. (If this sounds like Greek to you, and you don't speak Greek, don't worry; but theoretical computer scientists really do get quite jazzed about this sort of thing.) The Java Lambda Calculus Interpreter home page is at `http://www.cs.nott.ac.uk/~cjt/eval/Lambda.html`.

Per Bothner's Kawa Scheme compiler, Version 1.4, compiles R4RS Scheme source code into Java byte code. It provides Scheme access to Java objects, fields, and methods. The gnu.bytecode package is used to generate and manipulate .class files. The Kawa home page is at `http://www.cygnus.com/~bothner/kawa.html`.

KB Sriram's Jinstall 0.1 is an application that packs a directory into a single class file, which can then be run as an application to unpack itself on another machine. In fact, Jinstall itself is distributed as a Jinstall class. To unpack it, copy the install.class file to your hard drive and run *java install* from the command line. The JInstall home page is at `http://www.sbktech.org/jinstall.html`.

KB Sriram's Hashjava 0.3 is a java package which obfuscates symbols in your bytecode, making it a little harder to decompile. The Hashjava home page is at `http://www.sbktech.org/hashjava.html`. Hashjava is distributed as a jinstall class. To install it copy the hjinstall.class file onto your hard drive, and run *java hjinstall*.

KB Sriram's Jas 0.4 is a java package to generate java bytecode. It includes a scheme like scripting language to drive the package and generate bytecode. The Jas home page is at `http://www.sbktech.org/jas.html`.

Finally, all the source code for the examples in this book is included. Please feel free to reuse any or all of this source code in your own projects. No specific permission is necessary or required.

Note: It is best to view files on the CD with Microsoft Word, as Wordpad and Notepad may display some characters incorrectly. Note that some files with .PCX extensions may display an Invalid File Header message if viewed with MS Image Viewer. Finally, some .bat files that are included with software products may need to be edited by users for their specific setup to run properly.

INDEX

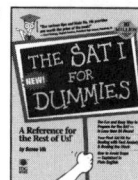

Title	Author	ISBN	Price
The Internet For Macs® For Dummies® 2nd Edition	by Charles Seiter	ISBN: 1-56884-371-2	$19.99 USA/$26.99 Canada
The Internet For Macs® For Dummies® Starter Kit	by Charles Seiter	ISBN: 1-56884-244-9	$29.99 USA/$39.99 Canada
The Internet For Macs® For Dummies® Starter Kit Bestseller Edition	by Charles Seiter	ISBN: 1-56884-245-7	$39.99 USA/$54.99 Canada
The Internet For Windows® For Dummies® Starter Kit	by John R. Levine & Margaret Levine Young	ISBN: 1-56884-237-6	$34.99 USA/$44.99 Canada
The Internet For Windows® For Dummies® Starter Kit, Bestseller Edition	by John R. Levine & Margaret Levine Young	ISBN: 1-56884-246-5	$39.99 USA/$54.99 Canada

MACINTOSH

Mac® Programming For Dummies®	by Dan Parks Sydow	ISBN: 1-56884-173-6	$19.95 USA/$26.95 Canada
Macintosh® System 7.5 For Dummies®	by Bob LeVitus	ISBN: 1-56884-197-3	$19.95 USA/$26.95 Canada
MORE Macs® For Dummies®	by David Pogue	ISBN: 1-56884-087-X	$19.95 USA/$26.95 Canada
PageMaker 5 For Macs® For Dummies®	by Galen Gruman & Deke McClelland	ISBN: 1-56884-178-7	$19.95 USA/$26.95 Canada
QuarkXPress 3.3 For Dummies®	by Galen Gruman & Barbara Assadi	ISBN: 1-56884-217-1	$19.99 USA/$26.99 Canada
Upgrading and Fixing Macs® For Dummies®	by Kearney Rietmann & Frank Higgins	ISBN: 1-56884-189-2	$19.95 USA/$26.95 Canada

MULTIMEDIA

Multimedia & CD-ROMs For Dummies® 2nd Edition	by Andy Rathbone	ISBN: 1-56884-907-9	$19.99 USA/$26.99 Canada
Multimedia & CD-ROMs For Dummies®, Interactive Multimedia Value Pack, 2nd Edition	by Andy Rathbone	ISBN: 1-56884-909-5	$29.99 USA/$39.99 Canada

OPERATING SYSTEMS:

DOS

MORE DOS For Dummies®	by Dan Gookin	ISBN: 1-56884-046-2	$19.95 USA/$26.95 Canada
OS/2® Warp For Dummies® 2nd Edition	by Andy Rathbone	ISBN: 1-56884-205-8	$19.99 USA/$26.99 Canada

UNIX

MORE UNIX® For Dummies®	by John R. Levine & Margaret Levine Young	ISBN: 1-56884-361-5	$19.99 USA/$26.99 Canada
UNIX® For Dummies®	by John R. Levine & Margaret Levine Young	ISBN: 1-878058-58-4	$19.95 USA/$26.95 Canada

WINDOWS

MORE Windows® For Dummies® 2nd Edition	by Andy Rathbone	ISBN: 1-56884-048-9	$19.95 USA/$26.95 Canada
Windows® 95 For Dummies®	by Andy Rathbone	ISBN: 1-56884-240-6	$19.99 USA/$26.99 Canada

PCS/HARDWARE

Illustrated Computer Dictionary For Dummies® 2nd Edition	by Dan Gookin & Wallace Wang	ISBN: 1-56884-218-X	$12.95 USA/$16.95 Canada
Upgrading and Fixing PCs For Dummies® 2nd Edition	by Andy Rathbone	ISBN: 1-56884-903-6	$19.99 USA/$26.99 Canada

PRESENTATION/AUTOCAD

AutoCAD For Dummies®	by Bud Smith	ISBN: 1-56884-191-4	$19.95 USA/$26.95 Canada
PowerPoint 4 For Windows® For Dummies®	by Doug Lowe	ISBN: 1-56884-161-2	$16.99 USA/$22.99 Canada

PROGRAMMING

Borland C++ For Dummies®	by Michael Hyman	ISBN: 1-56884-162-0	$19.95 USA/$26.95 Canada
C For Dummies® Volume 1	by Dan Gookin	ISBN: 1-878058-78-9	$19.95 USA/$26.95 Canada
C++ For Dummies®	by Stephen R. Davis	ISBN: 1-56884-163-9	$19.95 USA/$26.95 Canada
Delphi Programming For Dummies®	by Neil Rubenking	ISBN: 1-56884-200-7	$19.99 USA/$26.99 Canada
Mac® Programming For Dummies®	by Dan Parks Sydow	ISBN: 1-56884-173-6	$19.95 USA/$26.95 Canada
PowerBuilder 4 Programming For Dummies®	by Ted Coombs & Jason Coombs	ISBN: 1-56884-325-9	$19.99 USA/$26.99 Canada
QBasic Programming For Dummies®	by Douglas Hergert	ISBN: 1-56884-093-4	$19.95 USA/$26.95 Canada
Visual Basic 3 For Dummies®	by Wallace Wang	ISBN: 1-56884-076-4	$19.95 USA/$26.95 Canada
Visual Basic "X" For Dummies®	by Wallace Wang	ISBN: 1-56884-230-9	$19.99 USA/$26.99 Canada
Visual C++ 2 For Dummies®	by Michael Hyman & Bob Arnson	ISBN: 1-56884-328-3	$19.99 USA/$26.99 Canada
Windows® 95 Programming For Dummies®	by S. Randy Davis	ISBN: 1-56884-327-5	$19.99 USA/$26.99 Canada

SPREADSHEET

1-2-3 For Dummies®	by Greg Harvey	ISBN: 1-878058-60-6	$16.95 USA/$22.95 Canada
1-2-3 For Windows® 5 For Dummies® 2nd Edition	by John Walkenbach	ISBN: 1-56884-216-3	$16.95 USA/$22.95 Canada
Excel 5 For Macs® For Dummies®	by Greg Harvey	ISBN: 1-56884-186-8	$19.95 USA/$26.95 Canada
Excel For Dummies® 2nd Edition	by Greg Harvey	ISBN: 1-56884-050-0	$16.95 USA/$22.95 Canada
MORE 1-2-3 For DOS For Dummies®	by John Weingarten	ISBN: 1-56884-224-4	$19.99 USA/$26.99 Canada
MORE Excel 5 For Windows® For Dummies®	by Greg Harvey	ISBN: 1-56884-207-4	$19.95 USA/$26.95 Canada
Quattro Pro 6 For Windows® For Dummies®	by John Walkenbach	ISBN: 1-56884-174-4	$19.95 USA/$26.95 Canada
Quattro Pro For DOS For Dummies®	by John Walkenbach	ISBN: 1-56884-023-3	$16.95 USA/$22.95 Canada

UTILITIES

Title	Author	ISBN	Price
Norton Utilities 8 For Dummies®	by Beth Slick	ISBN: 1-56884-166-3	$19.95 USA/$26.95 Canada

VCRS/CAMCORDERS

Title	Author	ISBN	Price
VCRs & Camcorders For Dummies™	by Gordon McComb & Andy Rathbone	ISBN: 1-56884-229-5	$14.99 USA/$20.99 Canada

WORD PROCESSING

Ami Pro For Dummies®	by Jim Meade	ISBN: 1-56884-049-7	$19.95 USA/$26.95 Canada
MORE Word For Windows® 6 For Dummies®	by Doug Lowe	ISBN: 1-56884-165-5	$19.95 USA/$26.95 Canada
MORE WordPerfect® 6 For Windows® For Dummies®	by Margaret Levine Young & David C. Kay	ISBN: 1-56884-206-6	$19.95 USA/$26.95 Canada
MORE WordPerfect® 6 For DOS For Dummies®	by Wallace Wang, edited by Dan Gookin	ISBN: 1-56884-047-0	$19.95 USA/$26.95 Canada
Word 6 For Macs® For Dummies®	by Dan Gookin	ISBN: 1-56884-190-6	$19.95 USA/$26.95 Canada
Word For Windows® 6 For Dummies®	by Dan Gookin	ISBN: 1-56884-075-6	$16.95 USA/$22.95 Canada
Word For Windows® For Dummies®	by Dan Gookin & Ray Werner	ISBN: 1-878058-86-X	$16.95 USA/$22.95 Canada
WordPerfect® 6 For DOS For Dummies®	by Dan Gookin	ISBN: 1-878058-77-0	$16.95 USA/$22.95 Canada
WordPerfect® 6.1 For Windows® For Dummies® 2nd Edition	by Margaret Levine Young & David Kay	ISBN: 1-56884-243-0	$16.95 USA/$22.95 Canada
WordPerfect® For Dummies®	by Dan Gookin	ISBN: 1-878058-52-5	$16.95 USA/$22.95 Canada

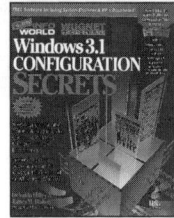

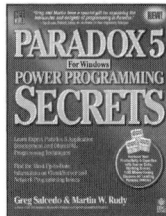

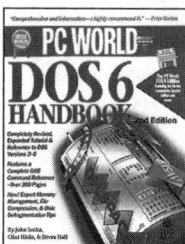

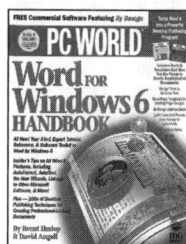

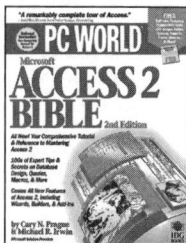

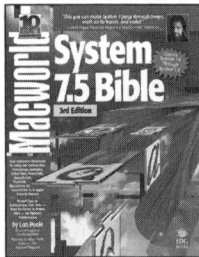

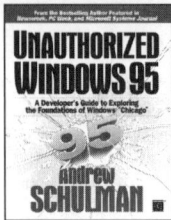

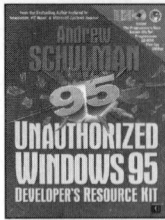

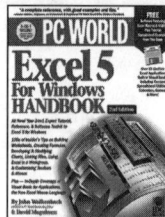

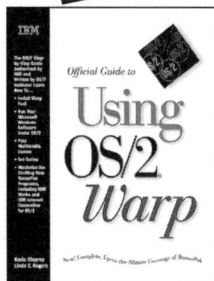

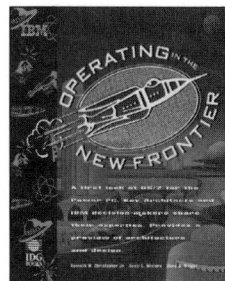

IDG BOOKS WORLDWIDE ™

Order Center: **(800) 762-2974** *(8 a.m.–6 p.m., EST, weekdays)*

Quantity	ISBN	Title	Price	Total

Shipping & Handling Charges

	Description	First book	Each additional book	Total
Domestic	Normal	$4.50	$1.50	$
	Two Day Air	$8.50	$2.50	$
	Overnight	$18.00	$3.00	$
International	Surface	$8.00	$8.00	$
	Airmail	$16.00	$16.00	$
	DHL Air	$17.00	$17.00	$

*For large quantities call for shipping & handling charges.
**Prices are subject to change without notice.

Ship to:

Name _____

Company _____

Address _____

City/State/Zip _____

Daytime Phone _____

Payment: □ Check to IDG Books Worldwide (US Funds Only)

□ VISA   □ MasterCard   □ American Express

Card # _____ Expires _____

Signature _____

Subtotal _____

CA residents add
applicable sales tax _____

IN, MA, and MD
residents add
5% sales tax _____

IL residents add
6.25% sales tax _____

RI residents add
7% sales tax _____

TX residents add
8.25% sales tax _____

Shipping _____

Total _____

Please send this order form to:
IDG Books Worldwide, Inc.
Attn: Order Entry Dept.
7260 Shadeland Station, Suite 100
Indianapolis, IN 46256

Allow up to 3 weeks for delivery.
Thank you!

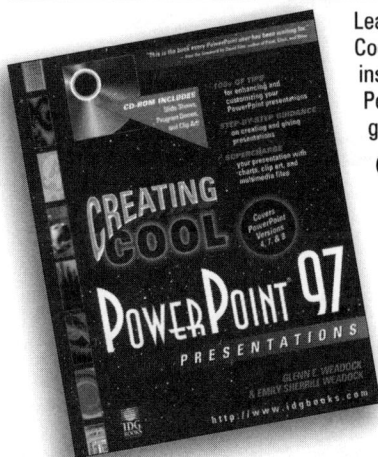

Bible Series
Comprehensive Tutorial/Reference Books with 100% of What You Need to Know

Bibles help readers reach higher skill levels by providing comprehensive information on a product or technology. Authors have extensive knowledge of the topic through years of experience and provide numerous step-by-step examples, real-live uses, and much more.

Office 97 Bible
Ed Jones & Derek Sutton
0-7645-3037-2
$39.99 U.S./$54.99 Canada
pp. 1200

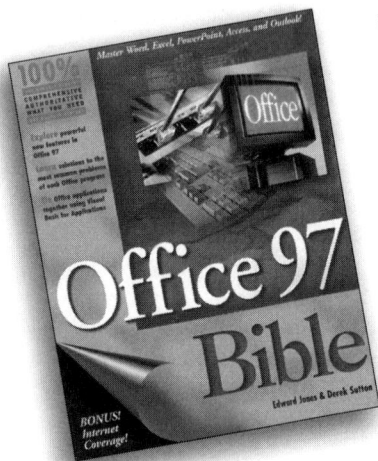

Excel 97 Bible
John Walkenbach
0-7645-3036-4
$34.99 U.S./$48.99 Canada
pp. 944

Word 97 Bible
Brent Heslop & David Angell
0-7645-3038-0
$34.99 U.S./$48.99 Canada
pp. 1008

Access 97 Bible
Cary N. Prague &
Michael R. Irwin
0-7645-3035-6
$49.99 U.S.
$69.99 Canada
pp. 1128
Bonus CD-ROM

Updated Bestseller

Intranet Bible
Ed Tittel & James Michael Stewart
0-7645-8013-2
$49.99 U.S.
$69.99 Canada
pp. 912
Bonus CD-ROM

To Order Call
800-762-2974

IDG BOOKS WORLDWIDE, INC. END-USER LICENSE AGREEMENT

3. <u>Restrictions On Use and Transfer</u>.

   (a) You may only (i) make one copy of the Software for backup or archival purposes, or (ii) transfer the Software to a single hard disk, provided that you keep the original for backup or archival purposes. You may not (i) rent or lease the Software, (ii) copy or reproduce the Software through a LAN or other network system or through any computer subscriber system or bulletin-board system, or (iii) modify, adapt, or create derivative works based on the Software.

   (b) You may not reverse engineer, decompile, or disassemble the Software. You may transfer the Software and user documentation on a permanent basis, provided that the transferee agrees to accept the terms and conditions of this Agreement and you retain no copies. If the Software is an update or has been updated, any transfer must include the most recent update and all prior versions.

4. <u>Restrictions on Use of Individual Programs</u>. You must follow the individual requirements and restrictions detailed for each individual program in the "About the CD-ROM" appendix (Appendix H) of this Book. These limitations are also contained in the individual license agreements recorded on the Software Media. These limitations may include a requirement that after using the program for a specified period of time, the user must pay a registration fee or discontinue use. By opening the Software packet(s), you will be agreeing to abide by the licenses and restrictions for these individual programs that are detailed in the "About the CD-ROM" appendix (Appendix H) and on the Software Media. None of the material on this Software Media or listed in this Book may ever be redistributed, in original or modified form, for commercial purposes.

5. <u>Limited Warranty</u>.

   (a) IDGB warrants that the Software and Software Media are free from defects in materials and workmanship under normal use for a period of sixty (60) days from the date of purchase of this Book. If IDGB receives notification within the warranty period of defects in materials or workmanship, IDGB will replace the defective Software Media.

   (b) **IDGB AND THE AUTHOR OF THE BOOK DISCLAIM ALL OTHER WARRANTIES, EXPRESS OR IMPLIED, INCLUDING WITHOUT LIMITATION IMPLIED WARRANTIES OF MERCHANTABILITY AND FITNESS FOR A PARTICULAR PURPOSE, WITH RESPECT TO THE SOFTWARE, THE PROGRAMS, THE SOURCE CODE CONTAINED THEREIN, AND/OR THE TECHNIQUES DESCRIBED IN THIS BOOK. IDGB DOES NOT WARRANT THAT THE FUNCTIONS CONTAINED IN THE SOFTWARE WILL MEET YOUR REQUIREMENTS OR THAT THE OPERATION OF THE SOFTWARE WILL BE ERROR FREE.**

(c) This limited warranty gives you specific legal rights, and you may have other rights that vary from jurisdiction to jurisdiction.

6. <u>Remedies</u>.

(a) IDGB's entire liability and your exclusive remedy for defects in materials and workmanship shall be limited to replacement of the Software Media, which may be returned to IDGB with a copy of your receipt at the following address: Software Media Fulfillment Department, Attn.: *Java SECRETS*, IDG Books Worldwide, Inc., 7260 Shadeland Station, Ste. 100, Indianapolis, IN 46256, or call 1-800-762-2974. Please allow three to four weeks for delivery. This Limited Warranty is void if failure of the Software Media has resulted from accident, abuse, or misapplication. Any replacement Software Media will be warranted for the remainder of the original warranty period or thirty (30) days, whichever is longer.

(b) In no event shall IDGB or the author be liable for any damages whatsoever (including without limitation damages for loss of business profits, business interruption, loss of business information, or any other pecuniary loss) arising from the use of or inability to use the Book or the Software, even if IDGB has been advised of the possibility of such damages.

(c) Because some jurisdictions do not allow the exclusion or limitation of liability for consequential or incidental damages, the above limitation or exclusion may not apply to you.

7. <u>U.S. Government Restricted Rights</u>. Use, duplication, or disclosure of the Software by the U.S. Government is subject to restrictions stated in paragraph (c)(1)(ii) of the Rights in Technical Data and Computer Software clause of DFARS 252.227-7013, and in subparagraphs (a) through (d) of the Commercial Computer—Restricted Rights clause at FAR 52.227-19, and in similar clauses in the NASA FAR supplement, when applicable.

8. <u>General</u>. This Agreement constitutes the entire understanding of the parties and revokes and supersedes all prior agreements, oral or written, between them and may not be modified or amended except in a writing signed by both parties hereto that specifically refers to this Agreement. This Agreement shall take precedence over any other documents that may be in conflict herewith. If any one or more provisions contained in this Agreement are held by any court or tribunal to be invalid, illegal, or otherwise unenforceable, each and every other provision shall remain in full force and effect.

IDG BOOKS WORLDWIDE REGISTRATION CARD

RETURN THIS REGISTRATION CARD FOR FREE CATALOG

Title of this book: Java™ SECRETS®

My overall rating of this book: ❏ Very good [1] ❏ Good [2] ❏ Satisfactory [3] ❏ Fair [4] ❏ Poor [5]

How I first heard about this book:

❏ Found in bookstore; name: [6] _____

❏ Advertisement: [8] _____

❏ Word of mouth; heard about book from friend, co-worker, etc.: [10] _____

❏ Book review: [7] _____

❏ Catalog: [9] _____

❏ Other: [11] _____

What I liked most about this book:

_____

_____

_____

What I would change, add, delete, etc., in future editions of this book:

_____

_____

_____

Other comments:

_____

_____

Number of computer books I purchase in a year: ❏ 1 [12] ❏ 2-5 [13] ❏ 6-10 [14] ❏ More than 10 [15]

I would characterize my computer skills as: ❏ Beginner [16] ❏ Intermediate [17] ❏ Advanced [18] ❏ Professional [19]

I use ❏ DOS [20] ❏ Windows [21] ❏ OS/2 [22] ❏ Unix [23] ❏ Macintosh [24] ❏ Other: [25] _____
(please specify)

I would be interested in new books on the following subjects:
(please check all that apply, and use the spaces provided to identify specific software)

❏ Word processing: [26] _____

❏ Data bases: [28] _____

❏ File Utilities: [30] _____

❏ Networking: [32] _____

❏ Other: [34] _____

❏ Spreadsheets: [27] _____

❏ Desktop publishing: [29] _____

❏ Money management: [31] _____

❏ Programming languages: [33] _____

I use a PC at (please check all that apply): ❏ home [35] ❏ work [36] ❏ school [37] ❏ other: [38] _____

The disks I prefer to use are ❏ 5.25 [39] ❏ 3.5 [40] ❏ other: [41] _____

I have a CD ROM: ❏ yes [42] ❏ no [43]

I plan to buy or upgrade computer hardware this year: ❏ yes [44] ❏ no [45]

I plan to buy or upgrade computer software this year: ❏ yes [46] ❏ no [47]

Name: _____ Business title: [48] _____ Type of Business: [49] _____

Address (❏ home [50] ❏ work [51]/Company name: _____)

Street/Suite# _____

City [52]/State [53]/Zipcode [54]: _____ Country [55] _____

❏ **I liked this book!** You may quote me by name in future
IDG Books Worldwide promotional materials.

My daytime phone number is _____

IDG BOOKS

THE WORLD OF
COMPUTER
KNOWLEDGE

❏ YES!

Please keep me informed about IDG's World of Computer Knowledge.
Send me the latest IDG Books catalog.

SECRETS™

...FOR DUMMIES™
COMPUTER
BOOK SERIES
FROM IDG

MACWORLD
MW
AUTHORIZED
EDITION

AUTHORIZED
PC WORLD
EDITION
★